A FABULOUS FAILURE

POLITICS AND SOCIETY IN MODERN AMERICA

*Gary Gerstle, Elizabeth Hinton, Margaret O'Mara,
and Julian E. Zelizer, Series Editors*

A FABULOUS FAILURE

The CLINTON PRESIDENCY and the TRANSFORMATION of AMERICAN CAPITALISM

NELSON LICHTENSTEIN
and JUDITH STEIN

PRINCETON UNIVERSITY PRESS

PRINCETON & OXFORD

Published by Princeton University Press
41 William Street, Princeton, New Jersey 08540
99 Banbury Road, Oxford OX2 6JX

press.princeton.edu

Library of Congress Cataloging-in-Publication Data

Names: Lichtenstein, Nelson, author. | Stein, Judith, 1940–2017, author.
Title: A fabulous failure : Bill Clinton and American capitalism /
    Nelson Lichtenstein, and Judith Stein.
Description: Princeton : Princeton University Press, [2023] |
    Series: Politics and society in modern America | Includes bibliographical
    references and index.
Identifiers: LCCN 2022040787 (print) | LCCN 2022040788 (ebook) |
    ISBN 9780691245508 (hardback) | ISBN 9780691245515 (ebook)
Subjects: LCSH: Clinton, Bill, 1946– | United States—Politics and government—
    1993–2001. | United States—Economic conditions—1981–2001.
Classification: LCC E885 .L53 2023 (print) | LCC E885 (ebook) |
    DDC 973.929—dc23/eng/20220823
LC record available at https://lccn.loc.gov/2022040787
LC ebook record available at https://lccn.loc.gov/2022040788

British Library Cataloging-in-Publication Data is available

Editorial: Bridget Flannery-McCoy and Alena Chekanov
Production Editorial: Kathleen Cioffi
Text and Jacket Design: Karl Spurzem
Production: Erin Suydam
Publicity: James Schneider and Kate Farquhar-Thomson
Copyeditor: Cynthia Buck

Jacket image: Joseph Sohm / Shutterstock

This book has been composed in Arno Pro with Balboa

Printed on acid-free paper. ∞

Printed in the United States of America

10 9 8 7 6 5 4 3 2 1

For Judith Stein

1940–2017

CONTENTS

PART IV. THE NEW DEAL IN ECLIPSE

PREFACE

This book may well have had its origins in the fall of 1993, when I held a Fulbright fellowship in Helsinki. Newspapers were not then online, so once or twice a week I would walk over to the United States Information Agency reading room and take a look at the *New York Times*. That paper was filled with dense reports on the emerging shape and fate of Bill Clinton's health care reform proposal, the most important effort to expand the welfare state since the 1960s. The *Times* followed every twist and turn: conflict between large insurance companies and small, between unionized manufacturing firms and low-wage retailers, between various factions in both the Democratic and Republican Parties. The *Times* coverage was like a set of X-rays revealing the hard structures of American capitalism.

I also thought the debate held an uncanny resemblance to the conflicts and compromises that had reconfigured business, labor, and the state during the early years of the New Deal, a historical moment upon which I was then writing. Presidents Roosevelt and Clinton were hardly soul mates, but both wanted to use government power to transform sectors of the economy that were clearly operating in a dysfunctional fashion. That was the task before FDR's National Recovery Administration, and whatever else one thought of the new Clinton administration, his health reform initiative, an ambitious effort to manage one-seventh of the US economy, might move America a step closer to the Nordic welfare states, in one of which my family was now temporarily ensconced.

That Clinton effort proved a failure, and inadvertently I later moved on to study one of the reasons why. I wrote a book on Wal-Mart, which by the end of the 1990s had replaced General Motors as the nation's largest company, by sales and employee count. Unlike GM, Wal-Mart was rural and Southern, low-wage, and hostile to unionism; indeed, Wal-Mart was unreconciled to even the most fundamental New Deal reforms. I held a conference and edited a book whose title told the tale: *Wal-Mart: The Face of Twenty-First-Century Capitalism*. This made me part of the generation of labor historians who were turning themselves into students of capital. No historian can understand one without the other, nor should they ignore the intellectuals and politicians who sought to make eschatological sense of the latest developments in technology, business, trade, and culture.

I was working on the shape-shifting character of the twentieth-century corporation when Judith Stein died in May 2017. I had been friendly with her for decades. We were interested in many of the same things. Indeed, when illness prevented her from participating on an academic conference panel that I had organized early that same year—entitled "State, Capital, and the Corporation: Ideological and Social Transformations of the Last Half Century"—I read her incisive comments to the audience.

Judith Stein was a determined and supportive inspiration to generations of grad students, scholars, and activists. She graduated from Vassar College in 1960 and in 1968 took her PhD in American studies from Yale. She began teaching at the City College of New York in 1966 and spent half a century at that institution. Her early work arose out of an engagement with African-American history; the analytical template she established linking class, race, and the structure of political economy would guide her scholarly career for decades. In her first book, *The World of Marcus Garvey*, Judith saw a social movement whose nationalist and petit-bourgeois ideology was often in tension—creative or destructive—with the proletarian social strata that sustained it. Likewise, when she turned to the political economy of postwar America, Judith probed the ideological fissures that weakened a racial liberalism that now had to contend with an increasingly globalized capitalism. Her studies of the steel industry and of the politics and political economy of the 1970s—a "pivotal decade," she called it—charted the dividing line between a four-decade-long New Deal order and the post-Keynesian era that structured the statecraft of both Ronald Reagan and Bill Clinton.[1]

In her preliminary work on the 1990s, Judith Stein wanted to know why a newly empowered generation of political operatives, policy mavens, and officeholders failed to transform the trajectory of American politics and the troubled economy that was already turning the industrial heartland into a "Rust Belt." Why was the Clinton White House unable to take advantage of a largely peaceful and prosperous decade in order to build a more equitable and stable economy and a political order powerful enough to challenge the forces mobilizing on the right?

After I published an obituary framing her work in terms of contemporary historiographic controversaries, I got an email from Sandy Dijkstra, her literary agent, asking if I would like to take over the writing project on which Judith had been at work.[2] Stein had done research in some of the presidential libraries and drafted a book outline and a couple of rough chapters, but the most important thing I took from her work was the topic itself: it would be less of a "presidential history" than a study of political economy in an era of capitalist transformation. Judith believed that Clinton's coming of age in an impoverished Arkansas was important to the story, and so did I; she also thought progressive intellectuals of that era wanted a post–Cold War variety of American capitalism to emulate some of the industrial policy innovations found in Japan and Germany. She had therefore begun to probe the contradictory character of US trade policy from Reagan through Clinton, an issue whose combustible importance Donald Trump seemed to ratify during his 2016 campaign.

Those issues are explored in this book, but as I began my own research and writing I vastly expanded the scope of the work and also tilted away from Judith's interpretation in notable ways. Chapters and sections on the politics of Wall Street and the Federal Reserve, on the collapse of Clinton's Health Security Act, on welfare reform and criminal justice, and on efforts to transform the American workplace, expand trade and investment with China, deregulate banking and telecommunications, and financially coerce East Asian regimes during the late 1990s offered me a broader canvas upon which to evaluate the Clinton years. I've entitled this book *A Fabulous Failure* because I don't think historians or journalists are justified in comfortably labeling Bill Clinton and an important slice of his team either centrist New Democrats or neoliberal ideologues on the day they marched into the White House. Clinton's failure lay in presiding over a tangible but thwarted progressive politics as well as a misguided effort to find market solutions to social problems.

Most of the research was conducted either at the Butler Center for Arkansas Studies in Little Rock, the Clinton Presidential Library, or the latter's invaluable online portal. I conducted phone interviews or email exchanges with Jeff Faux, Jeffrey Garten, David Kusnet, Robert Kuttner, Ira Magaziner, Clyde Prestowitz, Derek Shearer, Joseph Stiglitz, and William Julius Wilson. I found highly useful the extensive set of oral histories the University of Virginia's Miller Center conducted with many leading administration figures; also useful were interviews found at the University of California at Berkeley and the Corporation for Public Broadcasting.

Various chapters in this book were offered as papers delivered to prepandemic audiences at the University of Michigan Law School, Paris Diderot University, the Global Labor Migration Summit in Amsterdam, and the Universities of Nottingham and Birmingham in the United Kingdom. Life during the Covid-19 pandemic was no fun, but it did make Zoom presentations routine: I spoke at workshops and round-tables hosted by Clara Mattei at the New School for Social Research, Gary Gerstle at the University of Cambridge, Andrew Hartman and Elizabeth Shermer at the Newberry Library Seminar in the History of Capitalism, and Leon Fink at the Washington Labor History Workshop. I also received good feedback from a presentation delivered at a 2021 meeting of the Society for US Intellectual History.

Sandy Dijkstra and her entire team in San Diego, especially Elise Capron and Andrea Cavallaro, proved patient, hardworking, and resourceful. Sandy played a key role in helping me sharpen my argument, consider the audience, and find a publisher, even when "Clinton fatigue" seemed to stand against us. Samir Sonti and Andrew Elrod also helped me conceptualize the project in its early stages. Representing the Judith Stein estate, Jonathan Stein shipped to me four boxes of research materials assembled by his sister and proved cooperative and supportive as we worked out the legal and financial division of responsibilities.

During the fall of 2021 a group of recent PhDs in history and political economy offered me invaluable commentary as they discussed the nearly completed manuscript in a series of biweekly Zoom workshops. This intergenerational dialogue included Tim Barker, Andrew Elrod, Ted Fertik, Max Fraser, and Gabriel Winant. Gary Gerstle helped steer the book toward Princeton University Press and then offered an extraordinary reading that materially improved the work. Meg Jacobs also provided dozens of pages of commentary and correction, much of which I was able to assimilate into the final product. Kim Phillips-Fein read the entire manuscript, likewise an anonymous reader for Princeton. In addition, portions of the book were reviewed and suggestions offered by Eric Arnesen, Eileen Boris, George Cotkin, David Kusnet, Robert Kuttner, Clyde Prestowitz, Derek Shearer, Elizabeth Shermer, Kirsten Swinth, and Lee Vinsel.

At Princeton, Bridget Flannery-McCoy has been a wonderfully hands-on editor whose insightful, eminently constructive guidance has made the final revision of this book something close to a pleasure. Cynthia Buck edited the copy with much skill, Kathleen Cioffi pulled the manuscript into production, and James O'Brien once again caught last-minute errors as he prepared the index.

Eileen Boris played a crucial role as well. At our dinner table, as I waxed on about each topic and theme, she probed the narrative for elisions and contradictions. And Eileen, a keen student of the American welfare state, made sure I devoted ample space to two of the most controversial pieces of Clinton-era legislation, the 1994 crime bill and the welfare reform that followed two years later.

A FABULOUS FAILURE

Introduction

At the dawn of Bill Clinton's presidency, the management and reform of American capitalism stood at the top of his agenda. One could glimpse the progressive and expansive promise of a newly empowered generation when on December 14 and 15, 1992, the Clinton transition team assembled more than three hundred of the nation's leading economists, executives, politicians, and policy entrepreneurs in Little Rock for an "economic summit." Almost all agreed with strategist James Carville's now-famous catch phrase, "The Economy, Stupid," first posted on a wall of the Clinton campaign's "war room."[1] It was time for the government to offer a forceful set of initiatives designed to increase the productivity of capital and labor, transform key industry sectors, and enhance the quality of American life. "We must revitalize and rebuild our economy," said the president-elect, but "we clearly face structural problems that today threaten our ability to harness the energies of all of our people."[2] On display was an adventuresome range of ideas about what to do now that the Democrats once again controlled the White House and the Congress after nearly two decades of frustration, defeat, and economic dislocation under every president since Richard Nixon. There were plenty of corporate chieftains in attendance, not so much to balance the academics and think-tank liberals with a more conservative outlook as to demonstrate that the underperformance of the American economy was so debilitating that they too had a stake in efforts to rehabilitate industries and enterprises, especially those threatened by new competitors abroad and burdened by out-of-control health care expenses at home.

Those assembled would not make any decisions, but the conclave was more than just a well-choreographed show. Bill Clinton was an engaged and expert ringmaster. For nearly ten hours each day, he sat in a swivel chair at the head of a large oval arrangement of tables, taking notes, asking questions, and offering his views about topics ranging from infrastructure to interest rates, technology and taxes, and energy and the environment, plus trade policy, health insurance reform, and the economic impact of chronic budget deficits at the federal level. As the *New York Times* observed, Clinton was "teacher, student, preacher, the President-elect played all the parts well."[3] Even Republicans were impressed. "After four years of watching the Bush team amateurs, it's fun to watch the pros play again," said Martin Anderson, one of President Reagan's domestic policy advisers.[4] Although no one compared the 1992 Clinton victory to FDR's election sixty years before, there seemed to be an ideological and generational coherence to the Clinton cadre that evoked a fresh set of hopes and aspirations. James Tobin, who had served on President John Kennedy's Council of Economic Advisers, told the Little Rock conferees, "The excitement of this transition reminds me of the transition to the Kennedy Administration in 1960, which I enjoyed as well." And Robert Kuttner of *The American Prospect*, who would soon become disenchanted with the Clinton White House, told the same assemblage, "Words fail me in describing what an extraordinary event this is. . . . This is a magical moment."[5]

The reforms explored at the Little Rock economic summit were tangible and within an ambitious grasp. It did not seem impossible for Clinton and his allies to make health insurance nearly universal, to stimulate not just economic growth in general but specific industries and occupations that were socially and ecologically important, to manage trade so as to preserve factories and jobs, to enact a welfare reform that did not repudiate a New Deal entitlement, and even to regulate Wall Street finance. Structural reforms of this sort promised to break with Reaganite laissez-faire and renew the allegiance of blue-collar voters to the party of Roosevelt, Truman, Kennedy, and Johnson.

Moreover, during the 1990s the Clinton administration had the good fortune, and perhaps the actual skill, to preside over an economy that grew at a steady 4 percent a year. The economist Robert Gordon called it the "Goldilocks economy" because it was neither too hot nor too cold.[6] Real wages were rising, the stock market boomed, and for a few years at the end of the decade the federal budget actually ran a surplus. High tech was flying high, likewise real estate and finance. Declared *Fortune* in 1997, "Job prospects are terrific. Unemployment is lower than it's been in nearly a quarter century. Business sales and profits are growing handsomely."[7] Liberal Keynesians Alan Blinder and Janet Yellen, both of whom served in the administration, called those years "The Fabulous Decade."[8]

Today, however, Clinton's presidency wins little respect. Few liberals want to return the Democratic Party to that era because so many see his presidency as a betrayal of the progressivism that was once the hallmark of the New Deal and the Great Society. Bill Clinton was the first Democratic president since FDR to win two consecutive terms, but that accomplishment seems merely a product of his accommodation to an ideology that privileged trade liberalization, financial deregulation, and privatization of government services, while tolerating the growth of class inequalities. President Clinton has been labeled "the Democratic Eisenhower," the popular leader of a political party whose electoral success was predicated upon a wholesale accommodation to the ideology of its opponents. Clinton's 1996 declaration that "the era of big government is over" seemingly ratified Reaganite conservatism and in the process transformed Republican politics and policy into a hegemonic ethos that liberated global finance and eviscerated Keynesian liberalism.[9]

This general view made it easy enough for journalists and academics to simply declare the administration of Bill Clinton a neoliberal project and leave it at that. Lily Geismer, noting that the president described himself as a "new kind of Democrat," emphasized that he took a "market-based approach" to virtually all social and economic issues. Gary Gerstle wrote that after losing Congress in 1994 Clinton became "America's neoliberal president par excellence."[10] The journalist Ryan Cooper thought that "neoliberal ideas held hegemonic sway among the Democratic elite,"[11] while the *Guardian*'s George Monbiot concluded his story on the rise of neoliberalism by asserting, "The man who sank Hillary Clinton's bid for the presidency was not Donald Trump. It was her husband."[12]

The word "neoliberalism" is a "linguistic omnivore," as Daniel Rodgers reminds us.[13] Although hardly in use during the 1990s, it became shorthand in the next decade for the liberalization of trade, the deregulation of finance, the privatization of government services, reductions of taxes on the rich, and the evisceration of the labor movement and the welfare state. That the Clinton administration embarked on this path is without doubt. His presidency not only saw passage of the North American Free Trade Agreement (NAFTA) in 1993 but also the end of a New Deal entitlement in the welfare reform of 1996 and protests against the World Trade Organization (WTO)—and in particular against US support for China's entry to that organization—in the 1999 Battle of Seattle, which put environmentalists and union labor on the same side of the barricade. This book explores these Clinton administration forays, but it also illuminates some overlooked initiatives that trended in the same market-oriented direction: the effort to "reinvent" government championed by Vice President Al Gore, the deregulation of the telecommunications industry, the rise of a gargantuan market in financial derivatives, and the insistence during the financial crisis that wracked Mexico, East Asia, and other countries that the free flow of global capital, largely from Wall Street and London, would not be abridged regardless of the social or political consequences.

But the neoliberal project was never a seamless unfolding of an all-encompassing ideology, springing full blown from the mind of a Friedrich Hayek or Milton Friedman. Nor was it a Wall Street scheme foisted upon the nation through blunt financial power. Neoliberalism contrived to "fail-and-fall forward" declared the sociologist Jamie Peck, in a "churning and contradictory process."[14] The capitalist world "stumbled towards neoliberalization" through a series of "gyrations and chaotic experiments," wrote David Harvey, who more than anyone made the word popular. Harvey recognized that neither Bill Clinton nor Tony Blair was entirely a true believer, emphasizing the degree to which these two "Third Way" politicians found themselves in a political world where "their room for maneuver was so limited" that they could not help but advance the neoliberal project, if sometimes against their own better instincts.[15] As Stuart Hall famously put it, "Hegemonizing is hard work."[16]

Bill Clinton's path to power was not driven by an ideology that can be securely labeled "neoliberal." Much of his economic and social policymaking would eventually reside there, but the crucial question—and the central subject of this book—is the how and why of that transmutation. What was contingent and what was driven by the logic of politics and political economy, both global and domestic? Within the country, the Congress, the administration, and the mind of Bill Clinton himself, much was left unsettled between the time the Arkansas governor burst upon the national political scene in the 1980s and the chaotic aftermath of the election between George W. Bush and Al Gore in December 2000. Ideas and proposals were subject to intense debate, first among the ever-growing "Friends of Bill" and then within the White House, among Democratic officeholders, and in academe, think tanks, foundations, journals, and the Democratic Party in all its manifestations. "The lingua franca of this network was the language of policy, the specifics of governmental activism," wrote the journalist and White House aide Sidney Blumenthal, who first met the Arkansas governor at one of the "Renaissance Weekend" talkfests that Bill and Hillary attended almost every New Year's Eve in the 1980s. Blumenthal saw Clinton approaching new ideas and proposals like they were "jazz riffs," which he played "until he felt he had improvised the right composition. And then he would start again."[17]

When Bill Clinton came to power, none of his partisans, from the White House on down, were Cold War triumphalists. Many agreed with Senator Paul Tsongas, Clinton's most formidable opponent in the Democratic primaries: "The Cold War is over: Germany and Japan won." That there were other "varieties of capitalism" in the world—more competitive, dynamic, and socially cohesive than the version championed by Ronald Reagan and Margaret Thatcher—would prove a powerful motivating impulse for an effort to "manage" American capitalism during the first years of his presidency. Clinton had come from a poor, Southern, rural state, and he spent the bulk of his energy as governor seeking some way to attract industry, raise wages, and increase worker skills and education. He was therefore amenable to an "industrial policy" that deployed state policy, not just the market, to target economic development. Clinton's appointment of three of the highest-profile advocates of such a program—Robert Reich to head the Department of Labor, Laura Tyson to serve as chair of the Council of Economic Advisers (CEA), and Ira Magaziner to be in charge of the administration's ambitious health reform—was an indication of the degree to which the label "neoliberal" fails to capture the original ideological and policy thrust of his administration.

Clinton and his team sometimes found support among elements of the business community who saw a decline in profitability and international completeness as a problem that demanded a solution from an activist government. Chrysler's Lee Iacocca once declared that he was ready to become a socialist if that doctrine could reduce his company's bloated health insurance costs. Thus, Clinton and Ira Magaziner banked upon the support not only of liberals and organized labor but of an important slice of the business community—largely unionized manufacturers and big insurance companies—to muscle the health reform scheme through Congress. That scheme was a far more radical and market-regulating proposal than anything advanced by Barak Obama fifteen years later.

Likewise, Robert Reich thought high-tech industry could lead the nation toward policies that would create a far better educated workforce and might even be willing to accept a greater degree of unionism if, in return, companies had a free hand in boosting productivity and skills through new forms of German-style work organization. This would prove an illusion, but Reich was not alone in proposing that the government incentivize a "responsible" corporate leadership to avoid mass layoffs and excessive executive salaries. In similar fashion, trade policy also constituted a species of "industrial policy" since it was of vital importance, for ill or boon, to specific economic sectors and industry groups. Thus, in dealing with China, trade officials protected Hollywood and Silicon Valley from rampant pirating of their intellectual property (films and software). But the Office of the US Trade Representative, initially under the adept leadership of Mickey Kantor, an old Friend of Bill, also achieved agreements that enabled China to flood the

United States with consumer products advantaged by low wages and an undervalued yen, thus decimating many of the heartland towns and cities where toy, apparel, furniture, and appliance factories had once thrived. However, the American capacity to reshape the global economy had its limits. Much to the displeasure of Treasury Secretary Robert Rubin, a former Goldman Sachs executive, Wall Street did not win the open investment door in China that it had long sought. China was becoming an imperial power, one where neoliberal rules, especially those made in America, did not always apply.

This book explains why and how Clinton's expansive agenda ended in failure and why that failure haunts us still. The failure was actually twofold. In the first instance, Clinton faced defeat when seeking to enact progressive reforms, from health insurance to labor rights, not only because of fierce opposition from Republicans and conservatives but also because the political and economic terrain upon which he hoped to construct a more progressive America was growing smaller and more fragile. Clinton confronted a changing economy that was restructuring many of the old political and social categories—creating, for example, bitter divisions within the business community, eviscerating the labor movement, and heightening Wall Street influence. Clinton partisans thought a technologically advanced "new economy" would demand— and fund—a more highly skilled workforce, far greater employment opportunities, and a higher standard of living. But that Panglossian thinking was belied by the harsh dynamic still at work in the world of American capitalism. Reform-oriented manufacturers carried far less political and economic weight than either low-wage, low-benefit, anti-union firms like PepsiCo and Marriott or the Wall Street financial titans who championed capital mobility at all costs. Great fortunes were created in both Silicon Valley and booming northwest Arkansas, the latter home to Wal-Mart and Tyson Foods, but these avatars of the new economy were hardly allies when it came to either industrial policy at home or managed trade abroad.

The global terrain also tilted toward the right. The end of the Cold War had transformed the economic world in two decisive ways. First, the potential labor force available to make things had just about doubled

with the opening of Eastern Europe and East Asia to export manufacture. That would generate a nearly irresistible demand to globalize production that had once been solely domestic. And second, the end of the
Cold War had left no actually existing alternative to some sort of capitalism. There were "varieties" of capitalism, but the competitive absence
of any other noncapitalist system, authoritarian or democratic, now
constrained even an imaginative quest for a viable, radical alternative to
the status quo. The lack of alternatives had the pervasive impact of shifting economic discourse toward market solutions.[18]

But an even greater failure may well have arisen from what the Clinton administration did accomplish: creating a surplus in the federal
budget, downsizing the government workforce, enacting an ambitious
crime control law, passing NAFTA, constructing a pathway for China
to join the WTO, and deregulating both Wall Street finance and America's vast telecommunications infrastructure. Wall Street boomed and
unemployment dropped, but in the end none of these reforms moved
the nation toward the economic stability, social equality, and global
democratic resurgence that the president and his chief economic advisers had promised. Trade with China, they had prophesied, would undoubtedly create the conditions for a free press, the entrepreneurial
freedom, and the autonomy, both individual and organizational, necessary to sustain a robust civil society in that ancient nation. A democratic
effervescence was sure to accompany all those new cell phones, stock
markets, and supermarkets.

Moreover, virtually every legislative victory scored by the Clinton
administration, especially in the years after 1994, was achieved over the
strong objections of a substantial portion of his own party. On any issue
that involved an expansion of the welfare state or progressive taxation,
the Democrats stood well to the left of the Republicans—and increasingly
so after the rightward lurch of the GOP when Newt Gingrich became
Speaker of the House in 1995. But on many other Clinton initiatives,
especially those involving trade and financial deregulation, the White
House relied on Republican votes, while a large fraction of the Democrats, sometimes even a majority, stood in opposition to their own
president. Democratic Party loyalty saved Bill Clinton during the

impeachment crisis of late 1998, but his contradictory effort to win a measure of bipartisan support on highly contentious issues made him a dreadful party leader.

"Managing" the economy is usually thought of as a project of progressives, but Wall Street and its allies were even more potent and ambitious during the Clinton administration. Neoliberalism, whatever its form, was not laissez-faire. It required the deployment of sovereign power on a scale just as far reaching as that of any proposed by those on the left side of the polity. During the Clinton years two institutions of federal governance—the Federal Reserve and the Treasury Department—were powerful, nearly unaccountable managers of both the domestic American economy and that of the nation's trading and investment regime abroad. The Fed was virtually a fourth branch of government, a "central planner that dare not speak its name."[19] To accommodate Chair Alan Greenspan's requirement that the federal budget deficit decline in rapid and sustained order, Bill Clinton and his advisers cobbled together an austerity budget in 1993 that abandoned one progressive campaign promise after another. Then, in 1994, Greenspan's Fed unexpectedly raised interest rates, wreaking havoc from Orange County to Mexico, but two years later the Federal Reserve let the rates fall, despite full employment and a roaring stock market. That sustained American prosperity but also created a series of "asset bubbles" that distorted and endangered huge sectors of the US economy. This "asset price Keynesianism" helped advance the late 1990s boom, but it would prove unsustainable after the turn of the new millennium.[20]

Meanwhile, the Treasury Department became the most important institution of governance in the Clinton administration. The deregulation of Wall Street finance and the forced draft transformation of foreign economies from Mexico to South Korea and Indonesia came under the leadership of Wall Streeter Robert Rubin, a welfare state liberal who nevertheless argued that the mobility of capital in all of its baroque forms was the key to the low interest rates and booming asset values that he thought would ensure investment, profits, and full employment. At home, Treasury had a virtual free hand, especially in the second half of the 1990s, when the president was consumed with reelection, scandal, and impeachment. Abroad, Treasury pursued a strong-arm strategy during the Asian financial crisis against the opposition of the State Department, the CEA, and Bill Clinton himself. At home, another Treasury project, the "modernization" of American finance, facilitated even more mergers on Wall Street, while creating conditions for an explosion of derivatives, those highly volatile securities whose multitrillion-dollar collapse in 2007 and 2008 helped inaugurate the most severe financial crisis since the Great Depression.

Ideology, illusion, and interest shaped the Clinton presidency and the shifting economic structures over which it presided. If Clinton and like-minded Friends of Bill were hardly neoliberals when they first occupied the White House, they had moved far in that direction by the time they departed. But this shift in policy and rhetoric was not merely a product of defeat at the hands of corporate enemies and political foes. It was also bred by the set of seductive illusions explored in this book. The Clinton administration's assumption that a new world of technology and markets would lay the basis for both an era of prosperity and progressive statecraft proved sorely mistaken. Instead, the financialized capitalism that Bill Clinton came to champion generated inequality and crisis, opening the door to retrograde forces they had barely imagined. The path toward the management of a capitalist polity would prove far more difficult than Clinton's partisans could imagine, but it is only by grappling with the obstacles they faced and the choices they made that we might avoid such failures in the future.

PART I

"The Economy Stupid"

1

How Arkansas Educated Bill Clinton

Bill Clinton came of age in the segregationist South. His values were animated by the revolution in race relations that came out of the 1960s, by opposition to the Vietnam War, and by sojourns at the nation's elite universities. He was not a "movement" New Leftist, but rather a Southern progressive who had the good fortune to win office and influence during the unique political moment that followed the liberating impact of the civil rights movement, when Democrats in the South could rely upon a biracial electorate to sustain their ambitions. That era would end abruptly in the 1990s, but by then Clinton had vaulted to the national stage. The journalist turned White House aide Sidney Blumenthal labeled him "the leading meritocrat of America's first mass generation of college-educated meritocrats."[1]

However, his experience as an Arkansas politician—he spent far longer in the Little Rock governor's mansion than in the White House—remained a shaping influence. As the chief executive of one of the nation's most impoverished states, Clinton saw his main task as the transformation of the state's economy in an era when a booming "Sun Belt" seemed to promise a new prosperity based on a higher level of education, deployment of advanced technology in the region's workplaces, and sometimes even a more equitable level of taxation. To this end Clinton sought out the latest developmental ideas from Europe, the Far East, and a network of increasingly influential policy entrepreneurs and governmental colleagues at home. But if Clinton's political ambitions were virtually unlimited, his economic programs were always well constrained by the hard demands of the Arkansas business class, an often skeptical electorate, and the absence of either a vigorous civil rights movement or a powerful set of unions that might have backstopped his more adventuresome social policies. In Arkansas, Clinton was therefore an opportunist, sometimes creatively adventurous when the stars were fortuitously aligned, but just as readily a cynic and a cad, willing to abandon allies and promises when faced with the sort of opposition all too common in a state once loyal to the old Confederacy.

The Education of a Meritocrat

Bill Clinton was born right after World War II, the son of a mother determined to give herself and her offspring more of a chance in life than would ordinarily arise out of an upbringing in small-town Arkansas. Clinton's smarts and his striving ambition came from her. Meanwhile, his alcoholic stepfather created the tensions in a home life that Bill had to surmount as well. His extraordinary capacity for creating and maintaining a circle of friends, his instinctive desire to reconcile potential enemies, his charm and his empathy may well have arisen out of the boy's efforts to negotiate a productive adolescence threatened by a sometimes violent father figure. And like so many other successful sons of the South, Clinton sought meritocratic legitimacy elsewhere, even as he advertised his identification with its folkways—race being the great exception— and his determination to build a political career on home turf.

As an undergraduate at Georgetown University and a Rhodes Scholar at Oxford, Clinton was very much the cautious radical, the student who both worked within the mainstream and sought to lead it. At Georgetown he did not join the 1967 March on the Pentagon, nor did he work for Senator Eugene McCarthy, the insurgent, antiwar Democrat in the 1968 presidential primaries. He identified with Arkansas Senator William Fulbright, who used his chairmanship of the Foreign Relations Committee, where Clinton interned, to advance a measured critique of the war. Indeed, Clinton was voted out of his class presidency in the fall of 1967 because his campaign slogan, "A Realistic Approach to Student Government," proved so tepid.[2] At Oxford he lived amid other young people more activist in the antiwar movement than he was; on his return to the

United States in the summer of 1970, he joined Project Purse Strings, an attempt to persuade Congress to starve the war effort of funds.

Had Clinton not become a national political figure, his troubled encounter with the Selective Service System would have simply confirmed his membership in that large cohort of similarly conflicted young men who were desperate to avoid being drafted to fight an unpopular war. Contacted by his draft board while he was at Oxford, Clinton used his political connections to delay and defer a military obligation. He did not declare himself a conscientious objector or an outright draft resister but instead sought and obtained a spot in the ROTC at the University of Arkansas, where, he told home-state draft authorities, he planned to study law. But then fortune intervened. The government instituted a lottery to determine who would be drafted, Clinton lucked out with a high number, and he was off to Yale Law School with many of his Rhodes Scholar friends. His promise to join the Arkansas ROTC unit evaporated without a second thought—or so it seemed until it returned with a vengeance when Clinton sought national office twenty years later.

If the more outré examples of early 1970s antiwar radicalism held no appeal for Bill Clinton, campaign politics proved much more to his liking. Yale Law School was then in an exceedingly liberal phase and made few day-to-day demands on its enrollees. So Clinton had the time and opportunity to volunteer for the campaign of Joseph Duffey, a peace candidate and former McCarthy partisan who successfully challenged the hawkish Senator Thomas Dodd in the 1972 Connecticut Democratic primary. Because Dodd ran as an independent in the fall, Duffey lost to the liberal Republican Lowell Weicker in the general election, but the experience widened Clinton's circle of politically engaged friends and primed him for more campaigning. That came in the fall of 1972 when McGovern campaign manager Gary Hart sent Clinton and another novice from the South, the journalist Taylor Branch, to win Texas. That was a hopeless task, but one that confirmed Clinton's determination to return to his Southern home turf to test his own electability.[3]

With his Oxford and Yale pedigrees, Clinton had little trouble persuading a faculty hiring committee to give him a job at the University of Arkansas Law School at Fayetteville. He never took that job with any seriousness: from the start he was on the lookout for an opportunity to run for a political office. That task was soon advanced when he persuaded Hillary Rodham, his Yale classmate, girlfriend, and the woman he considered "the smartest person he had ever met," to join him in Fayetteville, where she also took a post at the law school. Their marriage would be tempestuous, but Hillary always put her considerable talents at the service of Bill's career. Even before they married, she told everyone she knew that Clinton was destined to be president. Hillary actually had the more accomplished résumé, capped by an exciting year working as a staffer with the House Judiciary Committee's impeachment investigation of Richard Nixon, but none could gainsay Bill's charismatic persona. Hillary stood just to the left of him on most issues, but she could be as flexible as her husband when political necessity demanded. When Rodham arrived in Arkansas, she was a firm opponent of the death penalty and while teaching at Fayetteville helped prepare the successful appeal of a prisoner on death row. However, by the time Clinton had become governor, with the power to grant or deny stays of execution, she had changed her position, if not her mind.[4]

The Burden of Arkansas History

When Clinton returned home in 1973, his state was then among the poorest in the nation, with a per capita income only 43 percent of the rest of the United States. Arkansas had been "Dogpatch" since the nineteenth century, when Mark Twain, in *Huckleberry Finn*, wrote of its residents as "Arkansaw lunkheads." A diagonal drawn from northwest Arkansas to the southeast divides the state and its history. The east and south, the delta and gulf plains, were part of the Deep South plantation economy, with a large African-American population. The highlands of the north and west, the rugged Ouachita and Ozark Mountains, were settled by small-scale and subsistence farmers who, lacking the capital, had no need for slaves. During the Civil War the Union Army recruited heavily in northwest Arkansas, which helped make Arkansas second only to Tennessee in the number of volunteers from a Confederate state who fought alongside the Yankees.[5]

Biracial politics retained a presence in the state well into the 1890s, when the planter elite, backed by railroad interests, displaced rivals of either a Republican or Populist lineage. Violence and fraud were built into this regime change. In the Ozarks, a wave of white brutality forced half of the local Blacks to flee the region. Thereafter, poll taxes, disenfranchisement, and one-party rule ensured that voting participation and civic life would remain depressed. In his classic *Southern Politics in State and Nation*, V. O. Key concluded in 1949 that "conservatives control without serious challenge. In Arkansas, more than almost any other Southern state, social and economic issues of significance to the people have lain ignored."[6] Although Arkansas had the lowest percentage of Blacks among all the old Confederate states—about 15 percent—race remained pivotal to state politics; the battle over the desegregation of Little Rock's Central High School in 1957, for instance, remained an open wound well into the 1960s.[7]

In a poor state, the few rich residents have an outsized influence. Even as the power of the Delta planters was beginning to wane in the postwar era, the decline of subsistence agriculture in the rest of the state was laying the basis for the rise of a new generation of entrepreneurs. By the 1970s Little Rock was still the only real city, with a metro area of 300,000 people, but northwest Arkansas, where fast-growing Wal-Mart and Tyson Foods were headquartered, was booming. The fortunes of these two companies were advantaged by a postwar agricultural revolution that swept the old Southwest, especially Missouri, Oklahoma, Arkansas, and Texas. In the Ozarks, mechanization and fertilizers helped consolidate thousands of farms and wiped out two-thirds of the rest, leaving many rural families, still farming or not, desperate for any local job. Both Wal-Mart and Tyson Foods needed a reliable delivery system, so Arkansas's J. B. Hunt Transport Services, a trucking company, also headquartered in the northwest quadrant of the state, grew along with them. Trucking wages, like those of retail workers and those who labored on the poultry disassembly line, were a notch lower in right-to-work Arkansas than in more heavily unionized Missouri. And all three of these big firms—Wal-Mart, Tyson Foods, and Hunt—were backed by the biggest investment group west of the

Mississippi, Little Rock's Stephens Investment Bank. The Stephens family made their initial fortune buying Arkansas bonds that had been heavily discounted during the Depression era; later they made even more money supplying credit to a region long neglected by Wall Street. The Stephens Investment Bank made its weight felt in state politics, backing cautious modernizers like Bill Clinton as long as they did not try to tax or regulate the big boys too intrusively.[8]

Elite control of Arkansas was not uncontested. During World War II organized labor won a solid foothold in the munitions plants, the paper industry, construction, and trucking, and by the end of the 1960s the state had the highest proportion of unionized workers—17.5 percent—in the South. Although Arkansas's planters, bankers, and utility executives pushed through stringent antilabor legislation, including the nation's first "right-to-work" law in 1944, the new political environment encouraged labor leaders to create a broad coalition, one including African Americans, that could challenge the power of the big mules, raise taxes, and pull the state more than one step above Mississippi on all the social indexes measuring literacy, income, welfare, and housing that had generated such condescension from the rest of the country. The movement found a leader in Sidney McMath, who won the first of his two terms as governor in 1948. McMath increased aid for Black schools, integrated the state's universities, extended electrification to rural areas, raised the minimum wage, and fought the Dixiecrat element within the Democratic Party. Allied with the labor movement, in state and out, McMath tried to end the poll tax and the election fraud long routine in the plantation districts. He lost those battles, as well as an effort to defeat Senator John L. McClellan in a 1952 Democratic primary, but the state gradually shed its gothic past. By 1968, just after the Twenty-Fourth Amendment abolished the federal poll tax, and in a state whose population had hardly increased at all, more than 600,000 voters, Black and white, flocked to the polls, up from less than a quarter million two decades before.

Arkansas labor stood in the vanguard of change, both racial and economic. Post-Brown racism in the state had pulled the newly elected governor, Orval Faubus, a socialist-bred politician who had come out of the

McMath administration, well to the right. When Faubus threw in his lot with opponents of integration at Central High School in Little Rock, the Arkansas AFL-CIO was the only white civic group to stand in public opposition to the governor. The building trades sided with the segregationists, but that merely enabled the rest of the Arkansas labor movement to shift leftward. These unionists were not radical, but they were the most important force in the state that consistently sought to democratize politics. In 1959 white Teamsters drove African Americans to the polls when the main issue was keeping public schools open, and in the 1960s some white unionists cooperated with the young radicals in the Student Nonviolent Coordinating Committee (SNCC) to organize workplaces in southwest Arkansas. Labor's greatest victory came in 1964 when Faubus finally agreed to support an AFL-CIO measure reforming the voter registration system and repealing the state's poll tax.[9]

Many veterans of the Arkansas freedom struggle went to work for the labor movement in the wake of the Central High crisis. Ernest Green, the de facto leader of the Black students who integrated Central High, later worked alongside Bayard Rustin at labor's A. Philip Randolph Institute. Championing interracial unionism, Green declared that if "we stand divided and separated, big business and big industry will triumph again in the South."[10]

This was a sentiment heartily endorsed by J. Bill Becker, a Chicago-born clothing union organizer who would come to lead the Arkansas AFL-CIO from the early 1960s through the late 1990s. By expanding the voter rolls and helping consign race-baiting to the margins of political discourse, Becker and other unionists opened the door for ambitious men and women of limited means and connections to win office by appealing to a biracial coalition of increasing weight within the state Democratic Party. This was the foundation from which Bill Clinton launched his meteoric career. Indeed, many from the ranks of labor and from the African-American community saw this young and cosmopolitan politician as the embodiment of their most expansive political and social aspirations. But their hopes would be subverted time and again by what Becker and many others saw as little more than Clinton's calculated betrayal. It was a calculation made by others as well, based upon a reading of what was politically and economically possible in post-1960s Arkansas, but it was a betrayal nonetheless.

Clinton's Rise

As a Southern Democrat of the Vietnam generation, Clinton ran for elective office at a most fortuitous time. The segregationist Democrats who had once dominated politics were clearly in retreat, African Americans were voting in record numbers, and a more moderate Democratic Party still held the residual loyalty of millions of lower-income white voters. To a degree this allegiance was based on their support of the New Deal economic liberalism, which had materially improved living standards throughout the South. Working-class white voters would eventually migrate to the GOP, but not in the 1970s.[11] The culture wars over sexuality, immigration, religion, and abortion had not yet been fully engaged; meanwhile, class politics still retained an animating power, especially during the sharp recession of 1973 and 1974. Across the South nine first-term Republicans lost in 1974, reversing much Nixon-era growth of the GOP in the region.[12] In Arkansas David Pryor, a young Democrat of modestly progressive views, was elected governor, while Senator J. William Fulbright lost his long-held seat when the sitting governor, Dale Bumpers, a far more liberal figure, defeated him in a Democratic primary and then went on to win his Senate seat in the general election that November. In Arkansas politics, Fulbright had been old guard, opposing most civil rights legislation, defending the oil industry, advocating for higher energy prices, and retaining the support of the state's utility interests. Bumpers easily outflanked him as a home-grown populist.[13] Two years later the Southern tide was still with the Democrats as Georgia governor Jimmy Carter won every Southern state save Virginia and Oklahoma in his campaign for president. By way of contrast, in the 1992 presidential contest Bill Clinton would win just five states in the South: Arkansas and Al Gore's home state of Tennessee, plus Louisiana, Kentucky, and Georgia.

In 1974 Bill Clinton ran a spirited campaign to unseat an incumbent Republican representative, John Paul Hammerschmidt, a conservative

FIGURE 1. Hillary Rodham and Bill Clinton campaigning, 1978.
(Butler Center for Arkansas Studies)

defender of President Nixon, who took good care of the timber, poultry, and trucking interests of northwest Arkansas. Clinton lost by just six thousand votes, but his charm, energy, and capacity to tap into Watergate-era disdain for corruption, gasoline rationing, and 1970s-era stagflation served him very well indeed.[14] In a speech to the state Democratic convention in September, Clinton, just twenty-eight years old at the time, denounced targets of a classic populist sort: Mobil Oil, New York banks, and the Arab kingdoms that had inaugurated the oil boycott. "The people want a hand up—not a handout," he said. Among those who thrilled to his campaign were the state's trade unionists, who whooped and applauded a speech Clinton delivered at the 1974 convention of the Arkansas AFL-CIO in Hot Springs. "Our people just fell in love with the guy," recalled the AFL-CIO's Becker in an interview several years later. His campaign jingle—by a country singer sounding very much like Arkansas native Johnny Cash—included the refrain "Bill

Clinton's ready, he's fed up too. He's a lot like me, he's a lot like you." Clinton raised at least 10 percent of his campaign funds from labor, whose contributions included volunteer door knocking by unionized steelworkers and teachers.[15]

Because Clinton had run such a terrific race in 1974, he had little trouble securing the nomination for state attorney general in 1976 and then winning the post with a healthy majority in the general election. Of course, Clinton was thinking about his next move, and in early 1977 he brought in a young political consultant, Richard Morris, who had once been active in New York City reform Democratic circles but was now well on his way to adopting a far more cynical, if highly effective, approach to politics. Backed by a set of convincing polls, Morris told Clinton that the governor's race would be a sure bet, while running for the Senate would be far riskier because he would have to campaign against the popular governor, David Pryor, who also sought election to the upper house. So Clinton campaigned for the statehouse and easily won. At thirty-two, he became the youngest chief executive of any state in nearly a century.[16] Throughout this climb to higher office, Clinton projected himself as an insurgent who targeted some of the most powerful interests in the state. As attorney general, he successfully challenged the regional telephone company when it sought to raise the price of a pay phone call from a dime to a quarter. When he was governor, his Energy Department forced Arkansas Power and Light to refund several million dollars in overcharges to its customers. Clinton thereby joined Pryor and Bumpers as reformers who divvied up the state's top positions into the 1990s. They were social liberals and administrative modernizers, appointing more women and African Americans to government than ever before.[17]

Although all three owed their good fortune to the labor movement's long struggle to expand the electorate, not to mention the money and precinct volunteers mobilized by the unions each time they ran for office, they all turned their backs on the trade unions in the political crunch. They did so both to accommodate the anti-unionism of the powerful set of entrepreneurs arising in northwest Arkansas and to undermine potential rivals on the left. Within labor circles Bumpers and Pryor are best remembered for their failure to back closure votes in

Congress, first in 1978 and then in 1994, when labor law reform bills stood their best chance of passage in decades.[18] Clinton traveled the same path. As attorney general, he spurned the unions by refusing to sign a petition to place an amendment on the ballot repealing the state's right-to-work law. Such statutes, common in the South and Mountain West, weakened organized labor by prohibiting unions from negotiating contracts that made union membership a condition of employment. Advised again by Morris, Clinton wrote a series of attack ads warning that unions were "disastrous for the economy of Arkansas." These televised advertisements were directed against Democrat Jim Guy Tucker, who in 1978 ran to the left of Pryor in the senatorial primary. Clinton rightly feared that Tucker might become a formidable rival in state politics. Later, during Clinton's first term as governor, he antagonized labor again when his administration highlighted the state's right-to-work status in a series of nationwide ads that sought to entice companies to relocate to the state.[19]

Clinton's disdain for the labor movement primarily reflected a political calculus about who held power and who did not in his state. There wasn't much industry in Arkansas, so the labor movement was relatively small. More important, the economic powerhouses emerging in northwest Arkansas—Wal-Mart, Tyson Foods, Hunt Transport—were militantly hostile to organized labor. But Clinton and many in his generation were also deeply ambivalent about the labor metaphysic itself, and certainly about the institutions that embodied the "industrial pluralism" that had once seemed so essential to American prosperity and democracy. Thus, in 1967, when Clinton was a junior at Georgetown, he was part of a panel discussion on the topic "Is Collective Bargaining Dead?" AFL-CIO president George Meany was the featured participant. Clinton avoided the attack mode of the other student panelists, all of whom were from the School of Business, but the query he addressed to Meany had its own sharp New Left flavor. "Many times institutions prove to be inflexible, restrictive and out of date," asserted Clinton. "Now, Mr. Meany, do you think that collective bargaining as an institutional arrangement may regiment men too far, and has become merely another institution against which man must assert himself?"[20]

State labor leaders thought Clinton's failure to back their campaign against right-to-work was a gratuitous ploy to use a well-publicized disagreement with a key part of the Democratic coalition in order to position himself as a centrist and thus as a more traditional white Southerner. Clinton seemed to agree, arguing that "this is a bad time because our people generally are in a conservative mood." But Clinton's rejection of any firm alliance with Arkansas labor was also a self-fulfilling prophecy. Hostility to unions was not in fact baked into the political cake of the mid-South in the mid-1970s. In nearby Missouri conservative proponents of a right-to-work law thought their well-funded efforts could put the union-crippling statute on the books in 1978. But the state labor movement fought back, and under the leadership of Jerry Tucker, a young and energetic UAW official, pro-union sentiments prevailed. For another generation Missouri remained a true border state, with higher wages than Arkansas and a far more robust labor-liberal presence than its neighbor to the south.[21]

The Arkansas elite saw Bill Clinton as another in a long line of young and ambitious politicians who could be groomed, they thought, to reconcile Arkansas poverty with elite hegemony. Even in 1974, as Clinton campaigned for Congress as something of a McGovern Democrat, the Tyson family financed a telephone bank for him, if only because Clinton denounced the Nixon grain deal with the Soviets that had jacked up feed prices for all those Ozark chickens destined for Tyson poultry processing plants. "He was young and he was impressive. I don't believe we ever talked about his politics," Don Tyson recalled years later. "The Arkansas system had always been to find some good young people and encourage them to work on the local level. The system kind of weeds them out. . . . It's like a horse race. You back three or four, so you always get a winner."[22] Clinton's alliance with Tyson Foods was sealed by Bill and Hillary's friendship with James Blair, an outside counsel for Tyson. It says a lot about the incestuous nature of small-state political life that Blair helped Hillary make a killing on the cattle futures market late in the 1970s even as she became an associate of Little Rock's prestigious Rose Law Firm, described by her biographer Carl Bernstein as "the ultimate establishment law firm" in the state. Its clients included Tyson

Foods, Wal-Mart, the Stephens brokerage business, and the *Arkansas Gazette*, then the state's largest and most influential newspaper.[23] This was how political and business life had been intertwined for generations in a state like Arkansas.

The Limits of Statehouse Liberalism

Clinton wanted to be the chief executive who began to pull his state out of the social cellar, but there were definite limits to what a reformer could do in a state that was still dominated by such a close-knit elite. When serving his first term as governor Clinton had promised Don Tyson that he would raise the weight limit on big trucks to eighty thousand pounds, a real boon for the company. That would put a burden on Arkansas roads, which were never in good shape to begin with, so Clinton wanted to raise vehicle taxes as well to pay for a more robust transportation infrastructure. The proposed taxes were proportional to the weight of the vehicle, so Tyson Foods, Wal-Mart, and other trucking-dependent companies would take a hit—a fair and progressive hit, thought Clinton, since these same firms would benefit directly from the higher weight limits. But they balked, mobilizing their minions in the state legislature against the weight-linked taxes. Clinton then shifted the weight of the new taxes to car owners. It was a characteristic maneuver: when confronting entrenched power Clinton would seek a way around, a compromise so as to take half a loaf rather than none at all. But such triangulation could also backfire, and it did so with disastrous consequences when Clinton ran for reelection in 1980. All those vehicle taxes now fell on the good old boys who drove their pickup trucks and heavy clunkers around rural Arkansas. They hated the cumbersome procedure that required them to get their vehicle inspected, prove they had paid last year's car tax, and then pay the higher car registration fees.[24]

Clinton lost his 1980 reelection bid to a conservative Republican. It was a humiliating defeat, a product of his own miscalculations on the car tax issue and the bad publicity that arose when several hundred Cuban refugees consigned to an Arkansas military base by President Carter—never a popular idea among the locals—escaped their confinement in a riotous breakout that was quelled only when Clinton sent in a large contingent of state police. Clinton had not publicly criticized Carter for settling eighteen thousand Cuban refugees at Fort Chafee, in part because they were both Democrats, but also because Clinton did not want to publicly challenge federal authority for fear that doing so would reawaken memories of segregationist defiance of the White House during the 1957 Central High School crisis. Of course, Clinton's gubernatorial opponent, Frank White, a former savings and loan executive and recent GOP convert, had no such hesitancy, using footage of rioting Cubans to indict Clinton for endangering Arkansas residents to placate a Democratic president.[25]

Clinton recaptured the governorship in 1982 after apologizing to the Arkansas electorate for past "errors." He was reelected in 1984, 1986 (now a four-year term), and 1990. His 1982 campaign, like his 1974 run for Congress, was fought in the midst of a recession, so Clinton campaigned as an anti-Reagan Democrat critical of high interest rates and job losses and anxious to do something about abysmal conditions in his state. "Our mission," said Betsey Wright, perhaps Clinton's most influential aide, "was to lift Arkansas out of its rut of poverty."[26]

More money for the schools became the defining issue of his second term. It had been forced on him after the Arkansas Supreme Court decided that the state's public education financing arrangements were unconstitutional because they denied equal opportunity to students in poor districts. Bill and Hillary Clinton became genuine enthusiasts for a reform. In the postsegregation era, a key element of elite sentiment in Arkansas was that government activism was legitimate as long as it enhanced economic development. This was especially true if a "new economy" based on high technology and global trade required a skilled and adaptable workforce. Thus, in his 1983 inaugural address Clinton declared that, "over the long run, education is the key to our economic revival and our perennial quest for prosperity." And a few months later, when he unveiled his educational reform, Clinton told the state legislature: "We see in the changing nature of the economy new opportunities long denied to Arkansas . . . not because of cheap labor, low taxes, and weak environmental laws, but because of the productivity of our people."[27] Poor and rural Arkansans knew, he would later claim, that education was the "only shot" they had "to liberate themselves from the ravages of the world economy."[28]

Clinton was hardly the only politician who staked the well-being of his constituents on the enhancement of educational opportunities. But it is also important to recognize that prioritizing educational issues displaced other ideas and programs that might also have boosted incomes and economic growth. The focus on education marginalized the idea of economic planning and targeted investments, an idea then in discussion among progressive Democrats. It elided the role played by both the welfare state and the trade union movement in raising incomes and labor costs, and it ignored the Federal Reserve's increasingly powerful role in setting employment policy. Manufacturing production in the state soared by over 300 percent between 1967 and 1980, before the educational reform. Per capita income, as a percentage of the nation, peaked in 1978.[29] All that growth came, however, in the years just before the Federal Reserve, seeking to break inflation's grip, precipitated a recession during which exceptionally high interest rates devastated US manufacturing and home building. That Fed strategy not only deindustrialized many of the cities bordering the Great Lakes but also put downward pressure on the labor-intensive branch plants that had proliferated in rural states like Arkansas. Nevertheless, by the time Clinton announced that he would run for president in 1991, the educational mantra had become an idée fixe. As he told a Georgetown University audience, "Education is economic development. We can only be a high-wage, high-growth country if we are a high-skills country. In a world in which money and production are mobile, the only way middle-class people can keep good jobs with growing incomes is to be lifetime learners and innovators."[30]

To build support for educational reform and the taxes to pay for it, Bill Clinton appointed his spouse as head of an educational standards committee that spent the summer and fall of 1983 taking testimony from small-town school officials and consulting with nationally known educational experts. After more than seventy-five meetings and hearings were held a consensus soon emerged: there would be lower class sizes, a more uniform and higher-quality curriculum, more money for teachers, and new hiring of nurses, counselors, and librarians as well as classroom teachers.[31]

But all this would require more tax revenue, a hard lift in Arkansas. Relying once again on polling conducted by Dick Morris, the Clintons found that if teacher testing was a requirement in the reform package—an idea the Clintons had begun to explore—at least 85 percent of the public and a large majority in the state legislature would support their legislation. There were some poorly educated teachers in Arkansas, mainly older African-American women who had once taught in the Jim Crow schools of the plantation districts. But teacher testing was also becoming popular among Republican conservatives and neoconservative educational "reformers" who sought to denigrate teacher unionism and find a cheap fix for the nation's underfunded and poorly performing schools. Frank White, Clinton's GOP predecessor in the governor's mansion, had been an advocate, as had the Walton family, the Wal-Mart heirs, who were beginning their foray into charter school advocacy. Thus, when in the fall of 1983 Hillary Clinton belatedly declared that competence tests for public school teachers constituted "the real heart" of the reform package, she caught her erstwhile allies—the Arkansas Education Association (AEA), the NAACP, and other liberals—by surprise that immediately turned to anger.[32]

It was "Treachery by the Governor" and a "War on Teachers," declared the Arkansas Education Association newsletter. Even the Educational Testing Service, whose tests would be used, condemned the idea. Said a spokesperson: "It is morally and educationally wrong, to tell someone who has been judged a satisfactory teacher for many years that passing a certain test on a certain day is necessary to keep his or her job."[33] Racial issues were quite obviously in the forefront of this charge. When in November 1983 Clinton bravely chose to address the AEA Assembly, "polite but stony silence greeted the Governor. . . . Teachers rose silently as he entered the stage. They listened silently as he spoke for nearly 30 minutes. The conclusion of his speech was met with silence by the 1,200 teachers who watched Clinton exit hastily through the wings of the auditorium stage instead of down the aisle. . . . The emotionally charged silence stretched another five minutes," after which the room "erupted with applause" as "delegate after delegate trouped to the floor microphones to denounce the offensive legislation and to blame the Governor for pushing it through."[34]

After his bruising battle with the AEA over teacher testing, Clinton admitted it had been "very painful," referring not so much to the implied insult to the competence of Arkansas teachers, but rather to the more pointed charge that such tests were designed to drive minority teachers from the classroom. "I can tell you with all my heart that's not true," Clinton told an audience of liberally inclined Southerners in 1985.[35] And from Clinton's perspective it was not. He could see, feel, and respond to racial disparities and insults; issues bearing on class, and especially the organizations representing the interests of working-class America, were not so well defined, either in Clinton's heart or on the sociopolitical map upon which he charted his future.

What were the lessons of this highly fraught episode? The new money Clinton put into the Arkansas school system was real. Although Arkansas ranked forty-seventh in per capita income at the end of the 1980s, it ranked twenty-third in state fiscal efforts to support public schools. The percentage of Arkansas high school graduates going to college jumped ten points, in part a function of the dramatic spread of instruction in the sciences to nearly all schools.[36] Arkansas still sent fewer high school graduates on to college than most other states, but average SAT scores moved higher after the Clinton educational reform.[37] In seeking to boost educational spending, Clinton threw down a progressive political marker, but by charting this course in opposition to an otherwise supportive labor movement, Clinton was also defining that liberalism in a contradictory fashion. This approach would not travel well on the national scene.

Think Global, Act Local

"Think global, act local." That idea would soon become a cliché on the ecological left, but it came naturally to Bill Clinton, whose appetite for novelty was endless. From his time at Oxford he had kept up with

European politics, especially on the left—social democratic and even Communist. He had visited Prague in 1969 to observe the dispiriting aftermath of the Warsaw Pact's suppression of Alexander Dubček's "socialism with a human face." In the 1970s he followed the Italian left's effort to construct an anti-Stalinist "Euro-Communism." He admired the Scandinavian social democratic model, which seemed to combine technologically advanced entrepreneurialism with a robust social safety net. As governor, he visited Germany four times on trade missions, badgering German contacts for material on that nation's apprenticeship system and its mixed public-private health insurance system. Clinton visited Asia four times as well, on trade missions to Taiwan and Japan. Clinton came to believe that the United States needed its own version of the Ministry of International Trade and Investment, the governmental institution that played such a powerful role in charting Japan's trade and investment strategy.[38]

Wal-Mart and other big-box retailers were booming in the 1980s, but as Clinton well understood, too many products were now being sourced from low-wage sweatshops in Mexico, Central America, and the Far East. As we shall shortly see, a high-wage "industrial policy," of which Clinton's Oxford companions Robert Reich and Ira Magaziner were now among the most prominent proponents, would soon come into ideological and policy play as the Arkansas governor moved toward a campaign for the presidency.

Clinton sought to deploy any and all of these foreign economic models on Arkansas soil so long as they proved politically feasible. For decades Southern politicians had sought to entice industry to their states by keeping taxes and wages low, avoiding environmental regulations, and offering to build or finance the roads, utilities, and factory space required by companies fleeing the high-cost North. Such industrial recruitment efforts amounted to "buying payroll." Led by local boosters and Chamber of Commerce men, the state in 1955 had created the Arkansas Industrial Development Commission with a sales pitch that largely focused on the virtues of cheap labor. An official in Fort Smith, Arkansas's second-largest city, assured an out-of-state air conditioning manufacturer, "There is plenty of darn good labor within commuting distance, now making the base minimum wage. These thousands of rural dwellers have little or no rent to pay and grow or raise most of the food they eat. . . . They will be with you and for you and listen to no leaders except your own."[39] Such a development strategy ensured that even as the South industrialized it would remain a low-wage, branch-plant colony to the more dynamic centers of entrepreneurship, both those still in the North and West and now others in Europe and even Japan. By the 1980s the stretch of freeway linking Atlanta and Charlotte was called "the autobahn" in recognition of the dozen or more German factories sited there. In Arkansas, the northwest quadrant of the state, headquarters of Wal-Mart, Tyson Foods, and Hunt Trucking, was booming, but the rest of the state, except for Little Rock, still relied on agriculture or the kind of light manufacturing enterprises that were easily shuttered when trade patterns shifted or the next recession arrived.

Like Clinton, the Southern Growth Policies Board (SGPB) rejected the low-road branch-plant strategy. Headquartered in North Carolina's Research Triangle, the SGPB had a far more progressive outlook than any other Southern industrialization initiative to that time. It wanted to foster homegrown entrepreneurship, a highly skilled workforce, good infrastructure, and the taxes necessary to pay for it all.[40] Led by Jesse White, a genuine Southern liberal, the SGPB linked its strategy for a Southern revival to the "industrial policy" ideas put forward by Reich, Magaziner, and Lester Thurow, an MIT economist who saw government playing a large role in guiding domestic investment. Clinton knew their work well.[41]

As critics of industrial recruitment, SGPB staffers tried to convince Southern politicians to give up on low-wage employers and instead focus on creating lots of smaller but more competitive firms that used advanced technology and employed highly skilled workers. As SGPB staffer Stuart Rosenfeld put it in an echo of the line advanced by Robert Reich, the South should "emphasize industrial competitiveness instead of competing for firms."[42] Jesse White therefore had little trouble persuading Bill Clinton to assume the chairmanship of the board in 1985, and it was during his tenure that the SGPB published one of its best-received blueprints for Southern development, "Half-Way Home and a Long Way to Go." This post–civil rights manifesto argued that "as manufacturing retools from low to high skill and relies less on labor and more on technology, the currents of rapid change will leave some of the South's labor force high, dry, and unemployed." Community colleges, better vocational education, improved child care—those were the solutions for "preparing a flexible, globally competitive work force."[43] The growth of trade unionism was conspicuously absent from this blueprint, even though the SGPB authors of the report understood—privately—that good intentions and a highly skilled workforce were not enough: a political mechanism was needed that could pressure Southern employers to take the high road that depended on human capital investment.

In his speech accepting SGPB leadership, Bill Clinton fully endorsed that vision even as he alluded to its limitations. "Can we at long last have the range of economic opportunities that our people certainly deserve and clearly need?" he asked. "If we do succeed in creating a genuinely competitive economic environment and a genuinely competitive educational system, can we do it uniformly?"[44] Clinton was here thinking as much about race as economic growth or social inequality. He recalled the day in 1963 when as a seventeen-year-old Hot Springs high school student he flipped on the TV and caught the prose poetry of Martin Luther King's March on Washington speech delivered on the steps of the Lincoln Memorial. Clinton ended the broadcast in tears and soon thereafter memorized King's entire speech. For the rest of his life Clinton would remain highly sensitive to, and often defensive about, the way racial disparities were ameliorated or exacerbated by any sort of social reform.[45]

For a brief historical moment in the late 1980s, Southern governors like Clinton, small-businessmen looking for more capital and connections, industrial policy advocates seeking to thwart the Japanese challenge, SGPB development technocrats, and even labor partisans looking for a new way to revive US trade unionism were all entranced by an explosive revival of microenterprise in once-obscure northern Italian towns like Modena, Parma, and Bologna in the province of Emilia-Romagna. There wages were high, production was booming, and innovation seemed built into the DNA of the thousands of small firms that had proliferated in little more than a generation. The MIT social scientists

Charles Sabel and Michael Piore were the first to put the region and its wondrously variegated set of small firms on the imaginative landscape of American industrial reformers. Especially influential was their 1984 book *The Second Industrial Divide*, which forecast that the digital revolution would create the material conditions for a new world of highly skilled, highly paid "flexible specialization" in manufacturing and other globally competitive economic sectors. One of these Italian companies, Benneton, a maker of colorful sweaters, had opened a store in New York in 1980 and was expanding rapidly in the United States. The Ford Foundation took notice as well, along with scores of business school academics and industrial consultants who had come to see the limits and costs of mid-twentieth-century mass-production Fordism.[46]

The artisanal renaissance in Emilia-Romagna was dependent on an abundance of skilled labor, a product not only of the guild tradition but of the decline and decentralization of the big industrial enterprises of Turin and Milan. Many of these workers became entrepreneurs in workshops that were networked together and, in some instances, financially sustained by business associations and local governments that offered loans, training, technical expertise, factory space, and even housing. These firms—many with less than twenty workers— did not try to compete with low-cost Far Eastern manufacturers but instead emphasized high-quality product innovation and intimate knowledge of customer wants and needs. Fiat had no factories in Emilia-Romagna, but Ferrari, Ducati, Lamborghini, Maserati, and Pagani all built cars there. Specialized leather, silk, and clothing enterprises also flourished. Piore and Sabel advertised the virtues of this region, arguing that with the waning of the era of Fordist mass production, northern Italy demonstrated the virtues of a nimble craft production regime wedded to both high technology and well-defined niche markets.

By all accounts Bill Clinton was entranced by his visit to the Italian region in the early fall of 1987. He visited factories, talked to academic experts, exchanged ideas with government leaders and the heads of regional business associations, and participated in a two-day Florence conference. In his autobiography Clinton wrote, "One of the reasons for the region's prosperity seemed to be the extraordinary cooperation of small business people in sharing facilities and administrative and marketing costs, as northern Italian artisans had been doing for centuries, since the development of medieval guilds."[47] Arkansas had already been doing some of this: the state's Seed Capital Investment Fund provided up to one-quarter of the capital required of high-tech start-up firms, and its Business Incubator Program sought to more closely link Arkansas institutions of higher education with technology-based businesses.[48] The Arkansas Development Finance Authority (ADFA) provided long-term, fixed-rate bonds for manufacturing plants and housing developers. Initially opposed by the Stephens Investment Bank, which saw it as a financial competitor, the ADFA was one of the few programs that Clinton pushed through the legislature against the wishes of one of the Arkansas "big dogs."[49]

About this same time Clinton had also become an enthusiast for the work of the Bangladeshi economist and social entrepreneur Muhammad Yunus, who would later win a Nobel Peace Prize for his effort to extend microloans to poor but entrepreneurially minded peasants. The governor believed that the state could both reduce poverty and spur rural development by providing "more capital to people who had the potential to operate profitable small business but couldn't borrow the money to get started." So he set up the Southern Development Bank Corporation in 1986, using state funds and money "from corporations that Hillary and I asked to invest in it."[50] Thus, Clinton's visits abroad seemed to confirm that regions of small towns and small enterprises, be they Emilia-Romagna or the Arkansas Ozarks, could transform themselves if the right combination of education, technology, entrepreneurship, and government assistance was on offer. Back in Arkansas, Clinton reported on his Italian trip to various Chambers of Commerce around the state, renewed efforts to get state government to support nascent entrepreneurs, and spread the gospel of small-scale, high-tech, flexible production. In his autobiography Clinton reported that he helped a "group of unemployed sheet-metal workers set up businesses and co-operate in cost- sharing and marketing as I had observed Italian leatherworkers and furniture makers doing."[51]

Clinton's efforts to reconfigure the Arkansas economy were genuine enough, but he had neither the financial tools nor the social infrastructure to do so. His search for development models, from northern Italy to Bangladesh, was an effort to evade rather than confront the obstacles that stood in the way of a more prosperous South—indeed, of the entire high-tech, high-wage America that his generation of development intellectuals and Democratic Party reformers projected. This would become clear enough when Clinton and his friends occupied the White House, but it could be glimpsed in Arkansas as well.

Once one probed beneath the surface, the differences between Arkansas and northern Italy were enormous and so great that it would have been impossible for any Southern politician to spearhead a similar industrial renaissance in the region without something close to a radical transformation of power, culture, and economy in Arkansas and similar states. Emilia-Romagna was home to a powerful trade union movement, and Bologna, the provincial capital, had long had Communist municipal leadership. For a century syndicalism, anticlericalism, and egalitarianism had been the social and cultural hallmarks of those skilled workers and craftsman entrepreneurs who populated the innovative industrial networks that created such unique and high-quality products. A purge of the left in Milan and Turin factories following Italy's "hot autumn" in 1969 had sent thousands of highly skilled workers back to the provinces, where, in the words of a Ford Foundation report, "they saw the establishment of small manufacturing concerns, not so much as investments but rather as a continuation of the individual entrepreneur's career as a worker."[52]

Moreover, the power of the union movement and the left-wing character of the local governments made large enterprises fear a loss of managerial control and predictable profitability should they attempt to make the province their home. But this was not a recipe for capital flight: instead, risk and production were pushed down to the microenterprise, whose financial health was backstopped by a left-wing government, a tradition of networked production, and a trade union federation that socialized many of the costs attendant on small enterprise. Examples of such networked, small-scale, and high-skilled enterprises were not foreign to the United States, but they were of another time and place: the tool and die shops of Detroit during the mid-twentieth-century era of United Auto Workers power, the Cincinnati machine tool industry that got its start in the 1880s, and the Philadelphia carpet manufacturers whose demand for skilled and creative craftsmen provided for the coexistence early in the twentieth century of a powerful set of craft unions and a set of small and medium-sized firms that were highly attentive to changing consumer tastes.[53]

All this was attractive to Bill Clinton as he searched for a set of solutions that might pull Arkansas out of its bottom rank on the US income and industry scale. He was creatively opportunistic when it came to the search for such new initiatives. Thus, when he ran for reelection in 1986—against both Orval Faubus, the ancient segregationist, and Frank White, who had defeated him in 1980, the Memphis *Commercial Appeal* reported that "Clinton's stump speeches in the area sound as much like seminars on the economy as pleas for votes and most political analysts agree that the strategy is working."[54]

Lessons from Wal-Mart

Clinton did win a handsome victory in 1986, but he could hardly speechify Arkansas onto an alternative economic trajectory. In his state a species of low-wage Fordism was still the preferred strategy of firms like Tyson Foods, Wal-Mart Stores, and the Stephens Investment Bank. None of these companies tried to emulate the actual mass-production regime that had powered American industrial growth a half-century before. Not only did these firms employ a non-union workforce at rock-bottom wages, but they fissured their supply chains so as to off-load risk and expense to a set of ostensibly independent suppliers. Thus, Tyson did employ tens of thousands of workers—many of them African-American and Latino—in a set of poultry processing plants and slaughterhouses whose work regime emulated the most hierarchical and brutal version of a 1920s-era Detroit assembly line. But Tyson also outsourced the production of millions of chickens and hogs to Ozark farmers whose hatcheries and feedlots were subject to the most exacting regulation and control. These farmers were little more than "sharecroppers" standing at the base of a late-twentieth-century supply chain. The same was true of Wal-Mart: store "associates" were direct employees of the fast-growing firm, but hundreds of supply-chain "vendors" were kept on an exceedingly tight leash that was at once financially precarious and entrepreneurially constraining.[55]

Clinton's dilemma was embodied in his relationship to Wal-Mart. By the early 1990s Hillary Clinton sat on the Wal-Mart board, where, in a business that had consciously avoided contact with the social currents arising out of the Sixties, she pushed for more equitable treatment of women and minority employees and sought to make the company more eco-friendly. But she stayed clear of labor issues, which had begun to vex management as Sam Walton's company outgrew its Southern roots. Her husband had another problem. Companies like Wal-Mart had begun to source an increasing proportion of the clothes, toys, shoes, kitchen appliances, and home electronics they sold from the Far East. More than 250 domestic garment factories closed between 1980 and 1985, and no region was hit harder by these closures than the rural South, where cheap labor had been the prime attraction before those minimum-wage jobs were outsourced to Central America and across the Pacific.

The closure of several Arkansas firms led to an outcry against the import practices of big retailers like Wal-Mart. Such was the case with Farris Fashions, an apparel manufacturer that nearly closed in 1984 when Phillips–Van Heusen decided to move its production of shirts offshore to meet demands from Sears and JCPenney for lower prices. In Brinkley, a small town deep in the heart of the Mississippi Delta, ninety jobs, largely held by African-American women, were at stake. So Governor Clinton got on the phone to David Glass, then head of Wal-Mart Stores, and asked if the big retailer could send some business to the locally owned Brinkley firm. This was the start of Wal-Mart's famous "Buy American" campaign, enthusiastically endorsed not only by Sam Walton but also by Clinton and his economic development department. Clinton and his administration hosted conferences and press events with the big retailer, encouraged some 2,500 local manufacturing firms to bid on consumer products that Wal-Mart sought to source at home, and advertised the Buy American program to other Southern governors. At a press conference announcing the Farris Fashions deal, Clinton pronounced Wal-Mart's Buy American program "an act of patriotism and it makes good economic sense in the long run."[56]

But *Discount Store News* described it best: "a public relations coup historic in its dimensions." There were two problems with the Buy American program. First, Wal-Mart and the other retailers that followed its lead were willing to buy at home only if their domestic vendors slashed production costs to a level competitive with East Asia and Central America. Doing so required low-wages, single-product production runs, with no money devoted to brand development, advertising, or searching for additional clients. "The problem is I have no access to markets other than Wal-Mart," admitted Farris Burroughs, owner of the Brinkley apparel manufacturer. Wal-Mart designed the shirts, sold them under its American Eagle label, found a Taiwanese supplier from which it purchased flannel in huge bulk, and bought the entire factory output. Employment rose to 350, but the jobs remained unskilled and poorly paid.[57] Not unexpectedly, most Arkansas manufacturers were unwilling or unable to participate in the Wal-Mart program, and despite energetic efforts by Clinton's economic development people, the response of Arkansas employers was a "disappointment."[58]

This was not northern Italy. When Farris Fashions workers signed up with the Amalgamated Clothing and Textile Workers Union (ACTWU) in 1990, Burroughs told them "to stop messing around with the union" because Sam Walton would turn the plant into "a chicken coop" before he would agree to "buy union goods."[59] Burroughs remained intransigent even after the union won a National Labor Relations Board (NLRB) election. When Jean Hervey of the ACTWU appealed to the governor, who was a friend of the extended Burroughs family, to mediate a settlement, a staffer sent Clinton a memo. "Do you want to try and get Farris to sit down with them to discuss an agreement?" In a marginal note, Clinton replied, "OK to see her but <u>very</u> doubtful I'll get involved."[60]

Such was the pattern. In 1990 union workers at Morrilton Plastics, a small minority-owned auto parts plant, went on strike. Shortly beforehand

Detroit automakers had advised the company to stockpile a large inventory of parts. To pay for the buildup, Morrilton applied for and received a $290,000 loan from the Arkansas Industrial Development Commission. "It was a clear case of siding with management," said Arkansas AFL-CIO's Bill Becker. "Clinton helped break a union." Clinton claimed his motivation was to keep the plant open and save jobs.[61] But such cheap jobs were highly mobile jobs, subject to globally competitive winds. The company soon went bankrupt when cheaper auto parts poured into the United States from Japan and Mexico; likewise, Farris Fashions closed down in 2005 after consumer demand for flannel shirts declined and Wal-Mart abandoned its Buy American campaign to source even more apparel from China and the Far East.[62] Such trade issues were also class issues, and Bill Clinton had not seen the last of them.

Bill Clinton's sojourn in Arkansas politics demonstrated the degree to which he wanted to be a progressive governor, raising educational standards and advancing the state's economic development and the living standards of its citizens. But market forces alone would not transform the state. Clinton faced enormous obstacles, largely emanating from a self-confident business class who combined the most advanced technological and organizational innovations with a low-wage, outsourcing employment strategy that would prove a social and economic dead end for the vast majority of Arkansans. Clinton understood this conundrum, but his disdain for organized labor left him without the most potent tool he could have wielded to counter that power. Instead, Clinton kept up a restless quest for any innovation, originating at home or abroad, that might enhance development without even the semblance of a conflict with the corporate behemoths of his state. This was a strategy that would grow even more fraught when deployed on the national stage.

2

"The Cold War Is Over: Germany and Japan Won"

Bill Clinton's frustrating efforts to transform the Arkansas economy were but a microcosm of the problems that confronted American liberals in the 1970s and 1980s. The new normal seemed to be recession, inflation, and deindustrialization, maladies that failed to respond to the tool kit of New Deal–era remedies that for a third of a century had propelled US economic growth, doubled the standard of living, and sustained Democratic Party hegemony. Beginning with the sharp recession that followed the 1973 oil crisis, the United States seemed to have entered an era of limits, both economic and political, that threatened the capacity of government to carry out functions that just a few years before had seemed routine. The 1970s were a dismal decade, with the slowest rate of economic growth and the lowest level of population increase since the Great Depression.

The road to a Reaganite ascendency was now open, and many liberals in academe and politics were also coming to see the virtue of the market as a mechanism that rewarded efficiency, spurred economic growth, and even enhanced democratic practice. But another ideological current was also present in the policy circles inhabited by Bill Clinton and his increasingly wide network of friends and collaborators. "Industrial policy," an effort to manage key enterprises and economic sectors, especially in terms of trade and competition with other industrial nations, was perhaps the most serious and politically realistic alternative to Reaganite conservatism during the 1980s and early 1990s. Policy entrepreneurs like Robert Reich, Laura Tyson, Ira Magaziner, and Jeffrey Garten, who would hold important posts during the Clinton presidency, welcomed the end of the Cold War with little of the triumphalism so well advertised by Margaret Thatcher and Ronald Reagan. These policymakers saw American capitalism as increasingly dysfunctional: it had not only bred economic stagnation and social inequality but failed to stay competitive with the set of rival economies, Germany and Japan especially, where the state played a far greater role in establishing the market rules and funding the industrial innovations necessary for growth, trade, and social well-being. Their ideas would play an important role in both the 1992 Clinton presidential campaign and in some of the most important debates and initiatives of the new president's first term.

Assault on the New Deal Order

To curb inflation and a huge trade imbalance, President Richard Nixon had imposed wage and price controls and a surtax on Japanese car imports. This was the "New Economic Policy" promulgated in August 1971. The dollar was devalued and eventually allowed to float, thus ending the system known as Bretton Woods, the name taken from the New Hampshire hotel where in 1944 finance ministers from the Allied governments had met to create an international currency structure designed to ensure that financial markets were clearly subordinate to governmental authority. While the wage and price controls were soon lifted, the "oil shock" of 1973, followed by the most severe recession since 1938, seemed to demonstrate that a Keynesian response to economic malaise was no longer an effective solution. Inflation reached double-digit levels even as unemployment followed suit.[1]

A reinvigorated conservative movement, hardly fettered by a liberalism grown tired and timid, saw its chance to begin the dismantlement of the old New Deal. An emerging generation of Republican politicians and business leaders, backstopped by a newly assertive cohort of market-friendly economists, argued that the welfare state destroyed entrepreneurial incentives; that government regulations of virtually every sort merely created new inefficiencies; that trade unionism constituted a "monopoly" just as pernicious as any trust; and that high taxes, especially on capital gains and high incomes, had proved a drag on the capacity of banks and corporations to create the new concentrations of financial resources necessary to boost economic growth and technological innovation. In the 1980 election, President Jimmy Carter straddled many of these issues in a vain effort to defend a pale economic liberalism, while his opponent, Ronald Reagan, embraced the emerging critique of the New Deal.

It was actually Carter who well and truly inaugurated the Reaganite economic future when he appointed Paul Volcker as Federal Reserve Board chair in 1979. Inflation, Volcker would later assert, "was a dragon that was eating out our innards, or more than our innards."[2] Whatever the cost, it had to be slain, so Volcker turned Fed policy toward an ultra-orthodox monetarism, limiting the money supply in just the fashion that Milton Friedman and other anti-Keynesians had long advocated. Interest rates soared to nearly 20 percent as the "Volcker shock" of 1979 engendered a double-dip recession in 1980 and then again in 1981–1982. This interest rate spike was designed to lower inflationary expectations by making anything bought with credit—houses, cars, commercial real estate, industrial equipment—prohibitively expensive. Layoffs and unemployment soon followed, decimating the bargaining power of workers, both unionized and the unorganized. Indeed, when Chrysler Corporation faced bankruptcy in 1979 and 1980, Volcker himself played a key role in bailing out the company, demanding painful UAW wage concessions in return for federal loan guarantees. Amid much internal turmoil, the union once known as "the vanguard in America" agreed to the concessions Volcker and Carter wanted. The result was a wage-reducing, two-tier contract that would soon become a template throughout blue-collar America.[3]

Volcker was demonstrating that the politics of inflation was about nothing less than the distribution of the national income—or, as the Cambridge economist Joan Robinson put it in 1976, inflation was an "expression of class struggle." This was a sentiment not at variance with Volcker's outlook. In his autobiography, the former Fed chair highlighted "one important but little-recognized contribution to the fight against inflation": Ronald Reagan's decision to fire thousands of striking air traffic controllers in 1981, resulting in the destruction of the Professional Air

Traffic Controllers Organization (PATCO), was a watershed moment in the modern history of anti-unionism. Consumer price inflation had been a pressing issue during the middle decades of the twentieth century because only during the heyday of the New Deal order had the working class had the power to make it one.[4] But now that era was over as corporation after corporation turned collective bargaining on its head, exacting concessions and pay cuts from their workforces, unionized or not. Alan Greenspan, Volcker's successor as head of the Fed, would characterize this generation of American workers as having accepted stagnant wages and insecure work because they were "traumatized."[5]

Saddled with the worst kind of stagflation, a hapless Jimmy Carter had little chance of defeating the former Hollywood star once it became clear in an October debate that Reagan had enough substance and steadiness to actually govern the country, despite his right-wing pedigree and economic ideas that a more orthodox Republican like George H. W. Bush had labeled "voodoo." Reagan's tax reductions for the wealthy and his deregulatory economic program not only increased inequality but also changed the structure of the economy, promoting finance, real estate, retail, and defense. Because of the high dollar, US exports were expensive and foreign imports amazingly cheap. American manufacturers therefore faced a crippling environment that would persist even after the 1985 Plaza Accord, which was designed to devalue the dollar against the yen and the mark. Interest rates, however, remained stubbornly high even after the Volcker shock abated, thus raising corporate expectations for what constituted an acceptable rate of return, a standard that many manufacturers could not meet. The result was a wave of takeovers, the outsourcing of much of the domestic supply chain, and a continual downward pressure on labor costs, which perpetuated the concession bargaining, if not outright union busting, that began with the destruction of PATCO and the Chrysler bailout. The fundamentals essential to long-term growth—high rates of saving and investment, competitiveness in world markets, high-quality education, a stable fiscal program—all deteriorated badly. By 1989, after more than six years of economic recovery, US factory jobs totaled two million fewer than ten years before. This inexorable shift from high-wage manufacturing jobs to lower-paid service-sector work proved foundational to the income stagnation that now pervaded the lives of so many American families. The economist Paul Krugman wrote that the 1990s in the United States would be an "age of diminished expectations."[6]

Reconfiguring American Liberalism

A reconfiguration of liberalism emerged from this new political and economic terrain. Initially called "neo-liberals" and "Atari Democrats" in the early 1980s, these erstwhile liberals sought to salvage progressive values in a global economy where the old paths to a good society seemed utterly blocked. The labor movement was in decline, tax revenues were growing paltry, and high-wage manufacturing was giving way to lower-paid employment in a vast retail, fast-food, and hospitality sector. Many thought that the New York City fiscal crisis signaled the end of an era when the most liberal constituencies could expand the welfare state; likewise, the tax revolts of the late 1970s in California, Massachusetts, and elsewhere proscribed any new round of social spending. Bill Clinton had failed to win reelection in 1980 largely because he hiked automobile registration fees to pay for new roads and highways, a fiscal lesson he would not forget.[7] Meanwhile, foreign competition offered a plethora of cheap goods but sucked well-paying jobs south of the border or across the Pacific. The favorite economist of this new liberalism was Joseph Schumpeter, who saw capitalism as an innovative, creative, and sometimes self-destructive system, not John Maynard Keynes, tribune of the intrusive state. Microeconomics had become more fascinating than macro.[8]

But economic growth was still essential, the predicate necessary to transcend the constraints so evident in the early 1980s. In his widely read book *The Zero-Sum Society*, Lester Thurow, a progressively inclined MIT economist, argued that in an economy of limited growth and fiscal constraint any benefit that one group or fraction enjoyed required that some other sector of the population accept a reduction in its standard of living. Protections against cheap imports saved manufacturing jobs but burdened millions of consumers. Schools and other municipal services would have to suffer when caps were put on the property taxes homeowners were required to pay. But there was a solution: "If you have a growing economy, you don't have to choose between his claims on the national pie and your claims on the national pie." Likewise, argued New Jersey Democrat Bill Bradley in 1980, "social issues *are* secondary . . . to the health of the economy." With Keynesianism in eclipse, it would be left to market forces—channeled and structured by this new generation of liberals—to transform an era of limits into one of abundance.[9]

The deregulation of airlines and trucking late in the Carter era is a case in point. In 1975 Senator Edward Kennedy began holding hearings on the airline industry that demonstrated the degree to which economic thinking had changed since the New Deal. Airline fares were fixed by the Civil Aeronautics Board in a cartel-like fashion. Having fares, routes, and profits determined by the government was good for the stability of the industry, for airline executives and shareholders, and for unionized pilots, mechanics, and flight attendants. Customers paid a lot to fly, though wide seats, hot meals, and half-empty cabins were partial compensation. By overseeing the deregulation of commercial aviation, the Cornell economist Alfred Kahn—a self-described "good liberal Democrat"—became something close to a celebrity during the Carter years. Among his allies were Senator Kennedy, the consumer activist Ralph Nader, and a future Supreme Court justice, Stephen Breyer, who had been the high-level staffer on Kennedy's Judiciary Committee most responsible for framing the Airline Deregulation Act that President Carter signed in 1979.[10]

Trucking, railroads, and the savings and loan industry were also substantially deregulated. Kahn, Kennedy, and Carter were encouraged by a rising generation of public-interest lawyers, largely on the environmental and consumer protection left, who attacked governmental power and administrative discretion. They saw the "tripartism"—the New Deal–style interplay between industry, labor, and governmental experts—that was ideologically and administratively inherent in so many government agencies as bankrupt. The cozy relationships between the Civil Aeronautics Board and the airlines, between the Federal Trade Commission (FTC) and trucking interests, and between

AT&T—Ma Bell—and various government regulatory agencies seemed both self-serving and economically constipated. Citizens and consumers had been disenfranchised, while the benefits that such a regime offered to airline workers, telephone linesmen, and truck drivers, whose wages had been sheltered from downward competitive pressures, merely ratified the extent to which big labor had become part of a stolid establishment. "There is administrative arrogance at every level," the lawyer Frederick Sutherland of the Center for Law in the Public Interest explained in 1975. Government agencies "need to have their butts kicked once in a while." A new kind of liberalism—skeptical and distrustful of government, yet still committed to a set of progressive social and economic goals—had emerged in the heart of the liberal establishment.[11]

Such a perspective also ratified the near-demise of traditional antitrust law and regulation, a movement propelled forward by the global competitive pressures now making life difficult for American steel, auto, aerospace, and telecommunications companies, which were once thought either part of an oligopoly or an outright natural monopoly. Thus, Lester Thurow argued that globalization had fundamentally altered the antitrust calculus: "In markets where international trade exists or could exist, national antitrust laws no longer make sense."[12] This put many liberals in the same camp as Robert Bork, the conservative legal scholar and government official who had helped orchestrate President Nixon's "Saturday Night Massacre" of Watergate infamy. Bork was also the author of a highly influential 1978 law review article, "The Antitrust Paradox," that would have a material impact on how the Reagan administration deregulated business and finance. Bork derided the tradition of economic liberalism associated with trustbusters like Theodore Roosevelt and Louis Brandeis, arguing instead that the sole criterion for antitrust action—or inaction—must be the welfare of the consumer. Corporate mergers and monopolies were no vice if they lowered prices and offered buyers more choice. In a world of global competition, technological innovation, and efficiency-generating economies of scale, the old antitrust ethos, which had feared the political influence and class power of big business, was outdated. Thus, when in 1987 Edward Kennedy spoke on the Senate floor in opposition to President Reagan's nomination of Bork to a seat on the Supreme Court, he warned that in Bork's America abortion would be outlawed, racial segregation legitimized, the teaching of evolution proscribed, and the censorship of writers and artists enabled "at the whim of government." But Kennedy failed to even mention Bork's hugely influential economic views.[13]

The Cold War Ends

The demise of the Cold War was a momentous event with ideological consequences among American liberals equal to the noisy triumphalism arising from the right. "The collapse of socialism, not merely as a ruling ideology, but as an idea with the power to move men's minds," wrote Paul Krugman not long after the fall of the Berlin Wall, was the "fundamental political fact of the 1990s."[14] That ideological collapse was not merely a product of the fall of the Soviet Union. It had begun decades before when Soviet suppression of Hungarian, Czech, and Polish efforts to reform communism in Eastern Europe punctured any illusions that Western liberals or leftists might have still held about those noncapitalist regimes. Then, to sustain social peace in the 1970s and 1980s, virtually all of these Communist states took out huge loans from the West. And even more telling was the decision by Chinese leaders to take the capitalist road, to abandon even a rhetorical Marxism in governing the billion people under their command. Then came the largely bloodless but swift demise of the Soviet regime and its chaotic replacement by a corrupt and predatory capitalism that enabled a generation of commissars to transform themselves overnight into a ruling oligarchy that was half mafia and half manager.[15] A few intellectuals tried to argue that the demise of Stalinism did not consign democratic socialism to the dustbin of history, but that was a hard argument to make, at least for the generation that witnessed the Soviet collapse. As in the Victorian era, capitalism seemed secure, not so much because of its success— there would be recessions, scandals, panics, and meltdowns—as because there seemed to be no plausible alternative.

The Communist threat, even if operative only in the Third World, had nevertheless helped constrain an entirely "liberal" deployment of market forces in both the West and the global South. Now the end of the Cold War had transformed the economic world in two decisive ways. First, the potential labor force available to make things had just about doubled with the opening of Eastern Europe and East Asia to world trade, finance, and export manufacturing. With near-lightning speed, Western capital flooded these new labor-rich countries, creating almost overnight a web of low-wage export rivals whose productive output soon made life difficult for North Atlantic workers, firms, and left-of-center political parties.[16] And second, the moral and economic ignominy into which the Communist regimes had descended even before their demise seemed to ratify Margaret Thatcher's famous declaration that "there is no alternative." A triumphalist mood soon erupted among Anglo-American conservatives and some not so conservative. This was the meaning of Francis Fukuyama's celebrated essay "The End of History," published in the summer of 1989. Fukuyama argued that "a remarkable consensus concerning the legitimacy of liberal democracy" had emerged throughout the world, marking "an end point of mankind's ideological evolution" and the "final form of human government."[17] Although the word "neoliberalism" is absent from his essay, Fukuyama was certainly endowing that concept with a large sense of global inevitability. It would take almost two decades—until the publication of David Harvey's *A Brief History of Neoliberalism*, followed by the world financial collapse in 2008—for the word to achieve widespread currency and the explanatory power it so often holds today.[18]

The idea that capitalist markets are essential to, or even define, the democratic idea has always been present in the West, but this sentiment achieved far greater power after 1989. In a maddening piece of ideological larceny, market triumphalists invoked the ultimate sanction, once the principal asset of the left: the stamp of historic inevitability. Words like "reform" and "liberalization" came to denote the process whereby an open market in labor and capital now replaced the regulatory regimes, either social democratic or autocratic, that had been erected earlier in the century. Fukuyama wrote that "liberal democracy combined with open market economics has become the only model a state could follow." Indeed, markets were thought both less coercive than government and more powerful. Part of the neoliberal appeal was that it offered individuals who had the right sort of educational and cultural preparation a world of cosmopolitan freedom, a transnational capacity to create new identities and build new careers. Writing in *Forbes*, columnist Peter Huber added a libertarian twist, arguing that it was "market forces and the information age" that had beaten the Soviets and would soon force the dissolution of America's largest economic organizations. He advised those who had "grown accustomed to a sheltered life inside a really large corporation" to take care: "The next Kremlin to fall may be your own."[19]

Neither progressive intellectuals nor many in the Democratic Party bought into this sort of triumphalism. Communism might have fallen, but American capitalism often seemed less the winner than the survivor of the Cold War. Indeed, it was Paul Tsongas, a Massachusetts Democrat often identified with market solutions to US economic problems, who famously declared during his campaign for the 1992 presidential nomination that "The Cold War Is Over: Germany and Japan Won."[20] In a similar vein Bill Clinton used the Little Rock inauguration of his presidential campaign to announce that "our competition for the future is Germany and the rest of Europe, Japan and the rest of Asia."[21] Those rivals had "productivity growth rates that were three and four times ours because they educate their people better, they invest more in their future, and they organize their economies for global competition while we don't."[22] Wrote Denis MacShane, a Labour Party MP, "For years socialists used to argue among themselves about what kind of socialism they wanted. But today, the choice of the left is no longer what kind of socialism it wants, but what kind of capitalism it can support."[23]

Varieties of Capitalism?

These politicians were sloganizing the "varieties of capitalism" debate that during the 1970s and 1980s had animated academic scholarship, generated an outpouring of sensationalistic novels, and engendered much left-of-center political discourse. That debate was predicated on, and politically energized by, not just the undoubted success of some European and East Asian economies but also the left-of-center argument that in Reagan's America or Thatcherite Britain there were alternatives to the inequities inherent in Anglo-American political economy. Looking abroad to Germany and Japan, it seemed apparent that there were ways of organizing and regulating a capitalist polity that generated far higher degrees of income, growth, and social stability. The set of governing ideas, institutions, and underlying economic structures that made these different capitalisms seem so distinct reached their apogee just as Bill Clinton and other Democrats were seeking to claim the White House. As we shall see, the argument would play an important role in Clintonian economic statecraft early in his administration. But soon thereafter, this way of structuring US economic debate would fade, a result largely of the stagnation that plagued Japan, the unexpected financial crisis that enveloped a number of the East Asian "Tiger" economies, and the multiyear US boom that crested at the turn of the millennium. Thereafter, the global economic crisis of 2008 consigned the "varieties of capitalism" debate to the university seminar room.[24]

Jeffrey Garten, a Lehman Brothers banker with wide experience in the Far East and later a Clinton administration trade official, explained that American liberals had traditionally sought to steer their economy with Keynesian macroeconomic measures—taxes and spending—but now European and Japanese methods, a mixture of trade subsidies and targeted industrial policies designed to protect and advance key industries, seemed a remarkably successful economic model that the United States might emulate. In his 1992 *A Cold Peace: America, Japan, Germany, and the Struggle for Supremacy*, Garten hardly saw an "end of history" in the victory of the West, but rather a new set of conflicts in which the distinction between foreign and domestic policies would vanish and "what goes on among nations will be shaped more heavily than ever by what happens *within* them."[25] Although he ignored the rise of China, Garten was among the increasingly large cohort of academics, trade experts, unionists, and politicians who saw a renewed era of competition between the United States, Japan, and Germany as a function of the "contending models" of capitalism that these nations represented. In terms of growth, trade, and even living standards, US capitalism, especially when guided by administrations like those of Carter, Reagan, and Bush, was in danger of falling behind because the schools, factories, banks, and government policies of Japan and Germany had combined to create two distinctly different but highly successful models of capitalist dynamism, elements of which the United States needed to emulate if it was to maintain its influence in the world and create democratic prosperity at home.[26] Neither Garten nor Tsongas nor Clinton actually used the phrase "varieties of capitalism," but their arguments hinged on a comparative referencing that both helped explain America's inequitable and substandard economic performance and challenged the idea, à la Fukuyama, that world capitalism was proceeding in one inevitable direction.

Japan's rise to become the second-largest economy in the world and an export powerhouse that challenged American dominance in automobiles, steel, computer chips, and electronics demonstrated the point and generated much alarm, some of which was tinged with traditional American fear of a "yellow peril." The title of Ezra Vogel's 1979 bestseller, *Japan as Number One*, epitomized that anxiety, as did novels like Michael Crichton's 1992 *Rising Sun*, which exposed the murderous and politically well connected rule of the Japanese executives in control of a powerful Los Angeles corporation, and Tom Clancy's 1994 thriller *Debt of Honor*, which detailed how a bitter trade dispute turned into a new Japanese-American war in which economic sabotage proved as potent as military hardware.[27] One 1991 survey found that Japan had become the principal embodiment of voters' economic fears.[28]

The Japanese state had long played a central role in the management of the island nation's economy. Until the 1980s, elite bureaucrats at the Ministry of International Trade and Industry (MITI) determined how capital was allocated by picking winners, selecting favored industries, and then ensuring that state-controlled banks funneled money to the preferred companies and projects. As in the United States, subsidies to the agricultural sector reinforced conservative rule in many districts, but Japan also shielded industry from foreign competition, kept the yen artificially low to favor exports, and encouraged cartelization. In the United States consumer welfare was the highest priority of both trade and antitrust policy; for the Japanese, producer interests reigned supreme, just as had once been the case in the high-tariff America of the late nineteenth century, when the nation was also a "developmental state." Weak private-sector unionism in Japan was tolerated by a once-radical working class because many core firms offered workers something close to lifetime employment. By the end of the 1980s Japan was the world's largest creditor nation and the United States had become the world's leading debtor. In high-profile industries like steel, auto, electronics, and semiconductors, Japan was a clear innovator, and nations that pursued a similar strategy, like South Korea, Taiwan, and Singapore, were not far behind.[29]

Although a fear of German economic success generated no best-selling murder mysteries, that nation's social market economy seemed another alternative to US-style capitalism, and one particularly favored by the policy entrepreneurs who would soon constitute a Clintonite left. Germany was an export powerhouse, rivaling and sometimes besting the East Asian economies, especially when it came to producer goods. Like the United States, the German state was not as interventionist as Japan, and the country was open to foreign investment. But substantial inter-firm collaboration in research and development, combined with an engineering culture from the shop floor to the management office, enhanced German manufacturing technology beyond what pure market forces might have engendered. Unions were strong in Germany, and firms were much more willing to train rather than poach the skilled labor they needed. The German apprenticeship program, now extended from the traditional metal-bending industries to high-tech and office work, excited many observers. Robert Reich, soon to become Bill Clinton's Secretary of Labor, wanted every large firm to devote 1.5 percent of sales to worker training, an idea that Clinton would advertise in campaign speeches.[30] Likewise, American progressives looked favorably upon the works councils and codetermination boards that offered workers a voice, or at least informed consent, when it came to production and productivity inside German firms. Liberals hoped that some elements of this collaborationist Rhineland capitalism might be transferable to the United States. If the big problem on this side of the Atlantic was stagnant productivity and a chronic trade imbalance, then the German model seemed to hold win-win solutions for both labor and capital.[31]

Managing American Capitalism

The phrase "industrial policy" first emerged in the late 1970s. By that time cracks in the American industrial base had become all too visible, setting off a debate over the extent to which the government should construct a policy for supporting manufacturing industries (of the right kind)—in other words, "industrial policy."[32] The concept differed from New Deal–era planning in two respects. First, it would work mainly by creating a series of economic and regulatory incentives that private-sector firms would find it advantageous to accommodate. There would be no government-built projects along the lines of a Tennessee Valley Authority or the extensive war production facilities constructed with federal dollars during World War II. Second, the industrial policy of the late twentieth century was driven as much by the competitive challenges that the United States faced from Germany, Japan, and other export countries as by the kind of developmental programs and projects that characterized New Deal and Great Society efforts to raise living standards in the South and Appalachia and to provide jobs for inner-city youth. Industrial policy advocates wanted American capitalism to succeed, but they thought that the macroeconomic policies pursued by the Keynesian liberals from the 1940s to the 1960s were no longer working. They wanted to focus industrial policy on those strategically crucial corporations and industries that nurtured so many traditionally good-paying jobs and upon which American trade prowess depended.

Thinking of this sort, and not only among Democrats, first crested in the late 1970s. By this point Felix Rohatyn, the banker who had played such an influential role in managing the New York City fiscal crisis, was already a well-published advocate of a new federal lending entity modeled on the Reconstruction Finance Corporation, the powerful New Deal agency that had played such an important role in developing the American South and West. MIT's Lester Thurow used more leftist language, but he basically concurred with Rohatyn: "We need the national equivalent of a corporate investment committee," he wrote. "Major decisions have become too important to be left to the private market alone, but a way must be found to incorporate private corporate planning into this process in a nonadversary way."[33] The high-profile Trilateral Commission endorsed the concept in a lengthy report, *Industrial Policy and the International Economy*, published in the late 1970s after two years of discussion among dozens of academics and government officials. Among the coauthors was William Diebold, the US automation theorist who, as an industry-oriented technocrat, had never put much faith in macroeconomic Keynesianism or other forms of society-wide regulation. Instead, the authors of the Trilateral Commission report wanted the government to adopt programs aimed "directly to affect the structure of industry."[34] Bolstered by this kind of advocacy, presidential candidates Jerry Brown and Edward Kennedy challenged Jimmy Carter with a call to "reindustrialize America," prodding the president to propose an economic revitalization board during the 1980 campaign.[35]

Many of the initiatives in this direction first occurred at the state level; in Arkansas, for instance, Bill Clinton's efforts to use state agencies and regulatory incentives to stimulate the creation of a series of small and medium-sized enterprises was very much in line with such thinking. The "Massachusetts Miracle" touted by Governor Michael Dukakis was based in part on the $4 billion in reindustrialization bonds the state had issued between 1978 and 1985. Scores of states had created industrial programs; some were comprehensive planning initiatives, while others were little more than tax subsidies to business. By 1991, states and localities had established some 116 new research parks, most based on the example pioneered by North Carolina's Research Triangle, which featured proximity to a good university, cheap land, tax abatements, and little unionization.[36] These state-level initiatives demonstrated that there was a large constituency, even among some Republican officeholders, for an industrial policy that either sought to revitalize old industries or targeted the creation of new, higher-wage, higher-skill enterprises.

Still, it would take a group of well-connected policy entrepreneurs to put the industrial policy idea on the national agenda and then insert it into the debates that shaped Bill Clinton's campaign and his first term in office. Four are profiled here: Laura Tyson, who would become the first chair of Clinton's Council of Economic Advisers; Ira Magaziner, who led the Clinton effort to restructure the nation's system of health provision; Robert Reich, the president's first Secretary of Labor; and Clyde Prestowitz, a Reagan administration trade official who would play an influential role in the 1990s advocating for a system of "managed trade," especially with Japan.

How Industrial Policy Fosters "Managed Trade"

One of the key nodes of industrial policy scholarship and advocacy arose in the Bay Area, where the Berkeley Roundtable on the International Economy (BRIE) proved an exceptionally vigorous incubator of policy proposals designed to enhance US manufacturing capacity and strategically manage foreign trade. Organized in the early 1980s, the BRIE list of academics included the Asian expert Chalmers Johnson, a Cold Warrior who in the aftermath of Vietnam turned into a sharp critic of American empire; he subsequently published some of the earliest and most influential studies of MITI and Japanese economic development more generally. He was joined by younger scholars—like the political scientists Stephen S. Cohen, who got his start as a student of French economic planning, and John Zysman, who coauthored numerous books and articles with Cohen, and the economist Laura Tyson—in analyzing the crisis confronting American living standards and the important role that would be played by a new trade regime in restoring US prosperity.

Tyson had been trained at MIT in the early 1970s, when many New Leftists like herself were looking to Communist Yugoslavia, where a seemingly non-Stalinist government encouraged experiments in "workers' control" and a kind of market socialism. Tyson's mentor was Evsey Dormer, a Russian-born, left-wing Keynesian economist who argued that economic growth is inherently unstable without sustained government encouragement. Tyson wrote her dissertation on how Yugoslav planners and central bankers sought, or should have tried, to control inflation in an economic system that had begun to decentralize and offer workers real participatory power. Believing that an evolution toward some kind of social democracy was possible in Eastern Europe, she wanted to help chart its trajectory.[37]

By the early 1980s, however, the evident dysfunctionality of all the Eastern European economies, including Tito's Yugoslavia, robbed that region of any imaginative hold on social or economic reformers in the West. Tyson described herself as "bored" with those regimes.[38] After joining the Berkeley faculty in 1977, she therefore turned her attention to a far more successfully planned economy, that of Japan, and its trading relationship with the United States. Team teaching a class with John Zysman, whom she met as a graduate student at MIT, Tyson cofounded the Berkeley Roundtable, wrote extensively on US-Japan trade rivalry, and in 1992 published *Who's Bashing Whom? Trade Conflict in High-Technology Industries*. There Tyson argued for a tough new "managed trade" policy toward the Japanese if the United States was to finally penetrate the all-but-closed Japanese market and prevent the evisceration of the industries in which Americans had been an innovation pioneer but lagged in low-cost manufacturing technique.[39]

Tyson's book was provocatively entitled and would win the attention of Bill Clinton and his circle, but BRIE's most important intervention was *Manufacturing Matters: The Myth of the Post-Industrial Economy* by Stephen Cohen and John Zysman, published five years before. That book took aim at those, both left and right, who saw America and other advanced industrial economies transitioning to a post-factory, service-oriented economy in which knowledge workers—or in the words of Robert Reich, "symbolic analysts"—would create value by manipulating data, ideas, sentiments, and interpersonal relationships. Education, health provision, entertainment, and data manipulation of all sorts would now stand at the heart of the economy.[40]

Daniel Bell, the erstwhile socialist, had first popularized the knowledge worker concept in his 1976 prognostication *The Coming of Post-Industrial Society*, a book that saw manufacturing and its millions of blue-collar workers going the way of American agriculture, which now employed but 2 percent of the US workforce. As services and other "post-industrial" occupations replaced the making of things, production would either be offshored or become so well automated that manufacturing, though still nostalgically celebrated, would fade away like the family farm. Bell's perspective gained much traction to his right. In 1984 a report from the US Trade Representative, published under President Reagan's signature, set out a comforting framework for understanding America's contemporary—and hopefully temporary—trade situation. "The move from an industrial society toward a 'postindustrial' service economy has been one of the greatest changes to affect the developed world since the Industrial Revolution. The progression of an economy such as America's from agriculture to manufacturing to services is a natural change." Likewise, a New York Stock Exchange report of the mid-1980s asserted that "a strong manufacturing sector is not a requisite for a prosperous economy." And *Forbes* magazine agreed: "Instead of ringing in the decline of our economic power, a service-driven economy signals the most advanced stage of economic development."[41]

In rejoinder, the BRIE academics argued that the United States was far from a post-industrial economy. Transitions from one mode of production to another were neither natural nor inevitable, and indeed they may not even have taken place. Thus the United States had never moved out of or beyond agriculture; farming just became immensely more productive and less labor-intensive. But it remained a major component of the American economy and an even more important driver of commodity exports, generating both foreign exchange and political influence throughout the late twentieth century and rivaling aircraft, earth-moving equipment, and even finance. Moreover, just as agriculture required the development of industries to produce farm and food-processing equipment, fertilizers, and transport, so too was contemporary manufacturing linked at the hip to a wide variety of service occupations and industries, including scientific research, product engineering, advertising, and sales. The service sector was therefore not a successor economic stage beyond the production of actual things, but a necessary component of a sophisticated manufacturing regime. Of course, the United States had created millions of really low-paying McJobs unrelated to industrial production, but the offshoring of more factories was no solution to that problem.

Instead, Cohen, Zysman, and Tyson advocated an industrial policy that combined strategic investment in key industries—they did think it possible to separate the winners from the losers—with an aggressive program of managed trade with industrial rivals, above all Japan. Indeed, they argued that the island nation had not become such a threat because it enjoyed any "natural comparative advantage," nor because of some cultural tradition that enabled managers to organize work more efficiently, but rather because the Japanese government, often sustained by US foreign policy, offered key industries effective protection in the home market. Japan's striking ability to produce consumer goods did "not emerge from the mists of Japanese history" but from the kind of raw protectionism so widely eschewed by mainstream American economists. Free trade, they argued, existed only in the minds of economists and Washington policymakers.[42]

Ira Magaziner sought to operationalize such industrial policy insights. Like the BRIE academics, he came of age in a world whose ideological landscape had been saturated with New Left attitudes and atmospherics: Brown University in the 1960s. There a Magaziner-led effort to reform the undergraduate curriculum captured both the tenor of the times and his own place within it. His reform proposal, a 455-page manuscript written during the summer of 1967, won the respectful engagement of university administrators. He wanted to perfect institutions, not overthrow them. As a Rhodes Scholar at Oxford, he became good friends with Robert Reich and joined the Friends of Bill club. Reich got a law degree from Yale, while Magaziner, who would later make millions as a business consultant, took a seemingly more radical turn. He dropped out of Oxford to organize against the Vietnam War, and then, back in America, he moved with several of his Brown classmates to gritty, deindustrializing Brockton, Massachusetts, which they sought to transform in much the same spirit in which they had earlier left their imprint on undergraduate life at Brown. These ex-students were part of a larger New Left migration from college towns to industrial cities, where they took factory jobs, joined unions, and agitated for radical change. Magaziner and his friends sought to influence city politics and policies by publishing a newspaper and supporting liberal candidates for local office. But it did not take long for the Brown crew to abandon the project: they soon recognized that competition with local manufacturing, from the low-wage South and abroad, would undercut their revitalizing efforts in any single town.[43]

In 1973, at age twenty-five, Magaziner began working for the Boston Consulting Group (BCG), one of the premier management consultants in the United States. They hired him as part of an effort to reap some of the energy and insights that had emerged from the Sixties generation at a time when the industrial malaise enveloping America made clear that BCG needed something new in the way of managerial advice. Magaziner's first client was LTV, the big Texas conglomerate. That firm had just bought America's sixth-largest steel company, Jones & Laughlin of Pittsburgh. As the youngest member of a six-man consulting team, Magaziner was tasked with exploring the degree of foreign competition, mainly from Japan. BCG and LTV thought they knew what was happening. Despite the backwardness and inefficiency of its steel mills, Japan was undercutting US prices by "dumping" excess tonnage in the States, that is, selling for less than production costs. This was a problem, but steel executives thought it merely a temporary one, because all the experts told them that a world steel shortage was looming over the next few decades. LTV's recent purchase of Pittsburgh's Jones & Laughlin was sure to pay off.

Magaziner flew to Japan and soon discovered that the conventional wisdom was worthless. The Japanese had already built a second wave of postwar mills, all basic oxygen ovens, while the Americans were still making steel in the same mills constructed during the era of Andrew Carnegie and Elbridge Gary. Equally important, up-to-date mills were being built in Brazil, South Korea, and Mexico, often with technical assistance from the Japanese. There would be no steel shortage in the near future, but rather a glut generated by the new mills coming on line and by the substitution of aluminum and plastics for the thinly rolled sheet steel so long purchased in such enormous quantities by Ford, GM, Maytag, and other durable goods manufacturers.[44]

LTV executives dismissed Magaziner's warnings and went on to purchase still more US steel companies rather than using its capital to modernize the old ones. Magaziner was first bewildered by and then contemptuous of this kind of insular US management. "American steel was a closed circle, where a few experts and executives talked only to each other."[45] They blamed foreign government subsidies and low wages abroad for the inefficiencies and financial shortsightedness that made domestic American mills vulnerable to global competition. LTV filed for Chapter 11 in 1986, the largest bankruptcy in US history to that point. Magaziner may have felt a certain sense of schadenfreude, but he was never a mere critic of corporate management. He blamed government's hands-off policy and the free market ideology that stood behind it for the overall troubles faced by US manufacturing enterprises. Based on his BCG experience, he published *Japanese Industrial Policy* in 1980; two years later he coauthored, with Robert Reich, *Minding America's Business: The Decline and Rise of American Prosperity*.[46]

In the famous Plaza Accord of 1985 the United States let the dollar fall by 40 percent. That made American exports less expensive, but it would not solve any real problems, argued Magaziner. The devaluation did not make US industry more efficient, and the cheap dollar policy had an ominous side effect: it made US assets a bargain for those with stronger currencies, creating a temptation for foreign takeovers, not only of firms and factories but of iconic real estate like Rockefeller Center, the Exxon Building, 666 Fifth Avenue, and Arco Plaza in Los Angeles.[47] "Clearly, to outsell the world, we need a strategy far more complex than a lowered currency." Magaziner's conception of industrial policy was to urge upon governments, and especially the US government, the same kind of strategic thinking that consulting groups like BCG had proffered to individual companies. Management, after all, was still a visible hand, a planning apparatus that mobilized capital where it was thought to do the most good. The same outlook might well work for nation-states. "My idea," remembered Magaziner, "was to devise economic-development strategy based on business-strategy concepts."[48] To pursue this idea he turned to politics and policymaking, an even more unpredictable terrain, and a far less remunerative one than private industry consulting work.

Magaziner and his coauthor Robert Reich had very different personalities. Magaziner was brash and sometimes abrasive. Reich was no less

FIGURE 2. Robert Reich and Ira Magaziner in the early 1980s.
(Courtesy of Ira Magaziner)

smart and ambitious, but because he was just four-foot-eleven, he had "learned at an early age that the way to stop getting beat up was to make alliances with bigger guys" when confronting schoolyard bullies. Throughout his work and writing he would therefore seek points of commonality with his opponents, always looking to construct a mutually beneficial outcome.[49]

After prestigious clerkships with a number of influential judges, and a stint at the Justice Department, Reich was appointed by President Jimmy Carter to chair the Policy Planning Staff at the Federal Trade Commission. There he came into intimate contact with the same industrial problems facing US industry that Magaziner was encountering at the Boston Consulting Group. He discovered that many of the companies being prosecuted by the FTC for antitrust violations had been losing ground to the Japanese and other competitors. He met with European officials in charge of industrial policy and with the even more powerful set of men who ran the Japanese Ministry of International Trade and Industry, the state agency that had used a combination of loans, regulations, and persuasion to shape the "state capitalist" renaissance in that island nation.[50]

With Jimmy Carter's defeat, Reich took a post at Harvard's Kennedy School and then burst upon the national scene with a stream of articles and opinion pieces promoting an American version of the "industrial policy" he had seen deployed in Europe and Japan. "Robert Reich is red hot," said one top aide to Walter Mondale, who had already spent a weekend reading a manuscript copy of Reich's new book, *The Next American Frontier*, as part of his successful campaign for the 1984 Democratic Party presidential nomination. "This should do it for the Democrats in 1984," Mondale is said to have remarked to his spouse after turning the last page.[51] "There's no question that every one of the Democratic candidates has been looking at Reich," said Michael Pertschuk, the FTC chairman when Reich served there. Then identified with the "Atari Democrats" who looked to Silicon Valley for new votes, visions, and jobs, Reich certainly thought his industrial policy ideas would be central to any Democratic Party revival. Mondale's campaign, focused on deficit reduction, nevertheless proposed an "Economic Cooperation Council" to help transition the economy toward a high-tech future. Said Reich in 1982, "If you look back 12 years from now, you will say that Reagan was the best thing that happened to the [Democratic] party in terms of forcing it to redefine what it stands for and come up with new solutions."[52]

At the Federal Trade Commission, Reich had encountered the same kind of insular managerial thinking that had so vexed Magaziner. The solution was to "increase the competitive productivity of our industry" through the creation of a "coherent and coordinated industrial policy" that would improve the pattern of investment rather than merely focusing on "aggregate investment levels."[53] Success would be based on "gaining and sustaining a competitive advantage in specific business segments" in the international marketplace.[54] Organized labor played virtually no role in all of this. "I have a great deal of admiration for Bob," said Robert Kuttner, then the editor of the left-liberal *Working Papers for a New Society*, "but labor is his Achilles' heel. If you switch from steel to semiconductors, you go from union to nonunion and I don't see how you can get [AFL-CIO president] Lane Kirkland to sign onto that bargain."[55]

Reich and the other industrial policy advocates were seeking to give that variety of economic thought denominated as "institutionalism" a new lease on life. Because they thought markets were constructed—and in any event highly distorted by the growth of large organizations, from corporations to unions and multilayered government—they stood in a tradition stretching back to Thorstein Veblen, John R. Commons, Rexford Tugwell, and John Kenneth Galbraith. After World War II economists and politicians had turned away from institutionalism, with conservatives renewing their faith in the market while liberals thought macroeconomic incentives, largely along Keynesian lines, would suffice to make the nation and its citizens prosper. Neither thought that institutions—unions, businesses, government rules and regulations—played central roles in determining the contours of economic life. But now Reich and his cohort believed the key to economic success, both for American companies and workers, depended on a conscious effort to reshape "the way the nation organizes itself for production." The "paper entrepreneurialism" that had infected corporate America was an utterly wasteful if not cancerous danger to the real economy in which wages were paid and real things built and sold.[56]

But mass production of the old Fordist sort was not the answer. Instead, Reich and the other industrial policy advocates thought that the rise of computer-assisted manufacturing techniques might well lead the way to a nimble new regime of "flexible specialization" predicated upon automation, skilled labor, and an imaginative managerial culture. Reich projected a future in which a new generation of well-educated workers would find themselves in such demand by companies determined to counter the Japanese or German threat that neither unionism nor tariff protections would be necessary to ensure their incomes, their job security, or their dignity.[57]

Reich was here popularizing one side of a debate then taking place among economists: Was income stagnation and inequality a function of labor's tepid market power in an era of union decline and increasing world trade, or was it a product of "skill-based technological change," a concept that was so widely popular, within the academy and without, that it was often simply labeled SBTC? Reich would resolve the SBTC inequities by offering far more Americans the necessary education and training to handle the new technologies. His solution was a techno-cratic, largely conflict-free vision that elided the contours of raw insti-tutional power then reshaping the political economy. By the early twenty-first century most economists had concluded that enhanced levels of education could not shield either workers or professionals from endemic income stagnation and the growth of societal inequality. But in the meantime the Reichian prescription was highly attractive: Bill Clinton, who read everything his old friend published, would as presi-dent confidently assert, "For more and more, the income gap in Amer-ica is a skills gap."[58]

By the end of the 1980s Reich had staked almost everything on the effort to create an environment so attractive to capital that corporations, both foreign and domestic, would find it to their advantage to invest in the United States. Unlike conservatives, who emphasized deregulation and low taxes, Reich's incentives were indeed "supply side," emphasizing good infrastructure, government-assisted R&D, and the development of a pool of tech-savvy workers—or "symbolic analysts," as he called them in his 1991 book *The Work of Nations*.[59] Market-oriented conservatives had pounded the industrial policy proponents with the charge that they were "picking industrial winners and losers," a task best left to managers and the market. Casper Weinberger, Reagan's secretary of Defense, called it "socialism with a business face—part of the same socialism which has failed wherever tried."[60] Likewise, Murray Weidenbaum, chair of the Council of Economic Advisers under Reagan, cited the history of the Depression-era Reconstruction Finance Corporation, which some advo-cates of a new industrial policy wanted to reconstitute, as an example of a government money-lending institution that descended into corruption and crony capitalism. Instead, the "most effective strategy for encouraging economic growth is no secret," argued Weidenbaum. "It is to reduce gov-ernment barriers and achieve a better functioning market economy."[61]

These ideological attacks were backstopped by two high-profile industrial policy failures. The bailout of the Chrysler Corporation at the end of the Carter administration had proven successful by the mid-1980s, and Reich, who had been a close observer of it all from his perch at the FTC, thought this government-industry-labor collaboration might provide a template for a set of industrial New Deals.[62] But no one celebrated. Conservatives thought the multibillion-dollar bailout set a terrible precedent: tax dollars and government guarantees rescued union labor, preserved the least robust of the old Detroit "Big Three," and ignored a set of market signals that were clearly flashing red. Meanwhile, liberals and many labor partisans denounced the wage concessions forced upon the UAW, the mass layoffs—disproportionately of African-American workers—and the plant closures that helped trim the company's debt and fixed costs. Under the flamboyant leadership of Lee Iacocca, Chrysler did survive and would pay off its government loans and other debts well ahead of schedule, but Detroit remained a symbol of American industrial decline in a region that was just then coming to be labeled "the Rust Belt."

Rhode Island, a New England version of Rust Belt America, was potentially small enough to be a manageable and fixable test case. By the early 1980s Ira Magaziner had resigned from BCG to start his own firm, Telesis (Greek for "intelligently planned progress"), with offices in Paris, Melbourne, and Providence, where Magaziner retained strong personal and political ties from his days at Brown University. In 1983 he volunteered the services of Telesis to help the state's Strategic Development Commission. The result was a vast scheme, in the form of a thousand-page report called The Greenhouse Compact, to revitalize Rhode Island's struggling economy. The state would create sixty thousand new jobs by spending $250 million, in part through a series of nonprofit research "greenhouses" for fledgling industries. Remarkably, the compact, finalized in early 1984, won overwhelming support from the entire Rhode Island political class. It passed the legislature by a landslide, had the endorsement of the governor and leading bankers and businesspeople, and scored well in early public opinion polls.

But in a 1984 referendum voters rejected the compact four-to-one, in part because it included a modest tax increase, but probably more importantly because of a mounting Reagan-era skepticism about any government scheme of large ambition and uncertain outcome. And in Rhode Island the plan seemed ripe for the corruption long identified with the Democratic Party insiders who ran the state.[63] "Industrial policy," wrote Reich, "is one of those rare ideas to have moved swiftly from obscurity to meaninglessness without any intervening period of coherence." As for Rhode Island, industrial planning was fine so long as it built on contemporary policies and institutions. "But wrap it in an elaborate plan and assign it to a new 'strategic commission' comprised of Big Shots, and you can stuff it. Which is what Rhode Island did."[64]

By the end of the 1980s such travails moved Reich and Magaziner to deemphasize the "micro interventionist," industry-specific thrust of any industrial policy and to seek a broader and more systematic approach. Magaziner chaired a high-profile commission whose report, "America's Choice: High Skills or Low Wages!," advocated US adoption of European-style apprenticeship and job training programs.[65] Reich doubled down on skill enhancement with a series of articles and books that appeared in the early 1990s. The most controversial was "Who Is Us?," which appeared in a 1990 issue of the *Harvard Business Review*. Here Reich sought to sever the link between the competitiveness of American-owned or -headquartered corporations and US prosperity. "Who is Us? The answer is the American workforce, the American people, but not particularly the American corporation."[66] Instead of wanting the government to make decisions about what were the most strategic industries in which to invest, or how a better trade policy could nurture or protect key companies, Reich now called for a stepped-up set of spending policies designed to improve infrastructure, worker training, and research in order to make the United States a more attractive place in which foreign companies would invest and produce. Big firms like IBM and Coca-Cola, among many others, earned most of their profits outside the United States. So these companies were not so much abandoning America as joining the world. An industrial policy designed to regulate them or channel their investments would be pointless and self-defeating. Therefore, the United States needed open invest-ment borders and government policies that would promote enhance-ments to human capital. "The American corporation is simply no lon-ger 'us,'" wrote Reich.[67]

This new iteration of industrial policy therefore stood both to the left and to the right of an older liberalism. Reich was right that the interests of corporations and workers were hardly the same. Chrysler had sur-vived, but only by slashing employment and wages. If American living standards could be maintained and improved, it mattered little for whom the American people actually worked. But Reich was also now siding with the global marketeers who had long sought the maximum freedom for capital and the devaluation of any government effort to guide the investment program of any individual company. Not unex-pectedly and perhaps to Reich's embarrassment, his new outlook won a respectful notice on the *Wall Street Journal* editorial page.[68]

Ultimately, the Reich perspective would carry the day as a policy preference in the Clinton administration, but at the time it encountered resistance, and not only from liberal Democrats. Laura Tyson took to the pages of *The American Prospect*, a journal Reich had helped found and a fount of industrial policy advocacy, to put forward a twofold ob-jection to the Reichian idea that corporate nationality hardly mattered anymore. First, she argued, it was premature at best, a view endorsed by Paul Krugman, then an MIT economist with a flair for popular writing on trade topics.[69] The overwhelming majority of all corporations and virtually all the small and medium-sized ones were inexorably rooted on the soil and employing the people of a specific country. R&D spend-ing in particular, the generator of all those good jobs, was almost always linked closely to corporate headquarters.[70] It was the branch assembly plants, employing low-wage, low-skill labor, that were emplaced abroad. And second, Reich assumed that globalization implied a symmetry of national economic policies, when in reality there were wide disparities in law and policy, often to the disadvantage of US companies. Japan put its "transplant" factories in the United States because of domestic content rules and trade friction in the auto and auto parts industry. Consequently, Tyson thought Reich foolishly sanguine to think that the United States could just foster the best possible workforce and then rely on market forces to bring high-wage jobs to our shores.[71] Much to her surprise, Clinton followed the debate and endorsed Tyson's perspective, which was one reason he would select her as his first chair of the Council of Economic Advisers.

Not Laissez-Faire: Reaganite Trade Policy

Had this industrial policy–cum–trade policy debate been taking place entirely within the progressive wing of the Democratic Party, its import might have been less weighty. But a parallel conflict also engaged Republican insiders. During the administration of Ronald Reagan, the US government had been far from passive when it came to managing trade and protecting American industry. Although free trade was the official ideology, relationships with industry groups and individual businesspeople often generated an ad hoc industrial policy that managed trade on a sectorial basis. Commerce Secretary Malcolm Baldrige and his deputy, Clyde Prestowitz, challenged the free trade orthodoxy still favored by the State Department and the economists on the CEA. Many complaints came from older industries that had long been bastions of GOP or Dixiecrat support, like textiles, steel, auto, and motorcycles. They were being inundated by Far Eastern imports.[72] Reagan himself was hardly an ideologue on this issue: while he had been a free trade advocate when still a New Deal Democrat thirty years before, the president owed much of his early financial and political backing to executives from the textile industry and other labor-intensive firms, and these strongly protectionist manufacturers disliked both trade unions and foreign competition. General Electric, which employed Reagan as he transitioned from Hollywood to GOP politics, was a prime example of an American firm that preached free enterprise but for almost a century participated in an array of cartels, price-fixing schemes, and other arrangements designed to eliminate actual price and market share competition.[73]

Clyde Prestowitz proved a forceful advocate for a managed trade program. Although a Republican who got his start in the Goldwater movement, Prestowitz came to have much in common with the industrial policy advocates among the liberal Democrats. His father, a chemical engineer, had advised him to study Japan, because even in the early 1960s it was apparent that the Japanese "made things." As both a student and a businessman in Japan, Prestowitz appreciated the unique features of the capitalist juggernaut he saw arising there. The government played a decisive role in picking winners and losers, but not necessarily in terms of immediate profitability. Instead, the Japanese looked for industries with high technology content; costs in such industries decline rapidly with increases in production. They also required that these new techno-industries be ones that had a "ripple" effect on other sectors of the economy. Prestowitz was therefore a follower of Joseph Schumpeter, the Austrian economist, who coined the famous phrase "creative destruction," a concept that embodied far more than mere price or market competition by one firm with another. The idea stood for something much closer to a near-revolutionary deployment of a new technology that would create an entirely new industry. With stakes this high, argued Prestowitz, government had to play an active role, financial, regulatory, or otherwise. He agreed with the high-ranking MITI official, Naohiro Amaya, who told him in 1986, "If the invisible hand cannot drive the enterprise to research and development, the visible hand must."[74]

Prestowitz was therefore a strong proponent of the Reagan administration's most ambitious industrial policy foray, a half-billion-dollar initiative that sought to parry Japanese efforts to dominate the computer chip industry. The initiative created a new research consortium, SEMATECH, a government-sponsored cartel that dampened domestic competition and stressed manufacturing prowess. And then US trade negotiators pushed through a tough new bargaining strategy that sought to use the Japanese state itself to penetrate that nation's market. Instead of trying to write a set of new rules for "fair" trade—these always failed when US companies encountered resistance from the Japanese cartels and their interlocking network of supplier firms—the United States would insist that the Japanese agree to a target share of their home market that MITI would enforce. Under this new regime Japan would stop dumping its chips on the US market and mandate that Japanese companies purchase 20 percent of all their chips from foreign (i.e., US) producers.[75]

Laura Tyson found much to like in this Reaganite accord. It was the first major US trade agreement in a high-technology, strategic industry, and the first one motivated by concerns about the loss of competitiveness rather than concerns about employment. It was also unique in that it was the first US trade agreement dedicated to improving market access abroad rather than merely restricting it at home, which had been the thrust of the Reagan administration's earlier motorcycle and auto import deals.[76] Perhaps most important, wrote Tyson in *Who's Bashing Whom?*, it was an agreement that moved trade in semiconductors from "manipulated" to "managed," in that the Japanese finally, if reluctantly, agreed to a quantitative target for the minimum share of their market to be supplied by foreign producers. Combined with the support the government was now offering the US semiconductor industry, this was an example of industrial policy designed to avoid American defeat in the "rigged game of international competition."[77] The trade historian Steve Dryden agreed. The accord was "the greatest American departure from free trade ideology in the postwar period."[78]

The battle over how far the United States should depart from free trade ideology to manage international commerce and target business investment was far from over. It would erupt throughout the 1990s, with far more energy and consequence, as Bill Clinton and his rivals sought to reshape the contours of American capitalism.

3

Winning the Presidency

Bill Clinton was ambitious—and lucky. He was elected chair of the National Governors Association in 1986, chair of the Education Commission of the States in 1987, and chair of the Democratic Governors Association in 1988. In 1987 *US News & World Report* found Clinton to be one of the nation's best governors, citing him as a "national spokesman for governors on education and welfare reform" and his reputation as "probably best-liked chief executive among his peers."[1] He almost ran for president in 1988 but settled for a high-profile appearance nominating Michael Dukakis at the Democratic National Convention. That speech turned into a long-winded disaster—the Dukakis people had insisted on adding a good deal of additional material—but it was not a fatal mishap once Clinton deployed a large measure of self-deprecating humor, on The Johnny Carson Show among other venues, to extract himself from that rhetorical debacle.[2]

Bill Clinton campaigned for the presidency as a progressive. Historians and journalists would later highlight his identification with the resolutely centrist Democratic Leadership Council, but Clinton was not its creature. He readily used the DLC political network and often adopted its rhetoric, but when it came to his campaign and to many of his presidential appointments, Clinton deployed the arguments and outlook prevalent among those who sought a vigorous management of the economy. The sharp recession that enveloped the nation in the early 1990s provided a near-perfect context in which his campaign could showcase an economic liberalism that was more robust and innovative than that of any other Democratic presidential candidate since 1964.

That posture would not last, but it got him elected president of the United States.

Three Strikes against George H. W. Bush

When Bill Clinton announced his candidacy in the fall of 1991, he faced an opponent whose apparent popularity cleared the Democratic field of a set of otherwise formidable primary opponents, even as George H. W. Bush so divided his own party that he destroyed his credibility among many conservative Republicans. As president, George Bush had three strikes against him. The recession, precipitated by a Federal Reserve still fearful that low unemployment was a dangerous sign of an overheated economy, officially ended in early 1991, but the recovery was painfully slow, with layoffs ravaging once-secure white-collar jobs. Sears Roebuck laid off fifty thousand workers and once-mighty IBM, for the first time in its seventy-nine-year history, cut over five thousand jobs in New York. The recession felled Michael Dukakis's high-tech "Massachusetts Miracle," but it hit hardest in California, where the state lost three hundred thousand jobs, many in an aerospace industry made obsolete by the end of the Cold War. There were still lots of fast-food and retail jobs out there—McDonald's and Wal-Mart were booming—but the recession of the early 1990s confirmed once again that income stagnation was now a permanent feature of American life, at least for the vast majority of those who traded their labor power for a paycheck.[3]

The second strike against Bush came at the GOP convention in 1988 that nominated him to run for president. Determined to assure skeptics that he walked in Reagan's footsteps, Bush had famously pledged, "Read my lips. No new taxes!" But the recession slashed tax revenues, thereby doubling the federal government's projected budget deficit. Bush therefore faced a conundrum: the Gramm-Rudman-Hollings Balanced Budget Act that President Reagan had himself signed in 1981 stipulated that if Congress and the White House could not agree on a budget that balanced by 1993, then an automatic sequestering of funds would begin on October 1, 1990, requiring at least a partial government closure, which in those days even Republicans sought to avoid. So Bush broke his tax pledge, relying on Democratic votes for a compromise budget deal. Although Ronald Reagan had raised taxes at least four times during his presidency, the Bush transgression seemed a stark betrayal to all those Republicans who had already begun to recast the Reagan presidency's complex history of sometimes messy statecraft as self-justifying myth. Conservative rage thereby opened the door to the rise of Georgia Representative Newt Gingrich and the 1992 primary challenge of culture warrior Pat Buchanan.[4]

The president might have counterbalanced both the recession and the tax controversy if his administration had advanced almost any sort of domestic agenda. But George H. W. Bush had no such program. As his chief of staff, John Sununu, told a conservative audience in November 1990, "There's not another single piece of legislation that needs to be passed in the next two years for this president. In fact, if Congress wants to come together, adjourn, and leave, it's all right with us."[5] The division and incoherence within the Bush administration was temporally masked by the short, sharp, and militarily successful Gulf War, which pushed the president's popularity to a stratospheric 92 percent in the early spring of 1991. With prospects for his reelection so high, many heavy-hitting Democratic politicians—among them Governor Mario Cuomo of New York, Senator Bill Bradley of New Jersey, Senator Edward Kennedy of Massachusetts, and House Majority Leader Richard Gephardt—decided that this was not their year. Thus was the presidential door opened to an Arkansas governor whose only previous national exposure had been an abysmal appearance at the Democratic National Convention two and a half years before.

Enter Stage Right: The Democratic Leadership Council

Clinton was winning many admirers beyond the state of Arkansas. One of the most important, and controversial, was Al From, the founder of the Democratic Leadership Council. Some historians have found it convenient to label Clinton a product of the DLC, but as this chapter and others will indicate, the relationship was actually far more ambiguous.[6]

Clinton often called himself a "New Democrat," which was a phrase the DLC used as well, but the Arkansas governor also drew support and ideas from a much broader range of people, some of whom were intensely hostile to From's organization and outlook.

Al From had once been a youthful Great Society liberal, but he soon identified with those who saw many of the social and cultural impulses arising out of the Sixties as harmful to the Democrats. He was a Senate staffer for Ed Muskie during most of the 1970s, after which he served as staff director of the House Democratic Caucus from 1981 to 1985, working for Louisiana Representative Gillis Long, its newly elected chair. Although Long was moderately liberal, one of his most important goals was to keep the Southern "boll weevils" inside the Democratic Party, even if they backed Reagan's military buildup, tax cuts, and hostility to the welfare state.[7] This would become a central concern for From and like-minded operatives when they formed the Democratic Leadership Council in the aftermath of Walter Mondale's forty-nine-state loss in 1984. A self-admitted "organization of political elites for political elites," the DLC made little effort to build a grassroots constituency or to hide its funding sources. Indeed, friendly corporations and wealthy individuals were often consulted when policy discussions took place.[8]

The DLC believed that the Democrats had to disengage from the unions, embrace markets more than government, and eschew anything that smacked of racial or gender rights militancy. Above all, the DLC argued that the key to Democratic Party political success was to accommodate the cultural conservatism that had seemingly created the Reagan Democrats, the Northern, white working-class voters fearful of racial and cultural change. As the DLC's 1989 manifesto, "The Politics of Evasion," put it, the next Democratic nominee for president would have to "convey a clear understanding of, and identification with, the social values and moral sentiments of average Americans." That tract, the DLC's most elaborate and influential policy statement, had been written by the well-respected political scientist William Galston, whose work had a communitarian flavor, and Elaine Kamarck, a more hard-nosed political operative. Both would find their way into the Clinton administration.

What Galston and Kamarck considered an "evasion" was modern liberalism's focus on issues of economic fairness and its defense of the welfare state, plus the Democratic Party's dependence on "interest groups." The DLC never explicitly spelled out which groups these were, but it was obvious: organized labor, the civil rights community, environmentalists, and advocates for women's rights. They called this "liberal fundamentalism" and rejected the idea that "it's all economics" when it came to the Democratic Party's core appeal. This was an evasion because "it allows Democrats to avoid dealing with problems of vulnerability on national defense and social issues." This was Republican culture war terrain, and until the Democrats contested it the party would never get a serious hearing from millions of white, suburban, and working-class voters. Galston and Kamarck also rejected the idea that the traditional class appeal put forward by the Democrats could mobilize new elements of the electorate, a viewpoint then being advanced by Jesse Jackson and his Rainbow Coalition. Instead, the DLC manifesto insisted that an electoral strategy based on traditionalist values had to take precedence. In practice this meant that the New Democrats would emphasize crime control, welfare reform, and a "reinvention" of government to make it both smaller and more efficient. The DLC saw shrinking the deficit as a cultural values marker in and of itself, and one of far greater import than any economic stimulus or welfare state enhancements that a Keynesian program might offer all those alienated Reagan Democrats.[9]

Al From and other leaders wanted to make the DLC a hegemonic presence within the Democratic Party, but after 1988 the organization actually took on an increasingly factional character rejected by much of the party. Take the case of Richard Gephardt. He won election to Congress in 1976 representing a German-Catholic working-class neighborhood in St. Louis. Early in his career, his moderate credentials were impeccable: he opposed abortion rights and affirmative action and voted in favor of Ronald Reagan's legislative agenda on 69 percent of all key votes, including the big tax cuts of 1981. Gephardt was therefore the perfect first chair of the DLC, a post he took in 1985. But as he geared up to run for the Democratic presidential nomination in 1988, he understood that his electoral base must be the industrial Midwest. That meant supporting union labor, and especially its critical view of unmanaged global trade, a far more progressive tax program, and a decided shift to the left when it came to the culture wars over gender and race. In 1990 Senator Howard Metzenbaum of Ohio, another Midwest liberal, took the lead in founding a coalition of officeholders to counter DLC influence by demonstrating that "the future of the Democratic Party does not lie in the fine tuning of Reaganism."[10] By the time Bill Clinton became president, Gephardt, by then Majority Leader in the House, would lead the bloc of liberal Democrats that rejected fiscal austerity, NAFTA, and welfare reform.

The DLC fight with Jesse Jackson and the wing of the Democratic Party for which he spoke was of even more consequence. In reality, Jackson was one of the more conservative figures to come out of the civil rights movement. By the 1970s his Operation Push, headquartered in Chicago, emphasized something close to a Black capitalism that linked education, self-discipline, homeownership, and entrepreneurial achievement. With Reagan's victory he shifted leftward, organized the interracial Rainbow Coalition, and ran for the Democratic presidential nomination twice, in 1984 and 1988, winning numerous primaries and actually doubling his support among both voters and convention delegates. With nearly seven million primary votes in 1988, he offered Michael Dukakis a strong challenge. His appeal was that of a militant New Dealer, updated to include contemporary issues of racial justice, as well as support for Palestinian statehood. Jackson called for a coalition of "working people" to counter the "merger maniacs" of corporate America. His campaign thereby evoked genuine enthusiasm, not only on the party's urban left but also among some of those Reagan Democrats the DLC saw as its natural constituency.[11]

The Jackson insurgency threw a monkey wrench into DLC plans. One of Al From's greatest accomplishments was to lobby successfully for an early, multistate Southern primary that would favor a presidential candidate from that region. But From's efforts could not ensure a victory for the kind of candidate his party faction wanted. In 1988 Jackson split the Southern primary vote with Tennessee Senator Al Gore, then a DLC favorite. Black voters in that region had become just as important as whites when it came to filling Democratic primary ballot boxes. Thereafter, the DLC went to war against Jackson and his wing of the Democratic Party, declaring his campaigns "the purest version of liberal fundamentalism" and excluding him from those meetings to which the DLC invited other prominent party figures. In response, Jackson described the New Democrats as modern "Dixiecrats," proposing that the letters DLC stood for "Democrats for the Leisure Class."[12]

From flew down to Little Rock in April 1989. To the DLC, Michael Dukakis had not been an "interest group liberal," but his campaign had inspired few Democrats, new or old.[13] From was therefore looking for a fresh and dynamic figure. "I've got a deal for you," he told Clinton in the governor's office on the second floor of the Arkansas State Capitol. "If you agree to become chair of the DLC, we'll pay for your travel around the country, we'll work together on an agenda, and I think you'll be president one day and we'll both be important."[14] From liked Clinton for many reasons—his vibrancy, intelligence, capacity to talk about ideas, and, of signal importance, his Arkansas educational reforms pushed forward against the opposition of the "powerful" Arkansas Education Association. Because he could not decide if he would run for governor again, whether he would run for president, or how he would craft his campaign, Clinton took nearly a year to accept From's oft-repeated importuning. In truth the DLC would serve as a vehicle for Clinton's aspirations, not the other way around. The DLC chairmanship gave Clinton plenty of national exposure, positioned him as a fresh new voice within the Democratic Party, helped him consolidate his support in the South, and validated his centrist bona fides. In later years Clinton always credited the DLC for helping develop his political posture, writing in his autobiography, "I believed the DLC was furthering the best values and principles of the Democratic Party with new ideas."[15]

In its earliest incarnation, the Clinton campaign did look like a DLC operation. The Arkansas governor hired the DLC's Bruce Reed as one of his first staffers. The Idaho-born Reed was a former speechwriter for Al Gore who had grown up in a politically liberal family that had been appalled as Republicans weaponized a set of culturally inflected wedge issues—crime, Cuba, welfare, and school prayer—to defeat in 1980 the liberal icon Senator Frank Church and then move Reed's home state rightward. So Reed signed on to the DLC culture-as-politics agenda and came to see Bill Clinton as the talented figure who would deploy this perspective in a successful presidential campaign. It was Reed who wrote the programmatic Georgetown University speeches of October 1991 that kicked off the campaign. Reed helped Clinton come up with the label "New Covenant" to describe the New Democrat emphasis on personal responsibility that his administration would seek to engender. Although neither the idea nor the words ever caught on, Clinton liked it because of its communitarian and vaguely religious flavor. More controversially, Reed was also the wordsmith who came up with the "End welfare as we know it" phrase, whose policy implications, racial and otherwise, would inaugurate years of infighting during Clinton's first term.[16] For now, however, those DLC-inspired portions of Clinton's speeches remained largely rhetorical.

But some things were not just wordplay. By the middle of Clinton's campaign to capture the presidency it had become apparent that this candidate had a deep and genuine engagement with African-American culture, more so than any other white politician of his time. He knew by heart the words to "Lift Every Voice and Sing," the "Negro National Anthem." He had a decades-old reservoir of Black friends and colleagues, many of whom would join his administration. In the Super Tuesday primary, he won 80 percent of the Black vote across the South. And he could play the sax.[17]

But none of this stood in the way of the calculating decisions Clinton made in the first half of 1992. In January he made a point of returning to Arkansas to oversee the execution of Ricky Ray Rector, who had murdered two people, including a police officer, eleven years before. The Rector case was controversial because a suicide attempt had left this Black man mentally impaired, both during his trial and at the time of his execution, when he famously asked that his jailers put aside the pecan pie dessert from his last meal, "saving it for later." Then in early March, just before the Super Tuesday set of Southern primaries, Clinton held a campaign event, at which he announced his support of a tough crime bill, at a prison near Stone Mountain, Georgia, the notorious site of

KKK rallies and Confederate revivals. In a widely distributed photo, dozens of Black prisoners form a backdrop for Clinton and other white Southern politicians.[18] And then in June 1992 Clinton took a page from the DLC handbook when he used his own speaking time at a Jesse Jackson Rainbow Coalition event to chastise rap artist and community activist Sister Souljah for intemperate remarks a month earlier—in the aftermath of the Rodney King riots—that seemed to condone Black-on-white violence.[19]

Clinton Moves Left

Despite all this, Clinton's campaign was not that of a DLC New Democrat. By 1992 one key pillar of the DLC perspective had been sharply discounted. With the end of the Cold War, no one thought military experience or the projection of a strong national security posture important to the success of a presidential candidate. Clinton's reputation as a draft dodger did not help, but his manifest disinterest in most of the classic dilemmas of the Cold War proved inconsequential. His campaign proposed substantial cuts to military spending, both to reduce the budget deficit and to free up the funds needed to invest at home. Like the New Democrats, Clinton said he wanted his presidency to focus on economic growth, not income redistribution, but that idea was hardly at variance with the industrial policy advocates who had become influential in the Clinton brain trust. A warmed-over Keynesianism was not enough. In a global economy, growth would require the kind of governmental investment programs, regulatory reforms, trade negotiations, health provision, and progressive changes in the tax law that were essential if a form of managed capitalism was to be put on the agenda. At a May 15, 1992, Little Rock meeting chiefly concerned with figuring out how to counter Ross Perot's appeal, Al From claimed to have "stopped the headlong dash into social democracy" by the likes of Robert Reich and Ira Magaziner, who had led the discussion. But this was braggadocio. Despite all of the DLC's best efforts to "make traditional Democrats who guard the Democratic status quo unhappy enough to scream," the Clinton campaign was shifting leftward and stayed there right through the election.[20] Magaziner thought Clinton was a "master politician" trying to bring together a "majority coalition." He therefore had few qualms about Clinton's DLC membership. He was "in" that organization, but hardly its "creature."[21]

Campaign aide James Carville achieved a certain political immortality by coining the slogan "The Economy, Stupid!" It was posted on the wall of the Clinton campaign's Little Rock war room early in the fall of 1992 to keep campaign strategists intently focused on the economic welfare of working America. But it was also a cautionary injunction: stay away from the social controversies and cultural flashpoints that an increasingly desperate George Bush was seeking to highlight. Of course, most Clinton Democrats were social liberals who favored affirmative action, a process for allowing gays to serve in the military, and various energy conservation measures, which by the early 1990s were as much cultural markers as economic programs. The GOP naturally sought to turn such views into wedge issues that would divide the Democrats, and all too often the Republicans had a willing partner among DLC office-holders, like Georgia Senator Sam Nunn, who helped create the damaging contretemps over gay men and women serving in the military during the first few months of the Clinton presidency. And as we shall see, on a wide variety of Clintonite issues, including the legislative fight to preserve a stimulus program early in the first term as well as health care reform, progressive taxation, and a tax on carbon emissions, DLC stalwarts proved far less loyal to the new administration than the liberals from labor, the civil rights community, and the left academy, who more often than not muted their criticism in the interest of preserving a solid progressive front.

By late in the spring of 1992 Bill Clinton was winning the Democratic presidential nomination, but he was briefly in third place overall because Ross Perot, the eccentric Texas populist, was stealing the economic limelight. This spurred the progressives among the Friends of Bill to put out a campaign manifesto remarkable for its ambition. Derek Shearer, an advocate of "economic democracy" who had been active in Tom Hayden's 1976 Senate campaign, put forward the idea for the pamphlet that became *Putting People First*. Written largely by Reich and Magaziner, the thirty-one-page pamphlet had plenty of input from other domestic policy advisers. There was much advocacy of training and education, including a very German-style proposal that every employer spend 1.5 percent of payroll on apprenticeship and training programs for their workers, both blue-collar and white-collar. The call in *Putting People First* for $50 billion a year in new "investments," though designed to boost productivity, including a "Rebuild America Fund," was not merely Keynesianism: the pamphlet's subtitle was A National Economic Strategy for America. Americans had once earned higher wages than anyone else in the world, but US workers were now in tenth place, it reported. "In Europe and Japan our competitors' economies grew three and four times faster than ours—because their leaders decided to invest in their people and Washington did not. . . . Today we have no economic vision, no economic leadership and no economy strategy."[22] In a video accompanying the plan's launch, Clinton declared, "I asked the rich to pay their fair share, so the rest of America can finally get a break."[23]

Organized by Jeff Faux of the left-progressive Economic Policy Institute, five hundred liberal economists endorsed *Putting People First*.[24] Although the Clinton plan promised to cut government employment by one hundred thousand people, there was no discussion of shrinking entitlement programs and only the briefest mention of the eventual need to move the federal budget into balance. Indeed, the campaign document proposed a new entitlement, "by guaranteeing quality, affordable health care." Remarked Alan Blinder, who would join the new administration's Council of Economic Advisers, "Clinton did not really run on reducing the budget deficit in any strong way."[25] Speechwriter David Kusnet, who also had a hand in writing *Putting People First*, concurred. "Fiscal conservatism had not been part of Clinton's appeal during the campaign." Deficit reduction had been a Tsongas issue and would be a Perot call to arms. "The title of our campaign document was Putting People First. It wasn't Getting America's Fiscal House in Order."[26]

Indeed, "The Calls for an Industrial Policy Grow Louder." That was the headline for a July 1992 *New York Times* story on why all three presidential candidates were now entertaining targeted investments in what Bill Clinton called "cutting edge products and technologies." Even the

Bush administration budget director, Richard G. Darman, no fan of big government, was boasting that the Republicans had increased the federal budget for nonmilitary research by 7 percent over the last year. "Industrial policy is an idea whose time has come," announced Clyde Prestowitz, now president of his own Washington think tank. "Even the Bush Administration is going that way."[27] The communitarian writer Amitai Etzioni declared in the midst of the presidential campaign, "Whoever the next President may be, industrial policy (by one name or another) is coming." Therefore, the real question was "but what kind."[28]

But an industrial policy would cost billions, and that expenditure clashed with the deficit issue still looming over the 1992 campaign. In some instances, the candidates debated the deficit as a concrete issue that would necessarily constrain expenditures. But more often, and more pervasively, the deficit had become a metaphor for all that was wrong in America. That was certainly the way Paul Tsongas saw things. A former Massachusetts senator who had resigned to battle cancer and then made what seemed like a full recovery, Tsongas was focused as much on the nation's economic maladies as the Arkansas governor. He hailed from Lowell, a declining mill town, but Tsongas was not a Keynesian or industrial policy partisan. Instead, he wanted self-sacrifice. America may have won the Cold War, he pronounced, but Japan and Germany were gathering up the spoils. To compete, the United States had to freeze the federal budget, cap expenditures, and avoid tax cuts even for the middle class. When asked why he had not offered a tax cut similar to that proposed by Bill Clinton, Tsongas retorted, "I'm not trying to play Santa Claus."[29]

All this sounded like the Walter Mondale of 1984, whose promise to raise taxes in the face of Reagan's sunny economic optimism had lost him every state in the union except Minnesota and the District of Columbia. But Tsongas, who beat Clinton in the New Hampshire primary, had a message that resonated in a political season that saw both rising unemployment and a budget deficit four times higher than that which greeted Ronald Reagan twelve years before. Clinton countered by arguing for a targeted investment program, including specific tax and credit incentives for specific industry sectors rather than the across-the-board reduction in capital gains taxes favored by the Massachusetts senator. After Tsongas criticized Clinton for "pandering" to the middle class, the Arkansas governor replied that such tax relief was just compensation, given the "class warfare" waged by the GOP during the 1980s.[30]

Bedeviled by charges that he was an adulterer and a cad, Clinton would declare his second-place finish in New Hampshire evidence that he was "the comeback kid." He then went on to trounce Tsongas in Illinois and Michigan, winning the working-class vote, both Black and white. Clinton's strength in the South and among African Americans helped him survive and then defeat a handful of once-promising challengers. Tom Harkin of Iowa was labor's candidate, but he left the campaign in early March. Senator Bob Kerry of Nebraska was a decorated Vietnam War veteran, but he ran a lackluster campaign. Jerry Brown, the former California governor, ran as an eccentric, poorly funded candidate who nevertheless took advantage of liberal misgivings about Clinton, both moral and economic, to win six states, including New York. But Brown had to drop out in June after Clinton beat him in his own state of California.

The Perot Factor

Clinton had yet one more rival on his "left." That was Ross Perot, who in 1992 would run the most successful third-party campaign since Theodore Roosevelt eighty years before. A conservative Democrat turned Republican from Texarkana, Texas, Perot was a short wiry man with the didactic manner of someone used to commanding subordinates. An ardent supporter of the Vietnam War and a high-profile champion of American POWs, Perot had become rich in the 1960s after he founded Electronic Data Services (EDS), which used high-pressure salesmanship and a well-funded lobby operation to win multimillion-dollar contracts to administer Medicare and Medicaid at both the state and national levels.[31] When GM bought most of EDS in 1984, Perot joined the automaker's board. There he was appalled by the bloated bureaucracy, the managerial complacency, and the Wall Street influence that thwarted long-range investment. After he went public, denouncing the

"GM system," company president Roger Smith persuaded GM to buy him out and then throw him off the board.[32]

Perot rejected the phrase "industrial policy," but the swashbuckling Texas entrepreneur was very much an advocate of managed trade, government efforts to guide new investment in US plant and equipment, and a thorough reform of the managerial ethos, which he saw as shortsighted and greedy. "I don't want to live in a country that can't make its own television sets," Perot told the journalist John Judis in June 1992, shortly after he decided to run an independent campaign for president. He shared with the Clintonite industrial policy theorists both a fear of Japan's trading prowess and an admiration for MITI and other East Asian efforts to stake out leading-edge technologies. He wanted changes in the tax and regulatory laws designed to persuade— or force—CEOs to plan "ten years ahead, not ten minutes ahead."[33] Although the press often condescended to Perot as something of an untutored Texas wildcatter, his money and fame made it possible for him to tap into and enhance a discontent with America's economic prospects that was not dissimilar from the message advanced by Clinton, Reich, Magaziner, and Prestowitz.

Perot used his fortune to broadcast a series of didactic infomercials highlighting his determination to eliminate the budget deficit and balance the federal budget. But his most famous contribution to political discourse came in an October 15, 1992, presidential debate when Perot weighed in against a prospective Mexican-US free trade agreement. "If you're paying $12, $13, $14 an hour for factory workers and you can move your factory south of the border, pay a dollar an hour for labor . . . have no health care . . . have no environmental controls, no pollution controls and no retirement, and you don't care about anything but making money, there will be a *giant sucking sound* going south."[34] Perot won almost 19 percent of the vote in November; his supporters were as much from the North as the South, overwhelmingly working-class, and mainly motivated by economic rather than cultural issues. In analyzing the 1992 vote—which was exceptionally large by historic standards—social scientists argued that Perot had taken as many votes from the Democrats as the GOP. But most Republicans thought Perot had cost their party the election, and in the next few years they would make strenuous efforts to win over his base.[35] Bill Clinton might well have forestalled this GOP gambit had he been able to win over much of Perot's constituency to a program of economic reconstruction. But Clinton's policy failures during the first two years of his presidency thwarted that hope; over time Perot's economic nationalism, authoritarian disdain for congressional politics, and fixation on the budget deficit foreshadowed the GOP sweep in the 1994 congressional elections, the rise of the Tea Party in 2010, and the appeal of Donald Trump five years later.

Indeed, the fetishization of deficit politics, which Perot did so much to advance, would prove an albatross around Clinton's neck. Deficits had been of little concern to the Reaganites during the 1980s, and in most recessions Democrats had welcomed a Keynesian excess of spending over taxes as a spur to the economy. But now the very existence of a budget deficit was associated with governmental dysfunction, the increasingly severe recession, and the prospect of much more inflation. Fighting those price increases, phantom or not, was the ostensible reason the Federal Reserve had tightened the economic screws almost from the onset of the Bush presidency. Economists hostile to Keynesianism, including Milton Friedman and his heirs, thought that any economic stimulus generated by a budget deficit was negated by "crowding out" in the bond market, because funding the deficit necessarily used up savings that might otherwise have bought bonds, thereby raising interest rates and making new investments prohibitively expensive.[36] Interest rates were at about 7 percent in the early 1990s, with unemployment rising to 7.8 percent, the highest level since the recovery from the Volcker shock of a decade before. To much of the public, budget deficits and high unemployment had become linked at the hip, regardless of protests from left-of-center economists. Ross Perot and Paul Tsongas had put deficit reduction at the core of their presidential bids, while President Bush adopted the classic GOP denunciation of all Democrats as tax-and-spend profligates.

FIGURE 3. Bill Clinton, Ross Perot, and George H. W. Bush at the Michigan State University presidential debate on October 19, 1992. (Mark Cardwell / Reuters Pictures)

All this was encapsulated by the query put forth by an anxious voter during the second of three televised presidential debates in October 1992. "How has the national debt personally affected each of your lives?" asked Marisa Hall Summers, a twenty-five-year-old African-American woman then working for a downsized engineering firm. "And if it hasn't, how can you honestly find a cure for the economic problems of the common people if you have no experience in what's ailing them?" Bush took the question literally and flubbed the answer, but Clinton understood its ill-defined if more poignant meaning. The issue was economic insecurity and stagnant wages. He took a couple of steps toward Summers, asking her if she knew people who had lost their jobs and their homes. When she said yes, he launched into an empathetic account of how hard times impacted the people of Arkansas, workers and families in a small state, many of whom he had actually gotten to know during his twelve years as governor. And he told Summers he had a plan to fix things by reinvesting in the skills of the American people and escaping "the grip of a failed economic theory" emanating from Washington.[37] The exchange proved a stellar moment in the Clinton campaign, for the candidate understood that Perot's fixation on the national debt was but a metaphor for a far larger set of economic and social issues facing the polity.

After Victory: Putting Some Liberals on the Team

Clinton's victory in 1992 had a bifurcated character. On the one hand, his election was not impressive. He won with 43 percent of the vote, a mere plurality, as the Republican Senate leader, Robert Dole, was quick to point out on the morning after the election. Despite his 370 electoral votes, only Woodrow Wilson had entered the twentieth-century White House with a lower proportion of the popular vote. Of course, George Bush polled disastrously, at 37.5 percent, even as Perot helped boost overall turnout to a substantial 55 percent. Still, Clinton's mediocre showing was reflected in the Congress, where the Democrats made no gains in the Senate and actually lost ten seats in the House. Virtually every Democrat who won their district in a two-person race did so with a larger margin than Clinton did. The new president's legislative affairs director, Charles Brain, was faced with a Congress in which "nobody felt particularly indebted to Bill Clinton for getting there." The party retained majorities in both chambers, but they were "unruly," as Clinton CEA member Alan Blinder later put it.[38] The ranks of Democratic women and racial minorities rose substantially, moving the Democratic caucus several degrees to the left, even as the party retained an unreliable cohort of Southerners, some of whom would decamp to the GOP when the going got rough.

But liberals were enraptured by the 1992 results. Twelve years of conservative governance seemed to be finished. "The American public thundered yesterday for, above all, change," editorialized the *New York Times* on the morning after the election.[39] "Democrat Bill Clinton's victory marks the end of the age of heroic conservatism," wrote *Washington Post* columnist E. J. Dionne, "a time when the right sought to remake the world through market economics, traditional values and military superiority.

The president-elect has thus been offered the opportunity Ronald Reagan was accorded 12 years ago: To name and define a new age, a turning point in the nation's life."[40] And Walter Dean Burnham, the political scientist who practically invented critical elections theory, wrote that the 1992 returns were a "landside vote of no confidence in the conservative regime that Ronald Reagan and his allies had sought to create. . . . Rejections of this order of magnitude have not happened very often over the course of American political history."[41] Still, Clinton and his team had to move quickly to take advantage of this rare progressive opportunity. As the *Times* editorialists put it, "If he is to avoid the fate of Jimmy Carter, the last Democrat to follow a failed Republican Administration, he'll have to set out a short list of clear goals—and work fast to meet them, before the political concrete dries."[42]

At first glance, it seemed that the new Clinton administration might well fulfill the more interventionist and adventuresome campaign promises embodied in Carville's "The Economy, Stupid" slogan. Both Robert Reich and Ira Magaziner got important posts in the new administration. Magaziner would lead the task force writing the administration's health insurance reform, a project that, as we shall see, was conceived as an industrial policy initiative as much as an expansion and reform of the American welfare state. Reich, whom the *New York Times'* Louis Uchitelle mistakenly called "Clinton's Point Man on Economics," became the new Secretary of Labor.[43] This was a second-tier cabinet post, but Reich expected—well, hoped anyway—that in the new administration the Labor Department's clout might be enhanced because he would have a voice on the new National Economic Council (NEC). That was a coordinating body for domestic social and economic policy analogous to the older, and powerful, National Security Council (NSC), which had just played such an effective role coordinating the Gulf War. The NEC had been an idea put forward by Reich and Shearer.

Reich was also unorthodox because he was the first Democratic secretary of Labor who had no ties, institutional or academic, with any wing of the American labor movement. When Reich's appointment was announced, Tom Donahue, the AFL-CIO's second in command, called up Jeff Faux to ask, "Who is this guy?"[44] Many in the Clinton circle saw such distance as a potential advantage, especially since Reich had been wont to identify trade unionism with an "old economy" based on static industries, low-skilled jobs, and an aversion to global trade and commerce. His passion was for training, education, and new technologies. The recipe for a prosperous working class therefore lay in the creation of a skilled workforce that could keep companies in the United States and lure other firms there from across the globe. Reflecting upon the growth of wage inequality over the past fifteen years, Reich opined that "the solution isn't to stop technological progress or to block global trade and investment (even if such moves were possible, they'd impoverish every-one). The main answer is to improve education and job skills. The other part of the answer is to renew the compact between companies and their workers. Encourage profit-sharing. Strengthen unions." If his en-dorsement of unionization seemed an afterthought, it was. Even after spending four years at the Labor Department he caricatured labor's trade program, claiming in his 1997 memoir *Locked in the Cabinet* that unions wanted to "erect walls around America and produce inside our borders everything we buy."[45]

Clinton chose the forty-five-year-old Berkeley economist Laura D'Andrea Tyson as chair of his Council of Economic Advisers. They had first met in August 1992 when Clinton hosted a group of economic ad-visers in Little Rock. The least academically distinguished of the group, which included Nobel laureate James Tobin, Lawrence Summers of the World Bank, Alan Blinder of Princeton, and Paul Krugman of MIT, Tyson nevertheless made a huge impression on Clinton, if only because her unorthodox, industrial policy–oriented views complemented his own. During a wide-ranging discussion, Blinder, Krugman, and Summers downplayed the degree to which the decline of traditional manufactur-ing was a critical problem for the United States. Tyson disagreed, and relying upon a very concrete understanding of the specific industries and firms studied by her colleagues at the Berkeley Roundtable on In-ternational Economics, she pressed home the point. "That was clearly the meeting where she outshined the other folks," recalled Derek

Shearer, who, along with Reich, had pushed for the Tyson CEA appointment. "She scored a lot of points" with Clinton on the question of reviving US manufacturing, remembered Blinder. Her advocacy of "managed trade" was particularly appealing to the president-elect. "It would be a mistake to underestimate her," said Krugman.[46]

Historically, a president's CEA chair had been, in the words of Sylvia Nasar of the *New York Times*, "the most mainstream of mainstream economists," but Tyson broke that mold. She advocated using government policy to make sure the United States maintained its economic edge: giving subsidies to industries that were developing new technologies, using tougher "managed" trade tactics, and channeling money into commercial research. Although Tyson differed with Reich on trade policy—she hardly thought that enhanced job skills alone would bring industry back to the United States—they worked in tandem when it came to the need for a large stimulus program and new "investments" in training and infrastructure, even if the budget deficit remained high during the early years of the new administration.[47] Not a macroeconomist—and not a man either—Tyson set off alarm bells when Clinton chose her over the World Bank's Larry Summers, whose academic prestige, policy experience, and network of powerful advocates was far superior to hers.[48] Alan Blinder, who also wanted to be chair of Clinton's CEA, was therefore reluctant to come on board as a mere member: "The notion that I would sit as second fiddle . . . well, it took a long time for my male ego to swallow that." After entreaties were made by increasingly senior members of the new administration, Vice President-Elect Al Gore made a phone call. "I said something about playing second fiddle," remembered Blinder, "and he said, 'Tell me about it.'" Blinder signed up and soon enjoyed a highly cooperative relationship with Tyson.[49]

Tyson's appointment—and the policies she would pursue—were backstopped at Clinton's Little Rock conference by high-profile economists, including James Tobin and Robert Solow, who were not afraid of an activist role for the government when it came to ending the stagnation that had doomed the Bush presidency. Solow, who had practically invented growth economics in the 1950s and won a Nobel Prize for it, was the kickoff speaker at the economic summit. Most attending

FIGURE 4. In 1995 President Clinton promoted Laura Tyson from chairwoman of the Council of Economic Advisers to head of the National Economic Council. (Clinton Presidential Library)

agreed with him that the decline in productivity, wages, and economic growth during the previous two decades could not be solved by a shot of Keynesian stimulus. "This is not just a short-term glitch," announced Solow. Putting on the Clinton agenda the inequality and stagnation that had attenuated the capacity of the Democratic Party to win working-class votes, Solow told his listeners that "family incomes used to double every 30 years: at current rates they'll double in 200."[50] Such was the challenge. Could Bill Clinton and his talented team muster the will to tackle it?

PART II

Market Managers

4

Managing Health Care Capitalism

At the onset of Clinton's presidency there were two initiatives that most clearly reflected the ideas of his advisers and other policy mavens who saw the US economy as a system that needed a large measure of governmental management if employers and their workers were to thrive. The first effort centered on the universalization of American health provision, a truly gigantic task and the great unfulfilled promise of the New Deal. The second was the contentious attempt to "manage" trade with Japan, then thought to be America's most formable economic rival. Both initiatives would prove to be highly instructive failures, revealing a great deal about how and why liberal efforts to reconfigure even a slice of the US economy faced such political, ideological, and economic obstacles.

Losing the Corporate War on Health Care Costs

By the 1990s many thought the time had finally come when a universal system of health provision commanded the support not only of those who had long sought a New Deal–style expansion of the welfare state but of those within the worlds of business, insurance, and medical provision, sectors of the economy once historically hostile to such a social innovation. Not only were health care costs increasing far more rapidly than inflation, but the burden was falling with greater weight upon big business and government. In 1965 households funded 60.5 percent of the nation's health care expenses, with employers paying but 17 percent and government a few percentage points more. A quarter-century later, each sector paid about one-third, with the largest increase being felt in the corporate ranks.[1] Meanwhile, health care costs were eating up an alarmingly larger proportion of the entire gross domestic product. In 1970 both Canada and the United States devoted about 7 percent of their GDP to the medical sector. Twenty years later, the United States was spending more than 12 percent of GDP on health care, compared to 9 percent in Canada, where a remarkable restructuring of health care finance had imposed a "global budget" on hospitals and physicians, thus constructing a ceiling on spending and fees. In the United States, by contrast, there seemed to be few limits on health care expenses. In just the last half-decade before Clinton's inauguration, private insurance premiums had increased by 90 percent, far outpacing the growth in wages.[2]

And of course, all that additional health care money generated a remarkably dysfunctional payoff. Nearly forty million Americans were without health insurance in 1992, an increase of five million in just three years. Infant mortality in the United States, a key index of good health care provision, trended higher than in Europe or Japan, while racial disparities in longevity were shamefully large and growing. An "industrial policy" that would rationalize this huge economic sector seemed a pressing necessity.

Corporations were hurting. In 1965 health benefits for employees really were "fringe benefits," accounting for but 2.2 percent of salaries and wages, but by 1989 they were a major drain on corporate profits, at more than 8 percent of payroll. US automakers routinely complained that they were paying more for health insurance than for steel. At first management responded by seeking to shift more of these costs onto their employees, either through higher deductibles when they visited the doctor or by having workers foot a higher proportion of their annual insurance premium, an additional cost reflected each month in their paycheck. Of course, many companies, especially those in the booming retail, hospitality, and food service sectors of the economy, subsidized health insurance so poorly that most employees could not afford it. The percentage of workers participating in employer- or union-sponsored group health plans declined from 61.2 percent of the total workforce in 1979 to 54.2 percent in 1992.[3]

The employer effort to shift these health insurance costs amounted to a wage cut, a breach of trust that enraged unionized workers. By 1989 health insurance issues were the cause of nearly 80 percent of all strikes involving more than a thousand workers. The most spectacular came at the Pittston Coal Company in southwest Virginia. Hard-pressed by a decline in coal prices, Pittston doubled health deductibles in 1988, lowered the proportion of medical costs its insurance plan would cover from 100 to 80 percent, and discontinued benefits to miners who retired before 1974. When the United Mine Workers (UMW) and the company failed to reach a new contract the next year, 1,500 people, including widows and disabled miners as well as those still digging coal, were left without health care. During the eleven-month-long strike that followed, workers occupied Pittston facilities, blockaded roads, and courted mass arrest. Walkouts of forty thousand other miners convulsed southwest Virginia and nearby coal-producing states. A settlement restored health insurance coverage to most working miners, but the UMW incurred $60 million in fines from a notably hostile Virginia judiciary, while Pittston Coal staggered through the 1990s until it was purchased by a larger mining entity in 2002.[4]

If many a business executive reserved the right to "take a strike" in order to hammer down their health insurance costs, even more sought the same end through some combination of internal health benefit efficiencies and political engagement with the federal government. Under the high-profile leadership of Lee Iacocca, the Chrysler Corporation was perhaps the most celebrated example of a company that came to embrace a large and intrusive governmental presence in the health insurance marketplace. It was in the vanguard of those companies that sought a "corporatist" resolution of the crisis in health provision finance. Chrysler was not a company beloved by liberals or labor. Industrial relations had always been contentious, no more so than during its brush with near-bankruptcy in 1979 and 1980, when it shuttered plants, laid off forty thousand workers, and forced the UAW to take a series of wage and benefit cuts that soon set off a round of "concession bargaining" in the auto industry and beyond. Chrysler was again making money in the mid-1980s, but with an aging, unionized workforce and thousands of retirees also benefiting from its health insurance program, its cost per employee was four times the national average. The company wanted to break the back of the inflationary fee-for-service medical insurance system by channeling workers into health maintenance organizations, where doctors were on salary and companies paid a fixed monthly fee per enrollee.

But even that would not be enough. In the 1980s Iacocca had put his good friend Joseph Califano on the Chrysler board as chair of a new committee to do something about health care costs. Califano had helped push Medicare through Congress as a special assistant to President Lyndon Johnson and later served as secretary of Health, Education, and Welfare in the Carter administration, where he irritated the president in a vain effort to ratchet down health care costs. On the Chrysler board, Douglas Fraser, a former UAW president, worked closely with Califano and Iacocca. They all saw the inexorable rise of health care costs as a cancer that sapped profitability and bred conflict. Despite a determined effort to pressure Detroit-area hospitals, doctors, and insurers, Iacocca concluded that without a revamping of the nation's system of health care, "You'll see a lot of broke companies." Iacocca told the *New York Times*, "If I want to buy steel, I can go to the lowest seller, but in health, the buyer-seller relationship doesn't exist." With Califano and Fraser, Iacocca wanted to create "an orderly system and if that means some kind of national health insurance, then I'm for it." The Chrysler CEO struck a chord that would soon motivate much of the Clinton-era health reform impulse: "For businessmen like me, the issue is competitiveness. . . . We've got three times more health costs baked into our cars than Japan"[5] The UAW's Fraser quipped that Iacocca spent so much time talking about the need for universal health care that he was beginning to sound like an Italian socialist.[6]

In the capital Chrysler proved instrumental in the formation of the National Leadership Coalition for Health Care Reform (NLC), which put unions and corporations in the same lobby organization. Both saw their health care costs approaching crisis levels. The companies were often unionized, but that hardly meant that their labor relations were placid: International Paper, Caterpillar, Safeway, Georgia-Pacific, and

Bethlehem Steel had taken or would soon experience bitter strikes. The NLC endorsed a plan, similar to that of Senate Democrats, under which employers would have to provide health insurance for workers—the "employer mandate"—or pay a tax to finance such coverage. This plan, called "pay-or-play," was designed to ensure universal coverage and was now supported by longtime health insurance advocates like Senator Edward Kennedy. Supervising the system would be a European-style tripartite board composed of labor and business representatives, along with government officials, to set rates and benefit guidelines.[7]

This would help stop the cost-shifting among companies that saddled high-wage, high-benefit companies with the costs of employees' family members who worked at retailers, restaurants, and other firms that offered skimpy coverage or none. Wal-Mart, Pizza Hut, Marriott, and thousands of other low-wage service-sector firms shifted the health care costs of their employees to the state, to charity, or to other firms' payrolls. Wal-Mart, for example, provided a health insurance package that was so burdensome and inadequate that fewer than 50 percent of its employees subscribed to it. Such cost-shifting was the "Achilles' heel" of industry efforts to contain health insurance costs, concluded a 1991 study published in *Business & Health*. It "completely overwhelms the well-intentioned efforts of employers" to control their health insurance costs.[8] A survey commissioned by the National Association of Manufacturers (NAM) that same year found that $11.5 billion had been cost-shifted onto its members.[9] "Right now, big companies pay all of the health costs of small companies that are not providing insurance," argued one pro-reform businessman. "It's another form of tax."[10]

Health care is "the issue of the hour, the No. 1 concern of our members" said Sara Hillgrove, a NAM spokeswoman.[11] A 1991 survey published in *Health Affairs* found that 80 percent of 384 Fortune 500 executives believed that "fundamental changes are needed to make it [the health care system] better."[12] Companies offering generous health benefits were even taking a hit from Wall Street, with Standard & Poor's lowering its credit rating for General Motors, Navistar, and Bethlehem Steel on those grounds. High health care costs increased the cost of capital and created tensions in the workplace and at the bargaining table.[13]

Health Reform Becomes a Clinton Issue

This was a remarkable transformation of elite business sentiment. National health reform, albeit of some as yet undefined sort, had become associated with keeping corporate costs and taxes down, rather than driving them up. Liberals and labor were no longer the only ones who saw an expansion of the welfare state as a solution to some of America's most pressing problems. "The federal government needs to be involved," affirmed an industry lobbyist.[14] All this was music to the ears of a staunch liberal like Edward Kennedy, chair of the Senate Labor and Human Resources Committee. Kennedy now welcomed the business community's openness to reform, even if it did not quite measure up to the universal, Medicare-like system he had long championed. "The health issue is back on the American agenda," he told the *New York Times*. "At last the cost is hitting the middle class, and American business is understanding the effects on the bottom line."[15]

Clinton liberals also saw corporate America's newfound commitment to health insurance reform highly encouraging. For the moment, the fact that so many old-line firms stood in the vanguard seemed to ratify their own commitment to a revival of the nation's manufacturing prowess. Companies that made things on US soil still loomed large in the imagination of those who had been exponents of an industrial policy road to a revival of the American economy. Robert Reich had written a book that saw Chrysler's survival in the early 1980s as one of the "New Deals" that could emerge when government, labor, and corporate management sought a collaborative solution to the industrial crisis. Ira Magaziner had devoted his time at the Boston Consulting Group to saving steel firms from bankruptcy, and at Berkeley Laura Tyson and her colleagues had published one study after another emphasizing the continuing importance of manufacturing in a world of growing international trade. A manufacturing revival would be at the center of the effort to penetrate the Japanese market and recast the relationship between workers and managers at home.[16] So, despite all the talk of a New Democrat mentality that embraced corporate globalization, when it came to their imaginative mapping of the

US economy, old-line manufacturing still commanded outsized, even unwarranted, attention.

This would become a problem later on, but in the meantime a special election in Pennsylvania demonstrated that the health insurance issue had a powerful reach within the electorate. When Republican Senator John Heinz died in a helicopter crash, Governor Robert Casey, a Democrat, chose Harris Wofford to fill the seat until a special election could be held in the fall of 1991. Wofford was a sixty-five-year-old educator who had last seen high-level government service in the Kennedy administration. He seemed like the kind of liberal whose time had passed, and in the early polls he trailed Dick Thornburgh, the Bush administration's well-regarded attorney general, by three-to-one.[17] Wofford had been Pennsylvania's Secretary of Labor and therefore understood that "increasingly, every labor dispute, every strike, turned in whole or in part on the issue of health care." And not only blue-collar workers but also well-employed middle-class people were becoming vulnerable to a radical erosion of their access to health provision.

Wofford therefore started using a line, in union halls and churches, that won a huge, unexpected response. "If criminals have a right to a lawyer, I think working Americans should have the right to a doctor." Campaign consultants James Carville and Paul Begala, then an unknown team hungry enough to take on loser clients, were soon persuaded of the enormous power carried by a robust health reform message. "I don't think we can win this election any other way," remarked Carville of his underdog candidate. Wofford's advocacy of national health insurance was "definitely the long bomb, the Hail Mary. But it's a pretty damn good Hail Mary," said Carville.[18] In November 1991 Wofford defeated Thornburgh by ten points, the first Democrat to win a Pennsylvania Senate seat in thirty years. Carville and Begala promptly went to work for Bill Clinton. After he posted his famous slogan "The Economy, Stupid!" on a bulletin board at the Clinton campaign's Little Rock headquarters, Carville also penned an additional line beneath it: "Don't forget health care."[19]

Wofford's victory advanced the aura of inevitability that now enveloped health insurance reform. "If the Iron Curtain can be lifted, the

Warsaw Pact dissolved, and East and West Germany politically re-united," wrote George Lundberg, editor of the *Journal of the American Medical Association*, "surely we in this rich and successful country can manage to provide basic medical care because it too is the right thing to do, and the time has come."[20] Wofford's victory precipitated a stunning increase in attention to health care reform, with even the Bush White House proposing a set of tax credits to help individuals purchase an insurance policy. The Democrats were much bolder. Every major presidential candidate invoked Wofford's victory in declaring support for a universal program of national health care reform. Nebraska's Bob Kerrey not only advocated a scheme close to that of single-payer but made an aggressive critique of Bill Clinton's maddingly imprecise health care reform ideas in the run-up to the New Hampshire primary.[21]

Indeed, Clinton had a problem. Critics of play-or-pay, not to mention a Canadian-style single-payer system, argued that such schemes were a de facto tax hike. In the case of play-or-pay, those companies that did not provide health insurance to their employees would have to pay a tax to fund a public health insurance plan that would finance health care for uncovered workers. To guarantee insurance coverage to all citizens, those not covered through employment would also be provided with public-funded insurance. President Bush denounced play-or-pay as little more than a backdoor attempt by liberal Democrats like Edward Kennedy and West Virginia Senator Jay Rockefeller to create a universal system of public insurance. This was the kind of damaging accusation that as a "New Democrat" Bill Clinton sought to parry.

Thus, Clintonian health reform rhetoric during the spring and summer of 1992 offered little more than a sense of populist aspiration. In *Putting People First*, the campaign's manifesto issued that June, the section on health care promised to "cap national spending," "take on the health insurance industry," "stop drug price gouging," "establish a core benefit package," "develop health networks," and "guarantee universal coverage."[22] But any outline of a funding mechanism was purposefully omitted, as was a discussion of how universal coverage would actually be implemented. "Play-or-pay got tagged as being a payroll tax," recalled a top staffer for Senator Edward Kennedy. "Clinton was scared to death of being portrayed as a guy who wanted to impose new taxes, so he needed something else."[23]

From Jackson Hole: "Managed Competition"

That something else would be "managed competition." Neither Bill Clinton nor any of his advisers were much aware of the idea when he began campaigning, but the concept was germinating in influential circles. If any health reform could be slotted as neoliberal, this was it, because it preserved private insurance, avoided new taxes, and relied on the competitive market to deliver a needed public good. But managed competition also derived some of its rationale from the idea, prevalent among industrial policy advocates and other critics of the status quo, that market failure in this important segment of the American economy required that the government construct a new set of economic incentives and administrative guidelines to actually make competition work.

The Jackson Hole group comprised the most prominent proponents of managed competition. Meeting periodically in the vacation home of Paul Ellwood, who had been active in health policy circles since the Nixon administration, this study group–cum–health industry cabal put in the same room high officials from the most powerful insurance companies and representatives of the hospitals and other providers with whom they were often in contention. The guiding spirit was Alain Enthoven, a Stanford economist and Pentagon defense intellectual under Robert McNamara who sought to deploy Rand Corporation systems analysis in forming welfare state public policy. He was one of the architects of the whole rational expectations school of economic policymaking. Enthoven understood that individual consumers of medical services were both powerless and ignorant when it came to making health care choices. Consumer choice had to be exercised when purchasing insurance, not when seeking medical care. But at this point in the market exchange, consumers needed organization if they were to participate on any sort of equal or efficient basis.

The Jackson Hole group therefore favored governmental management of the insurance market. This would take place not at the level of the individual or firm, but between giant health insurance purchasing cooperatives (HIPCs) and the large insurers, which would now offer standardized plans that met federal benefits standards. All companies would be mandated to offer health insurance to their employees, although the HIPCs would be particularly beneficial to small employers. Universality would also be advanced because the managed half of managed competition—the HIPCs, the standardized benefit package, and the national guidelines for hospitals and physicians—was designed to prohibit coverage denial for preexisting conditions and prevent nonprice competition among plans on the basis of other forms of risk selection. Corporate leverage in the health insurance market would therefore be greatly enhanced. Meanwhile, Enthoven also sought to put downward pressure on insurance premiums by limiting their tax deductibility. The required employer contribution would be excluded from taxable income only up to the premium of the lowest-cost plan in a region. The unions hated this idea, but they were not represented among the Jackson Hole conferees. Nor were advocates of a Canadian-style single-payer system, one of whom called the Jackson Hole version of managed competition "a last-ditch effort to preserve a role for the insurance industry in health care."[24]

Clinton was put in touch with the ideas emerging from the Jackson Hole group by John Garamendi, the California insurance commissioner who was also the campaign manager for the Clinton campaign in America's largest state. Garamendi, who wanted to run for governor, knew Enthoven and other Stanford economists working on health care provision, and he saw their scheme as a distinctive pathway to universal coverage without the ideological baggage or insurance industry opposition that single-payer plans had acquired. His own deputy, Walter Zelman, was a health policy intellectual also committed to many of the ideas emanating from Jackson Hole. But they wanted the HIPCs—the regional purchasing cooperatives—to be even more powerful than envisioned by Enthoven: they would give these new institutions the quasi-governmental authority to regulate insurance premiums and establish a set of regionally applied "global budgets" that would collectively flatten the nation's health care spending curve. With Paul

Starr, the Princeton health care sociologist and historian, Zelman wrote policy briefs backing this more statist version of managed competition and circulated them within Clinton campaign circles. Editorialists at the *New York Times* soon legitimized this once-obscure academic idea. It was the most effective road forward for health insurance reform.

The discussants meeting in Paul Ellwood's vacation home did indeed work to make universal health provision congruent with the interests of corporations, insurers, hospitals, and other influential components of the medical-industrial complex. To Garamendi, Zelman, Starr, and others in the Clinton camp, however, this corporatist accommodation to the big stakeholders was a feature, not a bug. Most Clintonites who cared about health provision were temperamentally and ideologically inclined toward a much more robust governmental program to ensure universal health insurance and the cost and profit containment that came with it. But the stalemate that had stymied health reform for the previous third of a century had also convinced these liberals that the only viable reform possible required preservation of and support from those health industry stakeholders with the greatest economic power and political influence. When Hillary Clinton met with single-payer advocates as first lady, she was wont to tell them, as she did in a West Wing meeting of early 1993, "You make a very convincing case that single-payer would be a good reform, but is there any force on the face of the earth that would counter the money the insurance industry would spend to defeat it?"[25]

By August 1992, Bill Clinton had delegated to Ira Magaziner the task of working out a health care program that would accommodate these powerful stakeholders. Magaziner had been involved in Rhode Island efforts to expand Medicaid coverage; in the process he had observed enormous inefficiencies and rent-seeking behavior among regional hospitals and insurers. His consulting experience had convinced him that with the proper economic and organizational regulations, both private businesses and government entities could be incentivized to eliminate waste, increase product quality, and lower costs. Of his first encounter with the concept of managed competition, Magaziner remembered, "I came across some of the stuff that Walter Zelman had been doing with Garamendi in California, and, as I read it, I said, 'Boy, this fits a lot with what we've been thinking.'" Shortly thereafter, in the early summer of 1992, Robert Reich sent Magaziner an *American Prospect* essay by Paul Starr that explained how a new Democratic administration could thread the health care needle to win the political support of both an anxious middle class and those insurance companies and medical providers (hospitals, doctors, and health maintenance organizations, or HMOs) that had been most fearful of government regulation. From all this Magaziner concluded that the Clinton health care plan would have to be more "private-sector oriented and more reliant on competition."[26]

This was a posture to the right of virtually all the health policy activists and experts in the Democratic Party, many of whom remained either single-payer stalwarts or adherents of the play-or-pay program championed by Senators Kennedy and Rockefeller. On August 10, 1992, Magaziner convened a meeting in Washington to bring these liberals on board. They did not have much choice, because Bill Clinton was now the party candidate. Moreover, despite Magaziner's effort to emphasize competition rather than governmental regulation as the road to cost control, the liberals with the most experience, like Henry Aaron of the Brookings Institution and Judith Feder, staff director of the Congressional Commission on Comprehensive Health Care, chaired by Jay Rockefeller, thought the turn toward managed competition something close to a rhetorical gesture. If Magaziner and Clinton included in their program the idea of a global budget, with a ceiling on total health care expenditures, then the federal government would have a muscular arm with which to bend the health care cost curve and regulate insurance premiums and hospital costs.[27] As we shall see, the Clintonites did come to rely upon a global budget and a de facto set of price controls, but they were exceedingly shy about advertising that degree of market regulation. This equivocation would have a disastrous impact on the fate of the health reform they sought to advance.

But in the meantime, campaign rhetoric had its uses and potency. Flanked by Senators Rockefeller and Wofford, Bill Clinton unveiled his health care initiative on September 24, 1992, in a speech delivered to employees at Merck Pharmaceuticals in Rahway, New Jersey. An employer mandate would expand coverage and stop cost-shifting; smaller firms would benefit from tax credits to help them purchase coverage from the regional HIPCs, which were expected to use their immense buying power to ratchet down insurance costs in a market where underwriting tricks were prohibited and community rating the new norm. "The forces of the marketplace" would drive down costs, asserted Clinton, even as he also proposed a government-imposed cap on the total spending of each purchasing cooperative. "We've got to quit having the federal government try to micromanage health care," said Clinton. "This is a private system. It is not play or pay. It does not require new taxes. It will preserve what is best about the present health care system."[28] When President Bush and others criticized Clinton for still relying too much on a global budget to hold down costs, the Democratic candidate issued a press release that contained what the *New York Times* called a crystal-clear statement: "Managed competition, *not price controls*, will make the budget work and maintain quality." That was enough for the *Times* to editorialize, "The debate over health care reform is over. Managed competition has won."[29]

Bill, Hillary, and Ira: Constructing a Health Plan

Most voters did not see health insurance per se as the central issue in the 1992 campaign season. Jobs, trade, and economic recovery were more important, which is why Clinton artfully sought to link those issues together at the December 1992 Economic Summit in Little Rock. There Ford CEO Harold Poling was given a high-profile slot on the program to argue that "our health care costs jeopardize our ability to compete, to preserve just the existing jobs, and create additional jobs." Poling estimated that Japanese automakers held a $500 per car cost advantage because of the US failure to get its health insurance system under control. The United States could "no longer delay in assuring that Americans have access to affordable health insurance," said the Ford executive.

Clinton eagerly embraced Poling's warning, so reflective of the alarm prevalent throughout the old manufacturing economy. Pounding the table, he sermonized, "One of the reasons real wages have gone down is that more money is going to health care . . . if you spend more money on this, you can't spend it on research and development and plant and equipment. . . . If you want America to maintain a manufacturing base, we have to do it."[30] To Clinton, health policy was industrial policy and it was trade policy; in virtually every presidential speech he gave to advance it, he emphasized that curtailing health care costs could liberate hundreds of billions of dollars in new investment while reducing the federal budget deficit. The president hoped that health care reform might constitute his most important legacy, and like FDR and LBJ, who were reelected on the basis of the epic domestic social legislation they put on the statute books, Clinton saw health care reform as key to a second term.[31]

Five days after the inaugural, Bill Clinton announced that his wife would lead the Task Force on National Health Care Reform, "an unprecedented effort" that would "work constantly night and day until we have a health care plan" ready to submit to Congress. The appointment surprised the nation, not to mention many staffers in the West Wing. Hillary knew a lot less about the topic than either Donna Shalala, the new secretary of the Department of Health and Human Services (HHS), or Judith Feder, who had headed up Clinton's health care transition team. But Hillary had the star power, the smarts, and, when necessary, the thick skin to replicate on a national canvas the success she had enjoyed a decade before when her championship of Arkansas educational reform had so enhanced Bill Clinton's reputation as a progressive Southern governor. Appearing before a congressional committee or at a public forum, Hillary Clinton poured on the charm, but she left no one in doubt that she was in utter command of a field whose complexities escaped many a politician.[32] When her old Arkansas friend Diane Blair visited Hillary in March, her journal recorded a slice of the first lady's schedule: From March 9: "HC absolutely exhausted after another day on the Hill." March 11: "Another exhausting day on the Hill, dealing with Senate Republicans; HC endlessly patient." March 12: "Another

FIGURE 5. Hillary Clinton explains the Health Security Act to House Democrats. Majority Leader Richard Gephardt is seated to her left. (Clinton Presidential Library)

day on the Hill; HC coiffed but looks beat."[33] By one White House count, Hillary Clinton had more than four hundred meetings with members of Congress over the next year and a half, with at least one hundred of them on Capitol Hill.[34]

But the devil was always in the details, and these were largely the province of Ira Magaziner. Hillary and Ira made a pretty good team: he was driven, ambitious, and in command of all the details, while Hillary had the charisma to be an effective public ambassador for the initiative. Magaziner was not an easy man with whom to work. With disheveled hair and suit, he kept meetings running for hours, hectored subordinates and congresspeople, and consolidated power unto himself. But he did the bidding of Bill and Hillary. "In the language of consulting, my 20-year profession, they were my clients," he told *Washington Post* journalists Haynes Johnson and David Broder. "The President wanted comprehensive reform. My job was to carry out his wishes."[35] Magaziner recognized that he needed to assemble a large coalition of experts and politicians who could agree on a plan, but all his instincts remained those of a sharp-elbowed business consultant who won the confidence of the boss by controlling the flow of information to the senior decision-makers and rolling over adversaries. Thus, Magaziner never lost the confidence of either Hillary or Bill, but constructing a health plan that would satisfy the Clintons was the least of his problems in the Washington political maelstrom.[36]

That became apparent on the very day that Bill appointed his wife head of the health reform task force. A one-column story on her new post appeared on the front page of the *Washington Post*, but the paper gave far more prominence to another issue confronting the new president. "Joint Chiefs Voice Concern to Clinton on Lifting Gay Ban" ran the top-of-the-page headline. Clinton had run on a pledge to end discrimination against gays in the military, but he had wanted to postpone for at least six months a public codification of this potentially controversial new policy. A military-run study commission would keep it under wraps. But now the top military brass, with a combined "200 years of experience," made clear their immediate and steadfast opposition. So too did Georgia Senator Sam Nunn, chair of the Senate Armed Services Committee. An ostensible DLC ally, Nunn helped keep the issue boiling all through the winter and spring of 1993, culminating in a photo-op visit to the Norfolk naval base, where he led a legislative delegation that inspected the tight living quarters on submarines and other ships where straight and gay enlisted men might be expected to mingle. Before the end of January, the *Washington Post* had run a dozen front-page stories on the issue, published two editorials, and filled the inside pages with culture-war stories that put the Clinton presidency under a microscope. Bill Clinton finally defused the problem with his awkward "don't ask, don't tell" policy, issued as a Department of Defense directive late in the fall of 1993. Few were pleased. "The military resented the intrusion," recalled George Stephanopoulos, "Democrats were furious, the public was confused, and the gay community felt betrayed."[37]

The contretemps over gays in the military would be followed by one scandal, real or imagined, after another. Nor was the chaos and controversy that bedeviled the Clinton White House imposed only from without. His staff was inexperienced and prone to missteps. The president himself was too often an indecisive decision-maker, if only because he could grasp all too well two, or three, or four sides of any question or personnel decision. The attorney general nominations of Zoe Baird and Kimba Wood floundered during the first weeks of the administration when it became known that both had hired undocumented domestic workers; Janet Reno proved a more successful pick, but her tenure turned to tragedy in April 1993 when FBI agents stormed the Waco, Texas, compound of David Koresh, leader of a fringe religious sect. Ninety-four of his followers died in a fire of uncertain origin. Reno took responsibility for the incident, but Clinton's reputation for forthright leadership suffered as well.

Then Hillary Clinton came under fire when she abruptly dismissed the staff of the White House Travel Office, which handled arrangements for reporters flying with the president. Inheriting the office from previous administrations, financial malfeasance may have been present, but the incident generated running headline recriminations, eventually prompting investigations by the FBI, committees in both houses of Congress, and two special prosecutors. That was followed by a growing furor over the Whitewater land deal in which the Clintons were thought to have exerted improper influence back in Arkansas. On July 20, 1993, came the suicide of Vince Foster, Hillary's old friend and a Rose Law Firm partner. A special prosecutor was appointed to investigate Whitewater in early 1994, after which Paula Jones filed an exceedingly well-publicized lawsuit against the president. Shortly thereafter, Hillary Clinton confided to Diane Blair, "He can't fire people, exert discipline, punish leakers—throws tantrums, but then does nothing." The president had failed to effectively tackle the seemingly endless series of scandals then breaking into the media. "Self-inflicted wounds. Inability to organize, make tough choices, drives her nuts."[38]

Public controversy focusing on the personae of Bill and Hillary might seem but tabloid froth divorced from the hard political and economic calculations that drove construction and debate over a reform involving one-seventh of the American economy. But the erosion of the cultural and moral power wielded by the first couple became part of the calculus by which the fate of their health reform, as well as their many other initiatives, would be decided. It came to matter, in both Congress and with the public, that the administration's Health Security Act (HSA) was often denoted as "Hillarycare" or, more plainly, the Clinton health care plan. When the going got rough, that identification generated a polarizing, partisan response to elements of the reform that might otherwise have been found acceptable, or even popular. The fate of health care reform was bound up in the way Americans evaluated the lives of the first couple. No other piece of Clinton-era legislation was so burdened.

In February 1993 Ira Magaziner began assembling an army of health care experts, who soon numbered over five hundred. They would not write the Clinton health care bill, but they would amass the data, arguments, pitfalls, and priorities that had to be analyzed and identified before the HSA could make its way to Congress. Laboring long into the night, they soon produced a stream of papers, presentations, and slide shows. All this came out of Magaziner's experience as a business consultant. If a corporate restructuring was imperative, that required thinking through innumerable options and meshing previously uncoordinated activities and groups into a coherent plan. At lengthy "tollgate" meetings, held in the majestic Indian Treaty Room of the Old Executive Office Building, Magaziner and Hillary Clinton presided over large conclaves where their work was offered up for criticism by "contrarians" and "auditors." The Magaziner operation was actually an enormously inclusive project that enlisted the expertise of a huge swath of knowledgeable and well-connected people, many already on the government payroll. And that was just the problem: for every insider there were a dozen others who wondered why they had been excluded from the deliberations. "If I'm not part of it, it must be a joke or a plot" is the way Chris Jennings, one of Hillary's key aides, summarized their outlook.[39] The congressional committees that would have to mark up and pass a health reform bill did not play much of a role, nor did the interest group stakeholders most impacted by the reform: leaders of the medical profession, insurance executives, Big Pharma, and corporate chieftains.

"Managed competition," whatever its faults or virtues, therefore assumed shape within an insular world of economists and health care specialists. Unlike other great reforms of equal magnitude—Social Security, the Wagner Act, Medicare, and the two epochal civil rights laws of 1964 and 1965—the Clinton health reform had shallow roots. Those historic laws had been subject to decades of debate, in the streets as well as in the legislative chamber. The quest for universal health provision had an equally rich history, but "managed competition" was something brand-new. Designed to placate all the powerful interest groups clamoring to preserve both their power and their profits, and to do so with no general tax increase, this scheme had few defenders who were both knowledgeable and committed. Even Robert Reich, an old friend of both Hillary Clinton and Ira Magaziner, confessed, "It's unwieldy. I still don't understand it. I've been to dozens of meetings on it, defended it on countless radio and TV programs, debated its merits publicly and privately, but I still don't comprehend the whole."[40]

"A Single-Payer System in Jackson Hole Clothing"

Ideologically, managed competition was designed to embrace the market, but politics and political economy drove it to the left. Although the unwieldy Magaziner task force was soon denounced for secrecy and high-handedness—it disbanded in May 1993—that effort did leave one important legacy: it shifted the managed competition scheme toward more comprehensiveness, universality, and government guidance. Indeed, that was part of the Magaziner strategy: creating a plan that incorporated the ideas and evoked the enthusiasm of American liberals, so that when the inevitable horse-trading became necessary in Congress, the progressive wing of the Democratic Party would remain on board. Meanwhile, to the administration's budget hawks Magaziner argued that the alarming increase in federal health care expenditures would "make it almost impossible to reduce the federal deficit" unless the health reform, and the savings it would generate, were part of the first Clinton budget. "Radical action is needed now," he asserted.[41] Robert Rubin, the former Goldman Sachs executive then emerging as a leader of those economic advisers seeking an austerity budget, did not buy into that argument, but a more prosaic legislative rationale nevertheless held sway in the White House. Incorporation of health reform into a budget resolution would avoid the use of the filibuster by GOP senators, and it would take supervision of the hearings away from the Senate Finance Committee, whose chairman, Daniel Patrick Moynihan, wanted to take on welfare reform first and then get to health care reform in Clinton's second term.[42]

The Democratic leadership on Capitol Hill was all in favor of this budget reconciliation strategy, but West Virginia Senator Robert Byrd, the respected guardian of Senate traditions, took umbrage at such legislative opportunism; he declared that the health care plan was not germane to Clinton's budget bill then working its way through the Congress. The Clintons and Magaziner knew that Byrd's objections would make passage of health care legislation much more difficult and probably delay it well into 1994. But there was one silver lining. Had the health reform bill been folded into the budget process, Treasury Secretary Lloyd Bentsen, Robert Rubin, and other budget hawks would have had a direct hand in shaping it and undoubtedly would have transformed it into a law far less generous and universal. Rubin, for example, just wanted catastrophic coverage: a bare-bones package of health benefits with high cost-sharing requirements. This was an essentially Republican approach to the issue that would reappear time and again during the health care debate of 1993–1994 and afterwards. But since Byrd insisted that health care had to advance on its own, the Clinton budget conservatives would now keep their distance from the proposed law, thus ensuring that health care would be one of Bill Clinton's few legislative initiatives shaped by progressives within his administration.[43]

The Clinton health plan was also pushed to the left by the Congressional Budget Office (CBO). When Clinton and Magaziner used the phrase "managed competition under a global budget," they expected that market competition between hospitals, insurers, and other parts of the health care system would be primarily responsible for driving down overall costs to companies, to consumers, and to the federal government. This mechanism was essential if the Clinton administration was to slow the proportion of the gross national product being eaten up by health care costs. But it was a new and untested social experiment that needed a backup mechanism to make sure total costs really were constrained. That is where the "global budget" came into play. It was a non-market assurance that costs would be held in check, especially as the Clinton health plan was first rolled out. After that the budget cap would, in theory, be rendered superfluous by the market forces that would assuredly ratchet down overall health care costs.

But the CBO refused to buy into this market fantasy. By the early 1990s CBO "scoring" of any prospective law was politically and fiscally essential, to gain some sense of both its cost and the taxes that might be needed to pay for it. CBO scoring had become a seemingly nonpartisan certification that could and would be deployed as a statistical bludgeon by friends or foes of the legislation on offer. Thus, the February 2, 1993, appearance of CBO director Robert Reischauer before the House Committee on Ways and Means was of considerable interest. Reischauer had helped set up the CBO in 1975 as a congressional—and hence liberal—counterweight to the Nixonian efforts to manipulate the federal budgeting process. Reischauer was a health care financing expert ("meticulous, widely respected," wrote the *Christian Science Monitor*) who had plenty of experience measuring how difficult it could be to contain such expenditures.[44]

Reischauer could not say if "managed competition" would flatten the ever-rising cost curve. Certainly that effect could not be predicted in the first few years, when insurance coverage for at least twenty million new clients was sure to increase costs, and it was also hard to say what would happen in the out years. "We are talking—with respect to the managed competition model—about a structure that does not exist anywhere in the world, and it would be wrong for me to say, I know what is going to happen, I know how this is going to play out." The whole experiment was a "pig in a poke." Reischauer said he did not want to take Congress on "the budgetary equivalent of a bungee jump, where one day we report a certain proposal could save billions and then a month later, when the details are more fully specified, we estimate that national health care costs would increase significantly under that proposal."[45]

But Reischauer made clear that it was not really the nascent quality of the managed care legislation that made a cost estimate difficult. The

problem was much more fundamental. Markets were inherently indeterminate, subject to political and economic winds involving "thousands of decisions" among multiple actors. In contrast, the CBO was far
more confident that, in a system of "global budgeting for hospitals and
other large providers," it could "score" the cost of a single-payer mechanism. Experience with Medicaid and Medicare had shown that "the
more effective mechanisms for holding down costs are also the more
intrusive ones."[46] Markets were fuzzy and indeterminate: the CBO
judged a health plan's cost containment mechanism on "how clear, specific, automatic, and enforceable the regulatory provisions were."[47] Hillary Clinton may well have agreed. After a February 23 White House
dinner at which Diane Blair conversed with the first couple, the political
science professor from Arkansas wrote in her journal, "At dinner, HC
to BC on complexities of health care—thinks managed competition a
crock; single payer necessary; maybe add to Medicare."[48]

In a 1995 postmortem on the failure of their health care plan, Magaziner told Hillary that CBO scoring ended up shaping "some of the more
controversial aspects of our proposal," so "we had to put in place mechanisms which would be scored, or the bill would lose all credibility."[49]
Magaziner's first impulse was to impose price controls for two or three
years, a view endorsed by the otherwise cautious Leon Panetta, head of
the Office of Management and Budget, who thought the regulation of
prices, perhaps by extending Medicare rates to private patients, much
more straightforward than the "complex business of designing a system
of 'managed competition.'" After Hillary criticized drug prices and profits as excessive, her husband took up the same theme, describing vaccine
costs as "shocking." Magaziner and other White House officials soon met
with executives of Merck and SmithKline to directly negotiate the supply
and price of their products sold to the federal government. Health care
stock prices took a beating.[50]

Magaziner retreated, but not by much. To hold down insurance costs
to businesses and individuals, he called for premium caps imposed by
the government. And his iteration of the Clinton health plan would
mandate that virtually all firms—those below five thousand employees—
participate in the HIPCs. This would give the health insurance purchasing

alliances the power to enforce the premium caps—price controls by another name—and police the global budgets assigned each HIPC. "These
measures were among the most controversial in our bill," Magaziner admitted, "and contributed significantly to the characterization of our bill
as 'big government' and bureaucratic."[51] Liberals understood this as well:
Paul Starr sent Magaziner a memo in June 1993 complaining that his accommodation to CBO scoring requirements made the global budget the
"centerpiece of the new system, not a backup." That in turn "effectively
makes price controls permanent."[52]

The Jackson Hole group now bailed on the Clinton plan, and not in
a confidential memo. Alain Enthoven entitled his well-publicized critique "A Single-Payer System in Jackson Hole Clothing" because the
Clinton plan not only relied on a global budget to limit health costs but
transformed the regional insurance purchasing alliances into powerful,
quasi-governmental regulators. Instead of simply "taking" the market
price for small-scale purchasers of insurance, they would incorporate
virtually all employers, small and giant, and thereby function as a monopsony—a statelike agency that could set insurance prices for millions.
"In effect," charged Enthoven, that was "a single payer system."[53] Others
who were not then unsympathetic to reform could see this as well. The
Chamber of Commerce, though in frequent contact with Magaziner,
was nevertheless "astonished" that his team "could be moving toward a
single payer system." Business would not countenance such a system,
"even one which purports in the short run to cost business less than
current premiums."[54]

That was the view of Reischauer himself when he reviewed the Clinton plan in early 1994. Although the president cringed, calling the CBO
analysis a "policy wonk deal," those liberal Democrats favoring a radical,
government-led restructuring of US health provision might well have
exulted. The CBO concluded that the Clinton plan could indeed slow
the growth of health spending for government and business, while
moving the nation toward universal coverage. But in his congressional
testimony Reischauer minced no words about how this would happen.
The Clinton plan, he said, "would establish a universal entitlement to
health insurance that would be largely financed by mandatory payments

resulting from an exercise of sovereign power." And as Enthoven had charged, the health alliances, said Reischauer, "would operate primarily as agents of the Federal government," not as private market-making entities.[55] Market failure, or its prospect, had driven Clinton's managed competition scheme toward something resembling a single-payer system.

It was a testimony to the apparent inevitability of health care reform that both conservative Democrats and moderate Republicans put forward their own plans in 1992 and 1993. These plans were also based on the managed competition idea, but they were decidedly more business- and insurance-friendly. The scheme developed by Rhode Island Senator John Chafee substituted an individual mandate for an employer mandate but was otherwise relatively compatible with the Clinton idea. More threatening was the plan championed by Democratic Representative Jim Cooper of Tennessee, which became a cat's paw for those who wanted to sink health insurance reform in its entirety. The Cooper plan eschewed an employer mandate, did not seek universal coverage, and gave the insurance companies much more freedom to set prices and select their clients. In a December 1993 memo entitled "Why We Started Left of Center," Magaziner explained to Bill and Hillary why accommodating liberals and labor was essential. "The die was cast in May when Cooper and others allied with him made clear that they would not support universal coverage in this bill . . . and when the Chafee group decided to produce their own bill with as broad Republican support as possible. . . . This left us no choice but to go center left to ensure a firm base of support for our bill upon introduction."[56]

Bill Clinton also pushed leftward in a high-profile appearance introducing his health care reform to a joint session of Congress. The September 22, 1993, speech proved a tour de force, even though Clinton winged it for the first fifteen minutes because his teleprompter scrolled the wrong text. The president again emphasized the importance of bending the medical cost curve to US industry competitiveness, but he ignored the Rube Goldberg–like details governing the Magaziner health plan. "Managed competition under a global budget" had no appeal to the general public, among whom the universalist simplicity of Social Security and its Medicare offspring reigned supreme. Clinton therefore devoted two passionate paragraphs to the health security card that all Americans would henceforth carry. Holding one aloft, he declared, "With this card, if you lose your job or you switch jobs, you're covered. If you're an early retiree, you're covered. If someone in your family has unfortunately had an illness that qualifies as a preexisting condition, you're still covered." Driving home this universalism, Clinton ended with an evocation of FDR's greatest and sturdiest domestic achievement: the creation of the nation's Social Security retirement system. "Forty years from now, our grandchildren will also find it unthinkable that there was a time in this country when hardworking families lost their homes, their savings, their businesses, lost everything simply because their children got sick or because they had to change jobs."[57] Clinton would double down four months later, even as his health security plan faced stiffening headwinds in early 1994. In his second State of the Union address, the president warned Congress, "If you send me legislation that does not guarantee every American private health insurance that can never be taken away, you will force me to take this pen, veto the legislation, and we'll come right back here and start all over again."[58]

In the fall of 1993 the Clinton health care plan, or some closely related version, still seemed all but inevitable. "The reviews are in and the box office is terrific," the political analyst William Schneider wrote just after Clinton unveiled his plan.[59] The *New York Times* declared health reform "Alive on Arrival" after Hillary Clinton "dazzled five Congressional committees" in the days following her husband's speech.[60] "I'm here as a mother, a wife, a daughter, a sister, a woman," she told the House Ways and Means Committee. Sitting forward in her chair, and never consulting notes or the aides sitting behind her, she answered 150 questions. She was charming, humorous, and willing to joust with conservatives and liberals alike. The *Washington Post*'s Mary McGrory called her a "superstar."[61] House Majority Leader Richard Gephardt, then gearing up for the bitter fight in opposition to passage of the North American Free Trade Agreement, nevertheless declared that when it came to health reform, "the launch of this couldn't have been better." Like other moderate Republicans, Senator John Danforth of Missouri wanted changes, but he saw no obstacle to constructive negotiations with Hillary Clinton and Magaziner. He predicted, "We will pass a law next year." Polls showed the plan had broad support.[62]

The Opposition Mobilizes

But it was all downhill from there. The initial release of the Clinton plan came in a premature and unfinished fashion when a Ways and Means Democrat, Representative Pete Stark, demanded that Magaziner and Hillary Clinton provide a copy of it. They sent him a technical outline, with a huge number of provisions and no overall explanation of the framework. Portions were soon faxed all over town. It was long, 1,342 pages, but not out of the range of other draft legislation. The NAFTA treaty was equally detailed, and John Chafee's own health care proposal clocked in at a good 850 pages. But the impression that the proposal was impossibly complicated had been firmly established.

And it was not just an impression. When Hillary sent Ira a request to explain to administration insiders why their plan had so much baggage, Magaziner frankly admitted that its length was a problem: "The complexity of our bill undermines our chances for success," he wrote, "but without complexity success is impossible." That paradox arose out of the fundamental choice the Clinton campaign made well before the inauguration. The simplest and least bureaucratic system was single-payer, admitted Magaziner. However, that scheme would require $300 billion to $400 billion in new taxes; substituting an employer mandate as the main financing mechanism obviated that requirement, but it introduced a host of new issues—collection mechanisms, subsidies for the unemployed, "extraordinary measures" to regulate the insurance market—that added layer after layer of complexity and bureaucracy.[63] Magaziner actually saw a silver lining in all this. The plan was "constructed as a negotiating document," with "dozens of moveable parts which can be changed and still bring successful health care reform." The administration would have plenty of room to compromise, and so too would the congressional committees when they marked up the bill. Most members of Congress, lobbyists for business, and leaders of the medical professions would be able to fight for the interests of their constituents and then actually alter the plan more to their liking.[64]

Bill Clinton was a brilliant speaker who could explain such statecraft in easily understood, morally compelling language. The architects of the health care plan scheduled him to spend most of October on the stump, but as he was flying to his first event, a labor convention in California, the news arrived that US soldiers had been killed in Somalia. Clinton flew back to Washington immediately after his speech and spent most of the next two months engaged with that East African country, with the NAFTA fight, and with the chaos engulfing Haiti. Complained Magaziner, "So we literally had one and a half days of presidential time on health care between September 27 and January . . . when the plan was being attacked . . . we just did not have the ability to define our proposal." The first lady was on the road, but other top Clinton administration officials who might have campaigned with her never grasped, nor entirely supported, all the intricacies of managed competition.[65] On his most important domestic initiative, the president was both isolated and AWOL.

This gave the opposition time to mobilize, and they did so on two fronts. The first was inside the Republican Party, where those hostile to the Clinton plan were determined to marginalize any moderate Republican efforts to dicker with Clinton, Magaziner, or key congressional Democrats. There would be no bipartisanship on this bill. And the second front was within the business community, where the support upon which Bill Clinton had counted would dissolve into acrimony and disaffection.

In the celebratory atmosphere that surrounded Hillary Clinton's appearances on Capitol Hill, one Cassandra-like voice stood in sharp dissent. "In the midst of the largest power grab by the Government in recent history, most Republicans are either nowhere to be seen, fawning approvingly or asking questions about the fine print," asserted William Bennett, a neoconservative writer who had served as Education Secretary and then drug czar in the administrations of Ronald Reagan and George Bush. "Here is a monumental assault on the private sector, on individual liberty, and those sworn to its defense are largely silent."[66]

Everyone knew who Bennett was talking about: not just Senator John Chafee, who had his own health care plan and much backing among other GOP moderates, but also Robert Dole, the Senate minority leader and prospective Republican candidate for president three years hence. Dole's chief of staff was Sheila Burke; as a true health policy expert, she was a rare find on the GOP side of the isle, the kind of figure who could craft an intelligent and principled bargain with the Democrats. Dole had many objections to the Clinton plan: "We don't like price controls, we don't like mandates on small business people, we don't like these mandatory health alliances," but in the late fall of 1993 Dole could still assert, "I would say that about in April of next year, there will be a new plan. It will be sort of a consensus plan: some of this plan . . . some of the Clinton plan. And if that happens, we'll have broad bipartisan support." To make it happen Burke stayed in touch with Magaziner and his team. Much alarmed, the conservative columnist Robert Novak wrote that many Republicans saw Dole "moving inexorably" toward compromise with Democratic congressional leaders.[67]

Bill Kristol was also determined to stop all this. In a series of short position papers addressed to "Republican Leaders," Kristol and his newly created Project for the Republican Future explained that obstructionism, not compromise, was a strategic imperative. Kristol was a second-generation neoconservative, the son of two "New York intellectuals," Irving Kristol and Gertrude Himmelfarb. While his parents had moved sharply to the right during and after the 1960s, they still thought of themselves as proponents of a modestly calibrated welfare state. Their son did too during the 1970s, when he worked in Daniel Patrick Moynihan's 1976 Senate campaign. But by the mid-1980s he was a partisan Republican, later serving as Vice President Dan Quayle's chief of staff. After Clinton became president, Kristol found himself just as alarmed as Bennett. Far too many Republicans were likely to partner with the president in crafting a health care plan that was both universal and highly regulatory. It was not just that they would provide the votes to pass some version of the Clinton plan. Far more damaging was the ideological subversion of such collaboration. The Health Security Act was the boldest effort to expand the welfare state that Democrats had launched in three decades. Any success they might have, Kristol wrote in a December 1993 memo faxed to GOP influentials, would "relegitimize" the Rooseveltian state. Clinton's plan "will revive the reputation of the party that spends and regulates, the Democrats, as the generous protector of middle-class interests." It would thereby "strike a punishing blow against Republican claims to defend the middle class by restraining government."[68]

Kristol therefore warned Republicans against any effort to make the Clinton bill more to their liking. Any Republican urge to win "concessions" from the Democrats instead of outright "surrender" had to be forestalled. "The conventional effort to negotiate a 'least bad' compromise with the Democrats, and thereby gain momentary public credit for helping the president 'do something' about health care," had to be sidetracked. Kristol urged Republicans to reject the insurance-friendly bill put forward by Representative Cooper, as well as the plan developed by Senator Chafee, whose most notable feature was the substitution of an individual mandate—an idea that first emerged at the conservative Heritage Foundation—for the employer mandate, which was already encountering resistance from most employers of low-wage, part-time labor. Both of these plans accommodated virtually all the complaints made by insurers, employers, hospitals, and their Republican allies. In practice they were either unworkable or ineffectual. But to the extent that these initiatives claimed to move the nation toward universal coverage and a regulated insurance market, Kristol found them just as ideologically dangerous as the plan put forward by Bill Clinton.[69]

Kristol's memos had enormous impact inside the Republican political universe. For example, in the fall of 1993 the Heritage Foundation journal, *Policy Review*, had published articles outlining a set of market-oriented health plans—the individual mandate was featured—that nevertheless achieved universal coverage in a way that many in the GOP could support. But after the publication of his memos, the Heritage Foundation featured an interview with Kristol, who made clear to conservatives that he thought Republicans "have been too timid and defensive so far in their reaction to Clinton's plan." Instead, their goal over the next several months must be "to defeat the Clinton plan root and branch." Indeed, Kristol wanted the health care debate to be a "model for routing contemporary liberalism and advancing an aggressive conservative activist agenda." That would put an end to right-wing tinkering with the HSA.[70]

Senate minority leader Bob Dole also felt the impact of the GOP lurch to the right. In 1993 he had made clear that he was ready to bargain, and in early 1994 he was still looking to endorse "mainstream" health reform efforts. By late May 1994, however, Dole had aligned himself with the hard-line views of Kristol and Gingrich. Both wings of the GOP had concluded that big victories in the off-year elections would be assured by a refusal to compromise with the Democrats. Operationalizing Magaziner's compromise strategy, the Clinton administration and its congressional allies sought to accommodate Republican moderates, but Dole and the rest of the GOP leadership backed away at every crucial stage. Senator Chafee continued to explore a compromise with the Democrats, but in the face of Dole's opposition, not to mention that of the Gingrich insurgents, failure was inevitable.[71]

There was never a set-piece battle, a high-profile vote in either house of Congress that put GOP opposition on public display. Defeat of the Clinton health security plan was therefore the "perfect crime," wrote Paul Starr, because Democratic Party disarray seemed the prime suspect.[72] But that murder was not just a legislative debacle. As we shall see in the next chapter, intractable divisions within the corporate world truly sealed the victim's fate.

5

Health Care Corporatism in Failure and Success

The ideological mobilization of conservative Republicans might well have been for naught had Clinton's Health Security Act retained support from those sectors of American capital that it had been designed to serve. Almost a generation later, wall-to-wall Republican hostility to President Barack Obama's Affordable Care Act did not derail that health reform scheme because in 2009 and 2010 all the key players—doctors, hospitals, insurers, Big Pharma, old-line manufacturers, and retail and fast-food employers of low-wage labor—remained on board. But in 1993 and 1994 most would defect. Their interests had stood at the center of Magaziner's calculations because no grand corporatist bargain could be constructed without accommodating the core economic and organizational interests of US business, which was still responsible for two-thirds of all health provision enjoyed by American families. Corporate defection was never just a question of economics—it was not about the red ink some companies saw flooding their balance sheet if and when a major overhaul of US health care came to fruition. This defection had ideological roots as well, because corporate support for the Clinton health plan would legitimize the law's cross-class character and open the door to the kind of managed capitalism that Bill Clinton and a good slice of those who held policymaking posts in his administration sought to advance.

A Capitalist Calculation on the Clinton Health Reform

American capitalism has never been a monolithic entity, and certainly not when a fragmented business community came to calculate the impact of the HSA on their financial prospects. In the early 1990s some of the most important employer groups wanted to be players when it came to the new health care politics. In contrast to the approach many business conservatives had taken when Social Security and Medicare were debated, the most important business associations, including the Chamber of Commerce, the Business Roundtable, and the National Association of Manufacturers, initially saw a new law as both inevitable and capable of being shaped to their liking. Magaziner saw this as all to the good, and he was ready to deal.

The Chamber and NAM had been historically hostile to the New Deal impulse, but both groups were now led by men who sought to nudge them toward an accommodation with the Clinton administration. With twelve thousand member firms, largely in manufacturing, NAM had long been a reliable anchor for the conservative wing of the Republican Party and a steadfast foe of trade unionism and the welfare state. But the failure of Reaganism to ameliorate the crisis facing US manufacturing made NAM open to industrial policy ideas. In 1990 Jerry Jasinowski, a Democrat looking to enhance productivity and competitiveness, became president. Because 97 percent of all member firms offered health insurance benefits, NAM affiliates were big losers in the cost-shifting game, which slashed 31 percent of their profits, according to a report commissioned by the organization. Jasinowski was therefore ready to work with the new administration. NAM, he said, would be "flexible" in reviewing administration reform proposals and would judge "the plan as a whole as opposed to rejecting individual provisions which we may not favor." In a May 1993 press release Jasinowski declared, "The manufacturing community is supportive of the general thrust of the administration's thinking."[1] An important sweetener for large companies, mainly unionized, was the Clinton promise to bail them out of 80 percent of the rapidly rising health costs they were providing for about five million early retirees not yet eligible for Medicare. In 1993, employers had a $412 billion

liability on this score, nearly double that of four years before. GM attributed the record losses it sustained in 1992 to the $22 billion it spent on
medical expenses for early retirees.[2]

NAM's leadership in Washington had to be attentive to the instinctive hostility of most members to any federal regulatory scheme, especially one emanating from the Democrats. Magaziner therefore met
frequently with Jasinowski, seeking accommodations to NAM concerns
that could be reached within the managed competition context.[3] Key
issues, including a longer phase-in, the degree to which all firms had to
join a health alliance, and the size of the employer contribution to the
premiums paid under the mandate (most employers wanted 50 percent,
not the 80 percent called for by the Task Force on National Health Care
Reform), would be open to some horse-trading. In not-so-subtle fashion, Magaziner, Jasinowski, and others in the NAM Washington office
formed an alliance against the more traditionally skeptical and conservative NAM membership. When a version of the Clinton plan was
leaked in September 1993, Jasinowski issued another press release prais-
ing the plan, downplayed the controversial mandates, which many in
NAM saw as a hidden tax, and told Magaziner that he would continue
to raise "our strongest criticisms of the plan with you privately" because
"the bulk of my members are open but undecided about the plan at this
point and require a great deal of education and selling."[4]

Far larger and more important than NAM was the Chamber of Commerce, an eighty-year-old business organization with 215,000 member
firms and 600 full-time employees. It was one of the top political lobbyists and campaign contributors in Washington, but Chamber political
influence also derived from the hundreds of local Chambers that made
their voices heard in so many cities and towns. Richard Lesher had revitalized the organization in the 1970s, quadrupling its membership and
making it an aggressive proponent of the version of capitalism preached
by Milton Friedman and Lewis Powell, the conservative jurist who urged
the business community toward more political engagement.[5] In the late
1980s, however, Lesher turned the Chamber toward something more
than knee-jerk hostility to taxes and regulation. The Chamber had been
bitterly divided in its attitude toward Reagan's tax policy, which slashed

rates on individuals but actually increased them for many corporations. Moreover, the same sense of economic crisis that drove debate over industrial and health policy filtered through the Chamber as well.[6] Lesher's shift had been advanced by the hiring of William Archey, a registered Democrat whose last federal job had been with the Reagan Commerce Department, where managed trade ideas were often in vogue. Archey wanted to make the Chamber a "player" in Washington by being less "ideological." He was known to refer to those who categorically opposed any government regulation as "whackos" or "fanatics."[7]

Archey worked closely with Robert Patricelli, the CEO of Value Health, a managed health care company whose clients included Chrysler and Ford. Patricelli chaired the Chamber's Health Policy Committee, from which he purposefully excluded insurance and pharmaceutical companies, which had long subverted the cost control efforts of benefit managers like himself, many of whom now looked to the government as a partner in this quest. Patricelli would meet with Magaziner and other Clinton administration figures on almost a weekly basis, telling Magaziner that the Chamber would back "shared responsibility," the organization's phrase for the employer mandate, "if there is an appropriate government subsidy mechanism to assist low-wage workers and their employers."[8] To this end the Chamber practically wrote the HSA payment schedule that capped employer premiums at 7.9 percent for the largest firms with high wages. Late in March 1993 a unanimous vote of the Chamber's board backed the health care framework that Archey and Patricelli had put forward.[9] Thereafter, Patricelli would back the Clinton plan in his frequent appearances before Congress.

The Chamber's willingness to engage in constructive discussions with the Clinton administration infuriated the increasingly powerful right-wing bloc among House Republicans. In March 1993, after a series of Chamber meetings with GOP leaders ended in acrimony, Newt Gingrich, Tom DeLay, Dick Armey, and other firebrands wrote to Lesher: "Your current posture is unacceptable." The Chamber "appears now to be a lap dog of the Administration," complained Ohio Representative John Boehner a few months later.[10] Although the Chamber eventually came to oppose Clinton's first budget—the higher taxes were a deal killer—most in the right wing of the House GOP thought it did so in a tardy and tepid fashion. Armey, Boehner, and other House conservatives contacted local Chambers to organize opposition to the policies of Archey and Patricelli, even urging that they leave the national organization. These tensions burst into public view in July 1993 when the Chamber prepared to give its annual Spirit of Enterprise Awards to about one hundred mainly Republican members of Congress. A boycott, organized by Gingrich, Boehner, and the rest of the seventy-five-member House Conservative Opportunity Society, limited GOP attendance to just thirty-two.[11]

The GOP conservatives worked hand in glove with the Chamber's chief rival, the fast-growing National Federation of Independent Business. Unlike NAM and the Chamber, the 600,000-strong NFIB was a staff-driven enterprise. It thrived in a political culture that linked GOP partisanship to a regime of low taxes, low wages, and union avoidance. Under the leadership of lobbyist John Motley, the NFIB issued "Action Alerts" to its membership that inundated targeted legislative offices with letters and telegrams, sometimes backed up with a mobilization of the membership against an incumbent considered too liberal on labor or taxes. The typical NFIB business employed less than a dozen workers and was unlikely to provide health insurance for its workers. But like the National Restaurant Association, which also boasted of its mom-and-pop membership, the NFIB had close ties to some much larger firms, like General Mills and PepsiCo, whose heavily franchised fast-food subsidiaries were dependent on the low-benefit business model typical of many NFIB entrepreneurs. The NFIB denounced unionized manufacturers as "tired old industries that gave away the store to their workers by providing health benefits in lieu of wages."[12] Not unexpectedly, the NIFB rejected not only the employer mandate that was key to financing the Clinton plan but any subsidies that might have made insurance expenses palatable for small business. NFIB opposition to the entire HSA was "nonnegotiable," declared Motley.[13] To this end the NFIB waged a war against the Chamber for new recruits. "We were getting creamed in the field by the NFIB," a Chamber health policy staffer told John Judis.[14]

The NFIB took on the American Medical Association (AMA) as well. In decades past the AMA had spearheaded opposition to virtually any health reform that involved federal funding or regulation. That included Medicare and Medicaid in 1965, but by the 1990s the AMA membership included a lot of physicians who worked for HMOs, battled the insurance companies, complained of high drug prices, and came out of the Sixties. Most members were still small businesspeople, however, and although the organization now supported universal coverage, many doctors feared that if employers of low-wage workers were required to pay for insurance, then these same companies would be more likely to support government efforts to control physician salaries and fees to hold down costs. Working through Texas and other conservative state AMA delegations, the NFIB successfully lobbied the organization's House of Delegates to reject the employer mandate as a viable way to pay for health care reform. That vote took place on December 7, 1993. "When administration officials go in to talk to members of Congress, they can no longer say, 'The AMA supports what we're doing,'" said Motley. "That's big. It removes a shield."[15]

Contemporary surveys found that about half of all small enterprises would have welcomed a properly subsidized employer mandate. But those voices were muted, and not only by NFIB ideologues. The US occupational structure was undergoing an enormous transformation, with industrial manufacturing in relative decline and retail, restaurant, and other service-sector companies rising to commanding heights in the political economy. When in 1995 *Fortune* magazine finally allowed retailers onto its list of the five hundred largest "industrial" companies, Wal-Mart popped up as number four, with Sears, K-Mart, and PepsiCo also among the top twenty. GM, Ford, and Exxon still had more sales than the Arkansas retailer, but low-wage Wal-Mart already employed more workers than those three corporations combined.[16] And when it came to health insurance coverage, executives at such "new economy" firms saw the world far differently as well.

Pizza Hut, a PepsiCo subsidiary, became a high-profile case in point. The bottling company was moving rapidly into fast food, opening a new restaurant every day, thereby nearly doubling overall employment in just five years. Pizza Hut paid health insurance to the 3,000 salaried, full-time, white-collar workers it employed. But another 100,000 hourly, part-time workers directly employed at the 4,720 restaurants owned and operated by Pizza Hut were left in the cold. It was theoretically possible for these minimum-wage employees to have health insurance, but the plan offered by Pizza Hut was both paltry and expensive. In Europe and Japan, health care advocates pointed out, the company was required to pay 50 percent of employee premiums, but in the United States it got off scot-free. As a consequence, cost-shifting was massive: more than 71 percent of all hourly employees had health insurance from another source, either a parent, a spouse, or the government. Only 14 percent of the company's hourly employees actually enrolled in the Pizza Hut plan. When at a congressional hearing in late 1993 a Ford Motor Company benefits manager complained of the "hidden taxes" his company paid because of such cost-shifting, PepsiCo executive David Scherb replied that it would be "absolutely wrong" to transfer more of the health care costs from firms that employed older and more highly paid workers to those in the service sector, where workers were younger and healthier.[17]

This same sense of righteous indignation–cum–balance sheet calculation put virtually all retail, restaurant, and hospitality firms in militant opposition to the Clinton plan. Although manufacturers would see their cost of providing health insurance fall by 35 percent under the HSA, retailers would have to absorb a 165 percent increase, or $1,303 an employee.[18] Sears calculated that it would spend $300 million more a year because of the Clinton plan's corporate mandate. Federated Department Stores said that its health care costs would nearly double if it had to cover its part-time workers.[19] PepsiCo's David Scherb estimated that under the Clinton plan labor costs would rise 20 percent for the typical $5-an-hour employee. The Magaziner task force thought a 10 percent increase was more likely, but by this point in the health care debate the calculation of monetary gain or loss was far less salient than the politics and ideology that framed those accounting figures.[20]

The Insurers Divide and Defect

By the last decade of the twentieth century the American insurance industry had become a giant force and was well represented on the Fortune 500 list of the largest US corporations. At first, insurers had good reason to think well of the Clinton health initiative. Managed competition made them an integral part of the quasi-governmental mechanism that would deliver health provision, while at the same time adding tens of millions of new clients to the insurance rolls. Insurers had no objection to the employer mandate if that would generate funding for the premiums to be paid on behalf of these new millions. But the insurance industry was itself divided. A handful of very large companies saw many elements of the Clinton plan, including guaranteed issue, community rating, and managed competition, as profitably congruent with their emerging business model. These "Big Five" companies—CIGNA, Aetna, Travelers, Met Life, and Prudential—had once been leading members of the all-inclusive Health Insurance Association of America (HIAA), but as the Clinton plan took shape they quit, complaining that the HIAA was "paralyzed by small insurers who are opposed to national health care reforms." That left the HIAA controlled by some 270 small and medium-sized insurers, who represented about one-third of the 180 million holders of private health insurance policies in the United States.[21]

The industry fissured because the very definition of an insurance company was being recast. The Big Five insurers saw health maintenance organizations as the key to the future of their business. These HMOs would provide a range of health care services in return for a fixed monthly fee paid by employers, the state, or individuals subsidized by the government. By the early 1990s 45 percent of the country's 562 HMOs were owned by the Big Five insurers, the two largest for-profit hospital chains, or the 71 nonprofit Blue Cross Blue Shield associations. "Our role has changed dramatically from providing the standard type of insurance to being a manager of care," said a Met Life executive.[22] "Ninety-nine percent of the insurance companies are going to be wiped out because they're only prepared to be insurance companies," concurred Paul Ellwood of the Jackson Hole group.[23] "Cherry-picking" healthy clients would no longer constitute a road to profitability; from this point on insurance premiums would stabilize, but the largest insurers would make up the difference through the larger volume and increased stability of the provider networks they now operated.

Nevertheless, the Big Five held many of the same concerns about the Clinton plan as did Alain Enthoven and others from the Jackson Hole group. Led by Robert Winters, the Prudential CEO who chaired the Business Roundtable's Health Care Policy Group, the big insurers feared that if the health alliances became too large, they would become a price-setting monopsony, something close to a single-payer bureaucracy that could ratchet down health insurance premiums and set regulatory standards for the hospitals, laboratories, doctors, and pharmacies that the big insurance companies sought to own or manage. Like NAM and the Chamber, they wanted the health alliances limited to a smaller set of employers—those with just a hundred or fewer workers—and they even began to worry that the employer mandate, a mechanism designed to generate tens of millions of new clients, might also give the insurance-purchasing alliances even more of the moral and administrative leverage necessary to cap the premiums jointly paid by employers and their employees. These disagreements were the subject of frequent meetings during the spring and summer of 1993 between Winters, Magaziner, and the Clintons, but they rarely broke into the news.

Not so the conflict between the HIAA and the Clintons. For most of these smaller insurance companies, managed competition was an existential threat destructive of their business model. Ironically, they were much more comfortable than the Big Five with the employer mandate, and the resultant threat of price controls, because HIAA companies made their money by carefully selecting the most advantageous clients. "We meet them in the marketplace all the time," said a Blue Cross Blue Shield executive, "and that's their competitive niche. Give me your healthy and your young."[24] Guaranteed issue and uniform community insurance rates would subvert that business model.

Early in 1992 the HIAA prepared for battle by hiring as its new president Willis Gradison. The politically savvy former congressman was a moderate Republican from Cincinnati with nearly twenty years of health policy experience on the Ways and Means Committee. Unlike the NFIB, the HIAA was not run by right-wing Republicans. It endorsed universal coverage and the idea of an employer mandate, sent officials to meet with Magaziner and Hillary Clinton, and seemed ready to bargain. But the appearance of an accommodation could not mask the irreconcilable conflicts for this insurance industry segment whose very existence was predicated upon the redlining practices that the Clintons, the Big Five, and many employers were determined to eliminate. If they succeeded, job destruction at HIAA member firms would be catastrophic among the 100,000 underwriters who assessed risk, denying coverage to individuals likely to get sick, and the 200,000-plus health insurance brokers, an occupation destined for liquidation under the HSA.[25]

Democratic Party rhetoric, from President Clinton on down, sought to demonize insurers, regardless of size. When Bill Clinton accepted the presidential nomination of his party in the summer of 1992, he told a cheering convention that he would "take on" the insurance industry, and six months later Ira Magaziner told Gradison, "Bill, I'm not a politician but our pollsters at the White House tell us that it will help sell our plan if we identify as enemies the pharmaceutical industry, the physicians, and the health insurers."[26] But the HIAA insurers actually faced little pushback in their efforts to delegitimize the Clinton health care initiative. The Clinton administration was distracted and off-message. The budget battle was not won until August 1993, and the NAFTA fight jumbled political alignments. Supporting the treaty were many Republicans who were Clinton's fiercest health reform foes, but the administration's NAFTA push strained relations with the very constituent groups that should have been bedrock partisans campaigning for health reform. The AFL-CIO's Lane Kirkland had approached the White House in August 1993 with a message: "We have $5 million to spend. We can either spend it supporting health care or fighting NAFTA."[27] Labor chose the latter.

Meanwhile, the health care debate inaugurated after Clinton's September 1993 speech to a joint session of Congress unleashed a tidal wave of interest group spending: at least $100 million from late 1993 through the summer of 1994. By far the biggest spenders were the Pharmaceutical Research and Manufacturers of America ($20 million), which was determined to stop any semblance of government price controls, and HIAA ($14 million), which devoted most of its money to TV ads. Spending slightly more than $4 million, the Kaiser Foundation, a generally pro-reform entity, came in a distant third. Opponents did not try to blanket the nation: HIAA's Gradison sought to target the districts of conservative Democrats, whose defection would indeed prove fatal to the Clinton scheme.[28] On at least two occasions Gradison offered to suspend his advertising campaign if advantageous concessions could be won from either the Magaziner White House operation or Dan Rostenkowski's powerful Ways and Means Committee. But these gambits came to nil because what HIAA wanted—the elimination of what it called "pure community rating," for example—entailed the evisceration of the entire Clinton health reform policy. Sometimes a corporatist compromise is simply beyond reach.

The famous "Harry and Louise" ads were developed by a Republican-connected Southern California PR firm. After HIAA officials saw drafts of the still-unfinished Clinton plan in late August, they quickly put these clever commercials on the air and kept them there, on and off, through the summer of 1994. Sitting at their kitchen table, actors Harry Johnson and Louise Clark portrayed a middle-class couple who looked worried and confused as they read through a copy of the Clinton health security plan. "There's got to be a better way," Louise opined for the camera as their dialogue ticked off HIAA talking points emphasizing "choice," a veiled attack on the HMOs favored by the Big Five, and higher insurance premiums for healthy people like themselves, a critique of community rating. The Harry and Louise advertisements struck a nerve because they leveraged a generation's worth of rhetoric denigrating the idea that government could muster the capacity to solve the acute problems that had eroded the quality of life for tens of millions of ordinary

Americans. In one ad, the dialogue conflated the idea of managed competition with an overweening government:

> LOUISE: This plan forces us to buy our insurance through those
>   new mandatory government Health Alliances.
> HARRY: Run by tens of thousands of new bureaucrats.
> LOUISE: Another billion-dollar bureaucracy.[29]

These TV ads almost immediately achieved iconic status, so much so that at a Gridiron Club dinner in the spring of 1994, the president of the United States and the first lady sought to spoof them by putting out a comic video in which they sat around a kitchen table dressed as Harry and Louise. Mocking the shock of the HIAA characters, Hillary/Louise finds disturbing provisions and requirements hidden deep within the text of the plan:

> LOUISE: On page 12,743—no, I got that wrong—on page 27,655,
>   it says that eventually we're all going to die.
> HARRY: Under the Clinton health plan? You mean after Bill and
>   Hillary put all those new bureaucrats and taxes on us? We're still
>   all going to die?
> LOUISE: Even Leon Panetta.[30]

The humor was good, but it did not work. In the six months immediately following the unveiling of the Clinton plan, the percentage of Americans supporting it dropped eighteen points. Senator Jay Rockefeller called the HIAA commercials "the single most destructive campaign I've seen in 30 years."[31] Inside the White House the ads were viewed as so damaging that on November 1, 1993, Hillary Clinton weighed in, denouncing the Harry and Louise claim that the Clinton plan "limits choice." Insurance companies, she said in a speech to pediatricians, "like being able to exclude people from coverage because the more they can exclude, the more money they can make." Her assault made the front page of the big dailies and often led on the TV news shows. Although aimed at the cherry-picking smaller firms, that nuance was misplaced even by the *New York Times*, which headlined "Hillary Clinton Accuses Insurers of Lying about Health Proposal."[32]

The attack, or rather, the public reception of the critique, had two problems. First, it personalized the identification of the Clintons, and Hillary in particular, with the rough-and tumble of the health care fight. Long gone was the charm and humor of her September tour before the key congressional committees. But more importantly, the attack on the smaller insurance companies, whatever the impact of the Harry and Louise commercials, was off-target. The true fate of the Clinton plan would be played out among the Big Five insurers, the HMOs, and the giant manufacturing and commercial firms that the Clinton administration had relied upon to bring the rest of the business community on board and muscle the reform through Congress.

Big Business Abandons the Clinton Plan

The Business Roundtable stood at the apex of the American corporate economy. Founded in 1973 by manufacturing titans like US Steel and General Electric, the Roundtable sought to curb the regulatory reach of government, the power of labor, and the inflationary tide, which it mainly blamed on excessive trade union bargaining leverage. Composed of more than two hundred of the largest and most powerful corporations in the country, it represented a sophisticated business conservatism whose leading lights shifted from the founding generation of manufacturing executives to those in telecommunications, retail trade, insurance, airlines, and hotels. Unlike NAM or the Chamber of Commerce, the leadership was not bedeviled by thousands of smaller firms whose owners might have their views shaped by clever PR campaigns or partisan politics at the state and local levels. The Roundtable firms employed scores of HR professionals who could calculate the impact of the Clinton reforms on their bottom line. Some had played key roles in the Jackson Hole group, which big insurers had helped fund.

Since the mid-1980s Roundtable firms had seen health care reform as crucial to the vibrancy of US capitalism, and in 1985 the organization set up its own Health, Welfare, and Retirement Task Force, which became the focal point for debate over the Clinton plan. Three viewpoints were present, emblematic of the divergent perspectives framing corporate health care politics overall. The Big Three automakers and legacy steel producers, as well as older high-wage companies like IBM and Kodak, already offered generous health coverage, so they favored an employer mandate to fund universal access. They liked the idea of premium controls, and if they had any concerns, they arose from the need to preserve the Employee Retirement Income Security Act of 1974 (ERISA), which preempted states from microregulating employer health plans. These firms were so large that they could buy insurance or self-insure on terms negotiated by their own benefits managers.

Another influential grouping within the Roundtable were those firms directly involved in selling health care insurance or services. These included Prudential and CIGNA, drug companies like Abbott and Eli Lilly, and health care conglomerates like Humana. General Electric and other firms that supplied hospitals with expensive equipment were coming to fear price controls almost as much as the big insurers. In theory, the latter favored an employer mandate—which would generate millions of new customers—but as a quid pro quo, the mandate opened the door to premium caps. "If you get one, you were going to get the other," explained a consultant who worked with these businesses.

And finally, there were the employers, like PepsiCo, Marriott, and General Mills, the owner of Red Lobster and Olive Garden, whose business model increasingly depended on a low-wage, low-benefit, part-time workforce. They were ideologically hostile to any sort of governmental initiative that might curb the prerogatives they enjoyed in an unregulated market, now or in the future. This group was joined by CEOs from companies, including General Electric, AT&T, and Union Pacific, that feared the Clinton plan, whatever its cost savings, would set a precedent they would come to regret. Drew Lewis, a former secretary of Transportation under Reagan and now head of Union Pacific, told Magaziner that he was opposing the Clinton plan even though benefits managers at his company had "costed it out" and found that it would save millions annually.[33]

By the fall of 1993 the Roundtable was ready to defect. The key figure was Prudential's Robert Winter, a strategic thinker who had been actively engaged with the Jackson Hole group. He endorsed universal coverage, thought HMOs were the wave of the future, and wanted to abolish the cherry-picking schemes that sustained so many niche insurers. In the spring of 1993, when Prudential was still formally a member of HIAA, his company refused to help fund the Harry and Louise advertisements. The Clinton plan, Winters wrote to Hillary Clinton, "offers the best chance to open our excellent health care system to all Americans."[34] But Winters had the same profound misgivings as those in the Jackson Hole group: premium caps were nothing more than price controls; likewise, the large health insurance purchasing alliances, projected to buy more than 90 percent of all insurance, were nothing less than a government-regulated single-payer scheme. Even the biggest companies, which could still manage their own insurance coverage, feared that they would be turned into "small fish in the sea," muscled out of the market by the regional insurance purchasing alliances.[35] Chairing the Roundtable's Health Task Force, where at least eighteen of thirty-five companies were either in the health business or did not insure all their workers, Winters was in a strong position to swing the entire Roundtable against the Clinton plan.

His chosen weapon was a bill sponsored by Democratic Representative Jim Cooper of Tennessee. Almost a decade younger than the Clintons, Cooper had missed the Sixties and was well attuned to the rightward-drifting politics of his state. He had several relatives who were physicians, so Cooper focused on health issues and became a participant in the Jackson Hole discussions well before Bill Clinton had ever heard of them. He put a bill forward in 1992 that embraced the idea of health insurance cooperatives, but it included neither an employer mandate nor direct controls on insurance premiums, and it did not promise universal coverage. That made it popular among the retailers and restaurateurs, as well as most insurers. The hospitals found it harmless. Cooper called his bill "Clinton lite," but the whole exercise was a mirage. It was internally contradictory because the health alliances would fail unless a large cohort of employers were encouraged to insure their workers and seek out cheap insurance. And without some mechanism to lower or subsidize premiums, low-wage employers would continue their fierce resistance to providing health insurance. "Jim Cooper is a real fraud," Jay Rockefeller told journalists Haynes Johnson and David Broder. His plan, complained the liberal West Virginia senator, had "no discipline, no mandate, no budget or premium caps or anything of that sort. That is pure sham. . . . It has no substance to it." Lack of substance, however, was its political virtue, since it so easily served as an alternative, or at least a placeholder, that could rival the Clinton bill. Republicans hinted that it served as the basis for a bipartisan bill, conservative Democrats saw it as more favorable to small business, insurers liked its avoidance of anything that looked like premium caps, and big corporations could park their support with this potential law in the expectation that it would be modified to their liking when and if it became the basis for any bill wending its way through Congress.[36]

Although Hillary Clinton offered a conciliatory talk to the Roundtable in early December 1993, it did little good when the Winters Health Care Task Force held a conference call a few days later. Within just 45 minutes, they voted 14–1 to favor the Cooper bill, with the lone dissent coming from Chrysler. Many executives on the phone—including five consecutive speakers from the insurance or pharmaceutical industries— were dismayed by the regulatory character of the Clinton plan. "Have you ever tried to swallow a watermelon?" asked David Jones, the chairman of Humana, Inc., the hospital chain. "The insurance and pharmaceutical companies were going bananas over price controls," a Ford Motor Company official later remarked.[37]

The White House mobilized to keep the full Business Roundtable in the fold. Magaziner would compromise on the size of the alliances, the rigidity of the premium caps, and the extent of the mandates. And of course, corporate America would get a second chance to shape the health plan to their liking when Congress began serious deliberations and markup in 1994. Wall Streeters Robert Rubin and Roger Altman, both now with the Clinton administration, were enlisted to lobby their industry contacts, while others got in touch with auto and steel executives, urging them to staunch a Roundtable endorsement of the Cooper plan. Rubin reported to the *Wall Street Journal* that "most of the CEOs I talk to are in favor of universal coverage and cost containment." But there was nevertheless a "visceral feeling" among most of these executives that despite the Clintons' claims to the contrary, the administration was proposing a big government scheme to a problem better left to the market.[38] Such sentiments were stoked by Newt Gingrich and other GOP conservatives, who told Roundtable CEOs that "their interests were best promoted by being principled rather than going for short-term deals" that either Magaziner or congressional Democrats might proffer. This argument was especially compelling for the telecommunication companies: Congress was putting in place a new deregulatory framework for their industry. "If you are going to come back and ask for help in future areas," Gingrich warned these companies, "you should know that it's not in your interests" to support any part of the mandates in the Clinton plan.[39]

When the Roundtable's eighty-five-member policy committee held conference calls on January 13 and 14, voice after voice reported, "I got a call from Rubin." "I got a call from Altman." "I did too." Administration officials pleaded with the executives to delay taking public action until after Clinton's 1994 State of the Union address on January 25. The Roundtable did so, giving the first lady time to meet with ten sympathetic CEOs at the White House, while Rostenkowski and other heavy-hitting Democrats lobbed key businesspeople from Capitol Hill. But it did no good. By a 60–20 majority the Roundtable publicly spurned the White House on February 2 to endorse a resolution supporting the Cooper bill "as a starting point." Only the old-line manufacturers voted with the administration.[40]

The Clinton administration hoped that continuing support from the Chamber of Commerce and the National Association of Manufacturers might counterbalance the Roundtable's hostility. Neither insurers nor hospital chains had as much influence in either of those two organizations. Magaziner was counting on the Chamber's Robert Patricelli to endorse the most important features of the Clinton plan when he testified before the House Ways and Means Committee on February 3. Indeed, when Patricelli submitted a copy of his testimony prior to the hearing, he reaffirmed Chamber support for an employer mandate. "We accept the proposition that all employers should provide and help pay for insurance on a phased-in basis." But Chamber leadership was now subject to intense counterpressure both from GOP conservatives in Congress and from local Chambers bombarded with missives urging them to protest Chamber collaboration with the Clintons.[41]

Chamber president Richard Lesher broke under the pressure and abruptly ordered Patricelli to repudiate his cooperative posture at the Ways and Means hearing. A chastened Patricelli then testified that the Clinton plan had so many flaws that it could not serve as the basis for sound legislation. "If employer mandates become the vehicle for those who favor the trappings of a government-dominated system, we will not accept those mandates."[42] Later that month the Chamber's board of directors made it official when it voted to reject not only employer mandates but universal coverage as well. Lesher fired William Archey on April 5, and soon afterward Patricelli resigned as head of the Chamber's health policy committee. For the next several months the Chamber used its considerable resources to kill any health care bill, no matter how modest.[43]

The National Association of Manufacturers followed suit on February 6, the third business group to make its opposition known within a week. Facing many of the same pressures as the Chamber, NAM's board of directors voted, 56 to 20, not to support the administration package "in its present form." Said NAM president Jasinowski, "The Roundtable vote certainly caused a number of our people to feel we ought to take an even harder line."[44] Although NAM did not endorse the Cooper scheme, the eruption of so much corporate hostility to the HSA "has changed the environment in which the health care debate is taking place," said Jasinowski. "The Clinton plan is no longer as dominant as it was."[45]

The defection of big business, whose accommodation had framed the entire managed competition idea, proved decisive to the defeat of the Health Security Act. Led by Prudential's Robert Winters, the big insurers had been among the first to double-cross the Clintonite corporativists. After a White House meeting, Harold Ickes called Winters a "19th-century coal baron," and at a news conference immediately following the Roundtable vote Jay Rockefeller declared, "There's a special place in hell waiting for Robert Winters."[46] But it was the one-two-three punch of all the top business associations that proved so devastating.

"Our biggest setback in any area has been with the large business com-munity where we expected better support," Magaziner told Hillary and Bill Clinton.[47] "Clinton had staked so much on the support of business that the defection of the leading business lobbies represented an enor-mous blow," concluded Paul Starr.[48] Without big business support, wrote John Judis, "what would have been difficult became impossible. Health care reform was doomed."[49]

Collapse in Congress

All this had a notable and immediate impact in Congress. The Energy and Commerce Committee proved a case in point. Chaired by a veteran health reform advocate, John Dingell's committee was a bellwether on the issue because its members were highly representative of the entire House membership, with many hailing from the South or rural areas. They were helpful to Dingell, who represented a Detroit-area district, when environmental issues arose that might hurt the auto industry, but they could not be mobilized to support the kind of health care bill that the UAW and the car companies wanted. By the spring of 1994 there were no longer any moderate Republicans for Dingell to enlist in the cause; mean-while, a third of the twenty-seven Democrats on the committee were waf-fling because of hostility from their business constituents, large and small.[50] Dingell used all his horse-trading talents to co-opt opponents, but he still needed twenty-three votes. It all came down to the vote of Kansas Democrat Jim Slattery, a Dingell protégé. Slattery was watching which way the wind blew because he was spending a lot of time in his home state, where he was running in the Democratic primary for governor. The NFIB therefore sent out an "emergency alert" to eight thousand of its small business members in Kansas, urging them to contact Slattery. Pizza Hut, headquartered in Wichita, wrote to every local Chamber of Com-merce in the state, reminding them that Chamber leaders in Washington had rejected the Clinton plan. On April 21 Slattery took a four-hour visit from lobbyists for two of his state's largest employers: Hallmark Cards and General Mills. Later that same day Slattery came out against the em-ployer mandate. That ensured a committee stalemate, after which Dingell

FIGURE 6. The rivalry between Senator Robert Dole (left) and Congressman Newt Gingrich (right) helped torpedo Clinton's health care plan. (Clinton Presidential Library)

pulled the plug on any further effort. "When the president failed to get the [Business Roundtable], there was a big shift in sentiment inside the Committee," Dingell told *Washington Post* reporter Dana Priest a few months later. "That was a defining event."[51]

"Health care faded with barely a whimper," wrote the first lady in her memoir of the White House years.[52] By the summer of 1994 none of the several compromise proposals still floating about could generate enthusiasm from any part of the body politic. In a last-ditch effort proposed by Senate Majority Leader George Mitchell and John Chafee, most Clintonite innovations were stripped away. Participation in the insurance purchasing alliances would now be voluntary, and the sponsors gave up on premium caps and the idea of a global budget. The employer mandate was virtually dead, deferred to 2002. At that point, an employer requirement to pay 50 percent of premiums would be "triggered" only if insurance coverage had not yet reached 95 percent of the population in a state. A parallel effort by a "mainstream" group of centrist senators

financed an extension of coverage up to 92 percent of the population by
imposing a cigarette tax, a tax on high-cost health plans, and cuts in
Medicare.[53]

Neither of these schemes had a true constituency. Liberals scoffed at
their failure to achieve universal coverage, and labor hated the tax on
the "Cadillac" health insurance plans embedded in hard-won collective
bargaining contracts. Meanwhile, Magaziner and his crew were virtual
bystanders. Of course, hospitals, insurance companies, and drug companies were happy to wash their hands of any government-sponsored
cost containment experimentation, while partisan Republicans saw
electoral success in the fall well advanced by the ruin of even the most
tenuous and accommodating health reform. "Sight unseen, Republicans
should oppose it" was Bill Kristol's advice regarding the Mitchell-
Chafee effort at a compromise law.[54]

Big business, and in particular unionized manufacturing, was also
absent from this fourth-quarter endgame. Just two years before the
quest for cost-saving health reform in this sector had done much to
make Clintonite corporatism a solution to a pressing economic problem. But these firms and business associations had looked to the government only because private-sector efforts to constrain health costs
had proven a failure. By the summer of 1994 these avenues once again
beckoned. Executives in even the most hard-pressed companies knew
that they could still shave health insurance costs by renewing efforts
to put more of the burden on their employees. The 1994 defeat of a
bill to make the "replacement" of striking workers more difficult told
executives in every corner office that management would face less resistance when they renewed that stratagem. With the inexorable shift
of health care expenses from companies to their workers, even well-
unionized and highly paid workers, it was they who would now pay
more for insurance premiums, deductions, co-pays, and sundry medical expenses.

Even more important was a remarkable, if temporary, deceleration
in medical inflation. Why? The managed care revolution was in full
swing as employers corralled their workers into HMO arrangements
that were negotiating large-volume discounts with participating

doctors and hospitals. Big HMOs like Healthnet in New York and Kaiser in California sought no insurance premium increases. Indeed, employers playing hardball hammered third-quarter 1993 health provision costs down to their lowest growth rate in twenty years. Reform advocates were quick to call this a product of the "Hillary effect," which induced providers to restrain price increases so as to head off regulatory legislation. The decline in health care inflation might also have been merely a cyclic variation, the product of the austerity of the early 1990s, which created new efficiencies in health provision, followed by an expansive health care market that enabled hospitals and other providers to cut per client costs. The phenomenal disappearance of health care cost inflation proved ephemeral, but it had a profound impact while it lasted. Opponents of reform easily agreed with the Eli Lilly executive who declared that "the politicians are several miles behind the market."[55] Executives at companies like Chrysler and Bethlehem Steel were not so sanguine, but journalists and politicians noted the marked passivity of such firms during the legislative wrangling of 1994. Bethlehem, for example, never bothered to contact politicians on the health legislation it favored, all the while lobbying them on other issues like shipbuilding subsidies and steel imports.[56] Health insurance costs would rise again at the end of the 1990s, but until then corporate America knew that it did not have to make an accommodation with the state to resolve this chronic problem.

Coda: What Obama Learned

"I kinda think Hillary was right," Barack Obama remarked to an aide in July 2008, after he had finally secured the Democratic presidential nomination. He was referencing the importance of an individual mandate to purchase health insurance, a mandate that Hillary Clinton had championed during the primaries as the most effective and politically adroit mechanism for securing universal health insurance coverage when and if the Democrats reoccupied the White House. Unlike 1992, health care was front and center during the 2008 presidential campaign, and in more than twenty-one debates Clinton and Obama hashed out what a new law might entail. There was a path from the Clinton health care debacle to President Obama's successful passage of the Affordable Care Act in March 2010. It was not a superhighway, but the route was recognizable nonetheless.[57]

The Democrats derived four lessons from their defeat in 1994. First, President Obama would put health insurance reform at the top of his agenda, right after passage of an emergency economic stimulus. After that was enacted in February 2009 the field was clear for health care legislation. In contrast, the Clinton health insurance initiative had to share the limelight with the budget battle of his first year, with a huge intraparty conflict among Democrats over NAFTA, and with the series of unforced errors over personnel and culture-war policies that bedeviled his administration. Second, Obama let Congress do it. His majorities there were much larger than Clinton's, and they were more ideologically united. The White House had a plan, but in a decisive contrast to Magaziner's operation, Obama had Congress do most of the work of putting together the legislation. Such a strategy was possible because, in another stark contrast to 1993, most Democrats agreed on the essential elements of any health insurance reform in 2009. Even conservative Democrats were on board. These "blue dogs" knew that failure spelled certain defeat, as it had for the Southern Democrats who opposed the Clinton plan in 1994. So virtually all Democrats, even Representative Jim Cooper of Tennessee, were ultimately in favor of reform.[58] Such party unanimity was essential if the Democrats were to sustain a filibuster-proof sixty-vote majority in the Senate, even if only for a brief few months in the fall of 2009.[59]

The key congressional committee was Senate Finance, where Obama and Chairman Max Baucus had hoped to get some Republicans on board, in particular Iowa's Charles Grassley, who was on record favoring the individual mandate as a health care analogue to compulsory auto insurance.[60] This effort extended the negotiations for several additional months and ended in failure, but the orientation toward Congress and the Republican demonstration of intransigence probably served to keep conservative and maverick Democrats like Joe Lieberman and Jim Webb on board, even if the price was elimination of a government-funded "public option" among the health insurance plans from which the un-insured might choose.[61]

Third, Obama proved a more skillful corporatist than Clinton. The president's collaboration with key stakeholders proved crass and crude, but his administration avoided the betrayals that bedeviled Clinton when business, hospital, and insurance support for his plan collapsed. Although cutting deals could generate a political backlash, Obama's team thought it was a necessary strategy for dampening and dividing the opposition. As the *New York Times* put it, they would "keep power-ful groups at the table [and] . . . prevent them from allying against [Obama] as they did against Clinton." David Axelrod, who had orches-trated Obama's electoral victory in 2008, thought such accommoda-tions with these stakeholders were the price of "getting things done within the system as it is."[62]

An early deal was struck with the big drug companies. The industry had been a bitter and effective opponent of the Clinton health insur-ance plan, but now the drug companies would offer $80 billion over ten years in rebates, assessments, and contributions. In return it received a commitment from the administration to resist measures opposed by the industry, such as permitting the reimportation of drugs from out-side the United States or downward price pressure on pharmaceutical products from Medicaid and Medicare. The deal was immediately at-tacked by Republicans, who saw "corporate welfare" in the making, and by liberals, who saw low Canadian drug prices as proof that the federal governmental should use its purchasing clout to drive down market prices at home. But the deal stuck: Big Pharma refrained from attack-ing the Obama plan and in fact contributed some $150 million in advertising to support the reform, including a new set of commercials featuring Harry and Louise, touting the ACA.[63] A similar compact was reached with the hospital industry, which agreed to $155 billion in Medicare and Medicaid payment reductions in return for the vast new number of paying patients they would reap. The hospitals expected that once most people had some form of medical insurance, the ultra-expensive use of emergency rooms would sharply decline, as would their expenditures on charity care for those without insurance.[64]

The Obama administration never quite struck a bargain with the insurance industry, but the failure had a very different flavor from that in 1994. The HIAA, sponsor of the original Harry and Louise ads, no longer existed. This association of small and medium-sized insurance companies had merged early in the twenty-first century with a more potent group of HMOs and the large insurance companies with which they were intertwined.[65] It says a lot about the shape of insurance industry politics that the head of the merged organization, America's Health Insurance Plans (AHIP), was Karen Ignagni, the daughter of a Rhode Island firefighter, an AFL-CIO health benefit specialist during the early 1990s—naturally she had thought the Clinton plan too timid—and after 1993 the head of a community-oriented group of nonprofit HMOs. Ignagni was no Robert Winters. She made clear that she wanted her industry to be a "player," and the Obama administration and its congressional allies reciprocated.[66]

In exchange for guaranteed issue and community rating—no insurance company could henceforth deny an affordable policy to an individual because of a preexisting condition—the government would mandate that all individuals, including the young and healthy, purchase medical insurance if they did not already have it through a government program or through their employer.[67] They would buy it through a set of insurance exchanges—here we find an echo of Clinton's health insurance purchasing alliances—designed to be run by the states or, if these jurisdictions declined, by the federal government. The purchase of such insurance policies would be subsidized by the federal government, sometimes at a ratio of as much as eight or nine federal dollars for every dollar paid by an individual. The divisive employer mandate was not quite dropped, but it was made far less financially onerous, even to the low-wage, low-benefit service-sector firms that had revolted against the Clinton plan.[68]

The individual mandate had once been a Republican idea, put forward by some individuals associated with the Heritage Foundation in the early 1990s and then championed by GOP moderates like John Chafee. Its advocacy by elements of the Republican hard right in the early 1990s was almost certainly a cynical ploy to subvert the Clinton health insurance plan, but the Democrats thought that they could make it work fifteen years later with enough carrots—government-financed insurance subsidies for moderate-income people—and sufficient sticks, primarily the threat to slash tax refunds for all those who failed to purchase health insurance. That sort of individual mandate had succeeded in Massachusetts, where Governor Mitt Romney, a Republican, had proudly worked with a Democratic legislature to create a state-level insurance exchange that boosted insurance coverage to the highest in the nation.[69]

Although the insurance industry would make billions from the twenty million new policies they were expected to issue under the ACA, Ignagni could not quite bring all the elements of a sprawling industry into a pact with the administration. Many companies had a large stake in Medicare Advantage, a privatization scheme that gave insurers a lucrative slice of Medicare expenditures. It was overpriced, so Obama wanted a rebate. Ignagni offered $80 billion, but the Senate Finance Committee wanted nearly twice as much to help bring the total cost of the ACA under $1 trillion over the next decade. No ideological principle was at stake, but the impasse was real enough.[70] And finally, the insurance companies were not sure that in exchange for "guaranteed issue" enough healthy young customers would sign up through the exchanges. Indeed, it is telling that what ultimately prompted insurers to move into formal opposition was the September 2009 decision of the Senate Finance Committee—under pressure from Republicans—to reduce the planned penalties for Americans who, after 2014, did not obtain insurance. Insurers feared that a lot of younger Americans would not sign up, leaving the insurers with an older and ill client base. In subsequent years the industry was proven largely correct: even before a Republican Congress eliminated the individual mandate in 2017, millions of young singles chose to pay a penalty to the IRS rather than enroll for health insurance on an exchange. But the irony remains: despite all the criticisms of Obamacare as representing too much government, insurers became opposed to the bill only when they came to believe that too little government coercion was being applied to those they hoped would constitute a new set of customers.[71]

No formal compact was reached with the business community. Most of the major business associations, including the Chamber of Commerce, the National Retail Federation, and the NFIB, went on record in opposition to the Obama health insurance program. But their bark was much worse than their bite. The absence of a tough employer mandate lifted a large potential "tax" burden from retail, fast-food, and service-sector firms.[72] The major cost of Obama's health care plan would be borne by wealthy individual taxpayers, not by corporations per se. All firms with more than fifty workers that did not offer at least minimal creditable coverage were required to pay a penalty, in some cases up to $2,000 per employee. But this was not a mandate, which would have cost much more; meanwhile, the expansion and upgrading of Medicaid took many low-wage workers out of the insurance market entirely and therefore out of the calculations made by corporate benefits managers. For a company like Wal-Mart, whose own pre-Obama plan had been so unattractive that barely 45 percent of its employees signed up, the ACA relieved it of much responsibility and embarrassment. It was a de facto subsidy, which is one reason that Wal-Mart president H. Lee Scott could share a podium with Andy Stern of the Service Employees International Union (SEIU) at a 2009 press conference endorsing Obamacare's essential framework. PepsiCo and General Mills, once bitter opponents of the Clinton plan, were also on board, as were employers of low-wage labor such as Kelly Services and Manpower, Inc.[73]

While the absence of an employer mandate diluted business hostility to reform, it also compelled the Obama scheme to rely far more than the Clinton plan on a set of tax increases to pay for both a large expansion of Medicaid and the subsidies necessary to make the state insurance exchanges work. Here we have perhaps the most significant difference between the architectures of the two plans. Clinton was afraid of new taxes to pay for anything other than deficit reduction. But the taxes incorporated into Obama's ACA were large and highly progressive, representing the most consequential redistribution of income that Americans had seen since the imposition of World War II–era hyper-taxes on the very rich. Unlike the regressive payroll taxes used to fund Social

Security, Obamacare added a 3.8 percent tax on all incomes above $250,0000 per family not just on wages but on investment income as well, including the capital gains on stocks and real estate that have powered so many fortunes of the super-rich. In addition, Medicare payroll taxes were increased nearly 1 percent, with no upper limit.[74]

The revenue raised by those taxes paid for a dramatic expansion of Medicaid. In 1965, when the Johnson administration enacted Medicare, Medicaid seemed almost an afterthought. It was conceived as an addition to state-run welfare programs, and like other forms of "welfare," it was stigmatized, underfunded, and used as a political whipping boy. One conservative senator called it a "health care gulag."[75] Few members of Magaziner's task force thought it could be salvaged, so in the Clinton plan it was abolished: if unemployed, poor people would get subsidized health insurance through the alliances. But two things happened in the second half of the 1990s to make liberals see Medicaid as a program that deserved championship and expansion. In the bitter fight between the Gingrich Republicans and the Clinton administration in 1995 and 1996, the fates of welfare (Aid to Families with Dependent Children) and Medicaid became decoupled. Conservatives wanted to slash both and eliminate them as entitlements. As we shall see in a later chapter, President Clinton twice vetoed legislation that did just this, but on the third effort, the Republican majority in Congress sent Clinton the freestanding welfare bill he demanded. To the disgust of many liberals, the president signed it, ending a federal entitlement to welfare without the job training, child care, and guaranteed jobs that Clinton had once championed as essential to that project.

But Clinton's 1996 welfare law actually strengthened Medicaid. The president had fought long and hard to preserve that program as an entitlement that included not just families on welfare but a wider population of low-wage workers, the unemployed, and those outside the labor force. The federal government provided between 50 and 75 percent of Medicaid's funding, with the higher proportion going to the poorer states, whose criteria for eligibility and level of benefits nevertheless remained Dickensian. Meanwhile, Medicaid had won some powerful defenders. Like the food stamp program long sustained by agribusiness,

Medicaid secured the favor of many of the new HMOs as well as the nursing home industry, whose clientele included many elderly middle-class parents who became eligible for Medicaid funds by shifting assets to their adult children.[76] Medicaid was further strengthened by the creation of the Children's Health Insurance Program (CHIP) in 1997. Clinton's unexpected budget surplus gave liberals and their GOP adversaries room to cut a deal that provided grants to the states designed to extend health care services to low-income children. Governors of both parties, and especially conservatives, liked the plan because it was not an entitlement but a block grant, which gave them plenty of budgetary flexibility; liberals were enthusiastic about an expansion of the welfare state to a vulnerable and deserving population. Nearly eight million kids were covered by the early twenty-first century.

A decade later Obamacare's backers greatly transformed and improved the Medicaid program, moving it a considerable distance toward a national system of health provision. The ACA raised payments for physicians, expanded health care services, especially in Southern and Mountain states, and eased eligibility standards, opening the door to single-payer health care to anyone with an income less than 138 percent of the poverty line (not far below that of a full-time Wal-Mart clerk supporting one or two children).[77] And there was now much more money in the system: for participating states (a 2012 Supreme Court ruling made state cooperation voluntary) the federal government paid 90 percent of the cost of new Medicaid enrollees, and 100 percent in states that signed up right away.[78]

The expansion of Medicaid proved an outstanding success, with enrollments more than 50 percent greater than those projected by the Congressional Budget Office. By 2022 Medicaid and the closely linked Children's Health Insurance Program had enrolled over eighty-two million people, a thirty million increase since the plan was expanded in 2013. In Arkansas, which accepted ACA funding and expanded eligibility standards, enrollment in both programs rose by 81 percent; likewise, enrollments rose in West Virginia by 76 percent, in Nevada by 160 percent, in Kentucky by 158 percent, and in populous California by 79 percent.[79] Meanwhile, enrollment in the ACA health insurance marketplaces was

disappointing. Although the CBO once estimated that twenty-one million individuals would purchase health insurance through these regulated exchanges by 2016, the actual number was far lower, about thirteen
million, including eleven million with subsidized coverage and two million without.[80]

The Medicaid experience might well be something of a "natural experiment" in which a single-payer system has demonstrated its superiority
over that of the hybrid public-private ACA insurance exchanges. Unlike
the exchanges, there are no premiums and no deductibles, and one can
enroll in Medicaid at any time. Where state officials have championed
the program, especially on the West Coast, in New England, and in poor
states where liberals have been in charge, Medicaid constitutes something close to "socialized" medicine for the bottom half of the American
working class. In Kentucky almost one-third of all residents are in the
program, thus dropping the state's uninsured rate to 7 percent from
20 percent when the ACA went into effect. In some former mining
counties 60 percent of all residents are covered by Medicaid.[81]

Statistics like these demonstrate why the Democrats took Bill Kristol
to heart. If Republicans were so afraid of an expansion of the welfare
state under Democratic Party auspices, seeing it as a game-changing
ideological repudiation of Reaganism, why then the Democrats would
proceed full steam ahead, reasonably certain that once something approaching universal health insurance was in place its roots would sink
as deeply into the body politic as Social Security and Medicare. The
settled existence of these programs naturalized both the taxes needed
to pay for them and the benefits that tens of millions of citizens enjoyed
and expected. In the case of Obamacare, it would take almost a decade
for that dynamic to consolidate itself, to create a mass constituency that
in turn would sustain the new public policy and the loyalty of an electorate that benefited from that program. "New policies create a new politics" is the way some social scientists have put it.[82] Bill Clinton's failure
to do just that shaped everything else he tried to do for the remainder
of his tenure as president.

6

Opening Japan

A DETOUR ON THE ROAD TO NEOLIBERALISM

On the evening of January 8, 1992, Japanese prime minister Kiichi Miyazawa was hosting a state dinner for President George H. W. Bush. Present at the exquisitely prepared banquet was a large retinue of US businesspeople, cabinet officers, and other government officials who had accompanied the president on a twelve-day trade mission, which had already taken them to Australia, Singapore, and South Korea. The trade talks in Japan, which had the second-largest economy in the world and a huge trade surplus with the United States, were of course the most consequential on the entire trip. Indeed, the chief executive officers of Ford, Chrysler, and General Motors had accompanied Bush on Air Force One. They wanted the Japanese government to help them finally get an import foothold in the Japanese car market; even more importantly, they wanted to cajole Japanese automakers into buying more American-built auto parts and incorporating them into the cars they sold, both in Japan and in the vehicles the Japanese assembled in their newly built transplant factories in Kentucky, Tennessee, and other Southern states.

That effort would be championed by Bill Clinton. Just as his health reform initiative sought to use government power to reorganize an industry that constituted one-seventh of the US economy, so too did the attempt to manage trade with Japan rely upon a set of nonmarket mechanisms. The Japanese variety of capitalism was hardly based on laissez-faire. As with his health reform, this Clinton gambit failed.

To fathom the sources of that failure is to take a long stride toward an understanding of just how and why the economic and political structures sustaining neoliberal globalization proved so resistant to reform in the 1990s and after.

Prime Minister Miyazawa was condescending to the American delegation, who came, he noted, from a nation beset with AIDS, homelessness, declining educational standards, and a growing budget deficit. Unless the United States got its social and fiscal house in order, he cautioned, the quality of that nation's manufacturers was bound to remain second-best. The US effort to sell more in the Japanese home market was little more than special pleading, a form of collective begging ill suited to a once-great nation.[1]

President Bush seemed to ratify that weakness during the state dinner when he came down with an intestinal flu. Somewhere between the second course (raw salmon with caviar) and the third (grilled beef with peppery sauce) the sixty-seven-year-old chief executive pushed back in his chair and fainted. His chin slumped to his chest, his body reeled to his left, and he vomited onto the pants of Prime Minister Miyazawa. Horrified, Barbara Bush leaped to her feet and held a napkin to her husband's mouth, and a Secret Service agent vaulted over the table to catch the president before he tumbled. Bush soon recovered enough to stand, white as a sheet, but gamely smiling. He staggered out of the banquet hall to a limousine that sped him back to his guest suite at Akasaka Palace. A wan president slept in the next morning, but resumed his schedule in the afternoon.[2]

Video of the incident flashed around the world, likewise the failure of the Americans to win much in the way of any real concessions at a high-profile meeting where the victors of World War II were now the supplicants. It therefore took no time for many to see the president's embarrassment as a metaphor for that of industrial America. "Millions of Americans have got the flu right now, so people will be sympathetic," said Mike McCurry, then an adviser to presidential candidate Senator Bob Kerrey of Nebraska and later a Clinton White House press secretary. But the symbolism was too powerful to ignore. "It's the metaphor of our country's economy, being wobbly and being sick and needing some help from the Japanese. That's an image the American people find distasteful."[3]

Of course, the incident was not just a metaphor. On the eve of the trade mission, General Motors had announced that it would close twenty-one factories and lay off seventy thousand workers, capping a year in which the nation's most iconic auto company lost $4.5 billion, the worst annual loss for an American corporation in history. In all, the Detroit-headquartered Big Three automakers—Ford, GM, and Chrysler—lost $7.7 billion, a product of both the US recession and the onslaught from the Japanese, who had captured more than one-third of the American auto market. Cars and auto parts represented three-quarters of the record $41 billion trade deficit with Japan.[4] Indeed, the Japanese trade imbalance accounted for 60 percent of the US worldwide trade deficit. Some economists projected that by the year 2000 the Japanese GNP would surpass that of the United States.

The *New York Times* called the American trade mission a "fiasco," and Bill Clinton, then campaigning in New Hampshire, labeled it "an embarrassment . . . it was an opportunity lost." "The President goes to Japan with the heads of our auto companies—the evidence of our own failures—to complain to them that Americans are buying Japanese cars instead of American cars," Governor Clinton said. "The message seems to be: 'Please don't send these cars over here anymore; our people just can't help themselves.'"[5]

President Bush had no intention of putting up any import barriers to Japanese auto sales in the United States, but his delegation did want to open up the stubbornly insular Japanese market. After a set of long and bitter negotiations, the American delegation extracted from Prime Minister Miyazawa a Japanese pledge to purchase another twenty thousand US-made cars and increase from $9 billion to $19 billion a year the American-made auto parts sold in Japan. Agreements to increase Japanese purchases of paper products, computers, and insurance plans were also reached. But these "action plans" were closer to mere expressions of hope, since the Japanese government was unwilling to coerce or incentivize Japanese businesses, and certainly not consumers, to buy American products, many of which were ill suited to the island nation's market. "There is no agreement," said Harold Poling, chairman of the Ford Motor Company at virtually the same moment Bush administration officials sought to portray the Japanese pledges in a more positive light. Chrysler's Lee Iacocca was so disgusted that he took an early flight back to the United States, and Robert Mosbacher, the Commerce secretary in the Bush administration, dissented from the official comity. "We need specific results," he told Japanese negotiators. "And we need them now."[6]

What to Do about Japan

The disdain among American businesspeople for the Bush administration's ineffectiveness embodied a larger debate then taking place in the United States over both the character of Japanese capitalism and how American business and labor might accommodate or confront it. The traditional approach to Japan, normally espoused by Treasury and State in administrations both Republican and Democratic, had privileged the maintenance of a strong military alliance and cordial diplomatic relations. Japan hosted the most important US military bases in the Far East, and during the 1991 Gulf War the country had been among the most generous of allies who heeded American appeals for the financing needed to put half a million US troops in Saudi Arabia and Kuwait. American officials wanted Japan to expand its projection of military power and pay more for the upkeep of US bases in the Far East, but except for military-oriented high technology, most policymakers working under Reagan and Bush were little bothered by growing trade imbalances between the two countries.

Michael Boskin, chair of the Council of Economic Advisers under President Bush, was a case in point. The Stanford economist thought an aggressive posture toward Japan and other East Asian trading partners might well set off a trade war. But on an even more fundamental level, Boskin spoke for an economics profession that saw free trade as its own justification. Most thought that in a modern, complex economy there were no strategic sectors. Competition eliminated large deviations between what equivalent quantities of labor or capital earned in different industries. If the Japanese dominated world production of semiconductors and undercut US producers, well then that cheap plentitude constituted a boon to all those American consumers who were eagerly buying Far Eastern electronic products.[7]

This was the logic behind Boskin's alleged comment during the 1992 campaign season that when it came to world trade, "It doesn't make any difference whether a country makes potato chips or computer chips!" Boskin later denied saying this, but the statement's veracity did not matter, because the idea had plenty of support among economists who were influential enough to shape government policy. In their view, if the United States had a comparative advantage in the production of food snacks, capital was most efficiently deployed in that sector. Moreover, potato chips were not necessarily a low-tech product. Their manufacture was highly automated, and the production and repair of potato chip processing machinery required the kind of skilled workers that the advocates of a US industrial policy had long thought essential to American economic prowess. On the other hand, while computer chip design and manufacturing did employ a lot of highly skilled nerds, the production of these components engaged an army of circuit-board stuffers making little more than minimum wage in the United States and far less abroad.[8]

But Boskin's quip was cavalier even among Republicans. After all, the Bush administration had presided over a renewal of the 1986 semiconductor trade agreement, certainly one of the highest-profile transgressions of free trade principles negotiated with any nation. Most of the business executives serving on a government advisory panel thought the computer chip deal was a model that could be used by other American companies. They wanted a "results-oriented trade strategy" geared toward "concrete evidence that US-Japan negotiations are succeeding."[9] Those concerns did not go unnoticed in the Bush White House. Except for oil, farm products, and a few other commodities, the Japanese hardly bought anything made in America. Even Honda, Toyota, and Nissan, which had built a set of transplant auto assembly factories in Ohio and states to the south, imported almost half of the value of their components from the home country. Thus, between 1982 and 1987, the US trade deficit rose sixfold, with the bulk of that generated by the trade imbalance with Japan. The Reagan administration had negotiated a set of "voluntary export restrictions" against Japanese autos and steel, but such import quotas merely hastened Japanese efforts to increase the nation's production and export of higher-priced, higher-quality luxury brands. Meanwhile, in New York and California the soaring value of the yen made it easy for Japanese investors to purchase trophy properties, including Rockefeller Center, Saks Fifth Avenue, the Pebble Beach Golf Course, and Hollywood's Columbia Film Studio.

The solution assembled by the Bush administration was called the Structural Impediments Initiative (SII). The idea was to make free trade actually work by unearthing and then rooting out all of the industry-specific conventions and barriers that made it so difficult to sell American-made products in Japan. These were not tariffs or quotas, but regulatory rulings, supply-chain conventions, banking traditions, and government procurement practices that created an insular economy. For example, US auto parts were rarely sold in Japanese garages because they did not meet safety certification standards; big-box stores, a key to the sale of US consumer goods, were impossible to build in many cities because of Japanese zoning regulations; and American-made skis did not sell because Japanese officials claimed them unsafe for the island's snow. The Bush administration thought that once these barriers were identified and removed, "normal" market forces would be freed and imports into Japan would increase.[10] But the problem, wrote one US trade official, was more like a set of tangled roots in a swamp: "They are tied together and you really have little choice but go down there and start cutting away at the roots. . . . It seemed to us that whether the issue was—the distribution system, lack of enforcement of anticompetitive laws, the lack of openness in the direct investment system, the policies on land use—all of those really played fundamental roles."[11]

These SII talks never got very far. On the Japanese side, observed the US ambassador, "the bureaucracy, which detested the SII process, dug in its heels about making any new commitments." It was an "excruciating process," concluded Merit Janow, the Bush-era official responsible for carrying out the program. He thought the idea that the Japanese might be persuaded to transform a long-standing set of socially legitimized business practices so that US companies could sell into the Japanese market a pipe dream.[12] Something more robust and radical would be needed to recast international trade between the two largest economies on the globe.

How Different Was Japanese Capitalism?

The issue came down to understanding the nature of Japanese capitalism. During the 1970s and 1980s a cohort of voices had come to see it as fundamentally different from that practiced in the United States. And that difference had important implications, not only for the construction of a tough new trade strategy but for what was possible when it came to a restructuring of the US system of business and its relationship to labor and the American state. A 1989 *Business Week* cover story, "Rethinking Japan," attached the label "revisionism" to the set of ideas challenging the free traders' view that Japan's political-economic system was fundamentally the same as, or converging toward, that of other capitalist democracies. A small group of writers proved most influential: the political scientist Chalmers Johnson; Clyde Prestowitz, a former Reagan administration trade official; the editor and author James Fallows, whose 1989 *Atlantic Monthly* article "Containing Japan" cast US-Japan relations in Cold War terms; and the Dutch journalist Karel van Wolferen, author of *The Enigma of Japanese Power*.[13] The novelist Michael Crichton channeled the alarmist ideas of these writers when in 1992 he published *Rising Sun*, the number-one best-seller that year. "Japan has become the leading industrial nation in the world," wrote Crichton in an afterword to his techno-thriller. "But they haven't succeeded by doing things our way. Japan is not a Western industrial state; it is organized quite differently. And the Japanese have invented a new kind of trade—adversarial trade, trade like war, trade intended to wipe out the competition."[14]

Such ideas had gained traction among millions of Americans who saw Japanese economic prowess as a new version of the "yellow peril"—another Pearl Harbor that again threatened the homeland. Forty years after the end of the war, wrote the journalist Theodore White, who had witnessed the surrender ceremony on the deck of the battleship *Missouri*, "the Japanese are on the move again in one of history's most brilliant commercial offensives, as they go about dismantling American industry."[15] Such alarms could quickly get very ugly: Detroit autoworkers sledgehammered Japanese imports in union parking lots and sometimes beat up unsuspecting Asians unlucky enough to be caught in the wrong place at the wrong time.[16]

This species of orientalism was muted within the universe of industrial policy advocates. But the rise of an intense, popularly based anti-Japanese sentiment nevertheless raised the stakes when it came to transpacific economic conflict. Few Americans wanted to directly emulate the Japanese model—Germany and the Nordic countries were far more attractive—but the very existence of such a successful and threatening economic rival gave weight to the arguments of those in the United States who sought a more potent role for the state in any American industrial renaissance. The revisionist writers took the lead in asserting that Japan practiced a unique form of state-directed capitalism. Under that model, close relationships among business executives, bankers, and government officials strongly influenced corporate practice, especially in terms of investment and trade strategy. By allocating capital through a tightly controlled banking system, they argued, Japan would drive foreign competitors out of sector after sector, leading eventually to world economic domination.[17]

Chalmers Johnson, a UC San Diego academic who had also been associated with Laura Tyson's Berkeley Roundtable on International Economics, was perhaps the most authoritative and respected of the group of scholars, journalists, and policy entrepreneurs who came to wear the revisionist label. He first visited Japan as a naval officer during the Korean War; thereafter he was very much a Cold War intellectual, combining scholarly investigations of Chinese and Japanese nationalism with consulting work for the CIA. But the Vietnam War turned Johnson to the left and toward an increasingly acerbic critique of American empire and the political economy that sustained it. In his highly influential *MITI and the Japanese Miracle: The Growth of Industrial Policy, 1925–1975* (published in 1982), Johnson had made the case that an interlocking network of banks, corporations, and government bureaucrats had effectively subordinated market forces to the requirements of a "capitalist developmental state" that emphasized production over consumption, exports over imports, and rapid economic growth designed to nurture key strategic industries and innovations. It was a mercantilist, adversarial regime, but one whose managed capitalism held lessons for America. That island nation was dynamic because there managers could grow their companies "without having to serve the parasitic interests of shareholders or the passive interests of workers who have no stake in the viability of the company."[18]

"The Japanese economy is the product of a different history of industrialization from that of the United States," summarized Johnson in the midst of the debate over how US corporations could penetrate the Japanese market in 1992. Because that history was based on such a "different role for the state in economic affairs," American economic independence could only be maintained if the United States sought to "manage our trade with Japan—as the Japanese have always managed their trade with us to their advantage—and to implement an industrial policy to insure that US manufactured goods are attractive to American consumers."[19] Johnson was contemptuous toward professional economists ("an entrenched priesthood") because they were "more interested in defending articles of faith than in understanding what is going on in international economic relations."[20]

Laura Tyson's analysis of the character of Japan's business system was heavily influenced by Johnson. In 1989 they were part of an editorial team that published essays on how Japan's developmental state worked, focusing on the shaping of Japanese industrial policy by the persistent influence of a permanent, autonomous financial bureaucracy.[21] Three years later, when she published her influential account of US-Japan conflict in high-technology industries, her debt to Johnson was equally explicit: structural barriers to the Japanese market were rooted in the unique character of Japanese business organizations. A high degree of vertical integration, a tightly knit set of interlinked industrial groups (*keiretsu*), and a pervasive set of cross-shareholding relationships insulated many Japanese firms from market forces, made American-style takeovers and stock-price fluctuations rare, and kept foreign competition at bay. "The invisible hand is at work in Japan," wrote Tyson, "but it is not Adam Smith's invisible hand—it is the invisible hand of the government working with Japanese industry."[22]

Others sharpened the argument. The Dutch journalist Karel van Wolferen, who wrote frequently for *Foreign Affairs*, argued that the basic "fiction that hampers the formation of an effective policy toward Japan is the premise . . . that Japan belongs in that loose category known as capitalist free-market economies." And Clyde Prestowitz, who founded the Economic Strategy Institute—funded by GM, Ford, Motorola, and other corporations—to advance the revisionist argument, similarly held that "the Japanese society, market, government, and companies do not operate according to the rules and assumptions of Western logic."[23] In the *Atlantic Monthly*, James Fallows concluded that "Japan, and its acolytes, such as Taiwan and Korea, have demonstrated that in head-on industrial competition between free-trading societies and 'capitalist development states,' the free traders will eventually lose."[24]

The revisionist viewpoint had a large impact within the Clinton administration. Tyson's understanding of Japanese political economy was seconded by Alan Blinder, who spent much of his time on the Clinton CEA dealing with Japanese trade issues. Blinder thought that Japan, which he had recently visited to interview leading policymakers, was "a new and unique type of economic system that, while certainly not socialist, is not quite capitalist either." Writing in a 1992 issue of *The American Prospect*, Blinder hailed the island nation's "emasculation of the shareholder and concomitant deemphasis on profit maximization as the goal of the firm." This was certainly not "the American way," remarked Blinder. Indeed, the "locked-up" character of Japanese shareholding, a product of the extensive system of cross-corporate ownership among suppliers, banks, and insurance companies, made American-style financial manipulations much more difficult. These Japanese arrangements constituted a subversion of the idea that the animating purpose of corporate management was to increase "shareholder value."[25]

A Japanese banker told Blinder that "shareholders are almost nonexistent in the mind of the president of any large Japanese company." Such an attitude, wrote Blinder, was reminiscent of the managerial power posited by Adolf Berle and Gardiner Means in their 1932 classic work, *The Modern Corporation and Private Property*, in which the authors (who would both become prominent New Dealers) highlighted the demise of shareholder "ownership" in a corporate world in which CEO "control" reigned supreme. This could lead to self-dealing, but it also made clear that the modern corporation was a social institution legitimately subject to government regulation and also to the influence of other stakeholders, especially unionized employees and government-protected consumers. In Japan, Blinder hailed the degree to which such management autonomy stood athwart profit maximization and sustained both long-range corporate planning and a system of labor-management relations that Blinder thought "congenial, cooperative, *and productive.*" The result was not just a spectacular record of economic growth, but "one of the most equal distributions of income on earth."[26]

Derek Shearer agreed with Tyson and Blinder, but he was also a long-time Friend of Bill and a 1992 campaign partisan who put candidate Clinton in touch with revisionist thinking on how trade conflicts with Japan should be handled. A professor of international relations at Occidental College in Los Angeles, he had toured Japanese auto plants and fed Clinton memos and material on Japan-US trade issues, urging him to read the work of Prestowitz, Tyson, Lester Thurow (*Head-to-Head*), and Robert Kuttner (*The End of Laissez-Faire*).[27] He sent Clinton a copy of Michael Crichton's novel *Rising Sun* when it came off the press. Shearer convinced Clinton that the Bush administration's Structural Impediments Initiative was a failure. Because Japanese capitalism was so unique, Shearer thought, "it is futile and self-defeating for us to lecture and hector the Japanese to change how they do business. It makes much more sense and will make for more harmonious relations to simply negotiate market shares in industries that we believe are crucial to the economic security of the US."[28] After the inauguration, when Shearer was headed toward a post in the Commerce Department, his views sustained Clinton's increasingly hard-line policy. "The best way to approach trade with Japan is to give them the results we want and let them figure out how to do it," he told a trade conference. Of course,

Shearer also thought such a "managed trade" program was insolubly linked to the industrial policy initiatives that Clinton and Reich advocated during the 1992 campaign.[29]

Taking a Hard Line on Japan

Once Clinton took office virtually all of his key economic advisers were united in what they called a "results-oriented" approach to US penetration of the Japanese market. Robert Rubin, for example, was an opponent of anything called "industrial policy," but he also told John Judis, "We have all learned from our experience with Japan. I do believe in free trade, but I believe in two-way trade, and we have not had two-way free trade."[30] Larry Summers, then at Treasury, published a forceful defense of Clinton's unorthodox policy in the *Financial Times* in June 1993: "Strategic continuity in the relationship will require economic discontinuity. . . . The lesson of trade negotiations with Japan is that exceptional measures are sometimes necessary."[31]

Neither Ron Brown, who became secretary of Commerce, nor Mickey Kantor, the US trade representative, had been identified with revisionism, but both became operational partisans of the tough new agenda. Both had cut their ideological teeth in the civil rights 1960s, but afterward they were consummate "deal makers," Brown at the Democratic National Committee, Kantor in a big LA law firm. As Brown told the trade negotiator Jeffrey Garten when he joined the department, "We can't let a free market ideology get in the way" of making a "systematic" set of trade deals.[32] When it came to Japan, the Secretary of Commerce quickly signed on to the Shearer-Prestowitz line: the only "logical way" to reduce the US trade deficit was to have "measurable results, to in fact have some targets," he told a press conference on his first official trip to Japan in April 1993.[33] Brown saw the US-Japan semiconductor deal as a model that might be deployed both in the auto sector and in various other high-tech industries. "The Clinton Administration intends to end our American obsession with process," he announced to a meeting of the American Chamber of Commerce in Tokyo. "Markets will be considered open not when rules and regulations and arrangements change, but when we see that American products, successful all over the world, have an equal opportunity for success in Japan. . . . What we are doing, is freeing ourselves from the bonds of trade dogma."[34]

By the fall of 1993 Brown's point man on the crucial auto front would be Jeffrey Garten, author of *A Cold Peace: Japan, Germany, and the Struggle for Supremacy*. His biography was that of a classic free trader: a PhD from the Johns Hopkins University School of Advanced International Studies, work on trade issues under Henry Kissinger and Cyrus Vance in the 1970s, and then thirteen years on Wall Street at Lehman Brothers and the Blackstone Group, where he specialized in sovereign debt restructuring in Latin America and the Far East. He spent a lot of time in Hong Kong and Tokyo. But Garten—whose wife, Ina, was the celebrity cookbook author and Barefoot Contessa star—came away from his encounter with Japanese business very much a revisionist.[35] Garten was therefore an advocate of managed trade abroad and managed capitalism at home. "America is in the process of a fundamental shift in philosophy that goes beyond the degree of government intervention in any particular industry," he wrote in *A Cold Peace*. "It is moving towards a policy of managed trade—government-to-government agreements to regulate the volume of trade in a particular area."[36] Appointed undersecretary of commerce for international trade, Garten was ready to put into practice the hard-line trade posture put forward by Kantor and Clinton. The president "has put other nations on notice that America will no longer make trade concessions in deference to the NATO or US-Japanese security relationship," argued Garten in *Foreign Affairs*. "In abandoning the rhetoric of Adam Smith, President Clinton only recognized the reality that totally free markets are a myth."[37]

Mickey Kantor would be preoccupied with the NAFTA negotiations during most of 1993, but he was also on board when it came to Japan. Although Kantor had represented some big Japanese firms in his Los Angeles law practice, this experience probably did more to validate his instrumental approach to trade negotiations than anything else.[38] Thus, as early as March 1993 Kantor told Japan's minister of international trade and industry, Yoshiro Mori, that he considered the voluntary commitments made by Japanese auto companies to increase their purchase of US auto parts to be a non-negotiable "pledge" and asked the Japanese government to detail the steps it intended to take to meet it. He also insisted that the Japanese car companies increase from 50 to 70 percent the proportion of US-made parts that went into each car they built in the United States.[39]

Kantor needed an enforcer and Charlene Barshefsky filled that bill. Still in her early forties, she was a tough, experienced DC trade litigator whose portfolio included vigorous pursuit of "Section 301" disputes. Section 301 was a provision in US trade law that enabled companies that felt aggrieved to institute a legal action that would force the US government to retaliate against the offending trade partner. Few Section 301 disputes ever got that far; they were settled in negotiations, which was where Barshefsky demonstrated her tenacity and knowledgeability. She called herself a free trader, but she was sharply critical of those countries ("Japan was the classic case") that formally adhered to the increasingly liberal trade rules promulgated by the General Agreement on Tariffs and Trade and the new World Trade Organization, "but did not meet the spirit of their goals. Markets remained largely closed, opaque and driven more by informal cliques than by laws, rules and contracts."[40]

Managed trade was therefore the only route to equitable trade. And that required a capacity to stand up to Japanese prevarication. Confirmed by the Senate in June 1993, Barshefsky soon found herself in Tokyo, where she emerged as the de facto head of the Clinton administration team negotiating the new "Framework Agreement" with the Japanese. She came to be called "Stonewall," a moniker conferred on her by those who witnessed her "fulsome" and "painfully direct" response to a set of initially confident Japanese negotiators. After an early meeting, Larry Summers said, "You are Stonewall Barshefsky," to which she replied, "Just want to keep them on the straight and narrow. I hate sitting there listening to guff."[41] Three months later she was still at it. In talking points for a Clinton summit with the Japanese, Barshefsky insisted that the American president make the Japanese recognize that a "dramatic change" had to take place in their economic relationship with the United States. The "same old Kabuki" was pointless, and the Japanese prime minister, she stressed, needed to "walk away from talks with a crystal-clear understanding that bickering at the bureaucratic level must end."[42]

In contrast to the bitter NAFTA fight, business, labor, and congressional Democrats lined up behind the Clinton administration's hardline trade policy with Japan. House Majority Leader Richard Gephardt argued that "the unrecognized incompatibility of our economic systems is at the root of our current tensions and frictions."[43] John Young, CEO of Hewlett-Packard, told attendees at a 1993 conference hosted by Clyde Prestowitz that mere promises from the Japanese to liberalize their market were not enough. "If you can't measure it, nothing's going to happen," Young said.[44] UAW president Owen Bieber agreed, asserting that when it came to Japanese trade policy, "the sense of common purpose among industry, government, and union is surely greater than at any time since I assumed the presidency of the UAW in 1983."[45] One telling indication: in 1992 the Big Three automakers expelled Honda from the ranks of the Motor Vehicle Manufacturers Association so that the trade group would represent the interests of US firms alone.[46]

Bill Clinton concurred. "The Making of a Trade Hawk" was the headline that *US News & World Report* gave to Clinton's posture in the summer of 1993. As Arkansas governor, Clinton had made four trade missions to Japan. There he would exchange business cards with Japanese industrialists—"and return frustrated about his failure to open markets for Arkansas rice and poultry."[47] In the 1992 campaign Clinton saw trade issues and the absence of a US industrial policy as part of the same problem: both were necessary for the United States to "compete and win."[48] Once in the White House, the president left US-Japan trade policy formulation to the Deputies Committee, composed of the US trade representative and the second in command from Commerce, Treasury, and the CEA. But Clinton was on top of the details, catching both the overall negotiating strategy and the "nuance" of the day-to-day give-and-take. Even Barshefsky was impressed.[49]

When Clinton hosted Prime Minister Kiichi Miyazawa in April 1993, the dinner was uneventful. Not so the rhetoric. "The cold war partnership between our two countries is outdated," Clinton told a joint press conference. "Let's not paper this over," Clinton said as his chief foreign policy and economic aides watched from the sidelines. "There are still differences between the Prime Minister and me about what we should do. . . . The simple fact is that it is harder to sell in Japan's market than in ours."[50] Miyazawa was not moved: "There is no reason we should solve it overnight," he told reporters, and then he launched into a discussion of the Japanese word *gaiatsu* to describe the well-rehearsed cycle of American pressure and Japanese concessions that, while part of his country's culture and negotiating style, nevertheless bred resentment among Japanese officials and technocrats. This infuriated Clinton, and in a leaked comment to Russian premier Boris Yeltsin, he came down hard on the side of his most hawkish advisers: "When the Japanese say yes to us, they often mean no."[51]

Early in July 1993 Clinton and his negotiating team were in Tokyo, where the president and Prime Minister Miyazawa signed the much-touted Framework Agreement, which in effect was an invitation for more bargaining. The "framework" called for a decrease in the overall Japanese trade surplus, accomplished by increasing US firms' access to the Japanese market. To make that work, US and Japanese negotiators would target specific industries and services: medical and telecommunications equipment, insurance and financial services, direct government purchases, and, above all, automobiles and auto parts. "Objective criteria" would measure the "progress achieved in each sectoral and structural area." Announcing the agreement in Tokyo, Clinton called it "a framework to govern specific agreements yet to be negotiated." Reaching those would be difficult, admitted the president. "But now, at least we have agreed what the outcome of these negotiations needs to be: tangible, measurable progress."[52]

The sort of deal Kantor wanted was exemplified by the US-Japan "Arrangement on Cellular Telephone Systems," heralded by the Office of the US Trade Representative in March 1994. Beginning in 1985, Motorola had sought to convince the Japanese government to approve its cellular telephone system and assign it the necessary spectrum. But the Japanese pulled a fast one: welcoming Motorola to Japan but effectively denying the US company spectrum access in the lucrative mega-region of populous Tokyo-Nagoya. Through three administrations, arduous

negotiations had gotten nowhere. Then Kantor threatened formal sanctions against Motorola's Japanese rivals, who were anxious to penetrate
the US market. The agreement announced on March 12 "validates the
results-oriented-approach you have taken," Kantor crowed to the president. A private Japanese company would do the construction work, but
the Japanese government committed itself to 159 new base stations, containing an additional 9,900 voice channels; installation would begin in
April 1994 and be fully completed by December 1995. The Japanese
would monitor the agreement and meet quarterly with the US representatives to assess its progress.[53] Within eighteen months subscribers
to the North America–designed system grew from 22,000 to half a
million.[54]

The Japanese—and the Economists—Say No

The Clinton administration claimed that under the Framework Agreement it had negotiated twelve "results-oriented" trade agreements, most
notably covering medical technology, flat glass, and some agricultural
products. US exports to Japan did increase through the mid-1990s, although a fall in the value of the dollar may have been as important as
any trade deal. But when it came to establishing the principle that some
sort of managed trade regime should govern economic relations between the two countries, the new American administration was a decisive loser.[55] Japan's continuous political turmoil during the 1990s—
almost every year there was a new government—ensured that trade policy
would remain the province of the powerful permanent bureaucracy
housed at MITI and the Ministry of Finance. The experienced trade
negotiators in those two ministries had been temporarily sidelined
when, at the highest political level, the United States and Japan put together the Framework Agreement. But since the negotiation of industry-
specific trade agreements was now in the MITI/Finance portfolio, the
really tough bargaining work had barely begun.[56]

The Japanese did not just say "no." They denounced Clinton's "results-
oriented" trade initiative as "managed trade," a phrase closely associated
with the more militant revisionists and a term not too far distant from

"Japan bashing" and, beyond that, centuries of orientalist suspicion and fear of all things East Asian. US negotiators like Barshefsky were actually seeking a more nuanced set of trade guidelines than the revisionists had originally proposed, but officials at the MITI and Ministry of Finance almost always characterized US trade proposals as just managed trade. Rejecting that schema, the Japanese argued that the proper place for the resolution of trade disputes was inside a multilateral forum, and in particular the new World Trade Organization, of which the United States was a founding member and strong proponent. Although Tyson, Summers, and Blinder repeatedly asserted their free trade credentials, US pressure tactics—the only route the Clintonites saw toward creation of a genuinely open market in Japan—now seemed positively retrograde, subversive of the global internationalism embodied in the nascent WTO. An editorial in *Far Eastern Economic Review* opined, "Mr. Clinton, in his pursuit of numerical 'targets' has managed to do what no American president in recent memory has done before: give the Japanese the moral high ground on free trade."[57]

US trade officials were flabbergasted. "For the most managed economy in the developed world to level [managed trade charges] against the most open economy in the developed world is preposterous," complained Bowman Cutter, a top assistant to Robert Rubin and the chair of the interagency Deputies Committee that formulated the Japanese trade policy initiative.[58] Barshefsky admitted that "we have been put on the defensive"; having lost the "high road," the Americans were afraid to use the word "retaliation" when confronted by Japanese stubbornness and delay. "This is becoming a meaningful victory for the Japanese," she wrote her colleagues. She urged a "counterattack. . . . If we play by Japan's rules, we lose."[59]

But in this instance "Japan's rules" were those of virtually all economists, academic and lay, on either side of the Pacific. Virtually all Japanese economists sided with their government.[60] And so too did fifty of the most prominent US economists, including five Noble Laureates, who sent a letter to Clinton denouncing the targeted trade policy benchmarks advocated by the United States. Written by Columbia's

Jagdish Bhagwati, whom even Summers considered a "hyper–free trader," the letter urged the Japanese to continue to "say no" to any US demands for managed trade. "The world needs more market-based trade governed by internationally agreed rules, not targets set by bureaucrats, politicians, and self-interested complainants from industry." Although not mentioned in the formal letter, Bhagwati thought any analysis of the Japanese economy that singled out that nation as "deviant," "aberrant," "bizarre," or "predatory" just fed the "Japanophobia" that he thought Fallows, van Wolferen, and other revisionists deployed to stigmatize the Japanese. Even Clinton, whom Bhagwati thought "a good and decent man . . . uses the fear of Japan to kill the fear of Mexico in selling NAFTA."[61] Signers of the letter, who included liberals like Paul Krugman, Robert Solow, James Tobin, Jeffrey Sachs, Lawrence Klein, and Paul Samuelson, also thought it "myopic for the US to create the impression that Japan's [trade] surplus is harmful when its own past profligacy and current budgetary deficit have crippled its ability to finance its own needs, much less those of the rest of the world."[62]

The letter revealed a divide within the Clinton trade camp. While Kantor, Barshefsky, and Garten were indeed managed trade revisionists, Summers, along with Tyson, Blinder, Cutter, and Altman, came to see the demand for benchmark trade targets as but a mechanism for the transformation of the Japanese home market, not unlike the goal of the Bush-era Strategic Impediments Initiative. As Summers insisted to Bhagwati in an exchange that followed publication of the open letter, managed trade was not on the US agenda. Instead, "our goal is to unmanage trade in sectors where Japanese public policies have interfered with market forces to the substantial detriment of foreign firms." Given that the government's role in shaping the home market posed such problems for foreign competitors, "the last thing we want to do is encourage the Japanese government to take a more active role in the Japanese marketplace."[63] Summers's interpretation of administration policy was not that of Bill Clinton. Indeed, it stood diametrically opposed to the militant, if increasingly desperate, strategy that US trade negotiators still sought to deploy in the decisively important automotive sector of the Japanese market.

In the spring of 1995, the Clinton administration launched one final offensive, an effort to open the Japanese market to American cars and auto parts. This initiative was "the one that matters most," said a US trade negotiator.[64] In the mid-1990s the automobile industry remained a trillion-dollar bedrock of the world economy. Japan produced about as many cars as the United States, but the island nation had two decisive advantages: First, the transplant factories owned and operated by Nissan in Tennessee, Honda in Ohio, Toyota in Kentucky and California, plus others soon to come on line, had captured 30 percent of the US home market. These cars were assembled in the United States, but at least half of the parts came from Japan, and of course all the design work originated in Japan and all the profits flowed back there. Meanwhile, US and European penetration of the Japanese market was minuscule. US sales of cars and auto parts constituted about 1.5 percent of the market in Japan; the Europeans' share was slightly higher. Japanese exports, increasingly of high-quality luxury brands like Lexus, stood at 24 percent of the US market.[65] And of course, it was not just a question of US jobs; for three generations a unionized auto industry had anchored Democratic Party power in the Midwest. But the UAW had been unable to organize the Japanese transplant companies, so they were something of a Trojan horse, offering the promise of more US jobs but without the high wages, good benefits, and progressive working-class politics that had once seemed so closely linked. Clinton and other administration strategists saw some effort to shore up the US auto industry as imperative.

In a linked set of negotiations that started in British Columbia in May and ended in Geneva in late June, the United States made clear what it needed: more Japanese dealerships to sell American cars, more auto parts purchases by Japanese manufacturers, and a deregulation of the Japanese auto parts aftermarket, so that consumers in that island nation could purchase an American-made battery or tire from their local repair shop. Mickey Kantor insisted that the Japanese government guarantee that individual firms would boost their purchase of American automotive products, in much the same way as the Japanese increased their purchase of foreign-made computer chips. Clinton agreed, realizing that in the wake of both the NAFTA brawl and the sweeping Republican victories in the 1994 midterms, his team had to triangulate, but in this case to his left and especially toward American labor. "Eighty percent of American dealerships sold Japanese cars," Clinton wrote in his autobiography, while "only 7 percent of Japanese dealerships sold cars from any other country."[66] Polls showed that over 70 percent of the public supported the administration's side in its dispute with Japan. Basking in such public sentiment, one While House aide exulted that the "politics" of the auto dispute was "excellent."[67]

When the auto trade talks stalled in the spring of 1995, President Clinton doubled down, backing Kantor's hard-line negotiating stance. It is "my line," he told the *Detroit Free Press*. "It is my conviction."[68] Thus, on May 5, 1995, Clinton backed a decision by his National Economic Council to impose a tariff on luxury car imports, even with the knowledge that such American unilateralism would generate an immediate Japanese complaint at the new World Trade Organization. Unless Japan reached a satisfactory agreement by the end of June, the United States would impose a 100 percent tariff on thirteen Japanese luxury car models that accounted for nearly $6 billion in US sales. These tariffs, then the largest ever to be imposed by the United States against any trading partner, were designed to double the price of all those Lexus and Infiniti models rolling off Japanese transport ships. "[We'll] lose the Lexus vote in Greenwich," joked a Clinton political adviser. Kantor was just a bit more serious when he urged those Americans in the market for a luxury car to consider a Cadillac or Mercedes.[69]

The United States was violating its own long-standing commitment to a multilateral mechanism that could resolve international trade disputes. The Japanese would have won at the WTO, admitted Barshefsky, but "who cared?" The Japanese had been "so obdurate, that my view was that if retaliation might force them to the table, we should do it. . . . It would take two or three years before the case was resolved." In the meantime, the damage to their vehicle sales in the United States would have been considerable. "Extreme measures were justified," she said in a 2005 interview.[70]

The trade talks now moved to a showdown in Geneva, where Jeffrey Garten was the key US negotiator. There, the United States and the

Japanese would bargain with the American tariff deadline looming, exemplifying the way that economic conflict had now superseded traditional diplomatic or security interests. Geneva had hosted dozens of Cold War arms control talks when national power was measured in MIRVs and throw weights. Now another sort of high-stakes negotiations seemed to renew the Swiss city's reputation as a cockpit of big-power rivalry. The Japanese government would resist any formal agreement on a market share for US auto products, so Garten sought some kind of measurable indicator that could track the progress of US sales once an agreement had been reached.[71] Although "car parts never quickened Henry Kissinger's pulse," reported David Sanger of the *New York Times*, the Americans did seek to redeploy Ronald Reagan's decade-old determination to "trust but verify." As Garten put it, "As in arms control agreements, verification is going to be a crucial test of what we have negotiated."[72]

But the Americans blinked first. Just hours before the US sanctions were to go into effect on June 28, 1995, Kantor abandoned the Clinton administration's demand for specific numerical forecasts for Japanese purchases of American-made auto parts or imported automobiles. Garten tried to defend the accord, citing the "huge amount of monitoring" that would put "pressure on them in a way that would not have happened in previous trade agreements."[73] President Clinton gilded that lily by describing the agreement as one that "will begin to truly open" Japan's markets. "This agreement is specific. It is measurable. It will achieve real, concrete results."[74] But none of this was true. The government of Japan made clear that it would not be a part of any such agreement. Toyota, Nissan, and other Japanese auto giants would expand production at their American transplants, but there would be no "numerical targets," either in the United States or Japan, when it came to the sale of more American products.

In the *Washington Post* Jim Hoagland called it a "soft deal" in which the Japanese "successfully resisted Kantor's demand for binding numerical trade targets."[75] Chrysler chairman Robert Eaton thought any increase in Japanese purchases of American products "was going to happen anyway. As far as I'm concerned, nothing's changed at all."[76] Clyde

Prestowitz thought it a "a kind a normal US-Japanese agreement"—faint praise considering that "we have not cracked the keiretsu system." Chalmers Johnson summed up the revisionist assessment: "This is total victory for Japan."[77]

The automotive dispute largely exhausted the Clinton administration's appetite for high-profile initiatives designed to secure quantitative market access targets. All the key players suffered from what Garten called a "growing fatigue and weariness among the negotiators on both sides of the Pacific."[78] Laura Tyson, who had moved up to chair the National Economic Council when Rubin took the top Treasury spot, repudiated the idea that she had ever been an advocate of "managed trade."[79] Likewise, Garten, who had grown skeptical that any sort of numerical targets would work, told a Tokyo audience that "a relationship between the world's two biggest trading nations that is characterized by one trade confrontation after another seems as anachronistic as the old gunboat diplomacy." He would soon depart to head Yale's business school.[80] Barshefsky remained a forceful advocate for US interests when she became America's chief trade negotiator after Kantor moved up to Commerce Secretary following Ron Brown's death in a Balkan airplane tragedy. She stayed until the very end of the Clinton administration but never enjoyed the level of intimacy with the president to which Kantor's Friend of Bill status had entitled him. Concluded Robert Lawrence, a member of Clinton's Council of Economic Advisers, "For the Clinton Administration the era of major high-profile negotiations over trade barriers was over."[81]

Japan: Financial Implosion and Trade Relations Victory

But negotiating fatigue was hardly enough to eviscerate the Clinton administration's effort to confront the structural features of the Japanese polity that had made the world's second-largest economy seem such a threat to the United States and its version of market capitalism. By the middle of 1995 Japan was in the midst of a long-term economic collapse. The bust had begun as early as 1989, when an overvalued Tokyo stock market and insanely inflated real estate prices—at one point the land

and buildings in greater Tokyo were more valuable than all the real property in the United States—declined by 40 percent in a single year and then kept on falling. At first Wall Street analysists as well as Clinton administration officials thought the Japanese troubles were merely those of a cyclical downturn, soluble through governmental economic stimulus and more consumer spending. But Japan was caught in what Paul Krugman called a "liquidity trap" in which deflation, bad debts, and a paucity of consumer confidence drove a downward spiral.[82]

Treasury Department officials feared that the economy of their once-formidable rival might well implode, with a banking collapse precipitating massive bankruptcies and an outright depression. In June 1995 Summers told Rubin that a "protracted slowdown" was unfolding in Japan, reminiscent of "a 1930s type scenario" in which "high real interest rates, deflation, rising unemployment and yen appreciation reinforce one another and cause sharp declines in activity." A month later another Treasury official, Timothy Geithner, weighed in with a report from Tokyo that found "deep pessimism about the outlook for the real economy" among top finance officials there.[83] And in October Rubin sent the president a Treasury report, "Is Japan Ready for the 21st Century?" that, he wrote, "provides a useful counterpoint to those that still view Japan as the major economic threat to the United States." Japan was now in the midst of its most "serious post-war slump . . . that goes well beyond a cyclical downturn."[84]

In less than a decade the Japan problem had been completely redefined: from a need to contain Japan's economic power and penetrate its fortresslike internal markets to a focus on that nation's economic stagnation and chronic deflation. Larry Summers would soon quip to reporters: "Japan today is an island with 125 million people growing old, who haven't invented anything new since the Sony Walkman." At a time when the United States was recording its longest economic expansion since records began in the mid-nineteenth century, many Japanese began to bemoan what they called "Japan passing," a phrase that meant both that the United States was surpassing Japan economically and that it was bypassing Japan to pursue alliances with China and other Asian countries.[85]

The crisis in the Japanese economy had two significant consequences that went well beyond the fate of Japanese-American trade conflict. First, responsibility for US-Japan economic relations now largely devolved to Robert Rubin and other internationalists at Treasury. This was no time to try to bludgeon that nation into opening its markets; rather, Rubin and Summers came to see the maintenance of large Japanese trade surpluses as essential to that nation's financial health and the continuation of the low interest rates that were thought a key to American prosperity—and just incidentally, to Bill Clinton's 1996 reelection prospects. Rubin therefore sought to strengthen the dollar against the yen, a project that not only subverted any remaining US effort to reach a market-opening agreement with the Japanese but also ensured that American manufacturing would have even more difficulty surviving the onrush of ever more competitive Japanese cars, steel, and machine tools.

Here's how it happened. In 1971 the dollar was worth 360 yen, but on April 19, 1995, in the midst of increasingly bitter negotiations over trade in autos and auto parts, the greenback hit an all-time low: it could be exchanged for just 79.75 yen. To the Japanese consumer, that super-strong yen made American products super-cheap, which made Japanese government resistance to US car imports all the more difficult to sustain. But a strong yen and a cheap dollar also made Japanese purchase of US Treasury bonds a tricky proposition. If the dollar continued to fall, the Japanese would get a negative return on the hundreds of billions they were investing abroad, investments that helped keep US interest rates low and thereby sustain the economic recovery upon which Secretary Rubin had staked both the Clinton boom and the president's reelection prospects. With Japanese banks holding billions of nonperforming loans and the powerful yen threatening the trade surplus that had always helped Japan export its way out of recession, the Ministry of Finance opened a set of negotiations with Rubin and Summers to ensure that the Japanese would keep financing the still formidable US budget deficit. Eisuke Sakakibara, Japan's vice minister of finance, whose fluent English, economics PhD from Michigan, and stint as a Harvard colleague of Larry Summers made him a simpatico negotiator, told the Americans that unless the United States revalued the dollar, Japanese banks would be forced to cash in hundreds of billions in Treasury bills, thereby driving up US interest rates to make all those unsold bonds attractive to other foreign investors.[86]

Robert Rubin took the deal. The Japanese would continue to buy a huge proportion of all the bonds that Treasury put on the market; in exchange the United States would encourage the dollar to increase in value—it rose almost 40 percent against the yen in just one year—and downplay the resultant Japanese trade surplus. Japan would preserve its protected markets, the United States would continue to depend on foreign capital to fund its debt, and American manufacturing would struggle in a world where low interest rates fueled a consumption boom full of cheap imports, from both Japan and the rest of East Asia.[87]

Even more important were the ideological consequences of the Japanese bust. Clinton's domestic statecraft had been predicated, at least in its more ambitious moments, upon the prospect that American capitalism could be "managed." Japan's troubles seemed to eviscerate that idea and hardly provided an attractive challenge to the American free market model. American conservatives were therefore positively giddy. "Japan's bureaucratic bust amounts to one more trauma for those who want to believe that mandarins can outperform markets," wrote the *Wall Street Journal's* Paul Gigot. "First socialism was the god that failed. Then the European welfare state became a model. . . . Asian mercantilism was the latest great hope. All that's left now is American-style capitalism, more or less."[88] Writers at the libertarian Cato Institute drove home the point: "The revisionists claimed to have discovered a new and superior form of capitalism: the Japanese capitalist developmental state." But that was just another road to "crony capitalism," wrote Brink Lindsey and Aaron Lukas. "The revisionists' doom-and-gloom prophecies could not have been more wrong. All their errors trace back to a common source: an inability to understand and appreciate the power of free markets."[89] Chalmers Johnson thought this "the worst kind of American triumphalism," but Clyde Prestowitz conceded that in the late 1980s "the bubble was very powerful and it gave the impression of much greater momentum and power in the Japanese economy than ultimately proved to be the case."[90] Paul Krugman weighed in with an assessment: "The Future That Didn't Work: Japan in the 1990s."[91]

In actuality, Japanese capitalism retained many of its distinctive features. The *keiretsu* system remained largely intact, and the Japanese government continued to play an intrusive role in the nation's economic life. But the structural features that had once seemed to make the Japanese variety of capitalism both a threat and a model now seemed to be sources of weakness. The very economic guidance that Japanese technocrats offered the nation's banks and corporations did indeed breed cronyism, economic stagnation, and a chronic banking crisis. Lifetime employment commitments and long-term relationships among firms made Japanese business far less flexible than its US counterpart when responding to economic downturns. Close links among banks, firms, and government once helped to generate savings and allocate capital. In the economic environment of the 1990s, these links provided incentives for government to carry insolvent banks and for banks to continue to lend on the basis of connections and loyalty, even to borrowers who were insolvent.[92]

But if Japan no longer offered the West a model of capitalist development, it still played an enormously vital role in perpetuating the financialization and deindustrialization that had become so characteristic of American capitalism. The very market-thwarting mechanisms that the Japanese put in place to govern the home economy have repeatedly demonstrated their usefulness to a world that pivots around the financial hegemony of the United States. Japan's enormous trade surplus made it the world's top creditor, with external holdings worth close to $1 trillion in the late 1990s. By recycling so much of its trade surplus into US Treasury bonds, it played a major role in sustaining a decade of cheap American credit and the resultant era of Clintonite prosperity. This was a dynamic that Robert Rubin and Larry Summers understood all too well.[93]

PART III

Market Champions

7

Budget and Boom

A revival and modernization of New Deal–style liberalism was stillborn at the dawn of the Clinton era. If advocates of health care reform and the forceful guidance of the nation's Pacific trade sought a management of the market, their voices would become increasingly marginal to the central levers of economic statecraft—taxes, spending, financial regulation, and the Federal Reserve's manipulation of US interest rates—that consumed the Clinton administration even before the inauguration in January 1993. During the same months and years that Ira Magaziner, Jeffrey Garten, Charlene Barshefsky, and the first lady sought to apply a species of industrial policy to a large slice of the US economy, a far more powerful set of newly empowered men and women pushed the Clinton administration in a very different direction, convinced that the reduction of the budget deficit, the deregulation of American finance, and the creation of an unfettered regime of global trade constituted the path to prosperity. They won the battle over Clinton's first budget, slashing the deficit to create an employment boom predicated upon the surge of new investment made possible by the reduction of interest rates on long-term bonds. But that boom would be heading for a bust.

Clinton's Economic Team

Clinton moved into the White House having spent nearly two decades enmeshed in the politics of a small Southern state. His generation of forty-something friends and advisers did not quite have the connections or the confidence required to select cabinet personnel who would match many of the bolder policy prescriptions put forward during the campaign. And Clinton admired rich, successful, and well-connected people.[1] While still president-elect, he therefore relied on two consummate insiders, Vernon Jordan and Warren Christopher, to advise him on key appointments. Both men passed muster with the press and pundits. Jordan, a civil rights veteran and former president of the National Urban League, was one of Clinton's most intimate friends. By the early 1980s, his career embodied the degree to which a certain strand of racial liberalism could coexist with, indeed legitimize, corporate power at its most elite level. At the Urban League in the 1960s and 1970s, Jordan's job had been to persuade employers to diversify their workforce and lend support to philanthropies and educational institutions important to Black America. This experience eased Jordan's entry onto nearly a dozen corporate boards once Robert Strauss, the renowned Democratic Party power broker, had lured him to his law firm, Akin, Gump. Ron Brown, who worked under Jordan in the 1970s as director of the League's Washington lobby operation, followed the same path to a K Street law firm (Patton Boggs). Brown would become chair of the Democratic National Committee in 1989 and then Secretary of Commerce in the Clinton cabinet.[2]

Warren Christopher, a partner at O'Melveny & Myers in Los Angeles, had been in and out of government since the 1950s. He was Deputy Secretary of State under Jimmy Carter, a major figure in the Democratic Party in the years afterwards, and then Clinton's choice for the top State Department post, which he held until 1997. Both Jordan and Christopher knew all the players from the Carter administration and before, so Clinton's government would not lack for veterans who had held top posts when inflation seemed the most immediate and dangerous economic problem. Jordan and Christopher made sure that potential appointees were competent and well credentialed, which was another way of increasing the likelihood that those chosen upon their recommendation would stand at variance with the policies advocated by the industrial-policy liberals also making their way into the new administration.[3]

Thus, Clinton appointed Leon Panetta to head the Office of Management and Budget (OMB), the increasingly powerful agency whose key personnel were always present when the crucial economic policy decisions were being made. A former Republican, Panetta had been an assistant to Health, Education, and Welfare Secretary Robert Finch in President Nixon's first term. After he attempted a vigorous enforcement of the civil rights laws he was forced out. Panetta became a Democrat in 1971, ran for Congress in 1976, and rose to chair of the House Budget Committee in the late 1980s. Representing a suburban Bay Area district, he was a deficit hawk who had criticized Clinton on that issue during the presidential campaign. His deputy was Alice Rivlin, a Brookings scholar since the late 1950s, a Johnson administration official, and founding director of the Congressional Budget Office in 1975. A formidable figure, Rivlin would be appointed by Clinton to head the OMB after Panetta moved on to become his chief of staff in the summer of 1994. Rivlin had been a trenchant critic of Reaganomics, and she thought the GOP tax cuts of the early 1980s—and the supply-side theory that rationalized them—were irresponsible and dysfunctional. She was a Keynesian, but a moderate one, once calling herself "a fanatical, card-carrying middle-of-the-roader." In a 1992 book, *Reviving the American Dream: The Economy, the States, and the Federal Government*, Rivlin argued that deficits were the nation's biggest impediment to economic growth, and she wanted to devolve to the states much responsibility for the nation's economic well-being. Clinton rejected that strategy, but Rivlin would nevertheless be a militant voice when it came to blocking any sort of Clinton-era spending plans that deviated from her commitment to reduction of the budget deficit.[4]

For most of the twentieth century it had been a tradition of Democratic presidents to appoint Wall Street–friendly Treasury secretaries to reassure the financial markets. But under Roosevelt, Truman, Kennedy, and Johnson these appointees lacked the power (or in the case of FDR's Treasury secretary, Henry Morgenthau, the desire) to undercut the rest of the progressive program. In contrast, Clinton found himself a captive of fiscal orthodoxy. He was often an unwilling and resentful captive, but also one who was complicit in the execution of a program that stood athwart the promise of his campaign and the programmatic vision of all those who wanted to stimulate, regulate, and guide US capitalism along lines far more progressive than those of his immediate predecessors.

The two most important figures who would come to influence economic policy were Treasury Secretary Lloyd Bentsen and the Goldman Sachs executive Robert Rubin. Bentsen was a wealthy businessman and a conservative Texas Democrat who was chair of the powerful Senate Finance Committee. With the political elite of his state he had supported Reagan's aggressively expensive defense program as well as the initial round of tax cuts during that GOP administration. Bentsen used his chairmanship of the Joint Economic Committee to legitimize a conservative version of a supply-side investment strategy, arguing that "for too long we have focused on short-run policies to stimulate spending, or demand, while neglecting supply—labor, savings, investment and production."[5] Tall, graying, and in his early seventies, Bentsen looked like a man of authority and gravitas. As the vice presidential nominee in 1988, he had demolished in televised debate George Bush's running mate, the callow and pretentious Dan Quayle, who had compared himself to President Kennedy. "I knew Jack Kennedy," retorted Bentsen. "I was a friend of Jack Kennedy. You're no Jack Kennedy." Bentsen's deputy at Treasury was Roger Altman, vice chair of the Blackstone Group investment firm, who had served in Carter's Treasury Department. Larry Summers would take a post at Treasury as undersecretary for international affairs, an exceedingly strategic job given the financial upheavals that would wrack Mexico, Korea, Thailand, and Russia in the next few years. Altman thought Clinton's choice of Bentsen a shrewd one because of his intimate connections with Congress, where "the Senate Finance Committee was going to be, more than any other single place, where the action was."[6]

Bentsen did have influence on the Hill, but he did not always exercise it on Clinton's behalf. The new Secretary of the Treasury was at best a health reform skeptic, an opponent of any new energy taxes, and an outright opponent of those who wanted to pay for a stimulus program regardless of the continuing budget deficit. His real power was exercised by merely saying "no."[7] But even the Clinton liberals thought it was better to have Bentsen inside the administration rather than outside, where he could do even more damage.[8]

Robert Rubin

Robert Rubin was by far the most influential figure President Clinton would appoint to any policymaking post in his administration, and "Rubinomics" was the shorthand epithet many critics deployed to characterize the market-friendly policies of the Clinton era. With Bentsen's endorsement, Clinton appointed Rubin chair of the first National Economic Council, and after Bentsen, whose health was failing, resigned from the Treasury late in 1994, Rubin replaced him. For almost five years Rubin was one of the most powerful Treasury secretaries in US history. In Clinton's scandal-tarnished second term, Rubin was often the most influential figure in the administration. When he returned to Wall Street in mid-1999, his like-minded protégé, Larry Summers, took the post for the remainder of Clinton's term. Rubin and Summers steered through a vast deregulation of American banking; ensured that even in the wake of the 1997–1998 East Asian financial panic Wall Street capital would still flow smoothly throughout the globe; and presided over the growth of a new, multitrillion-dollar market in financial "derivatives," the complex but lucrative insurance instruments whose implosion ten years later would prove so instrumental to the financial collapse that triggered the Great Recession. Any second thoughts about Robert Rubin's leadership, however, would be largely consigned to the new century. Upon his retirement, Bill Clinton called Rubin "the greatest Secretary of the Treasury since Alexander Hamilton."[9]

Rubin was a Democrat of great charm and erudition. Although he had grown up in Miami Beach, his roots were in New York, where his grandfather, who had been a delegate to the 1936 Democratic National Convention, ran the most powerful political club in Brooklyn. Rubin's mother was a civil rights militant in South Florida. She voted for Henry Wallace in 1948, and her son would vote for George McGovern twenty-four years later.[10] Educated at Harvard in the 1950s, Rubin was by his own account something of a coffeehouse intellectual, a liberal who sought a "society that works for everybody instead of just a few." When serving in the Clinton administration he opposed the president's controversial welfare reform on the grounds that capitalism sometimes creates victims as well as victors. As Rubin wrote in his memoirs, "I felt strongly that some people on welfare are unable to work for reasons that are beyond their control, whether psychological, physical, or simply through lack of work skills and work habits."[11]

Rubin spent a year at the London School of Economics and then three more at Yale Law, but he found his subsequent sojourn practicing corporate law dispiriting. In 1966 he jumped at the chance to work at Goldman Sachs, where he spent the next quarter-century climbing to the top of that Wall Street firm. By the time Clinton appointed him to chair the NEC, Rubin had become an important fundraiser and adviser to Democrats, including presidential candidates Walter Mondale and Michael Dukakis. Warren Christopher had gotten to know him when both served on the board of the Carnegie Corporation, and Goldman Sachs handled many of Bentsen's investments, so Rubin was becoming a very well-connected Democrat.[12] But it was Robert Strauss who had proven to be Rubin's most important political mentor. As treasurer of the Democratic National Committee, Strauss had enlisted Rubin as a fundraiser as early as 1972, and by the late 1980s Rubin was the party's main fundraiser in New York and increasingly a policy adviser to Democratic candidates.[13] The *New York Times* called him "easily the most active Democrat on Wall Street."[14]

Rubin's money-raising success during the Reagan era was not just a tribute to the residual liberalism of some Wall Street high-flyers. Many thought that the government bond sales necessary to fund large deficits in the 1980s "crowded out" private investment and therefore sustained persistently high interest rates on ten-year Treasury bills. That threatened to hurt the stock market, reduce investment, and curb mergers. Bowman Cutter, Rubin's new assistant at the NEC, had been in the Carter administration when an unexpected rise in the projected budget deficit for 1981 sent the already elevated interest rates generated by the Volcker shock soaring and Carter's reelection prospects plummeting.[15] Four years later, when Reagan's tax cuts and increases in military spending generated chronic structural deficits, most Democrats, including presidential candidate Walter Mondale, abandoned their residual Keynesianism to become deficit-scolding critics. They wanted an "accord" with the Federal Reserve: lower interest rates in return for a lower budget deficit. This perspective was endorsed by none other than Martin Feldstein, Reagan's conservative CEA chair, who blamed the administration's cavalier attitude toward the deficit for crowding out investment and overvaluing the dollar, thereby crippling the competitiveness of American manufacturing.[16]

Thus, Reagan's determination to lower marginal taxes on individuals, strongly endorsed by the libertarian-tinged "movement conservatives" who animated much of his electoral constituency, did not win much applause on Wall Street, where capital gains were a more important source of wealth and income.[17] Among the economic sectors that were far more likely to support budget-balancing Democrats in the 1980s— and 1992—were real estate and investment banking. The former depended on federal aid for infrastructure and mass transit in order to keep the cities livable, while the Democratically inclined bankers feared that a new round of inflation would destabilize the bond market. Many Republicans on Wall Street feared budget deficits as well, but the Democrats there were realistic enough to know that the federal budget would never be balanced by slashing social programs. Taxes would have to go up. Thus, Rubin and Rodger Altman, then at Lehman Brothers, flew out to Minnesota to press Walter Mondale on the issue shortly before the 1984 Democratic candidate made his ill-conceived convention pledge to raise taxes and curb the Pentagon budget, while proposing virtually no increase in social spending. The *Congressional Quarterly* called the program on which Mondale ran "the most conservative platform in the last 50 years."[18] The Democrats, not the Republicans, were now the party of balanced budgets.

Through the remainder of the decade, Rubin thought the difficulties faced by both parties in raising taxes and confronting long-standing social and infrastructure problems had opened the door to a mediocre economy and the "risk of inexorable national decline." Therefore, when he met Clinton at a Wall Street dinner in mid-1991, Rubin was impressed with the candidate's acumen and his ability to engage in a serious dialogue, telling a colleague, "This guy Clinton is amazing. It's remarkable

FIGURE 7. Robert Rubin. (Clinton Presidential Library)

how well he understands this stuff." Rubin was on board, describing himself as a "validator" of the candidate's program when the press asked this highly visible Wall Streeter for his view of the potential president.[19] Equally important perhaps, Goldman Sachs employees and their spouses donated more to the Clinton campaign than any other single group in the country. Most of that help came early in the primary season, when Clinton was battling to stay alive. Rubin later raised millions more to help finance the party convention that summer.[20]

One cannot fathom Robert Rubin, however, without an understanding of what he did to make his money at Goldman Sachs. There, in the 1960s, he had been put on the "risk arbitrage" desk, what was then an innovative realm of finance that the *New York Times* called "a chancy, boom-or-bust corner of the securities market."[21] Rubin had never heard of it. However, the explosive and lucrative growth of risk arbitrage over the next several decades tells us much about how Rubin came to think about the world and also about the how and why of financialization and neoliberalism well before those concepts achieved a catchphrase currency.

Arbitrage had existed for centuries, largely as a means by which bankers and brokers could take advantage of slight variations in the price of currencies or commodities trading in two distinct markets. Buy at the lower price in one market and very soon thereafter sell at the higher price in another to lock in a profit. By the 1960s, however, commodity arbitrage was being overshadowed by the far more complex system of risk or merger arbitrage. By then, corporate conglomeration, mergers, and the quest for "shareholder value" had unleashed an unprecedented wave of stock swaps, cash tender bids, recapitalizations, divestitures of corporate divisions, and outright purchases when one corporation sought to acquire another. There were some thirty-five thousand mergers and acquisitions between 1976 and 1990, worth more than $2.6 trillion. One-third of the companies on the Fortune 500 list of major corporations in 1980 were no longer there a decade later. Goldman Sachs had hired Rubin because he was a lawyer who understood antitrust procedures and probabilities when it came to mergers and acquisitions. That was an important skill set at any time, but even more valuable after the Reagan administration relaxed antitrust restrictions on intra-industry mergers in 1982.[22]

Risk arbitrage was the investment technique that exploited transitory price disparities between securities whose prices, for one reason or another, should have been linked. Because there was normally a time lag between the announcement that one company sought to acquire the shares of another and the subsequent completion of the transaction, arbitrageurs made their money by purchasing, at a discount, the stock of one of the companies and then hedging their bet by selling short the stock of the other company. If the merger went through as expected—or in some instances failed, as they had shrewdly forecast—Goldman Sachs and other Wall Street firms made their money when the prices of the two firms reached parity. But there was much risk involved: hostile takeovers were far less successful than friendly ones, stock prices were unpredictable, lawsuits were frequent, and antitrust laws had to be taken into consideration. Arbitrageurs had to factor all these considerations into the price they were willing to pay. As Rubin put it in a 1977 essay explaining his then-exotic job, arbitrageurs were "the men in the middle and their job is to assess risk, reward probability, and try to make judgements enabling them to win often enough to absorb the inevitable periodic large losses and on balance come out ahead at the end of the year."[23]

Unlike traditional bankers, who took a long-range approach to financial problems and possibilities, "risk arbitrage required split second decisions about large sums of money." For Rubin it was "a matter of feel and of judgement—for both the market as a whole and for each individual situation."[24] It was a nerve-wracking profession, wrote Rubin in his 2003 memoir, "but somehow or other, I was able to take it in reasonable stride. Arbitrage suited me, not only temperamentally but as a way of thinking—a kind of mental discipline." As in governmental policy-making, "you had to be able to pull the trigger, even when your information was imperfect and your questions can't all be answered."[25]

Of course, Rubin was not just flying by the seat of his pants. At Goldman Sachs he developed a philosophy he called "probabilistic decision making." One was never certain, error was inevitable, and the point was to limit it. In 1983, therefore, Rubin made what *The Economist* later called "arguably the single most influential decision of his long career" by hiring the academic economist Fisher Black away from MIT. With Myron Scholes, Black had developed a mathematical model for pricing stock options, the newly popular financial mechanism that enabled investors to purchase a fixed number of shares at a fixed price salable after a certain date. Silicon Valley firms were particularly aggressive in their bestowal of options rather than high salaries to recruit top talent. For Goldman Sachs, options trading opened up a whole new market that enabled Wall Street firms to vastly increase the leverage, and hence the profits, intrinsic to their trades. The key financial insight in the Black-Scholes formula was that one could hedge an option by buying or selling the underlying asset and thereby virtually eliminate any risk. But the market had to be as frictionless as possible, and that required a deregulated and technologically sophisticated trading environment.[26]

Rubin would remain a culturally cosmopolitan advocate of the welfare state, but when it came to the fundamentals of financial capitalism,
he could see no other world than one that enhanced capital mobility,
financial deregulation, and the monetization of corporate assets. To
this end he would encourage the creation of a plethora of innovative
securities designed to hedge risk and leverage capital. He was a founder
of the Chicago Options Exchange and a pioneer at Goldman Sachs in
the creation and trading of derivatives. In this hyper-financialized environment, Rubin believed that "business confidence" had to be sustained to keep interest rates low and investment healthy. Maintenance
of the proper "market psychology" was therefore a responsibility of
government as well as Wall Street.[27] At the Little Rock economic summit he had already clashed, albeit in a gentlemanly fashion, with the
old Keynesian James Tobin, whose advocacy of a large economic stimulus Rubin thought a detriment to the "restoration of confidence,"
given the current worry about how the budget deficit could be tamed.[28]
Among Clinton-era policymakers there would be many paths to neoliberalism, but for Rubin it clearly would be one in sync with his work-
a-day world.

In the Shadow of the Bond Market

Even as the president-elect was broadcasting industrial policy ideas at
the Little Rock summit, Rubin, Bentsen, Rivlin, Panetta, and other advisers persuaded Clinton to trade away an economic stimulus package,
including targeted investments, for a deficit reduction plan built on
constrained social spending and higher taxes. Although the Clinton
economic summit had put on marvelous display a variety of progressive
opinions and personalities within the victorious Democratic coalition, it
soon became apparent that on the core issues facing the new administration, a balance-the-budget, conservative version of supply-side economics was in the ascendant. As one dispirited progressive told *The
Nation*'s William Greider, "Liberals are going to get projects. Conservatives are going to get the economy."[29] "The ideological balance of the
campaign, the Clinton self-presentation, was that he was a populist on

economics. Not a class struggle populist, but a populist," recalled his campaign speechwriter, David Kusnet. But now "the rhetoric begins to change," and "all of a sudden the more fiscally conservative people are running fiscal policy."[30]

Those voices urging budget austerity argued that a huge reservoir of investment money lay frozen and untapped. Lowering interest rates—long-term bonds were now at or above 7 percent—would free up investment and spending far beyond that which Robert Reich's $50 billion stimulus program had projected.[31] So Clinton's more orthodox advisers believed that deficit reduction was the first task of the new government, even if it erased Clinton's promise of a middle-class tax cut and a generous program of federal "investments" designed to enhance education and infrastructure. Deficit hawks believed that budget shortfalls bid up the cost of capital, thereby diminishing the pool of needed funds available to the private sector. These deficits, not trade globalization, diminished labor power, or the overweening power of finance, were thought to be the cause of America's economic troubles. Focused on the big, total investment picture, deficit hawks were complacent about manufacturing weakness. They believed such industrial decline arose from trends in global markets that government policy could not alleviate. Tyson, Reich, Magaziner, and many of the campaign "politicals," like Begala, Carville, and Gene Sperling, had seen the pamphlet *Putting People First* as a very different blueprint for the new administration, but they were outgunned in the debates that consumed the new administration in January and February 1993. Although Bill Clinton was sympathetic to their activist perspective, he believed he could not resist the more fiscally orthodox tide that flowed against him. Indeed, by the end of the decade Clinton was bragging that deficit reduction had freed up more than $1 trillion for private-sector investment.[32]

Events outside of Clinton's control also seemed to push him toward prioritizing deficit reduction. Although Clinton had promised to slash the budget deficit in half by the end of his first presidential term, the pledge had not been a centerpiece of his campaign. However, the remarkable Perot showing in November had put the issue of the federal deficit as a source of all that ailed the nation squarely in the public consciousness. It had a "very big effect on Clinton," thought Alan Blinder.[33] Meanwhile, the deficit the Bush administration bequeathed to the new president was roughly 40 percent higher than had been expected just a couple of months before. Clinton got that news on January 6, 1993, after Bush's OMB director, Richard Darman, told Robert Reich that the outgoing administration had underestimated the red ink by $60 billion in the coming fiscal year. Most on the Clinton team thought the estimate had been deliberately withheld to help Bush during the campaign, but the news made even more problematic any hope that a big stimulus program could survive the budget-making process.[34]

Alan Greenspan and the Federal Reserve

And finally, the Federal Reserve Board's Alan Greenspan made his considerable presence known as the Clinton economic team began to crunch the numbers. Clinton had not been amused when, a few weeks after the election, Alan Blinder congratulated the president-elect on having been elected to the second-most powerful economic policy position in America.[35] Greenspan's autonomy and power as chairman of the nation's central bank made him something close to a celebrity in the Clinton era. His famously Delphic pronouncements offered up to inquisitive congressional committees always generated headlines and speculation when it came to Federal Reserve monetary policy. Greenspan had once been a disciple of the libertarian novelist Ayn Rand, but his politics had become more conventionally conservative once he served in the Nixon White House and then went on to chair the Council of Economic Advisers under President Gerald Ford, with whom he was unusually close. Ronald Reagan made Greenspan chair of the Federal Reserve in 1987 and George H. W. Bush reappointed him four years later. By this point Greenspan's autonomy and that of the Fed were virtually unchallenged. This owed much to his intellect and forcefulness but even more to the emergence of monetarism—a manipulation of the money supply designed to raise or lower interest rates—as the most important instrument for governance of the US economy, and by extension that of many other nations as well.[36]

The modern Fed came of age in the Great Depression, when its ability to influence bond prices and interest rates became allied with the thrust of New Deal reform. During World War II the Fed happily subordinated itself to FDR's Treasury in the interest of a war production program that required federal borrowing and deficits on an unprecedented scale. Keeping interest rates low had become patriotic because it saved the US government many billions throughout the course of the war. Full employment and commodity shortages increased inflationary pressures during the war, but the bureaucratic allocation of scarce war matériel, wage and price controls, and high taxes on both workers and capitalists would keep higher prices in check. Bondholders and the rich would not get much of a return on their wealth.[37] This is what John Maynard Keynes called "the euthanasia of the rentier."[38]

But after World War II inflation came to preoccupy Fed deliberations. A conservative onslaught against the Office of Price Administration and other government agencies designed to regulate the economy allowed prices to leap forward by double digits in 1946 and 1947. The Fed wanted to jack up interest rates in order to dampen the postwar boom and fight the inflationary menace. Truman and the Treasury resisted, but as their own sense of progressive power and purpose waned, the administration struck a deal with the Fed in what became known as the Treasury–Federal Reserve Accord of March 1951. Although not a headline-making event at the time, the Accord rapidly proved a crucial juncture in the life of the Fed and the entire course of postwar economic policy. Under the leadership of William McChesney Martin, a former president of the New York Stock Exchange who would hold its chairmanship from 1951 to 1970, the Fed achieved a well-advertised independence from both Congress and the White House.

The Democratic Party liberals on the Fed, who wanted easy credit and low interest rates, were soon replaced by conservative Republicans anxious to defend a "sound money" policy. The influence of conservatives on the Fed grew even higher during the stagflation that characterized the 1970s because the tools of Keynesian fiscal regulation seemed so ineffective. By the end of that decade any effort to combat inflationary pressures with New Deal–style price controls or rationing had also been consigned to the dustbin.[39]

President Jimmy Carter's infamous "malaise" speech of July 1979— he never actually used the word—was predicated upon this rightward-drifting economic stalemate, both political and ideological, that had brought his presidency to a domestic dead end. With inflation heading above 12 percent in 1979, the highest since 1946, Carter appointed Paul Volcker chairman of the Federal Reserve. Volcker had served in both Democratic and Republican administrations since the Kennedy era, but he now inaugurated a policy that made him the most radically innovative central banker since the New Deal. On October 6, 1979, Volcker announced that the Fed would adopt the program of right-wing economists like Milton Friedman and impose strict targets on the money supply, thus spiking interest rates, which reached 20 percent in the summer of 1981.

This was class warfare of the sort not seen since the dawn of the postwar era. The industrial Midwest and its unionized workforce were dealt a hammer blow, while the rentier class and its Wall Street enablers moved to the center of the nation's political and financial life. Volcker would later describe President Ronald Reagan's breaking of the air traffic controllers union as "the single most important action of the administration in helping the anti-inflation fight."[40] This was because worker income constitutes a large majority of the entire GNP, so any government policy, be it high interest rates or outright union busting, that reduces labor's power to claim that large share reduces inflationary pressure. A double-dip recession that began in late 1979 did slay the inflationary dragon, but it also prepared the way for Ronald Reagan's capture of the presidency, a drastic reduction in union power, and the evisceration of investment in the things that had once made the nation an industrial powerhouse. In terms of productivity growth, the 1980s would be the worst decade in US history since the Industrial Revolution 150 years before.[41]

"The Fed is a central planner that dare not speak its name," quipped an economist reviewing the central bank's policies in these years.[42] This observation helps explain why Alan Greenspan's visit with Bill Clinton in Little Rock on December 3, 1992, was of more than ceremonial interest. Lloyd Bentsen had helped arrange the meeting; as chairman of the Senate Finance Committee, he had very cordial relations with Greenspan and certainly knew how powerful and autonomous a Fed chair could be. George H. W. Bush, for one, blamed Greenspan for keeping interest rates high in the year leading up to the 1992 election and thus prolonging the recession that bedeviled so much of his presidency. At Little Rock it is almost certain that Greenspan told Clinton, although not in so many words, that if the new administration exercised fiscal discipline, then the Fed would be more likely to lower its interest rate targets. Clinton later told his aides that "we can do business" with Greenspan.[43]

Deficit Reduction Politics

While Greenspan was jealously determined to ensure the autonomy of the Fed, he let the more fiscally conservative Clintonites know that a four-year budget plan that materially shrank the deficit would keep the Fed on their side. According to Rubin, Greenspan had "told a number of us that . . . he projected a reduction of 1/10 of one percentage point in long term rates for each $10 billion in annual deficit reduction."[44] And Bentsen had gotten Greenspan to actually put his name on a number: $140 billion in budget cuts would certify that Clinton was going to put forward a budget that the Fed would endorse and the bond market applaud.[45] No agreement with Greenspan was ever announced, "but one day it was kind of anointed," recalled Blinder in an oral history interview. "I remember one White House meeting . . . we were all around the table, and somehow it had been decided that 140 was the number. And Laura and I looked at each other, 'Where did that come from?'"[46] That an understanding of some sort existed was certainly well advertised when a smiling Alan Greenspan appeared in the front row of the House gallery during Bill Clinton's first State of the Union address in mid-February 1993. To his right sat Hillary Clinton and to his left Tipper Gore, spouse of the vice president.

But of course, slashing the budget deficit would be painful. It sacrificed so many of the training, infrastructure, and social programs, as well as the modest middle-class tax cut, that Clinton had campaigned on in the fall. Beginning at a January 7 meeting in Little Rock and continuing in a series of sometimes acrimonious Roosevelt Room sessions in the White House, Clinton and his key aides, both budget hawks and doves, wrestled with the painful choices that were necessary to cut the deficit. Alan Blinder later called it "root canal politics."[47] Deficit reduction eviscerated much of what Clinton promised in the campaign; indeed, the absence of a fiscal stimulus might possibly reduce economic growth by 1.5 percent, thus putting the United States at the edge of a recession.[48] But the hawkish argument for lower interest rates on long-term bonds carried the day. Roger Altman and Larry Summers had already sent Clinton a memo making that point: "Credible enactment of a deficit reduction package" would lower long-term interest rates, thereby "liberating a significant part of the pool of private savings that are now flowing into government debt rather than productive investment."[49] In his memoirs Bill Clinton wrote, "Bentsen, Altman, Summers, and Panetta bought the bond-market argument and believed deficit reduction would accelerate economic growth. Rubin was just running the meeting, but I knew he agreed with them."[50]

"After the presentations, I decided the deficit hawks were right," wrote Clinton. "If we didn't get the deficit down substantially, interest rates would remain high, preventing a sustained, strong economy. Al Gore strongly agreed."[51] This was a cold-blooded calculation, but during the next two months, as the full costs of deficit reduction became apparent, Clinton raged against the fiscal cage in which he had imprisoned himself: "You mean to tell me that the success of the program and my reelection hinges on the Federal Reserve and a bunch of fucking bond traders?"[52] Late in February 1993, once the markets began to take seriously the Clinton administration's drive toward austerity, interest rates on thirty-year bonds sank below 7 percent, a sixteen-year low. There was much cheering at the White House and among Democrats more generally, which prompted consultant James Carville to tell the *Wall Street Journal*, "I used to think if there was reincarnation, I wanted to come back as the president or the pope or a .400 baseball hitter. But now I want to come back as the bond market. You can intimidate everybody."[53]

Clinton campaign strategists like Carville, Paul Begala, Stan Greenberg, and Mandy Grunwald, as well as Hillary Clinton and Ira Magaziner, were equally incredulous. There were no guarantees that shelving campaign promises would continue to generate a positive response from the fickle bond market.[54] Begala, who attended many meetings of the economic team, thought budget reduction had turned into something close to a "religion." In a memo to the president, he concluded, "It's NOT the deficit, stupid." And later he complained, "Why are you listening to these people? They did not support you." Most actually did, but a figure like Alice Rivlin, who presented herself as a hard-nosed, apolitical technocrat, came to the table with a profile—and a long political history—wildly at variance with those of many of Clinton's liberal advisers. Before speaking at one of her budget presentations, she looked around the room and wondered, judging from their demeanor, why so many of the politicals already seemed so hostile and angry.[55]

Of course, not everyone in the Clinton White House accepted the bond market magic. Robert Kuttner never got a West Wing office, but he was editor of the then-influential magazine *The American Prospect*, in which Tyson, Reich, and others close to the administration put forth their policy prescriptions. In a memo to the president-elect, Kuttner summarized the arguments of the Clintonite left. Deficit reduction per se might well lead to lower interest rates, but easy money was not the problem: a paucity of demand—stagnant wages and high unemployment—gave private industry no incentive to invest. Moreover, deficit reduction was a political loser. Before the midterm elections it would generate no jobs and put no upward pressure on wages. A large stimulus, targeted to raise productivity, would have much more of a payoff, political and economic. If the country needed to shrink the deficit, a reform of the health care system was the way to go. Reducing medical inflation would generate $200 billion in savings over the next decade, more than enough to wipe out all other deficit reduction measures. "The paradox is this," summed up Kuttner. "You don't get deficit reduction by targeting deficit reduction. You achieve it—over time—by raising the rate of growth and by fixing the health system."[56]

As the new chair of the CEA, Laura Tyson agreed with this viewpoint. Writing to Rubin and Clinton a month later, both Tyson and Blinder, by then the CEA chief economist, argued that "deficit reduction at the expense of public investment is self-defeating." Blinder and Tyson wanted a gradual, multiyear program to lower the deficit combined with "a shift in government spending toward public investment programs." Importantly, and like the rest of the Clintonite left, they argued that "any plan to bring down the deficit by large amounts—and hold it there—in the late 1990s and into the next century will require changes in our health care system."[57] Magaziner and those tasked with health reform hoped and expected that spending caps on health care and the introduction of a system of managed competition would indeed have a long-range impact on federal spending, possibly by 1996.

Tyson thought the drive to cut $140 billion out of the budget something close to a fetish: "There is too much intuition going on here," she complained at a January 13 meeting of Clinton's budget planning group. And a month later she called the budget reduction target "magical"; "there is a point where the bond market will take your program seriously," she explained, but it was impossible to quantify it. "Maybe it's $135 billion or $140 billion or whatever. I can't tell you."[58] But Tyson was outgunned. In the budget showdown during Clinton's first winter, both the Office of Management and Budget (Alice Rivlin and Leon Panetta) and the Treasury Department (Lloyd Bentsen and Roger Altman) held that an insufficiently tough deficit reduction plan would send the wrong political and fiscal signal. This was an endorsement of the business "confidence" argument at the heart of Rubin's economic worldview.

The budget cuts and a large tax increase on the wealthy would indeed move the budget toward balance, but a residual stimulus program of some $16 billion remained as well as a BTU tax designed to reduce carbon emissions from many sources, not just coal and automobiles. While the carbon tax was championed by Al Gore and many conservationists, it had a larger ideological meaning: despite all the obstacles, the Clintonites could still advance an innovative program designed to reshape and incentivize at least a slice of the entire economy. Likewise, the $16 billion stimulus program, although now reduced far below the level

Robert Reich had once sought, nevertheless promised an immediate, if modest, economic boost, and one that was important given the fiscal drag generated by the large cuts to post–Cold War defense spending and the tax increases that Clinton proposed on corporations and high-income earners. (Family incomes above $250,000 would be taxed at 39.6 percent, up from 31 percent.) Unfortunately, the stimulus package lacked coherence. There was a little of this and a little of that—some highway funds balanced by a smattering for mass transportation, grants and loans for water treatment, maintenance at parks and forests, scholarships, job training, and summer jobs. Although Clinton called it a set of needed "investments," most Republicans and some Democrats thought it politically motivated pork.[59]

Clinton and the Democratic leadership were able to steamroll Republicans in the House, but in the Senate, whose procedures were more generous to the minority party, Republicans had more leverage, and also enough Democratic allies, to subvert Clinton's plan. Senate Republicans thought the $16 billion stimulus was too small to have much of an effect on the economy, and as the weeks of debate rolled on, their posture hardened; they finally killed the stimulus with a filibuster in April.[60] The only item that survived was $4 billion for additional unemployment benefits. The BTU tax also came to naught, replaced by a 4.3 cent a gallon increase in the federal gas tax, which Bill Clinton had campaigned against. On this vote key Senate Democrats, including David Boren of Oklahoma and John Breaux of Louisiana, cast votes with the GOP. Boren had been a protégé of Lloyd Bentsen, and Breaux was a frequent speaker at DLC events.[61]

When the Clinton budget came up for the decisive Senate vote on August 6, everyone in the White House knew two things. First, this was a make-or-break legislative event. Defeat would neuter the new administration in its very first year; victory would give the Clinton and his allies breathing room to reassemble their forces and fight again. For all the compromises and sausage-making that went into the budget, it still constituted a real break with Reaganism. The package raised taxes by $241 billion, of which more than 90 percent was expected to come from those with incomes over $100,000 (the equivalent of $205,000 in

2022). The top effective tax rate rose to nearly 40 percent, and the new law eliminated the income cap on Medicare taxes. Clinton also expanded the Earned Income Tax Credit (EITC), which provided wage subsidies and tax credits for the working poor, and he increased funding for food stamps and childhood vaccinations. New tax incentives promoted business investment in depressed areas, and the capital gains tax for people who made long-term stock investments in small and medium-sized businesses was reduced. Finally, in one of those fiscally inconsequential but ideologically progressive changes to the tax system, the new law slashed the tax deductibility of the business lunch from 80 to 50 percent.[62]

Of course, the second thing that everyone knew was that, until the last hour, no one in the administration could foretell the outcome of the roll-call vote. They certainly knew that all the Republican senators would vote no, but the Democratic ranks were hardly as solid. Bill Clinton's approval rating stood in the mid-40s during the summer of 1993, and every Democratic senator who had won reelection in 1992 did so with a far higher proportion of the vote than the president. So liberals as well as conservative Democrats were in a grousing mood. Bob Kerrey of Nebraska complained that the budget did not shift incentives from consumption to saving. Frank Lautenberg of New Jersey called the budget plan unfair to the middle class. Bill Bradley, also of New Jersey, opined that the American people wanted "bold action informed by principle. Judged against this standard, today's choice is somewhat disappointing."[63] Boren of Oklahoma did not like the gas tax. In the end six Democrats, including DLC founder Sam Nunn, voted against the budget. Aside from Lautenberg and Richard Bryan of Nevada, the other naysayers were from the South. Victory in the tortuous process was assured only minutes before voting began, when Senator Kerrey, a Hamlet-like holdout, announced that he would reluctantly support the budget plan so as not to "cast a vote that brings down your presidency." Cheering Democrats leapt to their feet, after which Vice President Al Gore cast the late-night deciding vote that gave Clinton a 51–50 majority.[64] Treasury's Roger Altman, who had lobbied hesitant legislators from the Oval Office, remembered that vote "as the most dramatic moment I ever experienced in six-and-a-half years of government service."[65] The stakes were enormous wrote Robert Rubin a decade later: "Had the President lost on his initial budget, not only might economic recovery have been stymied, but . . . the whole Clinton presidency might have been imperiled."[66]

The Clinton Boom

Did that narrow vote set the stage for the nation's greatest postwar boom? Republicans had long denounced the Clinton budget bill, with Newt Gingrich calling it a "job killer" that would "put us back in recession." Declared California Republican Representative Christopher Cox, "It will kill jobs, kill businesses, and yes, kill even the higher tax revenues that these suicidal tax increases hope to gain."[67] But "they were wrong," wrote Bill Clinton in his 2004 memoir. "Our bond market gambit would work beyond our wildest dreams, bringing lower interest rates, a soaring stock market, and a booming economy."[68] The economy grew for 116 months, economic growth averaged 4 percent a year, 22 million new jobs were created, almost all in the private sector, and unemployment fell to less than 4 percent, its lowest level in more than thirty years. The stock market almost tripled, with the Dow rising from 3,651 at the passage of the Clinton budget bill to 10,788 at the end of his term, almost 27 percent a year.[69] Homeownership reached its highest rate on record, inflation remained at levels not seen since the Kennedy administration, and real wages grew even for those at the bottom of the income ladder, thereby slashing the poverty rate from above 15 percent to less than 12 percent. And on top of all this, the federal budget generated increasingly large surpluses for the last four years of the Clinton administration, with some even forecasting that the entire public debt would be paid off by 2009. Virtually every one of these indexes compared favorably with what the Republicans had achieved during the Reagan era's "Morning in America."[70]

And yet the Clinton boom proved highly ambiguous and is today remembered, if at all, with a large dose of cynicism and disdain, perhaps among liberals even more than among those on the right. There were two phases to the history of the Clinton economy. In the first, which lasted until early 1994, the idea that an austere budget would generate confidence among investors seemed well confirmed. Interest rates did drop in the bond market, just as Rubin, Bentsen, and Greenspan had forecast. These declines coincided with the moments at which the Clinton program advanced: the introduction of the president's plan in February, House approval of the plan in May, and final approval in August.[71] In 1993 real GDP in the interest-sensitive sectors of the economy, such as housing and consumer durables, rose by 11 percent, while the non-interest-sensitive sectors showed virtually no growth. Unemployment dropped from 7.3 percent of the workforce at the start of Clinton's presidency to 6.4 percent in December 1993.[72]

And so it went until the fourth quarter of 1993, when growth in the gross domestic product came in at a surprisingly strong 6 percent. A reduction of the budget deficit might have been on track, with inflation remaining tepid, but from the Federal Reserve's point of view this robust level of GDP growth was a warning sign that it was time to raise rates to head off the inflationary surge that it surely heralded. The interest rate decline had propelled long bond prices into "bubble" territory, said Chairman Greenspan. Convincing himself as well as his colleagues, he told a meeting of his Federal Open Market Committee (FOMC), "We finally have to start moving toward a somewhat less accommodative path. . . . We haven't raised interest rates in five years, which is in itself almost unimaginable, especially in the context of strong economic conditions and historically low inflation."[73] Thus, on January 21, 1994, Greenspan met with Clinton in the Oval Office to warn the president about the Fed's impending quarter-point rate hike, scheduled for February 4. Announcement of the rate hike—for the first time in a press release—crashed the bond market. Hedge funds, a new phenomenon in the early 1990s, were highly leveraged in the bond market, so their scramble to sell exacerbated the decline in bond prices and concomitant rise in interest rates. Insurance companies, always heavy bond investors, lost as much money on their holdings as they had paid out for damages following Hurricane Andrew, which had devastated parts of South Florida fifteen months before. Wall Street dubbed the collapse in bond prices "Hurricane Greenspan."[74]

For the Clinton administration the rate rise seemed disastrous. With inflationary expectations so low, it had expected long bond rates to continue their fall, ensuring economic growth.[75] But now the return on a five-year bond was higher than it had been at the time of Clinton's election, and the ten-year rate stood at almost the same level. The president "was totally enraged," remembered Alan Blinder. "We said, 'It isn't so bad, it isn't going to kill the recovery.' . . . Interest rates were abnormally low."[76] Every time Greenspan raised interest rates in 1994, Clinton fumed privately, said nothing publicly, and asked for more clarification. Robert Rubin explained that long-term rates were only loosely tied to inflationary expectations, a rather more nuanced view than he had advanced during the budget debate a year earlier. Because the Fed's ability to figure out what made the market tick had been subverted by the speculative financialization of so much economic activity, Greenspan told the FOMC, "we pricked that bubble [in the bond market]."[77] But this was also an admission that the declining rates of 1993 were as much a product of hedge fund speculation as a salutary function of Clinton's deficit reduction politics.

Clinton tried and failed to cut Alan Greenspan down to size and tilt the Fed toward policies that would encourage higher employment, even if inflation notched up a point or two. In the summer of 1994, the president appointed Alan Blinder as vice chair of the Fed and Janet Yellen as a board member, hopeful that these two liberal Keynesians might moderate the series of interest rate hikes Greenspan had already begun to orchestrate. Yellen would eventually convince Greenspan and the rest of the board that a 2 percent inflation target, not zero, would best facilitate economic growth and low unemployment, while still ensuring a practical level of price stability.[78] But Blinder, whom Greenspan saw as a potential successor, was soon marginalized during FOMC discussions and then roundly criticized by the financial press when in August 1994 he gave a speech reminding the banking community of the Fed's actual legislative mandate: "The central bank does have a role in reducing unemployment." A *New York Times* headline soon announced, "A Split over Fed's Role; Clashes Seen after Vice Chairman Says Job Creating

FIGURE 8. Federal Reserve chair Alan Greenspan and the president in January 1997. (Clinton Presidential Library)

Should Also Be a Policy Goal." Greenspan did nothing to temper a controversy clearly advantageous to his standing.[79]

After Alan Blinder resigned in early 1996, Clinton wanted Felix Rohatyn to fill his slot, with Greenspan getting another term as chair. Rohatyn was also a Democrat, but of even more consequence, he was the kind of experienced investment banker–cum–public intellectual whose opinions and policy proposals were certain to be taken with far more seriousness in Congress, on Wall Street, and in the press than those of Alan Blinder, a mere academic. During the 1970s Rohatyn had been an advocate of an industrial policy investment bank, so he was likely to push not only for higher growth and lower unemployment but also for financial regulations that would discourage speculation and channel new investments. This was anathema to Greenspan and Rubin, both of whom encouraged, albeit in subtle fashion, the wall-to-wall Republican opposition that staunched the Rohatyn nomination. He pulled out in February 1996, after which Clinton persuaded OMB chair Alice

Rivlin, a more fiscally hawkish figure, to move over to the Fed. Greenspan, of course, easily won Senate confirmation for another term in June 1996, and four years later Clinton nominated him once again. Greenspan's longevity at the Fed was the personal and physical embodiment of a regulatory regime that privileged price stability above all else.[80]

As it turned out, both Clinton and Greenspan were riding a deflationary wave much to their liking. In the aftermath of the Volcker shock, interest rates were in a long decline, a product not of the budget, balanced or not, but of a larger set of forces, global and domestic. As Joseph Stiglitz, who would later serve as chair of Clinton's CEA, summarized the macroeconomic scene, interest rates "were falling even before Clinton took office. The forces taming inflation—weaker unions, increased international competition, increasing productivity—were already at play, and it was the lower inflation as well as the deficit reduction that lowered long-term interest rates."[81] But that interest rate decline held its own dangers, and not just for the rentiers who wanted higher returns on their static capital. As the industrial policy advocates of the 1980s and 1990s had argued, the market was a highly imperfect mechanism when it came to capital investment, especially with a species of "secular stagnation" limiting the genuine opportunities available to global capital in those last decades of the twentieth century. As an angry and frustrated Robert Reich wrote to the president when it had become clear that the Clinton left would lose the 1993 budget fight, American corporations would not use "resources freed by deficit cuts to invest in the future productivity of all Americans." Instead, Reich feared business would "speculate, pad executive salaries, hire consultants to bust unions, [and] build new factories abroad."[82]

Given its failure to find genuinely productive domestic investments—one consequence of working-class income stagnation—capital would flow toward a variety of speculative bubbles. This had begun with the hyper-expansion of US savings and loan institutions in the early 1980s and their mass bankruptcy at the end of that decade. In the 1990s the tripling of the stock market generated a "wealth effect" that sustained consumer purchasing power, but the tech-heavy "dot-com" bust of 2001 was also a near-inevitability. And of course, the frenzy of speculation in real estate and related financial instruments in the run-up to the crisis of 2008–2009 constituted yet another gigantic asset bubble that was sure to burst.

At the Fed, Greenspan and the other central bankers were well aware of these speculative possibilities. But the lesson the chairman took from Hurricane Greenspan was that the financial system was fragile and that a rapid deflation of an asset bubble could destabilize far more than the problematic asset in question. "If the financial system were to be ruptured, it would not be terribly difficult to bring the economy down very quickly," he told FOMC colleagues in March 1994.[83] Thus, the Fed did nothing to staunch ballooning values on the principal US stock exchanges. With inflation in check and interest rates still low, investors bid stock prices to seemingly unsustainable levels. In December 1996, at a time when the Dow had just crossed the 6,000 level, Alan Greenspan gave a speech in which he coined the phrase "irrational exuberance" to describe the mentality that stood behind the nation's soaring equity and commodity markets. But this rhetoric was not backed by any effort on the part of the Fed to discourage speculation by tightening credit or increasing margin requirements. When one of his colleagues asked Greenspan what he would do to curb the high-flying market, the Fed chair deadpanned, "I will make another speech." By mocking his own reluctance to manage an increasingly fragile asset bubble, wrote Sebastian Mallaby, Greenspan's otherwise sympathetic biographer, the Fed chair "had reduced the whole issue of stabilizing finance into something of a fatalistic in-joke."[84]

Indeed, Greenspan would conclude that it was impossible to know when the stock market, or any other asset, had entered speculative territory. As he told his FOMC colleagues two years later, "a bubble is perceivable only in retrospect." The Fed's job therefore was to clean up after a collapse, often by slashing interest rates to sustain stock market values. He would do so in the fall of 1998 after the implosion of a heavily leveraged hedge fund (Long-Term Capital Management) threatened the entire financial system, and then again in the wake of the dot-com collapse in 2001. Wall Street called this the "Greenspan put," a moniker describing his propensity to assure traders that the Fed stood ready to staunch any excessive market decline, thus acting as a form of insurance

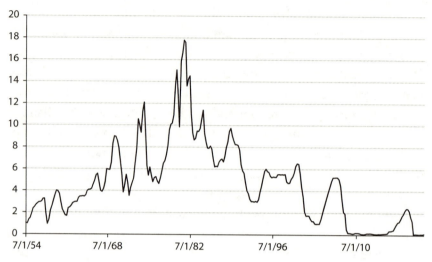

FIGURE 9. Federal Funds Rate, 1954–2021. (Federal Reserve Bank of St. Louis)

against losses, similar to a regular put option.[85] As one hedge fund manager put it, "If I get into big trouble, the Fed will come and save me."[86] Naturally, this assurance bred even more speculation.

Greenspan's New Economy

From 1996 to 2000 unemployment plunged to levels not seen since the late 1960s, but Alan Greenspan opted not to raise interest rates, a historic gambit that would make the Fed share responsibility for both the good times and the bust that was to follow. The conventional view among economists was that if the unemployment rate fell much below 6 percent, the inflation rate would begin to increase, and indeed would continue going up as long as the unemployment rate remained below this mark. Economists therefore sought a non-accelerating inflation rate of unemployment (NAIRU). The Fed had adhered to this doctrine closely over the prior decade. In the late 1980s, the Greenspan Fed raised interest rates sharply as unemployment fell, thereby inducing the recession that began in 1990, one of the factors that doomed George H. W. Bush's reelection prospects. And as we have seen, the Fed raised interest rates again in 1994 even before unemployment fell below 6 percent, engendering

Hurricane Greenspan. As unemployment fell, the Fed boosted interest rates again and again during the remainder of that year.[87]

But then it stopped. In the second half of 1995 Greenspan broke with the NAIRU doctrine. Although unemployment was falling below 6 percent, there were few signs of inflationary pressure. Normally, Fed economists would have taken that decline in unemployment as an important indicator of the inflationary surge soon to appear, but Greenspan, now praised by Congress and the press as "the Maestro," successfully argued that the Fed should just stand pat. A crucial moment came at an FOMC meeting in September 1996 when pressure to tighten monetary policy was widespread among the regional Fed presidents. Even liberal Janet Yellen declared that the economy was "operating in an inflationary danger zone." But Greenspan stood against the tide and kept rates steady. The unemployment level fell below 5 percent for the first time in May 1997, to 4.5 percent in April 1998, and then to 4 percent in December 1999, the lowest level in thirty years. But inflation failed to rise, and the Fed did not shift out of its new interest rate regime.[88]

There were two reasons that such low unemployment levels did not trigger a new round of wage-push inflation. By the mid-1990s Greenspan had taken a leaf from the industrial policy notebook to argue that a "new economy" characterized by high-tech productivity and global trade had made it possible to keep inflation in check even as wages rose in a full-employment economy. A new wave of productivity-enhancing computers and other machines finally enabled employers to raise wages while keeping prices in check. For years managers and economists had groused that the digital revolution had failed to fulfill its promise. As Robert Solow, a leading theorist of economic growth and its measurement, quipped in 1987, "We can see the computer age everywhere but in the productivity statistics."[89]

But the computer revolution finally kicked in during the 1990s, especially in the vast retail, health care, and food service sectors of the economy.[90] So Greenspan may well have been on to something. Although computerization hardly defined the entire economy, the linkage of the standalone terminal to the outside world through the internet and the World Wide Web did finally generate a large increase in the productivity of pink- and white-collar workers.[91] At Wal-Mart, for example, bar codes and checkout scanners had come into play during the 1970s, but these digital innovations had little impact on productivity until that technology was linked to a larger set of organizational transformations: supply chains that stretched from Bentonville to the Far East; a vast complex of hyper-efficient distribution centers in the United States; and a giant data warehouse in Bentonville that enabled the fast-growing retail giant to track every sale at every checkout counter among its thousands of retail outlets. These changes enabled top management to save money on inventory, squeeze its vendors, and deploy its workforce in precisely the most efficient and flexible manner. Combined with a multibillion-dollar increase in cheap imports from Central America and the Far East, they also enabled Wal-Mart—along with the other retailers that aped its business model—to brag early in the twenty-first century that the company saved the average family more than $2,500 a year compared to what a similar basket of goods would have cost twenty years before.[92]

Of course, Wal-Mart was known for its low-wage, low-benefit jobs. Indeed, real wages at the company had dropped since the 1970s, tracking the decline in the purchasing power of the minimum wage and the failure of the grocery unions to organize the Arkansas upstart. Writ large, the Wal-Mart story was that of American labor in general. Even with full employment, inflationary pressures were modest because US unions were weak and getting weaker. In the 1970s about 250 strikes involving 1,000 workers took place each year; by the 1990s that number had crumbled to less than 40, and many of these strikes were anything but triumphal confrontations.[93] Thus, in 1994 and 1995, during the very season when Alan Greenspan and his colleagues were concluding that the Fed could forgo an inflation-fighting interest rate increase, several thousand workers at Caterpillar, Firestone, and Staley in the central Illinois "war zone" were in the midst of long, bitter, and ultimately losing battles with a set of manufacturing firms determined to ratchet down their labor costs even if that effort created something close to a class war in heartland America.[94]

Greenspan and most other Fed officials saw union weakness and corporate downsizing as an altogether healthy development. Testifying before Congress in the summer of 1997, Greenspan saw the "exceptional" performance of the economy in the 1990s as a product not only of new technologies but of a "heightened sense of job insecurity and, as a consequence, subdued wage gains." Polls indicated that the proportion of workers in large establishments who were fearful of being laid off had risen from 25 percent in 1991 to 46 percent by 1996. A "lingering sense of fear or uncertainty seems still to pervade the job market," he told the Senate Banking Committee on July 22, 1997.[95]

But just a few weeks later the remarkably successful strike of 150,000 Teamsters against the United Parcel Service seemed for a moment to presage a transformation of worker consciousness and union power. The Teamsters not only won a healthy wage increase but a commitment from UPS that the company would create 10,000 full-time, full-benefit jobs, a signal victory for a union whose strike slogan had been "Part-time America Can't Work." Other unions and employers seemed likely to emulate that upward shift in labor costs. That specter cast a pall over the August 19 FOMC meeting. Robert McTeer of the Dallas Fed thought that "the strike has done a good deal of damage," with the settlement having undermined the "wage flexibility that we started to get in labor markets with the air traffic controllers' strike back in the early 1980s." Greenspan agreed, speculating that the real significance of the UPS strike was indeed a reversal of the "fundamental change" that President Reagan set in motion when he broke the PATCO strike sixteen years before. "It is conceivable that we will look back at the UPS strike and say that it too signaled a significant change."[96]

None of that happened: the UPS strike signaled neither a revival of the union movement nor an end to insecurity and wage stagnation. Militant, successful strikes in the 1980s and 1990s were not unknown, but they had few ripple effects, economic or political. The Fed could rest easy as the unemployment level drifted lower and lower. The import of cheap cars, clothing, and household goods from East Asia helped keep consumer prices low. This was the decade in which Wal-Mart, Target, and Home Depot all doubled in size. Families took on debt, not only as a result of low unemployment but also as a function of the "wealth effect" engendered by the rising stock market. Because of the rapid spread

of defined contribution pension plans—most were 401(k) accounts—
nearly half of all American families had some stake in the stock market
in 1998, up from 31 percent less than a decade before. This was a species
of "asset-price Keynesianism." Incomes might be stagnant, but as long
as the stock market, housing prices, and other assets were on the rise,
the consumption binge of the late 1990s did not falter.[97]

Thus, when the Dow collapsed in 2001, the impact was felt, at least
psychologically, by an enormous number of ordinary people, depress-
ing consumer confidence to a degree not evident in either the recessions
or bear markets of an earlier time.[98] Moreover, when asset bubbles pop
the government has few tools at its disposal to forge a recovery. For decades the Fed had engineered periodic recessions by raising interest
rates so that consumers delayed purchases of big-ticket items like automobiles and houses. The resultant pent-up demand would then be unleashed when the Fed once again lowered borrowing costs. But that sort
of boost is impossible when the downturn is caused by the collapse of
an asset bubble. With interest rates already low, the Fed cannot lower
them much more to engender a recovery. This was true in the years after
2001, when even a massive tax cut and huge increase in military spending could do little to revive economic growth, and even more so in 2008
and 2009, when the collapse in housing and banking values created a
crisis of such magnitude that the US government had to nationalize,
recapitalize, or subsidize many of the Atlantic world's most important
financial and industrial corporations.[99]

So, from the point of view of those who identified with the campaign
slogan "The Economy, Stupid!," what can we say about the Clinton
boom? Bill Clinton recognized that by the time Congress passed his
budget in August 1993, he had abandoned any effort to preside over an
investment strategy that made even the slightest effort to manage American capitalism. "I have a jobs program and my jobs program is deficit
reduction," Clinton confessed to Robert Rubin at that time. Instead of
seeking public investments in job training or the development of new
technologies, his administration had staked its hopes for economic
growth on the construction of a financial regime that engendered a
plentiful supply of cheap capital deployed by private-sector banks and

corporations.[100] Clinton's strategy "worked," but his success left the composition and trajectory of investment as much in private hands as it had been under far more conservative presidents. This was a sophisticated wager that relied heavily on the mentality of a few thousand traders in New York, Tokyo, Frankfurt, and London. Indeed, by the time he published his memoirs in 2003, Rubin had hedged his bet that lower deficits had generated the interest rate reductions vital to the boom of the late 1990s. "In retrospect, the effect of the Clinton economic plan on business and consumer confidence may have been even more important than the effect on interest rates. In important ways, the deficit had become a symbol of the government's inability to manage its own affairs—and of our society's inability to cope with economic challenges more generally. . . . The view that fiscal discipline was being restored contributed to lower interest rates and increased confidence, and that led to more spending and investment."[101]

All this was utterly self-serving, countered Joseph Stiglitz, a member of the Council of Economic Advisers during the 1993 budget controversy. Writing his own account of the Clinton era during the same year Rubin published his memoir, Stiglitz might well have been debating with the former Wall Street executive:

> I have become convinced that the confidence argument is the last refuge of those who cannot find better arguments: when there is no direct evidence that deficits directly promote recovery or adversely affect growth, then they do so because of confidence. When there is no direct evidence that lower tax rates stimulate growth, then they do so because of confidence. . . . We can measure deficits and assess their impact on growth; we can measure tax rates. . . . But confidence is too elusive to measure accurately. Thus, the businessman-turned-politician can assert his firsthand knowledge of how business thinks—and not be challenged.[102]

But perhaps even more important, Clinton's agonizing effort in 1993 to construct an austere budget may well have been pointless, given the larger historical forces that were pushing interest rates and the cost of capital lower and lower. From their apex in 1981, when the Volcker shock was in full force, to the end of the second decade of the twenty-first century, both inflation and interest rates were on a downward trajectory, impervious to either low unemployment or the enormous budget deficits that tax-cutting Republican administrations have been wont to create. Why this forty-year shift toward a lower cost of capital? Here we enter a realm detached from the statecraft of any single administration or the monetary program of any central banker, US or foreign. None of the Clinton administration policymakers, whether deficit hawks or doves, truly grasped the new reality. Many thought that America's "new economy" in the 1990s was based on a late-arriving era of technological innovation, fiscal discipline, and global economic integration. All true to a degree, but these same developments also masked a new era of secular stagnation, itself a product of the increasing weakness of organized labor, the shift of capital from manufacturing to finance and real estate, and the global mobility of capital, which increasingly made the United States a safe place for states, corporations, and the wealthy to park their surplus cash.

8

NAFTA and Its Discontents

Alan Greenspan's confidence that in the 1990s American workers exerted little in the way of upward wage pressure proved central to the Fed's capacity to keep interest rates low and speculative prices high. The next three chapters explore why and how the Clinton administration contributed importantly to this working-class weakness and consequent political marginality in the 1990s. The negotiation of a highly contentious trade pact with Mexico, the failure of the administration to reform a retrogressive labor law, and the evisceration of a key New Deal entitlement undercut the capacity of the working class, unionized or not, to make wage and welfare demands upon employers and the state.

Of all the trade agreements entered into by the United States in the last half-century, the North American Free Trade Agreement of 1993 remains the most politically and ideologically toxic. It was not the most economically consequential. The US failure to manage trade with Japan hobbled some of America's most technologically advanced industries, and the opening to China a few years later would gut a wide swath of US manufacturing. But NAFTA looms larger because Mexico stands at the US doorstep; because this regional free trade pact seemed to offer a template for the American approach to globalization; and of course, because of the racially tinged response NAFTA engendered when it became clear that mass immigration from Mexico was a necessary consequence of the trade agreement. And finally, NAFTA was a political blunder of the first order on the part of Bill Clinton: it split the Democratic Party, alienated working-class voters, and opened the floodgates to the Republicans during the 1994 congressional elections.

Originally, NAFTA had been a Mexican initiative, a product of the adverse economic winds sweeping through Mexico in the 1980s. For most of the twentieth century Mexico, along with other Latin American nations, had sought to industrialize via a program of import substitution. Deploying tariff barriers, state ownership, and controls on foreign investment, Mexico encouraged homegrown industries and sustained the living standards of the urban working class. It accepted foreign capital, but only if doing so fulfilled state goals. In 1962 Mexico prohibited car imports, forcing companies that wanted to sell in Mexico to assemble them locally. Over time Mexico expanded "domestic content" requirements to include the production of engines and transmissions. The government also established the *maquiladora* program in 1965, intending to use the country's low-wage labor and proximity to the United States to build export platforms that created jobs and earned foreign exchange. Maquila plants could bring in equipment, raw materials, and semifinished items duty-free as long as they were used to fashion products for shipment back to the United States, which in turn levied duties only on the value added in Mexico. Such measures worked, producing 6 percent annual growth rates from 1940 to 1980.[1] Mexico was therefore one of the Third World miracle economies: a successful, though occasionally troubled, example of import substitution industrialization. Real wages in manufacturing had risen for decades, surpassing those of the Asian Tiger economies. Peasant farming was subsidized with low-interest credit. Mexican governments were nationalistic and populist, if not social democratic, and they were certainly never anticapitalistic.[2]

The good times ended in the 1980s. Import substitution protected manufacturing, but productivity remained low. Likewise, high oil prices from government wells and refineries allowed federal spending to soar, but when the collapse of petroleum prices began in 1982, the country faced a debt crisis: Mexico and other Latin American nations were unable to meet interest payments on external debt. While US banks funded Latin American development with petrodollars (funds deposited from a Middle East flush with funds generated by high-priced oil), the rise of supply chains as the new organizational template for international business allowed companies to locate the lucrative stages of production—

research and development plus branding and administration—at home while transferring labor-intensive assembly to areas of the world where wages constituted a small fraction of those paid in the United States.[3]

With export earnings now essential to Mexico and other Latin American countries, the import substitution of an earlier era had become an anachronism. In its place at the end of the 1980s came the so-called Washington Consensus forged by the International Monetary Fund (IMF) and other US-dominated financial institutions. That policy consensus, designed to put debt-burdened Third World countries on a path to export-led growth, called for drastic reductions of social spending, the privatization of much of the state sector, unhindered capital mobility, and increasing degrees of free trade. In Mexico under the administrations of Miguel de la Madrid (1982–1988) and Carlos Salinas de Gortari (1988–1994) the old state-led import substitution strategy would give way to an export-oriented model that could underwrite payment of the country's external debt.[4]

The Mexicans accommodated the painful US demands, dismantling economic controls, privatizing state-owned firms, and reducing obstacles to foreign investment. Salinas, a Harvard-trained economist, exchanged the ruling party's nationalist bravado for a discourse favoring integration into the global economy. Clinton called Salinas "one of the world's leading economic reformers" and backed this free-trade technocrat to head the new World Trade Organization.[5] But there was a brutal underside to such cosmopolitan modernization. As *The Economist* reported from London, "The ugly truth is that Mr. Salinas and his band of bright technocrats, adored though they are by the great and good on the international-conference circuit, wield power courtesy of PRI-fixers and worse in the countryside." Scores of political opponents had been murdered in the years since Salinas came to power in a 1988 election corruptly manipulated by the Party of Revolutionary Institutions (PRI).[6] Crucial to Salinas-led "modernization" was a fundamental modification of Mexican property law, especially the repeal of Article 27 of the Mexican constitution, which had created the *ejido* system, long a cornerstone of Mexican social stability and political legitimacy. Under this system parcels of land were given in trust by the government to small farmers.

The demise of a landholding peasantry would have an immense impact on employment and migration patterns in years to come.[7] Some thought Salinas's goal was to "Taiwanize" the Mexican economy. But the Mexican government failed to observe that the ascent of the Asian Tigers depended not on the weakening of the state and the radical turn toward a neoliberal laissez-faire, but exactly the opposite: a robust, intrusive governmental effort to guide and enhance entrepreneurial activity.[8]

NAFTA in American Politics—and History

All this culminated in a proposal for a North American free trade agreement inspired by, if not modeled upon, the regional trade pacts then being forged in Europe and East Asia. The administration of George H. W. Bush was hardly sympathetic to a North American version of the liberalized immigration policies that accompanied European integration in the immediate post–Cold War moment, nor to the social compact that accompanied the European Union's free trade regime. And no one in the United States contemplated paying anything close to the one trillion marks that West Germany would eventually pony up to make the formerly Communist East an integral part of the Federal Republic. The Bush administration wanted fast-track congressional authority to negotiate an agreement with Canada and Mexico that was limited to lowering tariffs and protecting investment, not an industrial policy that guided capital flows, raised labor standards, or protected the environment.[9] Bush therefore hurried the NAFTA negotiations to a conclusion in August 1992 because he wanted to have the deal done in time for the GOP national convention and the presidential campaign that would follow. The NAFTA treaty negotiated with Mexico and Canada generated a thick document, consisting of more than one thousand pages of text organized into twenty-two chapters, most covering specific industries and economic sectors like energy, agriculture, telecommunications, financial services, and intellectual property. While lower tariffs facilitating cross-border trade were important, even more so were the guarantees baked into the NAFTA cake protecting the investment capital and intellectual property of American firms to "ensure a predictable commercial environment for business planning and investment."[10] Toward this end, the treaty ensured that future Mexican governments could not expropriate the property of US corporations or put in place restrictions on repatriating profits. Compared to the relative silence on issues related to labor and the environment, the elaborate set of guarantees extending patents and copyright protections into the Mexican market confirmed NAFTA's neoliberal character. Indeed, because of the Mexican government's determination to do whatever it took to attract foreign investment, the United States was able to win guarantees privileging the rights of US corporations well beyond those possible in other trade bargains.[11] This facilitated the extension of firm-specific supply chains into the Mexican heartland and thereby set up a model that might well be imposed on other developing countries through comparable agreements. Wal-Mart, among other US retailers, would soon build or buy hundreds of stores throughout Mexico.[12]

The Democrats were profoundly divided about NAFTA. Until the 1930s Republicans had been the party of high tariffs, while the Democrats were the free traders, anchored by cotton growers in the South, silver interests in the West, and a growing mass of urban consumers who wanted cheap products from abroad. FDR's New Deal therefore began a process of trade liberalization that would culminate in round after round of lower tariffs in the postwar era. This initiative was predicated on both the enormous strength of the American economy compared to its war-shattered trading partners and the Cold War foreign policy imperative that saw an open US market, even when not reciprocated by equally free markets in Europe and Japan, as essential to the battle against Soviet influence and nationalistic isolation. But the free trade regime was also sealed by a New Deal–style commitment to labor protections at home: government support for strong unions, infrastructure spending of both the military and commercial variety, and a general expansion of the welfare state. As the Republican Party developed its own powerful internationalist wing—anchored in New York banking, export-oriented agribusiness, and high-productivity manufacturing—the free trade consensus became virtually wall to wall by the 1960s. When Congress passed President John Kennedy's Trade Expansion Act in 1962, Senate Democrats backed it by 56–1 and Republicans by 22–7.[13]

This consensus evaporated in the 1970s and 1980s. It was not merely foreign competition or, from the late 1980s on, the waning of Cold War tensions that generated disquiet among those liberals and laborites who had once backed free trade. Equally important, the evisceration of New Deal social protections made the free trade compact inaugurated by Franklin Roosevelt an increasingly bad deal for those who might find themselves adversely impacted by imports from abroad or the offshoring of US services and manufacturing. When Ruy Teixeira and Guy Moly-neux published *Economic Nationalism and the Future of American Politics* in 1992, they found that 67 percent of Americans favored "restricting for-eign imports to protect American industry and American jobs." A Gallup poll reached similar conclusions in March 1993, when 63 percent were opposed to NAFTA and just 31 percent were in favor.[14]

The change of heart was soon reflected in US politics, especially among Democrats. As we have seen, Richard Gephardt had been con-sidered a fairly conservative Democrat during the early 1980s. But his working-class St. Louis constituency was being battered by imports and unemployment, even in the high summer of Reaganite prosperity. In 1988 Gephardt ran for the Democratic nomination as the proponent of "fair trade" and won the Iowa caucus before Michael Dukakis put an end to his candidacy in New Hampshire. Gephardt, who was by now the Democratic leader of the House, soon crystalized a constituency on trade issues, one more social democratic and pro-labor than those aligned with racial nationalists like Pat Buchanan or billionaire populists like Ross Perot. Because he still harbored presidential ambitions in the early 1990s, Gephardt backed George H. W. Bush's fast-track legislation that would give Congress just an up-or-down vote on NAFTA, but once Gephardt decided to forgo a presidential bid in 1992, his shift to an in-creasingly skeptical view of most trade issues became manifest.[15]

Clinton Equivocates

As his campaign for the presidency gathered momentum, Bill Clinton became more of a NAFTA skeptic as well. In late 1991, just before an-nouncing his presidential candidacy, Clinton voiced support for Bush's

NAFTA deal. This put Clinton to the right not only of the US labor movement but of many liberal Democrats, such as New York governor Mario Cuomo and Iowa Senator Tom Harkin. If Clinton was to have any hope of winning support from organized labor, he would have to reassure the AFL-CIO that he understood the potential impact of a NAFTA on US jobs and also offer a program that could ameliorate the "giant sucking sound" that Ross Perot would assert represented the lure of low-wage Mexican manufacturing on Rust Belt jobs and factories. Such a posture was particularly important as the Michigan primary approached in March 1992. In Flint, Clinton delivered a defense of NAFTA to a hostile UAW audience, but to avoid a break with labor, as well as to fend off the challenge from California governor Jerry Brown, who had denounced the trade agreement, Clinton said he was unlikely to support something a Republican administration had negotiated.[16]

Derek Shearer and Richard Rothstein, both veterans of the labor movement and the New Left, played key roles in working out the Clinton compromise position on NAFTA: "qualified support, but only with side agreements on labor and the environment." The real issue, of course, would be the content and enforceability of those side agreements. These left-wing Clinton aides thought capital mobility and factory relocation inevitable. It had been proceeding apace for almost two decades, but to make expansion into Mexico tolerable, a gradual "harmonization" of wages and environmental standards between the United States and Mexico was necessary, "so that firms are not tempted to relocate with the expectation that they will thereby gain a permanently exploited workforce." Something of this sort was taking place in Europe, where the incorporation of Spain, Portugal, and Greece into the European Union was linked not just to an absence of tariff barriers but also to the development aid necessary to pull living standards and labor standards to within hailing distance of those in northern Europe.[17]

Some Clinton liberals, like Reich, Tyson, and Magaziner, thought globalized production inevitable. The keys to a defense of American living standards were domestic investment in a highly skilled workforce and a hyper-productive set of industries, sustained by the social and physical infrastructure necessary for their success. Money for that was not forthcoming in any Clinton budget, but even had the United States inaugurated a massive program of industrial education and reskilling, unmanaged trade between high- and low-wage economies was still problematic. Overall, Mexican industrial productivity was indeed far lower than in the United States, but key export-oriented firms in the developing world had the capacity to produce high-quality goods with low-wage and poorly educated workers. During the 1980s, multinational corporations in Mexico—with world-class auto engine, stamping, and electronics plants—demonstrated levels of productivity and quality equal to that achieved in the United States. But Mexican workers reaped few benefits. Because of a devaluation of the peso in the early 1980s, the real purchasing power of Mexican wages had actually declined some 30 percent. "Why should companies invest in a high-skill, high-wage strategy in the United States," asked the widely quoted labor relations specialist Harley Shaiken in 1993, "when a high-skill, low-wage strategy is available in Mexico?"[18]

It is not surprising then that during the 1992 campaign season Bill Clinton held genuinely ambiguous views on NAFTA. As his speechwriter David Kusnet put it later, "Essentially, he had a lot of the assumptions of the anti-NAFTA people and the conclusions of the pro-NAFTA people and you really couldn't find any human being on earth except for him who saw it that way."[19] Thus, when Clinton gave a closed-door speech to an AFL-CIO executive board meeting on the eve of the California primary in June 1992, his sophistication earned him a warm reception. Echoing themes advanced by Shearer and other labor-oriented Clintonites, the presidential candidate made clear that he understood that a free trade pact alone was inadequate when it came to Mexico. He looked to the process of European integration and German reunification as a better model. "Globalization hurts working people," he told the unionists, but he also referenced the Federal Republic, a state that was trying to "provide better for their people and their workers without taking it on the chin the way ours are."[20]

Clinton's NAFTA disquiet did not go unnoticed by President Bush, who effectively criticized Clinton for "waffling" on the issue. So Clinton and his campaign aides knew he had to go public even before Ross Perot surprised everyone by reactivating his presidential campaign in early October. (He had abruptly and inexplicably withdrawn in July of that year.) When Clinton's campaign staff assembled at a Rosslyn, Virginia, meeting on September 29, most thought a NAFTA endorsement was a political loser, and even Clinton remarked of a recent bus trip through rural Georgia with Al Gore, "They loved us, but they don't want NAFTA." Stanley Greenberg, Clinton's chief pollster, thought that if the candidate supported NAFTA, Ross Perot would surge, throwing Michigan's electoral votes to George Bush.[21] But Clinton was still for the agreement, and he was backed by trade skeptics like George Stephanopoulos and James Carville, who wanted their candidate to just endorse NAFTA to neutralize it as a campaign issue. In an October 4 speech in Raleigh, North Carolina, Clinton did so, but he insisted that the trade deal had to be part of a "larger economic strategy" designed to raise the incomes of American workers and protect their jobs and the environment in which they lived and worked.[22] Clinton pledged to negotiate tough "side agreements" on labor standards and the environment. Thus, when the NAFTA negotiations resumed in February 1993, key figures from the Labor Department, some close to Robert Reich, were delegated to participate in the arduous series of negotiations, which would last until the late summer of 1993.[23]

Labor Standards Were Not a "Side" Issue

There were two key issues that emerged again and again in more than a half-dozen multiday negotiating sessions held between February and August 1993. Everyone agreed that each NAFTA signatory had to live up to and enforce its own labor standards and then move toward some kind of distant harmonization across borders. But Mexican labor standards and workers' rights guarantees were noble fictions, enshrined in the law by the Party of Revolutionary Institutions early in the twentieth century but then ignored and eviscerated as the PRI became a self-perpetuating machine controlled by regional strongmen and their collaborationist union allies. So the first issue put on the table by American negotiators was the creation of some sort of transnational commission that could, upon complaint, investigate, fine, and then sanction a nation that violated its own labor standards. Such a trinational institution was established for environmental issues, but when it came to labor both Mexico and Canada objected. The latter argued that its court system had long demonstrated sufficient independence and strength to handle such grievances. On the other hand, Mexico's courts were notoriously corrupt and ineffective, but the Mexicans argued that a defense of the nation's sovereignty forestalled creation of any such supranational institution. One Mexican trade negotiator denounced a labor side agreement proposal as "infamous, imperialistic, and aggressive. They wanted secretariats with powers to intervene and inspect business, oversee labor justice, and approve the constitutionality of labor laws. We told them to fuck off."[24] This response was highly ironic because the main virtue of NAFTA when it came to the protection of US property, and especially intellectual property, lay in providing new avenues by which US corporations could penetrate the Mexican legal structure.

But a challenge to Mexican labor standards was another question entirely, and one much more threatening to the continued rule of the PRI. What divided US and Mexican negotiators was not just the Mexican government's failure to enforce minimum-wage and health and safety laws, but also the extent to which the structure of Mexican trade unionism would conform to a standard that offered workers there a genuine chance of forming and running authentic unions. As one Mexican labor specialist put it, leaders of the PRI unions were "going to resist any changes that threatened their monopoly of representation of the labor movement."[25] This position became manifest at the very moment when Congress was debating NAFTA that fall. After workers at a small Tijuana coat-hanger factory sought to form a union, the company, a subsidiary of Boston-based Carlisle Plastics, contacted the government-aligned union in the maquiladora zone, signed a sweetheart contract, and then fired three employees who had led the drive for an independent organization. "Unions are just a legal fiction in the border area," said Harley Shaiken. "Workers are not even aware that their company is unionized until they start trying to form their own union. If they try to fight, they are fired." Both Gephardt and Senate Commerce Committee chair Ernest Hollings of South Carolina, a state vulnerable to apparel and textile imports, denounced Mexico's manipulation of the union organizing process.[26]

This was the real choke point when it came to the negotiation of the labor side agreements. If genuine unions were to flourish, Mexican workers would use the new standards enshrined in any NAFTA agreement to boost wages, working conditions, and their own militant unions. To Mexican negotiators, all drawn from the technocratic elite, opposition to such a radical reform was the crucial issue, while for Mickey Kantor and other American negotiators it was just a special-interest obstacle to the speedy conclusion of the deal. Kantor was impatient to reach a successful agreement, capped by a Rose Garden signing ceremony, that would boost his prestige and that of a hard-pressed administration as well, so he caved on August 8, 1993, dropping any demand that Mexico reform its industrial relations system.[27] This was the last hurdle to the "groundbreaking agreement" Kantor announced five days later.[28] The side agreements, bragged President Clinton, "turned NAFTA into a pathbreaking trade agreement . . . strongly in the interest of the United States. . . . The agreement helps our workers, our environment, our businesses and our consumers . . . [and] will create thousands of high-paying American jobs."[29]

It did not. The United States extracted a nonbinding commitment by the government of Mexico to tie its minimum-wage structure to increases in productivity and growth in the Mexican economy. Fines for violation of labor rights were possible at the end of a long process of consultation, but the tribunal set up by NAFTA would have no power to compel a government to pay or penalize a particular employer. By way of contrast, NAFTA protected the intellectual property rights of North American investors with "hammer force," asserting its sovereignty in the most intrusive fashion. The agreement forced Mexico to revise its laws and its judicial structure to impose sharp, swift sanctions on violators, including mandatory injunctive relief, border seizures, and destruction of counterfeit goods.[30] Nothing of this sort impacted either labor standards or the right of Mexican workers to free association.

Within hours a coalition of labor union leaders, consumer advocates, and environmental groups denounced the accord. If NAFTA passed, said Representative David Bonior, son of a Michigan autoworker, "we would be rewarding repression."[31] The AFL-CIO ridiculed the labor and environmental side agreements, pointing out that the transnational commissions designed to enforce them had "no real enforcement mechanisms, no power to impose trade sanctions and no effective remedies." Gephardt too rejected the side agreements as "not supportable," and in a speech to the National Press Club on September 21, 1993, he announced that he would vote against the pact. Gephardt argued that genuinely fair trade was a contradiction in terms when applied to societies whose social structures and economic policies were incompatible with US society. Although rich, Japan was such a nation. Likewise, the wage differential across the Rio Grande in far poorer Mexico was eight-to-one. Side agreements on labor and the environment would hardly have been enough to generate a truly level playing field between the two countries, their manufacturers, or their workers, and in any event they were always poorly enforced.[32] To indicate the scale of what he wanted, Gephardt looked to the European Union, where a $30 billion transitional adjustment fund eased the integration of Greece, Spain, and Portugal into the EU. And two-thirds of that fund was spent on training and social programs to boost living standards and wages in the southern European nations. The Clinton administration proposed nothing of the sort, and certainly not the "concrete, guaranteed, assured stream of revenue so that the people who lose their jobs know that there's going to be not only a training but a placement program there behind them." Yet even such amelioration would not have solved the even larger "psychological" problem: the specter of job loss "when our workers go to bargain for wages." That possibility, Gephardt argued, could "well be used as downward pressure on wage agreements, holding down our standard of living. And they faced that argument not only from Mexico, but from China and other places around the world."[33]

Splitting the Democrats

Labor Secretary Robert Reich campaigned long and hard for NAFTA that fall, arguing that jobs would be preserved and expanded in the United States. But his efforts were all fake, the reluctant duty of a loyal soldier. Three years later, in his diary-style memoir of his time in the Clinton administration, *Locked in the Cabinet*, Reich admitted his skepticism about the agreement. Labor was resentful and demoralized, job creation was a doubtful prospect, and there was "scant money for retraining."[34] Meanwhile, Clinton's own Council of Economic Advisers refused to endorse the president's oft-quoted claim that NAFTA would generate two hundred thousand new jobs each year. Said CEA member Alan Blinder, "Economists are free traders, to the man and woman basically. We were all big boosters of NAFTA," but the job benefits of NAFTA were "minimal" in the United States. The trade agreement would reduce prices on some consumer goods, but trade with a nation whose GNP was less than 5 percent that of the United States would generate few jobs. Thus, when the White House asked the CEA to estimate how many jobs would be created by NAFTA, the Council declined and pushed that task onto Mickey Kantor's Office of the US Trade Representative and the Commerce Department, both of which were "completely political agencies" from the CEA point of view. Blinder said that, on the NAFTA jobs issue, "we kept mum. This is what my mother always taught me. If you can't say anything nice about something, don't say it at all."[35]

Indeed, the highest-profile job creation estimate was a literal farce. When President Clinton presided over a signing ceremony for the newly revised NAFTA on September 14, 1993, his staff mistakenly put before him a speech that was still incomplete, especially when it came to an estimate of the number of jobs the agreement would create, since that number was both contested and controversial within the executive branch. So the speechwriter, Michael Waldman, inserted the word "million" as a placeholder, and that is the line Clinton read at the Rose Garden event: "I believe that NAFTA will create a million jobs in the first five years of its impact." Waldman and other White House aides were horrified, and Clinton sensed the problem as well. "His eyes bulged briefly when he realized something was amiss," Waldman later wrote. "He began to ad-lib." The White House scrambled to make amends, telling reporters that the million jobs figure was wrong "due to a staff error." Clinton admitted the mistake and soon told a news conference that he was only prepared to say that more jobs would be gained than lost. But the million jobs number stuck, taking on a life of its own that burdened Clinton in the weeks and years to come, especially as the whole NAFTA idea became increasingly controversial, and within a large slice of the Democratic Party absolutely toxic.[36]

Clinton knew he was in trouble getting NAFTA through Congress. He would have to rely on Republican votes because so many Rust Belt Democrats were following the lead of Gephardt and Bonior. Even pro-NAFTA White House aides, like Clinton's chief of staff Mack McLarty and William Galston, a deputy domestic policy adviser and a decided moderate representing the DLC point of view, hesitated to take the NAFTA plunge. Mickey Kantor recognized that there would be a huge price to pay. Hillary Clinton, Ira Magaziner, and Alan Blinder wanted to postpone NAFTA and tackle health care first. But Clinton felt committed to a course that had put his credibility on the line, and he wanted to shore up business support and perhaps push forward a bipartisan initiative after the hyperpartisan passage of his budget in early August 1993. Others in the administration, like Rubin and Kantor, saw Salinas as "our guy," a leader whose success would forestall the rise of a populist, protectionist left in Mexico.[37] So Clinton's ringing public adoption of NAFTA in September ended the political debate waged not only among his closest advisers but also within Clinton himself. Indeed, Clinton's decision-making style on the long road to NAFTA put on display his intellect and resolve, along with his capacity for calculation, his opportunism, and his deference to the corporate globalists.[38]

Because Majority Leader Gephardt and David Bonior, the House minority whip, were adamantly hostile to NAFTA and Speaker Tom Foley was lukewarm, Clinton had set up a White House war room, headed by William Daley, a banker and the youngest son of Chicago's legendary major. Side deals with representatives who had citrus, flat glass, wine, and other interests were crucial to securing their votes. "It's not a question of buying votes," explained Glenn English, a Democrat from Oklahoma. "This is the only way we could have supported the agreement." Said Assistant Treasury Secretary Roger Altman, "It was a cliffhanger. . . . There were deals being cut like crazy, deals on tomatoes, deals on Florida citrus. Everything imaginable. . . . There were probably twenty-five major separate deals negotiated to win passage."[39]

Polls showed that a majority of Americans still opposed the agreement and Clinton was short on votes in the House, Democratic votes especially. So, while not a Hail Mary, the administration put out the word that it wanted a NAFTA debate with Ross Perot, and the former third-party presidential candidate immediately snapped up the offer. Perot, who had been on a nine-month anti-NAFTA crusade that had taken him to ninety-one cities, was predicting that the treaty would cause nearly six million jobs to flee south.[40] This critique was not the one made by Gephardt, who rejected Perot's famous "giant sucking sound" metaphor. Like Clinton, Gephardt thought a lot of jobs were going to Mexico regardless of NAFTA's passage. The real problem was that if the pact was signed and the United States failed to get Mexico to raise wages and transform Mexican labor relations, then NAFTA would put "additional downward pressure on the wages of US workers and harm their standard of living."[41] Developments over the next two decades would demonstrate that Gephardt's forecast was far more accurate than Perot's. About a million jobs were lost to Mexico, but from the perspective of labor, organized or not, the greater dilemma proved to be the threat of capital mobility to both Mexico and Central America, and the blackmail that entailed for currently employed US workers.[42]

Thus, Al Gore and the rest of Clinton's NAFTA strategists were delighted that the vice president would confront the Dallas businessman and not the House majority leader or David Bonior, an even more formidable debater, on *The Larry King Show*. Gore was sometimes wooden and stiff, while Perot had a folksy ambience that led Republican consultant Ed Rollins to predict that the latter would "chew up Al Gore and spit him out. Gore will give intellectual answers, and Perot will hit the emotional buttons and spurt out sound bites."[43] But a Clinton briefing paper offered the better rationale for a Gore victory. "Many of the undecideds [referring to Democratic congresspeople] dislike Ross Perot almost as much as they crave labor support. By making Perot the voice of opposition, [people] should be reminded that NAFTA is opposed by demagoguery, more than anything else."[44] So Gore counterpoised expertise—and the

FIGURE 10. President Clinton signs the North American Free Trade Agreement with three former presidents in attendance. (Clinton Presidential Library)

support of every former president and fourteen Nobel Prize–winning economists—against Perot's sound-bite alarmism. Jobs had been lost, admitted Gore, but NAFTA would be a powerful spur to more employment. Perot, asserted Gore, exaggerated wildly when it came to any job losses, just as he had three years before when he mistakenly predicted that forty thousand US soldiers would die in the Persian Gulf War. Gore won the debate because he succeeded in making a testy Perot the face of NAFTA opposition. Public opinion now turned toward the administration.[45]

The House passed NAFTA by a vote of 234–200 on November 17, and the Senate followed three days later with 61 in favor and 38 against. In both chambers more Republicans voted for the trade agreement than Democrats, revealing an ominous fissure in liberal ranks. Edward Kennedy, hoping that NAFTA might be an updated version of his brother's Alliance for Progress, adopted the Clinton line: "All of the problems that working families face . . . will be even worse if NAFTA is defeated." The Clintonites thought they had secured a marvelous bipartisan victory, but many traditional Democrats, in both the Rust Belt and the textile South, spurned the trade compact. "This is a jobs program for Mexico, and my Lord, we need a jobs program for America," complained Michigan Senator Don Riegle.[46] Said David Bonior, who represented a working-class district full of Reagan Democrats, "There are a lot of people who are going to be put out of work here and those are the people we represent, that is the guts of who we are as a party. They are mad. . . . Perot is going after the Clinton base and people have their heads in the sand if they are not hearing from the grass roots of the Democratic Party on this."[47] The president "has seriously split the electoral base of the Democratic Party and has alienated swing voters," concluded Lawrence Mishel and Ruy A. Teixeira of the progressive Economic Policy Institute. "This is likely to interfere with his ability to win passage of future economic reforms, to keep control of the Congress in 1994, and, ultimately, to hold onto the White House in 1996."[48]

The 1994 Midterm Debacle

The NAFTA debacle, the unraveling of Clinton's health care initiative, and the near-constant scandalmongering by those seeking to take down the Clintons gave GOP conservatives the opportunity to take serious advantage of liberal disarray. Perot would run for president once again, and on the far right conservative pundit Pat Buchanan continued his denunciation of a Bush-Clinton "New World Order" that stood for globalization, multiculturalism, and a devaluation of American nationality. Most important, Newt Gingrich mobilized Republican opposition to both Clinton and four decades of Democratic control in the lower house by uniting most GOP candidates behind a "Contract with America" that repudiated all that was left of Clintonite liberalism. Whatever the cause, or combination of factors, the Republican takeover of the Congress profoundly altered the political terrain. Clinton would win an unexpectedly easy reelection two years later, but on the domestic policy front the GOP victory ended any possibility that the Democrats could fulfill an agenda that was anything other than defensive. In the 1994 midterms, fifty-four House seats shifted from the Democrats to the Republican column, giving the GOP a majority in that chamber for the first time in forty years. In the Senate, Republicans picked up eight seats, winning back the majority they had lost in 1986. In the South this was the first year that more Republicans (seventy-six) than Democrats (sixty-three) were elected to the House as well as the Senate (sixteen Republicans and ten Democrats).[49] Republicans from that region soon took over the top legislative posts: Georgia's Newt Gingrich became the House Speaker in 1995, and Mississippi's Trent Lott took over as Senate Majority Leader in early 1996, when Robert Dole stepped down to run for president.

Although Northerners like Bonior, representing union-heavy districts, were the most vocal critics of NAFTA, as well as being staunch supporters of health reform, the 1994 midterms had their most devastating political consequences in the white South. Until the early 1990s most Southern states had sustained a post-1960s two-party system. Lyndon Johnson had been wrong when he famously told aide Bill Moyers that the Democrats lost the South after passing the 1964 Civil Rights Act. Instead, and for nearly a quarter-century, the Democrats retained the allegiance of most working-class Southern whites, who voted for them for many of the same economic reasons as those living north of the Mason-Dixon Line. Their votes enabled Bill Clinton and a generation of white Southern moderates to win statehouses and legislative seats in the 1970s and 1980s. But NAFTA hit the South even harder than the North. Combined with the expiration of the Multi Fibre Arrangement, a 1970s treaty whose textile and apparel protections began to phase out in 1994, the South lost a disproportionately large number of manufacturing jobs. Textiles and apparel accounted for less than 10 percent of US manufacturing employment in 1990, but those two industries accounted for nearly one-third of the employment loss over the next decade.[50]

No demographic in the United States shifted more decisively to the GOP in the 1994 midterm elections than Southern whites, with Democratic Party identification falling most dramatically among those of a lower socioeconomic status. The sweeping GOP victory had many causes, of course. Redistricting in the South had created a sizable set of minority-majority congressional districts, greatly boosting African-American representation, while creating even more House seats that were heavily white and conservative.[51] At the same time the deindustrialization that swept the South—the rural small-town South in particular—undermined the biracial coalitions that had sustained Democratic Party moderation for nearly a generation. In the North and West, the Democrats would recapture some of the seats lost in 1994, but in the South the NAFTA debacle opened the floodgates to a GOP dominance that enlisted working-class whites in a partisan project that subordinated their economic interests to a set of fiery culture war crusades.[52]

NAFTA as Template

NAFTA proved a template for the trade deals that Clinton and the next two presidential administrations would enact. In contrast to Japan, a high-wage, fully developed nation where both American labor and capital sought a market-penetrating foothold, the trade deal with Mexico privileged north-to-south capital mobility and the consequent offshoring of much labor-intensive manufacturing. NAFTA's US employment impact was not great: there was no "giant sucking sound." Even the liberal, pro-labor Economic Policy Institute found that in the two decades after NAFTA took effect just 40,000 jobs were lost each year, a very small fraction of the nation's larger job churn. Of course, those jobs were concentrated in key manufacturing sectors—textiles and consumer electronics, for example. Meanwhile, Mexican employment in the apparel industry nearly tripled, to 762,000, in just four years after NAFTA's passage, leading to the demise of production at Levi Strauss and other old apparel firms in the United States.[53] And perhaps more important, managerial threats to move production to Mexico, especially during union organizing drives, suppressed wages and kept organized labor on the defensive.[54]

In the decade after NAFTA went into effect in 1994, Mexican exports nearly quadrupled. But the manufactured products shipped north were just as much a movement of cheap labor as were those individuals who walked or rode or flew, with papers or without, over the

US-Mexico border. This was because a huge proportion of all Mexican manufacturing constituted the low-wage foundation of the supply chains whose control and profit centers remained in North America. Despite the Clinton administration argument that NAFTA was an antidote to emigration, its underlying objective—its inner rationality— was the export of cheap, poorly trained labor, in the form of either physical goods or human bodies. At the US-Mexico border, the wage differential remained steep and massive; it was almost certainly the largest on the globe between two contiguous nations with a sizable cross-border trade in goods and people. In the early 1990s that ratio stood at about five-to-one in terms of wages, and it was larger if one considered the actual labor costs incurred by an employer on each side of the border. Despite the promise made by leaders of both nations when NAFTA was being negotiated that an increase in Mexican wages would lead to a convergence of such labor costs, no such leveling of the playing field took place.[55] There were few backward or forward "linkages" with the rest of the Mexican domestic market. In the expanding maquiladora sector, for example, the majority of US exports to Mexico were parts and components designed for assembly into the TVs, refrigerators, and other consumer products that were then shipped north of the border. Hundreds of thousands of Mexicans were employed in this low-wage border world, but the export boom generated few synergies of the sort that had once made Cincinnati, Providence, and Rochester, not to mention Detroit and Silicon Valley, centers of industrial research and manufacturing innovation.[56]

NAFTA helped generate a wave of Mexican migrants, many of whom had once been small farmers. Although Mexico's employed labor force increased by almost 10 percent between 1998 and 2007, it decreased in agriculture by almost one-quarter. During the NAFTA negotiations Mexican president Salinas personally took the decision to put maize—corn, the iconic staple sustaining millions of peasant farms and families—on the negotiating table. The subsequent liberalization of the nation's agricultural sector put peasant farming in direct competition with the immensely more productive US and Canadian agribusiness enterprises. PRI chieftains abandoned peasant Mexico because of their greater political and economic commitment to the large-scale, export-oriented fruit and vegetable growers who could take advantage of low Mexican wages to compete with Texas and California truck farming enterprises.[57]

When Mexican peasants fled rural bankruptcy, some got jobs in domestic manufacturing, but that sector of the economy could not take up the slack. Consequently, Mexico became the largest contributor to international labor migration in the world: between 2000 and 2005 more than two million people left the country, mainly to go to the United States. The dollar remittances that migrants sent back to Mexico became the second-largest infusion of foreign currency into the economy after oil revenues.[58] Mexico offered its farmers little in the way of financial support during this brutal transition. By one estimate Mexican farmers got $722 in annual subsidies from their own government, while US farmers collected more than $20,000 a year. Meanwhile, US producers, with their large, capital-intensive farms, boosted their exports of rice, cattle, apples, and milk by more than 15 percent a year in the decade after NAFTA took effect.[59] Mexico thereby became dependent on the importation of basic-subsistence grains, which had once been produced by smallholder peasant farmers.[60] Mexican efforts to deploy these "liberated" workers to attract foreign direct investment proved a failure, especially after the US economic slowdown in 2001, when Mexico lost six hundred thousand jobs during the first six months of the year as dozens of maquiladoras fled to even cheaper havens, including China and Vietnam. The pattern repeated itself even more dramatically with the deeper US recession of 2008.[61] Not unexpectedly, many of these displaced farmers and workers sought a better life north of the border.

Bill Clinton's decision to push NAFTA through Congress in the fall of 1993 was the product of a set of illusions: a wishful search for a moment of bipartisan consensus after the divisive budget battle; the promise of balanced growth and job creation between two economies starkly different in their structure, incomes, and wages; and a belief that in such circumstances free trade would not exacerbate the variegated set of class antagonisms and racial resentments that were generated by mass immigration, capital mobility, and an employer offensive against American labor that was gaining power and legitimacy even in the fabulous 1990s. In the next chapter we will see that illusions of this sort were equally present when the Clinton administration sought to engender a high-performance revitalization of the American workplace, in both technically advanced manufacturing and old-line government service, as well as in the great corporations of the mid-twentieth century that were now confronting new competitive threats at home and abroad.

9

Grand Illusions

REINVENTING THE AMERICAN WORKPLACE

In the Sherlock Holmes story "Sliver Blaze," the failure of a family dog to bark in the night is the crucial bit of evidence necessary to identify a horse thief. Likewise, the failure of the American labor movement to "bark," especially in the first few years of the Clinton administration, proved enormously consequential when the president and his aides stole from labor advocates much of the imaginative vision of how American work life might be revitalized. The theft was not difficult because the labor movement had rarely been more somnolent and thus offered to both its adversaries and its erstwhile friends the opportunity, ideological as well as political, to construct a set of reforms that would soon prove either feckless or illusionary. Clintonite efforts to encourage a more responsible corporate ethos and a consensual and innovative work regime lost traction when confronted by management intransigence, political hostility, and the diffidence of those administration insiders who saw the American labor movement as largely a spent force.

The New Industrial Relations

Robert Reich, Bill Clinton's new Secretary of Labor, identified stagnant US wages and insecure employment not only with fast and loose financialization but with the stolid and dysfunctional character of American industrial relations. Like health reform advocate Ira Magaziner and trade specialist Jeffrey Garten, Reich wanted the US government to

incentivize long-range planning and technological innovation throughout American enterprise. When it came to the beleaguered manufacturing sector, that effort would require not merely nifty new products and
investment in new machinery but a radical reform of authority and responsibility on the shop floor. This would be a cultural transformation
as much as an organizational reconfiguration of where power and initiative resided in the world of work. The "adversarial" labor relations that
had for three generations characterized the American workplace—both
unionized and not—would give way to harmony, efficiency, and shared
prosperity. Reich and his generation of industrial reformers, many of
them old Friends of Bill, thought that in a world of global competition
and technological change it was in the self-interest of capital to reform
the managerial structures that had governed the workplace for at least
a century. This vision would prove an illusion.

The enthusiasm for a new industrial relation had three sources. One
arose out of a long-standing managerial effort to generate loyalty and
productivity from an early-twentieth-century workforce too often
prone to strikes, absenteeism, and soldiering on the job. From Elton
Mayo of the famous Hawthorne Experiments in the 1920s to the psy-
chologist Douglas McGregor's 1950s-era critique of authoritarian management, a "human relations" approach to management sought to make
work more interesting and workers more cooperative. Such ideas were
largely confined to corporate HR departments until the early 1970s,
when a sharp drop in industrial productivity, combined with the dawning
of a new era of working-class discontent, exemplified by the well-reported
GM strike in Lordstown, Ohio, put issues of worker alienation and
white-collar anxiety on the national agenda. An exhaustive study by the
Department of Health, Education, and Welfare announced that "the
young worker is in revolt, not against work but against the authoritarian
system developed by industrial engineers" in thrall to the outdated ideas
of Frederick Winslow Taylor.[1] Sixties values had filtered down to the
working class.

The specter of deindustrialization in the 1970s and after provided a
second impulse for the creation of a new work regime. It gave to the
New Leftish critique of factory labor a new urgency that some old-line

managers soon appropriated. The United States, so it was argued, had entered a "post-Fordist" world in which high technology, greater international competition, and a cultural differentiation of product markets undermined the mass production/mass consumption regime that both Henry Ford and Walter Reuther once thought the key to a general abundance. In their influential 1984 book *The Second Industrial Divide*, the left-leaning MIT political scientists Michael Piore and Charles Sabel argued that America's celebrated devotion to a production regime based on mass production of millions of uniform products had become an economic albatross whose rigidities had stifled industrial creativity and rendered work in both factory and office oppressive.[2]

To prosper, workers and corporations must therefore accommodate themselves to a new world of "flexible specialization," which required a more highly educated workforce, rapid shifts in production technology, smaller firms serving specialized markets, and the creative deployment of skilled labor. Germany, Austria, and northern Italy were held up as the exemplars of this kind of production system, while Japan's capacity to penetrate US markets seemed to demonstrate the virtues of both a lifetime employment guarantee and a "non-adversarial" work regime. Thus, for unionized workers in the United States, whose elaborate collective bargaining agreements had once defined the meaning of democracy on the assembly line, the new world of post-Fordist labor required a radical shift in ideology and institutions. As Robert Reich put it in his 1983 best-seller *The Next American Frontier*, "This new organization of work necessarily will be more collaborative, participatory and egalitarian than is high-volume, standardized production, for the simple reason that initiative, responsibility, and discretion must be so much more widely exercised within it."[3] Reich would later celebrate the emergence of a powerful new class of factory-based "symbolic analysts" whose centrality to the innovation and production process dissolved many of the gritty conflicts endemic to the old industrial order.[4]

Liberal academics like Piore, Sabel, and Reich popularized this new industrial relations model. But they were not the heavy hitters. Old-line manufacturing managers were far more important, followed, with varying degrees of enthusiasm, by leaders of a trade union movement increasingly shell-shocked by factory closings, the rise of Reaganite anti-unionism, and the general disdain into which many AFL-CIO affiliates had fallen. In the 1960s and 1970s huge investments in automation machinery had failed to materially increase productivity in midwestern factories and mills. Thus, in a third iteration of the new industrial relations, managers turned to a set of innovations that went by a variety of names: "quality of work life" (QWL), "team production," "multitasking," "employee involvement," and "labor-management participation" were all designed to end the adversarial labor relations said to retard US innovation and productivity. Naturally, Japan seemed a model, both in terms of the enterprise unionism characteristic of the home islands and the non-union but high-productivity transplant factories that were being built in the American South. The new industrial relations sought to eliminate work rules, job classifications, cumbersome grievance procedures, and production bottlenecks. Higher productivity and cost cutting were the prime goals, with improved morale and shop-floor harmony the expected by-products.

In some instances, worker input did help create "high-performance" workplaces. But critics charged that the real agenda remained a form of old-fashioned "speedup" and layoffs, now cloaked in an industrial ideology that weakened union consciousness where it had long existed and staunched trade union organizing where it did not.[5] Top corporate executives did not disagree. Insecurity and unemployment proved a powerful spur to union willingness to accede to management schemes for work reorganization. As GM vice president Alfred Warren explained at a 1983 QWL conference, his company "always looked for plants that were in trouble because they were willing to do anything, so our greatest successes have always been with plants that were on the brink of failure."[6]

Bill Clinton was on board. Since his days as an Arkansas governor, he had struggled to grow high-wage, high-skill jobs in the nation's second-poorest state. It was hardly surprising that in 1992 he found the time to endorse a book that promised, "How a new approach to labor-management relations can help America compete in world markets." Written by the father-and-son team of Irving and Barry Bluestone, *Negotiating the Future: A Labor Perspective on American Business* seemed to complement much that Bill Clinton would seek to advance in his presidency. Barry Bluestone had been politicized in the 1960s, later wrote influential books on US industrial decline, and came out of the same industrial policy circles as Reich, Sabel, Magaziner, and Clinton. His father Irving had been a UAW vice president and confidant of Walter Reuther, the union's legendary president. Both were staunch and knowledgeable advocates of the new employee involvement schemes, which they saw as essential for unions to survive and companies to thrive. "Because of old-fashioned thinking and orthodox ways of doing things, America is failing to meet the global economic challenge," wrote the Bluestones. "The cornerstone in the rebuilding of America lies in reshaping the fundamental relationship between employees and management and creating a new work culture." Clinton's blurb appeared on the back cover: "The Bluestones offer a New Covenant for labor and management based on participation, cooperation, and teamwork," all necessary, Clinton added, "if America is to regain its competitive edge."[7]

The Dunlop Commission

To this end, Robert Reich persuaded the new president to authorize the Commission on the Future of Worker-Management Relations; charged with "recommending means for enhancing private-sector workplace productivity" through worker participation and labor-management cooperation, it would be sponsored by the Departments of Commerce and Labor. Commerce Secretary Ron Brown was "comfortable with the idea," as were key labor Democrats like Ted Kennedy and Howard Metzenbaum.[8] Creation of the commission solved a couple of immediate problems for both the labor movement and the administration. Reich saw the AFL-CIO's labor law reform agenda as a distraction, so the commission, whose report was not due until the summer of 1994, therefore offered a year's "breathing space" before an assuredly bruising battle would commence in Congress and on the airwaves when the administration sent labor's "striker replacement" bill to Capitol Hill. This was fine with AFL-CIO president Lane Kirkland because union leaders were divided over what kind of labor law reform they really wanted. Many from the old-line industrial unions, battered in the 1980s and early 1990s by lost strikes and membership decline, wanted legislation that would ban corporate use of permanent replacement workers during work stoppages. In contrast, service-sector trade unions seeking to expand membership in local government, hospitals, hotels, retail stores, and food service wanted a wholesale reform of the National Labor Relations Act so as to staunch employer opposition to their organizing efforts.[9]

The commission would be chaired by Harvard's John Dunlop. A founding father of the industrial relations field, Dunlop had been in and out of government service since the start of World War II. He was a legendary, consensus-building mediator who had served as secretary of Labor under President Gerald Ford. There Dunlop had distinguished himself by his way of leaving: he resigned in protest when conservative Republicans sabotaged his effort to cut a deal that would have limited inflationary wage pressures arising from the building trades in return for an incrementally more secure and powerful union presence in construction. Dunlop, whose name was soon attached to the commission, was therefore acceptable to both the AFL-CIO and the Chamber of Commerce. If anyone could prevent a debate over labor law reform from degenerating into a pitched ideological battle, Dunlop was the man. Otherwise, the commission tilted center-left: a set of pro-labor academics and three former cabinet officers (Ray Marshall and Bill Usery from Labor and Juanita Kreps from Commerce) would serve on it, alongside Douglas Fraser, the former president of the UAW, balancing Paul Allaire, CEO of unionized Xerox.[10]

Clinton, Reich, and Brown gave Dunlop and his associates a high-profile endorsement at a July labor-management conference in Chicago. There Reich had assembled a set of "showcase" companies, most from the unionized manufacturing sector, whose shop-floor practice exemplified the kind of cooperation and innovation that the Dunlop Commission hoped to codify.[11] Reich and Clinton moderated panels where workers and managers from Levi Strauss, Corning Glass, Xerox, AT&T, US West, and Magna Copper explained how they did it. Two General Motors ventures were also celebrated: Saturn in Kentucky and New

United Motors Manufacturing in Fremont, California, the latter a joint venture with Toyota designed to give GM practical experience adopting Japanese production techniques. Of the first venture, GM chairman Roger Smith announced, "In Saturn we have GM's answer—the American answer—to the Japanese challenge."[12] Most of these firms had struggled through the 1980s, when they sought help from their unionized workforce to improve efficiency, lower costs, and in many instances reduce overall employment. Bill Clinton proclaimed that these high-performance workplaces were establishing "the models, the rules, if you will, for our country's new economy."[13]

Because they needed a management buy-in on the Dunlop project, neither Robert Reich nor Ronald Brown used the kickoff conference to offer more than a tepid endorsement of the union idea. If the self-interest of workers and that of managers were now so intertwined, then trade unionism might no longer serve much of a purpose as the guardian of worker rights. "The jury is still out on whether the traditional union is necessary for the new workplace," Reich told *New York Times* reporter Louis Uchitelle. "Unions are OK where they are," said Commerce Secretary Ronald Brown. "And where they are not, it is not clear yet what sort of organization should represent workers."[14]

Corporate anti-unionism aside, the problem facing the architects of the new industrial relations was that even in those exemplary firms where greater productivity really was achieved by creating a participatory workplace, neither job security, high wages, nor even the survival of the company could be guaranteed. In a world of corporate mergers and spin-offs, outsourcing and planetary supply chains, the fate of all production and service enterprises had been thoroughly financialized and globalized. In the lead up to the conference Robert Reich had become enamored with L-S Electro-Galvanizing, a small Cleveland firm that made zinc-coated, rustproof sheet metal for the auto industry. Because many were former steelworkers who had lost their jobs in the great industry downsizing of the late 1970s and early 1980s, the union workers Reich met when he toured the factory were highly motivated and deeply invested in the success of the firm and its participatory work culture. Worker-management committees tasked with hiring, training, production quality, pay, and safety proved genuinely effective. Indeed, since the electroplating machinery deployed in the shop was readily available to any competitor, both workers and managers at L-S Electro-Galvanizing knew that their commitment to the firm constituted a signal competitive advantage. "I'd like to bottle L-S Electro-Galvanizing and sell it across America," wrote Reich in his 1997 memoir.[15]

The fate of L-S Electro-Galvanizing is therefore instructive. The firm was founded in 1986 as a joint venture between LTV, the big American conglomerate, and Japan's Sumitomo Metal Industries. LTV's bankruptcy in 2000—a product of overexpansion at home and cheap imports from abroad—ended the partnership, after which L-S Electro-Galvanizing was acquired by another joint venture, this one between Ohio-based AK Steel Corporation and Mittal Steel, a giant international with headquarters in India. A soft car market made production at the Cleveland works superfluous: AK Steel had other mills, equally efficient, that could turn out zinc-coated sheet steel; moreover, a write-off of the company's investment in L-S Electro-Galvanizing generated substantial tax savings. The mill was therefore shuttered in March 2006, abolishing the jobs of more than a hundred workers.[16]

Equally brutal was the fate of the far larger workforce at Levi Strauss, the century-old, family-run company that in the early 1990s converted all of its unionized North American plants to what it called "alternative manufacturing," or team-based systems. Fifteen-member teams would produce an entire garment more quickly and cheaply than under the old piecework regime of people separately performing one specific task. "The barriers to change [in our businesses] are things we can control," CEO Robert Haas told the Workplace of the Future conference. "It's management attitudes, it's traditional labor-management relationships. It's extending trust and responsibility so that we can empower our people."[17] Levi Strauss, the nation's largest apparel manufacturer, with thirty factories employing eighteen thousand workers, struck a deal with the Amalgamated Clothing and Textile Workers Union that facilitated unionization at all of the company work sites in return for labor's help in revamping its new production system.[18] This was just the sort of arrangement that Reich, Clinton, and the labor partisans on the Dunlop

Commission hoped to replicate throughout the hard-pressed world of American manufacturing.

It didn't work. Like Farris Fashions back in Arkansas, Levi Strauss contracted with Wal-Mart to get its product into every one of the giant retailer's three thousand stores. But Wal-Mart demanded a production regime that could fill orders quickly and at an ever-declining price. The San Francisco–based firm had to beat the competition from Central America and the Far East. By the end of the 1990s it was clear that a cooperative labor-management culture—and a de facto cut in actual wages—had failed this test. Levi Strauss did not go bankrupt, and the brand continued to supply its famous jeans to Wal-Mart and scores of other outlets, but none were manufactured in either the United States or Canada. By 2003 every North American Levi Strauss factory had been closed, with employment and production now shifted largely to India, Vietnam, and China.[19]

L-S Electro-Galvanizing and Levi Strauss were not the only "showcase" companies that ran into trouble. US West, a telecommunications company that Clinton took to be generative of secure and interesting jobs, was the scene of a bitter strike in 1998.[20] Likewise at Saturn, GM's "new kind of car company" with a radically simplified, "non-adversarial" collective bargaining contract, class tensions did not evaporate. In 1999 all of the local's officers who had endorsed this approach were turned out of office by unionists who wanted Saturn to stop linking pay to productivity and instead adopt many of the protective work rules and grievance procedures embodied in the national UAW-GM contract.[21] Although Saturn cars had been popular in the mid-1990s, the subsidiary never turned much of a profit, so GM—officially bankrupt in 2009—closed the factory that same year, just a few months after it pulled out of its joint operating agreement with Toyota in California.[22] The effort to reform US workplace culture could neither end industrial conflict nor staunch the recurrent financial hurricanes that wreaked such havoc on the rest of the economy.

These debacles were a few years down the road when the Dunlop Commission got to work in the summer of 1993. Most in the union movement, as well as most members of the labor-friendly commission, understood that the Dunlop project might succeed if it could redefine the terms of the debate over labor law reform. Dunlop himself was an earthy realist, but he also thought the commission represented "a unique opportunity that doesn't come along very often." Over the course of 20 months, it would hold 21 public hearings, interview 411 witnesses, and take more than 5,000 pages of testimony. This put it in the same league as the great social and labor investigatory commissions of the Progressive and New Deal eras.[23]

The labor liberals who dominated the Dunlop Commission saw two big problems. First, the Wagner Act had become utterly dysfunctional, not because of new technologies or organizational innovations in how business conducted itself, but simply because over the previous five decades the NLRB and the courts had opened wide the legal door to a plethora of corporate stratagems that enabled companies to run "union-free." As Richard Bensinger of the AFL-CIO told the commission, any employer "who expends maximum (and even not so maximum) effort to defeat a union can win, anytime, anywhere—without breaking the law."[24] During organizing campaigns, corporations fired one out of twenty union supporters. Legally or illegally, it made no difference, because the penalties for corporate transgression of the labor law were so paltry. All this and much more the Dunlop Commission documented in a comprehensive fact-finding report issued in June 1994.[25]

But trade unions faced a second, even more decisive problem. This was the implacable hostility of employers to unions and the social legitimacy that had attached itself to their anti-union intransigence. This increasingly routine defiance of the labor law was rampant in big-box retail, fast food, hotels, hospitals and nursing homes, banking and insurance, and other fast-growing and technologically innovative sectors of the economy. Starbucks and Microsoft were just as anti-union as the most retrograde old-line manufacturer. Hillary Clinton's service on the board of Wal-Mart, a company that used a combination of evangelically flavored paternalism and bare-knuckle, barely legal firings to squash any semblance of trade unionism, would become controversial when she spread her own political wings in the next century. But in 1992 and 1993 the Clinton family's friendship with Sam Walton and his successors passed

with little notice or notoriety. That told every corporate HR professional and "union avoidance" lawyer that little public opprobrium was
likely to attach itself to pushing the anti-union envelope.[26] The discharge
of so many union supporters during almost every union organizing
campaign caused no stir outside of those circles inhabited by the most
knowledgeable labor advocates.

Could the Dunlop Commission do anything about this wall of employer hostility and public indifference? Most labor partisans and their
allies in Congress knew that if the commission promoted labor law reform as a freestanding package designed to strengthen trade unionism,
it stood no chance of success. Such a reform had failed in 1978 when the
Democrats had much larger majorities in both houses of Congress. Instead, a reform of the National Labor Relations Act making union organization once again possible had to be sold as an integral part of a larger
quid pro quo that offered employers something they badly needed. If
that was a clear pathway to the high-performance workplace so hopefully
advanced by Clintonite liberals, then a bargain could be struck.

The deal Dunlop wanted would allow companies to set up
management-sponsored participation schemes in return for business
concessions that would make organizing easier. But if such committees,
funded and controlled by management, put wages and working conditions on the table, then they were "company unions" and hence illegal
under a long-standing NLRA rule. Dunlop, Reich, and most liberals on
the commission favored a revision of the Wagner Act that would facilitate the widespread and legal deployment of such productivity circles
as a trade-off that might entice employers to also change the labor law
to make union organizing less treacherous.[27]

The problem was that employers did not think the existing labor law
was much of an obstacle to the kind of involvement schemes that Clinton
and Reich had advertised at the Chicago conference. Employer spokespeople testifying before the commission often emphasized that, to their
mind, the replacement of top-down Taylorism by a cooperative management model was already taking place. That perspective devalued the notion that any aspect of the existing labor law precluded the diffusion of
employer-initiated participation schemes. Many quality circles and team

arrangements did in fact violate the Wagner Act, but as with so many aspects of labor and employment law, corporate executives did not care. Lawbreaking was rife. The vast majority of American workplaces had not been unionized, so whatever innovations top managers sought to deploy elicited few complaints from the workforce.[28] Even more important, employers would have been entirely willing to sacrifice employee involvement had it actually been part of a deal to make union organizing easier. The unions wanted to forestall corporate firings, threats, and "captive audience" meetings during the run-up to an NLRB election, but these were now routine union avoidance tactics deployed by virtually all employers faced with an organizing threat. And should a union actually manage to win NLRB certification as the bargaining agent for a newly organized group of workers, nearly half of all employers simply stonewalled the negotiating process. So unions wanted something the experts called "first contract arbitration" to make sure the union got on its feet with a contract, even one imposed by an outside arbitrator.[29]

But with 90 percent of the private-sector workforce union-free, reforms to facilitate organizing were simply too high a price for employers to pay in return for the encouragement of greater employee participation. Cyber-era Taylorism, based on scheduling algorithms, workplace surveillance, and a low-wage, high-turnover workforce, generated levels of productivity equal to or greater than those evoked by any system of worker participation with management. And in those few instances where participatory and cooperative labor relations led to high levels of productivity and innovation for more than one turn of the business cycle, researchers found that strong unions, secure employment, and high wages were essential.[30]

Employer spokespeople therefore dismissed any suggestion that they should agree to a deal reforming the NLRA's representation procedures. The status quo served the interests of the overwhelming majority of employers, union and non-union alike, and thus there was virtually no productivity carrot that the labor advocates on the commission—or in the Clinton administration—could offer that would counterbalance greater protection for trade union organizing and bargaining rights. The compact between Levi Strauss and Amalgamated Clothing Workers, highly touted at the 1993 Chicago conference, turned out to have been an industrial relations aberration. The larger impasse between unions and employer groups was held in rhetorical abeyance during the life of the commission: it was in the interests of both labor and management, as well as the Dunlop academics, to forestall any definitive admission of failure. But with the decisive GOP victory in the 1994 midterm elections, equivocations were cast aside. Jeff McGuiness, president of the anti-union Labor Policy Association, told the *Daily Labor Report* that "all deals are off, all swaps; whatever deals there might have been are now off." MIT professor Thomas Kochan, one of the most outspoken union advocates on the commission, could not disagree, then or a quarter-century later: "There was no deal, and there still is no deal."[31]

Reinventing Government

Many of the same ideas that led to the creation of the Dunlop Commission also animated the Clinton administration's "reinventing government" initiative, championed and directed by Vice President Al Gore. It is a now-forgotten project, but its ideological and administrative legacy had a lasting impact on employment norms and governmental functions, from the smallest city hall to the Pentagon and other giant federal agencies. Market incentives would guide government policy and services, privatization and outsourcing would be encouraged, and in the eyes of its proponents, citizens would become "customers." Officially entitled the National Performance Review (NPR), this multiyear effort to transform work in the federal bureaucracy was a product of two conjoined developments. First, it drew inspiration from the collaborative and participative managerialism championed by Reich, the Bluestones, and those corporate executives who saw a transformation of the work regime as a road to higher productivity and greater competitiveness. But equally important, the drive to transform the provision of government services was propelled by a chronic fiscal austerity that had overwhelmed state and local governments, thereby privileging the downsizing, outsourcing, and "flexibility" long championed by labor-intensive, anti-union employers. The reinventing government initiative was therefore the kind of "reform" that won an enthusiastic endorsement from both the DLC wing of the Clinton administration and the Gingrich Republicans who were soon ascendant in Congress and many a statehouse.[32]

"Should be read by every elected official in America," ran Bill Clinton's blurb on the cover of a book that in the spring of 1992 had spent eight weeks on the *New York Times* best-seller list.[33] The book was *Reinventing Government: How the Entrepreneurial Spirit Is Transforming Government*. Written by David Osborne, a public policy analyst and senior fellow at the DLC's Public Policy Institute, and Ted Gaebler, a Visalia, California, city manager, this guide to public administration, an otherwise deadly dull topic, had already persuaded candidate Bill Clinton that a campaign promise to slash one hundred thousand federal jobs during his first term would not be at odds with his administration's larger economic and social ambitions. The ostensible premise of *Reinventing Government* was not unlike that motivating those who sought a transformation of American industrial relations: The bureaucratic government established during the New Deal was broken. It was inefficient, expensive, and unable to carry out the basic functions that people demanded of it. The authors of *Reinventing Government* sounded like Robert Reich and Laura Tyson when they argued that the "emergence of a postindustrial, knowledge-based global economy has undermined old realities throughout the world, creating wonderful opportunities and frightening problems."[34] In this new world, frontline workers would be given much more latitude to do their jobs, bureaucratic hierarchies would be leveled, and cooperation and collaboration would replace hard, coercive enforcement of workplace regulations. Thus, almost every chapter in their book was packed with charmingly told anecdotes of plucky public-sector entrepreneurs reinventing their jobs in clever, cost-cutting ways.[35]

Yet for all their denunciation of a governmental bureaucracy that was slow to accommodate new technology, most of the tales of innovation arose from two economic disasters: the decay of America's cities beginning in the late 1960s, and the tax revolts–cum–economic austerity modeled on California's Proposition 13. This fiscal whip was the driving force behind the reinventing government idea. Above and beyond all the rhetoric celebrating participative management structures, Osborne and Gaebler wanted market mechanisms to be introduced into the governmental process as much as possible. They called it "competitive government" and labeled those using state services "customers." Such terminology legitimized outsourcing, or the threat of outsourcing, as a lever to drive down costs and break up what the authors called the governmental "monopoly."[36] The Osborne and Gaebler vision was therefore a governmental counterpart to the attenuated supply chains transforming the production and distribution of goods in the private sector. If Levi Strauss and Wal-Mart now sourced their apparel from overseas contractors, if General Motors and Ford were spinning off their automotive parts divisions—and forcing them to compete with the Japanese—then why not outsource a multitude of governmental services as well? Why not hand over to the private sector everything from garbage collection and schooling at the local level to the federal government's hiring of private security firms to protect overseas diplomats and Silicon Valley companies to construct departmental websites, aggregate electronic intelligence, and vet new employees?

In announcing the new initiative in March 1993, President Clinton declared, "Our goal is to make the entire federal government less expensive and more efficient and to change the culture of our national bureaucracy away from complacency and entitlement toward initiative and empowerment."[37] Six months later, when Gore delivered his first NPR report to the president, both men stood in front of a forklift bearing a ton of federal regulations they proposed to toss. Written with polish and flare by David Osborne, "From Red Tape to Results: Creating a Government That Works Better and Costs Less" made 384 recommendations and detailed 1,250 specific changes intended to save $108 billion in the next three years. The federal workforce would be reduced by 252,000 positions. Internal regulations would be cut in half.[38]

The Gore-Osborne "Reinventing Government" reports were always chock-full of horror stories, part scandal and part humor, recounting the

FIGURE 11. Clinton and Gore announce the elimination of forklifts full of government regulations in September 1993. (Clinton Presidential Library)

ridiculously elaborate regulations and guidelines developed by government agencies for the purchase of the most prosaic commodities. There were pages of instructions detailing how Army cooks should bake chocolate chip cookies; Bill Clinton took particular delight in recounting all the regs for government-cooked grits. The reinventing government initiative soon awarded a framed "Hammer" to vigilant employees who streamlined work or reduced costs in their agency, a backhanded tribute to the infamous—and actually fictional—$435 hammer whose Defense Department purchase came to light in 1985.[39] A legislative result was the Federal Acquisition Streamlining Act of 1994, which simplified the maze of government procurement regulations to make it easier for federal agencies to buy products and services from the private sector.

The push to "reinvent" government was not warmed-over Reaganism. That president's effort to diminish the nondefense side of the federal government had failed because of its ideological rigidity. "Government is not the solution to our problems. Government is the problem," announced Ronald Reagan at his 1981 inaugural. The GOP president even used the now-infamous phrase "drain the swamp" when he announced the formation of a commission, headed by industrialist J. Peter Grace, to root out waste and inefficiency in the federal government. While the Grace Commission emphasized the tax burden generated by unnecessary federal expenditures, it also deployed the kind of language Ayn Rand might have mobilized to smear civil servants: "Self-interested government workers will seek to maximize their pay [and] reduce their workloads."[40] Democrats and their union allies bristled at this kind of rhetoric. Likewise, Interior Secretary James Watt's effort to sell off public lands proved exceedingly unpopular because it seemed such an obvious favor for the oil, gas, and cattle interests that had been among Reagan's core supporters. Under the most conservative president since Calvin Coolidge, the federal payroll actually rose by 20 percent. And despite much rhetoric to the contrary, efforts to spin off government services to the private sector largely failed. In 1991 a *Newsweek* investigation concluded, "Privatization's greatest disappointment may have been Ronald Reagan."[41]

In contrast, Clinton's reinventing government initiative proved potent—and seductive to many liberals—because it rested upon a far more attractive ideological impulse. Osborne and Gaebler proclaimed, "We believe deeply in government." It was not a "necessary evil," they wrote, "How do we act collectively? Through government."[42] Therefore, the NPR reports put out under Al Gore's signature were not government-bashing documents: instead, they celebrated "effective, entrepreneurial governments" that "empower those who work on the front lines." Unionism was part of the equation if it was in a partnership that "transformed an adversarial labor-management relationship into a collaboration," thus generating a "high performing, customer-focused organization."[43] Unlike the Reaganites, who saw a decline in the public's trust in government as a vindication of their politics, the NPR sought just the opposite. If Democrats could make the administrative state cheaper and more efficient, then they could defang attacks on valued programs and ensure that a progressive agenda was ensconced in a new, streamlined administrative state.[44] Gore and Osborne were convinced that liberal efforts to advance virtually any program, no matter how modest, were fatally handicapped by the profound distrust in government that was baked into the DNA of the American people—from the Boston Tea Party forward—and that had risen dramatically in recent years. In the early 1960s, more than 75 percent of the public thought the federal government did the right thing most of the time; by 1993 less than 20 percent felt that to be true. As Al Gore put it in a 1994 video advertising the National Performance Review, "There is no way to reestablish confidence in government and confidence in ourselves as a free nation unless we can dramatically change the way the federal government works."[45]

Of course, such a posture fetishized a set of high-visibility, culturally inflected policies—welfare reform would be another—while devaluing the Clinton administration's ambitions when it came to health care reform, industrial policy, and other welfare state initiatives. Those programs required more government: new agencies staffed with experts willing and able to implement a set of far-reaching legislative advances. This was fine with at least one Clinton faction. While Osborne wrote up the propagandistic reports celebrating Gore's initiative, the real organizational work—and infighting—fell to Elaine Kamarck, soon dubbed "the high priestess of reinvention." Like Osborne, she was a DLC ideologue who thought the greatest accomplishment of the Clinton presidency was to "squeeze all the left-wing socialist junk out of the Democratic Party." Kamarck knew her way around government, so within six months she had a suite of offices and 70 staffers detailed from other government agencies. A year later 250 were working on the Gore project.[46]

Kamarck endorsed a participatory and flexible reorganization of work, but under her leadership and that of those who would follow the real cost savings came through layoffs and attrition. In some instances, a smaller workforce could indeed accomplish the job: for nearly two centuries the Government Printing Office had generated thousands of blue-collar jobs, most of them well paid and unionized. The advent of the World Wide Web, which blossomed during the Clinton years, meant that virtually every government report, map, and hearing transcript could now be transitioned to an electronic format, saving paper, ink, labor, and transport costs. Likewise, at the Internal Revenue Service the electronic filing of tax returns could save billions of dollars in labor and untold reams of paper—and also get refunds out to the public more quickly. "We were crazy fanatics about the concept of customers," remembered Kamarck's IRS project director.[47]

But the outsourcing of work was even more important. By the end of the Clinton administration, reported one student of public administration, "the blue-collar workforce in the federal government has . . . largely been contracted out."[48] There were plenty of janitors, cafeteria cooks and servers, construction workers, airport security personnel, and highway repairmen and women, but all were employed by contractors submitting the lowest bid. Many higher-paid workers, some of whom did work of a more technical or policy-implementing character, were employed by the "beltway bandits" whose offices proliferated throughout the Washington, DC, exurbs. Kamarck herself opposed most Clinton administration efforts to expand the welfare state: she thought the Clinton reform of the health care system premature, and she wanted to suspend the Davis-Bacon Act of 1931, which mandated union wage levels on federal construction contracts.[49] When "welfare reform" was enacted in 1996, she heartily endorsed it, cheering on the subsequent privatization of welfare services for millions of women and their children, with vast contracts going to IBM, Lockheed, and Ross Perot's EDS. To an extent, the public's faith in the federal government did improve during the 1990s, although the degree to which this was a product of the reinventing government initiative is impossible to know. In any event, Clinton always bragged in his stump speeches during his 1996 reelection campaign that he presided over the "smallest government since John. F. Kennedy."[50] This claim used the federal payroll count as a measuring rod, neatly excising the labor of all those working for outside contractors.

If all these Clinton administration efforts sound like part of a Republican agenda, GOP partisans did not disagree. Kamarck and other key NPR figures largely ignored the advice of academic specialists who thought she was hollowing out the governing apparatus; instead, her team found executives from the business world who sought to "reengineer the corporation" far more to their liking. "We really listened to them," she recalled in a 2006 oral history. Thus, when the Republicans won control of Congress in 1994, "the takeover was enormously helpful to us, and the reason was that we were fighting, essentially, an old Democratic mentality in the executive branch and in the Congress: Hey, what do you mean we have to cut people? What do you mean we have to balance the budget? What do you mean we have to be more efficient? . . . Against the Gingrich revolution, we looked like the voice of reason. . . . So Gingrich really helped us."[51] Indeed, from a conservative perspective, Bill Clinton's administration succeeded where those of Ronald Reagan and George H. W. Bush had failed. Writing in 1997, the Heritage Foundation's Ron Utt (who had been Reagan's "privatization czar") praised Clinton for pursuing "the boldest privatization agenda put forth by any American president to date."[52]

The "reinventing government" idea had even more success at the state and local levels. There the rhetoric of innovation and frontline creativity gave way to a more partisan and austerity-driven agenda that often took on an anti-union coloration. As early as 1993 Republican governors in Massachusetts and Michigan made rhetorical use of the Gore initiative to pummel Democratic legislators who resisted their plans to constrain budgets and cut payrolls. As Massachusetts Governor William Weld's director of strategic planning observed at the time, "Privatization is the quickest way to infuse all the other notions of reinventing government into your system."[53] *Governing* magazine did not dissent when a quarter-century later it summed up the lessons that local governments took from the reinventing government idea. "They should contract out more, embrace competition and insist on accountability; this aspect of Osborne's thinking became more pronounced as time went by."[54] Indeed, when Osborne was confronted with evidence that privatization eroded wages and created dead-end jobs far inferior to regular government employment, he was unrepentant: "We could subsidize higher wages than the marketplace provides, as we often do in the public sector, and tell ourselves we are all better off. But it would be a lie. The more of our dollars that go into taxes and fees to support public employees, the less we spend on other things, and the more demand we withdraw from the private economy. The end result: we are all poorer."[55]

By the last year of the administration, the Clinton-Gore initiative claimed a reduction in the federal payroll of 426,200. Those civil service slots really did disappear, especially among civilian employees at the Defense Department, where post–Cold War downsizing was dramatic. But there was "a bit of a shell game going on," concluded the public administration scholar Paul C. Light.[56] Taking into consideration the outsourced and grant-generated jobs, Light and other experts estimated that the true size of the government had actually increased by more than 300,000 during the Clinton years. In the early 1980s government procurement officers spent far more money on supplies and construction than services, but as a result of the National Program Review more money now went for outsourced services than for any other category. And many of these service contracts were ID/IQ (indefinite delivery/ indefinite quantity), which was just another way of hiding payroll. By 1999, Light estimated, the size of what he called the "shadow government" stood at 5.6 million, more than twice the number employed directly by the feds.[57] The "War on Terror" merely accelerated this trajectory, so that by 2009, 57 percent of all those deployed in Afghanistan were contracted employees of private firms. Although some of them made $100,000 or more a year, back at home poorly paid work for federal contractors was far more common: an estimated two million earned $12 an hour or less, or more than the number of low-wage workers at Wal-Mart and McDonald's combined.[58]

When President Clinton announced in his 1996 State of the Union address, "The era of big government is over," he was not seeking to merely triangulate toward GOP efforts to slash the budget and eliminate programs favored by the Democrats. He was also celebrating—in several paragraphs—the ideology and statecraft embodied within the "reinventing government" program. And in doing so he may have more profoundly subverted the liberalism he had episodically sought to advance. The Gore initiative's emphasis on market-based solutions and its hostility toward the federal bureaucracy helped delegitimize the New Deal–era governmental institutions that had sought to regulate and democratize the interaction between the market, the government, and the citizenry. As state capacity eroded, the ranks of those with institutional memory were thinned and federal functions once thought inherently governmental were put in private hands. There was little sense that government might aspire to become a site of democratic deliberation. Rather, it was simply a mechanism to deliver services.[59] Citizens became customers. And as with those who championed the high-performance workplace in the private sector, downsizing and outsourcing proved a spurious path toward that end in the public sector as well.

"He's on Our Side?": The Labor Movement and the President

If fantasies of work transformed had captured the imagination of some Clintonites, they still had to deal with the actually existing trade union movement. Regardless of the extent to which Bill Clinton sought to transform the electoral coalition that had constituted the backbone of his party, the American labor movement remained a core constituency whose agenda required a semblance of support. Labor leaders of all sorts were delighted that Bill Clinton was president, but that did not resolve their existential dilemma. Membership and power were draining away from almost all unions, and even those able to make some organizational advance were crippled by the increasingly hostile environment that now seemed a permanent feature of American political life. From Clinton's point of view, American trade unionism was a stolid interest group whose care and grooming might be necessary, but with a payoff of diminishing reward.

Still, unionists looked forward to working with the new administration. After twelve years of disdain and hostility from Republican presidents, the AFL-CIO had thrown itself into the election fray, once again playing a key role in keeping the industrial Midwest in Democratic hands. "Bill Clinton," declared the *AFL-CIO News* in September 1992, was "on our side."[60] With the exception of Indiana, voters in every state from Maine to Minnesota cast a plurality of their vote for Bill Clinton. Al Gore helped the Democratic presidential candidate win Tennessee and even Georgia, but the election was sealed in those places in the North and along the Pacific Coast where working-class Democrats returned to the fold. Fifty-five percent of all those in a union household voted for Clinton, more than twice the level supporting either George Bush or Ross Perot.[61]

Clinton did not disappoint. During the first weeks of his administration, he rescinded the obnoxious Bush-era executive order that had required the posting of signs in workplaces informing employees that they did not have to join a union; Clinton also rescinded an order that prohibited the use of project labor agreements, allowing the building trades to sign contracts, even before hiring took place, on federally financed construction jobs. Among other fruits, that order helped make virtually all the construction necessary for Atlanta to host the 1996 Olympics high-wage and union-built. Clinton also reversed the Reagan administration's lifetime ban that prevented former PATCO strikers from winning employment with the federal government. A 1994 hiring freeze at the Federal Aviation Administration (FAA) severely limited the actual impact of this executive order, but the symbolism was potent nevertheless. Most important, Clinton signed the Family and Medical Leave Act right after his inauguration, making it the first major piece of legislation Congress passed into law. It offered up to twelve weeks of unpaid—but job-protected—leave for family medical needs. While the law excluded small businesses and many part-time workers, it moved the United States a bit closer to the kind of social provision guaranteed in most other industrial democracies.[62]

For unionists the Clinton White House seemed a breath of fresh air. Robert Reich had never been a labor guy, but as an old Friend of Bill he enjoyed greater access to the Oval Office than labor secretaries in previous Democratic administrations. The NLRB got a strong pro-labor majority, and the White House staff was peppered with men and women who came out of the labor movement, including speechwriter David Kusnet and Joan Baggett, an assistant to the president for political affairs. "Nine to Five" founder Karen Nussbaum took over the Women's Bureau at the Department of Labor, and Steve Rosenthal played important roles on Clinton's 1992 election campaign and then worked with Reich at

Labor. AFL-CIO president Lane Kirkland had regular lunch meetings with presidential adviser George Stephanopoulos, and they were sometimes joined by Robert Rubin in 1993 and 1994. Of Clinton's first year, an AFL-CIO legislative aide remarked, "I've been to the White House about 40 times in the last nine months. Before I was there about twice in 12 years." When the AFL-CIO executive board held its annual meetings in Florida, Al Gore, often the featured speaker, offered reassurance where possible and soothed ruffled feathers when necessary.[63]

However, this early lovefest soon cooled. Battered and beaten throughout the Reagan era, most trade unionists had adopted an essentially defensive posture, seeking to preserve the industrial relations status quo and calling on the White House to expend political capital to this end. With virtually all unionists, Lane Kirkland had been hostile to NAFTA, threatening to withhold the AFL-CIO's financial and organizational support from any Democratic legislator who voted for the trade bill. As we have seen, White House lobbying and pork-barrel promises parried that gambit, but with elections looming within the year the greater danger was not active hostility from organized labor but disdain and apathy from a core constituency that Clinton would need to keep Congress in Democratic hands. And that demobilization reflected an even more difficult problem: the US union movement was no longer a force that Democrats could rely upon, whether to mobilize millions of voters on their behalf or to make corporate America think twice when choosing its legislative priorities or political alliances.

Robert Reich thought that "the AFL-CIO is dying a quiet death and has been doing so for years," a sentiment common among many in the Clinton administration. "It is intellectually brain dead," remarked Derek Shearer, who saw it as applying "no institutional political pressure on the Clinton Administration to pursue reformist politics." Lane Kirkland's stolid leadership, invisible to the public, merely confirmed the dour assessment. Kirkland had been a headquarters functionary for decades, the right-hand man of the gruff, cigar-smoking George Meany from the 1960s onward. In the Reaganite 1980s, after Kirkland slipped into the president's chair, he was far more excited by and engaged with the rise and travails of Poland's Solidarity movement than with anything going on at home. "Nothing about him suggests the leader of a *movement*," wrote Reich after a Bal Harbour meeting with the federation president in February 1993. "He looks and acts more like any other beefy, aging head of a special-interest lobbying group in Washington."[64]

The Clinton administration wanted a more vigorously led union movement, if only to bolster the troops in each election season. Perhaps Kirkland could be enticed out of the AFL-CIO's Sixteenth Street headquarters with an ambassadorship to an eastern European country where post-Communist regimes were still trying to find a stable democratic footing. Clinton himself broached the subject, but when Reich renewed the offer at an intimate, one-on-one Labor Department breakfast in April 1993, Kirkland understood well that accepting such an honorific post would implicitly acknowledge that the AFL-CIO was in desperate need of new blood. "Let me tell you something," Kirkland responded with a hardened gaze and tightened lips. "I love my job and I'm gonna die in it." As Reich recounted the incident, "The words came out slowly, deliberately, coolly. No explanation, no apologies," as if to say, "Fuck you, Mr. President, for even imagining that you could seduce me out of office with some cheap-ass-ambassadorship."[65]

The union movement's defensive posture was reflected in its number-one legislative priority: the Workplace Fairness Act, commonly known as "striker replacement." American employers had enjoyed the right to permanently replace striking workers since the Supreme Court's 1938 *Mackay Radio & Telegraph Co.* decision. But prior to the 1970s strikes involving permanent replacements were rare because most stoppages easily shut down the workplace; moreover, employers expected that, once the strike was over, they could maintain high levels of productivity only by getting along with a union that represented the vast bulk of the workforce. By the early 1980s, however, the rise of multifirm conglomerates and the persistence of high levels of unemployment made strikes at any one workplace less potent and strikebreakers an ever-present threat. This was a new world, ratified in spectacular fashion by President Ronald Reagan's destruction of PATCO and the firing of some eleven thousand air traffic controllers, who were replaced with military personnel, management staff, and a new levy of rapidly trained substitutes.

That hard line was soon replicated throughout industrial America, where "concession bargaining" sought to trim wages, pensions, and health insurance costs at some of the nation's most famous companies. Bitter strikes broke out—and were lost—at Phelps Dodge, Greyhound, International Paper, and Hormel Meatpacking. By 1992 employers hired replacements in 25 percent of all strikes. The issue proved divisive even in Bill Clinton's birthplace. In September 1991 a Champion Auto Parts factory in Hope, Arkansas, replaced its striking workers after they resisted company demands to gut their health coverage. That Governor Clinton's economic development people had approved a loan to the company just before the conflict seemed like yet another betrayal to the embattled Arkansas labor movement. "No issue is more important to the long-term future of organized labor," summarized a resolution at the 1993 AFL-CIO convention. "We must marshal all our resources to push for passage of the Workplace Fairness Act."[66]

The Caterpillar Strike

One of the most consequential strikes of this sort erupted in late 1991 at Caterpillar Inc., a leading manufacturer of heavy construction equipment headquartered in Illinois. In many ways CAT had been just the sort of company that the Clintonites hoped would prove a model for the revival of American manufacturing. CEO Donald Fites, an impatient, decisive executive with plenty of overseas experience, had written his master's thesis at MIT on how American firms could meet the Japanese challenge. After becoming Caterpillar president in 1985, he defined CAT's grand strategy as being "globally competitive from a US manufacturing base."[67] Indeed, from the early 1980s onward the company went head to head with Japan's Komatsu, the upstart manufacturer of heavy construction equipment. Caterpillar was one of the most aggressive corporations lobbying the Reagan administration to bring down the value of the dollar. The 1985 Plaza Accord did just that, enabling CAT to more effectively wage a price war with foreign rivals. Fites told reporters that his firm's export power was disproving the notion that "somehow manufacturing has been hollowed out and everybody is flipping hamburgers." By 1991 Caterpillar would be the worldwide leader in heavy equipment, with exports contributing 36 percent of all sales.[68]

Caterpillar was also heavily invested in the kind of employee involvement programs championed by the Bluestones and Reich. By the early 1980s the company had weathered eight strikes since the 1950s, including a particularly bitter 205-day walkout in 1982. Thereafter CAT and the UAW agreed to set up an "employee satisfaction process" with scores of "teams" that rooted out inefficiency and helped raise corporate productivity by nearly 30 percent within a decade. CAT used its reputation for labor-management cooperation as a marketing tool that, it claimed, guaranteed a quality product.[69] Caterpillar was also one of those high-benefit manufacturing firms that strongly supported the health insurance program that the Clintons would advocate. Since CAT already funded a generous health insurance benefit for its employees and their families, the employer mandate that lay at the heart of the Clinton scheme would cost the company nothing, and if the new law succeeded in holding down medical and insurance costs, so much the better.

That was the high road to manufacturing success and corporate profitability. But a low road beckoned as well, promising an even more immediate and tangible payoff. Fites saw a confrontation with the UAW as a matter of survival. He wanted an immediate downward shift in labor costs. "We're under tremendous competitive pressure," Fites said in May 1991. "We don't have time to take three years to change the culture of this company."[70] The recession, both at home and abroad, had cut sales and wiped out profits, even as health insurance costs continued to rise. And as the dollar strengthened again, CAT products would once more seem extra expensive. UAW bargaining demands, designed to recoup some of the damage inflicted by concession bargaining in the early 1980s, would erode the company's competitive stature and give the Japanese another chance at the US heavy equipment market. Explaining CAT's hard line just two months after President George Bush's disastrous Japan trip, Fites told reporters, "Hopefully, we will not get to the point where we have to get on our hands and knees to Japan, begging for pity."[71]

Fites precipitated a UAW strike in November 1991 when Caterpillar rejected the union's routine proposal that the big manufacturer agree to the "pattern" established by longtime rival John Deere and Company. Caterpillar negotiators told the UAW that the company now compared its labor cost structure to that of Komatsu, not John Deere's or that of any other US competitor. "I think the UAW leadership still thinks it is 1950," Fites told associates. "Times have changed, and they haven't changed with the times."[72] Fites wanted a wholesale revision of the collective bargaining contract: freedom to subcontract work to lower-wage, non-union companies, a two-tier pay scale at CAT that would put many new hires on track to a permanently lower standard of living; a weaker grievance procedure; and a general shrinkage of the union workforce.

With bargaining at an impasse, the union struck key plants, after which Caterpillar locked out the rest of the workforce of fourteen thousand, the largest among all Illinois manufacturers. The *Wall Street Journal* called the strike, which lasted five long hard months, "one of the most gut-wrenching, labor-management confrontations of recent decades."[73] The company put managers on the shop-floor production lines; hired security guards from Vance International, a late-twentieth-century heir to the Pinkertons of Homestead infamy; and used local papers to advertise for replacement workers ("scabs," in labor parlance), promising to pay triple what could be had at local fast-food restaurants. Calls from forty thousand people poured in from across the nation, and the company sent letters to all strikers telling them to return to work by April 6 or lose their jobs. By April 8, 1992, when candidate Bill Clinton visited the Peoria picket lines, workers were desperate and union resolve was shaky. To cheering picketers Clinton pledged that, if elected, he would sign a bill banning striker replacements. "People have the right to strike and they shouldn't lose their job because of it," Clinton said. That would have the "devastating effect" of giving other companies a "green light" to do the same.[74]

While in Peoria, Clinton spoke with Caterpillar executives as well, but he had no impact on their thinking. Fites's threat to hire permanent replacement workers proved to be a loaded gun. One thousand unionists crossed picket lines to return to work, prompting the UAW to abruptly end the 169-day-long strike. Not unexpectedly, tensions remained high in central Illinois, which by now had been declared a "war zone" by some unionists because of long and bitter nearby strikes at Britain's A. E. Staley Company, which operated a corn processing plant in Decatur, and Bridgestone/Firestone, the Japanese-controlled global tire company. Along with Caterpillar, these companies were determined to remain "globally competitive," and if that required hiring replacement workers to defeat a union and impose a new set of working conditions and wage standards, managers could and would adopt that strategy.[75]

This pressure drove a dagger through expectations that a participatory work culture at home could create the high-performance workplace enabling US companies to compete abroad. In the aftermath of the failed strike at CAT, union workers purposefully slowed production and let quality standards slip. "I used to give the engineers ideas," Lance Vaughan, a thirty-eight-year Caterpillar veteran told Louis Uchitelle of the *New York Times*. "We showed them how to eliminate some hose clips and save money. And I recommended larger bolts that made assembly easier and faster." But now, Uchitelle reported, Vaughan worked "to the rules" furnished by the company.[76] "Using the globally competitive argument is old around here," an East Peoria UAW leader remarked. "We swallowed the globally competitive bull hook, line and sinker. Then we get a new CEO. . . . They took every bit of our willingness to cooperate and laughed at us."[77]

At Caterpillar embittered labor relations lasted for years. Many workers wore T-shirts reading PERMANENTLY REPLACE FITES. After two years of guerrilla warfare and rising militancy inside the plants, the UAW again struck CAT, in June 1994. This strike lasted for more than eighteen months, but once again the company demonstrated that it could build product, turn a profit, and subvert union solidarity during a long and contentious work stoppage. This time Caterpillar hired hundreds of replacement workers.[78] By the time the UAW and CAT finally signed a contract in 1998 the company had blasted a hole in what remained of UAW pattern bargaining, won the right to outsource work, created a two-tier labor force, and held down wages. Meanwhile, during a long era of labor conflict, sales and profits nearly doubled and the stock price

FIGURE 12. The long Caterpillar strike generated a bitter class conflict in the American Midwest. (Jim West)

soared fourfold. "The union's concessions underscore the degree to which employers have the upper hand, despite jobless levels that are the lowest in a generation," wrote Arron Bernstein in *Business Week*.[79]

The Effort to Enact a "Striker Replacement" Law

Industrial unions like the UAW and the Steelworkers were desperate for some sort of legislative remedy that might thwart other companies deploying such draconian tactics. In 1991 a bill banning the wholesale replacement of a striking workforce passed the House. It quickly died in the Senate, even as President Bush threatened a veto. Although Clinton pledged to sign a "striker replacement" law, the new administration was far from enthusiastic; its budget bill, NAFTA, and a reform of health insurance were of far higher priority. And labor itself was divided. Reich and unions in the service trades, especially the rapidly growing Service

Employees International Union, would have preferred that the administration push for an increase in the minimum wage, but the high-wage unions in the building trades and manufacturing won the day. The Clinton administration formally delayed a push for a minimum-wage increase in June 1993, leaving the door ajar for legislative consideration of the striker replacement bill, its name now ideologically softened as the Cesar Chavez Workplace Fairness Bill, in commemoration of the farm union leader who died in April 1993.[80]

The existence of a law prohibiting striker replacements would have done little to give unions an advantage in the face of management militancy, but the stakes were nevertheless high. In congressional testimony offered during the summer of 1993, Labor Secretary Reich put forth the Clintonite case: "Without a viable right to strike, employers have less incentive to engage in serious bargaining with their unions, to hammer out mutually satisfactory solutions. And unions see no point in trying to work cooperatively with management." In the House Northern Democrats were nearly unanimously in support, and even among Southern Democrats the bill passed 52–32. Seventeen House Republicans voted for the bill as well—not a bad showing for a party increasingly militant in its anti-union posture.[81]

The real battle came in the Senate, where the votes of several Southern Democrats plus a few Republicans from the North would be crucial to reach the sixty votes needed for cloture. From the summer of 1993 on Clinton knew he did not have the votes, or rather, he was aware that only the most forceful expenditure of political capital would give the bill even an outside chance of success. But the decision to push for a tax increase in August 1993, then NAFTA in the fall, followed by a renewed application of executive branch energy to his health insurance scheme, all seemed to marginalize the chance that a striker replacement bill could be passed. Because two of the key Southern Democrats were from Arkansas—Dale Bumpers and David Pryor—many union leaders thought Clinton would put on the White House screws, but the president did little to win the votes of either of these two senators. Instead, Bumpers and Pryor were more than willing to accommodate the militant anti-unionism of the new business giants—Wal-Mart and Tyson Foods first among them—that had arisen in northwest Arkansas.

Thus, on inauguration day in 1993, when Don Tyson hosted a Washington breakfast for 1,200 Arkansans, the entire legislative delegation gladly attended. But eighteen months later, on the eve of the Senate closure vote, when a group of Arkansas trade unionists took a twenty-hour bus ride to Washington to participate in a press conference with the bill's sponsor, Ohio Senator Howard Metzenbaum, and to lobby their Arkansas senators, that meeting lasted all of twenty minutes. Recalled unionist Alan Hughes, the senators said that "if I vote for this I really get nothing in return. . . . There's gonna be this group [Arkansas business], they're going to come after me with everything they got and can y'all protect me?" They could not, nor could Bill Clinton, whose leverage in Arkansas politics had taken a sharp drop once he entered the White House.[82] Even the most committed labor partisans within the Clinton administration knew that sixty Senate votes for cloture were "unreachable."[83] The best that could be accomplished was for the administration to bloody itself a bit so as to use the striker replacement bill's defeat as an occasion to reknit the electorally vital alliance between the Clinton White House and the unions. As David Kusnet put it in a December 1993 memo to George Stephanopoulos, "This sense of insecurity—particularly among secondary leaders [local union presidents and others]—explains the priority the unions placed on NAFTA and are placing on striker replacement. This was and is not generals in Washington agitating the troops; it was and is the troops agitating the generals."[84]

In May 1994 Clinton had a revealing meeting with an angry cohort of top AFL-CIO unionists. With the bitter NAFTA battle now history, Robert Reich and the labor-oriented staffers at the White House had set up the East Room meeting as the moment for a reconciliation. Many in labor still thought that Clinton should be able to "produce" Democratic senatorial votes from his home state. "How you handle striker replacement is a symbol of your commitment to unions," an aide told the president. "They rightfully believe that no group is more loyal to you personally and to what you want to accomplish." But when Reich met

Clinton in the Oval Office, he found the president "red-faced." "Who the hell set this up? Why do I need to be yelled at about striker replacement? I can't ask senators to give me this one when I need them on health care, damn it."[85]

"They need to hear from you," said Reich as the two walked toward the West Wing. "What bugs them isn't that you didn't deliver striker replacement. They're angry because they think you didn't try. You might explain you got a majority in both the House and the Senate but couldn't get the last two votes you needed in the Senate to overcome a Republican filibuster." "How do I explain that those last two were the two Democratic senators from Arkansas?" said Clinton. It was a good question, thought Reich. Clinton proved an effusive host, emphasizing the agenda the White House shared with labor and the need for both to work together in the midterms. When pressed on striker replacement, Clinton affirmed that it was important to have a "law stopping companies from bringing in scabs when your members have to go on strike to get the companies to sit down and bargain with you."[86] Indeed, on the very eve of the Senate vote that would determine the fate of the bill, Clinton released a letter to Donald Fites asserting that "the threat or implementation of replacing striking workers has a poisonous effect on relationships between workers and employers." The UAW said it was "very grateful" for Clinton's last-minute effort, but the letter had no impact in either Peoria or the Senate.[87]

Thus, on July 13, 1994, a Senate effort to pass the striker replacement bill failed, with labor garnering only a 53–46 vote, far short of the filibuster-proof supermajority needed to end debate. The defeat revealed the same pattern that had stymied all legislation designed to strengthen trade unionism in virtually any fashion. A handful of Northern Republicans might well go along, but Southern Democratic senators were almost always hostile: in this case Dale Bumpers and David Pryor of Arkansas, Sam Nunn of Georgia, Ernest F. Hollings of South Carolina, Harlan Mathews of Tennessee, and David Boren of Oklahoma voted with forty Republicans against the striker replacement bill.[88]

The New York Times reported that the bill "never inspired the midnight phone calls and political arm twisting" that the White House had lavished on other difficult political issues, like NAFTA or the budget.[89] But this was not entirely fecklessness on the part of Bill Clinton, Robert Reich, or other administration officials. Trade unionists and liberals had also been disappointed with Presidents Lyndon Johnson and Jimmy Carter for their lackluster efforts on behalf of labor law reform. And fifteen years later Barack Obama would also abandon the labor-left when his administration did not prioritize congressional passage of the Employee Free Choice Act designed to aid union organizing. This multigeneration failure to strengthen trade unionism created a conundrum that has bedeviled liberal statecraft since the Roosevelt era. Although the heirs to the New Deal have been able to create coalitions that occasionally advanced the welfare state or offered a Keynesian spur to economic growth, a deep legislative freeze has blockaded virtually any sort of progressive labor law reform. That barrier has been continually constructed and reconstructed by the growing anti-union militancy of most employers, the rightward drift of the Republicans, and deep divisions within the Democratic Party, exemplified until recently by the outsized influence of the party's conservative Southern fraction. The incentive for any Democratic president to expend political capital on strengthening the labor movement is therefore minimal, but that abdication has come at enormous long-range cost. Union capacity to advance Democratic Party electoral fortunes declined in tandem with its institutional debilitation, even as labor's weakness opened the door, in 1994 and in later elections, for the demobilization or defection of millions of working-class votes from the party of Clinton and his Democratic Party successors.

Al Gore, Bill Clinton, and Labor's New Leaders

NAFTA's passage and the striker replacement failure had clearly sapped labor enthusiasm for Clinton and the Democrats. Some state labor federations in the North proved noticeably unenthusiastic in their support for pro-NAFTA Democrats, although the electoral carnage in 1994 slashed the ranks of both those in favor of the trade bill and those against it. In the midterm elections twenty-nine million fewer Americans voted than in 1992, and at least ten million of these missing votes were from union households. The percentage of union members voting Democratic dropped from 70 percent in 1990 to 61 percent in 1994.[90] "The real story of this election is that working people abandoned the Democrats because workers are hurting and we haven't done enough for them," Robert Reich told the president at an Oval Office meeting two weeks after the debacle. "Many of our traditional constituents simply didn't vote." Reich wanted Clinton to turn left, while most other counselors favored a rightward tilt.[91] But whatever the advice, the political devastation was indisputable. Every incumbent Republican gubernatorial, senatorial, and congressional candidate was reelected. The GOP picked up eight seats in the Senate and fifty-three in the House, gaining control of both chambers for the first time in forty years. When Al Gore undertook a damage control visit to the AFL-CIO executive board meeting in Bal Harbour in February 1995, a staff memo captured his daunting task: "Opposing NAFTA and passing striker replacement were at the top of labor's agenda. Hence, the administration's failure on both bills, connected in many union members' minds, is a big part of the problem the President has with this constituency. . . . The generally accepted view among rank-and-file union activists [is] that the Administration has been too pro-business and not pro-labor."[92] Commiserating with Clinton aide Harold Ickes at a post-election dinner, Tom Donahue, a Kirkland loyalist at the AFL-CIO, confessed, "Originally it was the labor leaders establishing Clinton's credibility with the membership. Now it is the leaders trying to retain their credibility with their membership."[93]

Al Gore would not seem to have been the most sympathetic figure to console the AFL-CIO. He was a deficit hawk in the Clinton administration's 1993 debate over the budget and a former DLC leader far closer to that grouping than the president; as head of the reinventing government initiative, he helped advance the influence of Elaine Kamarck, who favored a radical privatization of government employment. And yet Gore would be the unions' go-to guy in the White House, the high-ranking figure who, for example, leaned on the Pentagon to break off its contact with Avondale Shipyards, the intransigent New Orleans defense contractor that refused for half a decade to recognize the union that in an NLRB certification election had won an overwhelming majority of employee votes. Gore's labor-friendly focus reflected, in part, his determination to outflank, on the left, Richard Gephardt, the anti-NAFTA liberal who then seemed poised to be Gore's likely opponent in the 2000 Democratic primaries. But more importantly, Gore "had a political sense of the need to accommodate labor," judged a former AFL-CIO official. He had a better understanding of "the institutional relationship of labor to the Democratic Party than Clinton ever had."[94]

At Bal Harbour Gore won some cheers when he told those assembled that Clinton would sign an executive order penalizing federal contractors who replaced striking workers with scab labor. But the rest of his visit turned into a sideshow because top labor leaders were engaged in furious debate. Although the heirs of George Meany were not primarily responsible for the legislative and political debacle that had engulfed labor, their inside-the-beltway strategy seemed bankrupt, their fixation on foreign policy issues irrelevant, and their failure to take a more direct hand in union organizational work inexcusable. "With Bill Clinton's election in 1992," wrote SEIU president John Sweeney, a leading critic, "we had, for the first time in twelve years, a president who was not our sworn enemy. Yet labor continued to lose almost as many legislative battles in Washington as we won. . . . Our sense of alarm increased with the November 1994 elections."[95]

The year 1995 was therefore one of turmoil within the House of Labor. In an exceedingly rare upheaval, Sweeney and his "New Voice" slate ousted the AFL-CIO old guard and installed a set of leaders of a distinctly more progressive sort; they were far more open to the feminist, immigrant, and multicultural currents that were transforming the US working class. Sweeney was a Depression-born Irishman from the Bronx, but many on his team, like the new secretary-treasurer, Richard Trumka, who had won his spurs on many a United Mine Workers' picket line, and executive vice president, Linda Chavez-Thompson, from right-to-work Texas, had been animated by New Left currents in their youth. Indeed, the Sweeney leadership of the AFL-CIO finally breached the ideological and cultural Berlin Wall that had long divided organized labor from so many American progressives. Henceforth, the leadership of most US unions stood on the left side of American politics, not just in terms of economics but on issues of immigration, civil rights, sexuality, foreign policy, and the environment.

Clinton and many in his administration were far more comfortable with the new crowd. Two high-level staffers at the Labor Department, Karen Nussbaum of the Women's Bureau and the political strategist Steve Rosenthal, joined the Sweeney team, while David Kusnet, after leaving his White House speechwriting job in 1995, ghostwrote Sweeney's book-length manifesto, *America Needs a Raise*. Clinton may well have seen Trumka as a "kindred spirit," thought Kusnet. Both were striving small-town guys who left for an education but then returned to their roots to begin their real careers.[96] Because so many of the Sweeney group came out of unions in the service sector, an effort to organize low-wage retail, food service, home health care, and hospital workers rose to the top of their agenda, while the importance of global trade issues declined. Still, the new AFL-CIO desperately wanted Clinton reelected, and equally urgent to the new leaders was a return of the Democrats to majority status in Congress. In the 1996 campaign the degree of coordination between Rosenthal's AFL-CIO operation, the Clinton White House, and congressional Democrats was therefore continuous and energetic, far more than in previous presidential contests.[97]

Although Clinton famously "triangulated" in the months following the 1994 elections, he did not entirely abandon labor's agenda. He backed and signed a minimum-wage increase of 90 cents an hour—21 percent—that even the newly militant Gingrich Republicans had been unable to block in the House. In the Senate all the Southern Democrats were on board, plus several Northern Republicans, a tribute to the enormous popularity that virtually any increase in the minimum wage commanded. Meanwhile, the president vetoed a GOP-backed initiative called the Teamwork for Employees and Managers (TEAM) Act, a bit of leftover controversy from the Dunlop Commission. Designed by Republican hard-liners to give management the right to establish employee organizations to discuss workplace issues—including wages, hours, and working conditions—outside of union settings, this law contained none of the provisions that some unions had wanted in return, especially those that would facilitate efforts to organize new firms and members. In effect, the TEAM Act legitimized company-dominated "unions." Six hundred corporate executives signed a letter endorsing the law, but labor hated the whole concept, and Clinton vetoed the bill in July 1996, even as he continued to advocate for the kind of labor-management cooperation once envisioned by Reich and Dunlop.[98]

The president even tried to take some of the sting out of the striker replacement defeat by attempting an end run around Congress. After much lobbying by Reich, Clinton issued an executive order in March 1995 barring the federal government from doing substantial business with any firm that permanently replaced its workers during a strike. It was a "peace offering" to labor, editorialized the *Pittsburgh Post-Gazette*. The order may well have had enhanced potency, given the surge of outsourcing initiated by the reinventing government initiative.[99] Of course, the US Chamber of Commerce denounced the order as "a gross abuse of power," as did virtually all Republicans. "It is one of those gut, visceral issues for us," said a spokesperson for the National Association of Manufacturers. The Supreme Court agreed with the critics, letting stand a federal appeals court ruling that Clinton's order violated the National Labor Relations Act by creating a new industrial relations requirement that applied only to federal contractors. Throughout this long travail, the interests of organized labor had once again been stymied by two of the most antimajoritarian elements in the American political system: the Senate filibuster and the Supreme Court.[100]

Corporate Responsibility

Equally ineffectual was the Clinton administration's effort to promote "corporate responsibility." The idea had been around since the Progressive era, when "welfare capitalists" at National Cash Register, Kodak, Heinz Foods, Filene's Department Store, and elsewhere sought to retain the loyalty of their employees and stave off unionism by offering recreation programs, cheap lunches, sick leave, and even pensions. Unions and the New Deal had codified and upgraded many of these benefits, but the whole idea had more recently come under assault, inaugurated most famously by Milton Friedman in his *New York Times* opinion piece of 1970, "The Social Responsibility of Business Is to Increase Its Profits." Thereafter, the idea that corporations had a duty to anything other than the financial well-being of their stockholders faced a sustained challenge from those executives and Wall Street pundits who championed an enhancement of "shareholder value" as the supreme measure of corporate success.[101] In the crunch most Clintonites would not dissent, but they nevertheless paid homage to a broader conception of corporate success, if only to link a "high-road" social strategy to sustained profitability in the United States and competitiveness abroad.

Ironically, the quest for corporate social responsibility was enhanced by the very success enjoyed by the Clinton administration in putting the recession of the early 1990s behind it. Unemployment was dropping toward 5 percent, but profits and executive pay had risen far more rapidly than the real wages of the bottom two-thirds of the working population. Meanwhile, the "paper entrepreneurship" denounced by Reich and other industrial policy advocates had real consequences for working America. Even as the unemployment statistics trended lower in the 1990s the radical downsizings and layoffs ravaging some of the nation's most famous corporations captured newspaper headlines. "Chainsaw" Al Dunlop, the boastful CEO who slashed eleven thousand jobs at Scott Paper, proved a notable, well-remunerated corporate villain; likewise Robert Allen of AT&T, a company once known as Ma Bell, a steady and stolid employer of generations of lower-middle-class Americans. Telecom deregulation in the 1980s led to the breakup of AT&T, after which the phone company and its offshoots became Wall Street darlings. Mass layoffs led to savings that went straight to the bottom line. Thus, in early 1996, after AT&T announced that it was firing forty thousand employees, company stock soared 40 percent. Because of his stock options, Allen's compensation leaped upward as well. Both of these companies were featured in a widely noted *Newsweek* cover story of February 1996, "Corporate Killers." Call it "in-your-face capitalism," wrote Allan Sloan.

"You can practically smell the fear and anger in white-collar America, because no one in CEO-land seems to care."[102]

The issue was being politicized by Pat Buchanan, who unexpectedly beat Robert Dole in the 1996 New Hampshire GOP primary. Few thought Buchanan had a chance at the Republican nomination, but the cultural warrior of 1992 now found his denunciation of high-flying corporate executives winning much down-scale applause. In an uncanny prefiguration of the appeal that Donald Trump would ride into the White House, Buchanan linked hostility to NAFTA, disdain for immigrants, and contempt for Clintonesque cultural liberalism to a rhetorical assault on Robert Allen and other corporate Republicans. Even Dole began to make speeches calling on businesspeople to become more responsible.[103]

Robert Reich thought he saw an opening. He had always held that a corporate "high-road" strategy justified itself, even if a certain combination of incentives—public shaming for the highest-profile reprobates combined with economic incentives for the vast majority of firms— might nudge corporate behavior toward a more humane norm. The Labor Department had already begun to apply this strategy to the sweatshop production of clothing sold by some of the nation's best-known brands and retailers. And in the midst of the NAFTA debate Clinton had told corporate executives, "If you support free trade, it is your obligation to also support worker training. If you seek open markets for our products, you must support security for the workers who make those products."[104] Now Reich sought to use the ideological moment embodied in Clinton's "the era of big government is over" rhetoric as a lever by which to advance a "corporate responsibility" agenda. "If the government is to do less," Reich told a George Washington University audience in early February 1996, "then the private sector will have to do more." Indeed, if conservative Republicans were now demanding that film studios, TV networks, and record companies police themselves so as to forswear lewdness and violence, then the rest of corporate America might well enhance "family values" by limiting layoffs, raising pay, and providing health insurance and pensions for their workers. With unions and government now playing a lesser role, the restoration of America's "social compact"—this had long been one of Robert Reich's more illusionary historical constructs—would now depend on farsighted corporate executives.[105]

Of course, Reich had a fresh example readily at hand. When in December 1995 family-owned Malden Mills burned to the ground, owner Aaron Feuerstein pledged to keep his entire workforce on the payroll while the Massachusetts factory was rebuilt. It was a grand gesture, well celebrated in the media. But as with so many exemplary firms touted by Reich and Clinton, Malden Mills could not escape the merciless world of global commerce, where the textile industry was particularly vicious. Malden Mills went bankrupt in 2001, and its assets were sold to a new firm, Polartec, which slashed the workforce during the first decade of the twenty-first century. A few years later the new managers shuttered the ancient Massachusetts mill and moved most production to low-wage Tennessee.[106]

Reich was not oblivious to such economic turbulence. "Exhortation alone won't do the trick," he argued in a memo to President Clinton, "because top executives are under constant pressure from Wall Street."[107] He therefore worked with Senate Democrats, including Tom Daschle of South Dakota and Jeff Bingaman of New Mexico, to craft a bill that would encourage corporate "civic responsibility" by cutting the corporate tax rate from 18 to 11 percent for responsible companies that put 2 percent of their payroll toward employee training and 3 percent toward a portable pension plan impervious to downsizings and relocations. Such legislation had no chance in a Republican-dominated Congress, but Reich thought Clinton could use his bully pulpit to appeal to the nation's "anxious classes" and make the 1996 election a galvanizing effort to fulfill his "unfinished agenda."[108] Clinton was intrigued, and bits and pieces of the "corporate responsibility" idea appeared in his rhetoric. Profitability was essential to the maintenance and growth of jobs, conceded the president, but as he told a Michigan audience in early March, "We need people to really think about whether it's fair and the right thing to do when you see these downsizings."[109]

The corporate responsibility idea came under furious attack from Robert Rubin, Laura Tyson, and the rest of Clinton's core economic team. "At meeting after meeting," a White House aide told the *Washington*

Post, "discussions about corporate responsibility turn out to be Reich against everybody else." Tyson, who might have been expected to side with Reich, had become, as the new head of the NEC, much more of a Rubin-oriented team player. Despite Clinton's sometimes welcoming ear, Reich was therefore "off the reservation."[110] NEC deputy director Gene Sperling thought that "better times" were the only answer to lay-offs.[111] Rubin, who had moved up to Treasury, hated the phrase "corporate responsibility," which he found "inflammatory." Defending even the forty thousand AT&T layoffs, Rubin echoed Milton Friedman in a January memo to the president: "Notions that corporations should serve any constituencies or stakeholders easily lead to non-competitive companies, fewer jobs, and lower standards of living." Rubin advised Clinton to reject "class warfare language or criticism of economic success," in the president's upcoming State of the Union address.[112]

Tyson and the rest of the National Economic Council were equally adamant. Even the use of the word "principles" proved unacceptable because to many executives it conjured up the "Sullivan Principles," which had embarrassed many a firm that failed to hire enough minority workers at home or that engaged in business with apartheid South Africa abroad.[113] The president should base his reelection campaign on the economic success already achieved, not on any new anticorporate initiatives. "Listen," Tyson told a White House meeting the day after Pat Buchanan won the New Hampshire primary on February 25. "I don't think anyone should think that there is a reason for us to change our strategy one bit."[114] This view was in sync with that of Dick Morris, Clinton's influential—some would say Machiavellian—new strategist, whose advocacy of a small-bore, triangulated reelection strategy was then proving all too appealing to the president.

In the end it all came down to a farcical choice of phrases. Reich had always favored "corporate responsibility," if only because the president had used the word "responsibility" with so many other initiatives, including welfare, education, and family values. Rubin and Tyson thought the word implied that business had been irresponsible; they wanted to use the phrase "corporate citizenship" instead. When the White House held a Corporate Citizenship Conference in May 1996, it was clear who had won. Caterpillar's Don Fites was not invited, nor was Allen of AT&T, but the ideological downsizing of the conference was readily apparent. Instead of a discussion centering on mass layoffs, wage stagnation, and income inequality, which had inaugurated the corporate responsibility debate, the White House conference now emphasized a corporate voluntarism and paternalism that celebrated family-friendly workplaces, safety on the job, the voluntary maintenance of health insurance and pensions, and enough employee voice to generate a sense of transparent fairness "when restructuring and layoffs are essential to a company's long-term health."[115]

Bill Clinton was still uneasy, however, so soon thereafter he asked Joseph Stiglitz, his CEA chair, if anything could be done to stop the soaring compensation taken home by top corporate executives. The 1993 budget bill had tried to put a $1 million ceiling on the salaries that corporations paid their CEOs. Companies could pay more, but the excess would not count as a tax-deductible business expense. But that cap did not cover the "performance-based" executive remuneration that came in the form of stock options. Silicon Valley and Wall Street were adamant on this issue, and so were many of the otherwise liberal politicians who represented high-tech interests and New York finance. The salary ceiling had led to an explosion of corporate stock options, the exercise of which soon composed the bulk of executive pay.[116] Three years later, when Clinton asked if anything could be done to prevent companies from "getting around the $1 million cap," Stiglitz told him that any new regulations would be "ineffective and inefficient." In the absence of a radical legislative initiative, corporations would find some way to circumvent any pay cap.[117] Joseph Stiglitz was the most progressive economist to serve in a top post in the Clinton administration, but in this controversy he felt as trapped as Bill Clinton when it came to staunching the growth of income inequality and corporate power.[118]

Throughout the 1990s Clinton and his team thought that when it came to productivity and economic well-being a win-win solution might dissolve endemic conflicts between capital and labor, between workers and their managers. But this proved an illusion, albeit a useful one for an administration that found even the most stolid of labor

movements a political and economic distraction. Of even more consequence, when Clinton and his advisers recognized the wishfulness of
their vision, they had neither the political leverage nor the political will
to do anything about it. As we shall see in the next chapter, this set of
ideological illusions and political constraints would reappear in equally
tragic form when Clinton came to fulfill a campaign promise "to end
welfare as we have known it."

PART IV

The New Deal in Eclipse

10

Underclass Men and Welfare Mothers

In November 1993, in the midst of the debates over NAFTA and the Health Security Act, Bill Clinton flew to Memphis for a convocation of 1,500 African-American ministers. Speaking in the Temple Church of God in Christ, from the pulpit Martin Luther King Jr. had used to deliver his last sermon, Clinton trod lightly on the accomplishments of his first few months in office. Instead, he told the ministers that he wanted to talk about "the great crisis of the spirit that is gripping America today," an urban crisis of shuttered workplaces, fatherless children, and senseless violence that was destroying those American families trapped in poverty and despair. Clinton wanted Congress to pass a crime bill that would ban assault weapons, put more police on the streets, and stiffen prison sentences. But that law, enacted the next year as the Violent Crime Control and Law Enforcement Act, was not the real solution. Instead, President Clinton argued that the absence of work was at the heart of America's urban disarray. "I do not believe we can repair the basic fabric of society until people who are willing to work have work," Clinton declared to an appreciative and animated audience. "Work organizes life. It gives structure and discipline to life. It gives meaning and self-esteem to people who are parents."[1]

Clinton's ideas were shaped by the scholarship of William Julius Wilson, the African-American sociologist who had published *The Truly Disadvantaged: The Inner City, the Underclass, and Public Policy* (1987). Wilson argued that as deindustrialization and capital flight decimated good-paying industrial jobs, a generation of minority men had become economically and socially marginalized. They were therefore inadequate and erratic breadwinners for the women who bore their children. That problem was compounded by the migration from the inner city of middle-class Blacks taking advantage of new opportunities available with the end of legal segregation. This weakened institutions like churches, clubs, and schools, leaving the people who remained with few role models. Wilson recognized that the cultural pathologies associated with ghetto life were highly destructive of African-American well-being, but argued that crime and "welfare dependency" were consequences, not causes, of the dysfunctional economy in which so many were trapped.[2]

Clinton heartily agreed, and he would reference the Wilson thesis repeatedly during the 1992 campaign. At the Little Rock economic conference, Clinton called *The Truly Disadvantaged* "the best brief description of why the urban areas of the country are in the shape they're in that I have ever read." Wilson was "famous in our circles," Clinton told *NBC News* just before the Memphis speech, because *The Truly Disadvantaged* "graphically showed how the decline of the black family is associated not simply with the rise of welfare, but with the evaporation of jobs for black males."[3] New investment, public and private, was essential to create the income and work that would anchor social stability.

Not unexpectedly, Wilson found much to applaud when Clinton ran for president. The candidate had assembled a genuinely interracial coalition, "a progressive response to both racial and economic difficulties of the nation." And Clinton's ease with the Black community reflected a "respect for their judgement and an understanding of the depth and breadth of their concerns."[4] Naturally, Wilson was a frequent visitor to the Clinton White House for conferences and think-tank dinners, many to discuss "structural inequalities" and promote "affirmative opportunity."[5] As late as 1996 Wilson still thought Clinton's "vision" far superior to that of the GOP's Robert Dole, who did not have "the full understanding of what affects the life chances of these kids that Clinton has."[6]

During Clinton's first term the crime bill of 1994 and the welfare reform that would follow two years later were among the most controversial pieces of legislation backed by the president. Their passage opened a wide breach between the White House and many progressives, demonstrating how a combination of politics and ideology came to dilute, distort, and even repudiate the policy proscriptions that Clinton and social democrats like Wilson had advanced when they thought about how to solve "the urban crisis." Politics generally drove Clintonite social policy to the right, although a brief season of liberal leverage during the Lewinsky scandal successfully sidelined a Clinton-Gingrich effort to "reform" Social Security in 1997 and 1998.

The Rise of the "Underclass"

Although William Julius Wilson was one of the nation's most respected sociologists, he was not driving the social policy debate. The history of a single word, the "underclass," encapsulates how his views became contested and how a cohort of neoconservative intellectuals adopted and popularized a more culturalist approach to explain urban problems and the solutions required. Liberals and social workers had used the term "underclass" as early as the 1960s to emphasize the growth of a neglected and impoverished population sorely in need of money, jobs, and social stability. Both Gunner Myrdal, author of *An American Dilemma*, and William Julius Wilson had deployed the concept as well. But all that began to change after the 1977 New York City blackout, when looting and arson engulfed many parts of the city. Unlike the riots of the 1960s, which many racial progressives had thought of as disorderly and destructive but nevertheless as something close to a collective response to poverty and racism, the urban mayhem of the late 1970s seemed merely nihilistic and shameless, a manifestation of some underlying dysfunctionality that was both dangerous and willful. In a long *New Yorker* essay that popularized this neo-Victorian understanding of the "underclass," the journalist Ken Auletta described an urban world in which "waves of nomadic teenagers engulf city streets—out of work, out of hope. . . . These unemployed nomads are often choking with rage, which finds expression in broken windows, torched buildings, and acts of unimaginable violence."[7]

Charles Murray, James Q. Wilson, and John DiIulio were among the well-funded neoconservative intellectuals who in the 1980s and early 1990s helped push to the social policy forefront a set of ideas that broke sharply with the social liberalism that had long governed both criminal justice administration and welfare programs. Welfare—Aid to Families with Dependent Children (AFDC)—had been racialized and stigmatized for decades. The general public had long forgotten its origins as part of the Depression-era Social Security system.[8] Even before Ronald Reagan famously advertised the Cadillac-driving "welfare queen" as a symbol of endemic corruption and Black female presumption, AFDC had been an increasingly vulnerable target, especially for those who sought to demonize the sexual and social independence achieved by so many poor women in the wake of the feminist revolution and the civil rights movement. To Charles Murray, who wrote the highly influential *Losing Ground: American Social Policy, 1950–1980* (1984) while a fellow at the conservative Manhattan Institute, welfare programs trapped recipients in a culture of dependency that was detrimental to themselves and their offspring. The growth in welfare rolls was less a product of economic stagnation than a social index marking the decline of heterosexual marriage, the hedonism of young women, the irresponsibility of men, especially young Black males, and the devaluation of work among poor Americans more generally. With other neoconservatives, as well as most Republicans, Murray saw illegitimacy, teenage motherhood, and ghetto criminality as central to virtually all social problems facing the nation. The solution he proposed was draconian: orphanages and foster homes for the kids, an outright elimination of welfare for single mothers, and incarceration for youthful lawbreakers, with little regard for rehabilitation.[9]

These neoconservatives were not simply advancing in social science jargon the racist stereotypes propounded by Ronald Reagan and other conservatives. Instead, they were arguing that the young mothers caught up in the welfare system were victims, not thieves. In his characteristically extravagant language, GOP firebrand Newt Gingrich would channel this idea to declare that a radical reduction of welfare expenditures would "liberate" the American poor from a paternalistic bureaucratic state. He did not complain, as Reagan did, of corruption by welfare recipients; instead, he admitted that children were suffering but argued that the welfare system itself was to blame.[10] The phrase "culture of welfare dependency" soon became used with increasing frequency among liberals themselves. The idea of such a culture was not without some merit, for even progressive social scientists, like David Ellwood and Mary Jo Bane, both of Harvard, found in their surveys that single Black mothers thought welfare was demeaning and demoralizing and offered little chance for self-betterment.[11] This was a theme close to Bill Clinton's heart. He rejected Murray's neo-Victorian ethos, but nevertheless thought work was something close to spiritual redemption.[12] As governor and president, he was fond of telling audiences the story of Lillie Hardin, who had taken a job as a cook after years on the Arkansas welfare rolls. "I asked Lillie what was the best thing about being off welfare. Without hesitation, she replied, 'When my boy goes to school and they ask him, "What does your mama do for a living?" he can give an answer.' It was the best argument I've ever heard for welfare reform," wrote Clinton in his autobiography.[13]

An equally sharp break from past thought and practice was taking place on the criminal justice side of the neoconservative policy ledger. Violent crime had increased substantially since the late 1960s, peaking at 758 offenses per 100,000 people in 1991. Fear of crime was real, with 44 percent of all Americans afraid to walk alone at night even within a mile of their homes. Meanwhile, an overwhelming emphasis on punitive measures to combat crime resulted in dramatic increases in the nation's arrest and incarceration rates. The states were often the prime movers, but the federal government supplied much money and motivation. After Ronald Reagan signed the Anti-Drug Abuse Act of 1986, the "War on Drugs" dedicated more than $1 billion to state and federal law enforcement agencies, including an authorization of nearly $100 million for new federal prisons.[14]

James Q. Wilson and his former student John DiIulio were among those academics who not only agreed with Murray's critique of the welfare system but thought the remedies he proposed could work only when accompanied by an increased police presence in poor communities reinforced by the certain imprisonment of those ensnared (meaning fewer plea deals and far less probation). This approach, of course, would require a vast expansion of the prison system. Wilson became famous for his "broken windows" theory—the idea that low-level crime and disorder, such as breaking a window and leaving it unrepaired, created an environment that encouraged more serious criminality. Wilson and DiIulio both thought that the source of this lawbreaking was essentially cultural, reflecting the absence of two-parent families, the declining influence of church and school, and the pervasive sale and use of drugs.[15]

DiIulio, a product of South Philadelphia's scrappy streets, wrote that children become "criminally depraved when they are morally deprived." Street crime, often directed toward total strangers, was a product of a small but rapidly growing cohort of repeat offenders, he asserted, who "place zero value on the lives of their victims." These boys were "perfectly capable of committing the most heinous acts of physical violence for the most trivial reasons." Both Wilson and DiIulio became influential in circles far removed from traditional law-and-order Republicans. They thought recent trends in metropolitan demography forecast an exponential growth in the ranks of these lawless juveniles, white as well as Black, and perhaps an expansion of their range to encompass suburban districts and even the rural heartland. Absent a religious and moral renaissance, argued DiIulio, only more police, tough prosecutors, and a larger program of incarceration could get these "tens of thousands of severely morally impoverished juvenile super-predators" off the streets.[16]

William Julius Wilson had written *The Truly Disadvantaged* as a rejoinder to these neoconservatives, but by the early 1990s Wilson, Murray, and DiIulio were winning the criminal justice debate. They still represented a distinct minority of experts in the field, but their high profiles in the policymaking sphere lent legitimacy to an older set of racially motivated fears, even among liberals. A. M. Rosenthal, formerly the executive editor of the *New York Times*, channeled DiIulio's work in a *Times* opinion piece entitled "Prisons Save Lives."[17] Daniel Patrick Moynihan thought the rising number of out-of-wedlock births in the Black community was largely a cultural phenomenon that had little to do with the presence or absence of jobs for either men or women.[18] Thus, when DeIulio coined the word "super-predators" in a November 1995 cover story published by William Kristol's *Weekly Standard*, Hillary Clinton and others in the White House were paying attention.[19] "We need to take these people on," said the first lady two months later in a Keene, New Hampshire, speech that would bedevil her in later years. "They are often connected to big drug cartels; they are not just gangs of kids anymore. They are often the kinds of kids that are called 'superpredators.' No conscience, no empathy. We can talk about why they ended up that way but first we have to bring them to heel."[20]

Clinton's Crime Bill

Bill Clinton had campaigned on welfare-to-work issues in 1991 and 1992, but once in the White House he allowed any reform of AFDC to simmer on the back burner. A reform that envisioned elimination of one of the New Deal's most important entitlements engendered bitter opposition from feminists, liberals, and many of his closest friends in Congress and within his administration. William Julius Wilson and other Black sociologists were against it.[21] Only in late 1995 and 1996 would welfare reform become a high-profile issue.

In contrast, a change in the criminal justice system would be much easier to pass through a Congress still run by his own party. Unlike the health reform effort or NAFTA, the crime bill that Clinton outlined in August 1993 was based on the consensus views of most Democrats, including a majority in the Congressional Black Caucus (CBC) as well as Northern white legislators such as Brooklyn Representative Charles Schumer and Delaware Senator Joe Biden. "Crime has been transformed from an issue that generally divides Democrats into one that unites them," reported Schumer, who chaired the key House subcommittee on criminal justice.[22] "There's a virtual war on many of our streets," asserted the president in a radio address of that time, "and crime has become a national security issue to millions of Americans." Clinton thought "society has the right to impose severe penalties on the hardened criminals who commit the most heinous crimes."[23] If that sounded like a Republican talking point, so much the better: many liberals thought the defeat of Michael Dukakis had been a function of GOP efforts to paint him as soft on crime, so Clinton and most Democrats were determined to steal right-wing thunder and neutralize the issue.

Congress had been trying to clear a significant crime package for six years, but it took the election of a Democratic president to assure liberals that a new crime law would contain provisions not entirely inspired by the increasingly rightward tilt of criminal justice policymaking. Ron Klain, who had drafted an early version of the crime bill while serving as chief counsel on Biden's Judiciary Committee, orchestrated much of the White House approach. For the Clinton administration the funding of 100,000 more police was the "signature" provision of the bill. Liberals saw this $9 billion program as an advance toward "community policing" that would get more cops on foot patrol and out of their militarized cruisers. The legislation also included a ban on military-style assault weapons; more rehabilitation programs, such as funds for "Midnight Basketball," which the Republicans derided; and the separate Violence Against Women Act, long demanded by activists in the movement to protect battered women. VAWA provided $1.6 billion to investigate and prosecute sexual violence and domestic abuse.[24]

Conservatives also got what they wanted. Perhaps the most significant deal was trading the ban on assault rifles for the tough prison and sentencing provisions upon which the GOP insisted. Biden and Schumer were in accord, as was the president. They all relished the idea of standing on the side of the police—often literally in Rose Garden photo ops—while together they denounced the National Rifle Association, which still insisted that the public must be free to purchase military-style weapons.[25] Despite much disquiet from white Democrats representing Southern and rural districts, Clinton held fast and pushed through a ten-year ban, the very last federal gun control victory enjoyed by liberals until the third decade of the twenty-first century.[26] In return, the crime bill offered $12.5 billion in monetary incentives for the states to build more prisons, with nearly half earmarked for those that adopted tough "truth-in-sentencing" laws that scaled back parole. (Inmates had to serve at least 85 percent of the time for which they were convicted.)[27] Moreover, the crime bill added new mandatory minimum sentences to those that already existed. The bill was in some respects gratuitously cruel, reflecting the degree to which retribution had replaced rehabilitation as a penal policy goal. Thus, Pell grants were eliminated for inmates seeking college degrees. More ominously, some sixty new offenses were added to the roster of the federal crimes for which the death penalty might be imposed. Relatively few federal prisoners were actually executed, but the provisions that made some teenagers, even as young as thirteen, subject to the laws governing adult crime reflected the ideological influence of those conservatives in Congress and the academy who had so effectively legitimized some of the most repressive and alarmist impulses within the body politic.[28]

The inclusion of a "three-strikes" provision in the crime bill—life imprisonment or something close to it would be mandated for a third felony conviction—had not been part of Clinton's initial legislative package. But the idea was "sweeping the country," reported the Domestic Policy Council staffer Bruce Reed. Governors both liberal and conservative were touting it in their state-of-the-state addresses, followed by easy enactment in such otherwise liberal states as California and New York. Reed, who was one of the few DLC partisans then working in the White House, had little trouble convincing Clinton to get ahead of the movement by endorsing the concept in his 1994 State of the Union address. So Clinton told the nation, "When you commit a third violent crime, you will be put away, and put away for good; three strikes and you are out."[29] Based on the questionable supposition that a small minority of criminals were responsible for a majority of all violent crimes, the three-strikes concept proved a humanitarian disaster. Had the law been applied just to those with multiple convictions for crimes doing bodily harm, the numbers incarcerated would have been relatively low. But most states folded drug and property offenses into the three-strikes formula, thus vastly enhancing the pool of those ensnared in this draconian law. Long prison terms for minor offenses soon followed.[30]

The crime bill passed both houses of Congress in August 1994 and was signed into law the next month. In the weeks just before passage, those most hostile to the bill were not liberals but conservative Republicans, who wanted stiffer sentencing provisions, and Southern Democrats, who feared the assault weapons ban would doom their political careers. The Congressional Black Caucus had wanted to fold into the law a Racial Justice Act that would have enabled death-row inmates to offer evidence to appeals courts that the death penalty was being applied in a discriminatory manner. Like Title VII of the 1964 Civil Rights Act, which enabled petitioners to cite racially biased employment patterns on their behalf, the RJA would have had both practical and symbolic importance, reported Ron Klain, as an "explicit recognition that there is racial discrimination in the criminal justice system."[31] When President Clinton surrendered to Senate conservatives who wanted the RJA dropped, the *New York Times* called the concession "the last straw" that was enough to "pull the plug" on the bill. With Jesse Jackson, the NAACP was also opposed to Clinton's Violent Crime Control and Law Enforcement Act of 1994, calling it "a crime against the American people."[32]

But in the end the bill had the crucial backing of a coalition of ten African-American mayors, representing cities such as Detroit, Atlanta, Cleveland, Denver, and Baltimore. And members of the Congressional Black Caucus voted for the law 26–12, with South Carolina's James Clyburn, Texas's Eddie Bernice Johnson, and Maryland's Kweisi Mfume voting in favor, while John Conyers of Detroit, John Lewis of Atlanta, and Maxine Waters of Los Angeles were against. The CBC wanted to support the president on a crucial vote, but more importantly, many in the Black community were fearful of street crime and desperate to do something about it. When Clyburn explained to an all-Black audience that he opposed mandatory minimum prison sentences, he thought he was going to be physically attacked. "The atmosphere back then—the scourge of crack cocaine and what it was doing in these African American communities—they were all for getting this out of the community."[33]

With misgivings, Bernie Sanders, then a Vermont House member, cast a vote for the Clinton crime bill, in part because of his vigorous support for the Violence Against Women Act. Also in support were other high-profile white liberals in the House: Nancy Pelosi, Patsy Mink, Barney Frank, and Ed Markey.[34] They all disliked the harsh sentencing provisions, but Joe Biden had no qualms. He adopted the DLC line portraying the bill as a chance to rid his party of its soft-on-crime reputation and wrestle the issue away from the Republicans. "The liberal wing of the Democratic party is now for 60 new death penalties," he told the Senate. "The liberal wing of the Democratic Party is for 100,000 cops . . . 125,000 new state prison cells."[35]

The money and incentives in the new crime bill enabled the states, which housed almost 90 percent of all those incarcerated, to continue building prison after prison. The construction boom had begun in the early 1970s under President Richard Nixon, and now a Democratic president enabled it to continue apace. In 1968 the incarceration rate stood at just one inmate per 1,000 citizens. By the end of the second decade of the twenty-first century it had increased sevenfold, with 2.3 million people behind bars in jails and prisons and 4.5 million on probation and parole.[36]

Remarkably, just about all of this expansion took place while actual crime statistics were falling, having peaked in 1991. Rather than more policing, demographic transformations in the urban population— fewer young people, more jobs, gentrification—seems the probable cause. The idea that youthful "superpredators" would make urban life intolerable proved entirely mistaken. Juvenile arrests for murder—and juvenile crime generally—had already started falling during the years when John DiIulio achieved his greatest influence. By 2000, when tens of thousands more children were supposed to be out there mugging and killing, juvenile murder arrests had fallen by two-thirds. By then DiIulio admitted his error. "I'm sorry for any unintended consequences," he said.[37] Bill Clinton was contrite as well, telling an NAACP convention in 2016, "I signed a bill that made the problem worse. And I want to admit it."[38]

"End Welfare as We Know It"

The same toxic admixture of racial fear, partisan politics, and urban decay that had propelled Bill Clinton toward sponsorship of a draconian crime control regime also made him the architect of a welfare reform that seemed an even more controversial break with New Deal liberalism. As

Arkansas governor, Bill Clinton had been a welfare reformer. His state was so poor that even with a federal match, welfare payments were among the lowest in the nation. Even minimum-wage work in Arkansas generated more income than the paltry checks the state would cut. As chair of the National Governors Association in 1988, Clinton teamed up with Republican Mike Castle of Delaware to endorse a congressional initiative that promised training and government job opportunities to transition recipients from AFDC to a paying job. With President Reagan's endorsement, the Family Support Act squeaked through the national legislature. But it proved a bust. The new law was woefully underfunded: training and public-sector jobs cost money, much more than any savings that came from pushing people off the welfare rolls. Moreover, the recession of the early 1990s proved an inhospitable moment to tell mothers that they had to find a job. Welfare rolls swelled by one-third.[39]

Still, as a presidential candidate, Clinton had an issue that enabled him to outflank, sometimes on the left and sometimes on the right, both his interparty rivals and the Republicans. When Clinton declared his candidacy in October 1991, his vague call to move families "off welfare rolls and onto work rolls" generated few ripples. But when Clinton offered a much more detailed set of policy proposals, his pledge to "end welfare as we know it" gave his campaign a high-impact slogan that appealed to conservatives without entirely alienating the liberals. The phrase had been concocted by the DLC's Bruce Reed, one of Clinton's first speechwriters. Reed knew nothing about welfare, but he thought he knew what motivated Reagan Democrats who were disdainful of Democratic Party social liberalism. At a Cleveland meeting of the DLC in May 1991 Reed helped Clinton take a page from William Galston and Elaine Kamarck's "Politics of Evasion." Those two DLC social scientists had warned that Democratic Party "liberal fundamentalism has meant a coalition increasingly dominated by minority groups and white elites—a coalition viewed by the middle class as unsympathetic to its interests and its values."[40] Clinton channeled this argument when he told his DLC audience that middle-class voters—the fact that they were white was left unstated—no longer trusted Democrats "to put their values into social policy," and he used as a prime example the welfare checks that came from "taxpayer hides."[41]

But Clinton's campaign rhetoric on welfare reform was "cleverly ambiguous," thought Peter Edelman, a staunch liberal who began his career as an aide to Robert F. Kennedy in the 1960s. Edelman met his wife, Marian Wright, while touring impoverished parts of Mississippi with Senator Kennedy in 1967.[42] Six years later Marian founded the Children's Defense Fund (CDF) and hired Hillary Rodham to her first real job. For the next two decades, as they became good friends with the Clintons, the Edelmans were among the nation's most prominent advocates of child welfare and early childhood education. In 1993 Peter Edelman would take a high-level post in Clinton's Department of Health and Human Services.

A policy-heavy speech that Bill Clinton delivered at Georgetown University shortly after declaring his candidacy sustained Edelman's wry appraisal of the presidential aspirant's rhetoric. Among other issues, Clinton tried to spell out his welfare program, borrowing tropes and sentiments from both neoconservatives and liberals. "We need a New Covenant," he said, using a phrase formulated by Reed and others from the DLC,

> a solemn agreement between the people and their government, to provide opportunity for everybody, inspire responsibility throughout our society and restore a sense of community. . . . That means people who work shouldn't be poor. In a Clinton Administration, we'll do everything we can to break the cycle of dependency and help the poor climb out of poverty . . . we're going to put an end to welfare as we know it. I want to erase the stigma of welfare for good by restoring a simple, dignified principle: no one who can work can stay on welfare forever. We'll still help people who can't help themselves, and those who need education and training and child care.[43]

"End welfare as we know it" was a resonant slogan, but what did it mean? "End welfare" sounded definite and bold: most voters heard it as a cost-saving pledge that would penalize those welfare queens Reagan had made so infamous. But "as we know it" offered an all-purpose hedge: Clinton wasn't really proposing to abolish AFDC but instead was suggesting that if more welfare moms were to end up on a payroll, they would need training, child care, and other resources in order to make work, in government-created jobs if necessary, a realistic possibility. And that would cost upwards of $12 billion more than the current system. Clinton was here following the research of David Ellwood, as well as that of other liberals, who thought that an enhanced welfare state, including health provision, job training, child care, and public or nonprofit employment, would indeed enable many mothers of small children to enter the labor market, taking government-created jobs if necessary. In his 1990 book *Poor Support*, Ellwood had endorsed time limits on welfare, between eighteen and thirty-six months, but only as part of a larger expansion of aid. Reed, who had become a strategist as well as a speechwriter on the Clinton campaign, zeroed in on that most provocative issue—time limits—and chose a midpoint of two years, after which welfare mothers would have to work. Ellwood translated this to mean "two years and you work," but in campaign speeches Clinton often said, "Two years and you're off."[44] This line polled so well that the Clinton campaign, at the urging of George Stephanopoulos and other liberals, spent millions on TV ads touting it, along with the "end welfare as we know it" sound bite.[45]

The New Democrats: From Exile to Power

But Clinton did nothing with the welfare issue after his election. The Democratic leadership in Congress thought it divisive, the public employee unions feared that work requirements for welfare moms would erode wage standards and replace their members, and most liberals saw the whole issue as far too racially charged. And there were other pressing issues on the Clinton agenda: his first budget, NAFTA, and health reform, whose extension of insurance to low-income workers was an essential prerequisite to any welfare reform. The New Covenant language Bruce Reed had injected into Clinton's campaign speeches had flopped with focus groups and was little heard from again. Henceforth, the Clinton speechwriters would be liberals like David Kusnet and Michael Waldman.[46]

Meanwhile, at the December 1992 Little Rock economic conference, welfare reform went unmentioned. None of the economists or policy entrepreneurs associated with the Progressive Policy Institute or the DLC were on the program. But Clinton and Gore gave Marian Wright Edelman of the Children's Defense Fund a prominent slot at the first and most important plenary. Hillary had been a recent CDF chair, as had Donna Shalala, the new HHS secretary. The DLC thought Edelman's work was an example of "the failed Great Society mentality that was killing the Democratic Party . . . doomed-to-fail, bad-on-substance, bad politics."[47] But with her husband Peter, who played a key role in formulating Clinton's welfare program, Marian Edelman would be among the highest-profile opponents of a DLC-oriented "reform" of AFDC. Her Children's Defense Fund eschewed the moralistic critique of unwed mothers and deadbeat dads that conservative policy hawks sought to make central to the welfare debate.[48]

But Edelman's organization also offered ideological hostages to the conservatives. By emphasizing child welfare, the Children's Defense Fund purposefully deemphasized the status of the parent. By avoiding a forthright endorsement of the feminist argument that child raising was a worthy endeavor not just for the middle-class homemaker but for poor mothers as well, the Fund allowed conservatives to fill an ideological vacuum. Likewise, the idea that welfare programs enhanced the psychic and economic bargaining power of poor women, against both the men in their lives and potential employers, failed to gain much traction in the welfare debate that resumed in the mid-1990s.[49]

Still, Clinton marginalized DLC elements within his administration. Rob Shapiro, a DLC economist who had clashed with the Clinton liberals during the campaign, was not given a post, nor was Al From, who returned to running the organization he had founded. Clinton gave Bruce Reed and William Galston important-sounding posts on the Domestic Policy Council, but their roles were inconsequential when it came to the main domestic issues that confronted the White House.

None of the DLC partisans working in the administration, neither Reed nor Kamarck nor Galston, had anything to do with the budget tug-of-war that consumed administration insiders until August 1993, and they were not consulted in any way when it came to the health care fight that followed.[50] Reed's office was in a distant corner of the Old Executive Office Building. Indeed, when it came to the budget debate in the spring of 1993, Senate liberals like Ted Kennedy and Paul Sarbanes battled for Clinton's agenda, disappointing as it was to many of their constituents, while New Democrats like David Boren and John Breaux, both oil-state senators, were willing to sabotage Clinton's first-year presidency in order to protect fossil fuel interests.[51]

The DLC was funded by scores of wealthy individuals and corporations—including $250,000 a year from hedge fund manager Michael Steinhardt—but its operatives were not warriors for Rubinomics. Instead, both Al From and the New Democrat contingent within the administration took as their warrant a rather narrowly defined set of issues that they deemed central to a "Clinton Revolution." Welfare reform, a cultural and ideological marker of the first order, was by far the most important, closely followed by Al Gore's reinventing government initiative. The DLC "revolution" also called for a set of high-profile but low-budget innovations, like a youth-oriented national service program, to which Galston devoted his time, and the creation of a set of high school–based youth apprenticeships for working-class teenagers looking to enter the job market. When it came to criminal justice, the DLC's main interest was a community policing proposal to put one hundred thousand more cops on neighborhood streets by the end of the Clinton presidency. Not only would this "foster a new sense of community," From wrote Clinton, but it would "signal your willingness to put your mark on an issue that too many Democrats have ducked in the past."[52]

The striking feature of this agenda, and of Al From and Bruce Reed's interpretation of it, lies not in the policy innovations, which were often quite modest, but in the cultural and ideological weight they imputed to their proposals. "Vision is cheap," From told Clinton during the transition, "and it's exactly what we need."[53] DLC ideologues therefore advanced a set of "signature proposals" that graphically demonstrated how

New Democrats would repudiate an older liberalism that, in From and Reed's view, merely constituted the collective demands on the state by a set of aggressive "interest groups." They rarely spelled out who or what actually constituted the forces of "liberal fundamentalism," but everyone knew: civil rights organizations, labor unions, environmental groups that thwarted business investment, and those congressional liberals who defended the New Deal's social and regulatory legacy. Al From and others in the DLC circle were among the loudest critics of Lani Guinier, the affirmative action advocate whose nomination to head the Justice Department's Civil Rights Division generated a storm of opposition—from Republicans of course, but also from many conservative Democrats. Clinton abandoned Guinier, an old friend, in June 1993.[54]

As we have seen, Clinton and Gore did put the DLC "reinventing government" initiative into motion during their first year, but the rest of the New Democrat agenda languished. This agitated Al From no end. "You're just not dancing with the ones who brought you," he complained in April 1993. There was too much cooperation with the congressional Democrats, too much talk about "diversity," and not enough of the "New Covenant" rhetoric about "opportunity, responsibility, community" that had been prominent in Clinton's campaign speeches.[55] The president campaigned as a New Democrat, complained From, but he was "governing as an old one." Thus, From applauded those conservative Democrats who eviscerated the Clinton economic stimulus; indeed, he argued for more spending cuts, declaring them "essential to begin to change the tax and spend image" that now had Clinton perched "on the extreme left of the cultural divide."[56] Above all, From pounded away on the importance of welfare reform, which the DLCers saw as "the most important promise you made during the campaign" and "the single issue that demonstrates your willingness to break with old Democratic orthodoxy."[57]

But welfare reform stayed on the back burner. Galston saw himself as an "alien anthropologist" among the Clinton crowd, describing his New Democratic comrades as "a few raisins in a very large cake."[58] "Clinton had strayed from the DLC playbook," wrote Kenneth Baer in *Reinventing Democrats*, his semi-official history of the group. During the first two years of the Clinton administration, "the DLC increasingly found itself at odds with Clinton." The decision to pursue health care reform before welfare reform was particularly galling.[59] And Clinton was not the only renegade. During the 1993 budget negotiations the fiscal hawks, including cultural conservatives like Lloyd Bentsen and Alice Rivlin, dropped from the budget the $3 billion slated to implement welfare reform, perhaps the only austerity measure that truly displeased the DLC crowd.[60]

Clinton did hold fast to the full $26.8 billion cost of a campaign proposal to more than double the tax cut for millions of working families with incomes of less than $30,000 a year. This was the Earned Income Tax Credit, which pulled more than four million low-wage workers out of poverty during the next few years. The EITC offered genuine help for the working poor, in many instances refunding far more than the taxes deducted from their paychecks. But unlike an increase in the minimum wage, which had an impact on ten times as many workers, the EITC did nothing to alter the structure of the entire labor market by exerting upward pressure on wages immediately above the new minimum. And because it was also a subsidy for employers of low-wage labor, it won support from many Republicans as well as the DLC.[61] Bruce Reed calculated that the EITC transformed a $4.25 minimum-wage job into one effectively paying $6.00 an hour. Given normal turnover, reported Reed, McDonald's alone could hire all of the welfare recipients who would exhaust their two years on AFDC. "With the EITC and health reform," Reed advised Clinton, "any job is a good job."[62] Such advice was offered in the same the decade when the *Oxford English Dictionary* defined the word "McJob" as "an unstimulating low-paid job with few prospects."[63]

There was no consensus on welfare reform within the administration. In the working group the president established to write welfare legislation Bruce Reed was balanced by officials from the Department of Health and Human Services, including Peter Edelman, David Ellwood, and Mary Jo Bane, the last a Kennedy School political scientist with much expertise in family social policy. Bane and Edelman were surprised that Reed seemed to believe that "two years and you're off" was a reasonable approach to public assistance, but since the 1993 budget had eliminated new money for job training and more child care, Edelman and others from HHS, including Secretary Donna Shalala, assumed that the two-year limit was unworkable. Reed, on the other hand, said, "What's wrong with having hard time limits?" Those from the HHS were aghast.[64]

All this changed with the Republican sweep of the 1994 midterm elections. The Clinton White House was not just thrown onto the defensive but would soon accommodate the conservative onslaught. Southern Democrats, many of them identified with the DLC, were the chief victims of the GOP midterm victory. In the bitter aftermath, many blamed Bill Clinton's ideological transgressions, demanding that he get rid of the West Wing liberals and shift policy rightward. Clinton soon did so, although the inexorable polarization of US politics would demonstrate that DLC "centrism" had a questionable future.[65] In the meantime, however, the election was an "empowering experience," remembered William Galston. While Clinton was in a funk and the West Wing liberals were despondent, "I suddenly started getting invitations to political and strategic meetings from which I and others like me had been systematically excluded."[66] Newt Gingrich and his radical cohort of newly elected Republicans seemed, in the words of a *Newsweek* cover story, capable of altering "the basic course run by the government for the past 60 years." Al From agreed: "This election said the New Deal coalition is Humpty Dumpty and it isn't going to get put back together again." After the defeat the president stopped "taking orders from Democrats in Congress," recalled Reed with much satisfaction. "Now they weren't in a position to give orders anyway."[67]

The stealth appearance of Dick Morris did much to advance this transformation in politics and policy. Morris was the political operative who had known Clinton since the mid-1970s and worked for him as a campaign adviser and sometime confidant. He had played a key role in Clinton's gubernatorial comeback in 1982, when he had urged Bill to temper his liberalism and Hillary to accommodate herself to Arkansas cultural norms. This is when she changed her last name from Rodham to Clinton. The son of a New York City real estate lawyer, Morris had started his political career as a reform Democrat but soon became far more conservative in a poll-driven, even cynical fashion. "Morris is without a moral center," said Harold Ickes, who knew him from New York politics. Erskine Bowles, then deputy chief of staff and hardly a liberal, told George Stephanopoulos that he felt like "taking a shower" after every meeting with Morris.[68] Morris was so disliked by Clinton's inner circle that for several months in 1995 and 1996 he showed up on White House logs under the pseudonym "Charlie," after the heard-but-unseen character in the popular television program *Charlie's Angels*.[69]

Clinton had his doubts as well, but he was desperate to climb out from under the Gingrich landslide and this new Machiavelli seemed to have a strategy for the president: detach from any bold initiatives, accommodate the Republicans so as to steal their thunder, and, most famously, "triangulate" so as to stand apart from the Democrats, congressional or otherwise. Morris told Clinton to "fast-forward" the Gingrich agenda regardless of opposition from within his party.[70] Clinton would now thoroughly embrace the New Democrat ethos, advancing by executive order a series of small, largely symbolic reforms that were lifted from the DLC cultural politics arsenal: "V-Chips" to give parents control of the content viewed by their children on the internet, new efforts to keep cigarettes out of the hands of minors, and experiments with school uniforms so as to engender a more disciplined learning environment. When it came to welfare, Shalala's HHS issued dozens of waivers to the states, enabling them to put into practice elements of the welfare reform that House conservatives, as well as Reed and Clinton, now advocated. These included work requirements and time limits on how long AFDC recipients could stay on the welfare rolls and new regulations designed to force absent fathers to support their offspring. All this pleased the DLC contingent, but the linkage of their program to a flamboyant and unprincipled ally was also their "worst nightmare," confirming the left-of-center charge that the entire New Democrat project was "essentially a political tactic and not a governing agenda." Said Bruce Reed, "The price we paid for having Morris as our resident madman was that his presence made everything the president did look expedient."[71]

The DLC people were right to feel chagrined, because Dick Morris was such a scoundrel. His well-publicized dalliance with a prostitute came to light in the very midst of the 1996 Democratic National Convention, finally ending his access to the White House and the Clinton inner circle. Far more appealing to those advocating Bill Clinton's move toward a more austere social policy would be the idea of a "Third Way," which achieved much currency in 1994 and after as Tony Blair and his "New Labour" Party rose to prominence in Great Britain. Blair, who would take the premiership after winning a huge parliamentary majority in the general election of May 1997, had a youthful charisma that seemed the perfect complement to Clinton's persona. Together they generated a certain excitement when in November 1997 delegations from the White House and Blair's inner circle exchanged ideas at Chequers, the prime minister's country estate. Soon Third Way conferences were being held on the Continent and in the United States, with participation from social democratic heads of state, including Germany's Gerhard Schröder and France's Lionel Jospin. Al From played a large role in organizing these meetings.[72]

The phrase "Third Way" had once been associated with the policies of interwar Sweden and the New Deal, which offered a middle path between Soviet communism, German fascism, and nineteenth-century laissez-faire. Arthur Schlesinger Jr. had popularized the idea in his 1949 book *The Vital Center*, which staunchly defended an aggressive brand of Rooseveltian liberalism.[73] But Blair and Clinton downsized the concept, emphasizing the commitment of left-of-center parties to the social usefulness of markets and the modernization of government. Blair really did move Labour to the right, repudiating the party's commitment to the nationalization of key industries, limiting trade union influence, and continuing many of the privatization programs inaugurated by Margaret Thatcher. Clinton and the DLC were far more likely to use the Third Way idea as a rhetorical device designed, as Sidney Blumenthal put it, to give coherence to the "practical experience" of election-winning politicians who "operate in the real world." The historian Tony Judt called the concept "opportunism with a human face," but whatever the evaluation, the Third Way not only revalidated the DLC approach to politics and policy

but for the Clinton White House promised a high-minded internationalism even as scandal and stalemate bedeviled much of his second
term.[74]

Getting to a Welfare Reform

Newt Gingrich wanted a huge tax cut, drastic spending cuts, block grants
to the states instead of entitlements for welfare and food stamps, and a
budget that would balance in six years. Although a budget surplus would
become a reality by the end of 1997, no one in either party had initially
thought a balanced budget could be achieved without a radical reduction
of social programs, including Medicare, Medicaid, and AFDC. Clinton
therefore angered liberals when, in June 1995, he met the GOP partway
and agreed to balance the budget in ten years, cut discretionary spending
by 20 percent, and reduce the projected rise in Medicare costs. Three
months later Clinton let Congress know that he was willing to accept a
version of the welfare reform passed by the Senate, including the much
talked about two-year time limit, work requirements thereafter, and, perhaps most important, the block granting of AFDC.[75]

   This was the decisive moment in the welfare debate. Once word got
out that Clinton might endorse the "moderate" Senate bill, Donna Shalala rushed to the White House and hand-delivered to the president a
new Urban Institute study showing that the law would throw one million children into poverty. Edward Kennedy called the bill "legislative
child abuse," and Daniel Patrick Moynihan thought it would soon have
children sleeping on the street. But after Clinton made clear his support,
the bill passed the Senate by 87–12.[76] To the Children's Defense Fund
the potential loss of entitlement status for that federal program was the
"defining" issue of the welfare battle. "It would be the height of tragic
irony," Marian Wright Edelman wrote to the president, "for the New
Deal's most important legacy of national concern for the needy to be
dismantled during your watch."[77]

   But in late 1995 and early 1996 the Gingrich majority in the House
saved the president from having to sign on to the harshest sort of welfare
law. Enfolding the welfare reform in the GOP's larger austerity program,

Congress sent the president a version of welfare reform that cut funds for food stamps, disabled children, and foster care. Gingrich and Dole wanted to run a 1996 campaign against presidential hypocrisy: Clinton might talk welfare reform but would not deliver when he had the chance. So Gingrich demanded more spending reductions than even Clinton could stomach. Thus, on November 13, 1995, after the president vetoed a particularly austere GOP budget resolution, including the unacceptable welfare reform, the US government shut down, first for five days in November and then again for twenty-one days between late December and early January. More annoyance than actual crisis, the shutdowns were nevertheless the longest in US history, and national parks, museums, government civilian offices, and federal construction projects were operating with only skeleton staffs. Most of those who worked in the White House were sent home, replaced for the duration by unpaid interns. Thus was the stage set for the fateful encounter between Monica Lewinsky and Bill Clinton on November 15.

Both sides thought the other would blink first, but the Republicans had overreached and would take the brunt of public criticism. Gingrich created a self-inflicted wound when he told the press that one reason for precipitating the government shutdown arose out of his pique over being snubbed, he thought, by Clinton on the long flight back from Israel of the high-level delegation of US officials who had attended the funeral of Izsak Rabin after his assassination by a right-wing Zionist. The White House produced photographs showing Gingrich and Clinton in conversation on the flight, but in truth the House Speaker was right: Clinton and his inner circle wanted no further negotiations with Gingrich because they welcomed a showdown, if not a shutdown. Indeed, the 1995 government closure proved a decisive turning point in Clinton's political fortunes. His public approval ratings jumped into the mid-50s and never significantly declined before his reelection. Early in 1996, after Clinton had used his pen to again veto a Republican welfare law, he signed a budget resolution that ignored the welfare issue and tempered most of the Gingrich budget cuts. "We made a mistake," the Speaker told Clinton. "We thought you would cave." Henceforth, the GOP firebrand no longer seemed an invincible foe.[78]

The Era of Big Government Is Over

Clinton had won the battle for public opinion, but he would turn that victory into a profound ideological defeat in his 1996 State of the Union speech. In that address, Clinton sought to follow the advice of Dick Morris and strike a magnanimous note, balancing a recognition that his Republicans rivals had put forth a set of ideas and policies that had to be taken seriously with a defense of progressive verities about the role of government. After much consultation with Clinton and his inner circle, speechwriter Michael Waldman had written: "In the last thirty years it has become clear that government cannot solve all our problems for us. And in the last twelve months it has become equally clear that getting rid of government will not solve all our problems either. We don't need a program for every problem; we need citizens to rise to every challenge."[79]

Dick Morris wanted something with more punch. His edits transformed the Waldman text into the following: "The era of big government is over. But the era of every man for himself must never return." That pithy construct neatly balanced Gingrich against Clinton, offering something close to equal ideological weight to each. Even those staffers who were contemptuous of Morris had to admit it was better. But there was something wrong with the second sentence, and Ann Lewis, then communications director of the president's reelection campaign, quickly pointed it out. The language was sexist.[80]

Clinton's speechwriters searched for a substitute formulation but could find nothing with the right bite and balance. Thus, when Clinton delivered his 1996 State of the Union address on January 23, Republicans gasped, then jumped to their feet in applause when the president announced, "The era of big government is over." Clinton stood back, waved them silent, and then continued: "But we cannot go back to the time when our citizens were left to fend for themselves. Instead we must go forward as one America, one nation working together to meet the challenges we face together. Self-reliance and teamwork are not opposing virtues. We must have both."[81]

The meandering counterpoint fell flat. Virtually every newspaper and news show headlined "The Era of Big Government Is Over." No one paid attention to the rejoinder. The phrase was the best-remembered line delivered in any Clinton speech, and some journalists and historians declared that it put the 1996 State of the Union address among the five most noteworthy in US history.[82] Whatever the intentions of the Clinton speechwriters, or of Clinton himself, "the era of big government is over" embodied the accommodation of the president, and perhaps of an entire political class, not only to the policy setbacks of the Clinton administration's first three years but to the demise of the state-building ambitions advanced by the progressive men and women who had built the New Deal and the Great Society decades before.

The Welfare Decision

Before a drastic reform of the welfare system could be promulgated—one that did in fact repudiate its New Deal heritage—a last skirmish had to be fought. Bill Clinton was ready to sign a bill, but the Republicans were now the ones who were not quite sure they wanted a new law. Although Bob Dole was far more of a centrist than Gingrich, his campaign for president was predicated on making sure the public saw Clinton as a failure. That meant no Rose Garden ceremony where the president would sign the law with a bipartisan group of legislators standing behind him. So Gingrich inserted a "poison pill" in the 1996 version of the welfare reform bill: not only would Congress block-grant AFDC, but Medicaid, the means-tested system of health provision for the poor, would also cease to be an entitlement. Henceforth, each state would have wide latitude in its expenditure of those health provision dollars, but the annual grant would be capped and therefore would steadily decline as health care inflation galloped ahead.[83]

Why did Bill Clinton acquiescence to block-granting welfare but blanch when it came to Medicaid? As a governor, Clinton had been more sympathetic than other Democratic politicians to the block grant idea. Block grants offered budget flexibility and sometimes an opportunity for innovation. "We're not in the business of turning down waiver requests," Mary Jo Bane told Congress. "We are in the business of helping states do what they want to do." By 1996 forty-three states were operating their welfare programs under waivers from the Clinton administration.[84]

Block-granting Medicaid, however, was another story. In contrast to the welfare system, which allowed governors a great deal of discretion, the world of health provision was a hotly contested terrain where powerful entities—nursing homes, hospitals, pharmacies, insurers—competed for each dollar. From his Arkansas experience Clinton knew that if Medicaid were block-granted, then nursing homes and other long-term facilities for the elderly would secure an increasingly larger share of a shrinking monetary resource. Children and their mothers, as well as other very poor recipients, would soon be deprived of health support as each state scrambled to impose increasingly more stringent income standards for Medicaid eligibility. This was a message that Clinton carried to even the most conservative Republican governors, who in turn told Gingrich and other House leaders that not everyone in the GOP was eager to plunge their states into this Hobbesian jungle.[85]

Liberals like Peter Edelman were delighted at the new impasse: perhaps welfare reform was dead, at least until after the election, when the political landscape might be more favorable. But President Clinton was impatient to sign a bill, and Dick Morris insisted that passage of the law would add fifteen points to the president's popular vote margin, essential to victory in November.[86] So Bruce Reed and Rahm Emanuel spent much energy that spring lobbying Hill Republicans with the message: drop the Medicaid block grant idea and they could get a bill Clinton would sign. Robert Dole helped them out, albeit inadvertently. By April he had wrapped up the GOP presidential nomination, but his prospects looked increasingly dismal and threatened to subvert the reelection of many rank-and-file House Republicans. The GOP needed some conservative, culturally inflected legislative victories upon which to run in the fall. In June, therefore, more than a hundred representatives sent Gingrich a letter calling on the Speaker to decouple the prospective block grants for Medicaid and welfare reform.[87]

Gingrich did so, but the resultant welfare bill was still hard to swallow. It block-granted welfare funds to the states, ended most cash assistance to legal immigrants, cut back on food stamps, and imposed a five-year lifetime limit on federal welfare benefits in addition to the two-year cutoff. Although it continued the federal government's provision of more than half of each state welfare budget and actually increased child-care assistance by 40 percent over then-current levels, the bill failed to provide the level of support that Edelman, Ellwood, and others had wanted to assist welfare recipients in transitioning to the world of work. There was no guarantee, for example, of a public-sector job. The states had a free hand to set eligibility standards, punitively if they desired, and many soon did so. The bill easily passed both chambers of the national legislature, although there were probably enough Democratic votes in the Senate to sustain a veto.[88]

This was the context for a dramatic White House meeting on the morning of July 31, 1996. Almost every cabinet officer and high-level staffer who had struggled with the welfare issue was in attendance. Clinton opened the meeting by asking simply, "What should we do?" It was not an entirely sincere question. The presence of the DLC hard-liners Elaine Kamarck and Bruce Reed was indicative of Bill Clinton's inclinations. Hillary was absent, but she had told intimates, "We have to do what we have to do, and I hope our friends understand it."[89] However, President Clinton wanted to air the views of those opposed, if only to make them complicit in the ultimate decision. He railed against the provisions barring legal immigrants from food stamps and, in some states, from Medicaid as well. Robert Reich thought the president protested too much, and indeed, Clinton eventually told the group that he had gotten "a good welfare bill, wrapped in a sack of shit."[90] The rest of the room wanted a Clinton veto, whatever the political costs; after all, with Dole failing to gain traction in his campaign, those costs were probably not so enormous. Shalala and Reich were adamantly opposed to the bill; more circumspect were Robert Rubin and Chief of Staff Leon Panetta, the latter emphasizing the moral inequities inherent in the cutoff of aid to immigrants. Laura Tyson surprised Clinton by taking an entirely different tack: having concluded that AFDC, more than other entitlement programs, reacted to early signs of general economic stress with well-calibrated payments that stimulated recovery, she urged Clinton, quite apart from the moral or political issues, to veto the bill in order to preserve this recession-fighting tool.[91]

After the two-and-a-half-hour meeting, Clinton retreated to the Oval Office with just Al Gore and Leon Panetta. Gore told the president to sign the bill because the current system was just too damaged. Reed was summoned and once more emphasized the political imperative. "All right, let's do it," Clinton said. "I want to sign this bill." He made the announcement that same afternoon to reporters in the White House briefing room. By signing the Personal Responsibility and Work Opportunity Reconciliation Act, the most fundamental departure in federal poverty policy in six decades, Clinton had adopted the essential calculus advanced by the New Democrat/DLC contingent. At a Rose Garden ceremony in August the president said, "After I sign my name to this bill, welfare will no longer be a political issue. The two parties cannot attack each other over it. Politicians cannot attack poor people over it." Anyone who had ever said a disparaging word about welfare, he declared, should now say, "Okay, that's gone."[92] The welfare system—now called Temporary Assistance for Needy Families (TANF)—did become less of a "political football" in subsequent campaign cycles, but the underlying racialization of American social policy remained as divisive as ever. "I really believed that if we passed welfare reform," Clinton told the journalist Jason DeParle after he left office, "we could diminish at least a lot of the overt racial stereotypes that I thought were paralyzing American politics."[93]

History would prove Clinton very wrong, but controversy came much sooner. Once again, Bill Clinton had split the Democrats and signed legislation that could not have passed without solid Republican support. Equally significant, Clinton was soon confronted with the resignations of several high-level HHS officials, a rare instance of such public protest in official Washington. David Ellwood had resigned in 1995 when it became clear that Clinton wanted to sign a bill with definitive time limits. Wendell Primus, who had worked up the figures estimating that even a moderate welfare reform bill would push one million

A New Beginning
Welfare to Work

FIGURE 13. President Clinton signs the Personal Responsibility and Work Opportunity Reconciliation Act in August 1996. Over his right shoulder stands Lillie Harden, an Arkansas mother of school-age children and former welfare recipient whom Clinton frequently lauded in speeches on welfare reform. (Clinton Presidential Library)

children into poverty, left right after Clinton announced his decision to sign the 1996 law. And then Mary Jo Bane and Peter Edelman resigned in mid-September, just weeks after Edelman's spouse had published an open letter in the *Washington Post* that declared, "President Clinton's signature on this pernicious bill makes a mockery of his pledge not to hurt children."[94] William Julius Wilson weighed in as well, complaining that without a jobs program, "you're asking these welfare mothers who reach the time limit to sink or swim. It's a Draconian bill."[95] Peter Edelman wanted Clinton to be reelected, so he waited until the spring of 1997 to publish in the *Atlantic* his indictment, "The Worst Thing Bill Clinton Has Done." No one could ever say that Bill Clinton was still "an old liberal," wrote Edelman. "After all the noise and heat over the past two years about balancing the budget, the only deep, multi-year budget cuts actually enacted were those in this bill, affecting low-income people." President Clinton would award Marian Wright Edelman a Presidential Medal of Freedom before he left office, but the close friendship between the two couples was broken.[96]

From an economic standpoint, the passage of welfare reform did not have the disastrous consequences some of its opponents had forecast, in large part because of the uniquely favorable moment in which TANF was enacted. The EITC had been doubled in 1993, the minimum wage increased in 1997, Congress passed the Children's Health Insurance Program that same year, and in that same budget act Clinton was able to get many legal immigrants once again covered by Medicaid and the new welfare law. Most important, unemployment reached historic lows at the end of the 1990s, boosting real wages and job opportunities for those at the very bottom of the working class. Thus, many women were able to make the transition from welfare to work. Child poverty declined to 16 percent in 2000, the lowest rate since 1979, while welfare rolls dropped from above 12 million in 1996 to just 4.5 million a decade later. Of course, this did not mean that all those pushed off welfare actually had a job or that the intermittent work they did take was any more remunerative or steady than they would have been able to secure under the old welfare system. Still, a decade after passage of the law 60 percent of mothers who left welfare did find work.[97] That statistic would deteriorate during the Great Recession that began in 2008, when poverty made a substantial comeback, especially among the very poorest.[98] Nevertheless, welfare ceased to be a flash point in the world of high politics; indeed, to the degree that the economic and social problems facing poor single mothers remained a point of partisan and political contention, they were shared by many other working mothers, including those of middle-class income and education.[99] This reconfiguration of the welfare issue became particularly manifest by the time the Covid-19 pandemic began in 2020. Then virtually all Democrats and even a few conservatives put near-universal child allowances, income subsidies, and job programs on the policy agenda.[100]

So why did the Clinton welfare reform strike such a sensitive nerve and remain hotly contested for years thereafter? There were three reasons: First, the elimination of this New Deal entitlement came during the presidency of a Democrat and amid the opposition of most of the liberals still remaining in his administration, not to mention the sizable cohort in Congress. Second, Clinton was adopting the rationale of a set of conservative policy intellectuals, both those neoconservatives whose principal home was the Republican Party and the DLC factionalists among the Democrats. For both types of conservatives, welfare reform was a stalking horse for a far larger effort to delegitimize not only cultural and racial liberalism but virtually the entire welfare state that had emerged out of the New Deal and the Great Society. And finally, welfare reform was both highly racialized and implicitly paternalistic. It was not simply, or mainly, about how children could be fed, housed, and clothed. Instead, welfare reform was an assault on the autonomy of poor African-American women, a degradation of their personhood that limited the meaning of their citizenship. Public assistance benefits, however menial, had come to function like a social wage for unmarried women, offering them not so much dependency on the state as independence from unsuitable male partners and a measure of freedom and power within extended families. To a feminist community that hailed the appointment of Ruth Bader Ginsburg to the Supreme Court, welfare reform seemed an utterly misogynist step backward, "a war against poor women" that was "a war against all women."[101] Whatever the electoral advantage Bill Clinton might have temporarily won, his reputation as a heartless neoliberal was hereby well advanced within the ranks of progressive America.

"Monica Changed Everything"

Bill Clinton used welfare reform to help his reelection, but he was hardly finished with initiatives that would undermine key pillars of the New Deal state. The president saw himself as "modernizing" the banking system and "strengthening" Social Security, but by the onset of his second term such rhetoric had an increasingly Orwellian flavor.

If AFDC was a small yet highly symbolic program, Social Security, which sent checks to more than thirty-eight million retirees and their survivors each month, was a giant, collectivized entitlement that embodied both economic citizenship and a redistributive ethos. Although it was hugely popular, Social Security in the 1990s was no longer the "third rail" of American politics. It seemed an increasingly anomalous program as virtually every other institution of collective economic provision came under political and fiscal attack. Welfare and other means-tested forms of aid to the poor had become objects of disdain, many states were radically cutting back their unemployment compensation programs, and corporations were systematically eliminating their defined benefit pensions. These pensions were often replaced with 401(k) accounts for which the individual employee bore the risk, even if the long stock market boom made private investment decisions look easy and lucrative. Thus, Social Security was structurally isolated as the only part of the American system of social provision that was universal, guaranteed, and economically progressive.[102]

This opened Social Security up to ideological assault, often couched in terms of questioning its failure to remain solvent for the next generation of beneficiaries or to keep up with the returns found in the stock market. Those contributing payroll taxes to Social Security needed to make their own investment decisions, some maintained. Others argued that the system pitted one generation against another, the struggling young against comfortable retirees. Third Millennium, an inside-the-beltway privatization group with a twenty-something flavor, had little trouble winning support from Merrill Lynch, the Smith Richardson Foundation, and other Republican-aligned interests. It won enormous media attention for those claiming that Social Security was destined for bankruptcy when it sponsored a poll purporting to find that more young people ages eighteen to thirty-four believed in UFOs than thought Social Security would still exist by the time they retired.[103]

Liberals countered that the payroll tax generated an income stream sufficient to support the increasingly high proportion of retirees to contributors, but only if the real wages of American workers continued to rise at the historical rate generated during the era of postwar manufacturing prowess, union strength, and technological innovation. Since it was the stagnation in real wages and an actual decline in labor force participation that had produced a shortfall in Social Security's anticipated income, the solution required a very modest improvement in these underlying economic structures. For example, a reduction in the unemployment rate of just 1 percent or a shift in the distribution of income back to what existed in 1980 would have virtually eliminated the prospect of a long-range Social Security deficit. Lifting the cap on income subject to the Social Security payroll tax would also have gone a long way toward making the system solvent. In other words, there was no Social Security "crisis."

None of these arguments had much impact on the investment banks, think tanks, and legislative conservatives who sought to move the retirement system toward some sort of privatization. But what Wall Street meant by "privatization" was not unlike that proposed by Gore and Osborne in their "reinventing government" initiative: outsourcing and transforming a key government function. No one was proposing an end to Social Security payroll taxes so workers could invest as they saw fit the money they would have paid in taxes. Rather, Wall Street and every other privatization advocate would have had the Social Security Administration contract out a substantial portion of that multibillion-dollar income stream into the hands of the same banks, brokerages, and insurance companies that were simultaneously seeking a radical deregulation of their own financial affairs. These firms would then set up millions of private accounts, ostensibly controlled by individual Social Security enrollees. Thus, while much of the rhetoric behind the privatization movement had a libertarian flavor, Wall Street institutions would have used government taxing power to channel a huge stream of investment fees to their bottom line.[104]

Ironically, the federal government's unexpected budget surplus created a set of political and fiscal conditions that pushed Social Security to the top of Bill Clinton's agenda. In May 1997 the Congressional Budget Office announced that tax revenues generated by the 1990s boom and the higher taxes enacted four years earlier would create a $70 billion surplus in the next fiscal year and a $4 trillion surplus over the next decade and a half.[105] This astounding good fortune seemed to transform Washington politics; on August 5, 1997, the president and his onetime nemesis, Newt Gingrich, strolled proudly across the White House lawn to sign a budget deal and boast of their newly cooperative attitude. Republicans secured a modest set of tax reductions, $91 billion over five years, while the Democrats won $24 billion to fund health insurance for up to five million children from low-income families.[106]

That political rapprochement, though greased by the plenitude of new money, was also based on the Speaker's recognition that he had been outfoxed during the shutdown of 1995, forced to acquiesce in Clinton's version of welfare reform in 1996, and then compelled to watch helplessly as the president won reelection. The balance of power between Clinton and Gingrich had clearly shifted in the president's favor. But liberals could hardly celebrate because few remained in the second-term White House. Reich, Tyson, Blinder, and Stiglitz were gone. In the most significant move, Clinton replaced Chief of Staff Leon Panetta with Erskine Bowles, a North Carolina investment banker with close ties to many Southern Republicans. Bowles was among the most conservative figures Clinton would appoint to a high White House office. He had been hired to get a balanced budget deal with Gingrich and then to work out another one on Social Security. Bowles and Gingrich liked and trusted each other.[107]

Still, the White House worried that the newfound budget surplus would prove irresistible to GOP tax cutters, thus forestalling any social spending initiatives still on the administration agenda. In a series of unpublicized meetings, including a White House Treaty Room "summit" on October 28, 1997, Gingrich agreed to a scenario under which the Republicans would hold off pushing for a large tax cut in exchange for incorporating private investment accounts into Social Security. Clinton was not adverse to the idea. Private accounts evoked the opportunity and responsibility the president had touted during his campaign for welfare reform. Because the idea was so toxic to so many Democrats, however, another set of secret White House meetings to work out the complicated privatization details were given the code name "Special Purpose Meetings." Chaired by Gene Sperling and Larry Summers, they continued for several months in late 1997 and early 1998. Sperling and Summers thought individual accounts would be an effective means of "neutralizing Republican tax cut proposals" because the administration could portray them as a payroll tax rebate. The logic of the proposal, they argued, "is that we would be at a disadvantage if we only supported the Social Security Trust Fund, while the opposition was 'addressing' Social Security through accounts that provide a higher return."[108]

To make sure the White House held the high ground, Clinton used his 1998 State of the Union address to introduce the slogan "Save Social Security First." He would devote the entire budget surplus, or a very large portion of it, to making certain that Social Security remained solvent for multiple decades. This proved a politically attractive way to forestall even those Republicans who would not buy into the Gingrich-Bowles dealmaking, but it had two consequences that ratified the rightward drift of Clinton's second-term statecraft. First, the slogan asserted that Social Security was actually in need of saving. This legitimized the crisis narrative and conceded much ideological and policy ground to the austerity conservatives, whose interest in Social Security cutbacks was hardly satiated. Second, this was Rubinomics on steroids. Clinton was not just proposing to balance the federal budget but seeking to pay down the federal debt, even eliminate it, but without proposing any program of social, educational, or infrastructure investments of the sort he had sacrificed during the tumultuous budget debate of 1993. "By failing to consider any use for the budget surpluses other than saving Social Security, the President has finally raised the bar so high as to render any larger social agenda virtually unattainable," complained Robert Reich, now once again teaching at the Kennedy School. With the Democrats emasculating themselves, predicted Reich, "Republicans have found their platform for 2000 and beyond. The tax cutters will compete for floor space with the debt cutters. The conversation over the public good thus has been reduced to this cramped debate."[109]

This was the context, in January 1998, when the Monica Lewinsky scandal burst upon the nation. A special prosecutor, Kenneth Starr, had originally been tasked with investigating Whitewater, a bankrupt Arkansas development scheme in which the Clintons had invested in the 1980s. Eventually he extended his probe to the allegation that the president had lied under oath while testifying in a civil suit filed by Paula Jones, an Arkansas state employee, who had accused Clinton of sexually harassing her when he was governor. Acting on a tip generated by some of the president's right-wing opponents, lawyers for Jones asked the president if he had had a sexual relationship with Lewinsky when she was a White House intern. Clinton denied it, but when Starr summoned him to testify before a federal grand jury, the president admitted he had engaged in an "inappropriate relationship." By the summer of 1998 Lewinsky was providing explicit details of her intimate relationship with the president, all of which were contained in a 354-page report that Starr delivered to the House of Representatives in September. Two days later it was in the public realm, generating yet another wave of prurient excitement amid calls for the president's impeachment, on the grounds that he had lied under oath and obstructed justice by encouraging others to do the same.[110]

For more than a year the Lewinsky affair consumed the nation. The Associated Press assigned 25 full-time reporters to the story, who wrote more than 4,109 pieces, an average of 11 a day. Cable news coverage was almost nonstop, and on the evening news the three major networks devoted more time to the scandal than to the next seven topics combined.[111] Clinton called 1998 "the strangest year of my presidency." Nevertheless, he carried on, compartmentalizing the scandal and keeping to a schedule of White House meetings and the normal run of public appearances. Trips abroad, to Africa, China, and Europe, were long and welcome.[112] When, in the wake of the Starr report, Clinton convened a cabinet meeting to apologize, Robert Rubin spoke for many when he told him, "You know, Mr. President, there's no question you screwed up. But we all make mistakes, even big ones. In my opinion, the bigger issue is the disproportion of the media coverage and the hypocrisy of some of your critics." Rubin thought Clinton had remained remarkably focused and intent, doing the work while the storm raged around him.[113]

The Lewinsky scandal shifted the politics of Social Security in a decisive fashion. "We always knew that finding common ground on Social Security wasn't terribly difficult from a policy standpoint," recalled Ralph Reed. "Gingrich wanted to do it; Clinton wanted to do it," Bowles told the historian Steven Gillon, but "Monica changed everything."[114] With Republicans smelling blood, hoping to reap partisan advantage in the midterms, Clinton found that any détente he might have had with Gingrich and his faction was worthless.

By the time the House debated an impeachment resolution in the fall of 1998, the president had to rely, sometimes desperately, on the liberals and progressives with whom he had so frequently clashed. "I've stiffed organized labor on trade. I can't stiff them again," the president told William Archer, the Republican Ways and Means Committee chair. Archer wanted a deal, but now labor and the liberals had a veto.[115] So private Social Security accounts were out, and so was Erskine Bowles, replaced by the more liberal John Podesta. Triangulation seemed in abeyance. Fiery liberals like Maxine Waters, David Bonier, and Barney Frank led the Clinton defense in the House. Legislators close to the DLC were far more likely to condemn Clinton and then vote with the Republicans.[116] Most Democrats emphasized that the Lewinsky affair was a sexual tryst, while Republicans insisted that it was also about perjury and obstruction of justice. But as much as conservatives tried to make the impeachment effort about the rule of law, for most Americans the affair had been a consensual if embarrassing relationship between a powerful man and a female underling. That kind of relationship would raise much condemnation two decades later, but not so much in the era before "Me Too." Prominent feminists like Susan Faludi, Betty Friedan, and Gloria Steinem came to Clinton's defense.[117] His approval ratings stayed remarkably high through the fall of 1998, bolstering Democratic strength in the midterm elections. The party actually gained five seats in the House, a huge setback for Gingrich, who immediately resigned the speakership and then left the House entirely two months later.

Accommodation to the liberal wing of his party was apparent when Clinton's 1999 State of the Union speech unveiled a version of his Social Security plan. It was a "surreal" moment, thought Clinton, because his trial in the Senate had just begun. The president pledged that nearly two-thirds of the expected budget surplus would go to shore up Social Security, while another 15 percent would go to Medicare. About 20 percent of the new Social Security money would be invested in the stock market, generating returns more than twice the level of US government T-bills. Liberals were not displeased, because this was a collective wager on the equities market, similar to the way many cities, states, and corporations handled defined-benefit pension plans. Clinton nodded to the idea of individual retirement portfolios with a proposal for a set of 401(k)-like universal savings accounts that would take about 10 percent of the surplus to offer tax credits to Americans with incomes under $100,000. But this scheme was entirely separate from Social Security, whose payroll taxes and collective, governmental administration remained inviolate.[118]

President Clinton easily survived the Republican effort to impeach him. On February 12, the Senate vote on a perjury count failed by 22 votes, 45–55, and the vote on obstruction of justice, at 50–50, also fell well short of the two-thirds needed to convict. Social Security survived as well, largely unchanged. The Republicans still wanted a big tax cut—Clinton would veto that in September—and they fruitlessly backed individual retirement accounts carved out of the Social Security payroll tax stream. On the other hand, the idea that the Social Security trust funds might be invested in the stock market was anathema, tantamount to socialism. "No, no. A thousand times, no," declared the GOP's Archer. "If you thought a government takeover of health care was bad, just wait until the government becomes an owner of America's private-sector companies."[119] Greenspan was equally skeptical. Almost immediately following the announcement of Clinton's Social Security investment proposal, Greenspan effectively killed the whole idea when he told a Senate committee that he thought it "virtually impossible" to insulate investment managers from political influence.[120] Some liberals agreed. Labor-aligned writers at the Economic Policy Institute feared that Social Security trustees might become cheerleaders for a booming stock market, which was hardly the same thing as a full-employment economy.[121]

Did Monica Lewinsky save Social Security? Did she "change everything"? Unlike AFDC, Social Security had a far more powerful set of constituents serving as guardians of one of the New Deal's most potent and cherished legacies. The president's travail forced his reliance on labor and the liberals, but even in the absence of Monica's alluring smile, they would have given Clinton a bruising battle had he accommodated

Gingrich and the Republicans to "save" Social Security.[122] Still, the scandal distracted the president, slashed his moral authority, and once again polarized the polity. His promise to devote virtually all of the budget surplus to Social Security created stasis on the social policy home front. And with Clinton devoting ever more attention to foreign affairs—a settlement of the Irish troubles, Israeli-Palestinian peace negotiations, the war in the Balkans, and the terrorist threat in the Middle East—he proved far less engaged when it came to some of the most consequential trade and finance issues his administration would face at the end of the twentieth century. That vacuum would be filled by men and women whose ideology, and the deregulatory free market statecraft that flowed from it, did much to firmly stamp the label "neoliberal" on the Clinton presidency.

11

The China Price

The spectacular growth of trade with mainland China, culminating with that giant nation's admission to the World Trade Organization in 2001, was of enormous consequence, both in terms of how the American economy came to structure itself and as indicative of the emergence of a newly powerful player on the geopolitical stage. In contrast to Japan, which successfully sought to block American investment on the home island, or Mexico, whose entire economy was hardly larger than that of Los Angeles, China welcomed the Wall Street capital that helped privatize hundreds of huge state-owned enterprises, as well as the investments from American manufacturers seeking to establish thousands of joint ventures in coastal China capable of exporting a cornucopia of consumer goods back to the United States. American overconsumption thus sustained Chinese export-led development. Some called this increasingly entangled set of supply chains and financial relationships "Chimerica."[1]

Geopolitics and Chinese Human Rights

That close economic interdependence seemed highly unlikely in the aftermath of the 1989 Tiananmen Square massacre. A spirited democracy movement in the heart of Beijing had captured worldwide admiration, and the decision of the Chinese Communist Party (CCP) to respond by unleashing the People's Liberation Army against some one hundred thousand student demonstrators generated international condemnation of the sort not seen since the Korean War. So great was the outrage, both in the United States and elsewhere, that within two days President George H. W. Bush announced the imposition of a package of sanctions directed toward China, including the "suspension of all government to government sales and commercial exports of weapons" and a halt to all high-level visits between US and Chinese military and political leaders. Both the World Bank and the Japanese government blocked billions in loans designed to modernize Chinese transport and infrastructure development.[2]

It soon became apparent, however, that President Bush agreed with former secretary of State Henry Kissinger that "China remains too important for American national security to risk the relationship on the emotions of the moment."[3] In the summer and fall of 1989 Bush therefore sent high-level aides to assure Communist leaders that nothing fundamental would change in the relationship between the United States and China. In response, a coalition of liberal Democrats appalled at Chinese repression, conservative Republicans still hostile to "Red China," and neoconservatives who thought that the United States should not hesitate to impose its will in a post–Cold War world coalesced around a legislative mechanism designed to keep up the pressure on Beijing. Among the key figures in this effort were Nancy Pelosi, the San Francisco liberal whose district contained a large and sophisticated constituency of Chinese descent, and Winston Lord, a Reagan-era ambassador to Beijing who nevertheless rejected Bush administration "appeasement" of those Chinese "who predict America will be lulled by cosmetic gestures and return to business-as-usual."[4]

The Jackson-Vanik Amendment to the 1974 Trade Act, aimed largely at the Soviet Union, had denied most favored nation (MFN) status— normal trade relations—to nonmarket countries that prohibited or restricted emigration. Jackson-Vanik had therefore facilitated much Jewish emigration to Israel and the United States, so in subsequent years presidents of both parties had routinely issued waivers enabling the Soviets and the Chinese to enjoy MFN status. Now Pelosi and her allies weaponized the issue, insisting that any MFN waiver for China signed by the president must be "conditioned" on evidence that the Chinese regime was releasing student prisoners, respecting Tibet's cultural heritage, and allowing a modicum of free expression everywhere. In 1991 and 1992 waivers signed by President Bush that did not contain such human rights conditions were overridden by Congress, but then successfully vetoed by the president when the Senate failed to muster a two-thirds supermajority. Although many conservative Republicans still voted with Pelosi, because they either backed Taiwan or just wanted to bash a Communist regime, these battles became increasingly partisan as the voice of organized labor grew louder in linking human rights to labor's capacity for self-organization, both in China and at home.[5]

During the 1992 presidential campaign, the US relationship with China was a relatively marginal issue, but Clinton did make a point of meeting with Pelosi and Chinese student leaders still resident in the United States. Clinton considered the Bush China policy indicative of the Republican president's "indifference toward democracy." In his acceptance speech at the Democratic convention, Clinton accused Bush of "coddling aging rulers with undisguised contempt for democracy, for human rights." If he assumed the presidency, Clinton said, he would withdraw all trading privileges from China as "long as they're locking people up." Equally important, the end of the Cold War had radically altered the American geopolitical calculus. It "no longer made any sense to play the China card" and show "forbearance" toward Beijing, said Clinton, because America's Soviet opponents had "thrown in their hand."[6]

Chinese Mercantilism and US Business

Clinton was happy to let the State Department take the lead on Chinese affairs during the early months of his administration. Secretary of State Warren Christopher soon appointed Winston Lord as his Assistant Secretary of State for Far Eastern affairs. Christopher had played an active role in the Carter administration's human rights initiatives, and Lord promised to continue this effort, now with a bipartisan gloss. Lord got right to work, meeting with Pelosi and other Democrats on an MFN policy that Clinton and the Congress could endorse. Structured as an executive order, which gave the State Department more flexibility in carrying it out, Clinton signed a Chinese MFN waiver in

May 1993. Lord thought the conditions attached to the waiver "weren't so onerous that the Chinese couldn't meet them."[7] Pelosi agreed, calling the order a "very bold and historic move. . . . As long as we are united, the Chinese will get the message." And to a degree they did: more Tiananmen veterans were released from jail, the Chinese were more transparent about prison labor conditions, and a US-China dialogue on human rights conditions in general made some headway. With an MFN extension now linked to still greater liberalization of Chinese civil society, Lord and other State Department China hands were pleased that Clinton had embarked on a "much firmer policy than during the Bush Administration."[8]

All this would prove an illusion, because China's leaders were determined to maintain tight control of civil society even as it opened the door to a wide variety of capitalist institutions and trading relationships. China had been "opening up" its economy since the late 1970s, but in a disjointed and sometimes hesitant fashion that failed to generate anything close to the entrepreneurial capitalism and giant export trade that would later astound the world. The democracy movement of the late 1980s had in part been a response to layoffs in state-owned industries, rampant inflation, and corruption at the highest levels of the Communist Party. After Tiananmen Square, Chinese leaders such as Le Ping, who had been most instrumental in crushing the protest, thought that liberalization of either the economy or civil society was a dubious and dangerous experiment. If state-owned enterprises (SOEs) were privatized or allowed to go bankrupt, China's "iron rice bowl" would shatter, and with it the loyalty of millions of blue-collar workers. Like the American trade unionists who saw the defense of human rights as a step toward worker self-organization, Chinese autocrats also equated the end of outright repression in their nation with what they feared above all: the prospect of worker protest and radical independent unionism. This was one reason that in the immediate aftermath of Tiananmen protesting workers were treated even more harshly than students. Moreover, East Asian capitalism of the sort championed by the Chinese diaspora in Taiwan, Hong Kong, and Singapore might be dangerous. The joint manufacturing ventures the regime had encouraged in Guangdong and other coastal provinces now seemed a recipe for foreign influence and the fragmentation of party authority.

Such an economic posture, combined with worldwide revulsion against the crackdown, was hardly designed to generate much enthusiasm from American business. The *Wall Street Journal* thought China's economic prospects poor because that nation could not shake off "the stultifying bureaucracy of hard-line communism."[9] Wal-Mart, which was buying an increasingly large proportion of all its clothing, kitchenware, and hard goods from East Asia, including mainline China, started a separate Hong Kong buying operation, Pacific Resources Export Limited, so as to put some distance between Bentonville and the Chinese factories that filled shelf space in the US stores of the giant retailer. "The main reason" for setting it up, remembered a company executive, "was not to be exposed as going into Communist China."[10] A few other retailers, including such well-branded companies as Levi Strauss and Timberland, cut back on imports from China.[11] And whatever their involvement in the Chinese market, US companies remained marginal when it came to the most-favored-nation debate. The Chamber of Commerce and the National Association of Manufacturers were far more interested in the fate of NAFTA, from the time President Bush opened negotiations with Mexico until Clinton closed the deal in the fall of 1993, and US automakers, steel producers, and cell-phone companies were fixated on Japan.

Deng Xiaoping's "Southern Tour" of Guangdong Province and Shanghai in early 1992 proved a turning point, not just for unleashing an economic transformation in China but for activating the US business community as proxy lobbyists for the Chinese government in the MFN fight. Deng had been a hard-liner during the Tiananmen upheaval, but he thought the CCP could maintain its supremacy even as China inaugurated a set of developmental programs that would enable the nation to emulate the spectacular growth trajectory of the Asian Tigers. Because the economic reforms of the 1980s were mostly driven by the marketization of the rural-agricultural sector, requiring the importation of massive amounts of machinery, capital goods, and high-value consumer products, China often ran a trade deficit with the world. Communal farms were disbanded, village industries were encouraged, and peasants prospered, but these changes set off rampant inflation in the cities and a general economic chaos that was at least partially responsible for the Tiananmen upheaval.

Deng therefore wanted to shift China from a rural, consumption-driven economy to an urban, export-oriented manufacturing regime. In Shenzhen he told regional leaders to be "bolder in carrying out reforms" and to not act as "women with bound feet." Taking what seemed useful from Japan, Korea, and Hong Kong, the Chinese brand of capitalism would be far more mercantilist than neoliberal. The yuan would not float but remain undervalued, thus helping exports. Capital would flow largely where the government wanted it to go, and the state would still guide, consolidate, or disband the largest enterprises. Western investment would be welcome, however, often as part of joint operating partnerships with local government officials and well-connected entrepreneurs. In return for subsidized factories and cheap but competent labor, offshore investors were discouraged from selling in the domestic Chinese market and instead restricted to producing for export. China became the workshop of the world in the 1990s because it deployed a coercive industrial policy that put world markets at the service of a late-twentieth-century variety of the mercantilism that had first flourished two centuries before.[12]

Deng, still China's most influential figure, therefore championed the rise of Zhu Rongji, the mayor of Shanghai, who as vice premier would conduct many trade negotiations with the Clintonites. Deng also pressured Premier Jiang Zemin to move beyond the economic Stalinism endorsed by Li Peng and instead define China as a "socialist market economy."[13] China's growth rate leaped from little more than 4 percent in 1990 to more than 12 percent in 1992 and nearly 14 percent in 1993. Throughout coastal China a proliferating set of joint ventures, largely financed with overseas diasporic funds, nearly doubled the contribution of exports to China's GNP, which soared from 12 percent in 1989 to 23 percent five years later. China's trade surplus with the United States increased tenfold during these years. The International Monetary Fund released a study finding that if the Chinese economy were measured in terms of "purchasing power parity," it was now the third-largest in the world, ahead of Germany and behind Japan.[14]

American finance was in the vanguard of those taking advantage of China's opening after Deng's Southern Tour. Almost immediately the Chinese government invited US investment banks to restructure and recapitalize some of the biggest SOEs. They floated stock on the Hong Kong and New York stock exchanges and relied on Wall Street banks and accounting and auditing firms when their initial public offering (IPO) was put on the market. A fever of debt-financed investment by local governments was underway, with Goldman Sachs and Morgan Stanley playing a large role in creating scores of partially privatized, government-controlled corporations that soon poured onto *Fortune's* Global 500 list of the planet's largest firms. For example, Goldman Sachs was an aggressive suitor in the consolidation of China Mobile out of a disparate set of provincially based telephone companies. It was not an easy process, so the giant $4.5 billion IPO was delayed until 1997. But Goldman earned upwards of $200 million on the deal, and China Mobile soon became the world's largest wireless phone operator, with 776 million subscribers and more than 60 percent of China's market by the second decade of the twenty-first century. That wildly successful IPO catalyzed a series of blockbuster transactions that put Beijing front and center in the world's capital markets.[15]

Creating these new companies out of the old SOEs would have been impossible without international agreements codifying a set of global property rights. This was the bedrock imperative that sustained China's willingness to accommodate itself to the financial rules and intellectual property protections that had become increasingly central to the global standards negotiated by GATT and the WTO during the 1980s and 1990s. Initially, China wanted to enter GATT as a "developing nation," which would have enabled it to delay bringing its institutions up to Western standards. But under pressure from Wall Street, as well as from Hollywood and Silicon Valley, which sought to staunch the widespread piracy of films and software, both the Bush and Clinton administrations insisted that if China entered the WTO, it would be held to the financial and intellectual property standards of the most advanced nations.

As we will see, China would prove impervious to Clinton administration pressure on the broad question of human rights, but like Mexico, the Chinese regime was far more susceptible to US demands that intellectual property rights win legal protection. When in June 1994 Mickey Kantor's Office of the US Trade Representative threatened sanctions unless China shut down dozens of pirate software factories in Guangdong Province, the United States and China reached an IPR enforcement agreement the next year. At the provincial level there was much foot-dragging, so when Beijing still hesitated to crack down, the USTR, now led by Charlene Barshefsky, again threatened a new set of trade sanctions. In the summer of 1996 the central government finally put real pressure on provincial authorities in the South, who reluctantly closed some seventy outlaw factories. Thus, the US insistence that China could join the WTO only on "commercially meaningful terms" required an extensive, intrusive "reform" of the way China ran its domestic economy. Laws were changed to make some things legal and others not. Trade negotiations in the 1990s were a lever by which both the Chinese and the Americans transformed the mainland regime.[16]

US trade with China was growing, but except for a few large firms that produced unique and complicated products—such as Boeing and Caterpillar—the export of actual products from the United States to China was of little consequence, with the major exception of agricultural commodities. This was a huge shift in the nature of global trading patterns. Before 1980 the economies of the developed world exported manufactured goods to poorer nations. But during the next two decades the global South's share of all manufacturing exports rose from 27 percent to approximately 83 percent, with Chinese export industries in the vanguard.[17] By the early twenty-first century, therefore, the US commodity that filled more containers than any other on the return trip to China was trash, designed for recycling into the cardboard boxes and packaging that would protect all those consumer electronics, household appliances, toys, and sporting equipment that poured out of so many Chinese factories. These products were destined for retailers and brands—Wal-Mart and Target were the largest, Apple and Nike the best known—that now sourced an increasingly large proportion of their merchandise from Central America and the Far East. Most of the capital for these Chinese export manufacturers came from Japan and the Asian Tigers, but the real power in these supply chains—over pricing, product design, logistics, and even manufacturing technique—resided with the new set of US and European brands and retailers that distributed and sold the final products. "Designed in California" was the advertising slogan Apple deployed to codify this new reality. The low prices thereby generated—"the China price"—constituted the chief rationale for the MFN status that China sought from the United States. Supply chain economics thereby turned conventional trade theory upside down: instead of home-country manufacturers looking to expand their domestic production via exports, many iconic producers, including General Electric and Mattel, shrank domestic production, shifted manufacturing facilities offshore, and then imported the outsourced product.[18]

All this provided the global economic context for an unconditioned renewal of China's MFN status in 1994 and afterwards. But the Chinese hardly played a passive role. Instead, Chinese officials opened a concerted campaign to entice American business with a wide variety of trade and investment deals so as to turn US firms into proxies for the mainland regime. The Chinese showered key US firms with orders, collaborations, and promises of more. China placed a $4.6 billion jet order with Boeing; AT&T executives visited Beijing to sign a comprehensive cooperation agreement; Exxon Mobile won offshore drilling rights; and China bought $160 million worth of automobiles from Detroit and opened talks with General Motors and Ford to build a set of mainland factories. IBM chairman Louis V. Gerstner visited China to finalize plans for a set of joint-venture production projects. China signed 6,700 contracts with American companies in 1993, far more than in any other year.[19]

These transpacific economic ties soon created a new "China Lobby," composed of firms that wanted unfettered investment opportunities with the mainland. Thus, in early May 1994 the head of China's Export-Import Bank advised US business executives at a Chicago conference to "help solve the MFN issue once and for all," warning of "disastrous results" if they failed.[20] But such prodding was hardly needed. Just a month before, when President Clinton visited California for the funeral of Richard Nixon, a California business group presented him with a petition signed by nearly 450 West Coast companies warning that failure to renew MFN would be "an additional devastating blow" to a state whose aerospace industry had been radically downsized by the end of the Cold War.[21] Bill Gates of Microsoft, then the second-richest man in the world, was even more explicit. After he met with Chinese leaders in April 1994, he declared that the Chinese were right when it came to their critique of Clinton's effort to link that nation's respect for human rights to a renewal of MFN. "It is basically getting down to interference in internal affairs," he said, parroting the Chinese government line.[22]

The Human Rights Delinkage

Among those Americans visiting China late in 1993 was Representative Nancy Pelosi, who told the San Francisco Chronicle on her return, "I didn't see any progress in human rights at all."[23] Indeed, there was little to report. On occasion China would release a dissident or two from prison when the public outcry in the West reached uncomfortable levels, but the vast economic dynamism now engulfing much of urban China merely hardened the will of Chinese leaders. Millions of workers were losing their jobs as the SOEs downsized, millions more were migrating from rural villages to coastal cities, where they encountered all the stress, exploitation, and dislocation common to the creation of a new industrial working class. Strikes, protests, and public manifestations of discontent were on the rise. With the specter of Tiananmen never far from their minds, Chinese leaders faced an excruciating dilemma: they could not send a signal of accommodation to the United States without seeming to encourage dissidents at home, but they could not stifle dissent at home without further complicating relations with Washington.[24]

They gambled on repression and won. In the months following Clinton's 1993 executive order conditioning a renewal of Chinese MFN status on improvements in human rights on the mainland, top US officials held extensive talks with their Chinese counterparts. The Americans made clear that "overall, significant progress" would be essential if

MFN status was to be renewed once again.²⁵ But the Chinese rebuffed all efforts to accommodate the United States. In November 1993, when Clinton met with Chinese premier Jiang Zemin at a Seattle meeting of the Asian-Pacific Economic Council (APEC)—the first meeting between the US and Chinese heads of state since Tiananmen—the US president's handshake generated no response from China's premier. In their private ninety-minute meeting Clinton urged "early concrete progress" on Red Cross inspection of Chinese prisons, dialogue with Tibet's Dalai Lama, and the release of political prisoners. Premier Jiang made not even a verbal concession to Clinton's entreaties; meanwhile, on the very day Jiang Zemin arrived for the APEC meeting, newspapers reported that German chancellor Helmut Kohl was in Beijing, signing contracts for $2 billion in new business for German companies.²⁶

US-China relations did not improve as the May 1994 MFN deadline approached. When Secretary of State Warren Christopher visited China in March, he eschewed the normal round of banquets and toasts. Conversations with his hosts were "harsh and acrimonious exchanges" as Christopher bluntly told the Chinese that "overall significant progress on human rights remains necessary if I am to recommend the renewal of Most Favored Nation trade status for China."²⁷ But the Chinese did not budge. "China will never accept the US human rights concept," Premier Li Peng told Christopher. "It is futile to apply pressure on China."²⁸ They shipped chemical weapons to Iran and missile parts to Pakistan, continued their effort to turn Tibet into a Chinese province, and kept in jail an estimated three thousand political prisoners. That spring Chinese authorities amended the nation's public order law, broadening what were already sweeping police powers to detain, or restrict the activities of, democratic and labor union activists as well as leaders of religious and ethnic minorities.²⁹

At home the failure of the Christopher visit fell on the secretary's shoulders, not those of the Chinese. At a well-publicized forum sponsored by the Foreign Policy Association, former Secretary of State Cyrus Vance joined Kissinger and Lawrence Eagleburger, who had helped frame the Bush approach to post-Tiananmen China, in denunciation of the linkage policy. Congressional support weakened as well, with Jim McDermott, an otherwise left-leaning Democrat who represented thousands of Boeing workers, sponsoring a letter signed by 106 representatives that called for MFN renewal. Meanwhile, President Clinton made no public statement on behalf of his Secretary of State, which Winston Lord thought left "Christopher and the rest of us twisting in the wind."[30]

Robert Rubin had also begun undermining the State Department on the MFN issue. He thought China would become the largest economy in the world by early in the twenty-first century. Therefore, "I think probably everybody feels [trade and human rights] ought to be de-linked," he told reporters in late January 1994.[31] To Rubin "everybody" meant the vast bulk of the corporate executives seeking a footprint in China, plus all the principal players at Treasury, Defense, Commerce, USTR, and the National Economic Council. "Everybody" did not include, in Rubin's view, the State Department, the AFL-CIO, or even most Democrats in Congress. Lord thought that Rubin's rhetoric, an outright subversion of presidential policy, "totally undercut us with Beijing. Obviously, they could see the disarray within the US Government. It was a major failure of leadership by Clinton."[32]

After the Christopher trip, China trade policy was wrenched out of the hands of the State Department and given over to a White House team whose principal policy drivers were Robert Rubin and National Security Adviser Anthony Lake. The group met nine times from mid-March to late May 1994, with President Clinton far more engaged than he had been when Lord played the key role in formulating his 1993 MFN executive order.[33] For a time in 1994 Lord and other advocates of a tougher line on China—including Laura Tyson at the CEA—sought to apply a set of targeted sanctions that penalized trade with military-linked public enterprises while allowing easier trade with privately owned businesses. But given the increasingly complex character of economic life in China, such a disaggregation proved impossible, even when the CEA deployed the computer-based economic modeling techniques routinely used to analyze the US economy and its trade relations. Barber Conable, a former World Bank president, told Clinton and his advisers that, with respect to China, "you simply can't distinguish" between private and public sectors. "It's inconceivable."[34]

Bill Clinton threw up his hands, calling the linkage policy "nonsensi-cal" at one Roosevelt Room meeting on April 20. "Think about a country like Cuba or Haiti where you try and go in and foster human rights, even by aggressive acts. How successful have we been?" Describing those countries as "pin pricks on a map," Clinton said, "Think about China, its size, its history. . . . If we can't change these small countries, this is the way we're going to change China? No. The way you change China is you engage with them, you bring them into the tent, and you help mold them to the extent you can."[35] On May 26, just before Clinton an-nounced the new delinkage policy to the world, he called Pelosi, trying his charming best to keep the congresswoman's friendship. "I am an enthusiastic Democrat," Pelosi reminded the press after the conversa-tion. "But I cannot say one thing about George Bush's policy and an-other about Bill Clinton's when they are the same policy."[36] The *New York Times* editorialized that the United States had shown itself to be a "paper tiger" by abandoning its most powerful tool: "negotiating the terms of access to America's indispensable market."[37] "Realpolitik car-ried the day," wrote columnist Mary McGrory, the *Washington Post*'s acerbic liberal. "Clinton is being patted on the back by Democrats who say he did the 'wise' thing. Nobody claims it was right."[38]

Engagement Ideology as Wishful Thinking

Clinton argued that while a linkage between trade and human rights might have been constructive in the past, "we have reached the end of the usefulness of that policy."[39] The administration made no attempt to argue that China had met even the minimal human rights improve-ments urged upon it by the State Department. "Rose-colored glasses" had not been needed to reverse course, said the president. Instead, he put forward a historical and ideological rationale that would grow in-creasingly important in the latter half of the 1990s, especially during the contentious debates leading up to China's admission to the World Trade Organization. To those who argued for a revocation of China's MFN status, said Clinton at the press conference announcing the delink-age policy, "let me ask you the same question that I have asked myself. . . .

Will we do more to advance the cause of human rights if China is isolated or if our nations are engaged in a growing web of political and economic cooperation and contacts?"[40]

If neoliberal globalization had any popular appeal, even to the left, this was one of its central pillars. It was an argument derived from the Western triumphalism emergent at the end of the Cold War, the faith in the power of markets to erode state power, and the still-influential modernization theories that linked the rise of a bourgeois strata with pluralism, civil society, and democracy. Even Winston Lord thought that "economic reform produces—and requires—political reform."[41] This theme would appear again and again when the Clintonites defended "engagement" and deregulated trade with China. "China's economic growth has made it more and more dependent on the outside world for investment, markets, and energy," Clinton told the Asia Foundation in late 1997.[42] This was the "inexorable logic of globalization," asserted the president on another occasion.[43] Admitting that political reform had lagged behind economic change, the president was nevertheless confident that "computers and the Internet, fax machines and photocopiers, modems and satellites, all increase the exposure of people, ideas and the world beyond China's borders. . . . The more ideas and information spread, the more people will expect to think for themselves, express their own opinions, and participate."[44] A couple of years later Clinton doubled down, telling a Johns Hopkins University audience, "China is not simply agreeing to import more of our products: it is agreeing to import one of democracy's most cherished values: economic freedom. The more China liberalizes its economy, the more fully it will liberate the potential of its people—their initiative, their imagination, their remarkable spirit of enterprise."[45]

Panglossian rhetoric of this sort reached a triumphalist crescendo as the turn of the millennium drew closer. The *New York Times* columnist Thomas Friedman, whose best-selling *Lexus and the Olive Tree* encapsulated the most extravagant claims of Clintonite trade policy, proved to be the most widely read tribune of Chinese-American integration. "China's going to have a free press. Globalization will drive it," he wrote in 1999.[46] Friedman's argument was that capitalist marketplaces—and in particular the stock market, banking, and the investment protocols mandated by the WTO and other trade agreements—required accurate and unrestricted financial information to function. Once the Chinese media freely reported on the price of soybeans and software, how could news and opinion about protests, politics, and Communist Party leadership be far behind? Just as the Berlin Wall fell, Clinton remarked at a 1997 press conference, so too would China open up. "I just think it's inevitable."[47]

China was undergoing one of the great social transformations in world history. Abolition of the abject poverty that had long been the condition of hundreds of millions of peasants was reason enough to celebrate the "socialism with Chinese characteristics" being overseen by Communist Party mandarins. As these rural folk poured into the export manufacturing and urban construction zones incomes doubled and tripled. China was becoming rich, with new skyscrapers, fine apartments, and a vibrant consumerism arising in Shanghai, Shenzhen, and other coastal cities. Modernization theorists in academia and government had long argued that the rise of a middle class was key to social stability and the growth of civil society. Thus could Nicholas Kristof, a *New York Times* reporter on the scene during the bloody Tiananmen Square crackdown, now argue that the protesting students had in fact triumphed, with Western investment and domestic capitalism opening the door to "bourgeois freedom." Even hard-line Chinese leaders knew that when urban consumers struggled over what to order at Starbucks, "no middle class is content with more choices of coffees than of candidates on a ballot."[48]

This was wishful thinking. The prospect of a consumer society was hardly a compensation for the millions of workers and their families facing the new insecurities of the market. Both the new proletariat precariously employed in the export industries of the South and the old working class in the North, which was threatened by radical downsizing of the state-owned enterprises, were growing restless. Violent and illegal protests of all sorts—riots, factory occupations, and strikes—were more frequent during the 1990s, surpassing 120,000 a year in the new century.[49] But this dynamism from below was met by steadfast resistance from above. In contrast to the Soviet Union on the eve of its dissolution, Deng and other party leaders, many veterans of the Long March and the Civil War, retained a Leninist will to power. They had survived the Cultural Revolution, smashed the student uprising in 1989, and now were hardly willing to see either capitalist entrepreneurs or insurgent workers set their own course.[50]

The Chinese variety of capitalism was highly statist. It had never been as centralized as the Soviet command economy, but the continuing power of the CCP ensured China's avoidance of the sort of anarchic fragmentation that crippled Russia in the post-Communist era. In the export sector virtually all enterprises were joint ventures between provincial governments and Western or East Asian companies seeking a cheap labor force. Many state-owned enterprises were being "privatized" through the sale of stock and other financial instruments in the West, but genuine property rights, not to mention those of speech, press, and assembly, remained dependent upon the shifting politics of the regime. Periodic anticorruption campaigns launched by the Communist Party were a reminder to even the most prosperous entrepreneur that their status was insecure and contingent.

Meanwhile, Chinese growth and development were premised on the capacity of the state to suppress household consumption and worker incomes in order to aggregate investment capital for use either by a new stratum of regional entrepreneurs or by the government. China's rapid growth helped hide the scale of these transfers from ordinary citizens, but during the 1990s a variety of mechanisms were maintained to facilitate an upward transfer of wealth. In 1994 the yuan was devalued by about one-third, which helped juice US sales to and investment in the country during the crucial months when China was so intensely courting US business. But thereafter the yuan was progressively undervalued, making Chinese exports cheap for foreign consumers while simultaneously depriving ordinary Chinese of their ability to reap some fair portion of the productivity explosion generated by foreign investment, state-built infrastructure, and mass migration from near-subsistence agriculture to coastal export industries.[51] A system of "global labor arbitrage" enabled multinational corporations to base their supply chains in a country where cheap labor and efficient production methods made for an unbeatable "China price." The Chinese historian Qin Hui has called the state policy that suppressed worker income to subsidize investment the "comparative advantage of lower human rights."[52]

As a consequence, workers at nonfinancial corporations were paid only 40 percent of the value of what they produced, far below that in most other industrialized countries, where the labor share of corporate value added had been closer to 70 percent. The difference generated a new class of Chinese millionaires, paid for the nation's spectacular investment program, sustained a huge trade imbalance with the West, and generated the trillion-dollar current account surplus that the Chinese used to purchase US treasury bills. As with Japan, Chinese purchases of US bonds kept American interest rates low and the value of its own currency high, which in turn made Chinese exports cheap, perpetuating a trade surplus that was undercutting the competitive capacity of US industry. Powerful forces, both political and economic, were therefore at work negating the capacity of Clinton's program of trade and engagement to democratize Chinese society.[53]

America Rediscovers the Sweatshop

Both NAFTA and the delinkage of China trade from any human rights standard generated a howl of outrage from within liberal Democratic ranks. So too did welfare reform, which mandated work but offered few pay or employment guarantees. Clinton responded with a series of human rights and labor standard initiatives that, taken as a whole, were of minor social or economic impact in China or elsewhere. But they came to legitimize a critique of his own global trade policies that would reach an apogee at the Seattle WTO meeting in November 1999. Indeed, even as Clintonite globalization became entrenched in treaty and trade, popular hostility, on both the right and the left, became embedded in the cultural and political fabric of American life in the 1990s and after. This hostility became clear in both the renewed fight against sweatshop labor and the humiliating legislative defeat of the administration's "fast-track" trade bill shortly thereafter.

America rediscovered the sweatshop in the 1990s. In August 1995 California authorities raided an illegal garment shop in El Monte where seventy-two Thai women earned a subminimum wage in prisonlike conditions, sewing garments for some of America's leading brands. The next year human rights groups publicized the deplorable working conditions in Honduras under which the Wal-Mart clothing line of TV personality Kathie Lee Gifford had been produced. In carefully orchestrated appearances Gifford met with Robert Reich and then President Clinton to apologize and dedicate herself to the abolition of child labor in the factories where Wal-Mart subcontracted her brand. The owners of the El Monte sweatshop were jailed and their undocumented captives were assured a path to US citizenship. In 1998 the Smithsonian Institution even curated an exhibit on the history of American sweatshops and the efforts of reformers and regulators to abolish them.[54]

All this coincided with the Clinton administration's own anti-sweatshop initiative. That began with the delinkage announcement as Clinton sought to compensate for the human rights and labor rights leverage it had lost over renewal of China's MFN status. The United States, he said, would pursue "a new and vigorous American program to support those in China working to advance the cause of human rights and democracy." Hillary Clinton's celebrated appearance at the United Nation's Beijing Women's Conference in September 1995 was one element of this project. And the United States continued to pressure the Chinese regime to release political prisoners, not unlike the Cold War bargaining with the Soviet Union that periodically enabled prominent dissidents, including Aleksandr Solzhenitsyn, Natan Sharansky, and Andrei Sakharov, to escape prison, come out of internal exile, or immigrate to the West. Thus, Hillary's trip to the Women's Conference, where her speech in defense of women's autonomy, dignity, and human rights received a tumultuous reception, could only take place once the Chinese had released from prison Harry Wu, a US citizen and human rights advocate being held on trumped-up espionage charges.[55]

Labor standards could not be divorced from human rights, so after much interagency discussion, the Clinton administration announced a set of "Model Business Principles," a code of conduct for American businesses operating in China and other low-wage nations. These principles, though entirely voluntary, did lay down a set of aspirational markers, including standards that called for safe and healthy workplaces, a ban on child labor, nondiscrimination on the basis of race, gender, or religion, and respect for free expression. While human rights groups thought the codes were a limited step in the right direction, they were sharply critical of the voluntary nature of the administration proposal. "It's essentially milquetoast; it lacks political will," said Jim O'Dea, Amnesty International's Washington director. "It's designed to be as inoffensive as possible and the people most offended are those who are active in the field," a labor rights activist told the *Washington Post*.[56]

Indeed, when it came to the rights of workers to self-organization, the Clinton code was deliberately vague, on the grounds that China and other authoritarian nations would see such activity as an effort to undermine national laws governing labor relations. This was the view of the increasingly powerful US-China Business Council. In China the monopoly on worker representation was jealously guarded by officials of the All-China Federation of Trade Unions, a body that was integral to both party and state. "We're back to the same problem again," said Tony Lake, the national security adviser. "This time we're juggling the interests of the business community and human rights, and discovering that it's an impossible balancing act."[57]

Clinton's Model Business Principles never went anywhere, but after the El Monte and Kathie Lee Gifford revelations, Robert Reich put forward a much more sophisticated corporate code. The Apparel Industry Partnership Agreement, which Clinton announced in the summer of 1996 at a White House meeting with businesses, trade unions, and human rights organizations, sought to ameliorate sweatshop conditions both in the United States and abroad. Attenuated supply chains were the heart of the problem: few US brands or retailers were willing to take responsibility for working conditions among the contractors and subcontractors that produced the shirts, dresses, pants, and other apparel items that flooded US stores. Reaching back to the Progressive-era advocacy of Florence Kelley's National Consumers League, Reich wanted to create an AIP label that cooperating brands would sew onto their garments so as to make consumers aware that they were buying products produced by workers earning a living wage in a safe workplace. Reich also acceded to the demands of the anti-sweatshop activists who wanted to hold retailers and top-of-the-supply-chain manufacturers legally responsible for the labor practices of their subcontractors.

But the National Economic Council turned down Reich and the nongovernmental organizations (NGOs) backing him. Except for the Labor Secretary, every top figure on Clinton's economic team thought such a regulatory initiative would generate opposition from the garment industry and require new legislation, which was pretty much an impossibility. Moreover, Tyson, Barshefsky, and other NEC principals worried that such an enforcement mechanism might well violate WTO fair trade rules because exporting nations would label any effort to hold retailers and manufacturers responsible for their subcontractors' labor policies a barrier to free trade.[58] After Reich left the Labor Department, Gene Sperling, now NEC director, tried hard to prod AIP companies to participate in the Fair Labor Association (FLA), a more formal and permanent organization that would write and monitor a corporate code of conduct for the apparel industry. But this was not the New Deal era, when tripartite corporatism so often provided the governmental mechanism to resolve labor issues in steel and coal or on the railroads. In the 1990s the unions were too weak, employers too jealous of their prerogatives, and the government irresolute. The Union of Needletrades, Industrial and Textile Employees (UNITE), the US garment and textile union, soon quit the FLA, protesting that it provided but "the illusion of public oversight."[59] Whether under FLA auspicious or not, most international brands and retailers did put in place a seemingly elaborate social responsibility code, but observers from virtually every NGO and worker rights organization, as well as the eighty-year-old International Labor Organization (ILO), found them to be little more than public relations exercises to keep at bay the naming and shaming tactics deployed by the anti-sweatshop movement.[60]

The Fast-Track Debacle

If the administration's sweatshop initiative won it few plaudits, the fate of a 1997 "fast-track" trade bill demonstrated just how fragile was the political support for Clinton's brand of economic globalism. First passed in 1974, fast-track legislation was utterly uncontroversial until the end of the Cold War. It gave a president the authority to negotiate trade deals that Congress could approve or reject but not amend, thereby forestalling multiple negotiating rounds. In 1991 and 1993 fast-track authority was renewed, but the NAFTA fight in the fall of 1993 made it radioactive, turning the issue into a referendum on the impact of foreign trade on the United States. Clinton therefore let fast-track expire at the end of 1994, but his trade advisers soon pressed for a renewal if the administration were to negotiate a new set of Latin American trade agreements as well as a comprehensive deal with China, a prerequisite for that nation's long-sought admission to the World Trade Organization. Fast-track authority seemed vital because trade negotiators from other countries wanted assurances that Congress would not reopen whatever deals they could strike with the Americans. The measure enjoyed majority support within the GOP congressional delegation, on virtually every major editorial page, and among economists of nearly every political or methodological persuasion.

But the NAFTA legacy and the nasty squabble over the linkage between Chinese trade and human rights shadowed the fast-track debate. Labor and the Democrats were determined to deny it to Clinton if labor standards were not made an integral part of any new trade pacts. "Side agreements" would not be enough. Meanwhile, the collapse of the Mexican peso in 1995 ruined the administration's chance to make a clear-cut case that NAFTA benefited the United States. By making imports from Mexico dramatically cheaper than before, the peso crisis turned a small American trade surplus in 1993 into a $16 billion deficit in 1996. NAFTA critics argued that 420,000 US jobs were lost. US Trade Representative Barshefsky and others in the administration disputed those figures, but whatever the true statistics, public opinion was turning against any more trade deals.[61] The Clinton boom had slashed unemployment, so "a giant sucking sound" was not the main problem; instead, trade deals with low-wage countries offered employers "a tool" with which to threaten their employees, argued the AFL-CIO's Thea Lee. "To frighten them. To cow them. And this is the contradiction that people who live in Washington, who sell free trade for a living, don't understand. Managers across the country are beating workers over the head with the threat of globalization." The only way to forestall this kind of managerial leverage was to win "the same kind of binding dispute settlement for our concerns that business gets for things like intellectual property rights and investment rules."[62]

It was not just the Democratic left that was skeptical about increasing globalization. While most Republicans favored presidential fast-track authority, both Pat Buchanan and Ross Perot stoked anti-NAFTA sentiment on the right, often among working-class Democrats and disaffected Republicans. During the 1996 presidential primaries in Ohio, Buchanan had campaigned not in the traditionally Republican southwestern part of the state but in the industrial northeast, home to Akron, Cleveland, and Youngstown, where Perot did so well in 1992 and would again in 1996. Meanwhile, in California an increasingly right-wing Republican Party celebrated American "sovereignty," a code word that encompassed both hostility toward Mexican immigration and rejection of American participation in the World Trade Organization.[63]

As with NAFTA, Richard Gephardt served as a spokesman for those hostile to more trade deals. It was no secret that he hoped to be Al Gore's left-wing rival for the Democratic presidential candidacy three years hence. So Gephardt came out early and strong against fast-track authority, insisting that in all future trade pacts labor protections had to be made "equal in stature and force and linked to provisions on investment and trade."[64] Equally important—and radical, at least from the perspective of the US Treasury Department—was Gephardt's proposal that "capital flight and currency stability" be linked to future trade negotiations.[65] With Clinton, Gephardt was a featured speaker at a September 1997 AFL-CIO convention in Pittsburgh. The president got a cool reception, but when the House minority leader took to the podium nine hundred cheering delegates leapt to their feet. "If intellectual property and capital deserve protections in the core free-trade treaties, with trade sanctions to enforce it, so do labor laws and environmental laws, on an equal basis," declared Gephardt.[66]

The Clinton administration countered with a tepid, Republican-approved endorsement of labor and environmental protections, but only if "directly related to trade," whatever that meant. Clinton's own view—which was actually much closer to the AFL-CIO's and Gephardt's than the White House publicly acknowledged—was subordinated to a new reality: without substantial GOP support, fast-track would fail, thus limiting any presidential deviation from trade regime orthodoxy. To pass, House Speaker Newt Gingrich needed 150 Republicans in support and the White House wanted at least 70 Democrats. The administration tried to put on the same kind of lobby effort it had put into NAFTA. Corporate America was certainly on board, not to mention those who identified as New Democrats. But with many congressional Democrats resenting Clinton's effort to triangulate with Gingrich, on budget issues as well as trade, the votes were still not there.[67]

Shortly before midnight on November 9, 1997, Gingrich called Clinton to tell him the bad news. The Republicans could not muster enough votes to compensate for the crater into which Democratic support had fallen. So at 1:15 AM Clinton called back to ask the GOP leader to cancel the vote, which was scheduled for the next morning. The fast-track debacle generated few headlines, but Clinton's capitulation nevertheless constituted the first legislative rejection of an important free trade measure since Franklin Roosevelt and Secretary of State Cordell Hull had signed reciprocal trade agreements in 1934. And the opposition of four out of five House Democrats constituted the most divisive blow faced by Bill Clinton since Republicans had killed his health care plan three years before.[68] From this debacle Clinton took away some willingness to accommodate those who wanted labor and environmental concerns made integral to the deals his White House did negotiate. But in the remaining years of his administration Clinton's diminished, scandal-plagued stature, combined with continuing GOP control of Congress, made him but one player of many when China's admission to the WTO became a pressing issue.

A Trade Deal with China

The fast-track defeat, a concurrent financial crisis in East Asia, and chronic tensions over Taiwan delayed a final trade deal with China. But when Zhu Rongji, now the Chinese prime minister, visited Washington in early April 1999, the Chinese leadership had finally decided that they were willing to make important concessions in return for the WTO membership they saw as recognition of China's leading place in the world economic and political order. This would take place in two stages: First the Chinese and the Americans would reach agreement on an updated and permanent MFN agreement, now called permanent normal trade relations (PNTR). Then the Chinese would use the PNTR template to reach similar trade deals with the Europeans and other major players, a prerequisite to formal admission to the WTO. The Chinese saw WTO membership, which they had sought for over a decade, as a guarantee that their trading and financial relationship to the rest of the world would no longer be disturbed by the ebb and flow of domestic politics in the United States or the European Union.

US-China relations had been rocky during the previous five years. China had made no concessions on human rights, remained belligerent about any "recognition" that the United States might offer Taiwan, and was acquiring a military capability that sometimes entailed the theft of sensitive high-technology products from American companies. In the United States the usual contentiousness of the annual debate over reapproval of China's MFN status had been exacerbated during the 1996 election season by GOP charges that Clinton had accepted illegal campaign contributions from wealthy Chinese investors. But the stars seemed to align for a deal in the spring of 1999. Chinese president Jiang Zemin had visited the United States in 1997; The Clintons and a huge US delegation returned the favor in June 1998 with a nine-day state visit, the first presidential trip since Tiananmen Square. Although Barshefsky and her USTR team were unable to finalize a trade deal then, the visit generated headlines when, at a press conference with the Chinese president, Clinton took advantage of massive media attention to offer millions of Chinese an example of American-style political give-and-take, including a forthright call for the Chinese leadership to ensure religious liberty and human rights for its citizens.[69]

By April 1999 all seemed set. Everyone in the Clinton administration agreed that human rights would not be "the driving issue" that structured the entire relationship. "If the Chinese were carrying out massacres or some such, that would be a different story," argued the National Security Council China expert Kenneth Lieberthal. "But arresting a small number of the most active dissidents is not in the atrocity category."[70] Meanwhile, Zhu Rongji came to the United States with an agreement virtually in hand. It included a long series of outright concessions: lower tariffs and quotas on manufactured goods, of course, but also a set of guidelines that allowed much greater latitude for US financial institutions. Barshefsky was amazed and delighted at the Chinese accommodation, and both Secretary of State Madeleine Albright and the new NSC head, Samuel "Sandy" Berger, were for a quick signature. Their argument was that Premier Zhu was an economic "reformer," so any rejection of his efforts would undermine a cooperative negotiating partner and set back US efforts to open the Chinese economy to Western influence and ideas. That was a viewpoint hardly foreign to Bill Clinton, Gene Sperling, and others on the National Economic Council.[71]

But Clinton's economic team, including Rubin, Summers, and Sperling, now chair of the NEC, backed away. They thought, correctly, that congressional Democrats were still in a surly mood when it came to trade with China. Taking an agreement with Zhu to the Hill "could be as divisive w/in party & as consequential for rest of agenda as NAFTA," read one memo summarizing the White House discussions.[72] On the right, Republicans protested that if the Chinese were actually stealing nuclear secrets from Los Alamos—a Chinese weapons scientist had been arrested in March 1999—China's entry into the WTO "should be out of the question."[73]

Rubin's willingness to forgo the trade deal carried the most weight. By 1999 the unilateral tariff reductions that China offered, extensive as they might be, were no longer of particular appeal. The United States was not about to export any large basket of consumer products to China, and the exports it did make were intermediate goods destined for reassembly or reprocessing and then shipment right back across the Pacific and onto the shelves of American big-box stores. Textile exports from China remained a sensitive issue, as did the Chinese propensity to dump, at below cost, steel products and other manufactured goods. Barshefsky would finesse such traditional trade issues. But far more important were the investment opportunities opened up by any PNTR deal with China. "The key issue for us is not the [trade] deficit number, but the lack of access our companies have in China," wrote a Treasury official.[74] An economist with Morgan Stanley Dean Witter agreed: "The deal is about investment, not exports." US foreign investment would be the primary means by which American companies delivered "goods" to China. Few US jobs would be created by enabling Citigroup to take Chinese deposits or AIG to sell life insurance, but the creation of such a financial infrastructure would nevertheless supercharge the Chinese export machine. Said Thea Lee of the AFL-CIO: "Is it easier to have a factory in China producing toys or consumer electronics for the US market if you can also do your banking there, if you have more assurances that your investment there will be respected?"[75]

But one thing was missing. The Chinese steadfastly refused to make concessions on the unfettered ability of Wall Street investment firms to create and market Chinese securities. Almost immediately those firms told Rubin and Sperling they could not support the agreement if that market was closed to them. "We need to find some way of enabling foreign securities firms to engage in the domestic market without jeopardizing China's ability to determine its degree of openness to global capital markets," wrote Sperling.[76] Rubin wanted Wall Street to get almost immediate access to China's capital markets, if only to get the jump on European financial competitors.[77] But this was a politically sensitive issue. China's three hundred thousand state-owned enterprises, which still accounted for one-third of its GDP and employed upwards of seventy million, had been a centerpiece of Maoist industrialization. The SOEs were losing money, and the Chinese banks that bailed them out were in desperate shape, with more than 40 percent of all loans "nonperforming." Moreover, complying with WTO principles would require that China eliminate most subsidies to the SOEs. Indeed, the massive layoffs that began at the end of the 1990s would displace more than forty million workers, shred social welfare for even more, and generate widespread discontent.[78]

Wall Street saw the recapitalization of the SOEs as a huge potential securities market. And the reformers among the Chinese leadership also wanted the SOEs to downsize, consolidate, and secure Western funds. To a degree, therefore, Rubin and Zhu saw the SOE problem in the same way: without a recapitalization of these enterprises, a huge sector of the Chinese economy would remain inherently noncompetitive, China's banks would remain dysfunctional, and another East Asian financial crisis might well occur, but this time one creating instability within the world's third-largest economy. The problem was that Zhu and the other Chinese "reformers" did not have a free hand. The so-called conservatives in the Chinese government, many of whom had risen to power by climbing through the SOE ranks, understood all too well the social costs and political dangers inherent in the radical downsizing of this sector, where bankruptcies and cash shortfalls often made wage payments problematic.[79]

It would therefore take a separate trade negotiation for Wall Street to finally begin marketing the SOE initial public offerings in the West. The White House PNTR team thought that such investments would effectively marginalize "the entrenched state-owned manufacturing sector and those Communist officials clinging desperately to one-party control over how people work and live." The old heavy industries were "bulwarks of political conservatism and socialist economics." Once China slashed its tariffs to get into the WTO, these enterprises "will go belly-up. The government's ability to control workers and to purchase their loyalty will diminish," argued Sperling and Berger.[80]

Once again, this was wishful thinking. Although Western investors owned much stock, these firms remained firmly in the hands of the Chinese *nomenklatura*—indeed, even more so than when they were regionally based SOEs. As Carl Walter and Fraser Howie, the China-based authors of *Red Capitalism*, put it: "The investment banks put their reputations on the line by sponsoring these companies in the global capital markets, introducing them to money managers, pension funds, and a myriad of other institutional investors . . . Their professional expertise and skills put Beijing and the Communist Party of China in the driver's seat for a strategic piece of the Chinese economy for the first time ever."[81] The "reformers" were winning in China, but that hardly constituted a victory for economic pluralism, never mind political democracy.

It would take more than a year to reach a final PNTR deal with the Chinese. Within days after Rubin persuaded Clinton not to sign, the president had second thoughts. But the Chinese were not anxious to return to the bargaining table, especially after Zhu's opponents got wind of some of the concessions his negotiating team had offered Barshefsky. Then in May, during the US military effort against Serbia, a cruise missile smashed into the Chinese embassy in Belgrade. It was a mistake and the United States apologized, but the Chinese remained furious well into the summer. Although the attack strengthened the hand of "conservatives" in the Chinese leadership, who were already skeptical about the social discontent that privatization of the SOEs would generate, Zhu regained the upper hand by the fall. Barshefsky therefore flew to Beijing in November, accompanied by NEC chair Gene Sperling, whom the Chinese correctly saw as a commissar-like figure who would ensure that any deal struck in Beijing also stuck in Washington.[82]

Although these trade negotiations were hardly routine—indeed, at one discouraging point Barshefsky and Sperling had their bags packed and sent to the airport—the US negotiating team returned home triumphant, with the 250-page agreement in hand. Short on diplomatic language, the deal looked like a spreadsheet that listed the tariff and quota restrictions slashed by the Chinese. There were new safeguards against Chinese "dumping" and export surges that had been demanded by both labor and management in the steel industry, while textile producers won up to a decade of forbearance before US quotas on Chinese imports expired entirely. Bill Clinton later called the agreement a "one-way street."[83]

Despite all the tariff concessions made by the Chinese, the actual capacity of US firms to export physical goods to China was, except for agricultural products, construction machinery, and airplanes, largely a mirage. For example, the Chinese agreed to end import quotas and reduce tariffs on US automobiles from a prohibitive 80 percent to just 25 percent by 2006. US auto exports did rise to above two hundred thousand a year, but that was inconsequential in a Chinese market that would soon build and sell more than twenty million cars each year. Instead of exporting to China, General Motors built its own joint-venture assembly plants near Shanghai, established its own training facilities for a new generation of Chinese engineers, and contracted with local firms for most auto parts.[84] Within a decade China became an automobile production power in the same league with Japan, Germany, and the United States. China never exported many cars—the home market was gigantic enough—but virtually all other tradable goods crossing the Pacific were coming out of export-oriented Chinese factories tightly integrated into the supply chains that flooded American big-box stores with every variety of consumer durable, from washing machines and patio furniture to kitchen appliances and auto parts.

Moreover, permanent normal trade relations with the United States deprived Congress of its warrant to debate each year the degree to which China met American human rights or fair trade standards. Such issues would be handled by the WTO, to which China's admission was now virtually assured. Thus the United States would forsake its oft-invoked right to retaliate unilaterally against unfair Chinese trading practices. In the future, disgruntled Americans would have to seek redress from the WTO. To the press corps, Barshefsky justified this highly unpopular aspect of the deal by returning to themes the Clintonites had been pushing since delinkage in 1994. "Consider the broader picture," she said. China was being moved "in the direction of a rule of law" involving "basic obligations such as transparency, judicial review, the publication of all regulations, the notion that China will be held accountable to the contracts that it makes. These are extraordinarily important principles, which go well beyond the commercial."[85]

Congress finally got around to the PNTR agreement in the spring of 2000, when the debate proved a replay of all the other trade fights during the 1990s. But unlike fast-track authority, which had an ideologically abstract quality about it, the costs of rejecting the China deal were concrete and measurable. US business interests were therefore much more engaged, especially AIG, the big insurer, and Boeing, which would export much more product to mainland China. Wall Street was on the mark as well, with Goldman Sachs soon constructing IPOs for Petro-China, Ping An Insurance, and Bank of China; Morgan Stanley financing China Unicom (a telecommunications company), Aluminum Corporation of China, and China Construction Bank; and Merrill Lynch underwriting new stock for China National Offshore Oil, China Telecom, Air China, and the bank ICBC, whose IPO was a huge $21.9 billion.[86]

Because PNTR deprived Democrats of the yearly vote that gave them even a bit of leverage, they looked for a substitute mechanism that might influence trade relations with China. What they found was not much: a well-staffed, liberal-tilting US-China Economic and Security Review Commission, whose purpose was to keep in the public eye the costs and character of the China trade. Although Richard Gephardt once again led the Democratic faction hostile to any new trade agreement that lacked labor and environmental protections, the impulse to unite behind Vice President Al Gore's presidential candidacy made liberal trade skeptics reluctant to make the PNTR vote as divisive as that over NAFTA or fast-track. It wasn't, even though only 73 out of 211 House Democrats, just 35 percent, voted for PNTR when the agreement came to the floor in May 2000. Six and a half years earlier NAFTA had garnered 40 percent of the Democratic members. In September 2000 the Senate easily passed PNTR, but it would take another fifteen months for China to make its formal entrance into the WTO. China had to reach other trade agreements with the Europeans, Japan, Brazil, and a host of lesser economic powers, and of course the events of September 11, 2001, halted virtually all normal diplomatic interchange for several weeks. But later that year, on December 11, China became the 143rd member of the WTO, culminating a fifteen-year accession effort.[87]

The Battle of Seattle

Few noticed or celebrated because by then "the Battle of Seattle" had marked a transformative moment in the history of economic globalism. The November 1999 street protests against the WTO did nothing to stop the explosion of transpacific trade that coincided with China's WTO membership, nor were the labor and environmental protesters able to retard the wave of industrial job losses that swept America's old industrial districts. But Seattle, along with the large Democratic votes against NAFTA, fast-track, and PNTR, revealed for all the enormous dichotomy that Bill Clinton had created between the core of the Democratic electorate and the global trading regime his administration sought to construct. Over time this ideological and policy gap generated a class dealignment that opened the door to the right-wing populism that became manifest well before the appearance of Donald Trump on the national scene.

The first meeting of the WTO had been held in authoritarian Singapore. Bill Clinton's eagerness to host the second "millennium" round in liberal, environmentally attuned Seattle would showcase American commitment to an orderly and progressive globalism, but the meeting was also sure to spark a large set of marches, protests, and demonstrations. By the end of the 1990s the rise of an anti-sweatshop movement, the proliferation of organizations attentive to global environmental issues, the new leftward tilt of American labor, and the conflicts over NAFTA, China, and other trade deals had created a network of sophisticated and militant activists who saw the WTO as little more than a capitalist cabal that would put in place a trade regime antithetical to the moral sentiments and material interests of a majority of the nation's working population.[88]

A conflict over the protection of sea turtles seemed to encapsulate WTO overreach. When it became clear in the 1980s that hundreds of thousands of turtles were drowning in shrimp nets, a bevy of environmental groups prodded the Congress, and later the Clinton administration, to make an exclusion device—a sort of turtle escape hatch— mandatory on the nets used by most American shrimp trawlers. Foreign boats that sought to sell shrimp in the US market had to protect the turtles as well. But in 1996 Malaysia, Pakistan, and Thailand filed a complaint to the WTO claiming this was an unfair trade practice; two years later a WTO panel ruled that requiring these countries to use turtle conservation measures was arbitrary and unjustifiable discrimination.

FIGURE 14. Unionists joined environmentalists to protest a meeting of the
World Trade Organization in Seattle late in 1999. (David Bacon)

The United States would have no say over how the shrimp sold within its borders was caught. The case seemed exotic but had broad implications: if it was illegitimate for the WTO to inquire as to the "process" by which a good or service was created, then questions of environmental impact or labor standards might well be off limits as well. US laws that sought to govern the health, safety, and labor conditions under which imported products were produced—laws banning child or prison labor, for example, or requiring freedom of assembly—might well be in violation of WTO fair trade rules.[89]

Such was the social and ideological context that made it possible for a loose-knit group of activists to assemble tens of thousands in the streets of Seattle for the WTO meeting. The men and women there ranged from black bloc anarchists who smashed Starbucks windows and clashed with police to a far larger group of young environmentalists and an even larger cohort of trade unionists from both the Pacific Northwest and across the nation. Seeking to avoid violence and mass arrests, the Seattle mayor and his police force did too little to prevent the demonstrators from turning the area around the downtown convention center into a chaotic and sometimes dangerous no-go zone for WTO delegates. The Clinton administration sent a large delegation to the talks, but on the morning of November 30, the first day of the meeting, the US Secret Service kept Sperling, Barshefsky, Albright, Commerce Secretary William Daley, Agriculture Secretary Dan Glickman, and other officials confined to a downtown hotel. It would take several hours and a set of armored cars to drive them a few blocks to the back entrance of the Seattle conference center, where they finally greeted more than a thousand WTO delegates representing 135 countries.[90] Demonstrations and altercations continued for the rest of the week, but the WTO managed to hold scheduled sessions, now protected by a large police mobilization and two battalions of the Army National Guard.

The columnist Thomas Friedman denounced the protesters as "a Noah's ark of flat-earth advocates, protectionist trade unions and yuppies looking for their 1960's fix."[91] President Clinton, however, had hoped that the biannual WTO meeting in Seattle might provide the occasion for an amelioration of the tensions that had been growing with organized labor and a sprawling NGO community determined to eradicate sweatshops, protect endangered species, and defend the global environment. "Putting a Human Face on the Global Economy" was the label Clinton operatives attached to the administration's agenda for the Seattle WTO meeting. Privately, Clinton was even more emphatic. The year before he had told speechwriter Michael Waldman, "We did not create the WTO so that it could impose the economic theories of Milton Friedman on the rest of the world."[92] There were trade disputes, of course, and Barshefsky sought to put them at the center of the WTO's "Millennium Round": elimination of export subsidies in agriculture, more tariff cuts, encouragement of e-commerce, and a safeguard against import surges. But the Seattle meeting was also designed to bring a set of heretofore neglected voices into WTO debates. The day before the official start was set aside as "NGO Day," during which environmental and labor groups would have their say. In this context, the United States advanced an effort to put an ILO ban on child labor into WTO trade rules, and in a far more controversial gambit the United States proposed that the WTO create a working group to link higher labor standards with greater trade. Referencing Progressive-era and New Deal reforms, the USTR called for initial steps to "put a human face on the new, global information economy—to encourage a process parallel to our own national experience in the governance of the international economy."[93] Barshefsky herself thought the WTO exclusion of labor issues "intellectually indefensible, and it will over time weaken public support for the trading system."[94]

The AFL-CIO was encouraged. Indeed, early in 1999 Clinton appointed John Sweeney as one of three labor representatives on the Advisory Committee for Trade Policy and Negotiations, which had always been dominated by business leaders and lobbyists. In October 1999 Sweeney signed a committee letter backing Clinton's WTO agenda in exchange for the administration's commitment to promote the new WTO working group on labor rights. When he got to Seattle, Clinton told a union audience that for decades trade decisions had been "the private province of CEOs, trade ministers and the politicians who supported them."[95] That had to change if the WTO's rule-based system was to have any legitimacy. As tens of thousands of protesters created grid-lock and chaos in downtown Seattle, Clinton offered a sympathetic ear. Just before arriving in the city, he gave an interview to Seattle's *Post-Intelligencer* designed to mollify the WTO critics. Their presence in the streets was "healthy," said Clinton, later informing WTO delegates, "What they are telling us in the streets is that this is an issue we've been silent on."[96] For the first time, the president embraced one of labor's more advanced demands—that the WTO working group proposed by the United States should develop a set of core labor standards that would be part of every trade pact. "Ultimately I would favor a system in which sanctions would come for violating any provision of a trade agreement," he told the *Post-Intelligencer's* Michael Paulson.[97]

The interview became a sensation. "Nobody believed their eyes" when they read it, said Anabel Gonzalez, Costa Rica's vice minister of foreign trade.[98] If the United States pressed Clinton's idea, "we will explode the meeting," declared the Pakistani trade minister.[99] Barshefsky, who was trying to put together a "benign" labor text with several developing nations, told Clinton, "I'm not too thrilled with the newspaper today." In any event, Clinton's vision was not going anywhere. Leaders of developing nations, especially those from Egypt, Brazil, Malaysia, Indonesia, Pakistan, and India, saw any linkage between trade and labor standards as merely another form of rich-country protectionism, a payoff to homeland unions. "They literally hated the labor issue," remembered Barshefsky.[100] "It is past time for the police to round all of them up," a Malaysian delegate told a reporter from the *Wall Street Journal*, referencing the protesters. "These people should not be allowed to demonstrate."[101] Within days editors at *The Economist* would put a picture of an impoverished child on its cover under the heading "The Real Losers from Seattle."[102]

But Clinton could not satisfy American labor either. AFL-CIO president John Sweeney had stuck his neck out when he joined thirty-four business executives in signing the Advisory Committee letter. This did not go down well with industrial unions like the United Steelworkers and the United Auto Workers, whose leaders thought the formation of a WTO "working group" on labor standards was hardly enough to protect US manufacturing from the import surges and outright dumping sure to come from the Far East. Sweeney was outraged when Clinton signed on to the China PNTR deal that Barshefsky and Sperling had brought home in mid-November. There was nothing there on human rights or labor standards and no prospect that China would ever concede an inch. "It is disgustingly hypocritical of the Clinton Administration to pledge to put a human face on the global economy," said Sweeney in a scalding rejoinder, "while prostrating itself in pursuit of a trade deal with a rogue nation."[103] A couple of weeks later labor played a big role in orchestrating the Seattle demonstrations. The historically left-wing International Longshore and Warehouse Union called a one-day general strike, and the AFL-CIO sponsored a rally of twenty thousand where hard hats and environmentalists mingled in happy accord. "Teamsters and Turtles: Together at Last" proved a slogan that echoed widely.

Consequences

The Seattle WTO collapsed on multiple fronts. "We didn't need any help from protesters to fail," said Michael Moore, the New Zealand director general of the WTO. "We did it on our own."[104] The key WTO players—the European Union, Japan, the United States, and Canada—often plotted strategy in advance for big trade meetings, but they had been unable to reach any agreement that might resolve the always vexing issue of agricultural export subsidies, which American agribusiness wanted to slash. Meanwhile, developing nations wanted the United States to abolish its antidumping laws and accelerate the elimination of quotas on apparel imports, which the United States opposed in order to assuage the still-powerful players in Southern textiles and the Rust Belt steel industry. And of course, the United States made no progress on its "globalization with a human face" agenda. Thus, China would enter the new body largely unconstrained by any set of trade rules that might have tampered with either its export drive or its suppression of labor rights at home. The Seattle WTO delegates ended their acrimonious conclave without even a diplomatically worded final statement

FIGURE 15. On October 10, 2000, President Clinton signed the law granting
China permanent normal trade relations with the United States. Standing
behind him are Secretary of State Madeline Albright, Treasury Secretary Larry
Summers, US Trade Representative Charlene Barshefsky, National Economic
Council director Gene Sperling, and Speaker of the House Dennis Hastert.
(Clinton Presidential Library)

pledging some sort of cooperative negotiations in the new century. Indeed, the effectiveness of the WTO as a trade dispute mechanism faded
in the years following Seattle, and the organization never lived up to its
reputation as a capitalist cabal running roughshod over national interests, labor rights, and environmental protections. From this point on
"globalization" was a term that could not escape the pejorative connotations firmly affixed by those who had filled Seattle's streets with their
animated and creative voices.

But as a trade phenomenon, globalization proceeded apace, even as
its social and economic impact on US manufacturing subverted the rosy
expectations of Clinton administration officials. US manufacturing employment had fluctuated around eighteen million workers between 1965
and 2000 before plunging nearly 20 percent from March 2001 to

March 2007. Of the three and a half million jobs lost, at least half were a result of the import from China of products once made in the United States. At the time many economists and trade advocates questioned the degree to which the disappearance of all these jobs resulted from the opening to China, but today the verdict is in: China's accession to the WTO generated a "China Shock," as one team of economists entitled an academic paper. Another analyzed "The Surprisingly Swift Decline of US Manufacturing Employment."[105]

Aside from cheap labor, low tariffs, and a good manufacturing infrastructure, China had now achieved one absolutely essential element of export power: a decisive end to the uncertainty that had plagued the nation's trading regime during the previous decade. Between 1990 and 2001 Congress had each year debated China's MFN status, with opponents averaging 38 percent of all members in the House. But once Congress finally passed PNTR in the fall of 2000, the political anxiety that had bedeviled US firms seeking to construct integrated supply chains based in China was over. And when China joined the WTO it was required to phase out governmental requirements that had obligated many private Chinese companies to export through state intermediaries, thus greatly enhancing efficiency and flexibility. Within months more than eighty corporations announced their intention to shift production to China.[106]

Wal-Mart, America's largest retailer, was in the vanguard. In 2002 it moved its world purchasing headquarters to Shenzhen, where hundreds of Chinese-speaking supply chain experts put the company's US "vendors" in touch with mainland contract manufacturers ready to make and ship their branded products back to the firm's giant set of distribution centers in California, Texas, and the Carolinas. Wal-Mart, Home Depot, and other US retailers told scores of small and medium-sized US manufacturers that if they could not meet "the China Price"—a phrase Business Week called the "three scariest words in US industry"—they could either close up shop or transfer production to the mainland.[107] By 2006 Wal-Mart alone was responsible for $27 billion in US imports from China, up from $9.5 billion in 2001, accounting for 11 percent of the growth of the entire US trade deficit with that country. By then 80 percent of the six thousand foreign factories in Wal-Mart's supplier database were located in China. The company claimed, correctly, that it saved millions of shoppers upwards of $3,000 per family, a function not only of its cheap imports but also of the low wages it paid its US workers and the efficiencies it generated throughout its logistics system. Still, Wal-Mart alone was almost certainly responsible for the elimination of nearly two hundred thousand US manufacturing jobs in this period.[108]

China's share of global manufacturing output soon surpassed that of both the United States and the European Union. Its trade surplus exploded, rising from just $25 billion before it joined the WTO to more than $300 billion eight years later. The principal "beneficiary" was none other than the United States. To prevent China's enormous export earnings from fanning domestic inflation, the People's Bank had to mop up the foreign earnings of its exporters, and it bought more than $1 trillion of US Treasury bonds. This created a financial codependency between the United States and China and put downward pressure on US interest rates, fueling both stock market exuberance and a debt-heavy housing bubble. The road to the financial collapse of 2008 was paved in good part by China's admission to the WTO.[109]

12

The Committee to Save the World

In February 1999, at the start of the same year that would end with the Seattle debacle, *Time* magazine put Alan Greenspan, Robert Rubin, and Larry Summers on its cover over a caption that read "The Committee to Save the World." Written by Joshua Cooper Ramo, a prolific thirty-year-old staffer who would later join the Beijing office of Kissinger Associates, this infamous article encapsulated the power and hubris of an economic high command during a season in which US unemployment was reaching new lows and the stock market new highs, the federal budget was in surplus, and American global influence was at its height. Ramo called Greenspan, Rubin, and Summers, who had lunched together almost every week over the past four years, a kind of "free market Politburo" whose "faith is in the markets and their own ability to analyze them." They had "outgrown ideology," he asserted, even as "they all agree that trying to defy global market forces is in the end futile." Bill Clinton relied on these "Three Marketeers," as *Time* headlined them, "to a level that drives other Cabinet members nuts."[1]

The *Time* cover story was occasioned by the seemingly successful end of a financial crisis that had engulfed much of East Asia and then spread to Russia, Brazil, and, to a degree, even Wall Street. This "contagion," as it was often called, had its origins in the pervasiveness of the global financial market touted by Greenspan, Rubin, Summers, and so many others, on Wall Street and off. While trade with East Asia was booming, the circulation of financial assets and instruments was growing more rapidly still. Between 1987 and 1997 half a trillion dollars flowed into these "emerging markets" from international investors. The money seemed a godsend, as the once-impoverished nations of East Asia became integrated into a transnational financial system that was liquid, massive, and highly remunerative for both Western investment banks and the urban, cosmopolitan strata abroad who developed the real estate, ran the export factories, imported European luxury goods, and traded their local currency for dollars and yen. But this world of neoliberal finance would prove inherently unstable and elicit second thoughts even within the Clinton circle.

The very phrase "emerging markets" signified a transformation in how Western ministers and managers had come to think about the global South. The term was first coined in 1981 when a former World Bank official planned to start a "Third World Equity Fund." But that descriptor didn't work. The phrase "Third World" had Cold War, not to mention anticapitalist, connotations. Equally important, "emerging markets" was a better Reagan-era substitute for the older phrase "developing countries," an indication of the degree to which state-directed economic uplift was being eclipsed by a much heavier wager on market forces to do the same thing. And of course, the phrase "emerging markets" reflected the perspective of a bank or investor, most likely from Europe, North America, or Japan, searching for a venue where the profits and interest they earned could be repatriated with the tap of a keystroke.[2]

Moving at the speed of light through a globe-spanning set of fiber-optic cables, private capital flows to these emerging markets had increased more than six times from 1982 to 1994. And in the next few years these monetary currents would swell as Western and Japanese investors searched for bonds and other financial instruments that might earn double or triple the returns found in New York, London, or Tokyo. This global movement of capital was supercharged by the relatively low rates that prevailed in the United States, thanks to Greenspan's guidance at the Fed, and even more so because of the near-zero rates prevailing in Japan as the finance ministry there sought to gin up a stagnant economy. The United States sent nearly $1.3 trillion in private capital to developing countries in the 1990s compared to $170 billion in the previous decade. It was a measure of how far global capitalism had evolved that these private flows of capital now dwarfed the bilateral and multilateral state loans that had provided most of the money developing countries had invested in earlier decades. Banks and brokerages borrowed yen or dollars at relatively low rates and parked those funds in the high-return emerging markets. Called the "carry trade," most of these funds were "hot" money, endlessly seeking out the best return and turning skittish on any news of an unexpected risk; it was money as easily yanked out of an emerging market as it had once flooded in.[3] Such liquidity and mobility made Wall Street a truly global institution, but also one in which financial instability among low- and middle-income nations was necessarily endemic.

Mexico in early 1995 was the first big crisis and the one that set the template for the Clinton administration's response when two years later the Asian contagion threatened to plunge half a dozen economies into default and disarray. Following the contentious NAFTA debate in late 1993, Mexico had slashed public expenditures and pegged the peso to the dollar, thereby guaranteeing to foreign investors that it would not replicate the peso devaluation of a decade before, when foreign investments lost much value and the real buying power of millions of Mexican wage earners plunged disastrously. To maintain a high peso value, the Mexican finance ministry issued billions of dollar-denominated bonds—*tesobonos*—and from the proceeds they bought pesos, thereby sustaining the dollar-peso "peg." For the moment, Mexican consumers found that US imports were cheap, and to the Clintonites' delight that generated a US trade surplus with Mexico in 1994. Foreign capital poured into the country, much of it lured by those high *tesobono* interest rates.

But all this came crashing down by the end of 1994. After NAFTA's passage Mexico enjoyed no manufacturing boom because low-wage producers in East Asia proved formidable competitors. Millions of farmers were impoverished by the flood of US agricultural products now undercutting peasant agriculture. Some migrated to the United States, and others became radicalized; some of the latter joined an insurrection that had already begun in Chiapas. When Luis Donaldo Colosio, the presidential candidate of the ruling party, was assassinated in March 1994, Mexico seemed an increasingly risky venue for foreign capital. Indeed, Alan Greenspan's decision to double the Fed interest benchmark that same year (Hurricane Greenspan) slashed the relative premium that Wall Street bankers had enjoyed from their Mexican investments. In a pattern that would be repeated in the Asian crisis two years later, foreign bankers feared that unless they pulled their money out fast, they would be left holding a radically devalued investment. Capital flows therefore abruptly reversed during the summer of 1994. Despite a rapid increase in the interest rate that Mexico was willing to pay on *tesobonos*, the country faced a sharp recession and a currency devaluation, which came on December 20, 1994. Default—an "economic apocalypse" Summers called it—threatened when Mexico's treasury ran out of the hard currency reserves needed to fund its foreign financial obligations.[4]

The Clinton administration could not stand by. There was, first of all, the "Tequila effect": the fear that the Mexican crisis might spread to the rest of Latin America. "Mexico was hailed as a role model for developing countries," Robert Rubin wrote in his memoir. "The public failure of that model could deal an enormous setback to the spread of market-based economic reforms and globalization."[5] But equally pressing was the political calculation. Clinton's failure to pass health reform, followed by the 1994 midterm debacle, made NAFTA one of the administration's few signature accomplishments. Although the trade deal was not directly connected to Mexico's peso crisis, they were inexorably linked in the public mind. Chaos in Mexico might well have dire consequences along the border, where gang violence might increase and illegal immigration surge unless the country was bailed out.[6]

Larry Summers: The Kissinger of Economics

Larry Summers was the point man on the Mexican bailout and in virtually every other financial crisis, foreign and domestic, that engulfed the Clinton administration after 1994. In the years that followed, Summers achieved an outsized reputation as the neoliberal figure progressives found toxic: in Washington, where he held influential posts in two Democratic administrations; as president of Harvard, where a faculty revolt forced his resignation; and on the world stage, where he leveraged his academic reputation and political connections to advance his business interests. But to label Summers merely a neoliberal subverts the complexity and contradictions of his life, both in the academy and in government service.

Summers was a prolific author of influential economic papers on a wide variety of topics, earning a résumé that made him, at age twenty-seven, the youngest tenured professor in the modern history of Harvard University. As an applied economist, he was in his element discovering new analytic patterns within large realms of unconventional data. He thought the Reagan-era supply-side economists were "ignorant zealots," and he later authored papers that sustained important aspects of the progressive worldview. In one he took issue with the conservative argument that most unemployment is short-term, even voluntary; instead, Summers demonstrated, many of the same workers were repeatedly unemployed and long-term unemployment was far more common than most economists had thought. In other work he argued that higher minimum wages enhanced productivity. In the early 1980s he also launched a blistering attack on the efficient market hypothesis, which viewed financial markets as always rational and self-correcting. Examining the corporate takeover wave of the 1980s, Summers came down hard on those who saw the increase in the market value of target firms as representing an improvement in efficiency that would ultimately work to society's benefit. In the acrimonious debate on the merits of hostile takeovers—within economics as well as in politics—Summers showed that stockholder gains are hardly the same as social welfare gains, and certainly not for the workers in the target firms.[7]

During his Cambridge days, Summers often lunched with Robert Reich, whose ideas on the need for an industrial policy he rejected; instead, as he would later describe himself, he was "a market-oriented progressive. My belief is in a middle ground—not the invisible hand, not the heavy hand, but the helping hand of government."[8] Summers therefore understood that under stress self-correcting market mechanisms might well break down and require outside intervention. In the Mexican crisis and afterwards he thought a "bank run" mentality was transforming momentary market problems into a far larger crisis of

confidence. Governmental intervention was therefore essential to resolve it.[9]

But Summers was a fox, not a hedgehog. Unlike his Nobel Prize–
winning uncles—Paul Samuelson and Kenneth Arrow—his work could
not be summed up in one big idea. Said Brad DeLong, a former student
and colleague, Summers had "forty brilliant insights scattered around
whole bunches of literatures"—especially in finance, labor, and
macroeconomics—but no consistent body of work that would make a
singular impress on economic thought.[10] That failure to take his place
among the Nobel Prize aspirants of his generation may well have pained
Summers, but his empirically oriented, omnivorous mindset made the
messy and contingent world of politics and policy highly attractive, especially when factoring a fierce ambition, supreme self-confidence, and
a degree of opportunistic careerism into the mix.

Time's 1999 cover story had labeled Summers the "Kissinger of economics: a total pragmatist whose ambition sometimes grates but whose
intellect never fails to dazzle."[11] And like Kissinger, powerful mentors
helped Summers's rise. Martin Feldstein, his MIT dissertation adviser,
whom Ronald Reagan appointed chair of the Council of Economic
Advisers, gave Summers his first taste of government service as a staff
economist at the agency. Five years later Summers was an adviser to
the Dukakis presidential campaign. He made connections and in 1991
accepted an offer to become the chief economist at the World Bank,
a Washington-based institution created at Bretton Woods to support
economic development in the global South.

There Summers signed an infamous memo purporting to advocate
that high-income nations export polluting industries and toxic wastes to
poor nations. But the memo was not just an example of his economis-
tic hubris: it was originally written in a sarcastic tone by Lant Pritchett,
a young Summers assistant seeking to critique a World Bank report
that claimed trade liberalization would necessarily produce environmental benefits in developing nations. In an ironic aside, Pritchett suggested that if (in conventional economic terms) dumping pollutants
on poor countries would be "welfare-enhancing" for the world as a
whole, then the World Bank ought to endorse that policy. Among his

rhetorical provocations was the comment that "underpopulated countries in Africa are vastly underpolluted." Summers read the memo
quickly, noted the sarcasm, and signed it. Leaked and edited by an environmental activist, the memo may well have helped torpedo his appointment to chair Clinton's Council of Economic Advisers. In 1998
Summers told *The New Yorker*, "I learned to read a lot more carefully
what I sign. . . . The basic sentiment . . . is obviously all wrong."[12] Still,
the dirt stuck because in the world of market economics that Summers
would come to champion the idea that there might be painful trade-
offs between growth and the environment was hardly foreign to a man
who leveraged the power and influence of the US Treasury to make
Third World nations do America's bidding.

Despite the uproar over the toxic memo, Lloyd Bentsen hired Summers as an assistant secretary for international economic affairs. Two
years later Robert Rubin made him his deputy and closest adviser when
he became Treasury Secretary. Rubin had met Summers during the Dukakis campaign, hired him for a summer stint at Goldman Sachs in the
late 1980s, and came to see him as a protégé and successor. From Summers's perspective Rubin was the kind of Wall Streeter he had never
known: completely savvy about markets, but liberal when it came to
social policy. In turn Rubin respected Summers's brilliance as well as his
capacity for hard-nosed bureaucratic warfare. After Clinton's 1996 reelection, Rubin negotiated a confidential deal with the president. He
would remain as Treasury Secretary for at least two more years, and then
Summers would replace him. In the meantime Summers would attend
senior economic meetings at the White House, the only subcabinet official with that privilege. In those meetings, Rubin often made just the
briefest remarks outlining the Treasury position, then nodded toward
Summers, who would fill in the blanks to advance the argument.

The Rubin-Summers team was never reticent about exercising power.
When it came to virtually any financial issue, Treasury was by far the
most important institutional force in the Clinton administration. It originated most proposals and had an absolute veto over all others. Thus, the
high-profile economists at the Council of Economic Advisers—Tyson,
Stiglitz, Blinder, and Yellen—were often at odds with Summers and

Rubin, but the contest was far from equal. Said Blinder, "When the CEA comes nose to nose against Treasury, the CEA loses. Doesn't matter what the issue is, doesn't matter whether you're right or wrong, you lose."[13] And at Treasury Larry Summers exerted exceptional influence, even before Rubin made him heir apparent. A CEA spoof on the Treasury Department's organizational chart had Summers occupying every position under that of secretary, a post he would fill in 1999.[14]

By the end of the 1990s "hubris" was the only word to describe the way Summers saw America's place in the world. Both Europe and Japan were converging, he asserted, on the American economic model: a post–Cold War economy, based on the new technologies spawned by Silicon Valley and the financial innovations pouring out of Wall Street. That combination had vanquished both Communist-style planning and the command-and-control management characteristic of mid-twentieth-century American corporations. "The twin forces of information technology and modern competitive finance are moving us toward a post-industrial age," Summers told a San Francisco technology conference in early 1998. "And if you think about what this new economy means—whether it is AIG in insurance, McDonald's in fast-food, Wal-Mart in retailing, Microsoft in software, Harvard University in education, CNN in television news—the leading enterprises are American."[15]

The Mexican Bailout

On the evening of January 10, 1995, Bill Clinton swore in Robert Rubin as Treasury Secretary. Immediately afterward Rubin and Summers told an Oval Office meeting that with Mexico in near-default, the president should "support a massive, potentially unpopular, and risky intervention." Without US action, the flow of capital out of Mexico would accelerate and the peso would collapse, triggering severe inflation, a deep recession, and massive unemployment south of the border. The United States, Mexico's third-largest trading partner, would immediately feel the impact. Leon Panetta, the White House chief of staff, feared that a failed rescue effort might cost Clinton the 1996 election, a worry compounded by Summers when he suggested that the administration would have to ask Congress to approve a loan of as much as $25 billion to reassure Mexican bondholders that their investments would be honored. George Stephanopoulos said that surely he meant $25 million. No, Summers shot back. It was "billion with a B."[16] Bill Clinton approved because "we simply couldn't stand aside and let Mexico fail," and besides, "we would be sending a terrible signal of selfishness and shortsightedness throughout Latin America."[17]

Both Rubin and Summers thought the president's approval of this course exemplified his political courage, which was not always evident in his statecraft. In his decision to bail out Mexico Clinton was "defining America's international role," Summers would later assert. "He was very much committed to an expansive, inclusive, internationalist vision, even at very great costs."[18] As with his advocacy of an austerity budget in 1993, Rubin considered the restoration of "confidence" a "psychological matter." Both Rubin and Summers believed in the "Colin Powell financial doctrine." As in the first Gulf War, they wanted to deploy overwhelming force to ensure a quick and decisive victory. Rubin held that "the bigger and more certain the promise of official money, the less was likely to be needed."[19] Thus, the financing package that Treasury proposed was seven times larger than what was offered to Mexico in 1982 during an earlier near-default.[20] In all it was $50 billion: $20 billion from Congress, $18 billion from the International Monetary Fund, an additional $10 billion from Europe administered through the Bank for International Settlements, and smaller contributions from Brazil and the World Bank.[21] The Mexican bailout was the biggest financial aid project since the Marshall Plan.

In theory all the money would flow through the IMF. That Washington-based institution was a large bureaucracy run by Michel Camdessus, an ideologically dexterous French socialist who had helped orchestrate François Mitterrand's great U-turn in 1983, whereby a socially reformist government abruptly turned toward domestic austerity, privatization, and accommodation to Anglo-Saxon financial norms. Camdessus was not exactly a lapdog for Summers and Rubin, but in a crunch he felt he had no alternative but to cooperate with the Americans. On the IMF governing board, the United States had nearly three times the votes of any other nation, reflecting its outsized financial contribution, but even more important, the academic and financial networks upon which the IMF depended channeled an ever-growing stream of American-educated economists and administrators to high posts within the organization. The IMF's highly influential second-in-command was Stanley Fischer, who took his PhD from MIT. US influence was therefore paramount within the Fund, which *Time* called the "fire brigade" of the Committee to Save the World.[22]

The organization had been set up right after World War II as part of the Bretton Woods settlement. Until the early 1970s the IMF had provided loans and credit to backstop the system of fixed exchange rates linked to the US dollar. John Maynard Keynes and Harry Dexter White, the chief architects of Bretton Woods, had created a system designed to suppress the financial manipulations and autarkic trading regimes of the 1930s. Capital mobility was severely constrained, and there would be no competitive devaluations or financial gambits designed to take advantage of higher interest rates in one nation or another. Trade was growing, but each national economy maintained much autonomy: this was the golden era of Keynesian statecraft and rapid economic growth. As that system eroded in the 1970s, currency values floated even more wildly, and capital circulated ever more freely. The IMF became a crisis manager, helping to recycle revenues from petroleum-producing countries to developing countries and during the 1980s offering loans to resolve the Latin American debt crisis. Banking was no longer a boring occupation.

In 1989 the English economist John Williamson coined the term "Washington Consensus" to summarize the financial outlook commonly held by the IMF, the US Treasury, and the World Bank. Among its proscriptions, all directed toward client states attempting to emerge from the debt crisis of the 1980s, were privatization of state enterprises, trade liberalization, deregulation of financial markets, and much budget discipline. Not unexpectedly, the last often reduced funding for education, health care, and social services for the poor. Although the term "Washington Consensus" would eventually become nearly synonymous with neoliberal internationalism, Williamson was careful to exclude the idea of capital account liberalism—that is, the free and unfettered flow of capital between nations—in his Washington Consensus framework. The charge that IMF loans served as a "credit enforcer for Wall Street" would emerge under the watch commanded by Rubin, Summers, and Camdessus. No one in the Clinton administration actually argued that the advancement and protection of Wall Street investments was a prime objective; rather, Rubin and Summers thought that the idea of subjecting government policies within "emerging markets" to IMF discipline was, as Summers put it in a 1998 address to the libertarian Cato Institute, "the best means the world has found to ensure capital is well used." Anything else, including the targeted investment regimes so characteristic of the East Asian development model, were tantamount to "crony capitalism."[23]

Rubin and his Treasury team had a two-pronged strategy for salvaging Mexico and advancing its integration into the North American economy. The loan package was important, but they thought "the critical issue" was maintenance of high real interest rates on Mexican bonds and other financial instruments. These had already risen with the peso's devaluation and the subsequent flow of capital out of the country, but Summers and Rubin wanted to ensure that the Mexican government would hold the course. Rubin thought such high real interest rates were "the single most important aspect of this reform" because they "created confidence that credible policies were now in place to restore stability and, in the context of that confidence, it offered investors an attractive rate of return to induce them to hold pesos."[24]

The problem was that such hawkish interest rates were sure to engender a sharp recession as mortgages went unpaid, companies defaulted on their loans, and banks failed. Combined with a 35 percent inflation rate in 1995, real wages in Mexico would fall by over one-quarter and unemployment would double. Poverty increased and infant mortality rose sharply. Rubin was not sure the new government of Ernesto Zedillo could take the political beating dispensed by such high rates, some of which approached 50 percent annually. In Washington Mexico's economic team was notably reluctant to make the commitment, so Rubin dispatched Summers and another Treasury official, David Lipton—who had played a key role a few years earlier at the IMF in pushing Poland toward rapid marketization and Russia toward privatization of state enterprises—on a clandestine visit to Mexico City early in February 1995. Zedillo held a PhD in economics from Yale, and like his predecessor, Carlos Salinas (who had negotiated the NAFTA treaty and picked Zedillo as the PRI candidate for president), he was very much part of an elite stratum, both in Mexico and the rest of Latin America, who backed key elements of the Washington Consensus as their own. Holding the whip hand, Summers and Lipton therefore had little trouble in winning a high interest rate commitment from Zedillo's new government.[25]

The big bailout fund was also essential to Mexico's salvation, but the $20 billion that the administration requested from Congress soon became toxic on both the right and the left. Many saw it as a Wall Street bailout. At a hearing in late January Congressman Bernie Sanders told Rubin to "go back to your Wall Street friends, tell them to take the risk and not ask the American taxpayers."[26] Pat Buchanan also denounced the package as "not free market economics [but] Goldman-Sachsanomics."[27] Nor was uniform support in evidence on Wall Street, where many feared that Rubin was creating a US-funded "moral hazard." Deploying another military metaphor, James Grant, editor of the influential newsletter bearing his name, called the bailout "the Gulf of Tonkin Resolution of Finance"—in other words, an "open-ended commitment" to prevent a serious bear market in any country in which the United States had a strategic interest.[28] Given all this, the new Republican majority leader, Dick Armey, demanded that before the GOP leadership announced its support, the administration had to find one hundred House Democratic votes for the loan package.

Clinton could not do it. NAFTA had left a bitter taste, and beyond that the Clinton plan for Mexico was predicated on assuring global investors that the money they had poured into Mexican bonds would be repaid in full. Nothing less could ensure the restoration of the "confidence" that Rubin considered so essential. So Treasury came up with a (just barely legal) workaround to get the money from the heretofore obscure Exchange Stabilization Fund. That fund, entirely controlled by the Secretary of the Treasury, was designed to stabilize the value of the dollar and other currencies by way of short-term, relatively modest interventions. It was deployed in the peso crisis on a far larger and unprecedented scale, but congressional leaders—and certainly the Republicans now in control of all the key posts—were willing to stand aside, abdicating to the White House even more responsibility for international economic policy. Glory or shame for the Mexican bailout would now rest on the shoulders of Rubin, Summers, and Clinton.[29]

It took several months for the recovery to take hold. Reflecting bondholder skepticism, the value of the peso continued its decline, and both Rubin and Summers worried that the huge commitment of IMF and Treasury funds might well turn into a career-ending fiasco. On a February evening, after a day when the peso once again sank, Summers stepped into Rubin's office: "Bob, this doesn't look like this is working," he said, "and somebody should have to take responsibility . . . and so perhaps I should resign." Rubin would not let Summers hold the bag for the consensus Treasury decision; more important, in politics as well as on Wall Street confidence had to be maintained, even when the underlying economic situation failed to warrant it.[30]

Exemplifying the perverse logic of international finance, the severe recession into which Mexico plunged eventually generated the export earnings necessary to fund the *tesobonos*, stabilize the value of the peso, and even begin paying down the IMF loans. With unemployment on the rise and imported goods much more expensive, Mexicans had far less capacity to pay for foreign goods. Meanwhile, a cheaper peso made Mexican products far more competitive on the export market, helping the country to register a $7 billion trade surplus in 1995 and an even larger surplus the next year. Real wages remained depressed through the early years of the twenty-first century, but by 1997 Mexico's government had repaid the entire IMF loan—in the end it amounted to just over $10 billion—three years ahead of schedule. In contrast to the aftermath of the 1982 debt crisis, which inaugurated a "lost decade" during which Mexico struggled to secure access to outside capital markets, the purely financial dislocations engendered by the 1995 peso crash were over in a matter of seven months. Exchange rates stabilized, no financial crisis infected other Latin American countries, and US investors got their money back.[31] "Mexico moved from South America to North America," wrote Larry Summers, "in no small part, I believe, because of NAFTA and the financial rescue for Mexico."[32]

"Contagion" in East Asia

Whatever the merits of such IMF interventions—and they would come under increasing criticism at the end of the 1990s—the Mexican bailout set the template for all that would follow. Beginning in 1997, Thailand, Malaysia, the Philippines, Indonesia, and South Korea would all face the kind of hot money bank runs that almost brought Mexico to its knees. In each case, economic fundamentals were good in the years and months leading up to the crisis: for the most part East Asian countries were not running large budget deficits or trade imbalances, nor were their banking systems chronically unstable. Economic growth in the region was the envy of virtually every other emerging market.

It was the unfettered flow of capital, first into and then out of each nation, that turned a momentary financial embarrassment into a regime-shaking crisis. In Asia, Thailand was the first site of such a panic—a product, ironically, of the government's effort to ensure investor confidence by pegging the Thai baht to the US dollar. But as the US currency appreciated in the years after 1995—when Rubin and the Treasury inaugurated a "strong dollar" program to entice Chinese and Japanese purchases of US bonds and thereby keep US interest rates low—Thai exports suffered, leading to rumors of a baht devaluation. Foreign investors sold Thai currency, stocks plunged, and bankruptcies proliferated. When the baht was finally devalued in July 1997, the "contagion" spread, leading to capital flight and bank failures in nations whose economies had seemed robust just a few months before. South Korea, the world's eleventh-largest economy, was hit particularly hard late in the fall of 1997, after which both Russia and Brazil also came close to economic meltdown.[33]

The crisis inside South Korea combined elements of what had happened in Mexico and Thailand. A fixed-exchange-rate regime had led gradually to a serious overvaluation of the South Korean won. At the same time, South Korea's banks, often guided by the government, had made a practice of borrowing short-term money from foreign banks and lending it on longer terms to the domestic conglomerates known as "chaebols." With the Thai and Indonesian economic meltdowns spreading a sense of panic, foreign financial institutions, especially the cash-strapped Japanese, refused to roll over their short-term loans, imperiling the survival of South Korea's banks. Capital flight began in earnest, and the South Korean won plunged even as the government burned through billions in reserves trying to defend it.[34]

But to Rubin, Summers, and the IMF, Korea's economic difficulties were not just the product of a global bank run but the inevitable result of the country's stubborn insularity and its effort to follow the Japanese economic model of maintaining close linkages between banks, industry, and government. The Treasury Department's international staff had long urged Seoul to open up its financial sector—for example, to drop restrictions on competition from foreign banks and allow Korean companies to borrow on international bond markets and sell more stock to foreigners. Lobbying by American financial services firms that wanted to crack the Korean market was always a driving force behind Treasury's pressure on Seoul. In 1996, as a prerequisite to the country's triumphant entry into the Organization for Economic Cooperation and Development (OECD), the club for the most advanced industrial economies, South Korea grudgingly acceded to many of the American demands, but with a long phase-in period. Now, as the Treasury Department saw it, Korea was paying the price for its adherence to an Asian version of crony capitalism. A radical restructuring of the Korean economy would become an IMF "conditional" inseparable from the $55 billion in loans and backup credits advanced by the Fund and the G-7 financial powers.[35]

The IMF and US Treasury demanded Korean commitments to speed up liberalization of the country's financial system. These conditionals included doubling interest rates to 25 percent, allowing the entry of foreign bank subsidiaries and brokerage houses, and increasing the ceiling on aggregate foreign ownership from 26 to 50 percent. Insolvent banks, closely tied to the chaebol, would be shuttered. In Washington a Treasury spokesperson crowed that the program would "open up the Korean economy and move it toward one that is much more dependent on the operation of market forces." And in what can only be seen as a clear subversion of Korean sovereignty, the IMF insisted that all presidential candidates assent to these conditions before an aid package was put in place.[36] Like Mexico, the Korean rescue would eventually succeed, but it also demonstrated how the IMF and the US Treasury Department eroded the degree to which South Korea could construct an Asian "variety of capitalism." The Korean panic had been touched off, in part, by a three-week general strike in January 1997, followed by a series of chaebol bankruptcies; both of these developments signaled to foreign investors that a working class on the move was generating social and political conditions at variance with IMF austerity policies. Even before the Thai bubble burst foreign dismay was only increased when striking workers forced the government to legalize independent unionism and adopt a two-year moratorium on involuntary layoffs.[37]

When Korean officials first announced that their government would seek an IMF loan, *Dong-Ah Ilbo*, a leading Korean daily, lamented: "This is tantamount to losing our economic sovereignty."[38] This was very true, but Korean finance officials were not unhappy with the antilabor provisions in the reform package; these conditionals foisted onto foreigners the responsibility for restoring the unpopular legislation that allowed companies to undertake immediate mass layoffs. Indeed, when it seemed that the leading candidate for the Korean presidency, the social progressive Kim Dae Jung, might want to renegotiate IMF conditionality terms, Rubin sent David Lipton, the Treasury Department's "country doctor," back to Korea. Rubin gave Lipton marching orders: if the Koreans were willing to take decisive steps to change the way they ran their economy, the United States would help them, but "if they weren't willing, then aid wouldn't work and Lipton should make that clear." Most important, Lipton was to tell Kim that the labor issue was "key to Korea's situation." The high interest rates and bank closures demanded by the IMF and agreed to by the Koreans sent the country into a recession. Massive layoffs soon followed, pushing Korean unemployment up fourfold. The Korean economy would come roaring back in 1999, but the labor movement there never recovered the power and élan it had exercised during the 1990s, when it played the decisive role in making Korea a democratic polity.[39]

In the aftermath of the financial crisis, the American economist Rudi Dornbusch quipped that "the positive side" of these events was that South Korea "was now owned and operated by our Treasury." This was less a reference to American imperialism than an observation that power had shifted within the Clinton administration. Neither the State Department nor the Pentagon now wielded as much power as Treasury when it came to US foreign policy toward South Korea, Indonesia, or Russia, in all of which a regime-changing social crisis was a product of the financial policies imposed by the IMF and the US Treasury. The United States had thirty-seven thousand troops stationed in South Korea, facing a hostile foe to the north. But that geopolitical commitment did little to temper the IMF/Treasury effort to impose a transformative and potentially destabilizing new socioeconomic regime on an American military ally. The situation in Indonesia was even more dramatic. There the State Department and Clinton's National Security Council resisted Treasury efforts to impose far-reaching financial changes. As in the Cold War, these formulators of US foreign policy were willing to countenance de facto support for authoritarian regimes if the alternatives seemed worse and the ally was of sufficient strategic value. But Treasury saw Suharto and his family—corrupt, ineffective, and wedded to the economic status quo—as an absolute obstacle to any monetary support. "As long as Suharto is in charge," read a Treasury memo to the NSC, the IMF bailout package "is going nowhere." As the economy collapsed, riots and civil strife convulsed the nation, depriving Suharto of much traditional support. He resigned in May 1998, but the recovery of the Indonesian economy was far more difficult and much longer than the recoveries in Korea and Thailand.[40]

As these Asian financial meltdowns were coming to an end, the Treasury Department published a long report, *American Finance for the 21st Century*, with a preface by Robert Rubin. Written to advance the proposition that domestic banking mergers and deregulation were virtually inevitable in a world where opposition to market forces "is becoming an increasingly futile task," the report argued that the constraints of the New Deal were now entirely dysfunctional: "The goal of policy in the coming century should be to encourage rather than to suppress competition and innovation in finance."[41] Of course, in such a world financial markets, both at home and abroad, were far from perfect. Indeed, they were prone to periodic crisis. On Wall Street Rubin had made tens of millions of dollars from that insight. "When you have good times," Rubin later remarked, "there is an inherent tendency in markets, grounded in human nature and the pull of fear and greed, to go to excess."[42]

Robert Rubin had probably heard little of Hyman Minsky, who died in 1996, but the Treasury Secretary was here putting forth a sentiment that seemed schooled in the work of that radical economist. Minsky's explanation for capitalism's recurrent booms and busts seemed remarkably in tune with the economic reality that characterized the decades bracketing the turn of the millennium. Minsky thought financial instability emerged out of the logic of capitalist markets and the investor psychology that drove them. Following a crisis or slump, investors' expectations are at first cautious, but then become increasingly positive, even exuberant, leading to speculation, a drawdown of cash reserves, and an eventual crash. In an unregulated environment, Minsky explained, financial bubbles are inevitable. Thus, the crises, the bust, and the follow-on recession serve a purpose in the operations of a free market economy, even as they wreak havoc on the lives of hundreds of millions of ordinary men and women. Periodic panics—and the East Asian meltdown was a classic example—discipline investors and transform their mentality, if only temporarily. But governmental bailouts are also essential to this boom-and-bust cycle: without such infusions of liquidity, economic downturns might lead to permanent damage and in the process generate a countermovement hostile to markets, along the historic lines delineated by Karl Polanyi in his classic work *The Great Transformation*.[43]

Rubin and his comrades at Treasury understood this reality. Recognizing that global financial markets are bound to periodically implode, they argued that governments, operating through the IMF and the G-7 group of advanced industrial nations, had a vital role to play. As the

American Finance for the 21st Century report put it, they would administer the financial mechanisms necessary for "failure containment," which Rubin's Treasury Department counterpoised to "failure prevention." The difference was crucial, not because one regime favored a big, intrusive government role and the other did not, but because this example of neoliberal statecraft demonstrated that a coercive exercise of governmental power was absolutely necessary to "contain" the disruptive and dangerous upheavals that were endemic to the free play of international finance.[44] Larry Summers often analogized the emergence of global financial markets to the invention of the jet airplane. World travel was now rapid, comfortable, and cheap, and most of the time travelers could get to their destination in safety, "but the crashes when they occur are that much more spectacular. Governments can respond to the invention of the jet airplane by improving air traffic control and lengthening the runway or by banning jet landings. It is obvious which is better." Likewise, no set of prudential standards—sound banking regulations, bankruptcy laws, anticorruption statutes—could prevent countries from getting themselves into "very profound financial difficulties at the sovereign level. In short, we need systems that can handle failure, because until the system is safe for failure we will not be able to count on success."[45] And of course, those failures had another virtue: they gave the IMF and the US Treasury periodic opportunities to condition a rescue package that reshaped trade, banking, and governmental regulations to more closely conform to an Anglo-American model as the hegemonic norm.

Stiglitz in Dissent

Joseph Stiglitz was the leading opponent of the Rubin-Summers approach, both within the US government and outside it. The product of a Jewish lower-middle-class family from Gary, Indiana, Stiglitz shared classrooms with the sons and daughters of a steelworker generation for whom, even at the apex of America's postwar prosperity, life in the mills was arduous and unpredictable. He was a decade older than Summers and, if anything, even more rumpled in his persona. When he took his first teaching job at Yale, his contract included the proviso that he wear shoes, in and out of class, and show proof that he was leasing an apartment instead of sleeping on an office sofa. Like Summers, Stiglitz was a winner of the John Bates Clark Medal, but most economists also expected him to win a Nobel Prize, which came his way in 2001. His influential and practical work on "information asymmetry" demonstrated the many situations in which incomplete knowledge of relevant economic signals prevents markets from achieving social efficiency. Unlike Paul Samuelson, his MIT mentor, as well as other Keynesian liberals who treated periodic market failures as an exception to the general rule of efficient markets, Stiglitz argued that market distortions were the norm, so "that government could potentially almost always improve upon the market's resource allocation."[46] Of course, Stiglitz was not a socialist, but he saw market regulation as imperative, a viewpoint that would become even more pronounced as his conflicts with the Treasury worldview sharpened.

As a member of the Council of Economic Advisers, Stiglitz had written fruitless memos to Bill Clinton and the National Economic Council arguing that Treasury was acting as Wall Street's handmaiden and thereby taking insufficient account of the risks involved in exposing developing countries to the ebbs and flows of global money markets. With Alan Blinder, Stiglitz did not object to direct investment by multinational corporations overseas; both believed that the building of factories and other business operations in developing countries was positive for living standards. Instead, their problem lay with financial flows, especially the short-term flows that were so catastrophically susceptible to sudden reversals.[47]

Although Stiglitz thought the United States had handled the Mexican crisis boldly, he also believed Clinton's NEC, not to mention Treasury, had learned all the wrong lessons. Capital account liberalization created "risks without rewards," he wrote. Then the high interest rates the IMF imposed on Mexico and the drastic expenditure cutbacks it required had made the downturn worse. Mexico recovered quickly despite these IMF impositions—mainly by exporting commodities and light manufactured goods that were now seductively cheap—not because adherence to the IMF plan had restored the "confidence" that Rubin saw as

FIGURE 16. World Bank economist Joseph Stiglitz proved a sharp critic of the US Treasury Department and the International Monetary Fund during the East Asian financial crisis. (Ulf Andersen / Getty Images Entertainment)

the holy grail. Indeed, Stiglitz thought that capital account liberalization was the "single most important factor leading to the crisis" in Mexico, as well as in East Asia. Taiwan, Hong Kong, South Korea, and China "had been successful," he argued, "not only in spite of the fact that they had not followed most of the dictates of the Washington Consensus, but because they had not."[48]

Clinton would have been happy to have Stiglitz continue as CEA chair, but his ineffectuality at that post helped propel him toward the World Bank, whose president, James Wolfensohn, a financier, liberal, and Friend of Bill, asked him to become the senior vice president for development policy and chief economist. There Stiglitz quickly became a critic of IMF efforts to impose Treasury Department policy, whether on the floundering economies of the former Soviet bloc or the far more successful polities along the Pacific Rim. Traveling widely in Africa and Asia, Stiglitz thought the proscriptions embedded within the Washington Consensus had to fail because so many underdeveloped nations had not yet constructed the civic and governmental institutions necessary to sustain the kind of financial markets common in the West. In Asia, where governments helped shape and direct markets, the IMF's deregulatory program was entirely counterproductive. Indeed, Stiglitz thought that the spectacular success of the Asian variety of capitalism had served as an embarrassment and rebuke to proponents of the Washington Consensus.[49]

Stiglitz's unorthodoxy became clear in September 1997 at the annual joint meeting of the World Bank and the IMF in Hong Kong. On the one hand, this conference marked the apogee of IMF self-confidence, the high-water mark for the cause of globalizing money flows. Although the IMF had long been using its influence to urge countries to open their financial systems, Rubin pushed for more, for a definitive policy statement. Just a few months earlier the US Treasury secretary had orchestrated a proposal, endorsed at a G-7 meeting of finance ministers, to make capital mobility a core priority and had urged that the IMF charter be amended to that effect. Thus, at the Hong Kong meeting the Fund moved to formally repudiate the original Bretton Woods constraints by asserting that "the liberalization of capital flows is an essential element of an efficient international monetary system." Money, speculative or not, must have the freedom to flow to those investments returning the greatest profit and therefore the greatest efficiency. As Summers had put it just a few months before, "at Treasury, our most crucial international priority remains the creation of a well-funded, truly global capital market."[50]

At Hong Kong, however, Stiglitz found that the Asian finance ministers with whom he met were "terrified" about hot money flows, and he urged them not only to press ahead with plans to impose emergency controls on short-term funds but to act collectively to resist IMF strictures. To this end Stiglitz also supported a plan put forward by his friend and sometime collaborator Eisuke Sakakibara, the Japanese vice minister of finance for international affairs. Sakakibara had published widely to make the case

for Japan's "noncapitalist market economy," arguing that the financial turmoil of recent months was less an Asian crisis than a crisis in global capitalism. The United States and the IMF were "trying to change the Asian
system, without changing the international financial system." Sakakibara
therefore sought to create a $100 billion Asian Monetary Fund, backed by
Japan, China, and some of the East Asian Tiger economies, that would
operate independently of the IMF and the US Treasury.[51]

Little came of these anti-IMF initiatives. Early on, Summers got on
the phone to berate Sakakibara for proposing a plan that not only subverted IMF hegemony but threatened, he claimed, the entire US-Japan
alliance. But such setbacks did nothing to temper the Stiglitz critique
of the Treasury/IMF program. In February 1998, for example, he gave
a Chicago speech denouncing the IMF's use of high interest rates to
induce investors to keep their money in the host nation, arguing that
the resultant wave of bankruptcies would not only generate much economic misery for ordinary people but make outside investors even
more hesitant to invest. Later in the year that perspective was incorporated into a World Bank study he supervised. Contradicting the
Treasury/IMF perspective, the report offered a blow-by-blow account
of the East Asian crisis, blaming global investors who had lent money
to developing nations with such abandon. Said Stiglitz: "The heart of
this current crisis is the surge of capital flows." High interest rates were
no solution. There were just too many other factors that determined
currency values—political stability and manufacturing export capacity
being chief among them.[52]

Stiglitz's outspokenness exacerbated his feud with Summers, who
wanted Wolfensohn to rein him in. The World Bank president was hesitant to do so, however, in large part because he had a good deal of sym-
pathy for much of what Stiglitz was saying, especially insofar as the
economist emphasized the social devastation that seemed to inevitably
follow in the wake of IMF programs imposed on the less developed
nations. But Summers had his own bit of leverage. Wolfensohn wanted
a second term, perhaps to advance his claim to a Nobel Peace Prize, and the
US Treasury Secretary, a post now filled by Summers, had a veto over
top World Bank appointments. Summers therefore told Wolfensohn

that if he wanted that second term Stiglitz had to go. Wolfensohn agreed and Stiglitz formally resigned in early 2000, although the World Bank president announced that Stiglitz would stay on as a special adviser tasked with choosing a successor. Stiglitz told the *New York Times* reporter Louis Uchitelle, "Remaining silent when people were pursuing wrong ideas would have been a form of complicity."[53] So in April 2000, just a few months after the Seattle upheaval, he published a *New Republic* article, "What I Learned at the World Economic Crisis." It was timed to appear just a week before a joint meeting of the IMF and the World Bank, for which globalization opponents were planning a new round of street demonstrations. Stiglitz let Summers and the IMF mandarins have it. The demonstrators, he predicted, will "say the IMF is arrogant. They'll say the IMF doesn't really listen to the developing countries it is supposed to help. They'll say the IMF is secretive and insulated. . . . They'll say the IMF's economic 'remedies' often make things worse. . . . And they'll have a point. . . . I saw how the IMF, in tandem with the US Treasury Department responded. And I was appalled."[54]

This was treason, and Summers was livid because Stiglitz was not a lone ranger but had become the point man for a growing body of dissent, not just in the streets but within Clinton administration circles. Although now out of government, Alan Blinder, Laura Tyson, and Mickey Kantor had all made public their disquiet with IMF/Treasury policies.[55] Likewise, Jeffrey Sachs, the prominent Harvard economist and policy adviser to Eastern European countries, now repudiated his advocacy of an open market "shock therapy" for those nations. But such second thoughts were not for Summers. He ordered Wolfensohn to immediately sever all connections between Stiglitz and the World Bank. Within hours Stiglitz was well and truly fired, literally banished from the building. IMF staffers cheered the news.[56]

Orthodoxy in Trouble

The US Treasury, however, could not sustain the orthodoxy that Summers sought to uphold. Robert Rubin never endorsed capital controls, but he soon found himself a de facto practitioner. This became apparent as the South Korean financial crisis reached its endgame. On December 3, 1997, South Korea received the huge $55 billion bailout organized by Treasury and the IMF, an amount intended to calm the banks that had been yanking cash out of the country. But confidence remained in short supply, and on December 8 the Korean won resumed its free fall. Bribing creditors with sky-high interest rates was not working, so within a few days Rubin convened a dinner with Treasury and Fed officials at his DC abode, the Jefferson Hotel. The topic for discussion: Should the IMF rush more money to Korea to forestall a default, or would that merely ensure that frightened bankers in the West and Japan got their loans repaid in the weeks before the economy crashed?

The alternative was what Rubin called a bank "bail-in," which amounted to twisting as many financial arms as necessary to stop these bankers from draining Korea's hard currency reserves. In contrast to the Mexican crisis, Korea's foreign debts consisted mainly of bank loans, not bonds held by thousands of dispersed investors. Rubin and other Treasury officials therefore got on the phone cajoling old Wall Street friends to roll over their short-term loans. Instead of getting a bailout, the banks would have to recommit in order to give the Koreans time to restructure their economy—by slashing wages and employment and bankrupting the most vulnerable banks—and then generate the export earnings necessary to pay off the near-delinquent bank loans. Phone calls also went to Japan, where cash-strapped banks had also been pulling funds out of Korea.

Alan Greenspan remained chary of all this barely veiled coercion, but he gave his approval to a set of Christmas week meetings of the powerful New York Fed, to which its president, William McDonough, summoned the heads of the nation's six major banks—Citibank and J.P. Morgan were the largest—whose Korean exposure was second only to that of the Japanese. "I have been authorized by the international institutions and the United States government to tell you the game is over," McDonough told the bankers. Taxpayers were not going to pour more cash into Korea only to see it used to repay imprudent creditors. This was the threat: roll over your loans or the government will see to it that you lose everything. The Wall Street bankers called their capitulation "a market-oriented private sector financing initiative," but this capital flow blockage was tantamount to a government edict.[57]

Joseph Stiglitz might well have been pleased, but no tears could be shed for the US bankers who had not ceded an iota of formal authority to Korea or any other foreign financial ministry when it came to determining the mobility of their capital. Just a month later, in January 1998, they reached a broad agreement with Korean officials to reschedule $22 billion in short-term debt owed them by Korean banks. In exchange, they received high-yield bonds fully guaranteed by the Korean government. Wall Street lost not a penny, an outcome that Rubin justified in a speech delivered that same month just as the Korean crisis was abating. "We would not give one nickel to help any creditor or investor," he declared, ". . . [but] any action that would force investors and creditors involuntarily to take losses, however appropriate that might seem, would . . . cause banks to pull back from other emerging markets."[58]

Who Lost Russia?

Thailand and South Korea resumed their torrid growth within a year or two, and so too did Brazil, which faced a currency crisis in early 1999. But Russia was a far more dismal and dangerous story, one in which Clinton policymakers could not divorce the fraught geopolitics of post–Cold War Eastern Europe from the economic and social catastrophe creating a kleptocracy that, from a Western perspective, was "too nuclear to fail." In Russia the financial crisis was a decade-long affair, rooted in the all too rapid privatization—"theft" would be a better word—of Communist-era state property by a stratum of managers and ministers on the take. That seizure was propelled by the Russians themselves, but it was offered ideological guidance and financial support by the same Treasury circles that had played such an influential role in the IMF effort to transform Asian capitalism along lines more attuned to Wall Street standards. Indeed, the corruption that was so pervasive in Russia backwashed onto some of these same figures.

When it came to how Washington should approach the pace and character of the Russian transition to capitalism, the Clinton administration was divided between "reformers" and "gradualists." The former were advocates of what came to be called "shock therapy": price liberation, massive privatization of state assets, and an end to the subsidies, for both consumers and state enterprises, that had sustained working-class living standards and maintained employment in so many factories and firms. Rapid privatization was essential, even if those "grabbing" the former state assets were corrupt, incompetent, or former Communist insiders on the take. "*Privatisatsiya* (privatization) = *Prikhvatisatsiya* (grabbing)" ran the slogan of those hostile to the sale of state enterprises.[59] When Gazprom was privatized in 1994, a set of its managers from the Soviet era gained control at a cost of about $250 million. Three years later the Moscow stock exchange valued the company at $40.5 billion. But corruption was seen as a small price to pay if these new oligarchs constituted a bulwark against the return of the Communists, a potential threat in the early 1990s, when hyper-inflation and mass unemployment turned millions of Russians against the post-Soviet "reforms." By the end of the 1990s Summers knew that privatization in Russia, and his role in its advancement, had come in for much criticism, journalistic as well as expert. Millions of Russians had been bilked out of their patrimony. But the alternatives, he complained to Bill Clinton, were far worse, since they would have left "enterprises in the control of corrupt government managers whose incentives were to strip assets and preserve subsidies. . . . We did what we could to make privatization work."[60]

But even more important to its proponents in the Clinton administration was their expectation that privatization, whatever the temporary dislocations, would generate a set of laws and institutions to protect the wealth now in the possession of a new set of owners. The oligarchs would demand the establishment of the legal and administrative infrastructure necessary to make a market economy work. And that would help ensure the stability of the currency, enhance the rule of law, and facilitate the creation of orderly markets.[61] In the same way, they argued, that trade with China would encourage transparency and a democratic opening in that authoritarian country, the privatization of the Soviet command economy promised to open the door to a more pluralistic society in Russia.

Summers was very much in the "reform" camp, and so too, initially, was Jeffrey Sachs, who had been closely identified with the phrase "shock therapy" when he served as an adviser to the Solidarity movement in Poland and to the cohort of young Russian economists tapped by Boris Yeltsin to carry out the transition to capitalism. By the mid-1990s, however, Sachs had become disillusioned with Russian "reform," especially the decision to immediately privatize the extremely valuable oil, gas, and mining enterprises whose export sales were essential to funding the post-Soviet government. Sachs became a Stiglitz ally of sorts, but not so his sometime collaborator and fellow Harvard economist Andrei Shleifer, a Russian-born émigré, Summers's protégé, and the director of the Moscow-based Harvard Institute for International Development. The institute had the prime contract with the US Agency for International Development (USAID) to help with the post-Soviet economic transition. That facilitated the close contacts that Shleifer and other US reformers maintained with top Russian policymakers, including Deputy Prime Minister Anatoly Chubais. Rubin had once called Chubais "Russia's strongest and most effective reformer," even as his stewardship of the privatization program would soon make him, according to the *New York Times*, "the most despised man in Russia."[62] Both Sachs and Shleifer lobbied for a massive, Marshall Plan–style aid program for Russia. That never happened, even as the IMF doled out much smaller sums, all conditioned on adherence to Washington Consensus principles. It was shock without the therapy.

The Summers connection to the reformers, both American and Russian, had its smarmy side. In 1998 Shleifer, his wife, and another Harvard Institute associate, Jonathan Hay, lost their posts when a USAID investigation found that they had used insider knowledge to profit from investments in the Russian securities market. When the case was finally settled in 2004, Shleifer paid a $2 million fine to the US government; Harvard, then led by Summers, paid out $26.5 million, even as Shleifer remained a tenured professor there. Like his mentor, Shleifer was a winner of the John Bates Clark Medal, but the impression that Summers had offered his friend a degree of protection was one of the factors that led to his forced resignation from the university presidency two years later.[63]

The view of the gradualists, first among them Joe Stiglitz, was that before a market economy can be created, a nation needs institutions: the legal and regulatory framework to ensure that contracts are enforced, property rights respected, and disputes peacefully resolved. The oligarchs were hardly a stabilizing influence. Anyone smart enough to be a winner in the Russian privatization sweepstakes would be smart enough to get a large slice of their money into foreign bank accounts or the booming US stock market. Capital mobility in Asia had helped generate an investment boom in the years before the currency crisis. In Russia all that was missing, so capitalism there became capital flight, with perhaps half a trillion dollars fleeing the country in the 1990s. A large slice of every IMF loan ended up in London real estate or Cyprus bank accounts. After the fall of Communism, the GDP decline in Russia was greater than the Soviet Union had suffered in all of World War II. Industrial production had fallen by almost one-quarter when Nazi tanks rolled eastward; between 1990 and 1998 it dropped by over 40 percent.[64]

Stiglitz often compared the Russian debacle to the more measured marketization taking place in China. That large nation avoided the Asian contagion both because capital flows there were subject to much governmental restraint and because privatization was a far more gradual project. As we saw in the previous chapter, China, notwithstanding a fervent desire for WTO membership, had thwarted Robert Rubin's more ambitious efforts to open its financial markets to Western securities firms. Even more dramatic was the Malaysian case. Like Thailand, that much smaller nation had opened its doors to a flow of speculative, short-term money. Soon skyscrapers sprouted throughout Kuala Lumpur, but when the financial contagion hit, Malaysia rejected an IMF "rescue" and imposed tough capital controls, generating a howl of Western criticism. Like China, Malaysia was an authoritarian country; it was run by a mercurial strongman, Mahathir bin Mohamad, who saw IMF conditionality as not only an economic straitjacket but also a political threat. Whatever their motives, both China and Malaysia weathered the storm with short and shallow downturns. Neither country raised interest rates to the usurious levels imposed elsewhere, thus avoiding the widespread bankruptcies that engulfed Indonesia, Thailand, and South Korea.[65]

In Russia the Asian contagion struck like a hurricane battering a rickety house. As in so many East Asian nations, an overvalued currency was pegged to the dollar, so the Yeltsin government was rapidly running out of the hard currency it needed to avoid a ruble devaluation and the skyrocketing inflation that would follow. As the prospect of a default loomed ever larger, the yield on short-term government bonds rose to 60 and 80 percent during the spring of 1998. With strong backing from the Americans—Treasury, State, and even the Pentagon—the IMF cobbled together a $23 billion rescue package in July 1998. But the program was a failure from the start, with millions disappearing after the IMF deposited the first $4.8 billion in Russia's central bank. Shortly thereafter the Russian Duma, in a rebuke to both Yeltsin and the IMF, rejected a proposal to raise taxes and impose other austerity measures. Unlike Kim Dae Jung in South Korea, Yeltsin could not fulfill his side of the bargain.[66]

When Clinton administration officials discussed a disbursement of yet another multibillion-dollar tranche, Treasury's ascendancy was once again made clear, even on turf traditionally occupied by generations of Cold War Kremlin watchers. Meeting in the White House Situation Room, virtually the entire Clinton foreign policy team, including the secretaries of State and Defense, the chairman of the Joint Chiefs of Staff, NSC chair Sandy Berger, and Strobe Talbott, the State Department's chief Russia specialist, sought to convince Rubin that more money to sustain Yeltsin should be forthcoming. Russia, a nation with a poorly supervised nuclear arsenal and a disillusioned populace subject to appeals from the nationalistic right as well as the old Communists, was too geopolitically important to fail.

But Rubin held his ground. From the point of view of the international financial system he was trying to construct, there was something worse than a Russian default and the turmoil that was bound to follow. All those high-yielding Russian bonds had become a "moral hazard play," their payout predicated on the bet that neither the United States nor the Europeans were willing to see chaos engulf a nation with so many intercontinental missiles at the ready. However, such an outcome would have subverted the disciplined financial universe that Treasury and the IMF sought to construct. As Rubin put it, "Sending more money in the face of the Duma's defiance, in addition to almost surely being futile in terms of promoting recovery, would have undermined the credibility of the IMF in its efforts to apply conditionality elsewhere in the world." In the Russian crisis, this was where the real risk lay, asserted Rubin, now drawing a clear line in the sand. If the national security folks wanted to get another Treasury secretary who would force the IMF to act, "that was fine with me."[67]

Rubin prevailed. No more money went to Russia, so on August 17, 1998, the government there announced a unilateral suspension of payments on its bonds and a devaluation of the ruble. This was the same day Clinton gave his taped deposition in the Lewinsky affair, so the news was largely buried on the financial pages. But just a couple of weeks later the president flew to Moscow, once Talbott had assured him that Yeltsin was neither incapacitated by alcohol nor on the verge of resignation. Some progress was made there on denuclearization and a reduction of tensions in the Balkans, but there was no gainsaying the fact that the cost Rubin had exacted to sustain his vision of a global financial system had made a bad Russian situation worse. US efforts to reshape the Russian economy had come to a dead end. Yeltsin was in physical and mental decline, the oligarchs were ascendant, and foreign investors were outraged. In their briefing book for the summit, Sandy Berger and Gene Sperling told the president, "Average Russians are dispirited about their country's prospects and suspicious of US motives."[68] Later Clinton recorded in his memoir his encounter with a restive delegation from the Duma: "I tried hard to convince them that no nation could escape the discipline of the global economy, and that if they wanted foreign loans and investment, Russia would have to collect taxes, stop printing money to pay bills and bail out troubled banks, avoid crony capitalism, and pay debts. I don't think I made many converts."[69]

The mood was similar three months later when Summers was in Moscow for another meeting. Assistant Sheryl Sandberg took his downbeat phone call, which she passed on to Secretary Rubin: "He has seen no evidence to counter the proposition that some problems don't have answers."[70] That October a couple of other Treasury staffers reported from Russia, "The pervasive feeling is that Russia is in the eye of the storm." While the shock generated by devaluation, inflation, and the collapse of the banking system had passed, "the crisis appears to be driving Russians to look more urgently for a savior rather than a new ideology or strategy."[71] Eighteen months later, after Vladimir Putin, a former KGB officer, was elected president of Russia, Clinton put in a brief congratulatory phone call; he hung up "thinking he was tough enough to hold Russia together," and—with somewhat less expectation—"wise enough" to resolve Russia's festering border conflicts.[72]

Those geopolitical dangers would take a few years to unfold, but in the meantime Russia's August default came crashing home. That debacle quickly infected global markets as various hedge funds, banks, and other institutions that had borrowed heavily to buy once-attractive Russian bonds unloaded them to raise cash and purge their accounts of such toxic instruments. At the center of the storm was Long-Term Capital Management (LTCM), a four-year-old hedge fund that had mobilized academic brainpower and an extensive set of international connections to earn enormous returns—upward of 40 percent on equity in one year—for a small group of elite investors and investment banks. Utilizing the talents of dozens of economist PhDs and a couple of Nobel Prize winners in the same discipline, LTCM and its supposedly savvy clients thought it possible to deploy the latest econometric modeling to confidentially buy and sell derivative contracts worth more than $1 trillion. (We explore the spectacular rise of these unregulated financial instruments in the next chapter.) Since LTCM managed less than $5 billion of investor money, the leverage was extraordinary: 125-to-1. The Greenwich-based hedge fund thought it could manage such risk if historical patterns that had governed financial prices remained intact in a world of near-universal financial liquidity.

But that assumption proved faulty when almost every market, save that for the most liquid US Treasury bonds, went down in lockstep. This was an eventuality that LTCM's computer modeling had not foreseen. At the end of August the firm was down to about $2 billion of capital against $100 billion in debt. Now even small adverse movements in the price of its obligations would prove disastrous.[73] By mid-September

LTCM was effectively bankrupt; more important, its default threatened banks and other financial institutions if they could not recover the huge sums they had lent to the firm. The value of Goldman Sachs plunged 50 percent—$15 billion—in just over a month.[74] The Fed worried that these losses would spill over to investors with no relationship to LTCM, freezing credit markets almost everywhere. Alarmed, Robert Rubin warned, "The world is experiencing its worst financial crisis in half a century," and Alan Greenspan concurred. It was his "scariest moment in 50 years."[75]

As with South Korea the year before, this was a "too big to fail" crisis, one requiring government coordination if not outright coercion of the most important private financial institutions. Rubin and Greenspan hoped that the financial contagion spawned by the LTCM debacle might be staunched by Wall Street itself, so on September 23, 1998, New York Fed president William McDonough once again convened a meeting of the largest financial institutions, among them Bear Stearns, Chase Manhattan, Goldman Sachs, J.P. Morgan, Lehman Brothers, Merrill Lynch, and Morgan Stanley, all of which faced huge losses—collectively, some $20 billion—should LTCM simply liquidate. Together they put up nearly $3.65 billion to take over LTCM. If world markets stabilized, they might even get their money back; meanwhile, the panic would subside. Greenspan helped that along by cutting the Fed's short-term interest rate target three times in the next two months. This was the "Greenspan put" in action once again. It seemed to work: a worldwide financial crisis was averted, the Wall Street banks turned a profit on the LTCM gambit, and the lower interest rates fueled a soaring stock market. All this seemed yet another reason for *Time* magazine to put Rubin, Greenspan, and Summers on its cover just four months later.[76]

Consequences

Memories of both the Asian financial contagion and the LTCM rescue soon faded, superseded a decade later by a far greater meltdown of credit and confidence. Most of the nations impacted by the first crisis recovered smartly. Even Russia regained its footing when crude oil prices jumped higher early in the twenty-first century. But the events of 1997 and 1998 have had lasting consequences. Combined with the Seattle manifestation just a year later, this capitalist convulsion had two seemingly contradictory impacts: demonstrating that there were clear ideological and political limits to the neoliberal project, while at the same time globalizing an Anglo-American version of world finance as never before.

One immediate consequence was to put a large question mark next to the idea of unfettered capital flows. In one way or another, some of the most consequential nations affected by the panic—Russia, Malaysia, South Korea, Taiwan, and China—imposed constraints on the mobility of capital. Equally important perhaps, Stiglitz was joined by many other high-profile economists and investors, including Paul Krugman, George Soros, Dani Rodrik, Jeffrey Sachs, and Jagdish Bhagwati, in arguing that there was nothing fundamentally unbalanced about most of the Asian economies caught up in the crisis; instead, its depth and danger were a product of the same panicked herd instinct, now magnified on a globally electronic scale, that had generated bank runs on both sides of the Atlantic in 1931 and 1932. The LTCM debacle made clear that such financial turmoil was hardly limited to the less sophisticated banks and governments of East Asia and Latin America. That Bhagwati, a fierce advocate of free trade in goods and services, condemned the financial "panics and manias" of the late 1990s was almost as startling as the fact that in September 1998 Goldman Sachs published a note that seemingly endorsed the viewpoint of Joseph Stiglitz: "So far, countries whose currencies have not been freely convertible have done best" in weathering the crisis.[77]

Bill Clinton was not unsympathetic to this critique. Once he returned from Russia, he wanted to do something big: get the G-7 leaders to call a meeting, he proposed, perhaps to announce a "Bretton Woods II" in order to reorient IMF policies so as to moderate capital flows and ensure their close regulation. When in September 1998 George Soros sent Clinton the galleys for his new book, *The Crisis of Global Capitalism*, the president underlined it heavily and commanded NEC chair

Gene Sperling to read it. Soros thought reckless capital flows were a prime cause of the financial crisis. "Right now," argued Soros, "market fundamentalism is a greater threat to open society than any totalitarianism."[78] He advocated transformation of the IMF into a global central bank that downplayed the structural "conditionality" so important to Rubin, Summers, and Camdessus. Such a bank would serve as a lender of last resort and be available to otherwise stable economies in temporary distress. That Soros, who made billions betting against the pound and other currencies, would also penalize speculative investors proved as ironical as it was radical.[79]

Such themes soon appeared in Clinton conversations and speeches. As he told Tony Blair in a September 1998 phone call, "Bretton Woods assumed 50 years ago that no matter what, the issue would be to find enough money to facilitate trade and investment—not that money flows themselves would become a greater force of nature in the global economy."[80] To a meeting of the Council on Foreign Relations shortly thereafter, Clinton argued that "we need to consider ways to extend emergency financing when countries are battling crises of confidence due to world financial distress as distinct from their own errors in policy," a perspective at variance from Treasury's. Indeed, three weeks later he told an IMF/World Bank audience, "We must put a human face on the global economy." Evoking New Deal–era efforts to manage American capitalism and the stability that Bretton Woods had brought to world trade, Clinton asserted, "If global markets are to bring the benefits we believe they can, we simply must find a way to tame the pattern of boom/bust on an international scale."[81]

But such rhetoric was more sermon than plan. It was undercut by a congressional failure to appropriate more money for the IMF as well as Robert Rubin's own alternative advocacy of a "global financial architecture." Thus, when President Clinton broached the idea of a large international meeting, a "Bretton Woods II," that would discuss the creation of a set of new rules for international finance, Rubin nixed the idea. It would raise unnecessary expectations and open the door to critics seeking to undermine IMF hegemony, both in the developing nations and at home. Likewise, when Clinton asked Rubin and Summers to opine on the Soros proposal for a global central bank, they shot it down in a memo that just barely concealed their contempt for the whole idea. Meanwhile, the president found no takers for any version of an international New Deal. Rubin and Summers left Bretton Woods regulatory models on the shelf when they gave talks on the international financial crisis. For example, in a Rubin speech to a Wall Street conference that fall, he defended unfettered capital flows, blamed "the badly flawed and poorly regulated financial systems" of the emerging market economies for their own troubles, and emphasized "the capacity of markets to discipline governments to pursue the right policies for solid growth." Rubin's goal was a market-based "financial architecture which induces sound decision-making by investors, encourages capital to be used productively, and rewards governments that pursue sound policies."[82]

In practice this was a wager on the Anglo-American status quo that offered a modest set of best practices applied to the emerging markets. These emphasized transparency, risk assessment, routinized bankruptcy procedures, and open competition from the money centers of Europe and America. As he put it to a Brookings audience in April 1998, "When countries allow financial service providers into their markets—with all the competition, capital and expertise they bring with them—the strength of the financial system is greatly enhanced." Summers, in turn, told a meeting of economists late in 1998, "It would be a tragedy if the lesson learned from recent events was that the flow of capital from rich to poor counties was something that should be prevented, rather than encouraged."[83]

As in so many other instances, from the contretemps over his first budget in 1993 to the Seattle blowup in 1999, Clinton's progressive instincts gave way to a neoliberalism backstopped by all the ideological and organizational firepower mobilized on behalf of the US Treasury and its allies. Neither Clinton nor Rubin wanted to bring the conflict to a head: each relied upon the other, but there is little doubt that in August, September, and October 1998, as the Lewinsky scandal generated one headline after another, Clinton stood on the moral and political defensive.

Rubin, Talbott, Blumenthal, and other aides marveled at the degree to which the president remained sharp in meetings and briefings and while carrying out all the other duties of a chief executive. But the Lewinsky fiasco had pushed his reformist gambits to the back pages of even the most serious newspapers.[84]

As Clinton sank, Rubin's prestige rose ever higher. When Pete Peterson, the investment banker and former Commerce secretary, introduced Bill Clinton to the New York meeting of the Council on Foreign Relations, the release of the salacious Starr report three days before shadowed the president's appearance. The audience was polite, but Peterson made clear how diminished Clinton's stature was: "From Main Street to Wall Street," announced Peterson in his remarks introducing the president, "people sleep better because Bob Rubin is the secretary of the treasury." The applause was so vigorous that even Clinton had to muster a bemused half-laugh.[85]

Thus, little was done to moderate capital mobility in the remainder of Clinton's term or the decade that followed. When the next financial crisis struck, capital flows had soared from less than 5 percent of global economic output in 1999 to a peak of about 20 percent ten years later. By this point finally, the IMF formally—but modestly—shifted its "institutional view." Said the Fund: "The extent of the damage that large and volatile capital flows can cause to recipient countries has not been sufficiently recognized."[86] Paul Krugman put it more bluntly. Linking the Asian contagion of the late 1990s with the near-defaults of Greece, Cyprus, Iceland, Portugal, and Spain fifteen years later, Krugman wrote that the "unrestricted movement of capital is looking more and more like a failed experiment."[87]

Failure or not, the Asian financial crisis constituted a late-twentieth-century version of the "open door" policies that had animated American capitalists a century before when President William McKinley and Secretary of State John Hay had insisted on equal trading rights in China and the Far East for US firms. Now the International Monetary Fund and the US Treasury offered an even more powerful and intrusive version of that gunboat diplomacy. Neoliberalism was not laissez-faire. It required a powerful state willing and able to repeatedly restructure markets, on Wall Street as well as in distant capitals. Thus, economic development of a distinctly Asian variety would not be permitted to coexist with the Western variety if finance was to roam the world on a truly equitable basis. But such financial freedom, and the baroque innovations it catalyzed, bred its own set of dangers, at home as well as abroad.

13

Deregulating Finance

Precisely a decade after *Time* magazine put "the Committee to Save the World"—Rubin, Summers, and Greenspan—on its cover, the news-weekly indicted Bill Clinton as one of the politicians most responsible for the "free-wheeling capitalism" that engendered the economic crisis that began in 2008.[1] It was during the last years of his administration that financial deregulation ran rampant, setting the stage for the worldwide panic that liquidated trillions of dollars once thought safely stored in home mortgages, commercial loans, and stock market valuations. In the late 1990s the headlong rush toward financial irresponsibility had many powerful champions, with just a few contrarians. But the latter understood that at the very moment when a neoliberal worldview seemed to flourish as never before the seeds of its demise were taking root.

The Savings and Loan Debacle

The origins of the debacle lay in the Whitewater scandal, but not the one most people associate with Bill and Hillary Clinton. The failure of their make-a-quick-buck real estate venture on the White River in the Ozarks constituted just one minor but telling instance of a far larger financial debacle that engulfed thousands of savings and loan (S&L) institutions, many American banks and corporations, and some of the largest firms on Wall Street. However, by the time Congress, the White House, and key regulatory agencies finally came to legislative grips with these destabilizing financial problems at the end of Clinton's second term, the president was largely AWOL, still battling a prosecutor and an impeachment whose origins stretched all the way back to that abortive Arkansas land deal. After he left office, and in the midst of the even larger banking meltdown of 2008, Bill Clinton would bemoan his failure to pay more attention.

The Clintons were strapped for income in 1978. Bill's salary as Arkansas attorney general paid only $26,500 a year and Hillary was then earning even less at the Rose Law Firm. So when an old friend came along with a real estate scheme, they were all in. Bill had gotten to know James MacDougal when they both worked for Senator William Fulbright in the 1960s. MacDougal, a small-time land developer, proposed that the Clintons join him and his wife, Susan, in buying 230 acres of undeveloped land along the south bank of the White River in the Ozark Mountains. They would subdivide the property and sell the lots to retirees and visitors moving south from the industrial Midwest. The four borrowed $203,000 and then transferred ownership to a newly created Whitewater Development Corporation, in which they all had equal shares.[2]

The Ozark location turned out to be remote and inaccessible after a heavy rain. But the real disaster struck just as the Whitewater lots were ready for sale at the end of 1979. By then Fed Chairman Paul Volcker had begun his brutal assault on Carter-era inflation. Interest rates climbed to nearly 20 percent, slamming the brakes on the economy, sending a shock wave through the Northern manufacturing belt, and putting mortgage costs beyond the reach of the kind of people expected to build an Ozark vacation home. The Clintons were in hock for over $100,000, and although they were passive investors, conflict-of-interest entanglements were hard to avoid once Bill Clinton became governor, especially given MacDougal's fast and loose business practices.[3] But MacDougal's many financial indiscretions were not just a product of his good-old-boy persona. His speculative and sometimes illegal investments were a necessary product of the untenable financial dilemma the Volcker shock had created for thousands of small-town bankers and savings and loan owners.

At the depth of the early 1980s recession MacDougal bought a small savings and loan and renamed it Madison Guaranty S&L. The purchase was a gamble, because it was becoming impossible to run a profitable

S&L when the interest rate earned on a traditional thirty-year home loan was far lower than the rate necessary to attract depositors or borrow from other institutions. This happened because in the depths of the Great Depression, when more than five thousand banks had failed, the first New Deal Congress passed the Glass-Steagall Act, which, among other changes, established the Federal Deposit Insurance Corporation (FDIC), whose champion had been Representative Henry Steagall of Alabama. Middle-class depositors no longer needed to worry about being first in line at a troubled bank's door. If short of cash, these institutions could now borrow from the Federal Reserve, even when they could borrow nowhere else.

With these backstops in place, and with tax dollars now in play, Congress restricted bank activities to discourage them from taking excessive risks, another move intended to help prevent bank failures and irresponsible speculation. Virginia Senator Carter Glass, whose hostility to Yankee banking trusts was equaled only by his defense of a Jim Crow racial order in the South, was the chief sponsor of the provision in the law that prohibited banks from being "engaged principally" in nonbanking activities, such as underwriting securities or selling insurance. Firms were thus forced to choose between becoming a bank engaged in simple lending or an investment bank whose business was inherently riskier. J.P. Morgan & Co., the dominant Wall Street firm of that era, split in two following passage of the Glass-Steagall Act: several partners departed to form Morgan Stanley & Co. and focus on investment banking, while J.P. Morgan stuck with the lending business.[4] Furthermore, Congress let the Federal Reserve cap the interest rates that banks and thrifts—also called S&Ls—could pay depositors. This rule, known as Regulation Q, allowed S&Ls to pay slightly higher interest rates than banks so as to ensure the viability of thousands of local institutions whose prime mission was restricted to the financing of home mortgages, a bulwark of middle-class America.[5]

The system was stable as long as interest rates remained steady, which they did during the first two decades after World War II. Beginning in the late 1960s, however, inflation became a chronic problem, pushing up interest rates. Money market mutual funds, sponsored by brokerage firms and other financial institutions, offered higher rates than the S&Ls. To most of the public, consumer-oriented mutual funds and certificates of deposit might have seemed like another form of bank deposit, but they were actually uninsured securities, the kernel of a "shadow banking" sector that would soon balloon in size. And thanks to Regulation Q, the well-regulated banks and thrifts were at a disadvantage, stuck offering less than 6 percent on most deposits. This was an untenable bind for the depository institutions, and it became an existential crisis when Volcker sent interest rates sky high.[6] Congress responded by abolishing Regulation Q and also allowed the thrifts a much wider range of investment strategies to pay for the higher interest rates they now offered depositors.[7]

In this context, concluded the Whitewater counsel's final report, Madison Guaranty's failure was "entirely ordinary," with causes and consequences shared by hundreds of other S&Ls.[8] Rather than admit their insolvency, many S&Ls took advantage of lax regulatory oversight, itself a product of the Reagan era, to pursue highly speculative or fraudulent investment strategies. For example, Madison Guaranty employed a land appraiser who conspired with MacDougal and other executives to inflate estimates used to support the S&L's loans. One beneficiary in the mid-1980s was Jim Guy Tucker, who succeeded Bill Clinton as Arkansas governor. Tucker's illicit loans came to light a decade later, after which a jury convicted both Tucker and the MacDougals of conspiracy and mail fraud, thereby forcing the governor's resignation late in 1996. Even before Whitewater became a household name, FDIC chair L. William Seidman reported that "fraud had been found in [60] percent of the failed savings institutions. . . . Phony appraisals, self-dealing, loans to family and associates, kickbacks and payoffs were rife."[9] On March 2, 1989, Madison was seized by agents of the Federal Deposit Insurance Corporation and put into receivership. No one noticed because on that same day federal regulators took over 36 other ailing S&Ls in Alaska, Arkansas, Kansas, Louisiana, Maryland, and Texas, eight of which were in small-town Arkansas.[10] In all, some 1,043 out of more than 3,200 S&Ls would collapse between 1986 and 1995, costing the US government over $210 billion; the bailout of Madison Guaranty depositors alone clocked in at $73 million. None of the many investigations into Whitewater found that Bill or Hillary Clinton did anything criminal, but the epidemic of S&L scandals was real enough, generating 1,259 Justice Department indictments charging 1,955 defendants with "major" crimes relating to federally regulated savings and loans. Most were convicted and spent time in prison.[11]

Repealing Glass-Steagall

Those entangled in the S&L debacle were financial small fry. Wall Street thought it knew better. Even before the S&L collapse, many large, well-established commercial banks began to lobby Congress to loosen the Glass-Steagall restrictions. With the growth of money market mutual funds and other complex financial instruments that blurred the line between deposits and securities—checks could be written on a money market fund—the banking industry complained that the Glass-Steagall framework had become obsolete. They wanted to sell bonds, underwrite stock offerings, and compete with the unregulated foreign banks threatening to entice US corporations to invest their capital abroad. With a Reaganite deregulatory mindset in ascendance, it was not a surprise that the Federal Reserve began to accommodate such Wall Street pressures. In 1986 and 1987 the Fed ruled that a bank could derive up to 5 percent of its gross revenue from activities otherwise considered the province of investment banking firms, including commercial paper, municipal bonds, and mortgage-backed securities.[12]

Chairman Paul Volcker had actually been opposed to such liberalization, but his successor, Alan Greenspan, proved a relentless advocate of financial deregulation. Although the Fed's practice differed from Greenspan's Ayn Randish proclivities, the chairman often argued that regardless of the law or regulatory oversight, financial institutions had strong incentives to protect shareholders and customers, thereby ensuring that risk would be managed in a prudent fashion. Likewise, financial markets exerted strong and effective discipline: analysts, credit rating agencies, and investors would deploy the ever-rising stream of financial information and insight to police individual firms and industry sectors.

As a new generation of economists would argue, increasingly "efficient markets" precluded gross mispricing of all sorts of tradable assets, especially those bought and sold on Wall Street. Greenspan therefore argued that the urgent question about government regulation was whether it strengthened or weakened private regulation. Testifying before Congress in 1997, he framed the issue this way: financial "modernization" was needed to "remove outdated restrictions that serve no useful purpose, that decrease economic efficiency, and that . . . limit choices and options for the consumer of financial services." Removing the barriers "would permit banking organizations to compete more effectively in their natural markets. The result would be a more efficient financial system providing better services to the public."[13]

Early in Greenspan's tenure, the Federal Reserve reinterpreted Glass-Steagall to allow banks to deal in some debt and equity securities, so long as those activities did not exceed 10 percent of gross revenues. Later, in 1996, Greenspan's Fed issued an audacious ruling, allowing bank holding companies to own investment banking operations that accounted for as much as 25 percent of their revenues, a change that rendered Glass-Steagall effectively obsolete, since virtually any institution could arrange its operations to stay within that level. Alan Blinder, then the Fed's vice chair, thought that the new ruling amounted to "tacit repeal" of Glass-Steagall.[14]

Like other regulatory liberals, Blinder was less than enthusiastic about Greenspan's cozy relationship with Wall Street, and he thought that Congress, not the Fed, should take the initiative, but when it came to formal repeal of Glass-Steagall, there was little dissent from anyone inside the Clinton administration. Banking deregulation had a bipartisan flavor: when President Clinton signed the Riegle-Neal Interstate Banking and Branching Efficiency Act in September 1994, he was endorsing a Democratic bill designed to remove many of the restrictions that for seventy years had prevented money-center banks from establishing branches all across America.[15] "In effect, Congress has said let the merger mania begin," opined *The Independent*, a British paper that now expected UK banks to move into the American market.[16]

Within the administration, a high-level "working group on financial markets" took the lead on all the key regulatory issues. Chaired by Robert Rubin, this committee included the Fed's Alan Greenspan, NEC chair Gene Sperling, the Security and Exchange Commission's Arthur Levitt, and Brooksley Born, whose leadership of the once-obscure Commodities Futures Trading Corporation would soon become highly controversial. Rubin and Greenspan were first among equals, with Sperling an adept operative.[17] The views of President Clinton were not exactly an afterthought, but on many occasions memos on highly complex issues were passed to the Oval Office at almost the last minute. This was the case, for example, on the eve of a February 1995 speech in which Rubin, who had pushed for Glass-Steagall repeal when he was head of Goldman Sachs, would begin to advance the administration's case for revision of the Depression-era law.[18] Although Barings, a British investment bank, had just been wiped out over the previous weekend by risky futures trading, Rubin remained entirely self-confident: "The more diverse banks are by geography and by product, the better off the banking industry will be," he told a luncheon audience in New York. Rubin pointed out that "no other industrialized countries have the rules we have separating our commercial and investment banks, our insurance companies and our other financial industries."[19]

Although CEA chair Joseph Stiglitz was often a skeptic when it came to financial deregulation, he had transferred his talents to the World Bank by the start of Clinton's second term. Gene Sperling could therefore write the president a memo in March 1997 assuring him that "all your economic advisors believe financial modernization reform is long overdue."[20] The New Deal–era restrictions might remain on the books, "imposing needless regulatory and management costs, and impeding competition, innovation, and consumer choice," Sperling wrote. "Allowing financial firms of all types to affiliate holds promise that consumers will benefit as fair competition—less hindered by regulatory restrictions—will drive firms to achieve and pass savings on to consumers." Reflecting the Treasury view that a financial firm engaged in multiple lines of business was an inherently good thing, Sperling assured

Clinton that "increased affiliation will increase intra-firm diversification, which will almost certainly reduce the risk of institutional failure."[21]

Sperling was one of Clinton's more liberal advisers; he had been on Robert Reich's side opposing the austerity budget of 1993 and championed the Children's Health Insurance Program, a higher minimum wage, and an expansion of the Earned Income Tax Credit. His memoir of the Clinton era would be entitled *The Pro-Growth Progressive.* Sperling's endorsement of the bank mergers and acquisitions that would surely arise out of the repeal of Glass-Steagall was therefore all the more significant because it encapsulated the larger accommodation that American liberals were making with conservative, market-friendly jurists such as Robert Bork and Richard Posner, who had assimilated the Chicago School's market efficiency line of thought into their antitrust jurisprudence. Under this Reaganite dispensation, the only question that mattered when it came to economic concentration was not the potential political or market power wielded by such giant firms—the "economic royalists" that had "created a new despotism," in FDR's 1936 denunciation—but rather the impact of such a conglomerate on the price that consumers paid for goods or services. Big companies, in finance or elsewhere, would become problematic only when there was an overwhelming reason to think that they were gouging the public, and since size now seemed to equal efficiency, that was unlikely. Lower prices, not any worry over a rise in corporate power, was the single criterion by which antitrust action, or inaction, was to be judged. And since the rise of a globalized economy had thrust large American companies into competition with foreign rivals, the claim that even the largest US corporation was part of a price-fixing oligopoly seemed increasingly far-fetched.[22]

Since the 1970s a whole line of progressive thought had come to endorse deregulation. Ralph Nader had been but the most prominent figure to attack the "iron triangle"—the congressional committees supervising a particular industry, the executive branch regulatory agencies, and the corporations themselves—that sustained the self-interested, cartel-like governance of airlines, trucking, financial services, and traditional utilities such as electrical power transmission and telecommunications.

A Consumers Union spokesperson was aligned with this reformist, Naderite outlook when he told a Senate banking subcommittee in 1974, "In many ways, Regulation Q ceilings, like fair trade laws, are anti-competitive, anti-consumer vestiges of the Depression and have long outlived any usefulness they may once have had."[23]

The New Economy Comes to Telecom

The deregulatory ethos was greatly advanced by its linkage to the ideological power generated by those who foresaw an American "new economy" in the making. Heavily influenced by libertarian currents swirling out of Silicon Valley, both liberals and conservatives partook of this economic elixir, with Newt Gingrich as well as Al Gore sharing in the excitement. A case in point was the Telecommunications Act of 1996, which changed the fundamental rules governing the world of electronic and digital information, all in the name of deregulation and creation of an "information superhighway" traversing the "new economy." Gore, the administration's point man on this reform, asserted that the administration sought "open and free competition" that would "unleash consumer demand for the information products and services that will educate, entertain, and empower our people."[24] The 1996 act lifted many regulatory limits on cable television and allowed the regional telephone companies, the "Baby Bell" offspring of AT&T, to go into cable and long-distance service. Above all it ended most merger restrictions in an industry that accounted for more than 15 percent of the entire economy.[25]

Objections from some progressives might have been expected, but early in the legislative discussions Edward Markey, the liberal Democrat who then chaired the House telecommunications subcommittee, reported a "general conceptual agreement" between both parties and the White House.[26] The one important issue that divided the administration from Republicans arose over the degree to which the Baby Bells—which were actually huge companies championed by the GOP—would invade new markets without relinquishing their immensely profitable monopolies over local service. After a vague veto threat from Clinton, congressional Republicans made a few technical concessions on that issue, but within the administration's working group that framed the law CEA chair Joseph Stiglitz still thought deregulation was being taken too far. "Our deliberations were frequently contentious," he recalled. But Al Gore had long sought a reconfiguration of the telecommunications landscape, and Clinton was happy to champion a bipartisan piece of legislation that seemingly opened the door to a wonderous high-tech tomorrow.[27] Both houses of Congress passed the reform with but minuscule opposition.[28]

Thus, when President Clinton signed the Telecommunications Act of 1996 and then, three years later, the law repealing Glass-Steagall, he linked deregulation, markets, and the promise of a "new economy." The Telecom Act "will bring the future to our doorstep," he told a large audience assembled at the Library of Congress. The world was being remade by an "information revolution . . . so profound that it is changing the dominant economic model of the age." Outdated regulations reaching back to the New Deal had held back the revolution, Clinton asserted, but "with the stroke of a pen, our laws will catch up with our future."[29] Likewise, when Clinton put his signature on the law allowing commercial and investment banks to merge—"the most important legislative changes to the structure of the financial system since the 1930s"—the president assured the public that now banks and other firms would have "the freedom to innovate in the new economy."[30]

Innovation, as it turned out, meant something very close to a scramble for market dominance and creation of an industry oligopoly. In telecom the belief that deregulation would lead to more competition proved gravely mistaken. Deregulation put a premium on "first mover advantage"—the expectation that if a firm could secure an early, outsized position in a market, it would henceforth control it. It was to be a game not of continuous competition but of winner take all. This created an incentive to build market share through highly leveraged mergers, acquisitions, and heedless overinvestment, especially in fiber cable. Thus, the Baby Bells merged themselves from seven to three, the ten major media companies became six, and Clear Channel achieved a near-monopoly among rural radio listeners as the number of stations it controlled rose from 40 to 1,240 in just a few years.[31] Facing bankruptcy, AT&T—the old Ma Bell—was gobbled up by Southwestern Bell (SBC). Of this rapid series of consolidations Alfred Kahn, the father of Carter-era deregulation, remarked, "It just takes my breath away, the chutzpah of it."[32]

When the dust settled early in the twenty-first century, a series of bankruptcies had wiped out $2.8 trillion in stock market valuation, with WorldCom the single biggest bankruptcy in American history to that time. As the NASDAQ telecom index plummeted 92 percent from its March 2000 peak, more than half a million jobs were lost in this single industry, with unionized workers taking the biggest hit. Most of the new "wireless" and cable firms were resolutely anti-union.[33] This was a far larger debacle than the S&L crisis of the 1980s, and compared to the simultaneous dot-com crash the telecom bust was far more consequential. The swift fall among the high-tech stocks merely pricked a stock market bubble. After all, many Silicon Valley start-ups had no actual product, no income, and few employees. But the telecom collapse destroyed companies whose component parts—and the modestly good jobs that went with them—often stretched back a century. Consumers soon paid higher prices for telephone and cable service.[34] "Deregulation of the telecom industry—that was a mistake," concluded Laura Tyson some years after she left her NEC post.[35]

The Citigroup Authorization Act

The deregulation of finance and the repeal of Glass-Steagall were more politically difficult but of even greater consequence. The process had been frustrated not so much by traditional liberals hostile to Wall Street power as by the smaller stock brokerages, insurance companies, and banks fearful of their institutional demise at the hands of a new set of conglomerated financial institutions. Republican Representative James Leach, a moderate from Iowa who chaired the House Banking Committee, had long championed the interests of the small-town bankers who had been a backbone of heartland Republicanism for more than a century. Because Leach was being challenged by Christian conservatives back in Iowa, he led the House Whitewater investigation with an aggressive self-righteousness that put him at bitter odds with the Clintons.[36] But Whitewater was actually a sideshow for Leach: he was more concerned about the fate of the smaller banks, and he particularly feared that a big company, like Wal-Mart, might start a shopping spree for smaller financial institutions, putting them in a situation resembling that of the many Iowa mom-and-pop stores that found themselves unable to compete with the retail giant. William McQuillan, who ran an $18 million bank in Greeley, Nebraska, offered a representative sentiment from this quarter when, during a congressional appearance, he asked "why anyone would want to radically change our current banking system." To do so would create a "financial services world characterized by huge conglomerates which are being created as the Japanese model on which they are based is discredited."[37] Democrat John Dingell, who remembered the Depression-era bank runs and evictions in his youth, agreed. "There's been a great rush to create financial institutions that are at the same time too big to fail, too big to bother, and too big to care."[38]

The deadlock was broken in 1998, when Citicorp, itself the product of a series of Wall Street acquisitions, forced the issue by seeking a merger with the insurance giant Travelers. They would form Citigroup, a $70 billion financial conglomerate with more than one hundred million customers and four thousand branches around the world. Led by Sandy Weill of Travelers and John Reed of Citicorp, the megabank–cum–insurance broker was an enormous, flagrant transgression of even the most attenuated Glass-Steagall guidelines and would therefore require an extraordinary level of government acquiescence.

They got it. Because the Federal Reserve regulated the biggest banks, the deal went there for approval, but not before Sandy Weill had made heads-up calls to Greenspan, Rubin, and Clinton. Citing a technical exemption, Greenspan offered the bank a waiver from the law, with a two-year duration. This waiver was hardly unexpected given Greenspan's well-advertised commitment to the dismantling of Glass-Steagall, as well as his two decades of friendship with Weill, including stints as a consultant for Travelers in the late 1970s. But the waiver did not give the new conglomerate carte blanche: Citigroup would have to divest itself of many Travelers assets within five years unless Congress replaced Glass-Steagall with something far more accommodating to such giant mergers. The Clinton administration was all in, so Congress had to make a decision: Was it prepared to break up the nation's largest financial firm, or was it time to repeal Glass-Steagall once and for all?[39]

It wasn't much of a question. When Weill and Reed announced the marriage of their two firms on April 6, 1998, at a glitzy Waldorf Astoria press conference, the business media cheered and bank stocks lurched upward. The *New York Times* splashed the front page of its business section with a drawing of Weill and Reed as twin King Kongs, perched on the slanted roof of the Citicorp Center. Given the worldwide nature of finance, the *Times* editorialized, even if the new conglomerate was the largest such institution in the United States, it "threatens no one because it would not dominate banking, securities, insurance, or any other financial market." Within a week, other large banks were in merger mode: Banc One and First Chicago unveiled plans for a combine that would count as the nation's fifth-largest bank, and then North Carolina–based NationsBank and California-based BankAmerica announced an even bigger deal that, under the label Bank of America, would have nearly five thousand branches from sea to sea.[40]

The commission that would later probe the causes of the 2008 financial crisis reported that "the new regime encouraged growth and consolidation within and across banking, securities, and insurance." Bank-centered financial holding companies such as Citigroup, J.P. Morgan, and Bank of America would now compete directly with the "big five" investment banks—Goldman Sachs, Morgan Stanley, Merrill Lynch, Lehman Brothers, and Bear Stearns—in securitization, stock and bond underwriting, loan syndication, and trading in over-the-counter (OTC) derivatives. The strategies of the largest commercial banks and their holding companies came to more closely resemble the strategies of investment banks.[41]

In some Washington circles repeal of Glass-Steagall was called the "Citigroup Authorization Act."[42] Confirming the utter validity of this bon mot, Sandy Weill would later hang a four-foot-wide slab of wood on the wall of his office that proclaimed THE SHATTERER OF GLASS-STEAGALL, alongside an etched portrait of himself. But a more celebratory moment arrived in the fall of 1999, even before the formal congressional deconstruction of Glass-Steagall had been finalized. To a chorus of media applause, Robert Rubin had resigned as Treasury secretary in July after smoothly handing the reins over to Larry Summers. Almost immediately Weill began courting Rubin for a post at Citigroup. By early that fall the deal was set: for a reported $40 million a year Rubin would grace the new conglomerate with his presence. He was to be a consigliere, a minister without a portfolio who would lend a hand in many areas and be free to indulge in outside interests—such as the Hamilton Project, which sought to advance in the twenty-first century Rubin's brand of neoliberal welfarism.[43]

While all this was transpiring in Manhattan, the revocation of Glass-Steagall had one last act in the nation's capital. Texas Republican Phil Gramm, a former economics professor who allied himself with the most libertarian currents on Wall Street, wanted to use repeal of Glass-Steagall to limit consumer protections overall and in particular to sabotage the Community Reinvestment Act (CRA), which had been enacted in the 1970s to forestall bank "redlining" in minority communities. Gramm, who chaired the Senate Banking Committee, thought that Jesse Jackson and other civil rights activists used the CRA to "extort" banks into either providing unsound loans to minority-owned businesses and real estate projects or making philanthropic grants to community organizations like Jackson's Operation Push. Among other changes to the law, Gramm wanted to eliminate the requirement that banks seeking to merge with other financial institutions maintain a "satisfactory" CRA compliance record. The senator's retrograde militancy proved highly useful to the Clintonite deregulators, who were delighted to draw a line in the sand against destruction of the CRA.[44] In the five years after 1993 the number of home mortgage loans going to African Americans increased by 58 percent, to Hispanics by 62 percent, and to low- and moderate-income borrowers by 38 percent—all well above the overall market. With the president threatening to veto any financial reform that weakened CRA, this was a moral battle that could once again unite African-American activists, congressional Democrats, and the bank law deregulators at the Treasury and on the National Economic Council.[45]

In October 1999, as a House-Senate conference committee deadlocked over Gramm's hostility to CRA, Sperling and Summers, the latter now newly installed as secretary of the Treasury, kicked off a week of intense, on-again, off-again negotiations with Gramm to thrash out a deal to preserve bank community-lending requirements. They objected to key elements of Gramm's bill because it would reduce the frequency of CRA-compliance examinations for small banks and failed to penalize expansionist banks for having an unsatisfactory record helping minority communities. Gramm was handicapped by the fact that neither House Republicans, especially those led by James Leach, nor most of the big banks shared his hostility to this aspect of the law. "CRA is part of the way we do business—we don't have any problems with it," a Citigroup spokeswoman had told the *Wall Street Journal* a few months earlier.[46] Indeed, Sandy Weill and Jesse Jackson had a highly cooperative relationship, with Citigroup and other banks funding some of Jackson's Black capitalism projects.[47] Thus, in late night negotiations Gramm's hard line gradually dissolved, especially after the American Bankers Association and the Independent Community Bankers of America made clear that CRA was acceptable to them and indeed far less of a threat than the possibility that the big retailers or other nonfinancial companies might get into the banking business. With the CRA intact and the Wal-Marts of the world kept out, President Clinton was free to finally sign the Financial Services Modernization Act in mid-November 1999. It was a "historic agreement," he said, one that would "strengthen the economy and help consumers, communities, and businesses across America."[48]

How important was the repeal of Glass-Steagall, especially in light of the 2008 financial crisis? Before that cataclysm, few paid the Gramm-Leach-Bliley Act much heed. For most in the Clinton policy circle repeal of Glass-Steagall had been seen as close to inevitable. Alan Greenspan called it "an unsung moment of policymaking." In their memoirs, all written before the financial deluge, neither Gene Sperling, Robert Rubin, nor Bill Clinton even mention the demise of the law. Greenspan thought the Glass-Steagall divorce between commercial and investment banking had been a bad idea even in the Depression years. Congressional approval of a repeal was but a long-overdue correction and recognition that "awareness of the detrimental effects of excessive regulation and the need for economic adaptability has advanced substantially in recent years."[49]

The financial collapse of 2008 refocused attention on the law. Conservatives were quick to blame the CRA for the implosion in the housing mortgage market, but CRA-regulated mortgages actually proved safer than most others; in any event, they constituted too small a slice of the market to have any real impact. Liberals who directly pointed to the bank reform of 1999 as the chief culprit, such as Robert Kuttner, Elizabeth Warren, and Joseph Stiglitz, had a stronger case. Given his insider status, Stiglitz offered the most compelling indictment: even before 2008 he had highlighted the reckless, hyper-aggressive investment strategies of the giant financial institutions that arose in the wake of Glass-Steagall's repeal. He made the now-familiar argument that "when enterprises become too big, and interconnections too tight, there is a risk that the quality of economic decisions deteriorates, and the 'too big to fail' problem rears its ugly head."[50]

In contrast, Glass-Steagall had ensured that commercial banks, which made loans based on tangible collateral, provided a source of "independent" judgment on the creditworthiness of businesses. Without that autonomy, a full-service bank that made money by selling equities and bonds and arranging merger deals would be tempted to extend additional loans to a business that got into trouble. This is what happened at Enron, WorldCom, and other troubled companies early in the twenty-first century when banks continued to lend to them almost up to the day of bankruptcy. But it was not just a conflict-of-interest question: the repeal of Glass-Steagall helped transmit the risk-taking culture of investment banking to commercial banks and other ostensibly more prudent entities, including Fannie Mae and Freddie Mac, the quasi-governmental mortgage-makers that financed more than half the housing market. And like Theodore Roosevelt and the early-twentieth-century trustbusters, Stiglitz thought a concentration of financial power had spilled over into the political realm, with deleterious consequences for the governmental process.[51]

The problem with the Stiglitz argument was not that his critique was wrong, but that it did not require the repeal of Glass-Steagall to have a more general application. Most of the investment banks and other "shadow banking" firms that either collapsed or required giant bailouts—AIG, Bear Stearns, Lehman Brothers, and Merrill Lynch—were not the kind of financial holding companies engendered under the Gramm-Leach-Bliley Act. As Alan Blinder argued, "I have often posed the following question to critics who claim that repealing Glass-Steagall was a major cause of the financial crisis: What bad practices would have been prevented if Glass-Steagall was still on the books? I have yet to hear a good answer." The rise of a dangerous, unregulated, multitrillion-dollar market in complex derivatives and subprime mortgages did not require the repeal of Glass-Steagall but had its own perverse history, to which we now turn.[52]

Derivatives in Theory and Practice

Insuring against risk, now or in the future, is a good and ancient idea. The Egyptians constructed granaries to make certain they could bake bread even in those years when the harvest failed; Lloyds of London insured sailing ships on yearlong voyages, and Kansas farmers sold their wheat crop at a price made certain long before the seeds were even in the ground. Although it soon became easy enough to turn such bets on the future into a frenzied set of speculative trades—brokers yelling at each other on the floor of the Chicago Mercantile Exchange are forever etched in our imagination as the outré essence of capitalist performativity—the impulse to make the future predictable can also be stabilizing, a hedge against uncertainty, and even progressive if undertaken in a fully systematic fashion.

Thus, we find the Nobel Prize–winning economist Kenneth Arrow offering a Columbia University audience a 1978 lecture entitled "A Cautious Case for Socialism." Arrow was an uncle of Larry Summers and a pioneer in growth economics and the impact of asymmetric information on market outcomes. Arrow thought the absence of a full range of future markets a "severe shortcoming of the actual capitalist system compared with an ideally efficient economic system." These market uncertainties made efficient resource allocation, including the maintenance of full employment, impossible. Thus, mechanisms were needed, above and beyond the stock market and the Chicago trading pits, whereby the prices of future goods could be known today. This would generate "an efficient allocation of risk-bearing."[53]

Arrow's wish was soon fulfilled, but hardly as he expected. In the years after 1980, Wall Street firms, faced with Volcker shock instability, on the one hand, while also desperately seeking higher returns, on the other, made financial innovation a way of life—condoned, of course, by a Reaganite ethos that looked askance at any sort of governmental regulation. Derivatives thereby became the most rapidly growing part of the US financial system. All sorts of risks, from currency and interest rate volatility to outright bankruptcy, could be insured or "hedged." And since every player, on Wall Street or off, might well have unique interests, it was important that such hedging could be customized—a private agreement between two companies. Soon credit swaps—customized deals made "over the counter," that is, off the exchange—became the most heavily traded contracts in the world. As the journalist Michael Hirsh explained, "If one company had a lot of debt in fixed interest rates, and another had a lot of debt in adjustable rates, or if one company did heavy business by borrowing rubles and another relied on Mexican pesos, they could 'swap' some payment obligations so that neither would be wholly dependent on the fixed rate or the adjustable rate, or on the fortunes of the ruble or the peso."[54]

As we will see, such derivative trades were not transparent, they were often numbingly complex, and they involved huge amounts of leverage that soon proved dangerous to buyers, sellers, and the entire financial system. But most Wall Street firms were fiercely protective of this new form of speculation, resisting any and all efforts to make such trades part of a regulated and transparent market of the sort that sold equities in lower Manhattan or hog bellies in Chicago. These bespoke transactions—each one was uniquely structured—were far more lucrative for their creators than anything sold on a stock or bond exchange. Every share of IBM was identical, with a low, discounted commission for large blocs bought or sold. But a swap between IBM and AIG was one of a kind and hence generated much more revenue for the bank or broker who put it all together. Because there was no transparent market for such derivatives, their pricing was shrouded in mathematical complexity overseen by a new generation of "quants" (quantitative analysts) who were hired by Wall Street firms to develop models predicting how markets or security prices might change.

"It's a higher-margin product," said Joe Nocera of the *New York Times* in a PBS postmortem. "So one of the big problems with the rise of credit derivatives is that Wall Street was terribly resistant to the idea of standardizing contracts and allowing them to be traded on an exchange, because it would hurt their profits."[55] Robert Rubin concurred, at least in 2009 when he testified before the congressionally mandated Financial Crisis Inquiry Commission. Though he claimed that in the 1990s he favored some regulation of OTC derivatives, Rubin told the commission that "the very strongly held views in the financial services industry in opposition to regulation" were insurmountable.[56]

Derivatives were measured by their "notional" or face value—the reference amount against which interest rates were figured. The money actually changing hands, absent a total meltdown, was far less, but those notional sums were nevertheless astounding. By 1998 the global market for custom derivatives—the complex over-the-counter sort that became the object of much controversy—had risen to $70 trillion from almost nothing a decade before. This was at a moment when the entire US GDP was just over one-tenth that size.[57]

Derivatives burst on the public scene in February 1994 when Hurricane Greenspan took Wall Street by such surprise. Though he felt betrayed, Bill Clinton kept his mouth shut. Wall Street was more alarmed: this was the first interest rate increase since derivatives had become so pervasive and important. In just a few days, with the total damage to the bond market standing at upwards of $1.5 trillion, the impact of the Fed's seemingly minor rate adjustment had been costlier than any other market debacle since the 1929 stock market crash. It was "an Arctic blast through Wall Street," wrote the *New York Times*.[58]

The freeze-up soon wreaked havoc in Orange County, California. The conservative, sun-drenched exurb south of Los Angeles had nearly two million residents by the early 1990s. The home to Disneyland and Knotts Berry Farm, the county was still the abode of hundreds of thousands of white homeowners who had long anchored Republican political dominance in the state. Bill Clinton had managed to win California in 1992, in part because the post–Cold War collapse of the aerospace industry had sent a shiver across Southern California. Orange County was hit hard, but residents there had no appetite for raising taxes, even though Proposition 13, passed in 1978, had already drastically limited property tax increases on both single-family homes and commercial real estate.

Orange County treasurer Robert Citron was not worried. A nominal Democrat, Citron, then seventy years old, had spent his entire career in Orange County's treasury department, where, by the early 1990s, he was one of the largest investors in the country, managing $7.4 billion in taxpayer money. Citron, a college dropout, had no financial background: he kept many key records on index cards and a wall calendar, and though he claimed to understand the bond market, he more often than not blustered and bluffed when called to account by other county executives. But Orange voters loved him because of his seemingly magical capacity to leverage their tax dollars. Throughout the 1980s and early 1990s Citron had outperformed every other county investment manager, sometimes by several percentage points. Instead of putting money in plain-vanilla Treasury bonds, Citron bought structured notes, largely from Merrill Lynch. On paper these notes looked like very safe, AAA-rated investments, but they contained derivative formulas that were a big bet on interest rates remaining low and steady. For example, one $100 million note paid a coupon of 10 percent minus LIBOR—the London-based short-term interest rate index. So if the London interbank rate was 3 percent, Orange County would receive a 7 percent coupon. This was called an "inverse floater." As the financial analyst Frank Partnoy explained in a postmortem, Citron was effectively borrowing at short-term rates and investing at longer-term rates. The Orange County treasurer compounded the danger by borrowing another

$13 billion from various banks, including Merrill Lynch, which earned $62.4 million from the county in 1993 and 1994 alone.[59]

Given this leverage, the Fed's modest boost to short-term interest rates on February 4, 1994, had a devastating impact on the value of Orange County bonds. For nearly a year Citron was able to hide the true extent of the losses because of another feature of derivatives trading: the absence of "mark to market" valuations in an OTC arrangement that was shielded from public view. Although the real price of his investments had dropped, Citron and other such investors could continue to value them at the original cost—at least until the banks from which he had borrowed demanded additional collateral.

Orange County was not the only entity to lose big money investing in highly leveraged and unregulated financial instruments. Mutual funds, school districts, and other government jurisdictions, along with several high-profile companies, lost money in swap deals gone bad during Hurricane Greenspan and its aftermath. At one point eighteen Ohio towns lost $14 million and a Chicago college saw almost its entire $96 million endowment disappear. Bankers Trust, an aggressive derivative-dealing pioneer and a bank that was already pushing itself well past existing Glass-Steagall limits, used its expertise to construct interest rate swap deals so complicated and highly leveraged that they amounted to fraud. Gibson Greeting Cards and Proctor & Gamble, both century-old icons of midwestern commerce, were the "marks" in the early 1990s. Their unsophisticated executives lost millions in the swap deals that Bankers Trust constructed. P&G reported pretax losses of $157 million—the largest derivatives loss by a nonfinancial firm.[60]

In the ensuing uproar, George Soros, the billionaire investor, told the House Banking Committee in April that the new financial instruments were "so esoteric, that the risks involved may not be properly understood even by the most sophisticated investors." A month later the Government Accounting Office released a study that recommended a sweeping overhaul, including "federal regulation of the safety and soundness of all major OTC derivative dealers."[61] Meanwhile, a long, alarming investigation of these new financial instruments appeared in *Fortune* magazine. It was authored by Carol Loomis, the legendary financial journalist, who wrote, "Like alligators in a swamp, derivatives lurk in the global economy. Even the CEOs of companies that use them don't understand them."[62] Her Cassandra-like essay proved to be an uncanny prologue to the financial turmoil that would engulf Wall Street, first in the waning years of the Clinton administration and then on an even more disastrous scale in 2007 and 2008. "Most chillingly," she wrote, "derivatives hold the possibility of systemic risk—the danger that these contracts might directly or indirectly cause some localized or particularized trouble in the financial markets to spread uncontrollably . . . a chain reaction bringing down other institutions and sending paroxysms of fear through a financial market that lives on the expectation of prompt payments."[63]

But reform was stillborn in 1994 and 1995. Although four bills were proposed during the 1995 Congress, all died in the face of Wall Street pushback and GOP indifference. The new chair of the House Banking Committee, James Leach, was a notable exception. He knew enough to effectively battle Wall Street executives in committee hearings, but for most of this season his Republican colleagues were far more excited about his leadership of the time-consuming Whitewater probe.[64] Meanwhile, the administration was notably cool toward any enhanced regulation. Frank Newman, a banking executive who was acting secretary of the Treasury in the months before Rubin's confirmation, told a Senate committee that "the Working Group continues to find no need at this time for additional broad legislative grants of authority to regulators." At the SEC, Arthur Levitt, a former Citicorp stockbroker, thought it a grave error to "demonize derivatives." He favored industry self-regulation. Most importantly, the Fed's Alan Greenspan told the Senate Banking Committee that any effort to regulate derivatives would be both fruitless and inefficient. Regulations generated indirect costs that reduced essential liquidity, he argued. Moreover, Greenspan thought that derivatives' function—shifting risk to those who wanted to bear it—was now so vital that any set of new edicts would merely "create artificial incentives to structure transactions on the basis of regulatory rules rather than of the economic characteristics of the transactions themselves."[65] In other words, unfettered markets were so fundamental to economic life that any effort to reshape them was fruitless.

Enter Brooksley Born

To the extent that anybody was keeping a reformer's eye on these complex financial instruments, it was an obscure agency called the Commodity Futures Trading Commission (CFTC), created in 1974 just after the
Chicago Board of Trade opened the first public options market. The
CFTC had its origins in the regulation of futures in the corn, wheat, and
other agricultural product markets. Congressional oversight therefore
came from the less adept agriculture committees, not banking, so agency
"capture" was made all the easier. The SEC's Arthur Levitt thought the
CFTC was a "backwater commission, ill-funded and politically controlled."[66] For years the CFTC and the agriculture committees did the
bidding of traders from the Chicago Board of Trade. After derivatives
became important, they were equally in thrall to Wall Street. All this was
well approved by Wendy Gramm, the CFTC chair from 1988 to 1993.
Gramm, a sophisticated economist in her own right, shared the radically
deregulatory views of her spouse, Senator Phil Gramm. In the weeks just
after Bill Clinton became president-elect, Wendy Gramm issued an order
formally exempting most over-the-counter derivatives from CFTC
regulation, including derivatives in the oil and energy markets. These
exemptions were much appreciated by Enron, whose board she joined
immediately after vacating her Clinton administration post.[67]

After a short hiatus Gramm was replaced by Brooksley Born, whose
tenure as CFTC chair would soon generate a conflict that in subsequent
decades has been transformed into a morally compelling battle between
Clintonite neoliberals and a righteous woman seeking to stand against
the financial hubris of that era. At Stanford Law School, where she was
but one of seven women in her 1964 graduating class, Born was president of the law review, probably the first woman at any institution to
hold such a post. By the 1990s she had become a highly successful litigator for Arnold & Porter, the prestigious, historically liberal DC law firm.
There she specialized in finance, including derivative trading on the
London market. Born was a major figure in the American Bar Association and an important advocate for women's equality in that profession and
elsewhere. At Hillary Clinton's recommendation, she was a candidate

FIGURE 17. Brooksley Born, chair of the Commodity Futures
Trading Commission, clashed with Greenspan, Rubin, and
Summers over regulation of derivatives. (The Washington
Post via Getty Images)

for attorney general, but the interview in Little Rock did not go well. As
a consolation prize, Bill Clinton appointed her to a seat on the CFTC,
after which she became chair in mid-1996.[68]

Born was the most experienced and knowledgeable CFTC chair in
its short history, and she immediately put derivative traders on notice
that she meant to enforce the Commodity Exchange Act, a complex
and poorly structured law that nevertheless gave the CFTC a mandate
to ensure transparency and fairness. Born's parents had both been
workaday public servants—her father had been director of public welfare in San Francisco for thirty-five years and her mother was a high
school English teacher—so she was outraged at the way public entities,
from Orange County on down, had been "gambling with public
money" and then were fleeced by the complex and opaque financial

innovations pouring out of Wall Street. "These guys [the banks] are operating outside of the legal structure," she told associates. "Somebody's got to do something about it, because if they don't there's going to be a calamity."[69]

Alan Greenspan soon got wind of Born's activist posture and invited her for lunch in the Fed's august chambers. Greenspan knew that Born had been working on new regulatory guidelines for the derivatives market; as Born later recounted, "He explained there wasn't a need for a law against fraud because if a floor broker was committing fraud, the customer would figure it out and stop doing business with him." This was Greenspan's line, offered to Congress and the public at almost every one of his appearances: markets were self-correcting because honest—and even prudent—transactions were in the long-term interests of all participants. The latter were not naive consumers but highly skilled professionals who could police themselves and the markets they made. Born had a rather different view of the financial world, in part because she had spent much of the 1980s defending clients caught up in a vast conspiracy by the wealthy and unscrupulous Hunt brothers of Dallas, Nelson and William, who had duped investors while trying to corner the world silver market. To this Greenspan responded, "Well, Brooksley, I guess you and I will never agree about fraud."[70]

The key issue for Born and the CFTC was the regulation of over-the-counter derivatives, which were now six times larger than any of the financial instruments, including options and futures, traded on the far more transparent exchanges headquartered in Chicago and New York. She thought swaps and other derivatives were futures and therefore subject to CFTC oversight. Both Rubin's Treasury and Greenspan's Fed opposed such regulation and wanted derivatives excluded from CFTC jurisdiction, as did all the Wall Street banks and investment houses that were finding the world of customized and exotic financial instruments both highly opaque and extraordinarily remunerative. Shoehorning these derivatives into the kind of standardized products that could be traded on a regulated exchange would deprive Wall Street of the capacity for financial innovation and stymie its competitiveness in the global derivatives market. Rubin claimed that he was as concerned as Born about rogue trading; nevertheless, the Treasury Department would argue that any effort at regulation might generate "legal uncertainty" as to the validity of derivative contracts, opening the door to a flood of litigation from those who came out on the short end of the stick.[71]

Hardly dissuaded, Born proposed issuing a "concept release" that would raise the question of whether derivatives regulation should be strengthened. Her proposal, a thirty-three-page paper full of questions and analysis, was an otherwise unexceptional regulatory request seeking comment, public and governmental, on a potential change in agency rules. The paper asked: How could transparency be ensured? Should derivative traders be required to maintain adequate capital reserves? Innocuous as it might have seemed, Born's proposal did contain its share of zingers. Traders might be sophisticated, but somehow that was not enough to staunch allegations of fraud and misrepresentation. Moreover, the concept release pointed out that the giant OTC derivatives market was failing to achieve one of the bedrock virtues claimed for markets by virtually all orthodox economists: it "does not appear to perform the same price discovery function as centralized exchange markets."[72] Born's seemingly modest gambit soon provoked furious opposition, from both Wall Street and the economic heavyweights who occupied the commanding heights within federal government: Rubin, Summers, Greenspan, and Levitt. Summers placed an angry call to Born, telling her, "I have thirteen bankers in my office, and they say if you go forward with this you will cause the worst financial crisis since World War II."[73]

The debate came to a head on April 21, 1998, when Rubin convened a meeting of Clinton's working group on financial markets in an ornate conference room at Treasury. The room was packed and the atmosphere tense. The Asian financial crisis was still ablaze, so for most members of Clinton's economic policy high command the contretemps with Born's CFTC was a bothersome sideshow. Few had even met Born and the rest of her CFTC team. Levitt later recalled that all these men thought her an "irascible, difficult, stubborn, unreasonable" woman.[74] Born outlined her view that something had to be done to supervise the ever-growing derivatives market. Then Rubin, Greenspan. Levitt, and Summers all took their shots at her: The CFTC had no jurisdiction to regulate OTC derivatives. "Legal uncertainty" would therefore threaten to engulf contracts worth billions of dollars. Greenspan thought that merely inquiring about such regulation would drive much financial business offshore. Rubin said the financial community was "petrified" by the notion that OTC derivatives might fall under CFTC purview, an outlook echoed by Summers, who also thought Wall Street saw the CFTC initiative "as being disastrous for markets."[75]

Born would later blame Rubin more than Greenspan for the impasse, because the Treasury secretary had no ideological compulsion to think markets were not imperfect. His entire arbitrage experience was based on the contrary notion. Indeed, Rubin told Born that he did not disagree with the substance of what the CFTC wanted to do, but thought there must be a better way to proceed, one that did not create the legal uncertainty that Treasury officials claimed to worry about. If the CFTC won formal jurisdiction over the OTC derivatives market, all those swaps and other innovative financial instruments might well be considered "futures" that, by law, should be traded on exchanges. That would throw all OTC derivative bets into legal limbo, giving traders on the losing side the incentive not to pay off. Trillions of dollars were at stake. To this Born replied, "You are asking the CFTC not to uphold the law."[76] In truth Rubin was more concerned about fraud and manipulation than some of his allies. "Larry thought I was overly concerned with the risks of derivatives," Rubin wrote in his memoir, published five years before the 2008 financial crisis. "Larry's position held together under normal circumstances but it seemed to me not to take into account what might happen under extraordinary circumstances."[77]

Born was ashen at the conclusion of the hour-plus meeting, but a tentative agreement had nevertheless been struck to see if lawyers from the CFTC and the Treasury could work something out. Born did not see this as a turf battle: she was "flexible," willing to let another agency, most likely the SEC, write and enforce an enhanced set of regulations. But nothing happened. At first Treasury would not return a set of increasingly desperate phone calls and emails from the CFTC. Then Rubin's lawyers hedged on holding a meeting. "They can't just not talk to us," Born told an aide.

Exasperated and feeling betrayed, Born decided to formally publish the release. It appeared on the morning of May 7, 1998.[78]

That very afternoon Rubin, Greenspan, and Levitt put out an extraordinary press release repudiating Born's gambit. They had "grave concerns" about the possible consequences of the CFTC proposal, reiterating their worry that "the CFTC's action may increase the legal uncertainty concerning certain types of OTC derivatives."[79] Shortly thereafter they called on Congress to quickly pass legislation imposing a moratorium on any new CFTC regulatory activities in derivatives markets. Rubin's working group would take the lead when it came to any new initiatives on that score. With little controversy, Congress neutered CFTC powers in October, after which Born announced that she would not accept reappointment when her term ended in the spring of 1999. The president replaced her with Bill Rainer, the cofounder of Greenwich Capital Markets and an old Clinton friend from Arkansas. Greenwich would later become one of Wall Street's biggest bundlers of subprime mortgage-backed securities, another unregulated OTC derivative product.[80]

Deregulation at All Costs

The sensational collapse of Long-Term Capital Management in September 1998 demonstrated the degree to which Born's marginalization was a product of both a powerfully embedded ideology and Wall Street's immense financial self-interest. LTCM, like so many other hedge funds, was a "black box" (a term coined by Carol Loomis in a 1960s *Fortune* essay). Because it traded on the OTC derivative market, neither the SEC, the CFTC, nor its own banking partners knew the size of its positions or was aware that it had posted so very little collateral against those bets. This was the classic setup for a run: when an unexpectedly adverse event, such as the Russian default, made some losses likely, none knew who would get burned, confidence plunged, and LTCM's counterparties scrambled to liquidate their investments. That fall Brooksley Born would tell Congress that the collapse of LTCM was "exactly what I had been worried about."[81]

Despite the manifest example offered by LTCM, an instance of market failure if there ever was one, the impulse to do anything about runaway derivatives trading encountered as much resistance as ever. Bill Clinton's travails, which reached a climax that fall with the September release of the salacious Starr report and the subsequent trial and impeachment in October and November, distracted the public and consumed White House energy. When James Leach convened a meeting of the House Banking Committee in early October, TV cameras and reporters were scarce. Leach claimed that recent events had "vindicated" Brooksley Born, and he denounced hedge funds as "run-amok, casino like enterprises, driven by greed." Representative Bernie Sanders, among others, pilloried Greenspan with the accusation that the Fed had bailed out its Wall Street friends. Congressman Paul Kanjorski, a Pennsylvania Democrat, captured the moment: "I am just wondering, is there any way you can inject sex into this so we can get a little more national attention? . . . We are talking about the potential meltdown of the world's economic system instead of a fling at the White House, and yet nobody in the world seems to understand what may have transpired or may have been at risk in the last two weeks."[82]

Rubin's working group proceeded with extreme caution. Born, CEA chair Janet Yellen, and to a degree Rubin himself advocated greater transparency, capital requirements, and additional supervision of derivatives. One point of contention was financial innovation itself. Yellen and Born thought all those new and complex Wall Street instruments led to speculation and systemic risks, while Greenspan and Summers saw financial innovation as a competitive advantage that made the US economy more productive, capital readily available, and New York City first among the financial capitals of the world. After leaving office, Summers would call a critic of such derivative innovations "slightly Luddite."[83] Thus, a working group report that appeared in the spring of 1999, just before Rubin resigned as Treasury secretary, admitted that "excessive leverage can greatly magnify the negative effects of any financial market event," but it merely hinted that "direct regulation of [OTC] derivatives dealers" might be a "potential additional step" to ensure systematic safety.[84]

But that was as far as the Clinton administration would go. Six months later, with Larry Summers now installed at Treasury, another working group report slammed the door on reform. Most of its recommendations were included in a 262-page rider to an 11,000-page omnibus appropriations bill. Much of it was written by Senator Phil Gramm, who would soon join UBS, the multinational investment bank. There would be no administration fight with Gramm this time, so the Texas senator rushed the law through Congress on the last day of a lame-duck session; it was signed by President Clinton on December 21, 2000. The rider, entitled the Commodity Futures Modernization Act, removed what was by then the $95 trillion OTC derivative market from all federal regulation in a fashion even more deregulatory than that advocated by the Treasury in its fight with Born two years earlier. Both the CFTC and the SEC were barred from regulating most derivatives, and even the states were preempted from instituting any separate guidelines. OTC derivatives were exempted from capital reserve requirements, reporting and disclosure, regulation of intermediaries, and supervised self-regulation. Bars on fraud and manipulation were weakened. A huge slice of American finance was now wholly opaque to observation from government, the public, and many market participants themselves.[85]

All this set the stage for the disasters that would convulse the real economy during the first decade of the twenty-first century. The collapse of Enron and WorldCom in 2001 and 2002, up to then the costliest bankruptcies in US history ($63 billion and $104 billion, respectively), arose out of the fraudulent accounting practices attached to derivative investments whose leveraged complexity was visible to only a small circle of conspirators, and even they little understood these investments.[86] Those implosions did nothing to stem the growth and multiplication of derivative products, many now based on a booming housing market, itself the latest asset bubble sustaining the consumer-driven US economy. In the months between late 2000 and June 2008 the notional value of the OTC derivatives market grew sevenfold, peaking at $672.6 trillion—ten times larger than the GDP of the entire global economy.[87] Among the new financial innovations was the credit-default swap (CDS), a seemingly low-risk instrument whose monetary value increased a hundredfold in these years. Wall Street sold credit-default swaps to "insure" subprime mortgage investments, but unlike actual insurance policies, they were unregulated and therefore not required to post sufficient capital to support the "guarantees" they supposedly offered. They fell into the regulatory black hole created a decade before when Rubin and his colleagues had so contemptuously cast aside Brooksley Born's concept release. The upside potential of a CDS was modest, and the downside catastrophic, but of course no one thought that eventuality had much of a chance. When it did happen and the "insurance" payments were triggered, firms like AIG and Citigroup, in hock for hundreds of billions of dollars, required a bailout from Congress and the Federal Reserve to prevent their collapse and the financial chain reaction such an implosion was sure to engender.[88]

The financial and political trauma that swept the world economy in 2008 generated a momentary reconsideration of long-held ideas and practices. Brooksley Born reemerged as a near-celebrity, a Cassandra-like oracle whose fears had been cast aside by a set of arrogant men.[89] "All tragedies in life are always proceeded by warnings," said a chastened Arthur Levitt after the 2008 financial crisis had run its course. "We had a warning. It was Brooksley Born."[90] Robert Rubin also conceded that Born was "right about derivatives regulation" and that he too favored more oversight, especially by increasing monetary reserves in case of a loss. But Rubin excused his timidity with the rather remarkable assertion that he had been powerless: "All the forces in the system were arrayed against it," he told a reporter in the fall of 2008. "The industry certainly didn't want any increase in these requirements. There was no potential for mobilizing public opinion."[91] An odd claim from a member of the "Committee to Save the World."

The most remarkable mea culpas came from Greenspan and Clinton. Larry Summers, by now part of the Obama administration, projected no sense of contrition, though he did tell the Financial Crisis Inquiry Commission that "by 2008 our regulatory framework with respect to derivatives was manifestly inadequate."[92] However, Greenspan, the normally self-assured chair of the Federal Reserve, now finally retired, surprised listeners at a congressional hearing in October 2008 with the admission that he was in "a state of shocked disbelief" because the self-interest of lending institutions had failed to protect shareholders and the public. "The whole intellectual edifice" of the "modern-risk management paradigm" that he had defended for decades, Greenspan said, "collapsed in the summer of last year."[93] Bill Clinton had second thoughts as well. "I should have raised more hell about derivatives being unregulated," Clinton told the *New York Times* in May 2009. He remembered feeling "a little queasy about the derivative issue" during the collapse of LTCM in September 1998, but the former president largely blamed Alan Greenspan at the Fed, rather than Rubin and Summers, for insisting that OTC derivatives remain unregulated. "So I very much wish now that I had demanded that we put derivatives under the jurisdiction of the Securities and Exchange Commission and that transparency rules had been observed. . . . That I think is a legitimate criticism of what we didn't do."[94]

Epilogue

Bill Clinton often called his presidency a "bridge to the twenty-first century." But that arch would prove fragile and misaligned, with foundation pilons and suspension cables that could not bear the weight of the inevitable storms, political and economic, that swept the nation in the years after he left office.

Al Gore's campaign for the presidency demonstrated a set of barely hidden fractures. The "hanging chads" of south Florida have long haunted the effort to extend a Clinton presidential succession into the new millennium. Those ambiguous votes are one of the few things most remember about the 2000 election, along with the subsequent legal battle that culminated in the Supreme Court's 5–4 decision awarding George W. Bush a one-vote majority in the electoral college. But why was the election so close? Why didn't Gore sweep to victory on the peace and prosperity that Bill Clinton had bequeathed to him?

Both the vice president and his Republican opponent ran uninspiring campaigns, and voter turnout was at just over 50 percent, one of the lowest since the dawn of the New Deal. White House insiders were as bored as pundits and the public. It has been easy enough to declare Gore a stolid personality or to blame him for shunning Bill Clinton, presumably a morally tarnished figure, even though the president retained a remarkably high set of late-term approval ratings. But far more important from an electoral and policy posture were two legacies of the Clinton era that subverted Al Gore's presidential prospects. First, Clinton-era trade deals had alienated millions of Ross Perot voters, especially in the small manufacturing cities now being hollowed out by East Asian competitors. Gore may have won a notable victory against Perot in the televised NAFTA debate of 1993, but that soon proved Pyrrhic because neither Clinton nor Gore was able to incorporate the Perot constituency into the Democratic

Party fold. Those economically aggrieved voters might well have been Clinton's for the taking, but a plurality would now find their way into the ranks of the GOP, with many moving far to the right by the second decade of the twenty-first century.[1]

Second, the remarkable budget surpluses of the late Clinton years proved an albatross for Al Gore. Clinton's decision to plow most of that money into the Social Security trust fund—indeed, into actually paying down the national debt—was echoed by the candidate when he promised to "lockbox" the new tax revenues. Such fiscal "responsibility" offered nothing to the Democratic base. Even on climate change, his signature issue, Al Gore feared a fiscally bold proposal. The door was thus open for Ralph Nader, running on a leftist third-party ticket, to siphon hundreds of thousands of votes from the Democrats, ninety-seven thousand of which were cast in Florida. George Bush had none of Gore's fiscal scruples, telling voters, "The surplus is not the government's money. The surplus is the people's money." Therefore, he maintained, it should be promptly returned to them in a set of large tax cuts even if that led to the return of chronic deficits.[2]

Most Clinton policymakers, and certainly those remaining in his second term, had believed that a balanced budget and a deregulated economy were essential to the high levels of investment that would generate the high-performance economy necessary to increase living standards and open the door to progressive reforms of a structural sort. The Clintonites were neoliberals only inasmuch as their chief strategy was to coax the private sector into paying for all this. Fiscal discipline would send interest rates down, spurring on the Goldilocks economy of the late 1990s that kept employment high, the cost of capital low, cheap imports flowing, and GDP growth soaring well beyond historical norms. Many in the Clinton administration and many upscale liberals considered this a perfectly progressive agenda. Once faith in government had been restored, the politics of spreading the wealth to create a more egalitarian society could go forward. "FDR saved capitalism from itself," Clinton told Sidney Blumenthal in 1998. "Our mission has been to save government from its own excesses so it can again be a progressive force."[3]

But the Clintonites got both the economics and the politics wrong. Vice President Dick Cheney was right when in 2002 he declared, "Reagan proved deficits don't matter." At almost every inflection point since the Volcker shock, the Federal Reserve had determined the interest rate trajectory, not the bond market vigilantes both James Carville and Robert Rubin thought were so powerful. Until the Covid-19 pandemic disrupted global supply chains, interest rates had trended downward for more than three decades, regardless of the size of the deficit. Labor cost pressures had been weak, thus limiting inflationary pressures; moreover, the global role of the dollar as a stable reserve currency had also advanced this secular decline, since holders of foreign funds had usually been happy to take an interest rate discount for the safety inherent in American T-bills.[4] Of course, the capital thus generated was unguided by any of the industrial policy ideas envisioned by some in Clinton's early brain trust. During his administration and after, low interest rates did not create an investment boom, private or public, while capital's propensity to fund a series of cheap-money asset bubbles—in Silicon Valley startups, real estate, and the stock market—became endemic.[5]

Clinton and many Democrats also got the politics wrong in thinking that if an austerity budget led to prosperity and a budget surplus, then there would be time and opportunity for a socially progressive redistribution of all that new money, and voters would reward their propriety. This illusion persisted for decades. In 1984 Joe Biden, along with presidential candidate Walter Mondale, had supported a freeze on federal spending to deal with the "runaway deficits" of Reagan's first term. Nearly thirty years later Barack Obama felt the same constraints. Barely a month into his presidency he convened a "Fiscal Responsibility Summit," presided over by Vice President Biden, who saw "a real opportunity to both put our economy back on track and restore fiscal responsibility."[6] Obama remained hobbled by the issue, even going so far as to propose a "grand bargain" with the GOP that would have entailed significant cuts to Social Security, Medicare, and other programs in return for some modest tax increases.

That prospect never materialized, of course, because Republicans were hostile, but perhaps even more important, such fiscal austerity divided and demobilized the Democratic Party base. The lesson was plain: if progressives wanted to fix inequality, they could not wait around hoping that it would be easier once they got all their fiscal ducks in a row, and they could not assume that delivering strong economic growth would automatically generate an electoral victory. President Obama's decision to push for an overhaul of the nation's health care system in the midst of a financial crisis represented a partial lesson learned; President Joe Biden's effort to seek a massive infrastructure program in 2021, one that would generate a multitrillion-dollar deficit, constituted an even more profound shift in economic thinking.[7]

The idea that a "new economy" had transformed American politics proved an equally powerful illusion. When Clinton and Gore opened their Little Rock summit in December 1992, a sense of crisis pervaded the discussion of how the American version of world capitalism might be transformed. Seven and a half years later, in April 2000, Clinton convened a "White House Conference on the New Economy." A techno-triumphalism pervaded the conclave, with Clinton announcing, "We meet in the midst of the longest economic expansion of our history and an economic transformation as profound as that that led us into the industrial revolution."[8] At Little Rock the leadoff speaker had been Robert Solow, the Keynesian theorist of economic growth; at the 2000 White House conference it was Abby Joseph Cohen, a famed and hyper-bullish stock market analyst from Goldman Sachs.

Thus, by the end of the Clinton presidency this "new economy" construct had become a pervasive and powerful vision, offering a techno-social solution to virtually every problem confronting the nation. The idea that a globalized economy combining high technology and entrepreneurial innovation had generated a new sort of capitalism proved intoxicating, from the Apple headquarters in Cupertino to the corner office, the campus quad, and Capitol Hill. The concept became an all-purpose rationale for almost any sort of political or social program. For Robert Reich, the new economy promised to transform labor relations and worker skills; for Alan Greenspan, it would keep interest rates low because new economy productivity levels would mean that wage increases and full production were no longer inflationary; for Gene

Sperling, Charlene Barshefsky, and *New York Times* columnist Tom Fried-man, rapid communications and efficient transport networks linked together a new era of free trade and democratic reform. For Larry Sum-mers, Al Gore, and President Clinton, a technologically sophisticated new economy provided the "modernizing" rationale for the deregulation of telecom, banking, and international finance. Evoking the racially pro-gressive dreams engendered during his Arkansas youth, Bill Clinton told the White House conference, "I believe the computer and the internet give us a chance to move more people out of poverty more quickly than at any time in all of human history."[9] Ending the "digital divide" between internet haves and have-nots now seemed the key to a more equitable society, a rather more constrained and technocratic approach than any-thing proposed at the outset of the Clinton administration.[10]

Of course, America was generating a new economy, but it was far different from what Silicon Valley and its White House cheerleaders had imagined. Wal-Mart and McDonald's, Amazon and FedEx, Marriott and HCA Healthcare, all were giant growth companies. Software engineers and computer support specialists were among the fastest-growing oc-cupations, but when it came to sheer numbers, occupational growth was still concentrated in low-wage, low-skill jobs in retail trade, food preparation and restaurants, hospitals, nursing homes and home health care, janitorial services, and offices. These jobs were often structured and supervised by a new digital infrastructure—call center and ware-house work were prime examples—but they were hardly of the sort envisioned by "new economy" enthusiasts. Indeed, that phrase faded in the new millennium, replaced by descriptors of a far darker character: "the gig economy," "surveillance capitalism," and "the fissured work-place." Of course, none of this lessened the impact of high-technology companies on American politics and discourse. Silicon Valley's determi-nation to "change the world" had been backstopped by a tenfold increase in the amount of money Democrats raised from that sector between the 1994 and 2000 election cycles.[11]

If the new economy was not panning out, neither were the baroque financial innovations and deregulatory banking rules that Clinton's eco-nomic team had promulgated. Once the scale of the 2008 meltdown became apparent, virtually all of the key Clinton administration figures—Rubin, Greenspan, Levitt, Sperling, and Clinton—admitted that their faith in deregulated financial markets had been misplaced. For a moment it seemed as if the absolute collapse of the most important banks, brokerages, and insurance companies was leading to either the breakup or de facto nationalization of much of the US financial infrastructure.

It is a tribute therefore to the hegemonic power of Wall Street that in the very midst of this crisis, President Barack Obama, who had been elected by majorities far more decisive than those of Bill Clinton sixteen years before, nevertheless appointed to key economic posts, not the "left-leaning economists and activists" from his campaign, with whom he felt a sense of "kinship," but people who could "calm the markets in the grip of panic" even if they "might be tainted by the sins of the past."[12] Many had been protégés of a still influential Robert Rubin. Larry Summers returned to government as chair of the Obama National Economic Council; Timothy Geithner, who had played a prominent role managing the 1997–1998 East Asian financial crisis, won appointment as the new Secretary of the Treasury; Gary Gensler, a former Goldman Sachs partner who had served as a Treasury official during the era of derivatives deregulation, became chair of the Commodity Futures Trading Commission; and Peter Orszag, the new director of the Office of Management and Budget, had headed Rubin's Hamilton Project think tank in the years just before the financial crash.[13] Summers and Geithner were the "dominant voices," reported the new president, "men rooted in the centrist, market-friendly philosophy of the Clinton administration."[14]

Obama's team of Rubin acolytes did get a onetime stimulus through Congress that amounted to a modest public spending program linked to cheap and plentiful credit, but far from breaking up the big banks or removing their executives, the new administration bailed them out. Obama adopted Treasury Secretary Geithner's "stress test" to determine if the largest financial institutions would have sufficient capital reserves to weather an imagined crisis. If they did not, they would be required to take taxpayer money and remain subject to stringent government regulation. But once they could raise the necessary capital on their own, they were in the clear and free to go back to business as usual. None of the well-paid executives whose fraudulent products crashed the economy went to prison. Many used government bailout funds to pay the outsized bonuses to which most Wall Streeters had become accustomed. All this stands in stark contrast to the fate of hundreds of S&L executives who lost their shirt, lost their jobs, and went to prison in the late 1980s and early 1990s. Meanwhile, the economic recovery was exceedingly slow, with millions of lost jobs and unpaid mortgages. Legitimacy drained from the nation's economic and political system as the populist anger that might have been channeled against the twenty-first-century financial elite stoked Tea Party and Trumpist resentment toward the multiracial cosmopolitanism of the Obama era and the modestly social democratic initiatives of that moment, health care reform above all.[15]

Bill and Hillary Clinton escaped reputational fallout from the 2008 economic crisis, but their day of reckoning, and that of the politics they embodied, was soon to come. Hillary had been twice elected to the US Senate from New York and in the 2008 Democratic primaries had sometimes stood to Obama's left, winning more of the white working-class vote in Ohio, Pennsylvania, and elsewhere. Obama's appointment of Hillary Clinton as Secretary of State was a well-received olive branch extended to an important wing of the Democratic Party. Meanwhile, the former president's internationally oriented Clinton Foundation seemed a worthy endeavor designed to improve health and alleviate poverty in the developing world. At the 2012 Democratic National Convention, Bill Clinton offered an exceptionally effective defense of Obama's embattled health reform law. Obama soon called him the "Secretary of Explaining Stuff" and deployed Clinton's speech-making abilities in the battleground states that fall.[16]

But the polarization of American politics undercut the kind of politics practiced by the Clintons. During his years in power, even as the Republicans were lurching toward the right, President Clinton still had the capacity to cut deals with the congressional GOP on trade, crime, welfare, and financial deregulation. President Obama faced even more intransigent opposition, which had the effect of virtually eliminating the space for DLC-style centrism. Southern white Democratic politicians of a moderate persuasion had become an extinct species, one important reason Al From announced in February 2011 that a nearly bankrupt DLC would close down. The DLC's enthusiastic support for the Iraq War, alignment with Republicans on many culture-war issues, ongoing hostility to organized labor, and championship of Senator Joe Lieberman's increasingly conservative politics (he would campaign for John McCain, the Republican presidential candidate in 2008) alienated the vast bulk of the Democratic Party, including the new president.

But even more important than the demise of Democratic Party moderation was the rise of an energetic left. The Occupy Wall Street movement that began in 2011 put the increasingly stark economic and social inequalities engendered by global financialization on the party's political agenda. The rise of Black Lives Matter reinvigorated those who saw racism in the nation's police forces and carceral system as a chronic source of injustice. And the hollowing out of the American industrial heartland made clear that global trade was hardly a win-win economic proposition. Moreover, the idea that markets, trade, and democracy were inexorably connected had proved a fantasy. By the second decade of the twenty-first century the drift toward authoritarianism in Russia, Poland, Hungary, Turkey, Egypt, and India, all nations that had liberalized once-closed economies, was increasingly manifest. And in China, upon which Clinton had staked such hopes, a booming capitalist economy failed to weaken the Communist Party's tight control of civil society.

These new currents, ideological and political, became manifest when Hillary Clinton once again sought the presidency. Clinton had the support of the entire Democratic Party establishment, including President Obama, but her campaign inspired little genuine enthusiasm, even among young feminists. While Republicans renewed their decades-long assault on the Clinton persona, the most serious critique came from within her own party. The identification of both Bill and Hillary Clinton with the mass incarceration of Black and brown youth now constituted one of the principal indictments of their years in power. While the 1994 crime bill had not been particularly controversial in its day, the twenty-first-century movement against police brutality and the somewhat older effort to reduce the nation's bloated prison population put Bill Clinton's

$30 billion anticrime initiative in a troubling light. As he aided his wife's 2016 campaign the former president was repeatedly confronted by those charging him with signing a law that contributed to the inequitable imprisonment of more than two million, a majority of them people of color, in a prison archipelago that rivaled those of the twentieth century's most infamous regimes. When Joe Biden, a senatorial sponsor of the crime law, sought the Democratic nomination four years later, he faced many of the same accusations.[17]

Progressive contempt for Hillary Clinton's economic statecraft had less to do with her tepid campaign, however, than with the unexpected eruption of enthusiasm for Senator Bernie Sanders, a lifelong socialist who reanimated New Deal commitments to an expansive welfare state, the regulation of capital, and the tax-the-rich program necessary to pay for it all. His denunciation of the billionaire class reminded the public of the Clintons' accommodation to a global financial elite, exemplified not only by the Clinton Foundation's solicitation of contributions from a glittering cohort of wealthy individuals, foreign governments, and global corporations but also by Hillary Clinton's well-remunerated speeches to a Goldman Sachs audience after she left the State Department.[18] Candidate Clinton and her many seasoned advisers often seemed tone-deaf to this shift in political sentiment within their own party. While Clinton emphasized her commitment to a multiracial, LBGTQ- and immigrant-friendly America, she equivocated when it came to raising the national minimum wage to $15 an hour, a bedrock labor demand. Indeed, shortly after the 2016 election it was reported that she had chosen Starbucks CEO Howard Schultz as her prospective Secretary of Labor and Sheryl Sandberg, a Facebook executive and former Larry Summers protégé, for the top post at either Treasury or Commerce.[19]

Aside from being born in an outer borough of New York, Donald Trump and Bernie Sanders had virtually nothing in common except for a rhetorically robust repudiation of Clinton-era trade policy. Trump was an authoritarian ethno-nationalist, a crass and unscrupulous grifter who stoked populist anger of the most racist and misogynist sort. Sanders was a genuine heir to the democratic socialism of Eugene Debs. For almost his entire political life, in Vermont and then in Congress, Sanders had been a marginal figure, but now a wave of youthful enthusiasm greeted his challenge to Hillary Clinton in the Democratic primaries.[20]

Trump and Sanders were equally vociferous in their repudiation of the globalist free trade regime. Trump told Pittsburgh workers that "globalization has made the financial elite who donate to politicians very wealthy. But it has left millions of our workers with nothing but poverty and heartache. . . . We allowed foreign countries to subsidize their goods, devalue their currencies, violate their agreements, and cheat in every way imaginable." He called NAFTA one of the "worst legacies" of the Clinton years.[21] Sanders was equally outspoken. "I voted in complete opposition to every one of these disastrous trade agreements. Secretary Clinton voted for virtually all of them." Sanders called her an "outsourcer-in-chief." Both Trump and Sanders wanted new tariffs on Chinese steel imports, and both opposed the twelve-nation Trans-Pacific Partnership, championed by both President Obama and Hillary Clinton when she was secretary of State. During the campaign Clinton backtracked on that East Asian trade accord, but her assertion that "I do not currently support it as it is written" had none of the fire or indignation generated by her rivals.[22]

Trump's victory stunned everyone, but it had one salutary impact: for the first time since 1968 an electoral defeat reinvigorated Democratic liberals, pushing the entire party to the left rather than the right. This was partly a reaction to the authoritarianism and overt racism of a dangerous new enemy, but it also reflected the repudiation of Clintonite centrism and the emergence of a bolder new generation of social democrats who had risen to power by defeating more mainstream Democrats. They had ideas and programs ready to implement when the electoral terrain turned more favorable.

As a presidential candidate and then as a White House occupant, Joe Biden would accommodate this current, greatly aided by the Covid-19 crisis that for a moment in the spring of 2020 nearly shut down the US economy. When the pandemic struck, both parties quickly agreed on a massive relief program, the Coronavirus Aid, Relief, and Economic Security Act (CARES Act), which allotted $2.2 trillion to providing fast and direct economic aid to businesses, government entities, and tens of millions of newly unemployed people. While the GOP moved into near-unanimous opposition once Biden was in office, the new president and the vast majority of Democrats abandoned the ideological guard-rails erected during the Clinton era and became advocates of an expansive welfare state as well as a considerable level of economic guidance for the economy as a whole. Concern about budget deficits evaporated as the Biden team pushed forward one massive relief and reform package after another. In March 2021 came the $1.9 trillion American Rescue Plan, more than double the amount of Obama's 2009 stimulus effort, and in August of that year the new president signed a long-delayed infrastructure bill, costing another trillion dollars. Of equal significance, Congress passed two industrial policy bills in 2022 that appropriated more than $600 billion to advance domestically built computer chip production and develop a green energy infrastructure, while also providing funds to make Obamacare more universal and progressive.[23] These initiatives constituted the hard, physical component in Biden's even more ambitious Build Back Better program. As a whole the BBB was designed to move the United States a large step in the direction of a European-style welfare state, with billions spent on child allowances, an improved Obamacare, family and medical leave after the birth of a child or onset of an illness, and free kindergartens and community colleges.[24] Because of the dramatic and salutary impact on child poverty proposed by this near-universal program, the family-oriented BBB entirely marginalized the divisive Clinton-era welfare discourse that had once targeted non-working mothers.

Many of Biden's appointments represented an equally large break with the Clinton-Obama legacy. Brian Deese, Biden's first NEC chair, revived the industrial policy ideas once put forward by the Clinton left in the 1980s and early 1990s. He argued for an "American industrial strategy" that would use government regulations and money to strengthen supply chains, rebuild the US industrial base, enhance pubic investment, and fight climate change.[25] Katherine Tai, the Biden administration's Mandarin-speaking trade representative, was an advocate of a "worker-centered trade policy" that would sideline the WTO and constrain corporate influence.[26] And Lina Kahn, Biden's thirty-something chair of the Federal Trade Commission, won her spurs as a sharp critic of Amazon and other tech giants. She sought to return antitrust policy to the democratic antimonopoly tradition upon which it was founded late in the nineteenth century.[27]

In the Clinton era liberal aides like George Stephanopoulos, Derek Shearer, and Robert Reich bemoaned the absence of pressure from the left, especially from a potent and engaged labor movement. Even Bill Clinton complained that most of the voices heard by his administration were those defending the status quo. The problem remained in the third decade of the twenty-first century. Despite the tangible accomplishments of Biden's first years in office, an even more ambitious, New Deal–style program had been stymied by the thin and unsteady majorities upon which the Democrats relied in Congress. Thus, it was one thing to develop a bold program that expanded the welfare state and revived the industrial policy idea. It was quite another to marshal the army of voters to win the decisive legislative majorities necessary to vote such visionary plans into law.

Missing were the social forces that could mobilize not just on behalf of their own constituents, but with sufficient strength to transform politics and the political economy as well. A glimpse of what was possible came in the "red state revolt" of 2018, when a set of teacher strikes forced conservative legislatures to finally increase teacher salaries and overall funding for desperate school districts. Two years later the pandemic made clear the moral and economic centrality of tens of millions of frontline workers, thereby tilting the gigantic 2020 CARES Act in a progressive direction. Soon worker shortages, "resignations," and even walkouts pushed wages upward and renewed the union impulse among many young people. In contrast to the Clinton era, organized labor became both more popular and more aggressive. That's the sort of power—magnified a dozenfold—needed to recast American capitalism and enact the economic and social reforms offered by policymakers and politicians of even the most progressive sort. Its absence at the dawn of the Clinton administration opened wide the door to Wall Street and its like-minded minions. Today we need the transformational energy of such social forces more than ever.

NOTES

Preface

1. Her major works are *The World of Marcus Garvey: Race and Class in Modern Society* (Baton Rouge: Louisiana State University Press, 1991); *Running Steel, Running America: Race, Economic Policy, and the Decline of Liberalism* (Chapel Hill: University of North Carolina Press, 1998); and *Pivotal Decade: How the United States Traded Factories for Finance* (New Haven, CT: Yale University Press, 2011).

2. Nelson Lichtenstein, "Judith Stein, 1940–1917," *Dissent*, May 12, 2017.

Introduction

1. Bill Clinton, *My Life* (New York: Alfred A. Knopf, 2004), 425.

2. Bill Clinton, *President Clinton's New Beginning: The Complete Text, with Illustrations, of the Historic Clinton-Gore Economic Conference, Little Rock, Arkansas, December 14–15, 1992* (New York: Donald I. Fine, 1993), 4.

3. "A Valuable Economics Seminar," *New York Times* (hereafter *NYT*), December 16, 1992, A30; David Rosenbaum, "Clinton Leads Experts in Discussion on Economy," *NYT*, December 15, 1992, A1.

4. Sylvia Nasar, "Some Voices Missing at Clinton's Conference," *NYT*, December 21, 1992, D1.

5. Clinton, *President Clinton's New Beginning*, 225, 282.

6. Robert J. Gordon, "Foundations of the Goldilocks Economy: Supply Shocks and the Time-Varying NAIRU," *Brookings Papers on Economic Activity*, no. 2 (1998): 298.

7. Kim Clark, "These Are the Good Old Days," *Fortune*, June 9, 1997, 74.

8. Alan Blinder and Janet Yellen, *The Fabulous Decade: Macroeconomic Lessons from the 1990s* (New York: Century Foundation Press, 2001); see also Kurt Andersen, "The Best Decade Ever? The 1990s, Obviously," *NYT*, February 8, 2015, SR6.

9. Jonathan Chait, "The National Interest: How 'Neoliberalism' Became the Left's Favorite Insult of Liberals," *New York*, July 16, 2017; Gary Gerstle, *The Rise and Fall of the Neoliberal Order: America and the World in the Free Market Era* (New York: Oxford University Press, 2022), 255–65.

10. Lily Geismer, *Left Behind: The Democrats' Failed Attempt to Solve Inequality* (New York: Public Affairs, 2022), 4; Gerstle, *The Rise and Fall of the Neoliberal Order*, 156.

11. Ryan Cooper, "The Decline and Fall of Neoliberalism in the Democratic Party," *The Week*, January 2, 2018.

12. George Monbiot, "Neoliberalism: The Deep Story that Lies beneath Donald Trump's Triumph," *Guardian*, November 14, 2016.

13. Daniel Rodgers, "The Uses and Abuses of 'Neoliberalism,'" *Dissent*, Winter 2018, 78.

14. Ibid., 85.

15. David Harvey, *A Brief History of Neoliberalism* (New York: Oxford University Press, 2005), 13.

16. Quoted in George Lipsitz, "The Struggle for Hegemony," *Journal of American History* 75, no. 1 (June 1988): 147.

17. Sidney Blumenthal, *The Clinton Wars* (New York: Farrar, Straus and Giroux, 2003), 5, 24–25; see also David Maraniss, *First in His Class: A Biography of Bill Clinton* (New York: Simon & Schuster, 1995), 122–48, 233–45, for an account of how Clinton constructed his extensive friendship network at Oxford and Yale.

18. See Fritz Bartel, *The Triumph of Broken Promises: The End of the Cold War and the Rise of Neoliberalism* (Cambridge, MA: Harvard University Press, 2022). Bartel argues that massive Eastern Bloc indebtedness to the West generated an inexorable drive toward a neoliberal political economy even before the fall of the Berlin Wall.

19. J. W. Mason, "The Fed Doesn't Work for You," *Jacobin*, January 6, 2016. The idea that the Fed has been a planning regime became widespread after the Volcker shock in 1979.

20. Robert Brenner, *The Economics of Global Turbulence: The Advanced Capitalist Economies from Long Boom to Long Turndown, 1945–2005* (New York: Verso, 2006).

Chapter 1. How Arkansas Educated Bill Clinton

1. Blumenthal, *The Clinton Wars*, 24.

2. Maraniss, *First in His Class*, 58–59.

3. Ibid., 225–33, 265–86.

4. Carl Bernstein, *A Woman in Charge: The Life of Hillary Rodham Clinton* (New York: Random House, 2007), 96–97, 110, 127.

5. Brooks Blevins, *Hill Folks: A History of Arkansas Ozarkers and Their Image* (Chapel Hill: University of North Carolina Press, 2002), 147–78; Ben Johnson, *Arkansas in Modern America, 1930–1999* (Fayetteville: University of Arkansas Press, 2000) 200–202.

6. V. O. Key, *Southern Politics in State and Nation* (New York: Alfred A. Knopf, 1949), 185.

7. Blumenthal, *The Clinton Wars*, 33.

8. Martin Walker, *Clinton: The President They Deserve* (New York: Random House, 1996), 45.

9. Michael Pierce, "Odell Smith, Teamsters Local 878, and Civil Rights Unionism in Little Rock, 1943–1965," *Journal of Southern History* 134, no. 4 (November 2018): 955–56.

10. Ibid., 956.

11. Gavin Wright, "Voting Rights, Deindustrialization, and Republican Ascendancy in the South," Working Paper 135, Institute for New Economic Thinking, September 2020, 43.

12. Stein, *Pivotal Decade*, 115.

13. Diane Blair, "The Big Three of Late Twentieth Century Arkansas Politics," *Arkansas Historical Quarterly* 54 (Spring 1995): 53–79.

14. Clinton, *My Life*, 209.

15. Matea Gold and Tom Hamburger, "How Bill Clinton's Losing 1974 Race Helped Launch the Clintons' Donor Network," *Washington Post* (hereafter *WP*), November 20, 2015, A1. A handwritten copy of Clinton's speech is linked to this article.

16. Maraniss, *First in His Class*, 352–54.

17. Blair, "The Big Three of Late Twentieth Century Arkansas Politics."

18. Martin Halpern, "The Defeat of Labor Law Reform in 1978 and 1994," *Arkansas Historical Quarterly* 57, no. 2 (Summer 1998): 99–133. Then-governor Pryor was not yet in the Senate when the closure vote was taken in January 1978, but observers credited him with much influence on the sitting Arkansas senator, Kaneaster Hodges, whom Pryor had appointed upon the death of John McClellan late in 1977.

19. Michael Pierce, "How Bill Clinton Remade the Democratic Party by Abandoning Unions: An Arkansas Story," LABOR Online, November 23, 2016.

20. A longer discussion of this encounter can be found in Nelson Lichtenstein, *State of the Union: A Century of American Labor* (Princeton, NJ: Princeton University Press, 2013), 168–69. While at Georgetown, Clinton had been an intern in the office of Senator William Fulbright, then notable for his skepticism on the Vietnam War and related foreign policy issues. Back in Arkansas, however, Fulbright stood on the conservative, antilabor side of most state-level issues.

21. Maraniss, *First in His Class*, 348.

22. Walker, *Clinton*, 81–82.

23. Bernstein, *A Woman in Charge*, 128, 136; Maraniss, *First in His Class*, 369.

24. Walker, *Clinton*, 91.

25. Johnson, *Arkansas in Modern America*, 230.

26. David Maraniss, "Clinton's Record in Arkansas: Mixed Reviews," *WP*, February 3, 1992, A8.

27. "Making All the Difference," speech delivered October 4, 1983, in *Preface to the Presidency: Selected Speeches of Bill Clinton, 1974–1992*, edited by Stephen A. Smith (Fayetteville: University of Arkansas Press, 1996), 32–33.

28. Johnson, *Arkansas in Modern America*, 232.

29. Ibid., 188–89.

30. "A New Covenant for Economic Change," speech delivered November 20, 1991, in Smith, *Preface to the Presidency*, 102.

31. Bernstein, *A Woman in Charge*, 170–71.

32. Ibid., 172; Maraniss, *First in His Class*, 410–16.

33. Cited in David Owen, "Testing Teachers," Alicia Patterson Foundation, April 6, 2011, https://aliciapatterson.org/stories/testing-teachers.

34. "RA Delegates Adopt Plan to Fight Testing," *Arkansas Educator*, November 1983, 1, file 52, box 26, Bill Clinton Gubernatorial record group, Education series, Dan Ernst subseries, Butler Center for Arkansas Studies, Central Arkansas Library System, Little Rock (hereafter "Butler Center"). The Arkansas AFL-CIO also felt betrayed because Clinton reneged on an

agreement to pay for the reform with a sales tax that offered a rebate on the food portion of the tax for low-income people. Maraniss, "Clinton's Record in Arkansas."

35. "Governor Bill Clinton, Southern Growth Policies Board, June 28, 1985," file 35, box 7, Bill Clinton gubernatorial record group, Economic Development series, Bob Nash subseries, Butler Center.

36. Peter Applebome, "Clinton Record in Leading Arkansas: Successes, but Not without Criticism," *NYT*, December 22, 1991, A30.

37. Nina Martin, "Who Is She?," *Mother Jones*, November/December 1993.

38. Walker, *Clinton*, 15.

39. Cited in James C. Cobb, *Industrialization and Southern Society, 1877–1984* (Lexington: University Press of Kentucky, 1984), 47.

40. James C. Cobb, *The Selling of the South: The Southern Crusade for Industrial Development, 1936–1990* (Urbana: University of Illinois Press, 1993), 201–2.

41. Derek Shearer, email to the author, January 2, 2022.

42. Quoted in William Goldsmith, "An Equitable New South without Unions? The Worker Rights Lacuna of the New Economy Policymakers, 1980–1992," unpublished paper in the author's possession, 12.

43. Ibid., 8.

44. "Governor Bill Clinton, Southern Growth Policies Board, June 28, 1985," file 35, box 7, Bill Clinton gubernatorial record group, Economic Development series, Bob Nash subseries, Butler Center.

45. Ibid.

46. Michael Piore and Charles Sabel, *The Second Industrial Divide: Possibilities for Prosperity* (New York: Basic Books, 1984); see also Sabel's *Work and Politics: The Division of Labor in Industry* (New York: Cambridge University Press, 1982), which offers an even more expansive endorsement of artisanal production in Emilia-Romagna. In a June 21, 2022, phone interview with the author, Ira Magaziner confirmed that Clinton was familiar with this line of thinking.

47. Clinton, *My Life*, 337.

48. Bill Clinton, "Background Report for the International Forum, Region of Tuscany/The Bridge Association, Florence, Italy, September 22–24," 1987, file 19, box 11, Bill Clinton gubernatorial record group, Economic Development series, Phil Price subseries, Butler Center.

49. David Maraniss, "How Clinton Moved to Handle State's Economy," *WP*, October 18, 1992, A1.

50. Clinton, *My Life*, 328–29.

51. Ibid., 337–38.

52. "Ford Foundation Inter-Office Memorandum," November 5, 1986, file 15, box 11, Bill Clinton gubernatorial record group, Economic Development series, Phil Price subseries, Butler Center.

53. Philip Scranton, *Endless Novelty: Specialty Production and American Industrialization, 1865–1925* (Princeton, NJ: Princeton University Press, 1997), 193–230, 260–94.

54. Clinton, *My Life*, 325.

55. Steve Striffler, *Chicken: The Dangerous Transformation of America's Favorite Food* (New Haven, CT: Yale University Press, 2007); Bethany Moreton, *To Serve God and Wal-Mart: The*

Making of Christian Free Enterprise (Cambridge, MA: Harvard University Press, 2009); Nelson Lichtenstein, *The Retail Revolution: How Wal-Mart Created a Brave New World of Business* (New York: Picador, 2010).

56. Lichtenstein, *The Retail Revolution*, 210.

57. Ibid.

58. David Harrington to Bill Clinton, "Wal-Mart 'Buy American' Program," September 14, 1988, file 12, box 2, Bill Clinton gubernatorial record group, Economic Development series, Bob Nash subseries, Butler Center.

59. Lichtenstein, *The Retail Revolution*, 210.

60. Phil Price to Bill Clinton, "Call from Jean Hervey—ACTWU," March 15, 1991, file 7, box 3, Bill Clinton gubernatorial record group, Economic Development series, Phil Price subseries, Butler Center.

61. Maraniss, "Clinton's Record in Arkansas."

62. Lichtenstein, *The Retail Revolution*, 211.

Chapter 2. "The Cold War Is Over: Germany and Japan Won"

1. Jeffrey Garten, *Three Days at Camp David: How a Secret Meeting in 1971 Transformed the Global Economy* (New York: Harper, 2021); Stein, *Pivotal Decade*, 39–50; Jonathan Levy, *Ages of American Capitalism: A History of the United States* (New York: Random House, 2021), 551–60.

2. Paul Volcker interview, "The Commanding Heights: The Battle for the World Economy," PBS, September 26, 2000, https://www.pbs.org/wgbh/commandingheights/shared/minitext/int_paulvolcker.html.

3. Levy, *Ages of American Capitalism*, 587–611; Robert Reich and John Donahue, *New Deals: The Chrysler Revival and the American System* (New York: Times Books, 1985), 229.

4. Paul Volcker, *Keeping at It: The Quest for Sound Money and Good Government* (New York: Public Affairs, 2018), 113; Samir Sonti, "The World Paul Volcker Made," *Jacobin*, December 20, 2018, online.

5. Bob Woodward, *Maestro: Greenspan's Fed and the American Boom* (New York: Simon & Schuster, 2000), 168; Michael Perlman, "Sado-Monetarism: The Role of the Federal Reserve in Keeping Wages Low," *Monthly Review*, April 1, 2012, online.

6. Paul Krugman, *The Age of Diminished Expectations: US Economic Policy in the 1990s* (Cambridge, MA: MIT Press, 1990).

7. Brent Cebul, "Supply-Side Liberalism: Fiscal Crisis, Post-Industrial Policy, and the Rise of the New Democrats," *Modern American History* 2, no. 2 (2019): 13.

8. Leslie Wayne, "Designing a New Economics for the 'Atari Democrats,'" *NYT*, September 26, 1982, sect. 3, 6. At this time the phrase "neo-liberal" was often used to describe those who advocated various sorts of state-guided investment strategies, while marginalizing labor, minorities, and proponents of a renewed Keynesianism. See Randall Rothenberg, *The Neo-Liberals: Creating the New American Politics* (New York: Simon & Schuster, 1984), 221–23.

9. Quoted in Cebul, "Supply-Side Liberalism," 4, 14; Daniel T. Rodgers, *Age of Fracture* (Cambridge, MA: Belknap Press of Harvard University Press, 2011), 69–70.

10. Robert Hershey, "Alfred E. Kahn Dies at 93; Prime Mover of Airline Deregulation," *NYT*, December 29, 2010, A21.

11. Paul Sabin, "Environmental Law and the End of the New Deal Order," in *Beyond the New Deal Order: US Politics from the Great Depression to the Great Recession*, edited by Gary Gerstle, Nelson Lichtenstein, and Alice O'Connor (Philadelphia: University of Pennsylvania Press, 2019), 189, 202.

12. Quoted in Matt Stoller, *Goliath: The 100-Year War between Monopoly Power and Democracy* (New York: Simon & Schuster, 2019), 412.

13. Nicholas Lemann, *Transaction Man: The Rise of the Deal and the Decline of the American Dream* (New York: Farrar, Straus and Giroux, 2019), 146–47.

14. Paul Krugman, *The Return of Depression Economics* (New York: W. W. Norton & Co., 1999), 2.

15. Bartel, *The Triumph of Broken Promises*, 169–200; David Satter, *Darkness at Dawn: The Rise of the Russian Criminal State* (New Haven, CT: Yale University Press, 2003).

16. Richard Freeman, "What Really Ails Europe (and America): The Doubling of the Global Workforce," *Globalist*, March 5, 2010, online.

17. Francis Fukuyama, "The End of History?," *National Interest* 16 (Summer 1989): 3–18.

18. David Harvey, *A Brief History of Neoliberalism* (New York: Oxford University Press, 2005).

19. Quoted in Nelson Lichtenstein, *A Contest of Ideas: Capital, Politics, and Labor* (Urbana: University of Illinois Press, 2013), 168; see also Gary Gerstle, "America's Neoliberal Order," in Gerstle, Lichtenstein, and O'Connor, *Beyond the New Deal Order*, 268–69.

20. Cited by Kevin P. Phillips, "US Industrial Policy: Inevitable and Ineffective," *Harvard Business Review* 70 (July/August 1990): 104–12.

21. Smith, *Preface to the Presidency*, 81.

22. Ibid., 283. That comparison was made in a speech to the Economic Club of Detroit on August 21, 1992, but similar evocations of German and Japanese success can be found in Clinton's presidential announcement talk in October 1991 and in the more detailed "New Covenant for Economic Change," delivered at Georgetown University a month later. See ibid., 81, 99.

23. Lichtenstein, *A Contest of Ideas*, 168.

24. Some key contributions to this debate include Peter Hall and David Soskice, eds., *Varieties of Capitalism: The Institutional Foundations of Comparative Advantage* (Oxford: Oxford University Press, 2001); Wolfgang Streeck and Kozo Yamamura, eds., *The Origins of Nonliberal Capitalism: Germany and Japan in Comparison* (Ithaca, NY: Cornell University Press, 2001); Gary Herrigel and Jonathan Zeitlin, "Alternatives to Varieties of Capitalism," *Business History Review* 84, no. 4 (Winter 2010): 667–74; Travis Fast, "Varieties of Capitalism: A Critique," *Relations Industrielles/Industrial Relations* 71, no. 1 (Winter 2016): 133–55.

25. Jeffrey E. Garten, *A Cold Peace: America, Japan, Germany, and the Struggle for Supremacy* (New York: Times Books, 1992), 13.

26. Ibid., 16.

27. Ezra F. Vogel, *Japan as Number One: Lessons for America* (Cambridge, MA: Harvard University Press, 1979); Michael Crichton, *Rising Sun* (New York: Random House, 1992); Tom Clancy, *Debt of Honor* (New York: Putnam, 1994).

28. William Watts, "Japan: Focus of America's Worst Fears," *Japan Times*, July 15, 1991, 21.

29. Karel van Wolferen, *The Enigma of Japanese Power: People and Politics in a Stateless Nation* (New York: Alfred A. Knopf, 1989), 109–58 passim.

30. Smith, *Preface to the Presidency*, 103, 291.

31. Lester Thurow, *Head to Head: The Coming Economic Battle among the United States, Europe, and Japan* (New York: Warner Books, 1993); Garten, *A Cold Peace*, 113–14, 128–29.

32. Otis L. Graham Jr., *Losing Time: The Industrial Policy Debate* (Cambridge, MA: Harvard University Press, 1992).

33. Sidney Blumenthal, "Drafting a Democratic Industrial Plan," *NYT*, August 28, 1983, A31; Thurow, *The Zero-Sum Society*, 191–214 passim.

34. John Pinder, Takashi Hosomi, and William Diebold, *Industrial Policy and the International Economy* (New York: Trilateral Commission, 1979), 3.

35. Andrew Elrod, "What Happened to Planning? The New Left's Coming of Age under the Carter Administration," April 2018, unpublished paper in the author's possession.

36. Cebul, "Supply-Side Liberalism," 1, 16, 19.

37. Laura D'Andrea Tyson, *The Yugoslav Economic System and Its Performance in the 1970s* (Berkeley: University of California Press, 1980). Andrew Elrod explained Dormer's importance to me.

38. Harry Kreisler, "An Economist Goes to Washington: A Conversation with Laura D'Andrea Tyson," January 14, 1998, *Conversations with History*, http://globetrotter.berkeley.edu/conversations/Tyson/.

39. Laura D'Andrea Tyson, *Who's Bashing Whom? Trade Conflict in High-Technology Industries* (Washington, DC: Peterson Institute for International Economics, 1992).

40. Stephen Cohen and John Zysman, *Manufacturing Matters: The Myth of the Post-Industrial Economy* (New York: Basic Books, 1987).

41. Ibid., 5–6.

42. James Risen, "Manufacturing Matters: The Myth of the Post-Industrial Economy," *Los Angeles Times*, July 26, 1987. This was a view echoed by Susan Schwab, a Republican Senate staffer and Japan specialist, who wrote that editorial writers for the mainstream press constituted "one of the last great bastions of liberal trade philosophy" in the 1980s. Susan Schwab, *Trade-offs Negotiating the Omnibus Trade and Competitiveness Act* (Boston: Harvard Business School Press, 1994), 58.

43. Steven Pearlstein, "The Many Crusades of Ira Magaziner," *WP*, April 18, 1993, N12.

44. Ira Magaziner and Mark Patinkin, *The Silent War: Inside the Global Business Battles Shaping America's Future* (New York: Vintage Books, 1989), 3–4.

45. Ibid., 5–6.

46. Thomas Hout and Ira Magaziner, *Japanese Industrial Policy* (Boston: Policy Studies Institute, 1980); Ira Magaziner and Robert Reich, *Minding America's Business: The Decline and Rise of the American Economy* (New York: Harcourt Brace, 1982).

47. Ibid., 302; Tyson Freeman, "The 1980s: (Too) Easy Money Fuels a New Building Boom," *National Real Estate Investor*, September 30, 1999.

48. Magaziner and Reich, *Minding America's Business*, x, 16.

49. Perlstein, "The Many Crusades of Ira Magaziner"; "Transcript: Robert Reich's Speech at Occupy Cal," *Daily Californian*, November 18, 2011.

50. Sidney Blumenthal, "Drafting a Democratic Industrial Plan," *NYT*, August 28, 1983, A31.

51. Ibid.

52. Wayne, "Designing a New Economics for the 'Atari Democrats.'"

53. Magaziner and Reich, *Minding America's Business*, 4.

54. Ibid., 4–5.

55. Wayne, "Designing a New Economics for the 'Atari Democrats.'"

56. Robert B. Reich, *The Next American Frontier* (New York: Times Books, 1983), 140–72.

57. Graham, *Losing Time*, 65–66; Piore and Sabel, *The Second Industrial Divide*.

58. William J. Clinton, "Remarks and a Question-and-Answer Session with the Economic Club of Detroit," January 8, 1999, American Presidency Project, University of California, Santa Barbara. The American Presidency Project website has a comprehensive finding aid for all presidential speeches and news conferences. Paul Krugman, "Challenging the Oligarchy," *New York Review of Books*, December 17, 2015.

59. Robert B. Reich, *The Work of Nations: Preparing Ourselves for 21st-Century Capitalism* (New York: Alfred A. Knopf, 1991), 171 passim.

60. Clinton, "Remarks and a Question-and-Answer Session with the Economic Club of Detroit," 58.

61. Murray Weidenbaum, "Industrial Policy Is Not the Answer," *Challenge* 26, no. 2 (July/August 1983): 24–25.

62. Reich and Donahue, *New Deals*, 295–97.

63. Peter Petre, "A Liberal Gets Rich yet Keeps the Faith," *Fortune*, August 31, 1987; Jacob Weisberg, "Dies Ira: A Short History of Mr. Magaziner," *The New Republic*, January 24, 1994, 21.

64. Robert B. Reich, "How Not to Make Industrial Policy," in Reich, *The Resurgent Liberal: And Other Unfashionable Prophecies* (New York: Times Books, 1989), 255, 257; John Metz, "Good Policy, No Buyer: The Fall of Rhode Island's Greenhouse Compact," *Brown Political Science Review*, December 27, 2017.

65. *America's Choice: High Skills or Low Wages! The Report of the Commission on the Skills of the American Workforce* (Rochester, NY: National Center on Education and the Economy, June 1990).

66. Robert Reich, "Who Is Us?," *Harvard Business Review*, January/February 1990, 54. For a statistical analysis of the debacle, see William Hudson, Mark Hyde, and John Carroll, "Corporatist Policy Making and State Economic Development," *Polity* 19, no. 3 (Spring 1987): 402–18.

67. Reich, "Who Is Us?," 54.

68. "Review and Outlook: The Liberal Majority," *Wall Street Journal* (hereafter *WSJ*), March 26, 1990, A8.

69. Louis Uchitelle, "An Old Liberal, a New Sermon," *NYT*, April 12, 1990, D1.

70. Magaziner also disagreed with Reich on this issue. His study of R&D at Corning Glass convinced him that location mattered a lot. Author's phone interview with Ira Magaziner, May 17, 2022.

71. Laura Tyson, "They Are Not Us: Why American Ownership Still Matters," *American Prospect*, Winter 1991. In Sidney Blumenthal, "The Anointed," *New Republic*, February 3, 1992, Clinton counterpoised Ira Magaziner's more explicit advocacy of an industrial policy to Robert

Reich's. "You have to have an economic strategy that goes beyond just educating the work force," said Clinton.

72. Timothy Minchin, *Empty Mills: The Fight against Imports and the Struggle to Save the US Textile Industry* (New York: Rowman & Littlefield, 2013).

73. Steve Dryden, *Trade Warriors: USTR and the American Crusade for Free Trade* (New York: Oxford University Press, 1995), 270–71; Serge Ferreri, "General Electric vs. the Market," 2017, unpublished paper in the author's possession.

74. Clyde Prestowitz, *Trading Places: How We Are Giving Our Future to Japan and How to Reclaim It* (New York: Basic Books, 1988), 256–57. In my phone interview with Prestowitz (January 29, 2022), he said that he entered the Reagan administration as a Republican but left as a Democrat.

75. Larry D. Browning and Judy C. Shetler, *Sematech: Saving the US Semiconductor Industry* (College Station: Texas A&M University Press, 2000).

76. Tyson, *Who's Bashing Whom?*, 109.

77. Ibid., 133, 154.

78. Dryden, *Trade Warriors*, 319–20.

Chapter 3. Winning the Presidency

1. "The Best of State Capitols," *US News & World Report*, December 21, 1987, 52.

2. Maraniss, *First in His Class*, 444–47; Clinton, *My Life*, 339–43.

3. Erica L. Groshen and Donald R. Williams, "White- and Blue-Collar Jobs in the Recent Recession and Recovery: Who's Singing the Blues?," *Economic Review* (Federal Reserve Bank of Cleveland), 1992, quarter 4, 2–12; Jacques Steinberg, "Among the First to Fall at IBM: Thousands in Hudson Valley Told They Are Out of Work," *NYT*, March 31, 1993, B1; Michael Meeropol, *Surrender: How the Clinton Administration Completed the Reagan Revolution* (Ann Arbor: University of Michigan Press, 1998), 220–23.

4. Sean Wilentz, *The Age of Reagan: A History, 1974–2008* (New York: HarperCollins, 2008), 306–10.

5. Quoted in Michael Nelson, "Re-dividing Government: National Elections in the Clinton Years and Beyond," in *42: Inside the Presidency of Bill Clinton*, edited by Michael Nelson, Barbara A. Perry, and Russell L. Riley (Ithaca, NY: Cornell University Press, 2016), 37.

6. Patrick Maney, *Bill Clinton: New Gilded Age President* (Lawrence: University Press of Kansas, 2016), 42–44; Geismer, *Left Behind*, 106–15; Patrick Andelic, *Donkey Work: Congressional Democrats in Conservative America, 1974–1994* (Lawrence: University Press of Kansas, 2019), 173–76.

7. Al From, *The New Democrats and the Return to Power* (New York: Palgrave MacMillan, 2013), 33.

8. Kenneth Baer, *Reinventing Democrats: The Politics of Liberalism from Reagan to Clinton* (Lawrence: University Press of Kansas, 2000), 162.

9. William Galston and Elaine Ciulla Kamarck, "The Politics of Evasion: Democrats and the Presidency," Progressive Policy Institute, September 1989, 4, 16, 18, https://www.progressive

policy.org/wp-content/uploads/2010/01/Politics_of_Evasion.pdf; Jeff Faux, "The Myth of the New Democrats," *American Prospect*, Fall 1993.

10. Baer, *Reinventing Democrats*, 106–9, 184.

11. E. J. Dionne, *Why Americans Hate Politics* (New York: Simon & Schuster, 1991), 306–7; Michael Kazin, *What It Took to Win: A History of the Democratic Party* (New York: Farrar, Straus and Giroux, 2022), 272–76.

12. Galston and Kamarck, "The Politics of Evasion," 5; Baer, *Reinventing Democrats*, 81, 185–87.

13. From, *The New Democrats*, 97.

14. Ibid., 111.

15. Clinton, *My Life*, 381; see also David Greenberg, "The Reorientation of Liberalism in the 1980s," in *Living in the Eighties*, edited by Gil Troy and Vincent J. Cannato (New York: Oxford University Press, 2009), 65.

16. Baer, *Reinventing Democrats*, 198–200; Bruce Reed oral history, February 19, 2004, Miller Center, University of Virginia (hereafter "Miller Center").

17. Steve Kornacki, "1992: Bill Clinton Builds a Winning Coalition; Jackson Is Diminished," *NBC News*, July 29, 2019, https://www.nbcnews.com/politics/elections/1992-bill-clinton -builds-winning-coalition-jackson-diminished-n1029606; Suzy Hanson, "Why Blacks Love Bill Clinton," *Salon*, February 21, 2002.

18. Nathan Robinson, "Bill Clinton's Stone Mountain Moment," *Jacobin*, September 16, 2016.

19. Marshall Frady, "Death in Arkansas," *New Yorker*, February 14, 1993, 105–7; Richard Cohen, "Sister Souljah: Clinton's Gumption," *WP*, June 16, 1992, A21.

20. From, *The New Democrats*, 173–75.

21. Author's phone interview with Ira Magaziner, May 17, 2022.

22. Bill Clinton and Al Gore, *Putting People First: A National Strategy for America*, file 13, box 11, Bill Clinton gubernatorial record group, Economic Development series, Phil Price subseries, Butler Center; author's phone interview with Derek Shearer, January 4, 2022.

23. Stanley Greenberg, "The Real Lesson for All Factions of the Democratic Party," *American Prospect*, March 25, 2022.

24. Jeff Faux to "Fellow Economists," August 20, 1992, box 7, Derek Shearer Papers, Brown University Archives.

25. Russell Riley, *Inside the Clinton White House: An Oral History* (New York: Oxford University Press, 2016), 111.

26. Ibid.

27. Steven Greenhouse, "The Calls for an Industrial Policy Grow Louder," *NYT*, July 19, 1992, A5; author's phone interview with Clyde Prestowitz, February 1, 2022. Prestowitz endorsed Bill Clinton in the 1992 election.

28. Amitai Etzioni, "Caution: Industrial Policy Is Coming," *Challenge* 35, no. 5 (September/ October 1992): 58, 59.

29. Walker, *Clinton*, 125–26.

30. M. Kramer and J. F. Stacks, "Now That We're Face to Face. . . ." *Time*, March 23, 1992, 16–22.

31. Wilentz, *The Age of Reagan*, 316; Sidney Blumenthal, "Perotnoia," *New Republic*, June 15, 1992, 25, 27–28. Perot became a full-fledged conspiracy theorist when it came to the POWs and MIAs supposedly still imprisoned in Vietnam and Laos. He blamed Reagan and Bush for the "cover-up."

32. Doron P. Levin, "GM vs. Ross Perot: Breaking Up Is Hard to Do," *NYT*, March 26, 1989, B1; John Judis, "The Executive," *New Republic*, June 15, 1992, 22.

33. Judis, "The Executive," 20.

34. "The 1992 Campaign; Transcript of the 2nd TV Debate between Bush, Clinton and Perot," *NYT*, October 16, 1992, 4.

35. Ted G. Jelen, ed., *Ross for Boss: The Perot Phenomenon and Beyond* (Albany: State University of New York Press, 2001), 51, 80–82; Ronald B. Rapoport and Walter J. Stone, *Three's a Crowd: The Dynamic of Third Parties, Ross Perot, and Republican Resurgence* (Ann Arbor: University of Michigan Press, 2005), 147–55.

36. Allen J. Matusow, *The Unraveling of America: A History of Liberalism in the 1960s* (New York: Harper & Row, 1984), 53–54. Milton Friedman popularized the "crowding out" critique of deficit spending in response to President Kennedy's proposed tax cuts in 1963.

37. Sabrina Siddiqui, "Bill Clinton Won 1992 Town Hall Debate by Engaging with One Voter," *Huffington Post*, October 16, 2012; Jon Swaine, "US Election: 1992 Voter Who Stumped George H. W. Bush at Debate Criticizes Mitt Romney," *Telegraph*, October 17, 2012.

38. Quoted in Brendan Doherty, "Root Canal Politics: Economic Policy Making in the New Administration," in Nelson, Perry, and Riley, *42: Inside the Presidency of Bill Clinton*, 105–6; Wilentz, *The Age of Reagan*, 321.

39. "A Monumental, Fragile Mandate," *NYT*, November 4, 1992, A30.

40. E. J. Dionne, "After 12 Years of Conservatism, a New Era Emerges," *WP*, November 4, 1992, A27.

41. Walter Dean Burnham, "The Legacy of George Bush: Travails of an Understudy," in *The Election of 1992*, edited by Gerald M. Pomper (Chatham, NJ: Chatham House, 1993), chap. 1.

42. *NYT*, "A Monumental, Fragile Mandate."

43. Louis Uchitelle, "Clinton's Point Man on Economics," *NYT*, November 21, 1992, A33.

44. Author's phone interview with Jeff Faux, February 21, 2022.

45. Robert Reich, *Locked in the Cabinet* (New York: Alfred A. Knopf, 1997), 12.

46. Alan Blinder oral history, June 27, 2003, Miller Center, 18; Sylvia Nasar, "The Transition: An Unorthodox Choice for Economic Advisor," *NYT*, December 12, 1992, A1.

47. Nasar, "The Transition."

48. Peter Passell, "More Advisers, Less Council?," *NYT*, December 17, 1992, D2. Summers, who had worked at the World Bank, had been eliminated from consideration as head of CEA because he signed an infamous World Bank memo urging that one "comparative advantage" enjoyed by Third World nations would be their capacity for and receptivity to serving as dumping grounds for toxic waste from more advanced countries. The memo leaked, sending Al Gore and other environmentalists into orbit. See chapter 12 for a longer discussion of the memo.

49. Blinder oral history, June 27, 2003, 26.

50. Rosenbaum, "Clinton Leads Experts in Discussion on Economy."

Chapter 4. Managing Health Care Capitalism

1. Cathie Jo Martin, *Stuck in Neutral: Business and the Politics of Human Capital Investment Policy* (Princeton, NJ: Princeton University Press, 2000), 98; Peter Swenson, "Misrepresented Interests: Business, Medicare, and the Making of the American Health Care State," *Studies in American Political Development* (April 2018): 5–9.

2. Paul Starr, *Remedy and Reaction: The Peculiar American Struggle over Health Care Reform* (New Haven, CT: Yale University Press, 2011), 79–84.

3. Martin, *Stuck in Neutral*, 98; Marie Gottschalk, *The Shadow Welfare State: Labor, Business, and the Politics of Health Care in the United States* (Ithaca, NY: Cornell University Press, 2000), 123.

4. Richard Brisbin, *A Strike Like No Other: Law and Resistance during the Pittston Coal Strike of 1989–1990* (Baltimore: Johns Hopkins University Press, 2002).

5. Lee Iacocca, "Iacocca Says National Health Care Deserves a Closer Look," *Automotive News*, April 24, 1989, 14.

6. Martin, *Stuck in Neutral*, 122.

7. Robert Pear, "Conflicting Aims in Booming Health Care Lobby Help Stall Congress," *NYT*, March 18, 1992, A17; Walter Maher, "Rekindling Reform—How Goes Business?," *American Journal of Public Health* 93, no. 1 (January 2003): 92–95; Swenson, "Misrepresented Interests," 18.

8. Dean Coddington, David J. Keen, and Keith Moore, "Cost Shifting Overshadows Employers' Cost-Containment Efforts," *Business & Health* 9, no. 1 (January 1991).

9. Martin, *Stuck in Neutral*, 175.

10. Quoted in Colin Gordon, *Dead on Arrival: The Politics of Health Care in Twentieth-Century America* (Princeton, NJ: Princeton University Press, 2003), 252; Lichtenstein, *The Retail Revolution*, 286–95.

11. Milt Freudenheim, "A Health-Care Taboo Is Broken," *NYT*, May 8, 1989, D1.

12. Cathie Jo Martin, "Together Again: Business, Government, and the Quest for Cost Control," *Journal of Health Politics, Policy, and Law* 18, no. 2 (Summer 1993): 359 (Martin quote), 369 (statistics); Gottschalk, *The Shadow Welfare State*, 133.

13. Peter Swenson and Scott Greer, "Foul Weather Friends: Big Business and Health Care Reform in the 1990s in Historical Perspective," *Journal of Health Politics, Policy, and Law* 27, no. 4 (August 2002): 623.

14. Martin, "Together Again," 369.

15. Freudenheim, "A Health-Care Taboo Is Broken."

16. Reich and Donahue, *New Deals*, 288–97; Cohen and Zysman, *Manufacturing Matters*, 259–63; Laura Tyson, William Dickens, and John Zysman, *The Dynamics of Trade and Employment* (Pensacola, FL: Ballinger Publishing Co., 1988); Ira Magaziner and Mark Patinkin, *The Silent War: Inside the Global Business Battles Shaping America's Future* (New York: Random House, 1989).

17. Haynes Johnson and David S. Broder, *The System: The American Way of Politics at the Breaking Point* (Boston: Little, Brown,1996), 58–59.

18. Jacob S. Hacker, *The Road to Nowhere: The Genesis of President Clinton's Plan for Health Security* (Princeton, NJ: Princeton University Press, 1997), 11.

19. Johnson and Broder, *The System*, 60.

20. Quoted in Starr, *Remedy and Reaction*, 80.

21. Hacker, *The Road to Nowhere*, 39.

22. Ibid., 104–5.

23. Ibid., 114.

24. Robin Toner, "Hillary Clinton's Potent Brain Trust on Health Reform," *NYT*, February 28, 1993, A1.

25. Zaid Jilani, "In 1993 Meeting, Hillary Clinton Acknowledged 'Convincing Case' for Single-Payer," *The Intercept*, January 16, 2016. Ira Magaziner had invited David Himmelstein and Steffie Woolhandler to meet with the first lady, probably in March or April of 1993.

26. Johnson and Broder, *The System*, 78, 86.

27. Hacker, *The Road to Nowhere*, 111; Johnson and Broder, *The System*, 87.

28. Gwen Ifill, "Clinton Proposes Making Employers Cover Health Care," *NYT*, September 25, 1992, A1; Hacker, *The Road to Nowhere*, 113.

29. "The Bush-Clinton Health Reform," *NYT*, October 10, 1992, A20. There was a back story to the *Times* endorsement. Right after Clinton's Merck speech, Michael Weinstein, the *Times* specialist covering health care for its editorial board, wrote an editorial, "Clinton Waffles on Health Care," in which he correctly noted that the candidate could not quite decide whether price controls or competition would hold down health care costs. Thrown into a panic, the Clinton campaign had Paul Starr, John Garamendi, and others lobby Weinstein, while operatives put out a press release affirming that the government would regulate rates only during the transition to managed competition. That seemed to convince Weinstein. "Clinton Waffles on Health," *NYT*, September 27, 1992, A16; Hacker, *Road to Nowhere*, 115–16.

30. Clinton, *President Clinton's New Beginning*, 62–65.

31. Starr, *Remedy and Reaction*, 92.

32. Dana Priest, "Clinton Names Wife to Head Health Panel," *WP*, January 26, 1993, A1; Bernstein, *A Woman in Charge*, 394–97; Starr, *Remedy and Reaction*, 99–104; William Chafe, *Bill and Hillary: The Politics of the Personal* (New York: Farrar, Straus and Giroux, 2012), 211–12.

33. *Washington Free Beacon*, "The Clinton Files," Diane Blair journal entries, March 9, 11, and 12, 1993, available at Scribd, https://www.scribd.com/doc/205858605/The-Clinton-Files.

34. Hillary Clinton, *Living History* (New York: Simon & Schuster, 2003), 151; Chris Jennings and Jeanne Lambrew oral history, April 17, 2003, Miller Center, 29.

35. Ira Magaziner to David Broder and Haynes Johnson, April 10, 1995, "Retrospective on Health Reform" [1] folder, OA/ID 12503, First Lady's Office, Pam Cicetti, Health Care Materials 1993–1994 subseries, Clinton Presidential Records, William J. Clinton Presidential Library & Museum, Little Rock, Arkansas (hereafter "Clinton Library").

36. Insights here are taken, in part, from J. Bradford DeLong, "Review of Haynes Johnson and David Broder, *The System*," https://delong.typepad.com/hoisted_from_the_archives/2007/10/review-of-johns.html. DeLong worked in the Treasury Department during the early years of the Clinton administration.

37. Ann Devroy, "Joint Chiefs Voice Concern to Clinton on Lifting Gay Ban," *WP*, January 26, 1993, A1; Kent Jenkins, "Into Troubled Waters," *WP*, May 11, 1993; Maney, *Bill Clinton*, 79–81.

38. *Washington Free Beacon*, "The Clinton Files," Diane Blair journal entries, May 17, 1994.

39. Jennings and Lambrew oral history, April 17, 2003, 34.

40. Reich, *Locked in the Cabinet*, 166.

41. Ira Magaziner to Robert Rubin, "Healthcare and the Economy," December 28, 1992, OA/ID 10249, First Lady's Office, Lisa Caputo subseries, Magaziner Health Care Memos [1], Clinton Library.

42. Clinton, *Living History*, 150–52.

43. Hacker, *Road to Nowhere*, 127.

44. Marshall Ingwerson, "CBO's Hard Choice on Health Package," *Christian Science Monitor*, February 11, 1994.

45. US House of Representatives, Ways and Means Committee, "Overview of CBO Scoring for Cost Savings under Reform Proposals," February 2, 1993, 103rd Cong., 1st sess., vol. 1, 152, 179.

46. Ibid., 150, 162.

47. Linda T. Bilheimer and Robert D. Reischauer, "Confessions of the Estimators: Numbers and Health Reform," *Health Affairs* 14, no. 1 (Spring 1995): 48.

48. *Washington Beacon*, "The Clinton Files," Diane Blair journal entry, February 23, 1993.

49. Ira C. Magaziner to Hillary Rodham Clinton, April 17, 1995, 9, "Retrospective on Health Reform" folder, OA/ID 9145, First Lady's Office [Broder-Johnson interview], Jennifer Klein, Domestic Policy Council, Clinton Library.

50. Robert Pear, "Health Initiative Tilting toward Price Regulation," *NYT*, February 16, 1993, A14; Kathleen Day, "Executives Blast Health Cost Caps," *WP*, March 18, 1993, C15.

51. Ira Magaziner to Hillary Rodham Clinton, April 17, 1995.

52. Paul Starr, "A Critique of Our Plan," June 18, 1993, 3, as cited in Starr, *Remedy and Reaction*, 306.

53. Alain Enthoven and Sara Singer, "A Single-Payer System in Jackson Hole Clothing," *Health Affairs* 13, no. 1 (Spring 1994): 81–95.

54. Hacker, *Road to Nowhere*, 135.

55. Robert Pear, "Clinton Health Plan: Testimony Reveals the Government's Hand," *NYT*, February 10, 1994, D20.

56. Ira Magaziner to Bill and Hillary Clinton, "Why We Started Left of Center," December 1993, OA/ID 12503, folder Passing Health Reform [1], Pam Cicetti, Health Care Materials 1993–1994 subseries, First Lady's Office, Clinton Library; Hacker, *Road to Nowhere*, 133.

57. William J. Clinton, "Address to a Joint Session of the Congress on Health Care Reform," September 22, 1993, American Presidency Project. The symbolism of a universal health security card was not a speechwriting flourish. The White House had hundreds of sample cards printed up for distribution right after the speech. Starr, *Remedy and Reaction*, 102.

58. William J. Clinton, "Address Before a Joint Session of the Congress on the State of the Union," January 25, 1994, American Presidency Project.

59. Quoted in James Fallows, "A Triumph of Misinformation," *Atlantic*, January 1995.

60. Adam Clymer, "The Clinton Health Plan Is Alive on Arrival," *NYT*, A3.

61. Bernstein, *A Woman in Charge*, 395–96.

62. Clymer, "Alive on Arrival."

63. Ira Magaziner, "Passing Health Reform: Policy and Congressional Summary," December 10, 1993, 10, "Passing Health Reform [1]" folder, OA/ID 12503, First Lady's Office, Pam Cicetti, Health Care Materials, 1993–1994, Clinton Library.

64. Ibid., 2.

65. Ira Magaziner in Broder-Johnson interview, April 9, 1994, 6, "Retrospective on Health Reform" folder, OA/ID 9145, First Lady's Office [Broder-Johnson interview], Jennifer Klein, Domestic Policy Council, Clinton Library.

66. Clymer, "Alive on Arrival."

67. "Senator Bob Dole," "Passing Health Reform" [1] folder, OA/ID 12503, Pam Cicetti, Health Care Materials, 1993–1994, First Lady's Office, Clinton Library.

68. William Kristol to "Republican Leaders," "Defeating President Clinton's Health Care Proposal," December 2, 1993, "GOP—Kristol, William" folder, OA/ID 3582, Health Care Task Force series, Clinton Library.

69. William Kristol, "Why the Coming Clinton-Cooper Compromise Has to Be Defeated," *Washington Times*, February 10, 1994; William Kristol, "The Chafee Plan as a Trap for Republicans," *Washington Times*, May 13, 1994; William Kristol to "Republican Leaders," "Health Care Reform: The Next 100 Days," January 10, 1994; William Kristol to "Republican Leaders," "Health Care—The Principles of Conservative Reform," March 2, 1994; both in "GOP—Kristol, William" folder, OA/ID 3582, Health Care Task Force series, Clinton Library.

70. Theda Skocpol, *Boomerang: Clinton's Health Security Effort and the Turn against Government in US Politics* (New York: W. W. Norton, 1996), 147.

71. Ibid., 163.

72. Paul Starr, "What Happened to Health Care Reform?," *American Prospect*, Winter 1995, 20.

Chapter 5. Health Care Corporatism in Failure and Success

1. Martin, *Stuck in Neutral*, 175; Jerry Jasinowski to Ira Magaziner, "NAM President Praises Administration Health Care Leader's Remarks," March 18, 1993, "National Association of Manufacturers" folder, OA/ID 3304, Ira Magaziner, Health Care Task Force series, Clinton Library.

2. Peter Swenson, "Business Interests and the Health Care State: Medicare and Obamacare in Historical and Comparative Perspective," October 2015, 27 (no longer available online).

3. Martin, *Stuck in Neutral*, 176.

4. Johnson and Broder, *The System*, 317.

5. Benjamin Waterhouse, *Lobbying America: The Politics of Business from Nixon to NAFTA* (Princeton, NJ: Princeton University Press, 2014), 63–64.

6. Ibid., 218–20.

7. Paul Gigot, "Big Business Courts Clinton," *WSJ*, February 12, 1993, A14.

8. Martin, *Stuck in Neutral*, 177.

9. Starr, *Remedy and Reaction*, 115.

10. Newt Gingrich et al. to Richard Lesher, March 25, 1993; Ivan Gorr to Robert Michel, March 31, 1993, both in "Chamber of Commerce" folder, OA/ID 3304, Ira Magaziner, Subgroup Health Care Task Force series, Clinton Library; Boehner quoted in Jeanne Saddler and Rick

Wartzman, "Chamber of Commerce Is Roiled by Revolt within Rank and File," *WSJ*, April 15, 1994, A1.

11. Steven Pearlstein, "Chamber's Shift Hasn't Ended Fight; Hill Republicans Shun Group over Tax Tiff," *WP*, July 20, 1993, C1; John Judis, "Abandoned Surgery: Business and the Failure of Health Care Reform," *American Prospect*, Spring 1995, 67.

12. Robert Pear, "Business and Labor Call for Health Tax," *NYT*, November 13, 1991, A16.

13. Rick Wartzman and Jeanne Saddler, "Motley's Crew: A Fervent Lobbyist Rallies Small Business to Battle Health Plan," *WSJ*, January 5, 1994, A1; Motley quoted in Hilary Stout and Rick Wartzman, "Administration Is Trying to Woo Small Business in Bid to Overhaul Nation's Health-Care System," *WSJ*, March 29, 1993, A14.

14. Judis, "Abandoned Surgery," 68.

15. Michael Weisskopf, "Health Care Lobbies Lobby Each Other," *WP*, March 1, 1994, A8.

16. Thomas A. Stewart, "A New 500 for the New Economy," *Fortune*, May 15, 1995, 166–67.

17. US House of Representatives Committee on Ways and Means, "Effects of Health Care Reform on the National Economy and Jobs," 103rd Cong., 1st sess., December 15, 1993, 119, 133; Health Care Reform Project, "Do as We Say, Not as We Do: How Pizza Hut and McDonald's Fight Shared Responsibility in Congress While Paying for Better Health Insurance Overseas," July 1994, HEALTH—[Pizza Hut] file, OA/ID 13602, First Lady's Office, Health Care subject files subseries, P–Z series, Patti Cicetti, Clinton Library.

18. David Wessel, "Health Costs to Fall in Some Industries, Increase in Others, New Analysis Shows," *WSJ*, February 9, 1994, A3.

19. Hilary Stout and Christina Duff, "Big Retail Chains Are Speaking Out in Opposition to Clinton Health Plan," *WSJ*, October 11, 1993, A2.

20. House Committee on Ways and Means, "Effects of Health Care Reform on the National Economy and Jobs," 133; Health Care Reform Project, "Do as We Say, Not as We Do."

21. Skocpol, *Boomerang*, 136–37.

22. Sidney Wolfe, "Clinton Plan Rewards Big Insurers," *NYT*, November 7, 1993, A14; Robert Pear, "Leading Health Insurers into a New Age," *NYT*, December 6, 1992, A11.

23. Dana Priest, "A Health Care Primer: How 'Managed Competition' Would Work," *WP*, March 9, 1993, A1.

24. Rick Wartzman, "Insurance Industry Is Split over Level of Confrontation in Health-Care Debate," *WSJ*, March 15, 1994, A22.

25. Kathleen Day, "Health Insurance Shakeout; Higher Costs Push Industry to HMOs," *WP*, March 29, 1993, A1.

26. Johnson and Broder, *The System*, 201.

27. Magaziner and Kirkland quoted in Darrell West et al., "Political Advertising and Health Care Reform," paper presented at the annual meeting of the Midwest Political Science Association, Chicago, April 6–8, 1995, 7.

28. Ibid., 10–11, 35.

29. Quoted in Skocpol, *Boomerang*, 138.

30. Clinton, *Living History*, 229.

31. Center for Public Integrity, "Well-Healed: Inside Lobbying for Health Care Reform, Part I," *International Journal of Health Sciences* 25, no. 3 (1995): 413, 443.

32. Johnson and Broder, *The System*, 210.

33. Judis, "Abandoned Surgery," 70.

34. Robert Winters to Hillary Clinton, April 1, 1993, "Business Roundtable Health Task Force" folder, OA/ID 3304, Ira Magaziner, Health Care Task Force series, Clinton Library.

35. Hilary Stout and Rick Wartzman, "Why Clintons' Effort to Woo Big Business to Health Plan Failed," *WSJ*, February 11, 1994, A1. Staying independent of the purchasing alliances also would cost these companies a 1 percent payroll surcharge on top of the 7.9 percent they were required to spend on employee health insurance.

36. Johnson and Broder, *The System*, 309–15.

37. Judis, "Abandoned Surgery," 70.

38. Stout and Wartzman, "Why Clintons' Effort to Woo Big Business to Health Plan Failed."

39. Martin, *Stuck in Neutral*, 187.

40. Louis Uchitelle, "Manufacturers Oppose Clinton Plan," *NYT*, February 6, 1994, A26; Martin, *Stuck in Neutral*, 187.

41. Jeanne Saddler and Rick Wartzman, "Chamber of Commerce Is Roiled by Revolt within Rank and File," *WSJ*, April 15, 1994, A1; Judis, "Abandoned Surgery," 69.

42. Johnson and Broder, *The System*, 323.

43. Judis, "Abandoned Surgery," 69–70.

44. Stout and Wartzman, "Why Clintons' Effort to Woo Big Business to Health Plan Failed."

45. Uchitelle, "Manufacturers Oppose Clinton Plan."

46. Johnson and Broder, *The System*, 323.

47. Ira Magaziner to Bill and Hillary Clinton, "Health Care Reform," December 17, 1993, "Magaziner Health Care Memos" [4] folder, OA/ID 10249, First Lady's Office, Lisa Caputo, Clinton Library, FOIA 2006-0810-F (2).

48. Starr, *Remedy and Reaction*, 126.

49. John Judis, "Abandoned Surgery," 72.

50. Martin, *Stuck in Neutral*, 180.

51. Dana Priest and Michael Weisskopf, "Health Care Reform: The Collapse of a Quest," *WP*, October 11, 1994, A1.

52. Clinton, *Living History*, 247.

53. Starr, *Remedy and Reaction*, 120–21.

54. Bill Kristol, "Health: Congress Is Now More Dangerous than Mr. Clinton," *Washington Times*, July 27, 1994.

55. Swenson and Greer, "Foul Weather Friends," 624–25.

56. Steven Pearlstein, "Big Business Has Gone to Sidelines in Health Care Debate," *WP*, August 3, 1994, A10.

57. Obama opposed the mandate idea during the primaries, but by the time he assumed office he had been convinced by Hillary Clinton that her framework for health reform, including the necessity of an individual mandate, was the proper policy choice. Starr, *Remedy and Reaction*, 234.

58. Ezra Klein, "The Lessons of '94," *American Prospect*, January 20, 2008.

59. For good blow-by-blow accounts of the passage of the ACA, see Lawrence R. Jacobs and Theda Skocpol, *Health Care Reform and American Politics: What Everyone Needs to Know* (New York: Oxford University Press, 2016), 50–67; and Starr, *Remedy and Reaction*, 235–38.

60. John E. McDonough, *Inside National Health Reform* (Berkeley: University of California Press, 2011), 81.

61. Starr, *Remedy and Reaction*, 228.

62. Jacobs and Skocpol, *Health Care Reform and American Politics*, 69.

63. McDonough, *Inside National Health Reform*, 76; W. James Antle III, "The Irony of Obama-Care: How Liberals Came to Love Big Business," *The Week*, February 18, 2015.

64. McDonough, *Inside National Health Reform*, 164–66.

65. Sarah Lueck, "Health Insurance Trade Groups Plan to Merge," *WSJ*, September 23, 2003, B6.

66. Laura Meckler, "Democrats Turn Up the Heat on Insurance Industry," *WSJ*, July 16, 2009, A6; Jonathan Cohn, "Health Care Lobbyist Playing Nice," *New Republic*, June 2010.

67. Starr, *Remedy and Reaction*, 218.

68. John E. McDonough, email to the author, November 17, 2016.

69. N. C. Aizenman, "Health-Care Provision at Center of Supreme Court Debate Was a Republican Idea," *WP*, March 26, 2012. However, the conservative columnist Ramesh Ponnuru argued that the individual mandate was hardly a universally supported idea on the right even in the early 1990s; see "The History of the Individual Mandate," *National Review*, March 27, 2012.

70. McDonough, *Inside National Health Reform*, 78, 169. In August, with funds from large insurers, including Aetna, CIGNA, Humana, UnitedHealthcare, and Wellpoint, AHIP began secretly funneling financial support to the US Chamber of Commerce to bankroll a major advertising campaign against reform. In all, AHIP gave $86.2 million to the Chamber. The degree to which Ignagni was involved in this funding is not known.

71. Jacobs and Skocpol, *Health Care Reform and American Politics*, 73–74.

72. Starr, *Remedy and Reaction*, 220; McDonough, email to the author, November 17, 2016.

73. Not all retailers, however, were on board. Although the National Retail Federation represented many high-benefit, unionized firms, it condemned Wal-Mart's endorsement of the ACA as "quite possibly the most unwelcome development to date of the health care debate for us." The sense of betrayal carried over to the Chamber of Commerce, whose senior manager for health care policy denounced the Wal-Mart initiative as "the worst incarnation" of the mandate idea, "the most dangerous policy." Pamela Lewis Dolan, "Wal-Mart Backs Employer Mandate for Health Coverage," *American Medical News*, July 27, 2009; Janet Adamy and Ann Zimmerman, "Wal-Mart Backs Drive to Make Companies Pay for Health Coverage," *WSJ*, July 1, 2009.

74. Patrick O'Mahen, "Obamacare and Tax Reform: A Progressive Double Play (Part 1)," The Makeshift Academic, October 22, 2013, https://themakeshiftacademic.blogspot.com/search?q=Obamacare+and+Tax+Reform%3A+A+Progressive+Double+Play; Jacobs and Skocpol, *Health Care Reform and American Politics*, 135.

75. McDonough, *Inside National Health Reform*, 140.

76. Starr, *Remedy and Reaction*, 136–37.

77. Ricardo Alonso-Zaldivar, "As Medicaid Loses Stigma Election May Cloud Its Future," *Associated Press News*, October 20, 2016.

78. Ezekiel J. Emanuel, *Reinventing American Health Care: How the Affordable Care Act Will Improve Our Terribly Complex, Blatantly Unjust, Outrageously Expensive, Grossly Inefficient, Error Prone System* (New York: Public Affairs, 2014), 206–9; McDonough, *Inside National Health Reform*, 142–44.

79. "Medicaid & CHIP Enrollment Data Highlights" at Medicaid.gov offers a web portal for the latest state and national data. These figures were current as of October 2022. Another five million people would almost certainly have been enrolled if the Supreme Court in 2012 had not allowed states to reject Medicaid money and the new eligibility standards under ACA.

80. Kimberly Leonard, "Under Obamacare, Government Insurance Thrives More than Private Plans," *US News & World Report*, March 25, 2016; Timothy Jost, "CBO Lowers Marketplace Enrollment Projections, Increases Medicaid Growth Projections," *Health Affairs*, January 26, 2016.

81. Phil Galewitz, "In Depressed Rural Kentucky, Worries Mount over Medicaid Cutbacks," *Kaiser Health News*, November 19, 2016.

82. See, for example, Andrea Louise Campbell, "Policy Makes Mass Politics," *Annual Review of Political Science* 15 (June 2012): 333–51.

Chapter 6. Opening Japan: A Detour on the Road to Neoliberalism

1. Steven Weisman, "Bush's Painful Trip: Japanese Feel the Talks Will Not Help US Economy or Rapport with Tokyo," *NYT*, January 10, 1992, A1.

2. Bill Powell, "A Case of Political Flu," *Newsweek*, January 20, 1992; Michael Wines, "Bush Collapses at State Dinner with the Japanese," *NYT*, January 9, 1992, A1.

3. Osita Nwanevu, "Remember When George H. W. Bush Puked on the Japanese Prime Minister?," *Slate*, September 16, 2016.

4. Doron Levin, "General Motors to Cut 70,000 Jobs; 21 Plants to Shut," *NYT*, December 19, 1991, A1; Warren Brown, "GM Loses Record $4.5 Billion; Announces 12 Plant Closings, *WP*, February 25, 1992.

5. "Lost in Tokyo," *NYT*, January 10, 1992, A26; "Clinton Seizes on Asia Trip to Depict Bush as Beatable," *NYT*, January 15, 1992, A16.

6. David Sanger, "Chill Persists between US Car Makers and Japan," *NYT*, January 9, 1992, A 10; Michael Wines, "Bush Reaches Pact with Japan, but Auto Makers Denounce It," *NYT*, January 10, 1992, A1.

7. Dryden, *Trade Warriors*, 357–58.

8. Michael Schrage, "Potato Chips vs. Computer Chips—High Technology Any Way You Slice It," *WP*, January 22, 1993.

9. John Kunkel, *America's Trade Policy towards Japan: Demanding Results* (New York: Routledge, 2003), 131.

10. Robert M. Uriu, *Clinton and Japan: The Impact of Revisionism on US Trade Policy* (New York: Oxford University Press, 2009), 81.

11. Kunkel, *America's Trade Policy towards Japan*, 154.

12. Ibid., 158.

13. Robert C. Neff, "Rethinking Japan," *Business Week*, August 7, 1989, 44; Kunkel, *America's Trade Policy towards Japan*, 132–35; see also Brink Lindsey and Aaron Lukas, "Revisiting the

'Revisionists': The Rise and Fall of the Japanese Economic Model," Trade Policy Analysis 3, Cato Institute, July 31, 1998.

14. Crichton, *Rising Sun*, 349.

15. Theodore White, "The Danger from Japan," *New York Times Magazine*, July 28, 1985, 31.

16. "Killing of Vincent Chin," Wikipedia, last updated September 5, 2022.

17. Uriu, *Clinton and Japan*, 82–84.

18. Johnson, *Japan: Who Governs?* (New York: W. W. Norton & Co., 1995), 63.

19. Chalmers Johnson, "The 'Revisionist' Stance on Trade with Japan," *WP*, August 11, 1992, A16.

20. Kunkel, *America's Trade Policy towards Japan*, 137.

21. Chalmers Johnson, Laura D'Andrea Tyson, and John Zysman, *Politics and Productivity: How Japan's Development Strategy Works* (Cambridge, MA: Ballinger, 1989).

22. Tyson, *Who's Bashing Whom?*, 56–57.

23. Uriu, *Clinton and Japan*, 67. On corporate funding of the Prestowitz think tank, see Derek Shearer to Bill Clinton, August 26, 1993, box 7, Derek Shearer Papers, Brown University Archives.

24. Kunkel, *America's Trade Policy towards Japan*, 135.

25. Alan Blinder, "More Like Them?," *American Prospect*, Winter 1992, 51–52.

26. Ibid., 52–54.

27. John Judis, "Rougher Trade," *New Republic*, May 31, 1993, 28.

28. Derek Shearer to Bill Clinton, October 25, 1991; Shearer to Robert Reich, 1991; both in box 7, Derek Shearer Papers, Brown University Archives.

29. "Brown Lays Out Criteria for Sectoral Trade Negotiations with Japan," *Inside US Trade*, April 30, 1993.

30. John Judis, "Old Master," *New Republic*, December 13, 1993, 24.

31. Kunkel, *America's Trade Policy towards Japan*, 163.

32. Steven Holmes, *Ron Brown: An Uncommon Life* (New York: John Wiley & Sons, 2000), 250. Kantor had wanted to be Clinton's chief of staff, but settled for the trade job. Author's phone interview with Derek Shearer, January 4, 2022.

33. "Brown Lays Out Criteria for Sectoral Trade Negotiations with Japan," *Inside US Trade*.

34. Kunkel, *America's Trade Policy towards Japan*, 161.

35. Greg Rienzi, "Jeffrey Garten is a Financier, Academic, and Author—and Yes, He's Married to the Barefoot Contessa," *Johns Hopkins*, Spring 2016; Jeffrey Garten, email to the author, September 6, 2020.

36. Garten, *A Cold Peace*, 137.

37. Jeffrey Garten, "Clinton's Emerging Trade Policy: Act One, Scene One," *Foreign Affairs*, Summer 1993, 183, 185.

38. Author's phone interview with Derek Shearer, January 4, 2022.

39. "Kantor Says Auto Parts Commitments Constitute Pledge by Japanese Government," *Inside US Trade*, April 2, 1993.

40. Kunkel, *America's Trade Policy towards Japan*, 2.

41. Charlene Barshefsky oral history, March 2, 2005, Miller Center.

42. Charlene Barshefsky to NEC Deputies Group, September 24, 1993, "Japan" [1] folder, OA/ID 5059, Council of Economic Advisers, Clinton Library.

43. Uriu, *Clinton and Japan*, 75.

44. "Trade Officials, Senators Embrace 'Results-Oriented' Japan Policy," *Inside US Trade*, March 19, 1993.

45. "UAW President Says United with Carmakers Limited to Fighting Japanese Surplus," *Inside US Trade*, September 22, 1993.

46. Doron Levin, "Honda Cut from US Auto Group," *NYT*, November 26, 1992, D1.

47. Matthew Cooper and Jim Impoco, "The Making of a Trade Hawk," *US News & World Report*, July 12, 1993, 218–29.

48. David E. Rosenbaum, with Keith Bardsher, "Candidates Playing to Mood of Protectionism," *NYT*, January 26, 1992, A1.

49. Barshefsky oral history, March 2, 2005.

50. Gwen Ifill, "Clinton and Japanese Premier Scold Each Other on Trade Issues," *NYT*, April 17, 1993, A1.

51. David Sanger, "Head to Head with the Japanese," *NYT*, April 18, 1993, A5.

52. Kunkel, *America's Trade Policy towards Japan*, 169; David Sanger, "Clinton Achieves Trade Framework in Japanese Pact," *NYT*, July 10, 1993, A1. The devil, of course, was in the details. The Americans thought "objective criteria" were numerical targets, but the Japanese remained adamantly opposed to any sort of target, so that phrase, as well as its cousins like "benchmark," "yardstick," "measure," "standard," and "quantitative indicator"—all of which Barshefsky thought might serve as admittedly imperfect substitutes—appear nowhere in the text of the Framework Agreement. Charlene Barshefsky to NEC Deputies Group, June 16, 1993, "Japan" [2] folder, OA/ID 5059, Laura Tyson, Council of Economic Advisers, Clinton Library; Paul Blustein, "US-Japanese Trade Pact: A Deal That Nearly Wasn't," *WP*, July 11, 1993, A18.

53. Kantor to the President, "Today's Japan Cellular Telephone Agreement," March 12, 1994, "Japan" [5] folder, OA/ID 5059, Laura Tyson, Council of Economic Advisers, Clinton Library; "United States Japan Arrangement on Cellular Telephone Systems," March 12, 1994, "History of USTR" press releases, March/April 1994, Clinton Library.

54. "US Trade Policy with Japan: Assessing the Record," a report prepared by the Council of Economic Advisers, November 9, 1995, Michael Waldman Speechwriting Collection, Clinton Library, FOIA 2006-0461.

55. Ibid.

56. Edward J. Lincoln, *Troubled Times: US-Japan Economic Relations in the 1990s* (Washington, DC: Brookings Institution Press, 1998), 139–40; "Japanese Officials Balk at US Demands in Framework Negotiations," *Inside US Trade*, October 22, 1993.

57. Uriu, *Clinton and Japan*, 187.

58. Ibid., 188.

59. Japan Framework, June 18, 1993, "Japan" [2] folder, OA/ID 5059, Laura Tyson, Council of Economic Advisers, Clinton Library.

60. Takatoshi Ito to Laura Tyson, January 31, 1994, "Japan" [2] folder, OA/ID 5059, Laura Tyson, Council of Economic Advisers, Clinton Library.

61. Jagdish Bhagwati to Larry Summers, November 4, 1993, "Japan" [2], folder, OA/ID 5059, Laura Tyson, Council of Economic Advisers, Clinton Library; Joseph Stiglitz, then on the Clinton CEA, also thought that anti-Japanese "nationalism" was largely responsible for the Clinton trade posture. Author's phone interview with Joseph Stiglitz, February 22, 2022.

62. "Reject Managed Trade," *Far Eastern Economic Review*, November 4, 1993.

63. Larry Summers to Jagdish Bhagwati, October 20, 1993, "Japan" [2] folder, OA/ID 5059, Laura Tyson, Council of Economic Advisers, Clinton Library. Tyson agreed with Summers. Responding to a column by Peter Passell of the *New York Times*, she explained to President Clinton that, "in the presence of market access barriers, a managed trade deal that opens market opportunities in a closed foreign market is pro competition and pro trade—it is not protectionist." Tyson to the President, "US Trade Policy toward Japan," May 4, 1993, "Japan" [3] folder, OA/ID 5059, Laura Tyson, Council of Economic Advisers, Clinton Library.

64. Kunkel, *America's Trade Policy towards Japan*, 179.

65. Ibid., 108–9.

66. Clinton, *My Life*, 657.

67. James Shoch, *Trading Blows: Party Competition and US Trade Policy in a Globalizing Era* (Chapel Hill: University of North Carolina Press, 2001) 202–3.

68. Clay Chandler, "US Japanese Delegates Voice Pessimism in Trade Talks; Clinton Warns of Retaliation," *WP*, May 5, 1995, A30.

69. David Sanger, "100% Tariffs Set on 13 Top Models of Japanese Cars," *NYT*, May 17, 1995, A1.

70. Barshefsky oral history, March 2, 2005.

71. David Sanger, "US and Japan Open Crucial Auto-Trade Talks," *NYT*, June 23, 1995, D1.

72. David Sanger, "In Geneva, Diplomats Talk of Mufflers, Not Warheads," *NYT*, June 26, 1995, A2.

73. Paul Blustein, "A Bitter Fight Produces Little Real Change," *WP*, June 29, 1995, A1.

74. Kunkel, *America's Trade Policy towards Japan*, 182.

75. Jim Hoagland, "A Soft Deal with Japan," *WP*, July 5, 1995, A23.

76. Quoted in Kunkel, *America's Trade Policy towards Japan*, 183.

77. Blustein, "A Bitter Fight Produces Little Real Change."

78. Quoted in Kunkel, *America's Trade Policy towards Japan*, 178. Garten was annoyed that US automakers did little to build products Japanese consumers would buy. "I would meet with the big three CEOs regularly. They were delighted to have government bash Japan. They seemed totally unwilling to make cars Japanese wanted. I saw them as smug, entitled." Jeffrey Garten, email to the author, September 7, 2020.

79. Laura D'Andrea Tyson to Japan Deputies Group, " Reflections on Our Japan Trade Strategy," September 7, 1994, "Japan" [2] folder, OA/ID 5059, Council of Economic Advisers, Clinton Library.

80. Andrew Pollack, "US Trade Negotiator Urges Shift in Approach on Japan," *NYT*, August 1, 1995, D3. Although privately sympathetic to Garten, Commerce Secretary Ron Brown publicly repudiated Garten's dovishness. "All of us at the Commerce Department, Jeff included, ought to have absolutely unassailable credibility on the Japan issue; we were the tough guys," said Brown one day later. But Garten's sentiments proved more indicative of how the United

States would now approach other trade issues, especially with China. Keith Bradsher, "US Not Embracing Call for a Shift on Japan," *NYT*, August 2, 1995, D4; Garten, email to the author, September 7, 2020.

81. Robert Z. Lawrence, "International Trade Policy in the 1990s," in *American Economic Policy in the 1990s*, edited by Jeffrey Frankel and Peter Orszag (Cambridge, MA: MIT Press, 2002), 305–6.

82. Masao Yukawa, "Japan's Enemy Is Japan," *Washington Quarterly*, Winter 1999, 13; Krugman, *The Return of Depression Economics*, 74–78.

83. Larry Summers to Robert Rubin, June 9, 1995; Timothy Geithner to Larry Summers, July 13, 1995; both in "Japan and the United States: Diplomatic, Security, and Economic Relations, Part III, 1961–2000," National Security Archive, George Washington University.

84. Robert Rubin to the President, "Japan's Economic Outlook," October 3, 1995; Jeffrey Shafer, "Is Japan Ready for the 21st Century?," October 2, 1995; both in "History of the Department of the Treasury" supplementary documents [2] folder, OA/box 24124, Clinton Library.

85. John Judis, "The Sun Also Rises," *New Republic*, November 3, 1997, 22.

86. John Judis, "Dollar Foolish," *New Republic*, December 9, 1996, 23–24.

87. Ibid.; R. Taggart Murphy, "Japan's Economic Crisis," *New Left Review* 1 (January/February 2000): 25–52.

88. Paul A. Gigot, "The Great Japan Debate Is Over. Guess Who Won?" *WSJ*, January 31, 1997, A18.

89. Lindsey and Lukas, "Revisiting the 'Revisionists.'"

90. Paul Blustein, "US Looks Anew at Japan Inc.," *WP*, August 16, 1998, H1.

91. Krugman, *The Return of Depression Economics*, 60–82.

92. Michael Mastanduno, "Models, Markets, and Power: Political Economy and the Asia-Pacific, 1989–1999," *Review of International Studies* 26 (2000): 497.

93. R. Taggart Murphy, "A Loyal Retainer? Japan, Capitalism, and the Perpetuation of American Hegemony," *Socialist Register* (October 2010): 147–73; Murray Sayle, "The Social Contradictions of Japanese Capitalism," *Atlantic*, June 1998, 90.

Chapter 7. Budget and Boom

1. Author's phone interview with Derek Shearer, January 4, 2022.

2. Lloyd Grove, "The Man in Transition: Vernon Jordan, from Civil Rights and Big Business to the Clinton Team," *WP*, November 19, 1992, D1.

3. Warren Christopher, *Chances of a Lifetime: A Memoir* (New York: Scribner, 2001), 162. Mickey Kantor, a friend of Hillary's who worked at Christopher's LA law firm, had played the key role in securing Christopher's early endorsement of Bill Clinton. Author's phone interview with Derek Shearer, January 4, 2022.

4. Leon Panetta oral history, January 31, 2003, Miller Center; Walker, *Clinton*, 171; Robert Hershey Jr., "Alice Rivlin, 88, a Leading Government Economist, Is Dead," *NYT*, May 14, 2019.

5. Robert Collins, *More: The Politics of Economic Growth in Postwar America* (New York: Oxford University Press, 2000), 188–89.

6. Quoted in Doherty, "Root Canal Politics," 107.

7. David Wessel, "If Bentsen Has Clout, Prestige, and Clinton's Ear, Then Why Does Treasury Chief Seem So Glum?," *WSJ*, October 22, 1993, A16.

8. Author's phone interview with Ira Magaziner, June 21, 2022.

9. Telis Demos, "Robert Rubin's Legacy Up for Debate 10 Years after Citigroup Bailout," *WSJ*, June 8, 2018, A1.

10. Robert Rubin oral history, November 3, 2005, 3, Miller Center; William Cohan, *Money and Power: How Goldman Sachs Came to Rule the World* (New York: Random House, 2011), 141; John Judis, "Old Master," *New Republic*, December 13, 1993, 22.

11. Robert Rubin, *In an Uncertain World: Tough Choices from Wall Street to Washington* (New York: Random House, 2003), 200–201.

12. Roger Altman oral history, April 22, 2003 (no pagination), Miller Center.

13. Thomas Edsall, "'Victory Fund' Raises Millions for Party," *WP*, July 19, 1988, A21; Charles Babcock, "Names of 40 Who Gave Democrats $100,000 Each Disclosed," *WP*, November 3, 1988, A1; Cohan, *Money and Power*, 304–6.

14. Mary Billard, "The Executive Life: Wall St. Dems Find Little to Like in 1992," *NYT*, March 1, 1992, A23.

15. W. Carl Biven, *Jimmy Carter's Economy: Policy in an Age of Limits* (Chapel Hill: University of North Carolina Press, 2002), 11.

16. Jonathan Fuerbringer, "Mondale Picks His Deficit-Busters," *NYT*, August 19, 1984, C4; Paul A. Samuelson, "His Nagging Did Reagan a Good Turn," *NYT*, July 8, 1984, C2. Larry Summers, a protégé of Feldstein's, was on the CEA staff during this controversy.

17. Waterhouse, *Lobbying America*, 232–34; Leonard Silk, "Wall Street, Fearing Deficits, Finds Reagan Mixed Blessing," *NYT*, September 13, 1981, A1.

18. Thomas Ferguson, *Golden Rule: The Investment Theory of Party Competition and the Logic of Money-Driven Political Systems* (Chicago: University of Chicago Press, 1995), 243–53, 292–304; Steven Gillon, *The Democrats' Dilemma: Walter F. Mondale and the Liberal Legacy* (New York: Columbia University Press, 1992), 358–59.

19. Cohan, *Money and Power*, 308–9; Rubin, *In an Uncertain World*, 104.

20. Brett Fromson and Charles Babcock, "Politicians Mine a Rich Vein at Wall Street Firm," *WP*, October 5, 1992, A1. Partner Kenneth Brody, whose specialty was real estate financing, took the lead in much of the firm's fundraising. See also Stephen Labaton, "Angry at Bush, Republican Contributors Are Helping Clinton," *NYT*, September 22, 1992, A24.

21. Leonard Sloane, "Arbitrageur Takes the Big Chances," *NYT*, April 6, 1977, 79.

22. Lemann, *Transaction Man*, 116; Cohan, *Money and Power*, 129–31, 138.

23. Robert Rubin, "Arbitrage," in proceedings of the ABA National Institute, "The Role of the Takeover in the American Economy," *Business Lawyer* 32 (May 1977): 1315–18.

24. Sloane, "Arbitrageur Takes the Big Chances," 79.

25. Rubin, *In an Uncertain World*, 46, 75.

26. Michael Hirsh, *Capital Offense: How Washington's Wise Men Turned America's Future over to Wall Street* (New York: John Wiley & Sons, 2010), 96–97.

27. Rubin, *In an Uncertain World*, 80, 122.

28. Clinton, *President Clinton's New Beginning*, 247. Tobin's rejoinder was appropriately sarcastic: "I think confidence and expectations will be consistent with a plausible and actual, real

economic program. . . . I don't think we can try to outguess the way these things work in psychology." Rubin's responsibility, asserted Tobin, was to explain the program to the "gnomes of Zurich or of the Battery" to demonstrate that no increase in long-term bond rates was warranted.

29. William Greider, "Bill Clinton Goes Right toward Consensus," *The Nation*, February 4, 1993.

30. David Kusnet oral history, March 19, 2010, Miller Center.

31. The *Wall Street Journal* reported that Treasury secretary Bentsen calculated that a decline of just 0.9 percentage point in yields on thirty-year T-bills would translate into something like a $90 billion stimulus. David Wessel and Thomas Vogel, "Arcane World of Bonds Is Guide and Beacon to a Populist President," *WSJ*, February 25, 1993, A1.

32. Clinton, "Remarks and a Question-and-Answer Session with the Economic Club of Detroit."

33. Blinder oral history, June 27, 2003, 15.

34. *American Prospect* editor Robert Kuttner argued that almost all of that increase could be attributed to the savings and loan bailout, in which case it was largely an accounting arrangement and could not "crowd out" other investments. But his argument was a decidedly minority idea. See Robert Kuttner to President-Elect Clinton, December 24, 1992, "Deficit Reduction—Why?" folder, box 413, National Economic Council, Clinton Library.

35. Blinder oral history, June 27, 2003, 118.

36. The best biography is Sebastian Mallaby, *The Man Who Knew: The Life and Times of Alan Greenspan* (New York: Random House, 2016).

37. William Greider, *Secrets of the Temple: How the Federal Reserve Runs the Country* (New York: Simon & Schuster, 1987), 309–12.

38. Quoted in Paul Krugman's blog, "The Euthanasia of the Rentier," *NYT*, January 22, 2014.

39. Greider, *Secrets of the Temple*, 330.

40. Quoted in J. W. Mason, "The Fed Doesn't Work for You," *Jacobin*, January 6, 2016.

41. Mallaby, *The Man Who Knew*, 233; Robert Gordon, *The Rise and Fall of American Growth: The US Standard of Living since the Civil War* (Princeton, NJ: Princeton University Press, 2016), 547.

42. Mason, "The Fed Doesn't Work for You."

43. Bob Woodward, *The Agenda: Inside the Clinton White House* (New York: Simon & Schuster, 1994), 68–71; Walker, *Clinton*, 71.

44. Rubin, *In an Uncertain World*, 120.

45. Although Robert Rubin, in his memoir, rejected the idea than any agreement had been reached between Bentsen and Greenspan, Alan Blinder was convinced by Bob Woodward's many interviews—and a budget document upon which Bentsen had written "Greenspan says $140 billion"—that a deal had been struck to the effect that cutting $140 billion out of the budget by 1997 would be "creditable to the financial markets and likely result in lower long-term rates." And in his autobiography Greenspan admitted that he told Bentsen that the deficit would have to be cut by "not less than $130 billion a year by 1997." In the budget meetings that began on January 7, McLarty, Rubin, and Bentsen were all recommending a target reduction of at least $140 billion. Woodward, *The Agenda*, 121; Rubin, *In an Uncertain World*, 120–21; Alan Greenspan, *The Age of Turbulence: Adventures in a New World* (New York: Penguin Books, 2007), 147.

46. Blinder oral history, June 27, 2003, 39; Riley, *Inside the Clinton White House*, 119.

47. Riley, *Inside the Clinton White House*, 117.

48. Woodward, *The Agenda*, 83.

49. Larry Summers and Roger Altman, "Stimulus Options," December 23, 1992, "NEC—Economic Conference, December 1992" [7] folder, History of National Economic Council, Clinton Library.

50. Clinton, *My Life*, 460.

51. Ibid., 461.

52. Woodward, *The Agenda*, 84.

53. Wessel and Vogel, "Arcane World of Bonds Is Guide and Beacon to a Populist President."

54. Bob Woodward makes this narrative argument most strongly in *The Agenda*; Greenspan's presumptive bargain has subsequently been subject to much debate. See, for example, Blinder's view in Riley, *Inside the Clinton White House*, 118–19.

55. Woodward, *The Agenda*, 115–16, 126; Riley, *Inside the Clinton White House*, 121.

56. Kuttner to President-Elect Clinton, December 24, 1992, "Deficit Reduction—Why?"

57. Laura Tyson and Alan Blinder to Robert Rubin and President Clinton, "NEC—Deficit Reduction Plan of 1993" [1], February 1, 1993, "Why Deficit Reduction Matters," folder, National Economic Council, Clinton Library.

58. Woodward, *The Agenda*, 96, 130.

59. On the politics, see Julie Gibson and Kitty Higgins, memo to Rahm Emanuel and Joan Baggett, "Re Tier I Cities for Summer Jobs Program," February 24, 1993, box 12, OA/ID 6053, Department of Labor, Clinton Library.

60. Laura Tyson to the President, March 4, 1993, FOIA 2016-1158-F, Clinton Library; "Fiscal 1993 Stimulus Bill Killed," in *CQ Almanac 1993*, 49th ed. (Washington, DC: Congressional Quarterly, 1994), 706–9.

61. From, *The New Democrats and the Return to Power*, 83, 118, 123.

62. David Rosenbaum, "Clinton Wins Approval of His Budget Plan as Gore Votes to Break Senate Deadlock," *NYT*, August 7, 1993, A1.

63. Eric Planin and David S. Hilzenrath, "Senate Passes Clinton Budget Bill," *WP*, August 7, 1993, A1.

64. Karen Tumulty and William Eaton, "Gore Casts Tie-Breaking Vote as Senate OK's Clinton Budget," *Los Angeles Times*, August 7, 1993, 1; Douglas Jehl, " Rejoicing Is Muted for President in Budget Victory," *NYT*, August 8, 1993, A1.

65. Riley, *Inside the Clinton White House*, 122.

66. Rubin, *In an Uncertain World*, 131.

67. Pat Garofalo, "Flashback: In 1993, GOP Warned That Clinton's Tax Plan Would 'Kill Jobs,' 'Kill the Current Recovery,'" *Think Progress*, August 10, 2010.

68. Clinton, *My Life*, 537.

69. Louis Jacobson, "Bill Clinton Takes Credit for 'Flowering' of Economy in 1990s," *Politifact*, April 19, 2010.

70. Clinton White House, "The Clinton-Gore Administration: A Record of Progress," December 2000, https://clintonwhitehouse5.archives.gov/WH/Accomplishments/index.html.

71. James Galbraith, "The 1994 Council of Economic Advisers Report: A Review," *Challenge*, May/June 1994, 13.

72. Ibid., 84–85.

73. Transcript of FOMC meeting, February 3–4, 1993, 45. All FOMC meeting transcripts are available at the Federal Open Market Committee's website under "Transcripts and Other Historical Materials."

74. Mallaby, *The Man Who Knew*, 441–43.

75. Galbraith, "The 1994 Council of Economic Advisers Report," 14.

76. Blinder oral history, June 27, 2003.

77. Mallaby, *The Man Who Knew*, 444–45.

78. Ibid., 487–90.

79. Woodward, *Maestro*, 132–34; Mallaby, *The Man Who Knew*, 446–64; Blinder oral history, June 27, 2003.

80. Joseph Stiglitz, *The Roaring Nineties: A New History of the World's Most Prosperous Decade* (New York: W. W. Norton, 2003), 76–77; Woodward, *Maestro*, 154–65. Stiglitz opposed Clinton's renomination of Greenspan. Author's telephone interview with Joseph Stiglitz, February 22, 2022.

81. Stiglitz, *The Roaring Nineties*, 51.

82. Woodward, *The Agenda*, 133.

83. Mallaby, *The Man Who Knew*, 445.

84. Ibid., 507.

85. Transcript of FOMC meeting, December 22, 1998, 61; James Glassman and Kevin Hassett, "Stock Prices Aren't the Fed's Job," *WSJ*, January 5, 2001, A10.

86. Frederick Sheehan, *Panderer to Power: The Untold Story of How Alan Greenspan Enriched Wall Street and Left a Legacy of Recession* (New York: McGraw-Hill, 2010), 188–89.

87. Dean Baker, *The United States since 1980* (New York: Cambridge University Press, 2007), 144.

88. Mallaby, *The Man Who Knew*, 495; Baker, *The United States since 1980*, 144–45.

89. Gordon, *The Rise and Fall of American Growth*, 17.

90. Baker, *The United States since 1980*, 145–46.

91. Gordon, *The Rise and Fall of American Growth*, 574–84. In a single ten-year span, 1994 to 2004, increases in labor productivity rose well above the productivity levels of the 1970s and 1980s.

92. Lichtenstein, *The Retail Revolution*, 327; "American Families Now Save $2,500 a Year, Thanks to Wal-Mart," September 12, 2007, https://corporate.walmart.com/newsroom/2007/09/12/american-families-now-save-2-500-a-year-thanks-to-wal-mart.

93. US Department of Labor, Bureau of Labor Statistics, "Work Stoppages," https://www.bls.gov/web/wkstp/annual-listing.htm; US Department of Labor, Bureau of Labor Statistics, "15 Major Work Stoppages in 2016," February 22, 2017, *The Economics Daily*, https://www.bls.gov/opub/ted/2017/15-major-work-stoppages-in-2016.htm.

94. Stephen Franklin, *Three Strikes: Labor's Heartland Losses and What They Mean for Working Americans* (New York: Guilford Press, 2001).

95. Federal Reserve Board, "Testimony of Chairman Alan Greenspan: The Federal Reserve's Semiannual Monetary Policy Report before the Committee on Banking, Housing, and Urban Affairs, US Senate," July 22, 1997.

96. Transcript of FOMC meeting, August 19, 1997, 26, 72; see also Daniel J. Mitchell and C. L. Erickson, "Not Yet Dead at the Fed: Unions, Workers, Bargaining, and Economy-Wide Wage Determination," *University of California Postprints*, paper 1151 (2005): 565–606.

97. Robert Brenner may well have been the first to coin the term in his *Economics of Global Turbulence* (New York: Verso, 2006), 293.

98. Baker, *The United States since 1980*, 146–47.

99. Dean Baker, "Farewell to Bill," *Truthout*, September 10, 2012; Adam Tooze, *Crashed: How a Decade of Financial Crises Changed the World* (New York: Penguin, 2019).

100. Iwan Morgan, "A New Democrat's New Economics," in *The Presidency of Bill Clinton: The Legacy of a New Domestic and Foreign Policy*, edited by Mark White (London: I. B. Tauris, 2012), 70.

101. Rubin, *In an Uncertain World*, 122–23.

102. Stiglitz, *The Roaring Nineties*, 46.

Chapter 8. NAFTA and Its Discontents

1. Juan Carlos Moreno-Brid and Jaime Ros, *Development and Growth in the Mexican Economy: A Historical Perspective* (New York: Oxford University Press, 2009).

2. Kim Moody, "NAFTA and the Corporate Redesign of North America," *Latin American Perspectives*, Winter 1995, 100.

3. Patricia Fernández-Kelly and Douglas Massey, "Borders for Whom? The Role of NAFTA in Mexico-US Migration," *Annals of the American Academy* 610 (March 2007): 99–100.

4. Ibid., 101–2; Daniel Yergin and Joseph Stanislaw, *The Commanding Heights: The Battle for the World Economy* (New York: Free Press, 2002), 259–62.

5. Jeff Faux, *The Global Class War* (New York: John Wiley & Sons, 2006), 38–39.

6. Jeff Faux, "The NAFTA Illusion," *Challenge*, July/August 1993, 7.

7. Fernández-Kelly and Massey, "Borders for Whom?," 104.

8. Ibid., 104.

9. Maxwell A. Cameron and Brian W. Tomlin, *The Making of NAFTA: How the Deal Was Done* (Ithaca, NY: Cornell University Press, 2000), 62. For an excellent series of essays that compare NAFTA and EU trade regimes, see Kirsten Appendini and Sven Bislev, eds., *Economic Integration in NAFTA and the EU* (New York: St. Martin's Press, 1999).

10. Moody, "NAFTA and the Corporate Redesign of North America," 99.

11. Fernández-Kelly and Massey, "Borders for Whom?," 103; Cameron and Tomlin, *The Making of NAFTA*, 33–34, 41.

12. Baker, *The United States since 1980*, 131; Chris Tilly, "Wal-Mart in Mexico: The Limits of Growth," in *Wal-Mart: The Face of Twenty-First-Century Capitalism*, edited by Nelson Lichtenstein (New York: New Press, 2006), 189–212.

13. Andrew Wender Cohen, "Unions, Modernity, and the Decline of American Economic Nationalism," in *The Right and Labor in America: Politics, Ideology, and Imagination*, edited by Nelson Lichtenstein and Elizabeth Shermer (Philadelphia: University of Pennsylvania Press, 2012), 15–26; John Judis, "The Divide," *New Republic*, October 11, 1993, 26–32.

14. Judis, "The Divide," 30.

15. John R. MacArthur, *The Selling of "Free Trade": NAFTA, Washington, and the Subversion of American Democracy* (New York: Hill and Wang, 2000), 97–108; Faux, *The Global Class War*, 17.

16. Peter Behr, "Clinton's Conversion on NAFTA: President's Inner Struggle Mirrors the Battle Today," *WP*, September 19, 1993, H1.

17. Richard Rothstein to Governor Clinton, c/o Derek Shearer, March 11, 1992, box 7, Derek Shearer Papers, Brown University Archives.

18. Harley Shaiken, "Going South: Mexican Wages and US Jobs after NAFTA," *American Prospect*, Fall 1993.

19. Kusnet oral history, March 19, 2010.

20. Riley, *Inside the Clinton White House*, 128–29; Shearer to Clinton, August 26, 1993, box 7, Shearer Papers.

21. Peter Behr, "Clinton's Conversion on NAFTA." Campaign foreign policy adviser Sandy Berger remembers Greenberg arguing that although NAFTA was unpopular, Clinton should endorse the treaty in order to maintain "credibility" with a public that had come to see him as a free trade advocate. Samuel Berger oral history, March 24, 2005, Miller Center.

22. Gwen Ifill, "With Reservations, Clinton Endorses Free-Trade Pact," *NYT*, October 5, 1992, A16.

23. Cameron and Tomlin, *The Making of NAFTA*, 181–83.

24. Ibid., 188.

25. Ibid., 189.

26. Tod Robberson, "Mexico's Unions at Issue: Organizing Dispute Is Grist for NAFTA Debate," *WP*, October 28, 1993, A31. Of course, South Carolina textile mills were hardly places where independent trade unionism was flourishing.

27. Cameron and Tomlin, *The Making of NAFTA*, 197.

28. Keith Bradsher, "3 Nations Resolve Issues Holding Up Trade Pact Vote," *NYT*, August 14, 1993, A1.

29. Stuart Auerbach, "Key Hill Democrats Wary of NAFTA Side Agreements: Tough Fight Expected on Trade Accord," *WP*, August 14, 1993, A1.

30. Lance Compa, "Enforcing Worker Rights under the NAFTA Labor Side Accord," in "The Transformation of Sovereignty," *Proceedings of the Annual Meeting of the American Society of International Law* 88 (April 1994): 537.

31. Mary McGrory, "The NAFTA Disasta," *WP*, October 10, 1993, C1.

32. MacArthur, *The Selling of "Free Trade,"* 97–108.

33. "Gephardt Speech," in "NAFTA: Gephardt" folder, OA/ID 13660, Michael Waldman Speechwriting Collection, Clinton Library.

34. Reich, *Locked in the Cabinet*, 131.

35. Blinder oral history, June 27, 2003, 102–4. For a thorough debunking of Clintonite job creation claims, including two hundred thousand jobs in one year, see Thea Lee, "False Prophets: The Selling of NAFTA," briefing paper 56, Economic Policy Institute, July 1995, 10–11.

36. Glenn Kessler, "The Strange Tale about Why Bill Clinton Said NAFTA Would Create 1 Million Jobs," *WP*, September 12, 2020.

37. Faux, *The Global Class War*, 41; author's phone interview with Ira Magaziner, May 17, 2022.

38. Riley, *Inside the Clinton White House*, 130–33.

39. Ibid., 131.

40. MacArthur, *The Selling of "Free Trade,"* 233–40.

41. Dan Balz, "Gephardt's 'Quiet' Crusade against NAFTA," *WP*, October 6, 1993, A6.

42. Lori Wallach, "NAFTA at 20: One Million US Jobs Lost, Higher Income Inequality," *Huffington Post*, January 6, 2014; "NAFTA's Legacy: Lost Jobs, Lower Wages, Increased Inequality," Public Citizen, February 2018.

43. "The 'Great Debate' over NAFTA," *NYT*, November 9, 1993, A16.

44. Strategy memorandum, November 7, 1993, "NAFTA: Talking Points" folder, OA/ID 13660, Michael Waldman Speechwriting Collection, Clinton Library.

45. James Gerstenzang and Paul Richter, "Gore, Perot Tangle in Heated NAFTA Debate," *Los Angeles Times*, November 11, 1993, A1; MacArthur, *The Selling of "Free Trade,"* 236–49.

46. MacArthur, *The Selling of "Free Trade,"* 274; author's phone interview with Jeff Faux, February 22, 2022.

47. Thomas Edsall, "NAFTA Debate Reopens Wounds in the Body of the Democratic Party; Arguments Pit Traditional Coalition, Centrists in Battle for Soul," *WP*, October 24, 1993, A4.

48. Lawrence Mishel and Ruy A. Teixeira, "The Political Arithmetic of the NAFTA Vote," briefing paper 47, Economic Policy Institute, November 1, 1993, 7.

49. Peter Applebome, "The South: The Rising GOP Tide Overwhelms the Democratic Levees in the South," *NYT*, November 11, 1994, A27.

50. Gavin Wright, "Voting Rights, Deindustrialization, and Republican Ascendancy in the South," Working Paper 135, Institute for New Economic Thinking, September 2020, 22–28.

51. Applebome, "The South."

52. Wright, "Voting Rights, Deindustrialization, and Republican Ascendancy in the South," 29–30.

53. Gary Gereffi, David Spener, and Jennifer Bair, *Free Trade and Uneven Development: The North American Apparel Industry after NAFTA* (Philadelphia: Temple University Press, 2002), 33, 42. US apparel industry employment declined from 974,000 in 1994 to 633,000 in 2000.

54. Robert E. Scott, "Heading South: US-Mexico Trade and Job Displacement after NAFTA," briefing paper 308, Economic Policy Institute, May 3, 2011, 7–10.

55. Raúl Delgado Wise and James M. Cypher, "The Strategic Role of Mexican Labor under NAFTA: Critical Perspectives on Current Economic Integration," *Annals of the American Academy of Political and Social Science* 610 (March 2007): 120–22.

56. Ibid., 126, 129.

57. Cameron and Tomlin, *The Making of NAFTA*, 110–11.

58. Gerardo Otero, "Neoliberal Globalization, NAFTA, and Migration: Mexico's Loss of Food and Labor Sovereignty," *Journal of Poverty* 15 (2011): 391.

59. Geri Smith, "Farmers Are Getting Plowed Under," *Business Week*, November 18, 2002, 53–54.

60. Ibid., 385.

61. Otero, "Neoliberal Globalization, NAFTA, and Migration," 389. Mexican exports of fruits and vegetables to the United States and Canada did increase substantially, but this sector did

not generate nearly enough employment to absorb bankrupted peasants. Only about two thousand agricultural units, out of some seven million farms in all, export products to the rest of North America; of those, three hundred firms account for 80 percent of all exports.

Chapter 9. Grand Illusions: Reinventing the American Workplace

1. James O'Toole et al., *Work in America: A Report of a Special Task Force to the Secretary of Health, Education, and Welfare* (Cambridge, MA: MIT Press, 1973), 50.

2. Piore and Sabel, *The Second Industrial Divide*, 19–48.

3. Reich, *The Next American Frontier*, 246.

4. Reich, *The Work of Nations*, 182.

5. Donald Wells, *Empty Promises: Quality of Working Life Programs and the Labor Movement* (New York: Monthly Review Press, 1987); Mike Parker, *Inside the Circle: A Union Guide to QWL* (Boston: South End Press, 1985), 3–7; Mike Parker, "Industrial Relations Myth and Shop-Floor Reality: The 'Team Concept' in the Auto Industry," in *Industrial Democracy in America: The Ambiguous Promise*, edited by Nelson Lichtenstein and Howell John Harris (New York: Cambridge University Press, 1993), 249–74.

6. Quoted in Parker, *Inside the Circle*, 7.

7. Barry Bluestone and Irving Bluestone, *Negotiating the Future: A Labor Perspective on American Business* (New York: Basic Books, 1992), xiii, cover of hardback edition. Derek Shearer, a friend of the younger Bluestone, had served as the middleman who arranged for Clinton to see the galleys and perhaps even compose the blurb.

8. Robert Reich, "Memorandum to the President," March 12, 1993, "Labor Department Correspondence" [3] folder, OA/ID 5059, Laura Tyson, Council of Economic Advisers, Clinton Library; "Brown and Reich Announce Worker-Management Commission," *News: United States Department of Labor*, March 24, 1993, news release in the author's possession.

9. John Logan, "The Clinton Administration and Labor Law: Was Comprehensive Reform Ever a Realistic Possibility?," *Journal of Labor Research* 28 (August 2007): 612–14.

10. John Logan, "'All Deals Are Off': The Dunlop Commission and Employer Opposition to Labor Law Reform," in Lichtenstein and Shermer, *The Right and Labor in America*, 278–79; Taylor Dark, *The Unions and the Democrats: An Enduring Alliance* (Ithaca, NY: Cornell University Press, 1999), 173.

11. Since the transition, Derek Shearer had been an advocate for such a conference. Shearer to Robert Stein, US Department of Commerce, March 3, 1993, in the author's possession.

12. Mark Ritson, "Why Saturn Was Destined to Fail," *Harvard Business Review*, October 1, 2009, 90–91.

13. William J. Clinton, "Remarks to the Conference on the Future of the American Workplace in Chicago, Illinois," July 26, 1993, American Presidency Project; see also *Workplace of the Future: A Report of the Conference on the Future of the American Workplace* (Washington, DC: US Department of Labor, 1993), 19.

14. Louis Uchitelle, "Union Leaders Fight for a Place in the President's Workplace of the Future," *NYT*, August 8, 1993, A32.

15. Reich, *Locked in the Cabinet*, 113; Cash Powell Jr., "L-S Electro-Galvanizing: Factory without Walls," *Target*, July/August 1994, 45–48; US Department of Labor, *Workplace of the Future*, 5–6.

16. "Sumitomo Metal to End Steel-Sheet Making in US," *Nikkei Net Interactive*, July 16, 2002; Peter Krouse, "Soft Market Costs Half the Jobs at Mittal–AK Steel Operation in Cleveland," *Cleveland Plain Dealer*, June 29, 2005, C3; "Wainscott Seeks Fewer Workers, Job Classifications Here," *Middletown Journal*, January 25, 2006.

17. US Department of Labor, *Workplace of the Future*, 15.

18. Louis Uchitelle, "A New Labor Design at Levi Strauss," *NYT*, October 13, 1994, D1.

19. Kim Girard, "Supply Chain Partnerships: How Levi's Got Its Jeans into Wal-Mart," *CIO*, July 15, 2003; "As Levi's Work Is Exported, Stress Stays Home," *NYT*, October 19, 2003.

20. "34,000 Telephone Workers on Strike against US West," *NYT*, August 17, 1998, A8.

21. Keith Bradsher, "Saturn Plant's Union Leaders Are Voted Out," *NYT*, February 26, 1999, C1.

22. Ritson, "Why Saturn Was Destined to Fail"; Benjamin Gomes-Casseres, "NUMMI: What Toyota Learned and GM Didn't," *Harvard Business Review*, September 1, 2009.

23. Bruce E. Kaufman, "Reflections on Six Decades in Industrial Relations: An Interview with John Dunlop," *Industrial and Labor Relations Review* 55, no. 2 (January 2002): 342.

24. Quoted in Logan, "'All Deals Are Off,'" 283.

25. Dunlop Commission on the Future of Worker-Management Relations, *Final Report*, December 1, 1994, 40–45.

26. Lichtenstein, *The Retail Revolution*, 229, 240.

27. Jennifer Berkshire, *More Worlds to Negotiate: John Dunlop and the Art of Problem Solving* (Lanham, MD: Hamilton Books, 2019), 89–90; Logan, "'All Deals Are Off,'" 284–87. The UAW's Douglas Fraser dissented from the commission recommendation on the grounds that it was impossible to set up any kind of productivity-enhancing committee that did not also consider the issues of wages and working conditions that stood at the heart of the collective bargaining process. Dunlop Commission on the Future of Worker-Management Relations, *Final Report*, 32–33.

28. Ellis Boal, "Employee Participation or Labor Militancy: Remarks of Ellis Boal before the Commission on the Future of Worker-Management Relations," September 8, 1994, Cornell University Library, ILR School, https://ecommons.cornell.edu/handle/1813/77498.

29. Logan, "'All Deals Are Off,'" 288–89.

30. Maryellen Kelley and Bennett Harrison, "Unions, Technology, and Labor-Management Cooperation," in *Unions and Economic Competitiveness*, edited by Lawrence Mishel and Paula Voos (Washington, DC: Economic Policy Institute, 1992).

31. Logan, "'All Deals Are Off,'" 290; Berkshire, *More Worlds to Negotiate*, 90.

32. See also Lily Geismer's account of the "Reinventing Government" initiative in *Left Behind: The Democrats' Failed Attempt to Solve Inequality* (New York: Public Affairs, 2022), 115–18, 210–13.

33. David Osborne and Ted Gaebler, *Reinventing Government: How the Entrepreneurial Spirit Is Transforming the Public Sector* (New York: Penguin, 1992), quote on front cover of paperback edition.

34. Ibid., xvi.

35. Ibid., 166–80; Reuel Schiller, "Regulation and the Collapse of the New Deal Order, or How I Learned to Stop Worrying and Love the Market," in Gerstle, Lichtenstein, and O'Connor, *Beyond the New Deal Order*, 176.

36. Osborne and Gaebler, *Reinventing Government*, 1–5, 25–30, 76–107.

37. William J. Clinton, "Remarks Announcing the National Performance Review," March 3, 1993, American Presidency Project.

38. Vice President Gore's National Partnership for Reinventing Government, "From Red Tape to Results: Creating a Government That Works Better and Costs Less," 1993, https://govinfo.library.unt.edu/npr/library/nprrpt/annrpt/redtpe93/index.html.

39. Elaine Kamarck oral history, May 7–8, 2006, Miller Center. The pricey hammer was but one of four hundred items billed to the Pentagon in 1983 by an aviation electronics company that assigned an equal proportion of the firm's overhead and support costs to each line item. Hence $435 for one hammer. It was a bookkeeping procedure that rendered meaningless the cost assigned to each item. See Airon Mothershed, "The $435 Hammer and $600 Toilet Seat Scandals: Does Media Coverage of Procurement Scandals Lead to Procurement Reform?," *Public Contract Law Journal* 41, no. 1 (Summer 2012): 860–61.

40. Annelise Graebner Anderson and David F. Linowes, *Privatization: Toward More Effective Government: Report of the President's Commission on Privatization* (Washington, DC: President's Commission on Privatization, 1988), 243.

41. John McCormick et al., "Taking the Town Private," *Newsweek*, March 4, 1991, 54.

42. Osborne and Gaebler, *Reinventing Government*, xviii.

43. President Bill Clinton and Vice President Al Gore, "National Performance Review," Blair House Papers, January 1997, https://govinfo.library.unt.edu/npr/library/papers/bkgrd/blair.html.

44. Schiller, "Regulation and the Collapse of the New Deal Order," 176.

45. Quoted in John Kamensky, "The US Reform Experience: The National Performance Review," Conference on Civil Service Systems in Comparative Perspective, Indiana University, Bloomington, April 6, 1997, https://govinfo.library.unt.edu/npr/library/papers/bkgrd/kamensky.html.

46. Kamarck oral history, May 7–8, 2006; Stephen Barr, "'High Priestess of Reinvention' Changes Direction at Crossroads; Advisor's Departure Could Slow Gore's Government Reform Effort," *WP*, June 23, 1997, A17.

47. Charles S. Clark, "Reinventing Government—Two Decades Later," *Government Executive*, April 26, 2013.

48. Donald Kettl quoted in Carten Cordell, "5 Shifts That Transformed Federal Service," *Federal Times*, January 8, 2016.

49. Joan Baggett oral history, May 2006, Miller Center.

50. Kamarck oral history, May 7–8, 2006.

51. Ibid.

52. Quoted in Donald Cohen and Allen Mikaelian, *The Privatization of Everything: How the Plunder of Public Goods Transformed America and How We Can Fight Back* (New York: New Press, 2021), 27–28.

53. William Claiborne, "To Massachusetts Republicans, Gore Report Is Ammunition," *WP*, September 3, 1993, A23.

54. John Buntin, "25 Years Later, What Happened to 'Reinventing Government'?," *Governing*, September 1, 2016.

55. Timothy Noah, "How Privatizing Government Hollowed Out the Middle Class," MSNBC, June 3, 2014, https://www.msnbc.com/msnbc/government-privatization-hurts-middle-class-msna341956.

56. Paul C. Light, "Outsourcing and the True Size of Government," *Public Contract Law Journal* 33, no. 2 (Winter 2004): 312.

57. Ibid., 313; Laura Peterson, "Outsourcing Government," Center for Public Integrity, October 30, 2003, https://publicintegrity.org/national-security/outsourcing-government/.

58. Noah, "How Privatized Government Hollowed Out the Middle Class."

59. Schiller, "Regulation and the Collapse of the New Deal Order," 184–85.

60. Timothy J. Minchin, *Labor under Fire: A History of the AFL-CIO since 1979* (Chapel Hill: University of North Carolina Press, 2017), 185.

61. "How Groups Voted in 1992," Roper Center, Cornell University, https://ropercenter.cornell.edu/how-groups-voted-1992.

62. Minchin, *Labor under Fire*, 186.

63. Dark, *The Unions and the Democrats*, 163; Minchin, *Labor under Fire*, 190.

64. Reich, *Locked in the Cabinet*, 66; Derek Shearer, "Putting People First Is More Difficult than It Looks: A Realistic Assessment of the Clinton Administration," *Evatt Papers*, Summer 1993, 73.

65. Reich, *Locked in the Cabinet*, 107.

66. Minchin, *Labor under Fire*, 204–5.

67. Robert Rose, "Caterpillar Inc. Pledges It Won't Yield in UAW Strike; Union Vows to Fight On," *WSJ*, March 30, 1992, A5.

68. Quoted in Robert Rose, "Midwest Now Boasts Revitalized Factories—Its Heavy Capital Spending Pays Off in Productivity, New Manufacturing Jobs—but Wages Tend to Be Low," *WSJ*, January 3, 1994, A1; Robert Rose and Alex Kotlowitz, "Strife between UAW and Caterpillar Blights Promising Labor Idea—Worker Involvement Project Began with High Hopes but Was Killed by Strike," *WSJ*, November 23, 1992, A1.

69. Rose and Kotlowitz, "Strife between UAW and Caterpillar Blights Promising Labor."

70. Franklin, *Three Strikes*, 44.

71. Rose, "Caterpillar Inc. Pledges It Won't Yield in UAW Strike."

72. Franklin, *Three Strikes*, 42.

73. Dennis Farney, "Middle America in Clinton's First Year: To End an Impasse: Workers at Caterpillar Hope against Hope Clinton Will Be True," *WSJ*, July 26, 1993, A1.

74. Paul Gordon, "Candidate Criticizes Hiring of Replacements, Challenges President to Mediate 158-Day Strike," *Peoria Journal Star*, April 9, 1992, A1.

75. Franklin, *Three Strikes*, 89–116.

76. Louis Uchitelle, "Labor Draws the Line in Decatur," *NYT*, June 13, 1993, A1.

77. Quoted in Farney, "Middle America in Clinton's First Year."

78. Jason Kozlowski, "Will Globalization Play in Peoria? Class, Race, and Nation in the Global Economy," PhD diss., University of Illinois, Champaign-Urbana, 2011, 165.

79. Robert L. Rose and Carl Quintanilla, "Caterpillar Touts Its Gains as UAW Battle Ends," *WSJ*, March 24, 1998, A4; Bernstein quoted in Franklin, *Three Strikes*, 225.

80. Steven Greenhouse, "Clinton Delays Push to Increase Minimum Wage," *NYT*, June 3, 1993, A1.

81. Reich quoted in Louis Uchitelle, "Labor Has a Big Job for Its New Friend Clinton," *NYT*, June 27, 1993, A5.

82. Martin Halpern, *Unions, Radicals, and Democratic Presidents: Seeking Social Change in the Twentieth Century* (Westport, CT: Praeger, 2003), 168.

83. "Striker Replacement, February 21, 1994," box 23, OA/ID 4048, "Joan Baggett—Public Affairs," AFL-CIO, briefing book [2], Clinton Library.

84. David Kusnet to George Stephanopoulos, December 1993, David Kusnet Collection, Clinton Library.

85. Steve Rosenthal to Joan Baggett, "Issues Important to the AFL-CIO," May 9, 1994; Joe Velasquez, "Meeting with AFL-CIO Executive Council," May 9, 1994; both in box 23, OA/ID 4048, "Joan Baggett—Public Affairs," AFL-CIO, briefing book [2], Clinton Library; Reich, *Locked in the Cabinet*, 175.

86. Reich, *Locked in the Cabinet*, 176.

87. "Plus Business: Strike End Urged," *Chicago Sun Times*, July 14, 1994, 4.

88. Catherine S. Manegold, "Senate Republicans Deal a Major Defeat to Labor," *NYT*, July 13, 1994, D18.

89. Ibid.

90. Minchin, *Labor under Fire*, 209; John Sweeney, *America Needs a Raise: Fighting for Economic Security and Social Justice* (Boston: Houghton Mifflin, 1996), 104.

91. Reich, *Locked in the Cabinet*, 206.

92. "Memorandum for the Vice-President: Briefing for Your Appearance before the AFL-CIO Executive Council in Bal Harbour, Florida," February 15, 1995, "AFL-CIO—Labor 2/15/95" folder, OA/ID 10133, Don Baer series, Communications subgroup, Clinton Library. Joan Baggett wrote most of the memo to Gore. Joan Baggett to Leon Panetta, "Union Issues," December 14, 1994, box 14, "AFL-CIO general" [2] folder, OA/ID 9162, Ickes file, Clinton Library.

93. Harold Ickes, "13 December 1994 Dinner at Tom Donahue House," January 3, 1995, box 14, "AFL-CIO general" [1] [2] folder, OA/ID 9162, Ickes file, Clinton Library.

94. Harold Meyerson, "Union Man," *American Prospect*, April 24, 2000, 18–23; Jon Hiatt to John Podesta, "Avondale/NASSCO," December 20, 1996, box 21, "NEC—Sperling" folder, "AFL-CIO" [3] folder, Clinton Library; Steven Greenhouse, "US Issuing New Rules to Gain Contracts," *NYT*, July 9, 1999, 12.

95. Sweeney, *America Needs a Raise*, 90.

96. David Kusnet, email to the author, May 5, 2020.

97. Dark, *The Unions and the Democrats*, 185; Elizabeth Drew, *Whatever It Takes: The Real Struggle for Political Power in America* (New York: Viking, 1997), 69–78.

98. Dark, *The Unions and the Democrats*, 175. Secretary of Labor Reich wanted the administration to propose its own reform of the NLRA's section 8(a)(2), but Kirkland told Harold Ickes that "labor flatly opposed any changes." Harold Ickes to Leon Panetta, "Meeting with the President, Lane Kirkland, and Bob Georgine," February 21, 1995, box 14, "AFL-CIO general" [1] folder, Ickes file, Clinton Library.

99. Reich, *Locked in the Cabinet*, 241–42; "Laboring to Make Amends," *Pittsburgh Post-Gazette*, February 24, 1995, B2.

100. Catherine S. Manegold, "Clinton Is Challenged over a Plan for Labor," *NYT*, February 23, 1995, D2; Dark, *The Unions and the Democrats*, 176.

101. Milton Friedman, "The Social Responsibility of Business Is to Increase Its Profits," *NYT*, September 13, 1970, SM12.

102. Allan Sloan, "The Hit Men," *Newsweek*, February 26, 1996, 44.

103. Richard L. Berke, "Left, Right, Left: The Primaries Turn Politicians Around," *NYT*, February 18, 1996, E3; Elizabeth Kolbert and Adam Clymer, "The Politics of Layoffs; In Search of a Message," *NYT*, March 8, 1996, A1.

104. "NAFTA Remarks, Chamber of Commerce 'National Town Hall,'" October 29, 1993, "NAFTA: Talking Points" folder, OA/ID 13660, Speechwriting Collection, Clinton Library.

105. Robert Reich, "Pink Slips, Profits, and Paychecks: Corporate Citizenship in an Era of Smaller Government," George Washington University School of Business, February 6, 1996, "Corporate Responsibility—Harman International" [1] folder, OA/ID 10991, Carolyn Curiel series, Clinton Library.

106. Beth Germano, "Lawrence 'Double-Crossed' by Polartec Leaving Malden Mills, Former CEO Says," *CBS News Boston*, December 17, 2015, https://www.cbsnews.com/boston/news/lawrence-polartect-aaron-feuerstein-malden-mills/.

107. Reich, *Locked in the Cabinet*, 293.

108. Ibid., 294.

109. Clay Chandler and Frank Swoboda, "Reich's 'Responsibility' Issue Irritates Colleagues," *WP*, March 8, 1996, F1.

110. Ibid.

111. Louis Uchitelle, *The Disposable American: Layoffs and Their Consequences* (New York: Alfred A. Knopf, 2006), 166.

112. Reich, *Locked in the Cabinet*, 296; Robert Rubin to the President, "Your State of the Union Address," January 16, 1996, Michael Waldman Speechwriting Collection, OA/ID 13660, Clinton Library.

113. Gene Sperling and Laura Tyson to the President, "Update on Corporate Citizenship Plan," March 21, 1996, "Corporate Citizenship" folder, Alexis Herman series, Public Liaison subgroup, OA/ID 7478, Clinton Library.

114. Michele Frisby, "Buchanan's Populist Themes Threaten to Create Split among Democrats as Well as Republicans," *WSJ*, February 27, 1996, A24.

115. Laura Tyson, Alexis Herman, Gene Sperling, and Kate Carr to the President and the Vice President, "Update on Planning for Corporate Citizenship Conference," May 14, 1996, "Corporate Citizenship Conference" [3] folder, OA/ID 10707, David Shipley series, Clinton Library.

116. Stiglitz, *The Roaring Nineties*, 116–17; David Dayen, "Bill Clinton Created This Terrible Corporate Loophole. Will Hillary Close It?," *New Republic*, September 2, 2016.

117. Joseph Stiglitz to the President, "Comments on Weekly Economic Briefing," May 30, 1996, "BE" folder, OA/ID 21792, Records Management subject file, Clinton Library. Stiglitz did favor the "expensing" of options so as to make companies deduct their value from future profits, thereby inducing boards of directors to consider exercising some restraint when conferring stock options on top executives.

118. Uchitelle, *The Disposable American*, 161.

Chapter 10. Underclass Men and Welfare Mothers

1. William J. Clinton, "Remarks to the Convocation of the Church of God in Christ at Memphis, Tennessee," November 13, 1993, American Presidency Project.

2. William Julius Wilson, *The Truly Disadvantaged: The Inner City, the Underclass, and Public Policy* (Chicago: University of Chicago Press, 1987).

3. Clinton, *President Clinton's New Beginning*, 193; "Interview with Timothy Russert and Tom Brokaw on 'Meet the Press,'" November 7, 1993, American Presidency Project. Clinton's identification with the Wilson thesis is also evident in James Fallows, "A Visit with Bill Clinton," *Atlantic*, October 1992, 17.

4. William Julius Wilson, "The Right Message," *NYT*, March 17, 1992, A26.

5. William Julius Wilson, email to the author, July 15, 2022.

6. David Remnick, "Dr. Wilson's Neighborhood," *New Yorker*, April 29, 1996, 107.

7. Rodgers, *Age of Fracture*, 200–201.

8. Until 1962 it was called Aid to Dependent Children. In the social imagination, white widows and their children were thought to be the prime beneficiaries; thereafter African-American single mothers held center stage.

9. Elizabeth Hinton, *From the War on Poverty to the War on Crime: The Making of Mass Incarceration in America* (Cambridge, MA: Harvard University Press, 2016), 244.

10. Jason DeParle, *American Dream: Three Women, Ten Kids, and a Nation's Drive to End Welfare* (New York: Viking, 2004), 131–32.

11. Maney, *Bill Clinton*, 168.

12. For his views on Charles Murray, see "Interview with Timothy Russert and Tom Brokaw."

13. Clinton, *My Life*, 330. Geismer has a more extensive discussion of Clinton's use of the Hardin story in *Left Behind*, 182–85.

14. Lauren-Brooke Eisen, "The 1994 Crime Bill and Beyond: How Federal Funding Shapes the Criminal Justice System," Brennan Center for Justice, September 9, 2019, https://www .brennancenter.org/our-work/analysis-opinion/1994-crime-bill-and-beyond-how-federal -funding-shapes-criminal-justice.

15. James Q. Wilson, "What to Do about Crime," *Commentary*, September 1994, 25–34.

16. John DiIulio, "The Coming of the Super-Predators," *Weekly Standard*, November 1995; see also Bruce Shapiro, "How the War on Crime Imprisons America," *The Nation*, April 22, 1996, 17.

17. A. M. Rosenthal, "Prisons Save Lives," *NYT*, June 3, 1994, A27.

18. David S. Broder, "Illegitimacy: An Unprecedented Catastrophe," *WP*, June 22, 1994.

19. DiIulio's article "The Coming of the Super-Predators" was widely reprinted, and versions of it circulated in the White House; likewise the essays of James Q. Wilson. See "Academic Articles" folder, OA/ID 10441, Jonathan Prince, Speechwriting, Clinton Library.

20. Julia Zorthian, "Black Lives Matter Activist Confronts Clinton at Fundraiser," *Time*, February 25, 2016.

21. Felicia Kornbluh and Gwendolyn Mink, *Ensuring Poverty: Welfare Reform in Feminist Perspective* (Philadelphia: University of Pennsylvania Press, 2019), 61–63.

22. Gwen Ifill, "Clinton's Tightrope; Presidency Takes on Shifting Politics of US Role in Curbing Violent Crime," *NYT*, November 15, 1993, B8.

23. William J. Clinton, "The President's Radio Address," August 14, 1993, American Presidency Project.

24. White House Communications to House Majority Leader, "Crime Bill Promotion," July 22, 1994, "1994 Crime Bill Strategy Memos" folder, OA/ID 10441, Jonathan Prince, Speechwriting, Clinton Library; Marc Mauer, "The Fragility of Criminal Justice Reform," *Social Justice*, 21, no. 3 (1994): 22.

25. Rahm Emanuel, Bruce Reed, and Jonathan Prince to Mack McLarty, "Assault Weapons Ban," April 20, 1994, "1994 Crime Bill Strategy Memos" folder, OA/ID 10441, Jonathan Prince, Speechwriting, Clinton Library.

26. Emily Cochrane and Zolan Kanno-Youngs, "Biden Signs Gun Bill into Law, Ending Years of Stalemate," *NYT*, June 25, 2022, A1.

27. Eisen, "The 1994 Crime Bill and Beyond."

28. Hinton, *From the War on Poverty to the War on Crime*, 241.

29. Bill Clinton, "Address before a Joint Session of the Congress on the State of the Union," January 25, 1994, American Presidency Project.

30. Sasha Abramsky, *Hard Time Blues: How Politics Built a Prison Nation* (New York: Macmillan, 2011); see also "Three Strikes Laws Don't Prevent Crime," press release, Open Society Foundation, July 28, 2002, https://www.opensocietyfoundations.org/newsroom/paper-three-strikes-laws-dont-prevent-crime.

31. Ron Klain to Leon Panetta, "The Racial Justice Act," July 14, 1994, "Racial Justice Act" folder, OA/box 8413, Bruce Reed, Crime, Domestic Policy Council, Clinton Library.

32. "Pull the Plug on This Crime Bill," *NYT*, July 22, 1994; Todd S. Purdum, "The Crime-Bill Debate Shows How Short Americans' Memories Are," *Atlantic*, September 12, 2019.

33. Purdum, "The Crime-Bill Debate"; Adam Willis, "'I'm Not Sorry': A Quarter-Century Later, Eddie Bernice Johnson Stands by Her Crime Bill Vote," *Texas Tribune*, July 16, 2019.

34. US House of Representatives, "Crime Control and Prevention Bill" (HR3355), Final Vote Results for Roll Call 416, August 21, 1994, https://clerk.house.gov/evs/1994/roll416.xml.

35. German Lopez, "The Controversial 1994 Crime Law That Joe Biden Helped Write, Explained," *Vox*, September 29, 2020; Purdum, "The Crime-Bill Debate."

36. Eisen, "The 1994 Crime Bill and Beyond"; John Clegg and Adaner Usmani, "The Economic Origins of Mass Incarceration," *Catalyst* 3, no. 3 (Fall 2019): 25–26.

37. Carroll Bogert and LynNell Hancock, "How the Media Created a 'Superpredator' Myth That Harmed a Generation of Black Youth," *NBC News*, November 20, 2020.

38. Robert Farley, "Bill Clinton and the 1994 Crime Bill," FactCheck.org, April 12, 2016, https://www.factcheck.org/2016/04/bill-clinton-and-the-1994-crime-bill/.

39. Kornbluh and Mink, *Ensuring Poverty*, 40–41.

40. Galston and Kamarck, "The Politics of Evasion," 4.

41. DeParle, *American Dream*, 101–2.

42. Peter Edelman oral history, May 24, 2004, Miller Center.

43. Bill Clinton, "A New Covenant: Responsibility and Rebuilding the American Community," Georgetown University, October 23, 1991, in Smith, *Preface to the Presidency*, 89, 95.

44. David Ellwood, "Welfare Reform as I Knew It: When Bad Things Happen to Good Policies," *American Prospect*, May/June 1996.

45. Clinton, "A New Covenant," 103; George Stephanopoulos, *All Too Human: A Political Education* (New York: Little, Brown, 1999), 420–21.

46. Kusnet oral history, March 19, 2010, 72; Michael Waldman, *POTUS Speaks: Finding the Words That Defined the Clinton Presidency* (New York: Simon & Schuster, 2000), 20.

47. Kamarck oral history, May 7–8, 2006. A week before the Little Rock economic summit, Kamarck saw Clinton "having it both ways" when he showed up at a lobbyist-heavy DLC gala an hour late, delayed by a cocktail party at the Children's Defense Fund. Said Kamarck in her oral history interview, "We were shocked, thinking, Who is this guy?" See also Lloyd Grove, "Lobbyists Thermidor: Clinton Sups with Special Interests at Democratic Leadership Council Fete," *WP*, December 9, 1992, C1.

48. Marian Wright Edelman, "Investment in Children," in Clinton, *President Clinton's New Beginning*, 28–35; Peter Edelman oral history, May 24, 2004.

49. Kornbluh and Mink, *Ensuring Poverty*, 9–10, 67. This was a perspective put forward by a coalition of feminist academics and left-leaning officeholders led by Hawaii Congresswoman Patsy Mink.

50. William Galston oral history, April 22–23, 2004, 42, Miller Center.

51. Faux, "The Myth of the New Democrats"; Waldman, *POTUS Speaks*, 79.

52. Al From and Bruce Reed to the President- and Vice President-Elect, "Pursuing the Clinton Revolution," December 19, 1992, 1–3, History of the Domestic Policy Council, Documentary Annex II [6], Clinton Library; Baer, *Reinventing Democrats*, 137.

53. From and Reed to the President- and Vice President-Elect, "Pursuing the Clinton Revolution," 4.

54. Ibid., 4–6; Faux, "The Myth of New Democrats."

55. Al From to the President, "The Next 100 Days," April 16, 1993, Democratic Leadership Council folder, box 12, Rahm Emanuel Collection, OA/ID 3520, Clinton Library.

56. Al From to Bruce Lindsey, "The Economic Plan and the President's Politics," May 21, 1993, DLC folder, box 12, Rahm Emanuel Collection, OA/ID 3520, FOIA 2009-0140-F, Clinton Library.

57. Al From to the President, April 16, 1993; Al From to the President, "Improving Your Politics," May 4, 1993; both in DLC folder, box 12, Rahm Emanuel Collection, OA/ID 3520, Clinton Library.

58. Galston oral history, April 22–23, 2004, 46.

59. Baer, *Reinventing Democrats*, 210–11, 214.

60. Galston oral history, April 22–23, 2004, 60; Reed oral history, February 19, 2004, 10–12.

61. Clinton, *My Life*, 494; Eva Bertram, *The Workfare States: Public Assistance Politics from the New Deal to the New Democrats* (Philadelphia: University of Pennsylvania Press, 2015), 186.

62. Bruce Reed to the President, "The Politics of Welfare Reform," May 30, 1994, Domestic Policy Council, Documentary Annex 1 [4], Clinton Library.

63. "McJob," Wikipedia, last updated July 31, 2022.

64. Kornbluh and Mink, *Ensuring Poverty*, 62; Peter Edelman oral history, May 24, 2004, 128.

65. Baer, *Reinventing Democrats*, 242.

66. Galston oral history, April 22–23, 2004, 72.

67. Reed oral history, February 19, 2004, 160; Maney, *Bill Clinton*, 158; Baer, *Reinventing Democrats*, 233.

68. Stephanopoulos, *All Too Human*, 352.

69. Maney, *Bill Clinton*, 156.

70. DeParle, *American Dream*, 135.

71. Galston oral history, April 22–23, 2004, 119; Nelson, Perry, and Riley, 42: *Inside the Presidency of Bill Clinton*, 169.

72. Stephanie Mudge, *Leftism Reinvented: Western Parties from Socialism to Neoliberalism* (Cambridge, MA: Harvard University Press, 2018), 304–6, 344–50; From, *The New Democrats*, 239–48. Clinton and Blair had been simpatico in several meetings well before the latter became prime minister.

73. See Arthur Schlesinger Jr., "It's My 'Vital Center,'" *Slate*, January 10, 1997. The historian takes Clinton and the DLC to task for reinterpreting his famous phrase to mean "middle of the road" and therefore as closer to Reaganism than FDR's New Deal.

74. Mudge, *Leftism Reinvented*, 330; Baer, *Reinventing Democrats*, 258–59; Clinton, *Living History*, 422–30. Both Hillary Clinton and Blumenthal, often critics of the DLC, were Third Way enthusiasts because it cast President Clinton's statecraft in so much better a light.

75. Maney, *Bill Clinton*, 161–62.

76. Peter Edelman, "The Worst Thing Bill Clinton Has Done," *Atlantic*, March 1997, 43–58; Blumenthal, *The Clinton Wars*, 145.

77. Marian Wright Edelman to the President, January 30, 1995, Bruce Reed, "Welfare Reform" series, Children's Defense Fund [1], Clinton Library.

78. Clinton, *My Life*, 694; Maney, *Bill Clinton*, 163; Steven Gillon, *The Pact: Bill Clinton, Newt Gingrich, and the Rivalry That Defined a Generation* (New York: Oxford University Press, 2008) 168–72.

79. Waldman, *POTUS Speaks*, 107.

80. Ibid., 108.

81. Ibid., 111.

82. See, for example, Alison Mitchell, "State of the Union: The Overview; Clinton Offers Challenge to Nation, Declaring, 'Era of Big Government Is Over,'" *NYT*, January 24, 1996, A1; Jaime Fuller, "The 3rd Most Memorable State of the Union Address: Bye Bye Big Government," *WP* blog, January 26, 2014.

83. Bruce Reed to the President, "Democratic Governors and Welfare Reform," May 28, 1996, Domestic Policy Council—Documentary Annex [1] [5], Clinton Library.

84. Kornbluh and Mink, *Ensuring Poverty*, 50.

85. DeParle, *American Dream*, 148; Edelman, "The Worst Thing Bill Clinton Has Done."

86. Dick Morris, *Behind the Oval Office: Getting Reelected against All Odds* (Los Angeles: Renaissance Books, 1999), 595.

87. Nelson, Perry, and Riley, *Inside the Presidency of Bill Clinton*, 162.

88. Clinton, *Living History*, 368; Kornbluh and Mink, *Ensuring Poverty*, 76.

89. Morris, *Behind the Oval Office*, 300; Clinton, *Living History*, 369.

90. DeParle, *American Dream*, 152–54.

91. Rubin, *In an Uncertain World*, 201; Taylor Branch, *The Clinton Tapes: Wrestling History with the President* (New York: Simon & Schuster, 2009), 368.

92. William J. Clinton, "Remarks on Signing the Personal Responsibility and Work Opportunity Reconciliation Act of 1996 and an Exchange with Reporters," August 22, 1996, American Presidency Project.

93. Quoted in DeParle, *American Dream*, 152.

94. Barbara Vobejda and Judith Havemann, "2 HHS Officials Quit over Welfare Changes," *WP*, September 12, 1996, A1.

95. Gayle Pollard Terry, "William Julius Wilson," *Los Angeles Times*, November 3, 1996, M3.

96. Peter Edelman, "The Worst Thing Bill Clinton Has Done," *Atlantic*, March 1997, 43–58.

97. Scott Winship and Christopher Jencks, "Understanding Welfare Reform," *Harvard*, November/December 2004; Bill Clinton, "How We Ended Welfare, Together," *NYT*, August 22, 2006, A19.

98. Marianne Bitler and Hilary Hoynes, "Heterogeneity in the Impact of Economic Cycles and the Great Recession: Effects within and across the Income Distribution," *American Economic Review* 105, no. 5 (May 2015): 154–60.

99. Dylan Matthews, "If the Goal Was to Get Rid of Poverty, We Failed: The Legacy of the 1996 Welfare Reform," *Vox*, June 20, 2016.

100. Paul Krugman, "Ending the End of Welfare as We Knew It," *NYT*, March 12, 2022, A29.

101. Kornbluh and Mink, *Ensuring Poverty*, 72–73; Melinda Cooper, *Family Values: Between Neoliberalism and the New Social Conservatism* (Cambridge: Zone Books, 2017), 97.

102. Robert Kuttner, "Social Security and the Market," *American Prospect*, November 30, 2002.

103. Eric Laursen, *The People's Pension: The Struggle to Defend Social Security since Reagan* (Oakland, CA: AK Press, 2012), 256–60.

104. Ibid., 247.

105. Ibid., 342–43.

106. Gillon, *The Pact*, 200.

107. Ibid., 194.

108. Gene Sperling and Lawrence Summers, memorandum for the President, "The Unified Budget Surplus and Social Security," December 7, 1997, "NEC—Budget Surplus to Strengthen Social Security and Medicare" II [2], Clinton Library.

109. Robert Reich, "The Sham of Saving Social Security First," *Harper's*, June 1998, 392.

110. Maney, *Bill Clinton*, 194–95.

111. Gillon, *The Pact*, 226.

112. Clinton, *My Life*, 771, 780–84, 786–87, 792–95, 807–9.

113. Rubin, *In an Uncertain World*, 272.

114. Reed and Bowles quoted in Gillon, *The Pact*, 213, 224.

115. Ibid., 266.

116. Jackie Calmes, "Clinton's Best Friends Now Are the Liberals He Spurned in the Past," *WSJ*, October 9, 1998, A1.

117. Kevin Kruse and Julian Zelizer, *Fault Lines: A History of the United States since 1974* (New York: W. W. Norton, 2019), 227; Gloria Steinem, "Why Feminists Support Clinton," *NYT*, March 22, 1998.

118. Clinton, *My Life*, 842; Edith Rasell and Jeff Faux, "Fixing Social Security: The Clinton Plan and Its Alternatives," briefing paper 82, Economic Policy Institute, April 1, 1999.

119. Laursen, *The People's Pension*, 395; Eric Pianin, "Clinton Vetoes GOP Tax Cut Bill," *WP*, September 24, 1999, A1.

120. David Wessel, "Greenspan Frets over Outlook for Stocks: Fed Chairman Opposes Plan by Clinton to Invest Part of Social Security Fund," *WSJ*, January 21, 1999, A3. In this instance Robert Rubin broke with Greenspan and endorsed a limited Social Security investment.

121. Rasell and Faux, "Fixing Social Security," 6.

122. Richard Stevenson, "Social Security: Divergent Paths," *NYT*, March 24, 1999, A22.

Chapter 11. The China Price

1. Niall Ferguson and Moritz Schularick first coined the term in 2007. See their "Chimerica and the Global Asset Market Boom," *International Finance* 10, no. 3 (2007): 215–39. By the time of the financial crisis two years later these same authors, as well as many others, were doubting Chimerica's staying power.

2. Timothy Brook, *The Military Suppression of the Beijing Democracy Movement* (Stanford, CA: Stanford University Press, 1998).

3. Henry A. Kissinger, "China: Push for Reform, Not Rupture," *Los Angeles Times*, July 30, 1989, B1. This was also the column in which Kissinger made the infamous statement, "No government in the world would have tolerated having the main square of its capital occupied for eight weeks by tens of thousands of demonstrators who blocked the area in front of the main government building."

4. James Mann, *About Face: A History of America's Curious Relationship with China, from Nixon to Clinton* (New York: Random House, 1998), 213–24. Majority Leader Gephardt supported Pelosi's efforts. In his office was an ambitious young staffer named George Stephanopoulos who championed the cause of the thousands of pro-democracy Chinese students stranded in the United States.

5. Stewart Paterson, *China, Trade, and Power: Why the West's Economic Engagement Has Failed* (London: London Publishing Partnership, 2018), 18.

6. Michael Dobbs, "US Focuses on Better Ties to China: Policy Flip-Flops Roil Mercurial Relationship," *WP*, July 9, 1996, A1; Lawrence, "International Trade Policy in the 1990s," 306; John W. Dietrich, "Interest Groups and Foreign Policy: Clinton and the China MFN Debates," *Presidential Studies Quarterly* 29, no. 2 (June 1999): 280–96.

7. "Ambassador Winston Lord," Foreign Affairs Oral History Project, Association for Diplomatic Studies and Training, April 28, 1998, 544, 573, Library of Congress.

8. Daniel Williams and R. Jeffrey Smith, "Clinton to Extend China Trade Status, Future Action to Depend on Human Rights Progress," *WP*, May 28, 1993, A1; Keiji Nakatsuji, "Nancy Pelosi and Human Rights in China," *Ritsumeikan Journal of International Studies* 12, no. 2 (December 1999): 17.

9. Eric Morganthaler, "A Look at Tomorrow—A Centennial View," *WSJ*, June 23, 1989, 1; Claudia Rosett, "In China, Standard Communist Behavior," *WSJ*, June 23, 1989, 1.

10. Lichtenstein, *The Retail Revolution*, 156.

11. Louis Uchitelle, "Back to Business on China Trade," *NYT*, May 27, 1994, D1.

12. Ezra F. Vogel, *Deng Xiaoping and the Transformation of China* (Cambridge, MA: Harvard University Press, 2013); Robert Kuttner, "How Globalists Ceded the Field to Donald Trump," *American Prospect*, March 19, 2018.

13. Ho-fung Hung, "The Periphery in the Making of Globalization: The China Lobby and the Reversal of Clinton's China Trade Policy, 1993–1994," *Review of International Political Economy*, April 13, 2020, 5–6.

14. Mann, *About Face*, 284–85.

15. Ho-fung Hung, *The China Boom: Why China Will Not Rule the World* (New York: Columbia University Press, 2016), 61–63; Carl E. Walter and Fraser J. T. Howie, *Red Capitalism: The Fragile Financial Foundation of China's Extraordinary Rise* (Singapore: John Wiley & Sons, 2011), 178–79.

16. Lawrence, "International Trade Policy in the 1990s," 307–8; Walter and Howie, *Red Capitalism*, 182–83.

17. Thomas Palley, "Three Globalizations, Not Two: Rethinking the History and Economics of Trade and Globalization," FMM Working Paper 18, March 2018, Hans-Bockler-Stiftung/Macroeconomic Policy Institute, 11, https://www.boeckler.de/pdf/p_fmm_imk_wp_18_2018.pdf.

18. Ibid., 20.

19. Ho-fung Hung, "The Periphery in the Making of Globalization," 11–12.

20. Mann, *About Face*, 284; Richard Bernstein and Ross Munro, *The Coming Conflict with China* (New York: Alfred A. Knopf, 1997), 106.

21. I. M. Destler, *American Trade Politics* (Washington, DC: Institute for International Economics, 2005), 212.

22. Bernstein and Munro, *The Coming Conflict with China*, 101.

23. Nakatsuji, "Nancy Pelosi and Human Rights in China," 18.

24. Patrick Tyler, "China Sees Risk to Its Stability in US Demands," *NYT*, May 19, 1994, A1.

25. John Shattuck to the Secretary of State, "Status Report on China MFN Conditions," November 1993, Department of State; Office of Assistant Secretary for Human Rights, "China and the US"; both in National Security Archive, Georgetown University; Kerry Dumbaugh, "China-US Relations," Congressional Research Service Issue Brief, January 11, 1994, 7.

26. James Mann, "Our China Illusions," *American Prospect*, December 19, 2000.

27. Bernstein and Munro, *The Coming Conflict with China*, 99–100.

28. Elaine Sciolino, "China Rejects Call from Christopher for Rights Gains," *NYT*, March 13, 1994, A1.

29. Bernstein and Munro, *The Coming Conflict with China*, 100–101.

30. Destler, *American Trade Politics*, 212; Winston Lord oral history, April 28, 1998, 582.

31. Peter Behr, "Offering China a Carrot on Trade; in Exchange, US Would Insist on Human Rights Improvements," *WP*, January 29, 1994, C1.

32. Winston Lord oral history, April 28, 1998, 574.

33. David Lampton, "America's China Policy in the Age of the Finance Minister: Clinton Ends Linkage," *China Quarterly* 139 (September 1994): 616–19.

34. Marc Sandalow, "Clinton Must Soon Decide on China Trade Status," *San Francisco Chronicle*, May 16, 1994, A1.

35. Barshefsky oral history, March 2, 2005, 16–17.

36. Marc Sandalow, "Pelosi Says She'll Continue Fight on China," *San Francisco Chronicle*, May 28, 1994, A1.

37. "Shortchanging Rights in China," *NYT*, May 27, 1994, A26.

38. Mary McGrory, "The Price Is Rights," *WP*, May 31, 1994, A2.

39. Quoted in John W. Dietrich, "Interest Groups and Foreign Policy: Clinton and the China MFN Debates," *Presidential Studies Quarterly* 29, no. 2 (June 1999): 292.

40. John Broder and Jim Mann, "Clinton Reverses His Policy, Renews China Trade Status Commerce," *Los Angeles Times*, May 27, 1994, 1.

41. Winston Lord oral history, April 28, 1998, 524.

42. William J. Clinton, "Remarks to the Asia Society and United States–China Educational Board," October 24, 1997, 126–27, American Presidency Project.

43. William J. Clinton, "Remarks on United States Foreign Policy in San Francisco," February 26, 1999, American Presidency Project.

44. Clinton, "Remarks to the Asia Society," 127.

45. William J. Clinton, "Remarks at the Paul H. Nitze School of Advanced International Studies," March 8, 2000, American Presidency Project.

46. Thomas Friedman, *The Lexus and the Olive Tree* (New York: Farrar, Straus and Giroux, 1999), 204.

47. "Clinton's Containment Conundrum," *South China Morning Post*, March 24, 1997.

48. Nicholas Kristof, "The Tiananmen Victory," *NYT*, June 2, 2004, A19.

49. John Pomfret, "Chinese Workers Are Showing Disenchantment," *WP*, April 23, 2000, A23.

50. James Mann, "America's China Fantasy," *American Prospect*, February 19, 2007; Lawrence F. Kaplan, "Trade Barrier: Why Trade Won't Bring Democracy to China," *New Republic*, July 8, 2001. For a contrary view, see Ronald Inglehart and Christian Welzel, "How Development Leads to Democracy: What We Know about Modernization," *Foreign Affairs*, March/April 2009, 33–45. See also Perry Anderson's comparison of the demise of socialism in the Soviet Union and China in "Two Revolutions," *New Left Review* 61 (January/February 2010).

51. Matthew C. Klein and Michael Pettis, *Trade Wars Are Class Wars: How Rising Inequality Distorts the Global Economy and Threatens International Peace* (New Haven, CT: Yale University Press, 2020), 109.

52. John Bellamy Foster and Robert McChesney, *The Endless Crisis: How Monopoly-Finance Capital Produces Stagnation and Upheaval from the USA to China* (New York: Monthly Review Press, 2012), 112, 170.

53. Ibid., 113.

54. Reich, *Locked in the Cabinet*, 269–70, 314–16; Peter Liebhold, "25 Years Later: The Legacy of the El Monte Sweatshop Raid," National Museum of American History, July 31, 2020, https://americanhistory.si.edu/blog/el-monte-sweatshop-raid.

55. Todd Purdum, "Hard Choice for White House on Hillary Clinton and China," *NYT*, August 17, 1995, A1; "The Harry Wu Opening," *NYT*, August 25, 1995, A26; Bernstein, *A Woman in Charge*, 436–37.

56. Frank Swoboda, "White House Unveils Code for US Business Abroad," *WP*, May 27, 1995, F01.

57. Edward A. Gargan, "Business Objects to a Code in China," *NYT*, May 24, 1994, D2; David Sanger, "Clinton to Urge a Rights Code for Business Dealing Abroad," *NYT*, March 27, 1995, D1.

58. Laura Tyson to the President, "Proposed Garment Labeling Initiative," July 22, 1996, "Sweatshop Initiative" [3] binder, OA/ID 20237, Gene Sperling series, National Economic Council, Clinton Library.

59. Gene Sperling, *The Pro-Growth Progressive: An Economic Strategy for Shared Prosperity* (New York: Simon & Schuster, 2005), 100–101; Geismer, *Left Behind*, 282–83.

60. The contributions of Scott Nova, Jill Esbenshade, Robert Ross, Brishen Rogers, Jenny Chan, Pun Ngai, Anita Chan, and Jeff Hermanson detail the failures of the corporate social responsibility idea when confronted by the economic imperatives generated by the subcontracting universe that sustain contemporary global supply chains. See Richard Appelbaum and Nelson Lichtenstein, eds., *Achieving Workers' Rights in the Global Economy* (Ithaca, NY: Cornell University Press, 2016).

61. Julie Kosterlitz, "Muddy Track," *National Journal*, August 9, 1997, 1595.

62. Charan Devereaux, Robert Z. Lawrence, and Michael D. Watkins, *Case Studies in US Trade Negotiations*, vol. 1, *Making the Rules* (Washington, DC: Institute for International Economics, 2006), 207, 209.

63. Peter Beinart, "The Nationalist Revolt," *New Republic*, December 1, 1997, 20–26.

64. Devereaux, Lawrence, and Watkins, *Case Studies in US Trade Negotiations*, 212.

65. Destler, *American Trade Politics*, 263.

66. Devereaux, Lawrence, and Watkins, *Case Studies in US Trade Negotiations*, 220.

67. Ibid., 225.

68. Ibid., 226–28; Destler, *American Trade Politics*, 267. Consumed with the Lewinsky affair, Clinton did not reintroduce a fast-track bill in 1998, but Gingrich did, if only to embarrass the president in the midst of the impending impeachment hearings. As expected, it failed, with only twenty-nine Democrats in favor and no fewer than seventy-one Republicans joining the opposition.

69. "Administration Wrestles with Political Aspects of China WTO Deal," *Inside US Trade*, March 26, 1999; Clinton, *My Life*, 793; Joseph Fewsmith, "China and the WTO: The Politics behind the Agreement," *NBR Analysis* (National Bureau of Asian Research) 10, no. 5 (December 1, 1999), https://www.nbr.org/publication/china-and-the-wto-the-politics-behind-the-agreement/.

70. Kenneth Lieberthal to Richard Saunders, "Zhu Visit and Human Rights," December 28, 1998, "Asian Affairs—Lieberthal" [1] box, "Zhu Rongji Visit, April 1999" [8] folder, Clinton Library, FOIA 2014-1039F.

71. Helene Cooper and Bob Davis, "No Deal: Overruling Some Staff, Clinton Defies Zhu," *WSJ*, April 9, 1999, A1.

72. "China WTO Meeting," March 20, 1999, "NEC—Sperling" box, "China MFN—China WTO," 1998–99 [5] folder, Clinton Library, FOIA 2014-1039.

73. Senate majority leader Trent Lott quoted in Devereaux, Lawrence, and Watkins, *Case Studies in US Trade Negotiations*, 269.

74. "China: Trade Issues," April 1999, box 3, "China—Zhu Rongji" [1] folder, Clinton Library, FOIA 2014-1039.

75. Jacob Schlesinger, "China Trade Pact May Hinge on Unions' Stance," *WSJ*, April 12, 1999, A10.

76. "Improvements Sought in China's Financial Services Offer," "China—MFN and China—WTO" file, May 1999, "NEC—Sperling" folder, Clinton Library.

77. Joseph Stiglitz, *Globalization and Its Discontents* (New York: W. W. Norton, 2003), 64.

78. Richard Walker and Daniel Buck, "The Chinese Road: Cities in the Transition to Capitalism," *New Left Review* 46 (July/August 2007): 42–44.

79. "Robert Rubin Remarks for Opening Plenary China—US Joint Economic Committee—Eleventh Session," US Treasury Department press release, May 26, 1998, https://home.treasury .gov/news/press-releases/rr2476; Robert Rubin to the President, "Your Meeting with Premier Zhu Rongji: Key Economic Issues," April 7, 1999; Meg Lundsager to Timothy Geithner, "China's WTO Accession Negotiations: Status Report," May 6, 1999; both in "History of the Department of the Treasury—Supplementary Documents" [25], Clinton Library; Pomfret, "Chinese Workers Are Showing Disenchantment."

80. Gene Sperling and Samuel Berger, "Why PNTR Is Best Hope for Greater Openness in China," Spring 2000, "China" [3] folder, OA/ID 4022, Paul Orzulak, Speechwriting, Clinton Library; see also Peter Nolan, *China and the Global Economy: National Champions, Industrial Policy, and the Big Business Revolution* (New York: Palgrave, 2001), 210.

81. Walter and Howie, *Red Capitalism*, 182–83, 184.

82. Devereaux, Lawrence, and Watkins, *Case Studies in US Trade Negotiation*, 271–76.

83. William J. Clinton, "Remarks at the Paul H. Nitze School of Advanced International Studies," Johns Hopkins University, March 8, 2000, American Presidency Project.

84. "Summary of US-China Bilateral WTO Agreement," November 26, 1999, "Speechwriting—Paul Orzulak, China 11" [2] file, OA/ID 4022, Clinton Library; Lu Zhang, *Inside China's Automobile Factories: The Politics of Labor and Worker Resistance* (New York: Cambridge University Press, 2015), 35, 41.

85. "Interview with Charlene Barshefsky," *The News Hour with Jim Lehrer*, November 18, 1999, American Archive of Public Broadcasting.

86. Walter and Howie, *Red Capitalism*, 182–83.

87. Devereaux, Lawrence, and Watkins, *Case Studies in US Trade Negotiations*, 281–89.

88. Jeff Crosby, "The Kids Are Alright," *New Labor Forum*, Spring/Summer 2000, 35–39.

89. Janet Thomas, *The Battle in Seattle: The Story behind and beyond the WTO Demonstrations* (Golden, CO: Fulcrum Publishing, 2000), 18–19. However, in 2001 the WTO reversed itself when an appellate body released a report finding that implementation of the US sea turtle protection law was in fact "fully consistent with WTO rules." "US Wins WTO Case on Sea Turtle Conservation," Office of the United States Trade Representative, October 22, 2001, https://ustr.gov/archive/Document_Library/Press_Releases/2001/October/US_Wins _WTO_Case_on_Sea_Turtle_Conservation.html.

90. Sperling, *The Pro-Growth Progressive*, 43.

91. Thomas Friedman, "Senseless in Seattle," *NYT*, December 1, 1999, A20.

92. Waldman, *POTUS Speaks*, 231.

93. "The Clinton Administration Agenda for Seattle: Putting a Human Face on the Global Economy," November 29, 1999, "WTO—Seattle Ministerial 12/1/99 'Human Face' Lab/Envir./

Openness" folder, ID 21462, Jeff Shesol, Speechwriting, Clinton Library; Helene Cooper, "Clinton to Urge Protections on Child Labor at Meeting," *WSJ*, May 27, 1999, A10; Helene Cooper, "Corporate, Labor Leaders Both Trumpet Backing Clinton's Trade Talk Plan," *WSJ*, November 1, 1999, A6.

94. David E. Sanger, "Clinton Is Stymied on Trade Meeting," *NYT*, November 24, 1999, A1.

95. "Remarks by the President, Weyerhauser Facility, Port of Seattle," December 1, 1999, "China II" [2] folder, OA/ID 4022, Paul Orzulak, Speechwriting, Clinton Library.

96. David Sanger, "In Stormy Seattle, Clinton Chides World Trade Body," *NYT*, December 2, 1999, A1.

97. Michael Paulson, "Clinton Takes Strong Stand on Labor Rights," *Seattle Post-Intelligencer*, December 1, 1999, 1.

98. Robert Kaiser and John Burgess, "A Seattle Primer: How Not to Hold WTO Talks," *WP*, December 12, 1999, A40.

99. Steven Greenhouse, "US Effort to Add Labor Standards to Agenda Fails," *NYT*, December 3, 1999, A1.

100. Barshefsky oral history, March 2, 2005, 47. Of course, union representatives from some of those same countries did endorse a set of higher labor standards and blamed the WTO for avoiding the topic. At the labor rally organized by the AFL-CIO, South African miner Glen Mpufane, who called for a global minimum wage, shouted out: "Workers of the world unite— against the WTO!" Harold Meyerson, "The Battle in Seattle," *LA Weekly*, December 1, 1999, reprinted in *American Prospect*, November 29, 2019.

101. Helene Cooper, "WTO—Clash in Seattle: Poorer Countries Are Demonstrators' Strongest Critics," *WSJ*, December 2, 1999, A2:2.

102. "The Real Losers from Seattle," *The Economist*, December 11, 1999.

103. Mary McGrory, "Labor's Battle in Seattle," *WP*, December 2, 1999, A3; John Judis, "China's Going to Enter the WTO. Deal with It," *New Republic*, December 20, 1999, 18–21.

104. "The World Trade Organization: How Clinton Botched the Summit," *WSJ*, December 6, 1999, A34.

105. David Autor, David Dorn, and Gordon Hanson, "The China Shock: Learning from Labor-Market Adjustment to Large Changes in Trade," *Annual Review of Economics* 8 (2016): 205–14; Justin Pierce and Peter Schott, "The Surprisingly Swift Decline of US Manufacturing Employment," *American Economic Review* 106, no. 7 (July 2016): 1632–36.

106. David Autor, David Dorn, Gordon Hanson, and Jae Song, "Trade Adjustment: Worker Level Evidence," *Quarterly Journal of Economics* 129, no. 4 (November 2014): 1799–1800.

107. Pete Engardio and Dexter Roberts, "The China Price," *Business Week*, December 4, 2004.

108. Lichtenstein, *The Retail Revolution*, 211, 354; Robert E. Scott, "The Wal-Mart Effect," Issue Brief 235, Economic Policy Institute, June 26, 2007.

109. Barry Eichengreen, *Globalizing Capital: A History of the International Monetary System* (Princeton, NJ: Princeton University Press, 2019), 179–80; Stewart Paterson, *China, Trade, and Power: Why the West's Economic Engagement Has Failed* (London: London Publishing Partnership, 2018), 6, 59.

Chapter 12. The Committee to Save the World

1. Joshua Cooper Ramo, "The Three Marketeers," *Time*, February 15, 1999.

2. Paul Blustein, *The Chastening: Inside the Crisis That Rocked the Global Financial System and Humbled the IMF* (New York: Public Affairs, 2001), 43.

3. Leo Panitch and Sam Gindin, *The Making of Global Capitalism: The Political Economy of American Empire* (New York: Verso, 2012), 249; Rubin, *In an Uncertain World*, 17.

4. Levy, *Ages of American Capitalism*, 657; J. Bradford DeLong and Barry Eichengreen, "Between Meltdown and Moral Hazard: The International Monetary Fund and Financial Policies of the Clinton Administration," in Frankel and Orsag, *American Economic Policy in the 1990s*, 213; "Larry Summers Transcript: The Mexican Peso Crisis, 1994," *Conversations with Bill Kristol*, November 22, 2015, https://conversationswithbillkristol.org/transcript/larry-summers-transcript/.

5. Rubin, *In an Uncertain World*, 5.

6. DeLong and Eichengreen, "Between Meltdown and Moral Hazard," 214–15.

7. James M. Poterba, "In Honor of Lawrence H. Summers, Winner of the John Bates Clark Medal," *Journal of Economic Perspectives* 9, no. 1 (Winter 1995): 172–77.

8. John Cassidy, "The Triumphalist: Can Larry Summers Keep the Asian Economic Crisis at Bay?" *New Yorker*, July 6, 1998, 58.

9. Ryan Lizza, "Inside the Crisis: Larry Summers and the White House Economic Team," *New Yorker*, October 12, 2009, 80–95.

10. Ibid., 83. Summers, however, did win the John Bates Clark Medal, awarded every other year to the most outstanding economist under the age of forty.

11. Ramo, "The Three Marketeers."

12. "Toxic Memo," *Harvard*, May 1, 2001; John Cassidy, "The Triumphalist: Can Larry Summers Keep the Asian Economic Crisis at Bay?" *New Yorker*, July 6, 1998, 58.

13. Blinder oral history, June 27, 2003. See Noam Scheiber, *The Escape Artists: How Obama's Team Fumbled the Recovery* (New York: Simon & Schuster, 2011), 60, for a portrait of how Summers swapped one persona, that of a disheveled academic, for one that suited him better: an international diplomat.

14. Jonathan M. Orszag, Peter Orszag, and Laura Tyson, "The Process of Economic Policy-Making during the Clinton Administration," in Frankel and Orszag, *American Economic Policy in the 1990s*, 1021.

15. Lawrence Summers, "The Challenges of Success," Hambrecht & Quist Technology Conference, San Francisco, April 28, 1998, OA/ID 13660, Michael Waldman Speechwriting Collection, Clinton Library.

16. Rubin, *In an Uncertain World*, 1–3.

17. Clinton, *My Life*, 643.

18. Lawrence Summers, "Comments," in Frankel and Orszag, *American Economic Policy in the 1990s*, 264.

19. Panitch and Gindin, *The Making of Global Capitalism*, 252; Rubin, *In an Uncertain World*, 30.

20. Nora Lustig, "Mexico in Crisis, the US to the Rescue. The Financial Assistance Packages of 1982 and 1995," Brookings Institution, January 1, 1997, https://www.brookings.edu/articles/mexico-in-crisis-the-u-s-to-the-rescue-the-financial-assistance-packages-of-1982-and-1995/.

21. Rubin, *In an Uncertain World*, 12–13; Clinton, *My Life*, 644.

22. Blustein, *The Chastening*, 34; see also Ramo, "The Three Marketeers," for the "fire brigade" quote.

23. Larry Summers, "Building an International Financial Architecture for the 21st Century," remarks delivered at the Cato Institute, October 22, 1998, OA/ID 13660, Michael Waldman Speechwriting Collection, Clinton Library; Rubin, *In an Uncertain World*, 29.

24. Rubin, *In and Uncertain World*, 28.

25. Ibid.; DeLong and Eichengreen, "Between Meltdown and Moral Hazard," 214–15.

26. Quoted in Rubin, *In an Uncertain World*, 19.

27. DeLong and Eichengreen, "Between Meltdown and Moral Hazard," 213.

28. Brett D. Fromson, "Rescue Package Provokes Disagreement on Wall Street," *WP*, February 16, 1995, B13.

29. DeLong and Eichengreen, "Between Meltdown and Moral Hazard," 214.

30. "Larry Summers Transcript," *Conversations with Bill Kristol*; Rubin, *In an Uncertain World*, 33.

31. Stiglitz, *The Roaring Nineties*, 215; Rubin, *In an Uncertain World*, 34.

32. Summers, "Comments," in Frankel and Orszag, *American Economic Policy in the 1990s*, 261.

33. Levy, *Ages of American Capitalism*, 663. The term "strong dollar policy" was coined by Deputy Treasury Secretary Roger Altman in the summer of 1994; DeLong and Eichengreen, "Between Meltdown and Moral Hazard," 201. Summers was also a proponent, in contrast to those in the Clinton administration, including Mickey Kantor and Commerce Secretary Ronald Brown, who wanted a weaker exchange rate in order to aid US exports, especially to Asia.

34. Rubin, *In an Uncertain World*, 230–31.

35. Blustein, *The Chastening*, 143; Nicholas Kristof with David Sanger, "How US Wooed Asia to Let Cash Flow In," *NYT*, February 16, 1999, 1.

36. Blustein, *The Chastening*, 149; Panitch and Gindin, *The Making of Global Capitalism*, 257.

37. Panitch and Gindin, *The Making of Global Capitalism*, 259.

38. Blustein, *The Chastening*, 132, 149.

39. Panitch and Gindin, *The Making of Global Capitalism*, 259–60; Blustein, *The Chastening*, 143.

40. Panitch and Gindin, *The Making of Global Capitalism*, 261; Blustein, *The Chastening*, 138.

41. Robert E. Litan with Jonathan Rauch, *American Finance for the 21st Century* (Washington, DC: Brookings Institution Press, 1998), 6, 9.

42. Panitch and Gindin, *The Making of Global Capitalism*, 248; "Interview with Robert Rubin," *The Commanding Heights*, PBS, September 26, 2000, 9, https://www.pbs.org/wgbh/commandingheights/shared/minitext/int_robertrubin.html.

43. Gerald Epstein and Robert Pollin, "Neoliberalism's Bailout Problem," *Boston Review*, June 24, 2021. Timothy Geithner, who worked closely with Summers and Rubin, also thought that overconfidence ultimately breeds financial mania. Geithner would discover Minsky a decade later, when he became Obama's Treasury secretary; Timothy Geithner, *Stress Test: Reflections on the Financial Crises* (New York: Broadway Books, 2014), 68.

44. Litan and Rauch, *American Finance for the 21st Century*, 5–8; Panitch and Gindin, *The Making of Global Capitalism*, 248, 266.

45. Summers, "The Challenges of Success."

46. Peter J. Boettke, "Where Did Economics Go Wrong? Modern Economics as a Flight from Reality," *Critical Review* 11, no. 1 (Winter 1997): 29.

47. Blustein, *The Chastening*, 45.

48. Stiglitz, *The Roaring Nineties*, 215–17; Stiglitz, *Globalization and Its Discontents*, 91, 99.

49. Stiglitz, *Globalization and Its Discontents*, 92.

50. Blustein, *The Chastening*, 49; Kristof and Sanger, "How US Wooed Asia to Let Cash Flow In"; Robert Hunter Wade, "US Hegemony and the World Bank: The Fight over People and Ideas," *Review of International Political Economy* 9, no. 2 (Summer 2002): 227.

51. Stiglitz, *Globalization and Its Discontents*, 92–93; Blustein, *The Chastening*, 157–68; DeLong and Eichengreen, "Between Meltdown and Moral Hazard," 222.

52. David E. Sanger, "Decisions by US and IMF Worsened Asia's Problems, the World Bank Finds," *NYT*, December 3, 1998, 20; Louis Uchitelle, "A Pox on the High-Rates 'Cure,'" *NYT*, January 31, 1999, 4.

53. Louis Uchitelle, "World Bank Economist Felt He Had to Silence His Criticism or Quit," *NYT*, December 2, 1999, C1.

54. Joseph Stiglitz, "What I Learned at the World Economic Crisis," *New Republic*, April 17, 2000, 56.

55. Kristof and Sanger, "How US Wooed Asia to Let Cash Flow In."

56. Wade, "US Hegemony and the World Bank," 209.

57. Mallaby, *The Man Who Knew*, 519–21.

58. Blustein, *The Chastening*, 202–3.

59. John Lloyd, "The Russian Devolution," *New York Times Magazine*, August 15, 1999, 33.

60. Larry Summers to Bill Clinton, "US Policy toward Russia," September 9, 1999, "Russia" folder, OA/box 2191, Ted Widmer, National Security Council, Clinton Library. Summers offered his privatization defense in response to a Clinton query about Lloyd's article (see note 59).

61. Lloyd, "The Russian Devolution," 34; Robert Kuttner, "Was Putin Inevitable?," *American Prospect*, January 30, 2020; Stiglitz, *Globalization and Its Discontents*, 164. The beneficial impact of private property had been a core idea advanced by the economists Ronald Coase and Milton Friedman during the height of the Cold War.

62. Robert Rubin to Vice President Gore, "Background on Russian Economic Reform," January 26, 1996, "History of the Department of the Treasury—Supplementary Documents" [6] folder, OA/box 24124, Clinton Administration History Project, Clinton Library; Janine Wedel, "The Harvard Boys Do Russia," *The Nation*, May 14, 1998.

63. Robert Kuttner, "Falling Upward: The Surprising Survival of Larry Summers," *American Prospect*, July 13, 2020.

64. Stiglitz, *Globalization and Its Discontents*, 139–43; Lloyd, "The Russian Devolution," 34.

65. Stiglitz, *Globalization and Its Discontents*, 122–26. Mahathir's power rested on his appeal to and favoritism toward Malaysia's indigenous population, as opposed to those descended from Chinese immigrants. Since IMF conditionals would have made such favoritism more difficult, Mahathir feared the arrival of an intrusive "structural adjustment" mission from Washington. See DeLong and Eichengreen, "Between Meltdown and Moral Hazard," 224.

66. Panitch and Gindin, *The Making of Global Capitalism*, 263; Stiglitz, *Globalization and Its Discontents*, 148–51.

67. Rubin, *In an Uncertain World*, 277–79.

68. Samuel Berger and Gene Sperling to the President, "Your Trip to Moscow, September 1–2, 1998," August 27, 1998, "The President's Trip to Russia, September 1–2, 1998" folder, OA/ID 2593, Executive Secretary, Clinton Library.

69. Clinton, *My Life*, 807.

70. Sheryl Sandberg to Froman, Comstock, "LS from Russia," December 10, 1998, "History of the Department of the Treasury—Supplementary Documents" [7] folder, OA/box 241124, Clinton Library.

71. Deputy Assistant Secretary Medish and Nancy Lee to Larry Summers and Tim Geithner, "Russia Trip Report, October 13–16, 1998," "History of the Department of the Treasury—Supplementary Documents" [7] folder, OA/box 241124, Clinton Library.

72. Clinton, *My Life*, 904.

73. Financial Crisis Inquiry Commission, *Final Report of the National Commission on the Causes of the Financial and Economic Crisis in the United States* (Washington, DC: US Government Printing Office, January 2011), 57; Levy, *Ages of American Capitalism*, 664–65. The two Nobel laurates were Robert Merton and Myron Scholes, who had created a mathematical model in the 1970s and 1980s for pricing options. For a thorough account of the LTCM collapse, see Roger Lowenstein, *When Genius Failed: The Rise and Fall of Long-Term Capital Management* (New York: Random House, 2000).

74. Cohan, *Money and Power*, 405–6.

75. Frank Partnoy, *Infectious Greed: How Deceit and Risk Corrupted the Financial Markets* (New York: Public Affairs, 2009), 259; Greenspan quoted in "WGFM, December 7, 1998," "Working Group on Financial Markets" [1] folder, OA/box 23925, Jason Seligman, Council of Economic Advisers, Clinton Library.

76. Levy, *Ages of American Capitalism*, 666; Kathleen Day, *Broken Bargain: Bankers, Bailouts, and the Struggle to Tame Wall Street* (New Haven, CT: Yale University Press, 2019), 165–80; Ramo, "The Three Marketeers."

77. David Wessel and Bob Davis, "Less Cash Flow: Currency Controls Gain a Hearing as Crisis in Asia Takes Its Toll," *WSJ*, September 4, 1998, A1.

78. David Sanger, "Clinton Appeals for Joint Attack in Economic Crisis," *NYT*, October 6, 1998, A1.

79. Waldman, *POTUS Speaks*, 232; George Soros, *The Crisis of Global Capitalism: Open Society Endangered* (New York: Public Affairs, 1998); Jeffrey Frankel, "Restructuring the International Financial System: A New Bretton Woods?," Jeffrey Frankel's Blog, October 24, 2008, http://www.jeffrey-frankel.com/2008/10/24/restructuring-the-international-financial-system-a-new-bretton-woods/.

80. "Telcon with British Prime Minister Blair," September 11, 1998; declassified documents concerning Tony Blair, October 6, 1998, Clinton Library.

81. William J. Clinton, "Remarks to the Council on Foreign Relations," New York City, September 14, 1998; "Remarks at the IMF/World Bank Annual Meeting," Washington, DC,

October 6, 1998, both in American Presidency Project; John Harris and Helen Dewar, "Clinton Seeks Global 'New Deal' to End 'Boom and Bust' Cycles," *WP*, October 7, 1998, A16. The speech did not get much attention because on the day it was delivered the House Judiciary Committee voted to move forward with impeachment proceedings. Perhaps that explains why the *Washington Post* buried an account of Clinton's global New Deal idea on page 16.

82. Treasury Secretary Robert E. Rubin, remarks to the Dow Jones/*Wall Street Journal* annual conference on the Americas, New York City, October 1, 1998, "IMF—1998" [3] folder, OA/ID 14439, Michael Waldman Speechwriting Collection, Clinton Library.

83. Panitch and Gindin, *The Making of Global Capitalism*, 262.

84. Rubin, *In an Uncertain World*, 266, 272–73; Strobe Talbott, *The Russia Hand: A Memoir of Presidential Diplomacy* (New York: Random House, 2002), 277; Blumenthal, *The Clinton Wars*, 361.

85. Waldman, *POTUS Speaks*, 234.

86. Steven Pearlstein, "Rubin: US to Consider Reforms," *WP*, April 15, 1998, C12; Sudeep Reddy, "IMF Eases Its Blanket Opposition to Capital Controls," *WSJ*, December 3, 2012.

87. Paul Krugman, "Hot Money Blues," *NYT*, March 24, 2013, A23.

Chapter 13. Deregulating Finance

1. "25 People to Blame for the Financial Crisis," *Time*, February 23, 2009, 20–25.

2. Bernstein, *A Woman in Charge*, 353.

3. Ibid., 352.

4. Robert McGough, "The New Financial Landscape: Finally 1929 Is Put to Rest," *WSJ*, October 25, 1999, A20.

5. Matthew Sherman, "A Short History of Financial Deregulation in the United States," Center for Economic and Policy Research, July 2009, 4, https://www.cepr.net/documents/publications/dereg-timeline-2009-07.pdf.

6. Financial Crisis Inquiry Commission, *Final Report*, 29.

7. Federal Deposit Insurance Corporation, *History of the Eighties: An Examination of the Banking Crises of the 1980s and Early 1990s* (Washington, DC: FDIC, 1997), 179.

8. Robert W. Ray, *Final Report of the Independent Counsel in Re Madison Guaranty Savings & Loan Association* (Washington, DC: US Court of Appeals for the District of Columbia Circuit, Division for the Purpose of Appointing Independent Counsels, Division 94-1, January 5, 2001), appendix 2, iii, http://purl.access.gpo.gov/GPO/LPS67340.

9. Seidman quoted in David Rosenbaum, "A Financial Disaster with Many Culprits," *NYT*, June 6, 1990, A1.

10. Thomas C. Hayes, "US Regulators Seize 37 Ailing Savings Units in 6 States," *NYT*, March 3, 1989, D2.

11. Ray, *Final Report of the Independent Counsel*, iv–v.

12. Sherman, "A Short History of Financial Deregulation in the United States," 9.

13. Financial Crisis Inquiry Commission, *Final Report*, 35.

14. Sherman, "A Short History of Financial Deregulation in the United States," 9; interview with Alan Blinder, "The Wall Street Fix," *Frontline*, PBS, May 8, 2003.

15. Bill Medley, "Riegle-Neal Interstate Banking and Branching Efficiency Act of 1994," Federal Reserve History, https://www.federalreservehistory.org/essays/riegle-neal-act-of-1994.

16. Quoted in Ryan Chittum, "Bill Clinton on Deregulation: 'The Republicans Made Me Do It,'" *Columbia Journalism Review*, October 1, 2013.

17. Brett Fromson, "Plunge Protection Team," *WP*, February 23, 1997, H1. The working group had been set up in the aftermath of the sharp stock market drop of October 19, 1987. Dormant for much of the Bush administration, it was revived under Clinton and became especially active in his second term.

18. Bo Cutter to President Clinton, "Need for Decision Concerning Treasury's Proposed Approach to Financial Services Modernization and Repeal of the Glass-Steagall Act," February 21, 1995; John Podesta to the President, "Glass-Steagall Reform," February 24, 1995; both in folder 098309SS, OA/box 21860, FOIA 2010-0384-F, Clinton Library; see also Dan Roberts, "Wall Street Deregulation Pushed by Clinton Advisers, Documents Reveal," *Guardian*, April 19, 2014, 1.

19. Hirsh, *Capital Offense*, 182; Jonathan Glater, "Rubin Urges Changes in US Banking Laws," *WP*, February 28, 1995, C1.

20. Gene Sperling to Bill Clinton, March 1997, Financial Services Modernization Act and Community Reinvestment Act, FOIA 2010-0384-F, Clinton Library; also found in Lemann, *Transaction Man*, 166.

21. Sperling to Clinton, March 1997. Janet Yellen had taken over as CEA chair in February 1997.

22. Zephyr Teachout, "A Blueprint for a Trust-Busting Biden Presidency," *The New Republic*, December 18, 2020, 16.

23. Quoted in Stoller, *Goliath*, 354.

24. "Remarks of Vice President Al Gore as Delivered to the Federal-State-Local Telecomm Summit," Washington, DC, January 9, 1995, "OVP-Telecom" folder, OA/box 23867 [2], Clinton Administration History Project, Clinton Library.

25. Edwin Yoder, "Electronic Future: Law of the Jungle," *St. Louis Post-Dispatch*, February 21, 1996, 7B.

26. Sandra Sugawara and Paul Farhi, "Gore to Map out Telecom Blueprint—Bipartisan Support Exists on Major Issues," *Dallas Morning News*, January 11, 1994, 1D.

27. Greg Simon to Marcia Hale, "Telecommunications and the States," January 19, 1995, "OVP-Telecom" folder, OA/box 23867 [2], Clinton Library; Mike Mills, "Long-Distance Firms Oppose Reform Bill," *WP*, July 19, 1995, F1; Keith Bradsher, "Clinton Vows to Veto Bill on Telecommunications Decontrol," *NYT*, August 1, 1995, D1; Stiglitz, *The Roaring Nineties*, 96–99.

28. Pamela Samuelson and Hal R. Varian, "The 'New Economy' and Information Technology Policy," in Frankel and Orszag, *American Economic Policy in the 1990s*, 401.

29. William J. Clinton, "Remarks on Signing the Telecommunications Act of 1996," February 8, 1996, American Presidency Project..

30. William J. Clinton, "Statement on Signing the Gramm-Leach-Bliley Act," November 12, 1999, American Presidency Project.

31. Stoller, *Goliath*, 419.

32. Steven Perlstein, "Telecommunications Deals Are Setting off Antitrust Alarms," *Seattle Times*, May 29, 1997, D6.

33. Debbie Goldman, "Resistance in the Digital Workplace: Call Center Workers in Bell Telephone Companies, 1965–2005," PhD diss., University of Maryland, 2021, 243–67, 315.

34. Stiglitz, *The Roaring Nineties*, 92; Nomi Prins, "The Telecoms Disaster," *Left Business Observer*, no. 101, July 2002; Paul Starr, "The Great Telecom Implosion," *American Prospect*, August 19, 2002. After SBC acquired AT&T, it cloaked itself in the name of the iconic firm, but it was a very different company.

35. Maney, *Bill Clinton*, 166.

36. Blumenthal, *The Clinton Wars*, 94–95; Lemann, *Transaction Man*, 159–60.

37. "Testimony of William L. McQuillan, President of the Independent Bankers Association of America before the US House Committee on the Judiciary," June 3, 1998, National Economic Council History of Financial Modernization [3], Clinton Library.

38. Michael Schroeder, "Glass-Steagall Compromise Is Reached," *WSJ*, October 25, 1999, A2.

39. Mallaby, *The Man Who Knew*, 522–24; Financial Crisis Inquiry Commission, *Final Report*, 54.

40. Mallaby, *The Man Who Knew*, 525–26.

41. Final Crisis Inquiry Commission, *Final Report*, 56.

42. Robert Kuttner, "Friendly Takeover," *American Prospect*, March 18, 2007.

43. Rubin, *In an Uncertain World*, 304; Paul Beckett and Jacob Schlesinger, "Ex-Treasury Secretary Rubin Lands at Citigroup," *WSJ*, October 27, 1999, C1.

44. Gene Sperling, Bruce Reed, and Larry Stein to the President, "The Community Reinvestment Act," February 22, 1999, [03/03/1999–10/19/1999] folder, Financial Services Modernization and Community Reinvestment, Clinton Library.

45. Robert Rubin, Gene Sperling, Larry Stein, Chuck Ruff, and Bruce Reed to the President and the Vice President, "Community Reinvestment Act (CRA) Strategy Memo," April 7, 1999, [03/03/1999–10/19/1999] folder, Financial Services Modernization and Community Reinvestment, Clinton Library.

46. Jacob Schlesinger, "Gramm Crusades to Overturn Community Lending Act," *WP*, April 19, 1999, A24.

47. Geismer, *Left Behind*, 298–300.

48. Michael Schroeder, "Glass-Steagall Compromise Is Reached," *WSJ*, October 25, 1999, A2; Christopher Shaw, *Money, Power, and the People: The American Struggle to Make Banking Democratic* (Chicago: University of Chicago Press, 2019), 294.

49. Greenspan, *The Age of Turbulence*, 199, 376.

50. Stiglitz, *The Roaring Nineties*, 159.

51. Ibid., 160–61. Many of these same arguments are made in Joseph E. Stiglitz, "The Anatomy of a Murder: Who Killed America's Economy?," *Critical Review* 21, nos. 2/3 (June 2009): 329–39.

52. Carl Felsenfeld and David Glass, *Banking Regulation in the United States* (New York: Juris Publishing, 2011), 362; Jim Zarroli, "Fact Check: Did the Repeal of Glass-Steagall Cause the 2008 Financial Crisis?," National Public Radio, October 14, 2015.

53. Kenneth J. Arrow, "A Cautious Case for Socialism," *Dissent*, Summer 1978, 478.

54. Hirsh, *Capital Offense*, 176–77.

55. Financial Crisis Inquiry Commission, *Final Report*, 44; "Why Derivatives Were Created and What Went Wrong," *Frontline*, PBS, October 20, 2009. Statements of Joe Nocera and Joseph Stiglitz, among others.

56. Financial Crisis Inquiry Commission, *Final Report*, 49.

57. Simon Johnson and James Kwak, *13 Bankers: The Wall Street Takeover and the Next Financial Meltdown* (New York: Random House, 2011), 8.

58. Partnoy, *Infectious Greed*, 111–12.

59. Ibid., 114–15.

60. Ibid., 53–57; Hirsh, *Capital Offense*, 9.

61. Partnoy, *Infectious Greed*, 112, 148.

62. Carol Loomis and Erick Schonfeld, "The Risk That Won't Go Away," *Fortune*, March 7, 1994, 40.

63. Ibid., 41.

64. Partnoy, *Infectious Greed*, 152–53.

65. Senate Committee on Banking, Housing, and Urban Affairs, "Derivative Financial Instruments Relating to Banks and Financial Institutions," 104th Cong., 1st sess., January 5, 1995, 16, 18, 21.

66. Interview with Arthur Levitt, "The Warning," *Frontline*, PBS, October 20, 2011.

67. Lemann, *Transaction Man*, 170; Johnson and Kwak, *13 Bankers*, 95.

68. Rick Schmitt, "Prophet and Loss," *Stanford*, March/April 2009, https://stanfordmag.org/contents/prophet-and-loss.

69. Interview with Brooksley Born, "The Warning," *Frontline*, PBS, October 20, 2009; interview with Michael Greenberger, "The Warning," *Frontline*, PBS, October 20, 2009.

70. Manuel Roig-Franzia, "Credit Crisis Cassandra," *WP*, May 26, 2009, C1.

71. Robert Rubin to Senator Richard Lugar, February 3, 1997, History of the Department of the Treasury, supplementary documents [13], Clinton Library.

72. Commodity Futures Trading Commission, "Over-the-Counter Derivatives," May 7, 1998, in "Working Group on Financial Markets" [1] folder, OA/box 23925, Jason Seligman, Council of Economic Advisers, Clinton Library.

73. Johnson and Kwak, *13 Bankers*, 9; interview with Michael Greenberger, "The Warning," *Frontline*, October 20, 2009.

74. Interview with Arthur Levitt, "The Warning," *Frontline*, October 20, 2011; interview with Michael Greenberger, "The Warning," *Frontline*, October 20, 2009.

75. "Financial Markets Working Group Principals Meeting," April 21, 1998, "Working Group on Financial Markets" [1] folder, OA/box 23925, Jason Seligman, Council of Economic Advisers, Clinton Library; see also Michael Smallberg, "How the Clinton Team Thwarted Efforts to Regulate Derivatives," Project on Government Oversight, April 25, 2014, https://www.pogo.org/analysis/2014/04/how-clinton-team-thwarted-effort-to-regulate-derivatives.

76. "Financial Markets Working Group Principals Meeting," April 21, 1998, "Working Group on Financial Markets" [1] folder, OA/box 23925, Jason Seligman, Council of Economic Advisers, Clinton Library; Hirsh, *Capital Offense*, 18.

77. Rubin, *In an Uncertain Time*, 288.

78. Interview with Michael Greenberger, "The Warning," *Frontline*, October 20, 2009.

79. "Joint Statement by Treasury Secretary Robert E. Rubin, Federal Reserve Board Chairman Alan Greenspan, and SEC Chairman Arthur Levitt," US Department of the Treasury, May 7, 1998, https://home.treasury.gov/news/press-releases/rr2426.

80. Hirsh, *Capital Offense*, 18–19; Jerry Knight, "Agencies Try to Block Study on Derivatives," *WP*, June 6, 1998, E1.

81. Financial Crisis Inquiry Commission, *Final Report*, 57; Levy, *Ages of American Capitalism*, 664–65; interview with Brooksley Born, "The Warning," *Frontline*, October 20, 2009.

82. Woodward, *Maestro*, 208–9.

83. Lee Sachs to Secretary Summers, "Report of the President's Working Group on Financial Markets on OTC Derivatives Markets and the Commodity Exchange Act," October 15, 1999, History of the Department of Treasury, Supplementary Documents [13], Clinton Library; Levy, *Ages of American Capitalism*, 698.

84. Robert Rubin to the President, "Report of the President's Working Group on Financial Markets on Hedge Funds and Long-Term Capital Management," April 22, 1999, folder 302191SS, OA/box 21844, WHORM Subject File—General, Clinton Library; Partnoy, *Infectious Greed*, 260.

85. Lemann, *Transaction Man*, 178; Michael Greenberger, "Out of the Black Hole," *American Prospect*, April 25, 2010.

86. Financial Crisis Inquiry Commission, *Final Report*, 59.

87. Ibid., 48.

88. Greenberger, "Out of the Black Hole." Rubin's Citigroup required a $45 billion government loan.

89. Roig-Franzia, "Credit Crisis Cassandra."

90. Michael Hirsh, "The Comprehensive Case against Larry Summers," *Atlantic*, September 13, 2013.

91. Peter Goodman, "Taking Hard New Look at Greenspan Legacy," *NYT*, October 9, 2008, A1.

92. Financial Crisis Inquiry Commission, *Final Report*, 49.

93. Edmund L. Andrews, "Greenspan Concedes Error on Regulation," *NYT* blog, October 24, 2008.

94. David Leonhardt, "Bill Clinton, on His Economic Legacy, *NYT* blog, May 27, 2009.

Epilogue

1. Stan Greenberg, "The Real Lesson for All Factions of the Democratic Party," *American Prospect*, March 25, 2022.

2. "Full Text of Bush's Acceptance Speech," *NYT*, August 4, 2000.

3. Blumenthal, *The Clinton Wars*, 317.

4. David Dayen, "Donald Trump Is Right: Deficits Don't Matter," *New Republic*, May 11, 2016, https://newrepublic.com/article/133431/donald-trump-right-deficits-dont-matter; Adam Tooze, "Of Bond Vigilantes, Central Bankers, and the Crisis of 2008," in *A World of Public Debts*, edited by Nicolas Barreyre and Nicolas Delalande (New York: Palgrave Macmillan, 2020), 453–78.

5. Martin Sandbu, "The Investment Drought of the Past Two Decades Is Catching Up with Us," *Financial Times*, July 19, 2022.

6. "Why Joe Biden Isn't Afraid of Debt Any More," *The Economist*, March 29, 2021.

7. Ibid.

8. William J. Clinton, "Remarks at the First Session of the White House Conference on the New Economy," April 5, 2000, American Presidency Project; Richard Stevenson, "Conference on the New Economy Gives Clinton a Chance to Glow," *NYT*, April 6, 2000, A22.

9. Clinton, "Remarks at the First Session of the White House Conference on the New Economy"; see also Lee Vinsel, "What Was 'the New Economy'?," Medium, March 29, 2022, https://medium.com/@sts-news/what-was-the-new-economy-3744991c7cff.

10. Daniel Greene, *The Promise of Access: Technology, Inequality, and the Political Economy of Hope* (Cambridge, MA: MIT Press, 2021). Notable dissenters were Robert Rubin and Alan Blinder, but both were gone from Washington by the end of the 1990s.

11. Margaret O'Mara, *The Code: Silicon Valley and the Remaking of America* (New York: Penguin, 2019), 349.

12. Barack Obama, *A Promised Land* (New York: Crown, 2020), 211.

13. Jackie Calmes, "Obama's Economic Team Shows Influence of Robert Rubin—with a Difference," *NYT*, November 24, 2008, A1.

14. Obama, *A Promised Land*, 214.

15. Tooze, *Crashed*, 293–301; Geithner, *Stress Test*, 286–310; Gerstle, *The Rise and Fall of the Neoliberal Order*, 225–26.

16. Rosalind S. Helderman, "In Election's Last Weeks, Obama Campaign Deploys Bill Clinton to Battleground States," *WP*, September 11, 2012, A1.

17. Tamara Keith, "Bill Clinton Clashes with Black Lives Matter Protesters," *All Things Considered*, NPR, April 7, 2016; German Lopez, "The Controversial 1994 Law That Joe Biden Helped Write, Explained," *Vox*, September 29, 2020.

18. Jonathan Chait, "How 'Neoliberalism' Became the Left's Favorite Insult of Liberals," *National Interest*, July 16, 2017; Gerstle, *The Rise and Fall of the Neoliberal Order*, 255–65.

19. Ben Mathis-Lilley, "If Leaked List Is Accurate, Hillary's Cabinet Choices Would Have Enraged the Democratic Left," *Slate*, January 10, 2017.

20. Gerstle, *The Rise and Fall of the Neoliberal Order*, 259.

21. David Jackson, "Donald Trump Targets Globalization and Free Trade as Job Killers," *USA Today*, June 28, 2016, 1.

22. Chad Livengood, "Sanders Attacks Clinton's Support for Trade Agreements," *Detroit News*, March 5, 2016; Andrew Walker, "Are Donald Trump and Bernie Sanders Right about Trade?," *BBC News*, April 11, 2016; Doug Palmer, "Clinton Raved about T-PP before She Rejected It," *Politico*, October 8, 2016.

23. Catie Edmondson, "Senate Advances Expansive Industrial Policy Bill to Counter China," *NYT*, July 27, 2022, B3; Zachary Carter, "Democrats Discover Winning Feels Good," *American Prospect*, August 8, 2022.

24. Charley Locke, "How the $4 Trillion Flood of Covid Relief Is Funding the Future," *New York Times Magazine*, November 24, 2021, https://www.nytimes.com/2021/11/24/magazine/pandemic-aid.html.

25. "The Biden White House Plan for a New US Industrial Policy," Atlantic Council, June 23, 2021, https://www.atlanticcouncil.org/commentary/transcript/the-biden-white-house-plan-for-a-new-us-industrial-policy/.

26. Robert Kuttner, "After Hyper-Globalization," *American Prospect*, May 31, 2022, 20–22.

27. Nancy Socla, "Lina Kahn Isn't Worried about Going Too Far," *Intelligencer*, October 27, 2021.

INDEX

Page numbers in italics refer to illustrations.